Orlando Bump

Internal Revenue Laws

Internal Revenue Statutes Now in Force

Orlando Bump

Internal Revenue Laws
Internal Revenue Statutes Now in Force

ISBN/EAN: 9783337779641

Printed in Europe, USA, Canada, Australia, Japan

Cover: Foto ©Suzi / pixelio.de

More available books at **www.hansebooks.com**

INTERNAL REVENUE LAWS.

Internal Revenue Statutes

NOW IN FORCE;

WITH NOTES REFERRING TO ALL

DECISIONS OF THE COURTS

AND

DEPARTMENTAL RULINGS, CIRCULARS, AND INSTRUCTIONS,

REPORTED TO OCTOBER 1, 1870.

EDITED BY

ORLANDO F. BUMP,

REGISTER IN BANKRUPTCY.

NEW YORK:
BAKER, VOORHIS & CO., PUBLISHERS,
66 NASSAU STREET.
1870.

PREFACE.

The aim of the author in compiling this volume has been to collect all the existing statutes, departmental rulings, and court decisions, on matters of Internal Revenue, in one book, where all living, valuable law may be easily accessible to officials, attorneys, and business men. The matter to compose such a work consists of three kinds, to wit: statutes, decisions of courts, and rulings of the Office of Internal Revenue, including, under the head of rulings, all decisions, regulations, circulars, and instructions issued by the Commissioner. In order that these three kinds of material may be readily distinguished from each other, three kinds of types have been used; the largest for statutes, the next in size (open or leaded) for court decisions, and the smallest for departmental rulings.

For the sake of convenience, clearness, and accessibility, the court decisions and departmental rulings have been placed under the sections of the statute to which they relate, with proper references, so that the reader can readily determine whether or not there has been any decision or ruling upon the portion of the statute that he may be considering.

The arrangement of the statutes is similar to that of the well-known official compilation, and has been adopted both on account of its excellence and because the public are already familiar with it, and will thus more easily find the topics they may seek. The act of June 30, 1864, has been taken as the basis of this work, and the sections that are still in force are printed without brackets and in their original order, and are indicated by bold-face figures. The repealed sections are noted and a reference made to the repealing statutes. The dates of the acts by which a section has been amended are noted, and all merely verbal amendments have been incorporated in the sections, so that the wording in this work is that of the amended sections. Where a section has been modified or affected by subsequent acts, without being expressly or in effect repealed, the modifying sections have been placed under the section thus affected by them. A few sections have been also adopted and inserted from older statutes.

For the sake of printing the act of July 20, 1868, consecutively, the sections relating to fermented liquors have been placed first, and the act of July 20, 1868, inserted between them and the sections relating to special taxes. Those portions of the act of July 14, 1870, relating to income and corporations, have been inserted in the place occupied by the sections for which they are substituted, and the remaining sections have been either inserted under sections modified by them or placed at the end of the volume. In all cases, sections that belong to other acts than that of June 30, 1864, have been indicated by brackets. A table showing the pages on which sections of acts subsequent to the act of June 30, 1864, may be found has been prefixed for convenience.

Those who are in anywise familiar with matters of Internal Revenue will at once perceive that the labor involved in a work of this kind is neither small nor easy. Legislation has been frequent and not very systematic. Consequently it is difficult at times to tell how far an act has been affected by subsequent statutes. Thus the pith of the law in regard to manufactures was taken away by the acts of March 31, 1868, and July 14, 1870, and of the law in regard to special taxes by the act of July 14, 1870. This, of course, leaves other sections relating to those topics almost meaningless, and yet they may possibly affect some question that may arise hereafter. In all such cases it has been deemed safer to print the sections thus affected, and indicate the change, when necessary, by the index.

Decisions and rulings, moreover, have been rendered upon sections that have been repealed or modified, and yet they may have such a bearing upon existing sections that any work would be deficient without them. Thus the act of July 14, 1870, is entirely new, and yet its provisions are so nearly similar to those of the preceding acts that rulings and decisions under the old are applicable under the new act. Decisions were rendered under section 99 of the act of June 30, 1864, prior to the amendment of July 13, 1866, but no attorney would think a volume complete that did not refer to those decisions. Rulings under section 59 of the act of July 20, 1868, are similarly affected by the repeal of nearly all special taxes. Decisions of courts also frequently contain doctrines and principles or points of practice that do not depend upon particular statutes. In all such cases it has been deemed advisable to place the rulings and decisions under the proper sections.

The selection and collection of the rulings and decisions, of course, depend upon the judgment and discretion of the author, and others may at times differ from him. The object of the work, however, is not to present a treatise upon Internal Revenue law, or to state authoritatively what is law upon any particular topic, but to collect whatever may have a bearing upon existing statutes, arrange it so as to be convenient and accessible, and thus furnish to those who may desire it the means of finding out what is law.

It would be strange, indeed, if in such a mass of matter there should not be some mistakes. The critical examination inspired by interest in some special question may at times lead to a closer inspection, and thus to the detection of errors by the very microscopical character of the investigation. It is believed, however, that, in the main, the work will be found correct and reliable, and errors few in number and unimportant. To a public always grateful for faithful work and painstaking research, and generous toward mistakes that are incident to humanity, this volume is offered.

It seems scarcely necessary to acknowledge the author's indebtedness to the Internal Revenue Record, for this volume is full of references to it. It contains the only collection of rulings, and the best collection of decisions. Without it this work could hardly have been written.

ORLANDO F. BUMP.

BALTIMORE, *October* 1, 1870.

CONTENTS.

OFFICE OF INTERNAL REVENUE.

	PAGE.
Commissioner, duties and powers of	17
Organization of office of internal revenue	18

GENERAL PROVISIONS.

Commissioner to keep accounts and give bonds	18
Officers to pay over money daily	19
Duties of deputy commissioner	22
Revenue agents	22
Revenue agents	22
Inspectors	22
Collection districts	23
Appointment of collectors and assessors	23
Reduction of number of collection districts	24
Assessment districts	24
Appointment of assistant assessors	25
Reduction of number of assistant assessors	25
Designation of assistant assessor for specific duties	25
Collector's bond	25
Appointments of deputy collectors	26
Returns made to assistant assessors	27
When returns are to be made	28
Duties of assistant assessors	28
Returns where parties give information	29
Proceedings in case of failure to make returns or fraudulent returns	29
Returns to be in legal tender	35
Penalty for fraudulent returns	35
Property of non-residents of districts	37
Property lying out of district	37
Classification of lists	37
Appeals to assessors	40
Lists to be furnished collectors	41
Malfeasance in office by assessors and assistant assessors	43
Salaries of assessors and assistant assessors	43
Penalty for receiving money for appointment of assistant assessors	47
Accounts of assistant assessors	47
Compensation of collectors	50
Apportionment of commissioners	56
Receipt for lists and returns	57
Collection of tax by distraint	57
When returns shall be made	64

CONTENTS.

	PAGE
Penalty for failure to pay tax	64
Sale for taxes	65
Sale of real estate	66
Commissioner to have charge of real estate	69
Property of non-residents	69
Transmittal of lists to other collectors	70
Report of collections	70
Collectors charged with taxes	71
Delinquent collectors	74
Malfeasance in office by collectors or their deputies	75
Officers may enter buildings	76
Obstructing officer	76
Receiving money to compromise offences	77
Personating an officer	77
Conspiracy	77
Bribery	80
Deputy may act as collector during temporary disability	81
Deputy may act as collector during vacancy	81
Compensation of deputy acting as collector	82
Suits to recover taxes	82
Regulations in regard to suits	83
Perjury	88
Separate accounts at Treasury	89
Appeals to commissioner	89
When suits for taxes may be commenced	91
Bill of sale to be evidence	92
Insurrectionary districts	93
Direct tax	93
Seizures for fraud	93
Fraudulent removal or concealment	102
Search warrants	103
Seizure of property worth less than $300	103
Provisions for returns applicable to all liable to tax	106
Adoption of Act August 6, 1846	106
Embezzlement	106
Suits for money withheld by officers	108
Transcripts to be evidence	108
Who may administer oaths	109
Franking privilege	110
Officers not to be interested in distilleries, &c.	110
Rendering accounts of fees	110
Appointment of inspectors	111
Designation of officers to inspect spirits	111
Bonds of inspectors	111

FERMENTED LIQUORS.

Brewer's notice	112
Brewer's bonds	112
Tax on fermented liquors	113
Brewer's books	114
Verification of brewer's entries	116
Illicit brewing	117
Stamps on fermented liquors	117

CONTENTS. ix

	PAGE.
Affixing and cancellation of stamps for fermented liquors	119
Fraudulent removal of fermented liquors	119
Marks on vessels for fermented liquors	122
Fraudulent removal of stamps for fermented liquors	123
Non-payment of tax on fermented liquors	123
Bottling fermented liquors	123

DISTILLED SPIRITS.

Tax on distilled spirits	124
Proof spirit. Distillers of brandy from apples, &c.	124
Meters	129
Definition of distilled spirits	133
Registration of still	134
Notice given by distiller or rectifier	135
Distiller's bonds	137
Approval of bonds, Priority of lien	140
Consent of owner of fee not required	142
Plan of distillery	143
Survey of distilleries	144
Distilling not to commence till bond given	150
Where stills may be used	151
Capacity tax	152
Manufacturers of stills	152
Distillery warehouses	153
Receiving cisterns	154
Construction of doors, tubs, &c.	156
Signs of distillers, &c., of distilled spirits	157
Distiller's books	158
Computation of product of distilleries	161
Daily account of materials used by storekeepers	164
Suspension of work	165
Gauging and marking distilled spirits	167
Withdrawal of distilled spirits from warehouse	172
Payment of tax before withdrawal	174
Stamping and marking distilled spirits on withdrawal	175
Stamps for distilled spirits in book form	181
Stamps for distilled spirits, how made	181
Collector's account for stamps for distilled spirits	182
Fraudulent affixing of stamps for distilled spirits	184
Reduction of producing capacity	184
Inspection of worm tubs	185
Officers may enter distillery by day or night	185
Facilities for examination of distillery	186
Search to detect fraudulent distillation	186
Work on Sunday	187
Fraudulent removal of distilled spirits	187
Distilled spirits removed by day	189
Fictitious proof	189
Evasion of tax on distilled spirits	189
False weight, &c.	190
Detention of suspected spirits	190
Bonding seized distilleries	191
Obliteration of stamps, &c., on distilled spirits	191

CONTENTS.

	PAGE.
Distilling without payment of special tax	192
Books of rectifiers, &c.	194
Purchases of more than twenty gallons of spirits	196
Change of package	196
Sparkling wines	197
Supervisors	198
Detectives	200
Suspension of collectors and assessors	200
Storekeepers	201
Salaries of storekeepers	205
Collection of storekeeper's salary	205
Gaugers	206
Drawback on alcohol and rum	208
Regulations for exportation of alcohol and rum	209
Withdrawal of spirits from bonded warehouse	210
Extension of time for withdrawal	211
Stamping stock on hand	211
Sale of forfeited spirits	213
Special taxes	214

TOBACCO, SNUFF, AND CIGARS.

Mode of ascertaining amount of special tax	221
Amount of tax on tobacco	221
Packages for manufactured tobacco	223
Metallic packages	224
Manufacturers to furnish statements, give bonds, &c.	224
Manufacturer's signs	226
Record of manufactories	226
Inventories and books of manufacturers	227
Tobacco stamps	228
Labels for manufactured tobacco	232
Penalties against manufacturers	234
Absence of stamp evidence of fraud	235
Penalty for evasion of law	235
Destruction of stamp on emptying packages	236
Bonded warehouses	236
Transportation in bond to bonded warehouse	240
Actual manufacturer to affix stamps	242
Books of dealers	242
Stamps on imported tobacco	243
Stamping stock on hand	244
False representation on sales of tobacco, &c.	245
Sale of tobacco or snuff in bond	245
Tax on cigars	246
Cigar manufacturers to furnish statements, give bonds, &c.	246
Signs of cigar manufacturers	247
Record of cigar manufacturers and cigar manufactories	248
Mode of packing cigars	248
Inventories and books of cigar manufacturers	248
Stamps for cigars	250
Labels for cigars	250
Name on cigar labels	251
Fraudulent removal of cigars	251
Absence of stamp evidence of fraud	252
Manufacture of cigars on commission	252

CONTENTS. xi

	PAGE.
Penalties against manufacturers of cigars	252
Stamps on imported cigars	253
Inventory of cigars on hand	253
Refunding tax on cigars	254
Fraudulent representations on sales of cigars	255
Penalty for wilful violation of law	255
Fraud in distilling spirits	256
Officers not to be interested in distilleries, &c.	257
Malfeasance in office	257
Fraudulent bonds	258
Official misconduct	258
Collector's bonded account	259
Commissioner may make regulations	259
Compromising suits	259
Entering nolle prosequi	261
Regulations for time of assessment	261
Meaning of terms	261
Repeal of prior acts	261
Bill in chancery	262
Tax on all articles produced in United States	263
When act takes effect	263

SPECIAL TAXES.

Persons liable to special tax	263
Registration	264
Non-payment of special tax	264
Receipt for special taxes	265
No additional tax in case of death or removal	266
More than one pursuit by same person	267
Sales of auctioneers	267
Tax on partnerships	267
Special taxes	268
When gross receipts do not exceed $1,000	268
Wines of native growth	268
Refunding excessive taxes	269

ILLUMINATING GAS.

Statements of manufacturers	270
Time for making returns	270
Omission to pay tax	271
Assessment on evasion of tax	273
Full amount of actual sale	273
Tax on illuminating gas	274
Tax added to contract price	276
Purchase of goods free from tax	276
Tax on machinery	276
Exemption of naval machinery	276

BROKERS.

Sales made by brokers, &c.	277

xii CONTENTS.

BANKS AND BANKERS.

	PAGE.
Deposits, capital and circulation	279
Circulation of State banks	281
Notes of municipal corporations	282
When circulation of State banks exempt	282
Persons having more than one place of business	283

INCOME.

Persons liable to income tax	283
What is subject to income tax	285
Exemption from income tax	290
Deductions from income tax	291
For what time assessed	297
Income returns	297
Appeal to assessors	299
Declaration under oath	300
Foreign consuls	300
Dividends of corporations	300
Insurance companies	303
Return of dividends	304
Repeal of prior sections	304

STAMP TAXES.

Who shall affix stamp	306
Records of instruments	308
Use of more than one stamp	308
Official documents	309
Forged or counterfeit stamps	309
Mode of cancellation	311
Commissioner may prescribe mode	313
Omission of stamp, Collector may stamp	313
Foreign bills of exchange	324
Exemptions	324
Sale of stamps	324
Collector may determine amount	326
Unstamped documents no evidence	327
Provisions extend to Schedule C	328
Omission to stamp articles in Schedule C	328
Removing stamps from articles	329
Evasion of tax on articles	330
Exportation of articles	330
Exportation of matches, &c.	331
Transfer of matches, &c., to warehouse	332
Tax on imported articles	332
Medicines exempted	332
Certain officers to sell stamps	333
Collection of tax on omission of stamp	334
Schedule B	335
Schedule C	356

DRAWBACK.

	PAGE
On what drawback allowed	360
Drawback on cotton goods	360
What drawback on cotton goods	361
When allowed	361
Collector to superintend exportation	362
Fraudulent claim of drawback	362
Repeal of prior acts	363
Repeal of inconsistent acts	365
Regulations by Commissioner	365
Regulations for assessment, &c.	365
Foreign consuls	365
Prosecution of suits, Informers' shares	366
Fraudulent debt invalid	369
Disbursing agents	370
Meaning of terms	370
Removal of suits	370
Officers sued in State courts	373
Writ of error	874
Repeal of prior acts	374
Rewards	375
Fraudulent wrappers, &c.	375
Sales upon distraint or forfeiture	376
Repeal of prior acts	376

TAXES REPEALED.

Special taxes	377
Tax on sales	377
Various taxes	378
Stamp duty	378
Tax on barges, etc.	378
Legacy and succession	378
Provision dealers	379
APPENDIX	380

LIST OF CASES.

	PAGE
Adams v. Dale	307, 312
Aiken v. Blaisdell	264
Anderson v. Coble	342
Assessor v. Osborne	373
Bank for Savings v. Collector	281
Bayly v. McKnight	307
Ballard v. Burnside	307, 312, 336, 339
Baird v. Pridmore	316, 317
In re Blair Distillery	100
Blake v. Hall	341, 353
Blake v. McCartney	92
Blackwell v. Denie	319
Beebe v. Hutton	316, 317, 322
Boyd et al. v. Hood et al	307, 336
Belger v Dinsmore	335
Botkins v. Spurgeon	306
Bondurant v. Crawford	335
Bowers et al. v. Beck	342
Brown v. Crandall	322
In re Brown	33, 41
Blunt v. Bates	316, 322
Burnap v. Losey	328, 336
Cardell v. Bridge	343
In re Callicott	78, 79
Capps v. Watts	335
Carpenter v. Snelling	327, 328, 350
Clark et al. v. Gilbert	92, 278, 379
Craig v. Dimock	306, 316, 327
Celley v. Gray	307
Cedar Rapids & St. Paul R.R. Co. v. Stewart	312
City of Phila. v. Collector	61, 62, 92, 275, 373
Corry Nat. Bank v. Rouse	308, 312, 316, 317, 320, 323
Cole v. Bell et al	343
Commonwealth v. Hardiman	343
Colerick et al. v. Bowser	306
Commonwealth v. Casey	269
Commonwealth r. Holbrook	269
Commonwealth v. Keenan	269
Cooke v. England	323
Crocker v. Foley	316, 336
Cutting v. Gilbert	92, 373

	PAGE
Day v. Buffington	287
Day v. Baker	323
Deskin v. Graham	322
Desmond v. Norris	312
De Barre v. Livingstone	335
Dorsheimer et al. v. U. S	369
Dowd v. Wright	323
In re Doll	32, 33, 34
Dorris v. Grace	307, 316, 323
Dowler v. Cushwa	323
Dudley v. Wells	316, 317
East Haven v. Derby	343
Fifield v. Close	306
Ford v. Clinton	306
Garland v. Lane	323
Green et al. v. Lowry	321
German Liederkranz v. Schieman	306
Gibson v. Hibbard	323
Grover et al v. King	92
Goodwin v. Wands	316
Govern v. Littlefield	316
Groesbeck v. Seeley	345
Guyther v. Boury	336
Hallock v. Jaudin	316, 317, 318
Hawkins v. Wilson	328
Hardin v. Branner	320
Harshaw v. McCombs	320
Harper v. Clark	306, 307, 308, 316, 317
Hibbard v. Gibson	321
Hitchcock v. Sawyer	307, 316, 317, 318
Holyoke Machine Co. v. Franklin Paper Co	316, 323
Howe v. Carpenter	316, 317, 327
Hoppock v. Stone	320, 321, 323, 324
Hornthall v. Collector	372
Hugus v. Strickler	307, 316, 323
Hunter v. Cobb	327
Ins. Co. v. Ritchie	372
Israel v. Redding	319, 320

LIST OF CASES.

Jackson v. Northern Central R.R. Co.......................302
Jackson v. Allen.......806, 807, 335
Jacquin v. Warren.....318, 319, 339
James v. Blauvelt..............345
Jones v. Davis................317
Jones v. Pease.................320
Jones v. Keep.................306

Kelsey v. Dallon................372
Killip v. Empire Mill Co........323
Kimbro v. Colgate.............365

Lambert v. Whitelock...........320
Latham v. Smith..316, 318, 319, 320, 327
Lewis v. Campau...............208
Lee v. Chadwick.........82, 33, 34
Lewis v. Randall................306
License Tax Cases............269
In re Lippman..................83

Mandell v. Pierce..........92, 285
Mason v. Cheney...........307, 323
Maynard v. Johnson........316, 318
Magee v. Denton..............300
In re Meador & Brother...82, 33, 34, 199
Mechanics & Farmers Bank of Albany v. Townsend.........281
Miller et al. v. Morrow..........323
Miller v. Henderson........318, 353
Miller v. Larmon.........317, 343
Musselman v. Mauk............306
McAfferty v. Hale..........320, 322
McBride v. Doty. 308, 318, 323, 350
McCreedy v. Callahan..........308
McGovern et al. v. Hoesbeck....316, 342
McGuire v. Commonwealth......269
Mudd v. McElvain.........324, 327
McKnight v. McCulloch........336
Myers v. Smith........312, 322, 336
In re Myrick..................353

Nave et al v. King.............309
Nelson v. Carman..............92
New Haven & Northampton Co. v. Quintard...316, 317, 318, 336

O'Reilley v. Good................63

Pacific Nat. Ins. Co. v. Soule..85, 92, 284
Pacific Bank v. De Ro..........336
Patterson v. Eames............323

Prather v. Pritchard...........343
Pervear v. Commonwealth......269
Perry v. Newcome.......82, 34, 199
Plessinger v. Depuy............328
In re Philips...............32, 33
Pope v. Burns...........319, 339
Pullan et al. v. Kinsinger et al....92

Ritter v. Brendlinger..........320
Roback v. Taylor...............92
Robbins v. Deverill...........321
Roberts v. Murray..............328

Satterlee v. Bliss..............354
Sayles v. Davis............309, 345
Shaefer v. Ketchum.........92, 114
Sawyer v. Parker.........317, 323
State v. Elder.................269
State v. Garton............309, 341
State v. Haynes...............317
Stanwood v. Green et al..33, 34, 199
Stark v. Bossier................328
Stevens v. Mack...............373
Schermerhorn v. Burgess...317, 322
Sime et al. v. Howard et al.....345
Smith v. Short................306
Smith v. Waters..........307, 342
Smith v. Averill...............101
Sowell v. Sowell's Admr........353
In re Strouse...............83, 84
Sykes v. Bates................320

Thayer v. Barney..............317
Teagarden v. Grover et al......312
The Peoria Marine and Fire Ins. Co. v. Perkins........323, 335
Tripp et al. v. Bishop..........323
Toledo, Logansport & Burlington R. R. Co. v. Nordyke......343
Toby v. Chipman...............316
Towne v. Bossier..............328
Thompson v. Wilson...........328
Trull v. Moulton.........317, 318

U. S. v. Allen et al...78, 79, 80, 256
U. S. v. Abott.................329
U. S. v. Auja..................243
U. S. v. Barney................209
U. S. v. Balto. &. O. R. R. Co....317, 319, 335
U. S. v. Casks (46)............100
U. S. v. Cask (1)..........196, 256
U. S. v. Casks (8)............188
U. S. v. Casks (133).......181, 256
U. S. v. Callicott.....78, 79, 80, 258
U. S. v. Chassell..............368

LIST OF CASES.

	PAGE.
U. S. v. Hartwell	107, 108
U. S. v. Mathoit	193
U. S. v. Chaffee et al.	102
U. S. v. Harris	369
U. S. v. Farmers' Loan & T. Co.	281
U. S. v. Washington Mills	63
U. S. v. Mattingly	101
U. S. v. Walsh	329
U. S. v. Whalan	78, 79
U. S. v. Gallons (23,000)	368
U. S. v. Watson et al.	189
U. S. v. Blaisdell et al.	188
U. S. v. Wangarien & Son	128, 218
U. S. v. Vaporizer	134
U. S. v. Damiani	243
U. S. v. Garlinghouse	139, 140
U. S. v. Bbls. (36)	96, 99
U. S. v. Bbls. (37)	129, 181, 213, 256
U. S. v. Bbls. (8)	197, 368
U. S. v. Bbls. (50)	188, 195, 196
U. S. v. Bbls. (10)	192
U. S. v. Bbls. (469)	99
U. S. v. Bbls. (278)	100
U. S. v. Bbls. (8)	368
U. S. v. Bbls. (25)	98
U. S. v. Bbls. (34)	100, 368
U. S. v. Bbls. (35)	139, 161, 216
U. S. v. Bbls. (20)	100, 368
U. S. v. Bbls. (7)	97, 101
U. S. v. Bbls. (300)	101
U. S. v. Bbls. (95)	369
U. S. v. Bbls. (100)	368
U. S. v. Bbls. (33)	97
U. S. v. Bbls. (39)	106
U. S. v. Bbls. (78)	188
U. S. v. Bbls. (21)	100
U. S. v. Bbls. (153)	96
U. S. v. Bbls. (12)	368
U. S. v. Bbls. (6)	188
U. S. v. Bbls. (100)	368
U. S. v. Bbls. (20)	100
U. S. v. Bbls. (508)	188, 189
U. S. v. Bbl. (1)	195
U. S. v. Bbls. (56)	99, 100
U. S. v. Bbls. (396)	98, 100, 181
U. S. v. Bbls. (300)	369
U. S. v. Bbls. (69)	101
U. S. v. Bbls. (2)	134
U. S. v. Flecke et al.	152
U. S. v. Develin et al.	216, 265
U. S. v. Stern	81
U. S. v. Shea	216
U. S. v. McHenry	89
U. S. v. Develin	216, 265
U. S. v. England	186

	PAGE.
U. S. v. Fermenting Tubs (6)	256, 262
U. S. v. Sperry et al.	78
U. S. v. Rectifying Establishment	181, 194, 196, 197, 256
U. S. v. Rectifying Establishment	194, 196, 256
U. S. v. Learned	317, 319, 336
U. S. v. Bentz	36
U. S. v. Cigars (25,000)	368
U. S. v. Piece of land	140, 194
U. S. v. Whiskey, &c.	99
U. S. v. Simons	264
U. S. v. Fisk	63, 278
U. S. v. Still (1)	96, 134
U. S. v. McKim & Co.	156
U. S. v. Still (1), &c.	368
U. S. v. Distillery	194
U. S. v. Smith et al.	226
U. S. v. Fridenburg	196
U. S. v. Lindauer	263
U. S. v. Wright et al.	140
U. S. v. Singer	205
U. S. v. Findlay	36
U. S. v. Fox et al.	329
U. S. v. Howard	216
U. S. v. Hook et al.	368
U. S. v. Tons of coal (2)	101
U. S. v. Rosenfield	234
U. S. v. Frost et al.	287, 294
U. S. v. Thorn et al.	26
U. S. v. Blumgart	107, 108
U. S. v. O'Brien	140, 258
U. S. v. Cohn	250
U. S. v. Crosby	264, 319
U. S. v. Hoym	250
U. S. v. Lot Leaf Tobacco	101
U. S. v. Trobe et al.	216, 265
U. S. v. Mountjoy	27, 36
U. S. v. Smock	101
U. S. v. Strouse	84
U. S. v. Woolheim	253
U. S. v. Cutting	63, 278
U. S. v. Rumsey	36
U. S. v. Truesdell	216, 226
U. S. v. Quantity of distilled spirits	99
U. S. v. Quantity of spirits	102
U. S. v. Quantity of distilled spirits	100
U. S. v. Quantity of spirits	96, 99, 195
U. S. v. Quantity of spirits	256
U. S. v. Quantity of spirits	192, 195
U. S. v. Dutcher	196
U. S. v. Dutcher et al.	196

1*

LIST OF CASES.

	PAGE
U. S. v. Fullerton	79
U. S. v. Furlong	161
U. S. v. Tub (1)	369
U. S. v. Cutting Machines (4)	368
U. S. v. Quantity of rags	96
U. S. v. Sulzburger et al	78, 80
U. S. v. Fuers	116
U. S. v. Prussing et al	134
U. S. v. Mynderse	381
Union Bank v. Hill et al	306
Vail v. Knapp	307, 308, 323, 350
Veazie Bank v. Fenno	282
Violet v. Heath	342
Voerbeck v. Roe	316
Voight & Co. v. McKaim	307, 315
Walton v. Brien	306
Warren v. Paul	306
Wayman v. Torrenson	316, 319, 321
Wilson v. Carey	319
Whitehill v. Shickle	316
Wright v. McFaden	323

TABLE

SHOWING THE ARRANGEMENT OF THE SEVERAL SECTIONS OF THE ACTS AMENDATORY OF THE ACT OF JUNE 30, 1864, BY PAGES, IN THIS COMPILATION.

			PAGE				PAGE
March 8, 1865,	§ 1.	Amendatory of various sections of the act of June 30, 1864, and incorporated therein.		July 13, 1866,	§ 14.		102
				Do	15.		103
				Do	16.		375
Do	2.	Repealed by act of July 13, 1866, § 9, bis.		Do	17.		376
				Do	18.	Practically obsolete.	
Do	3.		19	Do	19.		91
Do.	4.		370	Do	20.	Amendatory of section 15, act of March 3, 1865, and so printed.	
Do	5.	Repealed by act of July 13, 1866, § 9, bis.					
Do	6.		281	Do	21.	Superseded by section 16, act of March 2, 1867.	
Do	7.	Omitted; relates to national banks exclusively.					
				Do	22.		
				Do	23.		
Do	8.	Repealed by act of July 13, 1866, § 9, bis.		Do	24.		
Do	9.			Do	25.		
Do	10.			Do	26.	Repealed by act of July 20, 1868.	
Do	11.		332	Do	27.		
Do	12.	Repealed by act of July 13, 1866, § 9, bis.		Do	28.		
				Do	29.		
Do	13.	Repealed by act of July 14, 1870, § 1.		Do	30.		
				Do	31.		
Do	14.		282	Do	32.	Superseded by section 14, act of March 2, 1867.	
Do	15.		362				
Do	16.		365	Do	33.		
Do	17.		276	Do	34.		
Do	18.	Expired.		Do	35.		
Do	19.	Repealed by act of July 13, 1866, § 66.		Do	36.		
				Do	37.		
Do	20.		22	Do	38.		
Jan. 15, 1866,	§ 1.		25	Do	39.	Repealed by act of July 20, 1868.	
Mar. 10, 1866,	§ 1.	Amendatory of two sections of the act of June 30, 1864, and incorporated therein.		Do	40.		
				Do	41.		
				Do	42.		
Do	2.			Do	43.		
Do	3.	Amended by act of July 13, 1866, § 9, bis., and printed as section 3...	35	Do	44.		
Do	4.			Do	45.		
Do	5.			Do	46.		112
July 13, 1866,	§ 1.			Do	47.		112
Do	2.	Repealed by act of February 8, 1868.		Do	48.		113
Do	3.			Do	49.		114
Do	4.			Do	50.		116
Do	5.			Do	51.		117
Do	6.		360	Do	52.		117
Do	7.	Repealed by act of February 3, 1869.		Do	53.		119
Do	8.			Do	54.		119
Do	9.	Amendatory of various sections of the act of June 30, 1864, and incorporated therein.		Do	55.		122
				Do	56.		123
				Do	57.		123
				Do	58.		123
Do	10.	Practically obsolete.		Do	59.		110
Do	11.		64	Do	60.		110
Do	12.	Repealed July 14, 1870, § 2.		Do	61.	Expired.	
				Do	62.		80
Do	13.		332	Do	63.		103

TABLE OF SECTIONS.

			PAGE
July 13, 1866,	§64		18
Do	65		110
Do	66.	Expired.	
Do	67		370
Do	68		373
Do	69		374
Do	70		374
July 27, 1866,	§1		269
Feb. 5, 1867,	§1.	Obsolete and repealed by act of July 20, 1868.	
Do	2.	Repealed by act of July 14, 1870, §1.	
Mar. 2, 1867,	§1		26
Do	2.	Repealed by act of July 14, 1870, §1.	
Do	3		83
Do	4		69
Do	5		334
Do	6		25
Do	7		375
Do	8		64
Do	9.	Amendatory of various sections of previous acts, and incorporated therein.	
Do	10.		
Do	11.	Practically obsolete.	
Do	12.	Repealed by act of July 20, 1868.	
Do	13.	Amendatory of various sections of act of June 30, 1864, and incorporated therein.	
Do	14.	Repealed by act of July 20, 1868.	
Do	15.		
Do	16.		
Do	17		111
Do	18.		
Do	19.		
Do	20.		
Do	21.	Repealed by act of July 20, 1868.	
Do	22.		
Do	23.		
Do	24.		
Do	25.		
Do	26		77
Do	27.	Repealed by act of July 20, 1868.	
Do	28		77
Do	29.	Does not relate to internal revenue.	
Do	30		111
Do	31.	Repealed by act of July 20, 1868.	
Do	32.		
Do	33.	Does not relate to internal revenue.	
Do	34		376
Mar. 26, 1867,	§1.	Obsolete.	
Do	2		262
Do	3.	Obsolete.	
Do	4.		
Jan. 11, 1868,	§1		174
Feb. 3, 1868,	§1.	Not printed.	
Mar. 31, 1868,	§1.	Amendatory of various sections of the act of June 30, 1864, and incorporated therein.	
Do	2		276
Do	3		361
Do	4.	Repealed by act of July 14, 1870, §2.	
Do	5		256
Do	6		258
Do	7		261
June 25, 1868,	§1		174
July 6, 1868,	§1.	Amendatory of act of June 25, 1868, and incorporated therein.	
July 20, 1868,	§1		124
Do	2		124
Do	3		129

		PAGE
July 20, 1868, §4		133
Do	5	134
Do	6	135
Do	7	137
Do	8	140
Do	9	143
Do	10	144
Do	11	150
Do	12	151
Do	13	152
Do	14	152
Do	15	153
Do	16	154
Do	17	156
Do	18	157
Do	19	158
Do	20	161
Do	21	164
Do	22	165
Do	23	167
Do	24	172
Do	25	175
Do	26	181
Do	27	181
Do	28	182
Do	29	184
Do	30	184
Do	31	185
Do	32	185
Do	33	186
Do	34	186
Do	35	187
Do	36	187
Do	37	189
Do	38	189
Do	39	189
Do	40	190
Do	41	190
Do	42	191
Do	43	191
Do	44	192
Do	45	194
Do	46	195
Do	47	196
Do	48	197
Do	49	198
Do	50	200
Do	51	200
Do	52	201
Do	53	206
Do	54	208
Do	55	209
Do	56	210
Do	57	211
Do	58	213
Do	59	214
Do	60	221
Do	61	221
Do	62	223
Do	63	224
Do	64	226
Do	65	226
Do	66	227
Do	67	228
Do	68	232
Do	69	234
Do	70	235
Do	71	235
Do	72	236
Do	73	236
Do	74	240
Do	75	242
Do	76	242
Do	77	243
Do	78	244
Do	79	245
Do	80	245
Do	81	246
Do	82	246
Do	83	247

TABLE OF SECTIONS.

		PAGE.
July 20, 1868, §84		248
Do	85	248
Do	86	248
Do	87	250
Do	88	250
Do	89	251
Do	90	252
Do	91	252
Do	92	252
Do	93	253
Do	94	253
Do	95	255
Do	96	256
Do	97	257
Do	98	257
Do	99	258
Do	100	259
Do	101	259
Do	102	259
Do	103	261
Do	104	261
Do	105	261
Do	106	262
Do	107	263
Do	108	263
Do	109. Repealed by act of July 14, 1870, § 2.	
Mar. 1, 1869, §1		82
Do	2. Expired.	
Mar. 3, 1869, §1		276
Mar. 29, 1869, §1		205
Apr. 10, 1869, §1. Amendatory of various sections of act of July 20, 1868, and incorporated therein.		
Do	2. Amendatory of section 155 of act of June 30, 1864, and incorporated therein.	

		PAGE.
Apr. 10, 1869, § 3		254
July 1, 1870, §1		82
July 12, 1870, §1		205
July 13, 1870, §1		303
July 14, 1870, §1		377
Do	2	377
Do	3	377
Do	4	378
Do	5. Amendatory of section 158 of act of June 30, 1864, and incorporated therein.	
Do	6	283
Do	7	285
Do	8	290
Do	9	291
Do	10	297
Do	11	297
Do	12	299
Do	13	300
Do	14	300
Do	15	300
Do	16	304
Do	17	304
Do	18	24
Do	19	25
Do	20. Amendatory of section 67 of act of July 13, 1866, and incorporated therein.	
Do	25	378
Do	27	378
Do	28	224
July 14, 1870, §1. Amendatory of Schedule C of act of June 30, 1864, and incorporated therein.		
July 14, 1870, §1		379
July 14, 1870, §1		361

ABBREVIATIONS USED IN THIS WORK.

A. L. Reg..............American Law Register.
A. L. Rev..............American Law Review.
A. L. T. (C. R.)........American Law Times, Court Reports.
A. L. T. (S. R.)........American Law Times, State Reports.
Bout..................Boutwell.
Blatch...............Blatchford's Reports.
Bt....................Benedict's Reports.
C. L. N...............Chicago Legal News.
I. R. R...............Internal Revenue Record.
Pitts. L. J.............Pittsburg Legal Journal.
s. c..................Same Case.

INTERNAL REVENUE LAW.

U. S. INTERNAL REVENUE LAWS.

AN ACT to provide internal revenue to support the government, to pay interest on the public debt, and for other purposes, approved June 30, 1864,

AS SUBSEQUENTLY AMENDED.

Duties of Commissioner.

Sec. 1. *Be it enacted by the Senate and House of Representatives of the United States of America in Congress assembled,* That, for the purpose of suprintending the collection of internal duties, stamp duties, licenses, or taxes, imposed by this act, or which may hereafter be imposed, and of assessing the same, the Commissioner of Internal Revenue, (*a*) whose annual salary shall be four thousand dollars, shall be charged, under the direction of the Secretary of the Treasury, with preparing all the instructions, regulations, directions, forms, blanks, stamps, and licenses, and distributing the same, or any part thereof, and all other matters pertaining to the assessment and collection of the duties, stamp duties, licenses, and taxes which may be necessary to carry this act into effect, and with the general superintendence of his office as aforesaid, and shall have authority, and hereby is authorized and required, to provide cotton marks, hydrometers, and proper and sufficient adhesive stamps, and stamps or dies for expressing and denoting the several stamp duties, or the amount thereof in the case of percentage duties, imposed by this act, and to alter and renew or replace such stamps, from time to time, as occasion shall require. He may also contract for or procure the printing of requisite forms, decisions, regulations, and advertisements; but the printing of such forms, decisions, and regulations shall be done at the public printing office, unless the Public Printer shall be unable to perform the work.

And the Secretary of the Treasury may, at any time prior to the first day of July, eighteen hundred and sixty-five, assign to the office of the Commissioner of Internal Revenue such number of clerks as he may deem necessary, or the exigencies of the public service may require; and the privilege of franking all letters and documents pertaining to the duties of his office, and of receiving, free of postage, all such letters and documents, is hereby extended to said Commissioner.

(*a*) A resignation by a Commissioner of Internal Revenue, to take effect upon the qualification of his successor, nominated by the President and confirmed by the Senate, has no official or legal force whatever, nor any operation upon the office, and the President's indorsement of acceptance thereon does not make the office vacant. 8 I. R. R. 54.

Organization of Office of Internal Revenue.

[SEC. 64. (July 13, 1866.) *And be it further enacted*, That the office of the Commissioner of Internal Revenue be reorganized so as to include—

One Commissioner of Internal Revenue, with a salary of six thousand dollars, and one Deputy Commissioner, with a salary of three thousand five hundred dollars; which offices are already created, and the duties thereof defined by law; and to authorize, under the direction of the Secretary of the Treasury, the employment of the following additional officers and clerks, and with the salaries hereinafter specified, namely:

Two Deputy Commissioners, each with a salary of three thousand dollars;

One Solicitor, with a salary of four thousand dollars;

Seven heads of divisions, each with a salary of two thousand five hundred dollars;

Thirty-four clerks of class four; forty-five clerks of class three; fifty clerks of class two; and thirty-seven clerks of class one;

Fifty-five female clerks;

Five messengers, three assistant messengers, and fifteen laborers.

And a sum sufficient to pay the additional salaries of officers, clerks, and employés herein authorized is hereby appropriated out of any money in the treasury not otherwise appropriated; and this section shall take effect from and after the thirtieth day of June, eighteen hundred and sixty-six.]

GENERAL PROVISIONS.

Commssioner to keep Accounts and give Bond.

SEC. 2. *And be it further enacted*, That it shall be the duty of the Commissioner of Internal Revenue to pay over daily to the Treasurer of the United States all public moneys which may come into his possession, for which the Treasurer shall give proper receipts and keep a faithful account; and at the end of each month the said Commissioner shall render true and faithful accounts of all public moneys received or paid out, or paid to the Treasurer of the United States, exhibiting proper vouchers therefor, and the same shall be received and examined by the Fifth Auditor of the Treasury, who shall thereafter certify the balance, if any, and transmit the accounts, with the vouchers and certificate, to the First Comptroller for his decision thereon; and the said Commissioner, when such accounts are settled as herein provided for, shall transmit a copy thereof to the Secretary of the Treasury.

He shall at all times submit to the Secretary of the Treasury and the Comptroller, or either of them, the inspection of moneys in his hands, and shall, prior to the entering upon the duties of his office, execute a bond, with sufficient sureties, to be approved by the Secretary of the Treasury and by the First Comptroller, in a sum of not less than one hundred thousand dollars, payable to the United States, conditioned that said Commissioner shall faithfully perform the duties of his office according to law, and shall justly and faithfully account for and pay over to the United States, in obedience to law and in compliance with the order or regulations of the Secretary of the Treasury, all public moneys which may come into his hands or possession, and for the safe-keeping and faithful account of all stamps, adhesive stamps, or vellum, parchment or paper bearing a stamp denoting any duty thereon, which bond shall be filed in the office of the First Comptroller of the Treasury. And such Commissioner shall, from time to time, renew, strengthen, and increase his official bond, as the Secretary of the Treasury may direct.

Officers to pay over Moneys daily.

[SEC. 3. (March 3, 1865.) *And be it further enacted*, That from and after the thirtieth day of June, eighteen hundred and sixty-five, the gross amount of all duties, taxes, and revenues received or collected by virtue of the several acts to provide internal revenue to support the government and to pay the interest on the public debt, and of any other act or acts that may now or hereafter be in force connected with the internal revenues, shall be paid by the officers, collectors, or agents receiving or collecting the same, daily into the treasury of the United States, under the instructions (*a*) of the Secretary of the Treasury, without any abatement or deduction on account of salary, compensation, fees, costs, charges, expenses, or claims of any description whatever, any thing in any law to the contrary notwithstanding.

And all moneys now directed by law to be paid to the Commissioner of Internal Revenue, including those derived from the sale of stamps, shall be paid into the treasury of the United States by the party making such payment; and a certificate of such payment, stating the name of the depositor, and the specific amount on which the deposit was made, signed by the Treasurer, Assistant Treasurer, designated depositary or proper officer of a deposit bank, and transmitted to and received by the Commissioner of Internal Revenue, shall be deemed a compliance with the law requiring payment to be made to the Commissioner, any law to the contrary notwithstanding: *Provided*, That in districts where, from the distance of the officer, collector, or agent receiving or collecting such duties, taxes, and revenues from a proper government depositary, the Secretary of the Treasury may deem it proper, he may extend the time for making such payment, not exceeding, however, in any case, a period of one month.]

(*a*) 1st. A collector, deputy collector, or agent, living in the same city or town with a United States depositary, must deposit his entire receipts at the close of each day.

2d. Where he lives away from a United States depositary, and daily deposits for that reason are impracticable, he shall forward funds for deposit as often as he receives $1,000, or at least once in each month, irrespective of the amount received.

3d. All collections must be deposited in a depositary nearest to the point of collection. When two or more depositaries are in the same city or town, he will distribute his deposits according to special instructions from the Treasury Department. The distribution of deposits among depositaries for the mere purpose of giving each deposit bank its share cannot be allowed.

4th. Deputy collectors or agents may deposit directly with a United States depositary, to the credit of the Treasurer of the United States, on account of and in the name of their principals.

5th. All officers charged with the collection, reception, or safe keeping of United States moneys, are forbidden to deposit the same, or any portion thereof, in any United States national bank depositary, or in any State or private bank, or with private individuals or bankers, to their private credit, or to the credit of what is known as a " collector's account."

All collectors, and their deputies or agents, are required, whenever they place moneys received for public dues in a United States depositary, to cause the same to be credited forthwith to the account of the Treasurer of the United States, and to take proper certificates of deposit therefor, and to forward the same at once to the Treasury Department.

The prohibition against keeping a " collector's account " is extended to all depositaries and depositary banks of the United States.

Deputy collectors, or agents, or acting collectors, will take certificates of deposit in the name of the collector whose agent or deputy they are, or for whom they are acting.

All moneys derived from compromises of frauds must be disposed of as directed in Circular No. 38. 3 I. R. R. 29. The same prompt depositing of these moneys is required.

All moneys advanced from the Treasury to a collector in his capacity as disbursing agent of the United States must be deposited to his official credit as such disbursing agent, and drawn upon only in such capacity. Deposits of such moneys must be made either with the Treasurer, or some one of the Assistant Treasurers, or regularly designated depositaries of the United States, or with a national bank depositary, when specially authorized by the Secretary of the Treasury for that purpose, under the act of June 14th, 1866, and not otherwise. 7 I. R. R. 173.

Moneys paid to collectors by delinquent taxpayers in lieu of penalties and forfeitures, or gross receipts paid for unascertained taxes and penalties, should be deposited to the credit of the Secretary of the Treasury, until the amount due the government is ascertained, when he will order it to be placed to the credit of the Treasurer of the United States. While the moneys remain deposited to the credit of the Secretary of the Treasury they should not be reported with the collections on Forms 22, 49, or 51, nor included in the receipt on Form 23½. 8 I. R. R. 205.

Whenever a deposit is made, the officer should accompany it with a clear and sufficient statement, showing not only the amount to be placed to the credit of the Treasurer of the United States, but also the source of internal revenue from which the amount is derived. He need not particularize in the certificate of deposit further than the following headings: viz., internal duties, sales of stamps, and also fines, penalties, and forfeitures. 2 I. R. R 4.

Adams' Express Company, The American Merchants' Union, United States, Southern, Texas, New Jersey, Eastern, United States and Canada, National, Central, Harnden, Howard, Hope, and Earle's Express Companies, should be employed for the necessary transportation of all moneys or stamps of the Treasury Department; said transportation to be made for the purposes of depositing the money transported with the Treasurer, or an Assistant Treasurer, or authorized Depositary of the United States; for transmitting moneys collected on account of internal revenue from deputy collectors to collectors, the Treasurer, Assistant Treasurer, or United States Depositaries; and for transmitting stamps for spirits, beer, and tobacco, from collectors to their deputies, and for special purposes, and under special circumstances, in accordance with instructions from the Treasury Department.

All moneys transmitted should consist of the sum of $1,000, or its multiples as near as possible, and should be sent by the shortest practicable route. The expenses of transportation will be paid by the Treasury Department, and not by the collectors. The use of the forms of vouchers and way-bills prepared by the Treasury Department to the exclusion of all others is imperatively enjoined. These forms are furnished by the Secretary of the Treasury, on whom requisitions for them should be made, and are bound in books. No more than one book at a time will be furnished to each officer entitled thereto. Changes in the forms, so as to show the facts in each case, must.be made, the object being to secure a full statement of the facts pertaining to every transaction.

The officers sending or receiving moneys or stamps will certify in this form of vouchers to bills for services rendered, stating the sum transported, its character, between what points and to what office the moneys or stamps were sent, the date, and that the services charged for were actually performed.

All officers or agents should carefully count and pack their moneys or stamps to be transported, securing them in strong packages, sealed with their own private seal in at least four places; and with the amount, their own name and title, and the name and title of the consignee, plainly marked upon the wrapper, and take receipts in the established forms from the express companies for all sums transmitted. 11 I. R. R. 9.

Duties of Deputy Commissioner.

Sec. 3. *And be it further enacted*, That the Deputy Commissioner of Internal Revenue, whose annual salary shall be twenty-five hundred dollars, shall be charged with such duties in the Bureau of Internal Revenue as may be prescribed by the Secretary of the Treasury, or as may be required by law, and shall act as Commissioner of Internal Revenue in the absence of that officer, and exercise the privilege of franking all letters and documents pertaining to the office of Internal Revenue.

Revenue Agents.

[SEC. 20. (March 3, 1863.) *And be it further enacted*, That the Secretary of the Treasury may appoint not exceeding three revenue agents, whose duties shall be, under the direction of the Secretary of the Treasury, to aid in the prevention, detection, and punishment of frauds upon the revenue, who shall be paid such compensation as the Secretary of the Treasury may deem just and reasonable, not exceeding two thousand dollars per annum. The above salaries to be paid in the same manner as are other expenses for collecting the revenue.]

Revenue Agents.

Sec. 4. (Amended March 3, 1865, § 1.) *And be it further enacted*, That the Secretary of the Treasury may appoint not exceeding ten revenue agents, whose duties shall be, under the direction of the Secretary of the Treasury, to aid in the prevention, detection, and punishment of frauds upon the internal revenue, and in the enforcement of the collection thereof, who shall be paid, in addition to the expenses necessarily incurred by them, such compensation as the Secretary of the Treasury may deem just and reasonable, not exceeding two thousand dollars per annum. The above salaries to be paid in the same manner as are other expenses for collecting the revenue.

Inspectors.

Sec. 5. (Amended July 13, 1866, § 9.) *And be it further enacted*, That the Secretary of the Treasury may appoint inspectors in any assessment district where, in his judgment, it may be necessary for the purposes of a proper enforcement of the internal revenue laws or the detection of frauds; and such inspectors and revenue agents aforesaid shall be subject to the rules and regulations of the said Secretary, and have all the powers conferred upon any other officers of internal revenue in making any examination of persons, books, and premises which may be necessary in the discharge of the duties of their office; and the compensation of such inspectors shall be fixed and paid for such time as they may be actually employed, not exceeding four dollars per day, and their just and proper traveling expenses. And any inspector or revenue agent, or any special agent appointed by the Secretary of the Treasury, who shall demand or receive any compensation, fee, or reward, other than such as are provided by law for or in regard to the performance of his official duties, or shall be guilty of any extortion or willful oppression in the discharge of such duties, shall, upon conviction thereof in any circuit or district court of the United States, having jurisdiction thereof, be subject to a fine of not exceeding one thousand dollars, or to imprisonment for not exceeding one year, or both, at the discretion of the court, and shall be dismissed from office, and shall be forever disqualified from holding any office under the government of the United States. And one-half of the fine so imposed shall be for the use of the United States, and the other half for the use of the person, to be ascertained by the judgment of the court, who shall first give the information whereby any such fine may be imposed.

Sec. 6. *Repealed* July 13, 1866, § 64.

Collection Districts.

Sec. 7. *And be it further enacted,* That the second section of an act entitled "An act to provide internal revenue to support the government and to pay interest on the public debt," approved July one, eighteen hundred and sixty-two, shall remain and continue in full force; and the President is hereby authorized to alter the respective collection districts provided for in said section as the public interests may require.

[SEC. 2. (July 1, 1862.) *And be it further enacted,* That, for the purpose of assessing, levying, and collecting the duties or taxes hereinafter prescribed by this act, the President of the United States be, and he is hereby, authorized to divide, respectively, the States and Territories of the United States and the District of Columbia into convenient collection districts, and to nominate, and, by and with the advice and consent of the Senate, to appoint an assessor and a collector for each such district, who shall be residents within the same: *Provided*, That any of said States and Territories and the District of Columbia may, if the President shall deem it proper, be erected into and included in one district: *Provided*, that the number of districts in any State shall not exceed the number of representatives to which such State shall be entitled in the present Congress, except in such States as are entitled to an increased representation in the thirty-eighth Congress, in which States the number of districts shall not exceed the number of representatives to which any such State may be so entitled: *And provided further*, That in the State of California the President may establish a number of districts, not exceeding the number of senators and representatives to which said State is entitled in the present Congress.]

Reduction of Number of Collection Districts.

[SEC. 18. (July 14, 1870.) *And be it further enacted*, That the President is hereby authorized to annex to, and unite with each other, two or more adjoining collection districts, whenever, in his opinion, it will reduce the expenses of collecting the internal revenue, without impairing the efficiency of the service; and thereupon shall retain but one collector and one assessor for such enlarged district. And the President is also authorized to consolidate in like manner, at his discretion, any two or more adjoining supervisors' districts, and to retain or appoint one supervisor for such consolidated district.]

Assessment Districts.

Sec. 8. (Amended, March 3, 1865, § 1; July 13, 1866, § 9.) *And be it further enacted*, That each assessor shall divide his district into a convenient number of assessment districts, which may be changed as often as may be deemed necessary, subject to such regulations and limitations as may be imposed by the Commissioner of Internal Revenue, within each of which the assessor, whenever there shall be a vacancy, shall appoint, (a) with the approval of said Commissioner, one or more assistant assessors, who shall be a resident of such assessment district; and in case of a vacancy occurring in the office of assessor by reason of death or any other cause, the assistant assessor of the assessment district in which the assessor resided at the time of the vacancy occurring shall act as assessor until an appointment filling the vacancy shall be made.

(a) The provision of this section, vesting the power of appointing assistant assessors in the respective assessors, is clearly unconstitutional. 1 I. R. R. 162.

The acceptance of a nomination to an elective office by any assistant assessor will be taken as evidence that he no longer wishes to retain his position. Assessors should promptly report the name of any assistant who may accept or who may be known to be seeking any nomination for such office, in order that a successor may be forthwith appointed. 4 I. R. R. 62.

Appointment of Assistant Assessors.

[SEC. 1. (Jan. 15, 1866.) *Be it enacted, &c.*, That the Secretary of the Treasury is hereby authorized to appoint any assistant assessors of internal revenue now provided by law.]

Reduction of Number of Assistant Assessors.

[SEC. 19. (July 14, 1870.) *And be it further enacted*, That as soon as practicable, after the passage of this act, the number of assistant assessors employed shall be permanently reduced by the discharge of all officers of that class who are assigned specially to the assessment of any taxes which shall have been abolished by law. And the Commissioner of Internal Revenue shall be required further to reduce the number of assistant assessors in proportion to any reduction of the service of assessment which has been made, or may hereafter be made, by the repeal of any portion of the internal taxes.]

Designation of Assistant Assessors for specific Duties.

[SEC. 6. (March 2, 1867.) *And be it further enacted*, That it shall be lawful for the Commissioner of Internal Revenue, whenever he shall deem it expedient, to designate one or more of the assistant assessors in any collection district to make assessments in any part of such collection district for all such taxes as may be due upon any specified objects of taxation, and in such case it shall be the duty of the other assistant assessors of such collection district to report to the assistant assessor thus specially designated all matters which may come to their knowledge relative to any assessments to be made by him: *Provided*, That whenever two or more districts or parts of districts are embraced within one county, it may be lawful for such assistant assessor or assessors to make assessment any where within such county upon such specified objects of taxation as he may be by said Commissioner required: *Provided further*, That such assessment shall be returned to the assessor of the district in which such taxes are payable.]

Collectors to give Bond.

Sec. 9. *And be it further enacted*, That before any collector shall enter upon the duties of his office, he shall execute a bond (*a*) for such amount as shall be prescribed by the Commissioner of Internal Revenue, under the direction of the Secretary of the Treasury, with not less than five sureties to be approved by the Solicitor of the Treasury, conditioned that said collector shall faithfully perform the duties of his office according to law, and shall justly and faithfully account for and pay over to the United States, in compliance with the order or regulations of the Secretary of the Treasury, all public moneys which may come into his hands or possession; which bond shall be filed in the office of the First Comptroller of the Treasury. And such collector shall, from time to time, renew, strengthen, and increase his official bond, as the Secretary of the Treasury may direct, with such further conditions as the said Commissioner shall prescribe.

(*a*) A collector may use the seal of his predecessor upon cutting the predecessor's name out. It is not considered necessary that the collector's name shall appear upon the seal. 10 I. R. R. 10.

Assessors should report in their quarterly returns any change of circumstances affecting the pecuniary responsibility of the sureties of the collectors in their respective districts. 10 I. R. R. 12.

The condition of the collector's bond is three fold: 1st, That the collector shall faithfully discharge the duties of his office; 2d, That he shall pay over to the United States all public moneys received by him; 3d, That any deputy collector he may appoint shall faithfully discharge the duties of such deputy collector. When the first condition only has been violated, it is not enough to allege generally that the collector has failed to perform all the duties of his office. It is necessary to go farther and state what were the specific duties which he has failed to perform. U. S. *v.* Thorn et al., 9 I. R. R. 65.

The omission to take bonds with good and sufficient sureties, as required by law, may render the collector and his bondsmen liable. This duty is one which requires for its faithful performance the exercise of the utmost care, caution, diligence and vigilance. It is not a mere clerical duty; it is a duty to be performed not so much in the office as out of it. It is a duty which can only be performed by the collector himself, or by a trusted and experienced deputy for whose acts he is responsible. Of all duties it is the one which cannot be trusted to a mere subordinate. It is for the jury to decide whether the collector, in taking bonds, faithfully discharged the duties of his office. U. S. *v.* Thorn et al., 9 I. R. R. 65.

Deputy Collectors.

Sec. 10. *And be it further enacted,* That each collector shall be authorized to appoint, by an instrument of writing under his hand, as many deputies (*a*) as he may think proper, to be by him compensated for their services, and also to revoke any such appointment, giving such notice thereof as the Commissioner of Internal Revenue shall prescribe; and may require bonds or other securities, and accept the same, from such deputy; and each such deputy shall have the like authority, in every respect, to collect the duties and taxes levied or assessed within the portion of the district assigned to him which is by this act vested in the collector himself; but each collector shall, in every respect, be responsible both to the United States and to individuals, as the case may be, for all moneys collected, and for every act done by any of his deputies whilst acting as such, and for every omission of duty.

(*a*) Minors should not be appointed to office, for they cannot be bound by their bonds. 10 I. R. R. 6.

An inspector cannot act in the double capacity of inspector and deputy collector. 4 I. R. R. 181.

Who must make Returns.

Sec. 11. *And be it further enacted*, That it shall be the duty of any person, partnership, firm, association, or corporation, made liable to any duty, license, stamp, or tax imposed by law, when not otherwise provided for, on or before the first Monday of May in each year, and in other cases before the day of levy, to make a list or return, (*a*) verified by oath or affirmation, to the assistant assessor of the district where located, of the amount of annual income, the articles or objects charged with a special duty or tax, the quantity of goods, wares, and merchandise made or sold, and charged with a specific or ad valorem duty or tax, the several rates and aggregate amount, according to the respective provisions of this act, and according to the forms and regulations to be prescribed by the Commissioner of Internal Revenue, under the direction of the Secretary of the Treasury, for which such person, partnership, firm, association, or corporation is liable to be assessed.

(*a*) This section simply requires yearly returns of incomes and articles subject to taxation. Yearly returns were thought to be sufficient in ordinary cases. But there were persons from whom it was believed that more frequent returns ought to be required, and these were to be provided for in subsequent sections. U. S. *v.* Mountjoy, 3 I. R. R. 159.

No returns required by law, or the instructions to be sworn to, should be received or filed until they have been thus verified. 7 I. R. R. 187.

Revenue officers are not permitted to make any charge for preparing the papers which the law requires taxpayers to furnish, and all fees accepted for such services must be refunded. 10 I. R. R. 193.

The publication of the annual list of income returns is prohibited. The public may inspect the list. 11 I. R. R. 113.

Criminal proceedings should not be instituted against any person who has filed his application or made his return and has at all times stood ready to pay the tax upon demand. 6 I. R. R. 130.

All special taxes are to be reckoned from the first day of May, or from the time of commencing the business subject to the tax, to the first day of May following. 7 I. R. R. 58.

When Returns are to be made.

[SEC. 1. (March 2, 1867, as amended Feb. 3, 1868.) *Be it enacted, &c.*, That all acts in relation to the assessment, return, collection, and payment of the income tax, special tax, and other annual taxes now by law required to be performed in the month of May, shall hereafter be performed on the corresponding days in the month of March in each year; all acts required to be performed in the month of June, in relation to the collection, return, and payment of said taxes, shall hereafter be performed on the corresponding days of the month of April of each year.]

Duties of Assistant Assessors.

Sec. 12. *And be it further enacted*, That the instructions, regulations, and directions, as hereinbefore mentioned, shall be binding on each assessor and his assistants, and on each collector and his deputies, and on all other persons, in the performance of the duties enjoined by or under this act; pursuant to which instructions the said assessors shall, on the first Monday of May in each year, and from time to time thereafter, in accordance with this act, direct and cause the several assistant assessors (*a*) to proceed through every part of their respective districts, and inquire after and concerning all persons being within the assessment districts where they respectively reside, owning, possessing, or having the care or management of any property, goods, wares, and merchandise, articles or objects liable to pay any duty, stamp, or tax, including all persons liable to pay a license or other duty, under the provisions of this act, and to make a list of the owners, and to value and enumerate the said objects of taxation, respectively, by reference to any lists of assessment or collection taken under the laws of the respective States, to any other records or documents, to the written list, schedule, or return required to be made out and delivered to the assistant assessor, and by all other lawful ways and means, in the manner prescribed by this act, and in conformity with the regulations and instructions before mentioned.

(*a*) Assistant assessors should call personally upon those who have not returned their incomes as required by law. If any person is not at home when the assistant calls at any time after the first Monday in March, the notice on the back of Form 24 should be filled up and the blank left. It is then the duty of the taxpayer to seek the assistant assessor and deliver his return. 7 I. R. R. 58.

The assessor should give definite and positive instructions to his assistants in relation to their duties, never avoiding his proper responsibility.

The assistant assessor should implicitly obey all instructions given by the assessor to the end that there may be an exact uniformity of practice throughout the entire district. 7 I. R. R. 187.

Duties of Assistant Assessor where Parties give the necessary Information.

Sec. 13. *And be it further enacted,* That if any person liable to pay any duty or tax, or owning, possessing, or having the care or management of property, goods, wares, and merchandise, articles or objects liable to pay any duty, tax, or license, shall fail to make and exhibit a list or return required by law, but shall consent to disclose the particulars of any and all the property, goods, wares, and merchandise, articles and objects liable to pay any duty or tax, or any business or occupation liable to pay any license, as aforesaid, then, and in that case, it shall be the duty of the officer to make such list or return, which being distinctly read, consented to, and signed and verified by oath or affirmation by the person so owning, possessing, or having the care and management as aforesaid, may be received as the list of such person.

Proceedings in case of Failure to make Returns.

Sec. 14. (Amended March 3, 1865, § 1; July 13, 1866, § 9.) *And be it further enacted,* That in case any person shall be absent from his or her residence or place of business at the time an assistant assessor shall call for the annual list or return, and no annual list or return has been rendered by such person to the assistant assessor as required by law, it shall be the duty of such assistant assessor to leave at such place of residence or business, with some one of suitable age and discretion, if such be present, otherwise to deposit in the nearest post-office, a note or memorandum, addressed to such person, requiring him or her to render to such assistant assessor the list or return required by law within ten days from the date of such note or memorandum, verified by oath or affirmation.

And if any person, on being notified or required as aforesaid, shall refuse or neglect to render such list or return within the time required as aforesaid, or if any person, without notice as aforesaid, shall not deliver a monthly or other list or return at the time required by law, or if any person shall deliver or disclose to any assessor or assistant assessor any list, statement, or return which, in the opinion of the assessor, is false or fraudulent, or contains any understatement or undervaluation, it shall be lawful for the assessor (*a*) to summon such person, his agent, or other person having possession, custody, or care of books of account, containing entries relating to the trade or business of such person, or any other person he may deem proper, to appear before such assessor and produce such book, at a time and place therein named, and to give testimony or answer interrogatories, under oath or affirmation, respecting any objects liable to tax as aforesaid, or the lists, statements, or returns thereof, or any trade, business, or profession liable to any tax as aforesaid. And the assessor may summon, as aforesaid, any person residing or found within the State in which his district is situated. And when the person intended to be summoned does not reside and cannot be found within such State, the assessor may enter any collection district where such person may be found, and there make the examination hereinbefore authorized. And to this end he shall there have and may exercise all the power and authority he has or may lawfully exercise in the district for which he is commissioned.

The summons authorized by this section shall in all cases be served by an assistant assessor of the district where the person to whom it is directed may be found, by an attested copy delivered to such person in hand or left at his last and usual place of abode, allowing such person at the rate of one day for each twenty-five miles he may be required to travel, computed from the place of service to the place of examination; and the certificate of service signed by such assistant assessor shall be evidence of the facts it states on the hearing of an application for an attachment; and when the summons requires the production of books, it shall be sufficient if such books are described with reasonable certainty.

In case any person so summoned shall neglect or refuse to obey such summons, or to give testimony, or to answer interrogatories as required, it shall be lawful for the assessor to apply to the judge (*b*) of the district court, or to a commissioner of the circuit court of the United States for the district within which the person so summoned resides, for an attachment against such person as for a contempt. It shall be the duty of such judge or commissioner to hear such application, and, if satisfactory proof be made, to issue an attachment, directed to some proper officer, for the arrest of such person, and upon his being brought before him, to proceed to a hearing of the case; and upon such hearing the judge or commissioner shall have power to make such order as he shall deem proper, not inconsistent with the provisions of existing laws for the punishment of contempts, to enforce obedience to the requirements of the summons, and punish such person for his default or disobedience.

It shall be the duty of the assessor or assistant assessor of the district within which such person shall have taxable property to enter into and upon the premises, if it be necessary, of such person so refusing or neglecting, or rendering a false or fraudulent list or return, and to make, according to the best information which he can obtain, including that derived from the evidence elicited by the examination of the assessor, and on his own view and information, such list or return, according to the form prescribed, of the property, goods, wares, and merchandise, and all articles or objects liable to tax, owned or possessed or under the care or management of such person, and assess the tax thereon, including the amount, if any, due for special or income tax; and in case of the return of a false or fraudulent list or valuation, he shall add one hundred per centum (*c*) to such tax; and in case of a refusal or neglect, except in cases of sickness or absence, to make a list or return, or to verify the same as aforesaid, he shall add fifty per centum to such tax; and in case of neglect occasioned by sickness or absence as aforesaid, the assessor may allow such further time for making and delivering such list or return as he may judge necessary, not exceeding thirty days; and the amount so added to the tax shall, in all cases, be collected by the collector at the same time and in the same manner as the tax; and the list or return so made and subscribed by such assessor or assistant assessor shall be taken and reputed as good and sufficient for all legal purposes.

(*a*) A revenue agent is empowered to examine the books and papers of any person whom he may have reason to suspect of attempting to defraud the revenue. The assessor has also the right to examine books and papers, and he may also require their production by a writ of summons, and he may also summon parties and witnesses to appear before him to give testimony. His authority in this respect transcends that of a revenue agent. The two officers may proceed separately or together in the investigation of a case. When evidence is obtained, it is the duty of the assessor to judge of its value. The revenue agent cannot make an assessment If the assessor connives at fraud, or refuses to make an assessment which evidence clearly requires, or in any other respect fails in his duty, the revenue agent should report the delinquency to the Commissioner. 2 I. R. R. 84.

An assessor may compel a stockholder and the officers of a corporation to appear and produce testimony and books, so that he can estimate the amount of profits to which the stockholder is entitled. The summons must grow naturally out of some actual case of understatement, or some statement which is false in the opinion of the assessor. In such examination parties who have conscientious scruples in reference to taking an oath may affirm. 1 I. R. R. 172, 180.

The assessor may summon a party, and make an investigation into the truth of his return, even after the annual list is transmitted to the collector. 3 I. R. R. 150.

The summons is not required to be issued in order to enable the assessor to assess the legal penalties for neglect, refusal, or fraud in making returns, but may be resorted to if the assessor deem it advisable. The place where the investigation is to be made should be within the district of the assessor who issues the summons.

The provision of section 19 provides for the rates at which witnesses should be paid when attending the appeals of assessors. As the practice of paying witnesses is universal, there seems to be no violence done in construing section 19 as applicable to the cases of witnesses summoned under this section. Expenses of this character will have to be paid by the collector as disbursing agent. 2 I. R. R. 101.

The statute does not prescribe the form, or contents, or manner of service of the summons to be issued by the assessor. 10 I. R. R. 20.

The summons should state with reasonable certainty the cause of its being issued, as that the assessor is dissatisfied with the returns, or the like, and the subject-matter of the inquiry. It is not like a mere subpœna to an ordinary witness to appear and give evidence in court, because that refers to the case pending in court, and thus enables the witness to ascertain what is required of him. It should be sufficiently explicit to enable the person summoned to decide whether he is bound to appear or not. Lee *v.* Chadwick, 11 I. R. R. 133; In re Phillips, 10 I. R. R. 107; s. c. 2 A. L. T. (C. R.) 154; Perry *v.* Newcome, 10 I. R. R. 20.

When a person has appeared in obedience to the summons, and the subject of inquiry has been made known to him, he must answer, and cannot then object to the insufficiency of the summons. In re Phillips, 10 I. R. R. 107.

The issuing of the summons is not a judicial act. Congress, in using the word "summons," did not intend it to be of the legal dignity of a writ or other judicial process, but simply a notice, and similar in its nature to a summons issued by overseers of roads, requiring persons to attend with the necessary implements, and to work upon the public highways. In re Meador & Brothers, 10 I. R. R. 74; s. c. 2 A. L. T. (C. R.) 140; In re Doll, 11 I. R. R. 36.

The acts of Congress and of the legislatures of the various States, conferring power not only upon committees, but upon officers, to send for persons and papers to be examined in furtherance of a stated purpose, have been so long acquiesced in, and the power so frequently exercised, without the right having been seriously questioned in the courts, that the constitutionality of the grant of such power to an assessor can hardly be disputed now. Perry *v.* Newcome, 10 I. R. R. 20.

The statute authorizes the assessor to examine the taxpayer's books. This is its whole scope and purpose. To effectuate this object, it adds agents and all other persons having care, custody, or even possession of the books. It is impossible to misunderstand it. No doubt, the books of every person with whom the taxpayer deals contain some entries which relate to his business, and if every such person were summoned, it might be within the bounds of possibility to make up his income, more or less accurately, from a detail of all the bargains which he has made with others. But the law does not contemplate any such absurd mode of proceeding. The trade of each person is to be shown by his own books, and he or his agent, or other person having custody of them, must produce them; but it is not the intention of the law to require A to produce his own book in order to discover incidentally the trade of B, C, or D, who may have dealt with him. Lee *v.* Chadwick, 11 I. R. R. 133.

The grant of this power to the assessor is constitutional. The proceeding is a civil proceeding, and in nowise partakes of the character of a criminal prosecution. No offence is charged against the party summoned. There is no likeness in principle between the summons and either general warrants or writs of assistance. In re Meador & Brothers, 10 I. R. R. 74; s. c. 2 A. L. T. (C. R.) 140; In re Strouse, 11 I. R. R. 182; In re Doll, 11 I. R. R. 36.

The party must answer, even though his testimony may tend to criminate himself. The disclosures and admissions made in the course of such an examination cannot be used against the party in any criminal or *quasi* criminal prosecution. It is no objection that the answer may point to other information, not otherwise to be obtained, that may be used against him. In re Meador & Brothers, 10 I. R. R. 74; s. c. 2 A. L. T. (C. R.) 140; In re Phillips, 10 I. R. R. 107; s. c. 2 A. L. T. (C. R.) 54; In re Strouse, 11 I. R. R. 182; In re Doll, 11 I. R. R. 36; Stanwood *v.* J. & T. Green, 11 I. R. R. 134; *contra*, In re Lippman, 9 I. R. R. 1.

When the assessor issues a summons, and the party served neglects or refuses to appear to testify under oath, or to produce his books, &c., his power is exhausted. For remedy to compel compliance with the exigency of the summons, he must make application in the prescribed manner to a judge or a commissioner. In re Meador & Brothers, 10 I. R. R. 74; s. c. 2 A. L. T. (C. R.) 140; Lee *v.* Chadwick, 11 I. R. R. 133.

The assessor has no power to summon a party before him after he has transmitted his annual list to the collector; and a party so summoned is under no obligation to answer any question put to him. There should be some limit of time beyond which the inquisitorial power of the assessor to examine into all the private business transactions of every person should not be exercised. In re Brown, 3 I. R. R. 134.

No inquiry can be made in regard to returns that were rendered before the passage of this act. In re Brown, 3 I. R. R. 134.

The use of any entries in books and of any testimony given is solely to furnish evidence for making a true return. If there are no entries in any book of account in the possession, custody, or care of the party summoned relating to his trade or business during the period named in the summons, he is not bound to produce them. But if there are any such entries, he is bound to produce the books. He is not obliged to submit the books, or any of them, at once to the inspection of the assessor, or of any other person. The entries, and not the books, are the things sought for by the section. When the books are brought, the party summoned must appear with them, under the summons, to give testimony. He must then be asked whether there are any such entries as the summons specifies. If he says there are, he must then be asked to exhibit any entry or entries relating to a particular point or matter to be named in the inquiry within the scope of the summons as to subject-matter and time. Such inquiries must be answered. In re Lippman, 9 I. R. R. 1; In re Strouse, 11 I. R. R. 182.

(*b*) The provisions of this section are not inconsistent with other existing laws for the punishment of contempts. The question of contempt will only arise for consideration when some process or lawful command of the judge is disobeyed. In re Meador & Brothers, 10 I. R. R. 74; s. c. 2 A. L. T. (C. R.) 140.

A merely "imaginary case" for the exercise of this power to summon ought not to be countenanced. To institute a proceeding or action, not to determine a right or controversy, but to deceive the court and raise a prejudice against third persons, is a contempt. A public officer is presumed to act in obedience to his duty until the contrary appears. In re Meador & Brothers, 10 I. R. R. 74; s. c. 2 A. L. T. (C. R.) 140; In re Strouse, 11 I. R. R. 182; Stanwood v. J. & T. Green, 11 I. R. R. 134.

The judge need not in all cases proceed to hear the application *ex parte*, and issue or refuse the attachment, as may appear to be just on such hearing. The power to issue the attachment includes the power to notify the respondent to appear and show cause against it, whenever such a course seems most reasonable. Lee v. Chadwick, 11 I. R. R. 133.

The proceedings for the attachment may be quashed for irregularities apparent upon their face. In re Doll, 11 I. R. R. 36.

The petition for the attachment may be amended. The proceeding is a civil, and not a criminal or *quasi* criminal action. Lee v. Chadwick, 11 I. R. R. 133.

If a person is of the opinion that a demand upon him is not authorized by law, it is his right to refuse compliance until the question shall be determined by the proper tribunal, and in the mode prescribed by law, and his non-production of the books and papers under such circumstances is by no means to be taken as an indication that he has been guilty of any omission or violation of the law. No doubt the court has power to punish a willful neglect or refusal to testify in this as in all other cases, but no judge would fine or imprison a person for vindicating his supposed rights in good faith. Lee v. Chadwick, 11 I. R. R. 133; Stanwood v. J. & T. Green, 11 I. R. R. 134; s. c. 17 Pitts L. J. 153.

A supervisor of internal revenue may compel obedience to his summons in the same manner as an assessor. Perry v. Newcome, 10 I. R. R. 20; In re Meador & Brothers, 10 I. R. R. 74; s. c. 2 A. L. T. (C. R.) 140.

Quære. Can Congress invest the commissioner with the authority, in a proceeding originally instituted before him, to summarily commit a citizen for an alleged contempt? This is an exercise of the judicial power which under the Constitution cannot be intrusted to an officer appointed and holding his office in the manner in which commissioners are appointed and hold their offices. In re Doll, 11 I. R. R. 36.

No writ of error will lie to review the decision of the judge on this application for an attachment. In re Meador & Brothers, 10 I. R. R. 74; s. c. 2 A. L. T. (C. R.) 140.

There is no law which authorizes the payment of an assistant assessor's traveling expenses or any other pay while in attendance as a witness before a United States commissioner or United States court than the per diem and mileage allowed to ordinary witnesses. 11 I. R. R. 113.

(c) The penalty imposed by the provisions of this section applies only to returns which should be entered upon the annual list. The assessed penalty is to be assessed upon the amount of tax found to be due and forms a part of the tax to be paid by the taxpayer, no portion of which is to be awarded to an informer as compensation for his services. 3 I. R. R. 60.

The assessor has no discretion, but must add the prescribed penalty. 11 I. R. R. 106.

Returns to be made in Legal-Tender Currency.

[SEC. 3. (March 10, 1866, as amended July 13, 1866.) *And be it further enacted*, That it shall be the duty of all persons required to make returns or lists of income and articles or objects charged with an internal tax to declare in such returns or lists whether the several rates and amounts therein contained are stated according to their values (a) in legal-tender currency or according to their values in coined money; and in case of neglect or refusal so to declare to the satisfaction of the assistant assessor receiving such returns or lists, such assistant assessor is hereby required to make returns or lists for such persons so neglecting or refusing, as in cases of persons neglecting or refusing to make the returns or lists required by the acts aforesaid, and to assess the tax thereon, and to add thereto the amount of penalties imposed by law in cases of such neglect or refusal. And whenever the rates and amounts contained in the returns or lists as aforesaid shall be stated in coined money, it shall be the duty of each assessor receiving the same to reduce such rates and amounts to their equivalent in legal-tender currency, according to the value of such coined money in said currency for the time covered by such returns. And the lists required by law to be furnished to collectors by assessors shall in all cases contain the several amounts of taxes assessed, estimated, or valued in legal-tender currency only.]

(a) This section denies to a person who has received in coined money, incomes, or other moneys subject to tax or duty, the right to return the amount thereof in the currency in which it was actually received and to pay the tax or duty thereon in legal-tender currency. It requires that the difference between coined money and legal-tender currency shall be added to the return when made in coined money, and that he shall pay the tax or duty upon the amount thus increased. Congress may prescribe the basis, fix the rates, and require payment as it may deem proper. Within the limits of the Constitution it is supreme in its action. No power of supervision or control is lodged in either of the other departments of the government. Pacific Ins. Co. v. Soule, 9 I. R. R. 185.

Penalty for Fraudulent Returns.

Sec 15. *And be it further enacted*, That if any person shall deliver or disclose to any assessor or assistant assessor appointed in pursuance of law any false or fraudulent list, return, account, or statement, with intent to defeat or evade the valuation, enumeration, or assessment intended to be made, or if any person who, being duly summoned to appear to testify, or to appear and produce such books as aforesaid, shall neglect to appear or to produce said books, he shall, upon conviction thereof before any circuit or district court of the United States, be fined (a) in any sum not exceeding one thousand dollars, or be imprisoned for not exceeding one year, or both, at the discretion of the court, with costs of prosecution.

(a) This section applies to both yearly and monthly returns. U. S. v. Mountjoy, 3 I. R. R. 159.

When persons who are partners in business make and sign a false return in their partnership name, they may be jointly indicted. The return was their joint act. If the return is false, they committed a joint offence and may be jointly indicted. U. S. v. Mountjoy, 3 I. R. R. 159.

A party cannot be tried both for perjury and for a false return as to the same return. The government must elect as to which it will prosecute. U. S. v. Rumsey, 5 I. R. R. 93.

When the statute which created the offence is repealed, the crime and its penalty are abrogated. The offence is gone, and no one can be punished for what is not a crime at the time of punishment. Nothing is more certain than that if a statute creating an offence is repealed, all proceedings under it fall. The act is no longer an offence; it cannot be indicted; it cannot be punished; it is taken from the penal code absolutely. U. S. v. Finlay, 9 I. R. R. 99.

Neither the oath nor the subscription to the return are needed to constitute a fraudulent return. If a party makes a return, knowing its contents to be untrue, and intending that it shall be acted upon by the officers of the government, an indictment will lie. U. S. v. Bentz, 7 I. R. R 25.

A return upon an old form which is not in compliance with the present law and the forms prescribed thereunder is no return, and no indictment will lie for making it. U. S. v. Mountjoy, 4 I. R R. 9.

Other returns than that in which the indictment is founded are admissible in evidence to show the defendant's fraudulent intent in making that return. The several returns are parts of a connected series of transactions forming the general business of the defendant, and, so far from being foreign to the case, is what both parties ought to desire to produce as being best calculated to elucidate the truth and affording the defendant the best opportunity of vindicating himself if innocent of fraud. It is admissible to show that the return on which the indictment is founded is not exceptional. U. S. v. Rumsey, 5 I. R. R. 93.

The limitation of fifteen months contained in section 20 does not affect the enforcement of the penalty provided for in this section. The failure of the assessor to assess the 100 per cent. penalty under section 14 does not relieve the guilty party from prosecution and punishment. 6 I. R. R. 155.

When Property is owned by Parties who do not Reside in the District.

Sec. 16. *And be it further enacted,* That whenever there shall be in any assessment district any property, goods, wares, and merchandise, articles or objects, not owned or possessed by, or under the care or management of, any person within such district, and liable to be taxed as aforesaid, and no list of which shall have been transmitted to the assistant assessor in the manner provided by this act, it shall be the duty of the assistant assessor for such district to enter into and upon the premises where such property is situated, and take such view thereof as may be necessary, and to make lists of the same, according to the form prescribed, which lists being subscribed by the said assessor, shall be taken and reputed as good and sufficient lists of such property, goods, wares, and merchandise, articles or objects as aforesaid, for all legal purposes.

Duties of Parties who own Property out of their Collection District.

Sec. 17. *And be it further enacted,* That any owner or person having the care or management of property, goods, wares, and merchandise, articles or objects, not lying or being within the assessment district in which he resides, shall be permitted to make out and deliver the list thereof required by this act (provided the assessment district in which the said objects of duty or taxation are situated is therein distinctly stated), at the time and in the manner prescribed, to the assistant assessor of the assessment district wherein such person resides. And it shall be the duty of the assistant assessor who receives any such list to transmit the same to the assistant assessor where such objects of taxation are situate, who shall examine such list; and if he approves the same, he shall return it to the assistant assessor from whom he received it, with his approval thereof; and if he fails to approve the same, he shall make such alterations therein and additions thereto as he may deem to be just and proper, and shall then return the said list to the assistant assessor from whom it was received, who shall proceed, in making the assessment of the tax upon the list by him so received, in all respects as if the said list had been made out by himself.

Classification of Lists.

Sec. 18. *And be it further enacted,* That the lists (*a*) aforesaid shall, where not otherwise specially provided for, be taken with reference to the day fixed for that purpose by this act, as aforesaid; and where duties accrue at other and different times, the list shall be taken with reference to the time when said duties become due, and shall be denominated annual, monthly, and special lists. And the assistant assessors, respectively, after collecting the said lists, shall proceed to arrange the same, and to make two general lists—the first of which shall exhibit, in alphabetical order, the names of all persons, firms, companies, or corporations liable to pay any duty, tax, or license under this act, residing within the assessment district, together with the value and assessment or enumeration, as the case may require, of the objects liable to duty or taxation within such districts for which each such person is liable, or for which any firm, company, or corporation is liable, with the amount of duty or tax payable thereon; and the second list shall exhibit, in alphabetical order, the names of all persons residing out of the collection district who own property within the district, together with the value and assessment or enumeration thereof, as the case may be, with the amount of duty or tax payable thereon as aforesaid. The forms of the said general list shall be devised and prescribed by the assessor, under the direction of the Commissioner of Internal Revenue, and lists taken according to such forms shall be made out by the assistant assessors and delivered to the assessor within thirty days after the day fixed by this act as aforesaid, requiring lists from individuals; or where duties, licenses, or taxes accrue at other and different times, the lists shall be delivered from time to time, as they become due.

(a) 1st. Special lists create liability to error, and therefore should be used only upon urgent occasions; but every effort should be made to get every tax liable to be assessed into each successive regular list.

2d. After an assistant assessor has completed his list, he should number the pages, and then he should number the top of the back of each return, which is the foundation for a tax, to indicate the page and the line where the tax may be found on his list. For instance, for page 1, line 15, mark the return, 1—15; for page 7, line 29, mark the return, 7—29; and so of any other pages and lines. And the returns should be regularly filed according to their numbers when transmitted with the list to the assessor. The assistant assessor should never omit to present all the returns to the assessor, with the list containing the taxes.

3d. The assessor or his chief clerk (who should be perfectly well qualified if assigned to this duty) should examine each and every return with positive care, in order to determine the correctness of the principle upon which the tax is assessed, and as to whether the rate is correct, and whether the computation, extending, and transfer of result to the list are correct. The assessor should be satisfied that every individual tax which he commits to the collector is correct in every respect. If he has good reason to doubt the correctness of a tax as assessed by an assistant assessor, and no reason to fear ultimate loss to the Government, he should erase it from the list and suspend its assessment until his inquiries have satisfied him as to the proper manner in which the assessment should be made, or whether it should be made at all.

4th. The collector's list on Form 23 should be made up in the assessor's office. Duplicates of Form 97 should not be made on Form 23 by the assistant assessors. The original lists made by the assistant assessors, when corrected by the assessors, are the proper ones to be placed on file in the assessor's office. Some assessors have wasted much labor, which ought to have been devoted to other objects, in making up a very nice copy for this purpose.

5th. The time which taxes for business or occupation are to cover should be stated in the list. Returns on Form 11 should be taken in duplicate in all cases. One of them should be sent to the assessor with the list and filed with the other returns; the other should be marked on the back, "duplicate," and it may be given to the taxpayer to be handed to the collector, or deputy collector, as the case may be. On the back of all these returns, below the date, should be noted the list in which the tax will appear, thus, "Annual List, 1868," or "April List, 1868," or any other list, as the case may be.

6th. Each individual tax should not be extended into the total column on the list when there is more than one entry against the same party, but only the aggregate of them all.

7th. Footings of pages should be carried forward from page to page on the lists, Forms 23 and 97; but the footings of the several pages for each division should be recapitulated on the last page. Errors are much easier corrected in the latter than in the former case.

8th. The lists for each annual or monthly tax to be placed on file in the assessor's office, should be fastened together in book form, including the report on Form 58, if any, and any thing else that goes to make up the amount for which the receipt on Form 23½ is to be taken; and recapitulation of the aggregates of the several divisions, together with any other items included in the grand total, should be made on the last page, and the grand total aggregate should agree exactly with the receipts on Form 23½ taken therefor. When the receipts on Form 23½ are received from the collector, one of them should be attached to the end of book list near the recapitulation, unless a receipt is taken upon the list itself.

9th. Taxes on the list should never be separated on account of their peculiar character, but all taxes for each division of every name and nature that are to be covered by the same receipt, should be entered alphabetically. Articles taxed should always be described in the same language on the lists that they are in the law or schedule of rates.

10th. Immediately after each list has been committed to the collector, the assessor should inform each assistant assessor of all the errors found in his work therefor; and he should notify him of any and all changes therein, to the end that he may correct his work accordingly.

11th. All returns, lists, and records should be compared and proved by every practical method, and be checked so as to indicate what has been done.

12th. All returns for special tax for business or occupation should be carefully examined in the assessor's office, and entered into the special tax book in alphabetical order (for each division separately would be best) before the tax is committed to the collector. All changes in relation to these taxes should be carefully noted in the record book. Each party specially taxed in one year should be reported by the proper assistant assessor for the next year, either for taxation, or with the reason why no tax should be assessed, in order that the assessor may have his record full and complete for the entire district. The record should be examined each year, and memoranda made indicating that several parties have again been taxed, or showing the reason why they have not. 7 I. R. R. 187.

The annual list will include the annual taxes upon income and special taxes dating from May 1st in each year. These items, and no others, will be entered on the annual list.

Each assistant assessor should complete his annual list and forward it to the assessor on or before the last day of March in each year, and the complete list should be delivered by the assessor to the collector on or before the 30th day of April in each year. 8 I. R. R. 201.

All monthly returns must be made by the taxpayers on or before the 10th day of each month, and all quarterly returns, and all those for which no provision is otherwise made, must be made on or before the tenth day of the month in which the return is required, or succeeding the time when the tax is due and liable to be assessed. All these returns which can be collected by the assistant assessor by the 15th day of each month, should be put on the monthly list and forwarded to the assessor; and the assessor should complete and deliver his list to the collector on or before the 20th day of each month.

Whenever the assessor deems it advisable, or the taxpayer requests it, any return may be certified to the collector, either singly or upon a special list, in order that payment may be made sooner than if the return was delayed until the completion of the monthly list. Assessors should retain copies or other complete records of all such returns or lists certified to the collector, and will exercise the utmost care that all such assessments are entered on the next monthly list, and receipted for by the collector on Form 23¼.

Whenever a change of collectors occurs, the assessor should take receipts on Form 23¼ from the out-going collector, for all special returns or lists transmitted to him, and for the unassessed penalties collected by him since his last receipt Such assessments should not be included in the monthly list presented to the new collector. 8 I. R. R. 201.

Appeals to Assessors.

Sec. 19. (Amended July 13, 1866, §9.) *And be it further enacted,* That the assessor for each collection district shall give notice by advertisement (a) in one newspaper published in each county within said district, and if there be none published in the district, then in a newspaper published in the collection district adjoining thereto, and shall post notices in at least four public places within each assessment district, and shall mail a copy of such notice to each postmaster in his district, to be posted in his office, stating the time and place within said collection district when and where appeals will be received and determined relative to any erroneous or excessive valuations, assessments, or enumerations by the assessor or assistant assessor returned in the annual list, and such notice shall be advertised and posted by the assessor and mailed as aforesaid at least ten days before the time appointed for hearing said appeals. And it shall be the duty of the assessor for each collection district, at the time fixed for hearing such appeals as aforesaid, to submit the proceedings of the assessor and assistant assessor, and the annual lists taken and returned as aforesaid, to the inspection of any and all persons who may apply for that purpose.

And such assessor is hereby authorized at any time to hear and determine in a summary way, according to law and right, upon any and all appeals which may be exhibited against the proceedings of the said assessor or assistant assessors, and the office or principal place of business of the said assessor shall be open during the business hours of each day for the hearing of appeals by parties who shall appear voluntarily before him:

Provided, That no appeal shall be allowed to any party after he shall have been duly assessed, and the annual list containing the assessment has been transmitted to the collector of the district. And all appeals to the assessor as aforesaid shall be made in writing, and shall specify the particular cause, matter, or thing respecting which a decision is requested, and shall, moreover, state the ground or principle of error complained of. And the assessor shall have power to re-examine and determine upon the assessments and valuations, and rectify the same as shall appear just and equitable; but such valuation, assessment, or enumeration shall not be increased without a previous notice of at least five days to the party interested to appear and object to the same if he judge proper, which notice shall be in writing and left at the dwelling-house, office, or place of business of the party by such assessor, assistant assessor, or other person, or sent by mail to the nearest or usual post-office address of said party:

Provided further, That on the hearing of appeals it shall be lawful for the assessor to require by summons the attendance of witnesses and the production of books of account in the same manner and under the same penalties as are provided in cases of refusal or neglect to furnish lists or returns. The costs for the attendance and mileage of said witnesses shall be taxed by the assessor and paid by the delinquent parties, or by the disbursing agent for the district, on certificate of the assessor, at the rates allowed to witnesses in the district courts of the United States.

(a) The notice for receiving and determining appeals must be advertised in each county, and posted in each assessment district, as directed in this section. 8 I. R. R. 201.

The fees for witnesses are $1.50 per day and five cents per mile from the place of residence to the place of trial or hearing, and five cents per mile for returning. 10 Stat. 167. These fees are to be paid by the party who is found to be delinquent; otherwise by the disbursing agent for the district, on the certificate of the assessor. 8 I. R. R. 202.

The power conferred upon the assessor by this section to re-examine and determine assessments and valuations, and rectify the same, is confined to cases of appeal. An examination of the whole section shows clearly that it has reference only to appeals, and was not intended to be extended beyond. In re Brown, 3 I. R. R. 134.

Assessors to furnish Lists to Collectors.

Sec. 20. (Amended July 13, 1866, § 9.) *And be it further enacted,* That the assessor of each collection district shall, immediately after the expiration of the time for hearing appeals concerning taxes returned in the annual list, and from time to time, as taxes become liable to be assessed, make out lists containing the sums payable according to law upon every subject of taxation for each collection district; which list shall contain the name of each person residing within the said district, or owning or having the care or superintendence of property lying within the said district, or engaged in any business or pursuit which is liable to any tax, when such person or persons are known, together with the sums payable by each; and where there is any property within any collection district liable to tax, not owned or occupied by or under the superintendence of any person resident therein, there shall be a separate list of such property, specifying the sum payable, and the names of the respective proprietors when known.

And the assessor making out any such separate list shall transmit to the assessor of the district where the persons liable to pay such tax reside, or shall have their principal place of business, copies of the list of property held by persons so liable to pay such tax, to the end that the taxes assessed under the provisions of this act may be paid within the collection district where the persons liable to pay the same reside, or may have their principal place of business.

And in all other cases the said assessor shall furnish to the collectors of the several collection districts, respectively, within ten days after the time of hearing appeals concerning taxes returned in the annual list, and from time to time thereafter as required, a certified copy of such list or lists for their proper collection districts.

And in case it shall be ascertained that the annual list, or any other list, which may have been, or which shall hereafter be, delivered to any collector, is imperfect or incomplete in consequence of the omission of the names of any persons or parties liable to tax, or in consequence of any omission, or understatement, or undervaluation, or false or fraudulent statement contained in any return or returns made by any persons or parties liable to tax, the said assessor may, from time to time, or at any time within fifteen months (*a*) from the time of the passage of this act or from the time of the delivery of the list to the collector as aforesaid, enter on any monthly or special list the names of such persons or parties so omitted, together with the amount of tax for which they may have been or shall become liable, and also the names of the persons or parties in respect to whose returns, as aforesaid, there has been or shall be any omission, undervaluation, understatement, or false or fraudulent statement, together with the amounts for which such persons or parties may be liable, over and above the amount for which they may have been, or shall be, assessed upon any return or returns made as aforesaid, and shall certify or return said list to the collector as required by law.

And all provisions of law for the ascertainment of liability to any tax, or the assessment or collection thereof, shall be held to apply, as far as may be necessary, to the proceedings herein authorized and directed. And wherever the word "duty" is used in this act, or the acts to which this is an amendment, it shall be construed to mean "tax," whenever such construction shall be necessary in order to effect the purposes of said acts.

(*a.*) The investigation may be made at any time within fifteen months after the list is delivered to the collector, without regard to the year or time when the assessment was made. 4 I. R. R. 76.

Penalties against Assessors and Assistant Assessors.

Sec. 21. (Amended July 13, 1866, § 9.) *And be it further enacted,* That every assessor & assistant assessor who shall enter upon and perform the duties of his office without having taken the oath or affirmation prescribed by law, or who shall willfully neglect to perform any of the duties prescribed by this act at the time and in the manner herein designated, or who shall knowingly make any false or fraudulent list or valuation or assessment, or shall demand or receive any compensation, fee, or reward other than those provided for herein for the performance of any duty, or shall be guilty of extortion or willful oppression in office, shall, upon conviction thereof in any circuit or district court of the United States having jurisdiction thereof, be subject to a fine not exceeding one thousand dollars, or to imprisonment for not exceeding one year, or both, at the discretion of the court, and shall be dismissed from office, and shall be forever disqualified from holding any office under the government of the United States. And one-half of the fine so imposed shall be for the use of the United States, and the other half for the use of the informer, who shall be ascertained by the judgment of the court; and the said court shall also render judgment against the said assessor or assistant assessor for the amount of damages sustained in favor of the party injured, to be collected by execution.

Salaries of Assessors and Assistant Assessors.

Sec. 22. (Amended July 13, 1866, § 9; March 2, 1867, § 9.) *And be it further enacted,* That there shall be allowed and paid to the several assessors a salary of fifteen hundred dollars per annum, payable quarterly; and, in addition thereto, where the receipts of the collection district shall exceed the sum of one hundred thousand dollars, and shall not exceed the sum of four hundred thousand dollars, annually, one-half of one per centum upon the excess of receipts over one hundred thousand dollars. Where the receipts of a collection district shall exceed four hundred thousand dollars, and shall not exceed six hundred thousand, one-fifth of one per centum upon the excess of receipts over four hundred thousand dollars. Where the receipts shall exceed six hundred thousand dollars, one-tenth of one per centum upon such excess; but the salary of no assessor shall in any case exceed the sum of four thousand dollars.

And the several assessors shall be allowed and paid the sums actually and necessarily expended, with the approval of the Commissioner of Internal Revenue, for office rent; but no account (*a*) of such rent shall be allowed or paid until it shall have been verified in such manner as the Commissioner shall require, and shall have been audited and approved by the proper officers of the Treasury Department. And the several assessors shall be paid, after the account thereof shall have been rendered to and approved by the proper officers of the treasury, their necessary and reasonable charges for clerk-hire; but no such account shall be approved unless it shall state the name or names of the clerk or clerks employed, and the precise periods of time for which they were respectively employed, and the rate of compensation agreed upon, and shall be accompanied by an affidavit of the assessor stating that such service was actually required by the necessities of his office, and was actually rendered, and also by the affidavit of each clerk, stating that he has rendered the service charged in such account on his behalf, the compensation agreed upon, and that he has not paid, deposited, or assigned, or contracted to pay, deposit, or assign any part of such compensation to the use of any other person, or in any way, directly or indirectly, paid or given, or contracted to pay or give, any reward or compensation for his office or employment, or the emoluments thereof; and the chief clerk of any such assessor is hereby authorized to administer, (*b*) in the absence of the assessor, such oaths or affirmations as are required by this act.

And there shall be allowed and paid to each assistant assessor five dollars for every day actually employed in collecting lists and making valuations, the number of days necessary for that purpose to be certified by the assessor, and three dollars for every hundred persons assessed contained in the tax list, as completed and delivered by him to the assessor, and twenty-five cents for each permit granted for making tobacco, snuff, or cigars; and the said assessors and assistant assessors, respectively, shall be paid, after the account thereof shall have been rendered to and approved by the proper officers of the treasury, their necessary and reasonable charges for stationery and blank-books used in the discharge of their duties, and for postage actually paid on letters and documents received and sent, and relating exclusively to official business, and for money actually paid for publishing notices required by this act:

Provided, That no such account shall be approved unless it shall state the date and the particular item of every such expenditure, and shall be verified by the oath or affirmation of such assessor or assistant assessor ; and the compensation herein specified shall be in full for all expenses not otherwise particularly authorized :

Provided further, That the Commissioner of Internal Revenue may, under such regulations as may be established by the Secretary of the Treasury, after due public notice, receive bids and make contracts for supplying stationery, blank-books, and blanks to the assessors, assistant assessors, and collectors in the several collection districts :

Provided further, That the Secretary of the Treasury shall be, and he is hereby, authorized to fix such additional rates of compensation to be made to assessors and assistant assessors in cases where a collection district embraces more than a single congressional district, and to assessors and assistant assessors, revenue agents, and inspectors in Louisiana, Georgia, South Carolina, Alabama, Florida, Texas, Arkansas, North Carolina, Mississippi, Tennessee, California, Nevada, and Oregon, and the Territories, as may appear to him to be just and equitable, in consequence of the greater cost of living and traveling in those States and Territories, and as may, in his judgment, be necessary to secure the services of competent officers ; but the compensation thus allowed shall not exceed the rate of five thousand dollars per annum. Collectors of internal revenue acting as disbursing officers shall be allowed all bills of assistant assessors heretofore paid by them in pursuance of the directions of the Commissioner of Internal Revenue, notwithstanding the assistant assessor did not certify to hours therein, or that two dollars per diem was deducted from his salary or compensation before computation of the tax thereon.

(*a*) The assessor's quarterly account, Form 82, must be transmitted to the Commissioner of Internal Revenue within fifteen days after the close of each quarter. Assessors will debit the United States as follows:

Salary (gross amount).
Commissions.
Clerk-hire.
Office rent.
Postage.
Express charges.
Stationery and blank-books.
Advertising and printing.

Assistant assessor's account for postage and stationery on Form 84.
Expenses of surveying distilleries.

They will credit the United States as follows:
Salary received of disbursing agent.
Clerk-hire received of disbursing agent.
Amount of tax on salary.

The several charges must, in all cases (except for salary and clerk-hire) be accompanied by the vouchers, regularly filled up and numbered and indorsed to correspond with the names and numbers in the account. All bills should be made out against the assessors in their official capacity.

Any accounts and vouchers which are not plainly and correctly stated, and properly receipted, will be suspended and returned for correction. If suspended, corrected vouchers must be furnished with the next quarterly account.

The law allows commissions to assessors on the excess over $100,000 of the receipts on the assessments for each fiscal year. The amount thus collected is taken from the collector's statement on Form 51, and is certified by the Commissioner to the Fifth Auditor. If the statements on Form 51 are not promptly and correctly made, the adjustment of assessor's commissions must necessarily be delayed, except in those districts where the receipts are known to be $1,200,000 or upward per annum.

The additional commission of one-fourth of one per centum on distilled spirits produced subsequent to July 20th, 1868, will be allowed only as provided by section 28, act July 20, 1868, upon the adjustment of the collector's account, and when he shall have returned the books of marginal stubs to the Commissioner of Internal Revenue, and shall have accounted for the tax on the number of gallons represented on the stamps and coupons that were contained in said books.

The proper vouchers for postage are the receipted bills of the postmaster, showing the number and amount of each denomination of stamps purchased during the quarter, and the date of purchase. The bills of assistant assessors for postage must be accompanied by the receipt of the postmaster, and be rendered on Form 84. In all cases the actual number of each denomination of stamps used and on hand must be stated.

Receipted bills, as vouchers, will be required for all payments made by assessors on packages forwarded or received by express.

Payments made for express charges during the quarter may be entered in one bill, with date and amount of each payment duly receipted by the agent of the express company; or the assessor may make his bill of the same items, which, with his receipt and the certificate of said agent that the bill has been by him compared with the accounts of the express company, and is correct, and has been paid, will be a sufficient voucher.

Notices of appeals should be published in only one newspaper in any county, as provided in section 19; but whenever a district is wholly within one county, as in New York and some other cities, said notice may be published in two newspapers.

The first voucher for office rent must be accompanied by the assessor's statement of the number and size of the room occupied by him as an office, with the name and number of the street, if any, where the same is located, and in what story of the building.

If the assessor is interested, directly or indirectly, in the building in which his office is situated, and in other cases when required, the vouchers for rent must be accompanied by the certificates of two disinterested persons of some official standing, stating their opinions as to the rent charged as compared with other rents in the same locality. No payments will be made to assessors for furniture, or rent of furniture, or for fuel and lights.

Vouchers for clerk-hire must be rendered as prescribed in Form 54, and they will be paid monthly by the collector, as disbursing agent of the district, to the assessor, or on his order to the clerk rendering the bill, after the estimate for the same has been made and approved by the proper officers of the Treasury Department.

Stationery and postage-stamps will be furnished to assistant assessors by assessors as far as practicable. When assistants find it necessary to purchase for immediate use, it must be done in limited quantities, and vouchers for the same must be furnished to the assessors, with their accounts, on Form 84. These vouchers must state date, quantity, and price of each article named. Assistant assessors will apply to their assessors for blanks and blank-books required by them.

The bills of assessors for surveying distilleries must be substantiated by a voucher for each expenditure, except for fare by railway, or other public conveyance, and for meals while traveling. The distilleries surveyed must be named, and the places visited stated, and the items of each day's expenses. Charges for travel by railway, or other public conveyance, must name the conveyance and the distance traveled.

An assessor going out of office will transfer to his successor all blanks, blank-books, stationery, postage-stamps, stamped envelopes, and all other property belonging to the Government, and must file with his final account an inventory thereof, in detail, with the receipt of his successor therefor. 11 I. R. R. 83.

An assistant assessor acting as assessor is not entitled to the fees and emoluments of an assessor, but only to the compensation allowed to him as assistant assessor. 5 I. R. R. 125.

(*b*) The chief clerk of an assessor is authorized to administer such oaths and affirmations, and such only, as the assessor might administer if present, but this can be done only when the assessor is absent; and the absence should appear upon the certificate, as also the fact that the clerk is the chief clerk of the particular assessor. 2 I. R. R. 2.

Penalties against Assessors for receiving Money for Appointment of Assistant Assessors.

Sec. 23. *And be it further enacted,* That if any assessor shall demand of, or receive directly or indirectly from, any assistant assessor, as a condition of his appointment to or continuance in his said office of assistant assessor, any portion of the compensation herein allowed such assistant assessor, or any other consideration, such assessor so offending shall be summarily dismissed from office, and shall be liable to a fine of not less than five hundred dollars upon conviction of said offence in any district or circuit court of the United States of the district in which such offence may be committed.

Accounts of Assistant Assessors.

Sec. 24. (Amended July 13, 1866, § 9; March 2, 1867, § 9.) *And be it further enacted,* That assistant assessors shall make out their accounts (*a*) for pay and charges allowed by law monthly, specifying each item and including the date of each day of service, and shall transmit the same, verified by oath or affirmation, to the assessor of the district, who shall thereupon examine the same, and, if it appear just and in accordance with law, he shall indorse his approval thereon, but otherwise shall return the same with objections. Any such account so approved may be presented by the assistant assessor to the collector of the district for payment, who shall thereupon pay the same, and, when receipted by the assistant assessor, be allowed therefor upon presentation to the Commissioner of Internal Revenue. Where any account, so transmitted to the assessor, shall be objected to, in whole or in part, the assistant assessor may appeal to the Commissioner of Internal Revenue, whose decision on the case shall be final.

And should it appear at any time that any assessor has knowingly or negligently approved any account, as aforesaid, allowing any assistant assessor a sum larger than was due according to law, it shall be the duty of the Commissioner of Internal Revenue, upon proper proof thereof, to deduct the sum so allowed from any pay which may be due to such assessor; or the Commissioner, as aforesaid, may direct a suit to be brought in any court of competent jurisdiction against the assessor or assistant assessor in default for the recovery of the amount knowingly or negligently allowed, as hereinbefore mentioned:

Provided, That in calculating the commissions of assessors and collectors of internal revenue in districts whence cotton or distilled spirits or other articles are shipped in bond to be sold in another district, one-half the amount of tax received on the quantity of cotton or spirits or other articles so shipped shall be added to the amount on which the commissions of such assessors and collectors are calculated, and a corresponding amount shall be deducted from the amount on which the commissions of the assessors and collectors of the districts to which such cotton or spirits or other articles are shipped are calculated.

(*a*) The bill of assistant assessors to be paid by disbursing agents, will include the per diem compensation and the three dollars per hundred persons assessed, and nothing else.

These bills must be made out in duplicate on Form 57, with all the blanks properly filled, and be scheduled on Form 56, with the vouchers for each month's service arranged by themselves, and in the order of the divisions according to the numbers on the Form, and all the columns footed. Assistant assessors will not be allowed for Sundays. In making charges for persons assessed on any list, each person will be counted but once, although his name may be repeated several times on the list.

The bills of assistant assessors must be completed in all respects (except the receipt of the assistant assessor) before coming into the hands of the assessor, and should be certified by him only in case they "appear to be just and in accordance with law." The assessor will be held to a strict accountability for his action; and before approving of the bill of an assistant assessor, should satisfy himself—

1. That the number of days charged are not disproportionate to the amount of work performed.
2. That the amount and names assessed are entered in the proper blanks.
3. That only the days upon which service was performed are entered, and the proper salary tax extended.
4. That the affidavit of the assistant assessor is legally executed.

It is the duty of the collector to see—

1. That the assistant assessor rendering the bill has been duly qualified.
2. That the certificate of the assessor has been properly filled, the amount for which he certifies being written in the body of the certificate.
3. That the bill is receipted by the assistant assessor.

If the collector knows or has reason to believe the account to be erroneous, he should refer the same to the Commissioner, stating his reasons for so doing, and should inform the assistant assessor of his action. When the disbursing agent of a district has paid a bill of an assistant assessor which shows upon its face that no names are added to the list, or that the amount of the bill is disproportionate to the amount assessed, the amount so paid will be passed to the credit of the disbursing agent, and be deducted from the salary or commissions of the assessor, unless he furnishes by indorsement upon the bill satisfactory reasons for the omission of names, or for the apparent disproportion between the amount of the bill and the amount of service rendered. If no indorsement is made by the assessor on the first presentation of the bill, the collector should return it to him to afford him an opportunity for explanation.

Claims of assistant assessors, other than for the per diem compensation and for persons assessed, should not be put on Form 57 or paid by the collector, but be sent to the assessor, and if correct, should be included in his quarterly accounts.

In case of the death of an assistant assessor the amount due him may be paid to his executor or administrator by whom the bills should be receipted. Such bills must be accompanied by certified copies of the letters of administration or letters testamentary under which the executor or administrator acts. The certificate of the assessor must be filled up as usual, and the blank for the assistant's oath should be filled, if possible, by some responsible person other than the assessor having knowledge of the service performed. 11 I. R. R. 83.

The ordinary work upon lists after they have been returned by the assistant assessor to the assessor does not form any part of the duty or labor of collecting lists and making valuations. Charges for such clerical services should not be allowed. Whenever it appears that an assessor has approved any voucher for such clerical services, the amount of payment thereon should be charged to the account of such assessor and deducted from any sum due him for salary and commissions 10 I. R. R. 6.

When the number of names reported upon an assistant assessor's account is small, or when the amount assessed is not six times as great as the amount charged for services, the assessor should indorse the reasons for his approval upon the account. All valuable services rendered in the line of duty should be paid for, whether such services increase the lists or not. 11 I. R. R. 50.

While collectors as disbursing agents are authorized to pay the accounts of assistant assessors when certified by the assessor, it does not follow that they are to pay any thing and every thing so certified. If the certified account contains illegal charges, or does not in other respects conform to the law, it is the duty of the disbursing agent to reject it, or to pay only such items and such amounts as are authorized by law. When a disbursing officer has made an error, he should correct it when making the next payment, or call upon the assistant assessor to correct it. 3 I. R. R. 133.

Compensation of Collectors.

Sec. 25. (Amended March 3, 1865, § 1.) *And be it further enacted*, That there shall be allowed to collectors, in full compensation for their services and that of their deputies, a salary of fifteen hundred dollars per annum, to be paid quarterly, and, in addition thereto, a commission of three per centum upon the first hundred thousand dollars, and a commission of one per centum upon all sums above one hundred thousand dollars and not exceeding four hundred thousand dollars, and a commission of one-half of one per centum on all sums above four hundred thousand dollars and not exceeding one million of dollars, and one-eighth of one per centum on all sums above one million of dollars, such commissions to be computed upon the amounts by them respectively collected and paid over and accounted for under the instructions of the Treasury Department.

And there shall be further paid, after the account (*a*) thereof has been rendered to and approved by the proper officers of the treasury, to each collector his necessary and reasonable charges for advertising, stationery, and blank-books used in the performance of his official duties, and for postage actually paid on letters and documents received or sent, and exclusively relating to official business; but no such account shall be approved unless it shall state the date and the particular items of every such expenditure, and shall be verified by the oath or affirmation of the collector: *And provided*, That the Secretary of the Treasury be authorized to make such further allowances, from time to time, as may be reasonable in cases in which, from the territorial extent of the district, or from the amount of internal duties collected, or from other circumstances, it may seem just to make such allowances.

(*a*) Collectors are required to render two quarterly accounts—a revenue account and a compensation account.

The *revenue account* must be rendered on Form 79, within fifteen days after the close of each quarter; in this account the collector will debit the United States with—

1. The balance due the collector per last account rendered.
2. Errors in former accounts.
3. Money deposited to the credit of the Treasurer of the United States during the quarter.
4. Orders for abatement of taxes issued by the Commissioner of Internal Revenue during the quarter.
5. Amount of taxes collected by successor on lists receipted for by himself.
6. Amount of taxes collected by predecessor on lists receipted for by himself.

7. Amount of 7½ per cent. discount on beer stamps sold during the quarter (this will be the aggregate of amounts reported on Form 103, for each month of the quarter).

8. Amount of stamps and coupons returned to the Commissioner during the quarter.

9. Amount of beer stamps, spirit stamps, tobacco and cigar stamps transferred to successor in office.

10. Balance due the United States, viz.,
    Cash.
    Tobacco and cigar stamps on hand.
    Spirit stamps on hand.
    Beer stamps on hand.
    Uncollected taxes.

These amounts will agree with the balances reported on Forms 49, 76, 90, 103, and 51, respectively.

He will credit the United States with

11. The balance due the United States per last account rendered.
12. Errors in former accounts.
13. Taxes collected on lists receipted for by predecessor in office.
14. Taxes collected on lists receipted for by successor in office.
15. The annual and monthly lists receipted for on Form 23¼.
16. The amount of beer stamps, and tobacco and cigar stamps received during the quarter.
17. The amount of stamps for distilled spirits received, and excess of gaugers' fees collected during the quarter.

The balance due the collector will be the collections made upon some list not receipted for by him during the quarter.

Under the head of cash deposited, no amount should be included unless the certificate of deposit for the same is dated within the quarter covered by the account.

If any item should accidentally be omitted in any account rendered, it may be entered upon a subsequent account under "Errors in former account."

A schedule of the certificates of deposit for the quarter must be forwarded with each quarterly account, showing the date, number, and amount of each certificate, the place of deposit, and the sum of the whole. The schedule may be readily made by copying the monthly returns on Form 49, with a recapitulation aggregating the three months.

The compensation and expense account must be rendered on Form 91, within fifteen days after the close of each quarter. In this account the collector will debit the United States with

1. His quarterly salary in gross.
2. Commissions for the quarter in gross.
3. Stationery and blank books.
4. Postage.
5. Express charges, and expenses for depositing money.
6. Advertising.

He will credit the United States with

1. The amount received from the collector acting as disbursing agent for salary.
2. The amount received for commissions.
3. The tax on salary.
4. The tax on commissions as shown by Form 63.

A statement of the expenses of administering the office should be made on Form 63, and forwarded with the account. The object of this statement is to enable the auditing officers to ascertain what portion of the commission is subject to tax; it should include only payments for deputies, clerks, rent, fuel, and lights. The name of each deputy and clerk must be given, together with the rate and amount of his compensation.

Commissions for the quarter should be calculated on the amount deposited to the credit of the Treasurer of the United States during the quarter, in the following manner, viz.:

Three per cent. on the first $25,000, one per cent. on the next $75,000, one-half of one per cent. on the next $150,000, and one-eighth of one per cent. on all over $250,000.

The commissions for the second and third quarters of the fiscal year will be computed the same as for the first quarter, and at the end of the fiscal year, a readjustment will be made at the rates prescribed by law for the year, and the amount found due passed to the credit of the collector. The commission for the fraction of a quarter should be computed in the following manner:

As the number of days in the quarter is to the number of days of service, so is $25,000 to the amount upon which commissions should be computed at three per cent.; three times the amount upon which commissions are to be computed at three per cent. will be the amount upon which commissions should be computed at one per cent.; twice the amount upon which commissions are to be computed at one per cent. will be the amount upon which commissions are to be computed at one half of one per cent.; and the remainder will be the amount upon which commissions should be computed at one-eighth of one per cent.

The additional commissions of one-fourth of one per cent. on distilled spirits produced subsequent to July 20, 1868, will be allowed as provided by section 28, Act July 20, 1868, upon the adjustment of the collector's account, and when he shall have returned the books of marginal stubs to the Commissioner, and shall have accounted for the tax on the number of gallons represented on the stamps and coupons that were contained in said books.

Assessors and collectors should make requisitions for stationery quarterly, when necessary, on Form 2, and are expected to include therein all articles that will be required for themselves and their deputies or assistants during the quarter for which the requisition is made. Supplemental requisitions for any quarter will not be approved except in extraordinary cases, when, for any reason, other than neglect, it becomes necessary; limited quantities may be purchased for immediate use until a requisition can be filled? Officers are authorized to purchase ink and mucilage, and their bills, if reasonable, will be allowed. Collectors are authorized to furnish store-keepers with such articles of stationery as they may require for their official duties.

Gaugers will be supplied with stationery at the expense of the United States.

Vouchers for stationery, blank books, postage, expressage, depositing money and advertising, must be entered on Form 85, and the affidavit on the Form must be made. The bills must, in all cases, be made out in detail, showing the date, price, quantity, and character of each article purchased or expense incurred, and be receipted. Bills given by a firm must be receipted by a member of the firm; the receipt of a clerk will not be accepted; express bills may be receipted by a regular agent of the company. The proper vouchers for postage are the receipted bills of the postmaster; these should show in detail the date, number, and amount of each kind of stamps purchased during the quarter. The receipt of a deputy collector for postage will not be accepted unless accompanied by the receipted bill of a postmaster; in all cases, the actual number of each denomination of stamps used and on hand must be stated with the bills.

Bills for depositing money will not be allowed to the collector unless he shows that it was impossible for him to deposit through the express companies under contract with the Treasury Department. Should it be impossible for a collector to deposit through such express companies, he must send the money to the depositary in the cheapest manner consistent with safety; the bills should show the amount deposited, the rates charged per thousand, and the points between which it was transported.

Collectors should, as far as possible, supply their deputies with stationery and postage stamps; when deputies are compelled to purchase for immediate use they must obtain receipted bills made out in detail. The same are required of the collector. These should be given to the collector.

Assessors and collectors must notify the Commissioner of all advertisements which they deem necessary to have published in their several districts, excepting such as are specially required by law, stating the number of newspapers in which they propose to have the same published, with the number of insertions and cost of the same; manuscript copies of all hand-bills or other matter not specially required by law must also be submitted to the Commissioner, with a statement of the quantity and cost of printing. The approval of the Commissioner must be obtained before any engagement for such advertising or printing is made, and the date of the letter authorizing the same must be indorsed on the vouchers, or a copy of the letter attached thereto.

Vouchers for advertising and printing must be accompanied by copies of the advertisements and the advertising rates of each paper, and printed copies of hand-bills and other printed matter.

Blanks and blank books will be furnished to assessors and collectors by the Commissioner.

No bill for printing blank forms, circulars, or blank books, or for binding will be approved, unless authority for the same is first obtained from the Commissioner and a copy of the letter giving the authority is filed with the voucher. Assessors and collectors, however, are authorized to have their assessment lists and Internal Revenue Record bound in an economical manner for preservation and reference, and the bills therefor will be approved without special permission by letter for the same.

Charges for furniture, gold pens, penknives, and for expenses of fitting up offices will not be allowed to collectors or assessors.

Assessors and collectors will, at the close of each fiscal year, and at such other times as may be required, render to the Commissioner an account or statement showing:

1st. The kind and quantity of stationery, blank books, postage stamps, and stamped envelopes on hand at the close of the preceding year.

2d. The kind and quantity received and purchased by them during the year for themselves and their subordinates.

3d. The quantity of each kind used by themselves and furnished to their subordinates.

4th. The amount of each kind on hand at the time of rendering the statement.

This statement should be in such detail as to show the quantity and character of each class of stationery, etc.

A collector, on going out of office, must transfer to his successor all blanks, blank books, stationery, postage stamps, stamped envelopes, and all other property in his possession, and must file with his final account, on Form 91, an inventory thereof, with the receipt of his successor therefor.

Assessors and collectors must retain in their offices duplicates of all accounts, schedules, abstracts, and vouchers which they send to the Commissioner.

All accounts transmitted by the assessor or the collector should be dated and signed by the officer who sends them. All the schedules or abstracts should show the number of the district and the name of the officer. 11 I. R. R. 81.

1. All such collectors of internal revenue as the Secretary of the Treasury may direct to act as disbursing agents—to pay the lawful expenses incident to carrying into effect the various acts relative to the assessment and collection of internal revenues—shall discharge their duties as such disbursing agents without increased compensation therefor, and give good and sufficient bonds and securities for the faithful performance of their duties as such disbursing agents in such sum and form as shall be prescribed by the First Comptroller of the Treasury and approved by the Secretary of the Treasury.

2. To meet the payments for the expenses of assessing and collecting the internal revenue in the several districts, money will be transmitted to the duly constituted disbursing agents of said districts at stated periods from appropriations in the United States Treasury.

3. The estimates of amounts required to defray the expenses in the said district, should be ascertained with judgment, and carefully prepared and transmitted monthly in advance to the Secretary of the Treasury. An account current, showing accurately the disbursements of such money for the preceding month, should in all cases accompany this estimate.

The Secretary of the Treasury will transmit these estimates of expenses to the Commissioner, who should carefully scrutinize them; if the proposed expenditures are found to be authorized, and judicious in amount the Commissioner should send these estimates for the proper amount to the First Comptroller of the Treasury, which estimates, if found to be correct by that officer, should be transmitted to the Secretary of the Treasury for warrants to be issued for the money. 2 I. R. R. 4.

The estimates of collectors, acting as disbursing agents, on Form 42, are to be made out monthly and transmitted to the Secretary of the Treasury on or before the 5th day of each month.

They will be for the amounts required to pay the salaries of the assessor and collector, the pay of assistant assessors, storekeepers and assessors' clerks, for the current month, and the commissions of the collector for the previous month.

The assessor will make to the collector, before the first of each month, a statement showing the amount needed to pay his clerk hire and assistant assessors for that month.

Disbursing agents will use the first column for dollars and cents in filling out the amount under each head, leaving the last column blank, to be filled out by the Commissioner, and will, as nearly as possible, enter the exact amount required.

The net amount of the salaries of assessor and collector, and of the pay of assistant assessors and storekeepers, must be entered under their respective headings.

Any balance of the disbursing fund remaining on hand should be deducted from the total of the estimate.

The amount on which commissions should be computed by collectors is the amount actually deposited during the previous month, and may often differ from the amount passed upon by the Commissioner, from the fact that all the certificates of deposit may not reach him during the month in which the deposits are made; the difference will be passed to the credit of the collector upon the quarterly adjustment of his compensation account. (Form 91.)

In estimating collectors' commissions the following rule should be observed:

For one month the limit is three per cent. on the first $8,333⅓, *one per cent. on the next* $25,000, *one-half of one per cent. on the next* $50,000, *and one-eighth of one per cent. on all over* $83,333⅓.

By a ruling of the accounting officers of the Treasury Department there will be withheld, on monthly estimates, ten per cent. of the amount of commissions computed for the first and second months of a quarter and the total commissions for the third month of the quarter until the adjustment of the quarterly account. The amount allowed on estimates is regarded simply as an advance on account,—for instance, on the estimate for February, ten per cent. of the commissions for January; on the estimate for March, ten per cent. of the commissions for February; and on the estimate for April the total commissions for March will be withheld. The total amount thus withheld will be allowed and passed to the credit of the collector on the adjustment of his compensation account (Form 91) for the quarter ending March, and he will be paid the same on the next estimate passed upon.

Promptness on the part of assessors in reporting to collectors, and on the part of collectors in forwarding their estimates to the Secretary of the Treasury, will insure promptness in the transmittal of their drafts.

The salary of an assessor or collector, by law, is $1,500 per annum or $375 per quarter, and the amount due per month will bear the same proportion to $375 that the number of days in the month bears to the number of days in the quarter.

In making payments to the collector and assessor for salary, and to assistant assessors and storekeepers, collectors acting as disbursing agents will pay only the net amount due in all cases. No tax should be deducted from the collector's commissions, as the amount of tax thereon will be adjusted in the settlement of the collector's compensation account (Form 91.)

No salary tax will be withheld from payments made to assessors' clerks, or from payments by collectors to their clerks or deputies, because they are not regarded as government officers in such a sense as to require the tax to be retained from their salaries; they should return the salaries thus received with their other income to be taxed on the annual list.

No deposit should be made for tax on salaries, nor any entry be made of the same on the account current. The amount found due, when the accounts are adjusted, will be transferred on the books of the Treasury to the credit of internal revenue.

The monthly account current (Form 44) should be transmitted to the Commissioner on or before the tenth day of each month, and should be made out for the month for which the estimate is made out and not for the month in which the disbursements were made,—for example, in Form 44, for March, the United States should be charged with—

1. Assessor's salary for March.
2. Amount paid assistant assessor for March.
3. Amount paid storekeepers for March.
4. Assessor's clerk hire for March.
5. Collector's salary for March.
6. Amount paid collector for commissions on amount deposited in February.
7. Any expenses that may have been ordered to be paid.

The United States should be credited with—

1. The balance from month of February (if any).
2. The draft sent for the amount allowed on the estimate for March.

This is the regular form of the account, and it will be readily seen that the object is to account for each separate draft each month; this necessitates prompt rendering of all bills of assistant assessors, storekeepers and assessors' clerks, as well as prompt payment; hence, assessors will see that all bills, which must be approved by them, are promptly made out and forwarded to the collector for payment. If, by any unavoidable delay, it should happen that bills for services rendered in any month could not be paid until after the Form (44) for that month had been made out and forwarded, they should be entered in the first (Form 44) made out after they are paid, but no efforts should be spared to have all bills paid and entered in the account to which they belong.

When bills are presented by assistant assessors, storekeepers, assessors or assessors' clerks for payment, which are for services in months or part of months covered by former accounts rendered by the collector, the collector must certify on the face of each voucher "not charged in any former account current." In no case should a duplicate charge be made in accounts current.

This account, accompanied by the proper vouchers and abstracts, should be sent promptly at the time prescribed; negligence or delay on the part of the collector in forwarding the same will cause delay in sending his draft, and may cause the total amount of his estimate to be rejected, if the records in the office of the Commissioner show a sufficient amount of money in his hands. 11 I. R. R. 82.

No appeal lies to the Secretary of the Treasury from the decision of the accounting officers upon the collector's account as disbursing agent. 3 I. R. R. 133.

Apportionment of Commissions.

Sec. 26. (Amended March 3, 1865, § 1; July 13, 1866, § 1.) *And be it further enacted,* That in the adjustment of the accounts of assessors and collectors of internal revenue which shall accrue after the thirtieth of June, eighteen hundred and sixty-four, and in the payment of their compensation for services after that date, the fiscal year of the treasury shall be observed; and where such compensation, or any part of it, shall be by commissions upon assessments or collections, and shall during any year, in consequence of a new appointment, be due to more than one assessor or collector in the same district, such commissions shall be apportioned (a) between such assessors or collectors; but in no case shall a greater amount of the commissions be allowed to two or more assessors or collectors in the same district than is or may be authorized by law to be allowed to one assessor or collector. And the salary and commissions of assessors and collectors heretofore earned and accrued shall be adjusted, allowed, and paid in conformity to the provisions of this section, and not otherwise; but no payment shall be made to assessors or collectors on account of salaries or commissions without the certificate of the Commissioner of Internal Revenue that all reports required by law or regulation have been received, or that a satisfactory explanation has been rendered to him of the cause of the delay.

(*a*) The apportionment should be based upon the amount collected, and the time served by each collector respectively, giving each collector commissions on his collections at each of the different rates prescribed by law on an amount proportionate to the whole amount for the fiscal year, according to the proportion his term of service bears to the whole year; taking care that no collector, from the comparatively large amount of his collections in proportion to his time, shall be given a lower rate of commissions than another until the full amount for the year at the higher rates shall have been exhausted; so that the several collectors in office in the same district during the same fiscal year shall receive precisely the same amount of commissions that one would have been entitled to on the same aggregate collections for the year. 11 I. R. R. 82.

Receipts to be given by Collectors.

Sec. 27. *And be it further enacted,* That each collector, on receiving, from time to time, lists and returns from the said assessors (*a*) shall subscribe three receipts: one of which shall be made upon a full and correct copy of each list or return, and be delivered by him to, and shall remain with, the assessor of his collection district, and shall be open to the inspection of any person who may apply to inspect the same; and the other two shall be made upon aggregate statements of the lists or returns aforesaid, exhibiting the gross amount of taxes to be collected in his collection district, one of which aggregate statements and receipts shall be transmitted to the Commissioner of Internal Revenue, and the other to the First Comptroller of the Treasury.

(*a*) All assessors in the several districts, at the close of each month, should transmit severally to the First Comptroller of the Treasury, and to the Commissioner, statements showing the true amount of the assessments certified by them to the collectors of their several districts for collection. 2 I. R. R. 4.

On or before the 15th day of each month, the collector should make out and furnish to the assessor a detailed statement, on Form 58, of all unassessed penalties and interest received by him during the calendar month next preceding, including all shares of penalties belonging to the Government, which are paid by order of court, and then placed to the credit of the Treasurer of the United States by order of the Secretary of the Treasury, the result of compromised suits of which the collector has received notice during the month. The collector should also report on the same Form all taxes which may have been allowed to him as uncollectible, after the same have been collected, and all taxes which may have been collected after the same have been allowed as uncollectible. These detailed reports will be kept on file in the assessor's office, and the amount will be entered on the next monthly list, and included in the aggregate thereof, for which the collector will receipt on Form 23¼. 8 I. R. R. 20.

Although returns are required to be made to the assistant assessor by brewers, distillers, and manufacturers of tobacco and cigars, these returns are not to be placed on any assessment list. nor included in the collector's receipt, Form 23¼. An assessment is only required when beer, spirits, tobacco, or cigars have been removed without stamps. 8 I. R. R. 203.

Proceedings by Distraint.

Sec. 28. (Amended March 3, 1865, § 1; July 13, 1866, § 9.) *And be it further enacted,* That each of said collectors shall, within twenty days (*a*) after receiving his annual collection list from the assessors, give notice, by advertisement in one newspaper published in each county in his collection district, if there be any, and if not, then in a newspaper published in an adjoining county, and by notifications to be posted in at least four public places in each county in his collection district, that the said taxes have become due and payable, and state the time and place within said county at which he or his deputy will attend to receive the same, which time shall not be less than ten days after the date of such notification, and shall send a copy of such notice by mail to each postmaster in the county, to be posted in his office.

And if any person shall neglect to pay, as aforesaid, for more than ten days, it shall be the duty of the collector or his deputy to issue to such person a notice, to be left at his dwelling or usual place of business, or be sent by mail, demanding the payment of said taxes, stating the amount thereof, with a fee of twenty cents for the issuing and service of such notice, and with four cents for each mile actually and necessarily traveled in serving the same.

And if such persons shall not pay the duties or taxes, and the fee of twenty cents and mileage as aforesaid, within ten days after the service or the sending by mail of such notice, it shall be the duty of the collector or his deputy to collect the said taxes and fee of twenty cents and mileage, with a penalty of ten per centum additional upon the amount of taxes. And with respect to all such taxes as are not included in the annual lists aforesaid, and all taxes the collection of which is not otherwise provided for in this act, it shall be the duty of each collector, in person or by deputy, to give notice and demand payment thereof, in the manner last mentioned, within ten days from and after receiving the list thereof from the assessor, or within twenty days from and after the expiration of the time within which such tax should have been paid; and if the annual or other taxes shall not be paid within ten days from and after such notice and demand, it shall be lawful for such collector, or his deputies, to proceed to collect the said taxes, with ten per centum additional thereto as aforesaid, by distraint (*b*) and sale of the goods, chattels, or effects, including stocks, securities, and evidences of debt, of the persons delinquent as aforesaid.

And in case of distraint, it shall be the duty of the officer charged with the collection to make, or cause to be made, an account of the goods or effects distrained, a copy of which, signed by the officer making such distraint, shall be left with the owner or possessor of such goods or effects, or at his or her dwelling or usual place of business, with some person of suitable age and discretion, if any such can be found, with a note of the sum demanded, and the time and place of sale; and the said officer shall forthwith cause a notification to be published in some newspaper within the county wherein said distraint is made, if there is a newspaper published in said county, or to be publicly posted at the post-office, if there be one within five miles, nearest to the residence of the person whose property shall be distrained, and in not less than two other public places, which notice shall specify the articles distrained, and the time and place for the sale thereof, which time shall not be less than ten nor more than twenty days from the date of such notification to the owner or possessor of the property and the publication or posting of such notice as herein provided, and the place proposed for sale shall not be more than five miles distant from the place of making such distraint. And said sale may be adjourned from time to time by said officer, if he shall think it advisable to do so, but not for a time to exceed in all thirty days.

And if any person, bank, association, company, or corporation, liable to pay any tax, shall neglect or refuse to pay the same after demand, the amount shall be a lien in favor of the United States from the time it was due until paid, with the interest, penalties, and costs that may accrue in addition thereto, upon all property and rights to property belonging to such person, bank, association, company, or corporation; and the collector, after demand, may levy, or by warrant may authorize a deputy collector to levy, upon all property and rights to property belonging to such person, bank, association, company, or corporation, or on which the said lien exists, for the payment of the sum due as aforesaid, with interest and penalty for non-payment, and also of such further sum as shall be sufficient for the fees, costs, and expenses of such levy.

And in all cases of sale, as aforesaid, the certificate of such sale shall transfer to the purchaser all right, title, and interest of such delinquent in and to the property sold; and where such property shall consist of stocks, said certificate shall be notice, when received, to any corporation, company, or association of said transfer, and shall be authority to such corporation, company, or association to record the same on their books and records, in the same manner as if transferred or assigned by the person or party holding the same, in lieu of any original or prior certificates, which shall be void, whether cancelled or not. And said certificates, where the subject of sale shall be securities or other evidences of debt, shall be good and valid receipts to the person holding the same, as against any person holding, or claiming to hold, possession of such securities or other evidences of debt.

And all persons, and officers of companies or corporations, are required, on demand of a collector or deputy collector about to distrain or having distrained on any property or rights of property, to exhibit all books containing evidence or statements relating to the subject or subjects of distraint, or the property or rights of property liable to distraint for the tax so due as aforesaid :

Provided, That in any case of distraint for the payment of the taxes aforesaid, the goods, chattels, or effects so distrained shall and may be restored to the owner or possessor, if, prior to the sale, payment of the amount due shall be made to the proper officer charged with the collection, together with the fees and other charges; but in case of non-payment as aforesaid, the said officers shall proceed to sell the said goods, chattels, or effects at public auction, and shall retain from the proceeds of such sale the amount demandable for the use of the United States, and a commission of five per centum thereon for his own use, with the fees and charges for distraint and sale, rendering the overplus, if any there be, to the person who may be entitled to receive the same :

Provided further, That there shall be exempt from distraint and sale, if belonging to the head of a family, the school books and wearing apparel necessary for such family; also arms for personal use, one cow, two hogs, five sheep and the wool thereof, provided the aggregate market value of said sheep shall not exceed fifty dollars; the necessary food for such cow, hogs, and sheep for a period not exceeding thirty days; fuel to an amount not greater in value than twenty-five dollars; provisions to an amount not greater than fifty dollars; household furniture kept for use to an amount not greater than three hundred dollars; and the books, tools, or implements of a trade or profession to an amount not greater than one hundred dollars shall also be exempt; and the officer making the distraint shall summon three disinterested householders of the vicinity, who shall appraise and set apart to the owner the amount of property herein declared to be exempt.

(a) Within twenty days after receiving the annual list from the assessor, the collector must advertise in one newspaper in each county in his district, and by notices to be posted in at least four public places, and mailed to every postmaster in each county, stating the time and place within said county at which he or his deputy will attend to receive the duties, which time must not be less than ten days after the publication of said notice.

At the expiration of ten days from the advertised time, it is the duty of the collector to serve demands upon all persons who have neglected to make payment. Form 9 has been prepared for this purpose, and for the issuing and service thereof the collector is entitled to a fee of twenty cents, and to four cents for each mile actually and necessarily traveled in serving the same. No travel fee can be charged when the notice is sent by mail, and none for the distance traveled in returning when personal service is made.

The interest imposed by the statute should always be collected. It is not regarded as a penalty, or as any part of a penalty, but as an amount paid for the use of money detained from the United States. If ten days have elapsed between the notice prescribed by this section and the time when a claim for an abatement is first presented to one of the three officers whose duty it is to add a certificate thereto (assistant assessor, assessor, or collector), or the person first applies to one of them for assistance in the preparation of such claim, the penalty, in case such claim is disallowed, should be collected. If, however, such steps were taken before the ten days elapsed, the ten days stopped running, and the period between such steps and an official notice of the rejection of such claim should not be counted. If the taxes are paid within ten days of the notice, exclusive of such period, the penalty should not be imposed. 10 I. R. R. 57.

If payment is not made within ten days after service of demand, the collector will proceed to collect the duties with the penalty of five per centum, and interest at the rate of one per cent. per month, and the proper costs and expenses by distraint. No interest is required for a fraction of a month. 8 I. R. R. 201.

The collector cannot remit the penalty of five per centum and one per cent. monthly interest. 9 I. R. R. 188.

In a case where the United States is a creditor of a bankrupt for taxes, the claim may be enforced in two ways:

1st. By a lien against the property where such lien attached before the proceedings in bankruptcy were commenced. In that case it is proper for the collector to demand, under the authority of a warrant of distraint, possession of the property of the bankrupt, to which such lien attached for the purpose of satisfying the warrant, and all lawful charges thereon. Should the officers of the bankrupt court refuse to deliver possession, the collector should then submit a motion to the court having jurisdiction of the case in bankruptcy, for an order to make the delivery as demanded. If the court refuse to make such order, but will direct that the claim of the United States be placed at the head of the list, and to be paid before even the costs in bankruptcy, then the collector may accept that order, or he may accept any other orders which the court may make, which will secure the collection of the whole tax and costs.

In cases where no such lien has attached, and also where the tax may be secured without resort to the remedy by lien, the collector should file the assessment with his certificate of non-payment among the claims against the estate of the bankrupt, with a further suggestion of the right of the government to priority among the creditors under sec. 5 of Act March 3, 1797, 1 Stat. 515, as well as by section 28 of the Bankrupt Act. It is safest to make this suggestion in writing on the claim itself, but it may be made otherwise if necessary. 6 I. R. R. 154.

A suit may be brought against the collector to recover back money paid under protest on account of duties or taxes erroneously or illegally assessed. The appropriate remedy is an action of assumpsit for money had and received. Where the party voluntarily pays the money, he is without remedy; but if he pays it by compulsion of law, or under protest, or with notice that he intends to bring suit to test the validity of the claim, he may recover it back, if the assessment was erroneous or illegal. City of Philadelphia v. Collector, 5 Wall, 720.

None of the internal revenue acts contemplate that collectors shall reimburse themselves for the amount of any judgment recovered against them on account of duties illegally or erroneously assessed and paid under protest. The direction is that all such judgments shall be paid by the Commissioner, including, by the later acts, costs and expenses of suit. A judgment against the collector in such a case is, therefore, in the nature of a recovery against the United States. It is not, therefore, material whether the collectors are required to account daily or monthly, or whether they are required to pay into the Treasury the gross or only the net amount of collections. City of Philadelphia *v.* Collector, 5 Wall, 720.

(*b*) The fees and charges to be allowed in all cases of distraint and other seizures are as follows:

Issuing warrant of distraint	$0 50
Service of warrant	1 00
Distraint without warrant, or seizure for fraud or violation of law	1 00
Traveling fees for service of warrant, or for making distraint without warrant, or seizure for fraud, etc., going only, for actual travel per mile	0 10
Custody of goods seized or distrained, allowed only in cases named below, per day of 24 hours for each keeper	2 50
Expenses of removal	Amount actually paid.
Storage	" "
Insurance	" "
Advertising sale by posting notices (not allowed when no notices are posted)	3 00
Advertising in newspaper	Amount actually paid.
Collector's commissions on proceeds of sale on amount demandable for United States	5 per cent.
Fee on sale of real estate	10 00
Drawing and executing deed	5 00

In no case will commissions be allowed to a collector on payments made before sale, as the law does not justify that charge.

The fee for custody is allowed only in cases where removal would be attended with great and unnecessary expense, or injury to the property, and where its safe keeping requires a custodian, as in the case of a distillery, a tobacco factory, a store containing a large quantity of goods subject to seizure, and like cases. In no case will a merely constructive charge for custody be allowed. When the property can readily and cheaply be moved to and kept in a warehouse owned by responsible business men, at the usual rates of storage, the latter only will be allowed, and no charge for storage will be allowed while the property is so stored. In such case the collector should take the usual warehouse receipt.

The fee for drawing and executing a deed to a private purchaser must be included in the bill of costs, and deducted from the proceeds of sale. But when the property is purchased for the United States, the fee for making and executing the deed to the government should be charged to the government.

The collector is entitled to the fee of $10 on the sale of real estate when the property is purchased for the government, and in such case may be included in the collector's bill of costs and expenses.

The fees for witnesses are $1.50 per day, and five cents per mile from the place of residence to the place of trial or hearing, and five cents per mile for returning. 10 Stat. 167. These fees are to be paid by the party who is found to be delinquent; otherwise by the disbursing agent of the district on the certificate of the collector.

In calculating mileage, the traveling is to be computed from the place of service, distraint, or seizure, to the office of the officer who makes service or seizure. When a warrant is issued against two or more persons (partners, for instance) for the collection of the same tax, the travel is to be computed from the office or dwelling of the serving officer to the place of service which is most remote, adding thereto the extra travel which is necessary to serve it upon the other.

In other cases the distraining officer is allowed to charge for the actual number of miles traveled for the purpose of serving the warrant. Thus, if the officer travels twenty miles to serve four warrants for four separate assessments, serving the first at a distance of five miles, the second ten, the third fifteen, and the fourth twenty, he will charge for five miles in the first case, ten in the second, and so on.

When Form 69 is used, it will be a warrant for each tax assessed, except when two or more assessments against the same person are included in one schedule. In the latter case, if distraint is made at the same time for two or more assessments against the same persons, only one charge for mileage is to be made.

Where the officer serving the warrant learns, upon reaching the place where the party recently resided, that he has removed, and follows to his present residence, he is entitled to charge for the entire distance actually traveled in order to complete the service.

The issuing of a warrant of distraint is the writing, signing, sealing, and placing the same in the hands of the officer for service.

The service of the warrant is not complete in the case of personal property, unless the officer actually takes possession of some piece or article of property. In the case of real estate, the distraining officer should make service of the warrant in the same manner that the sheriff levies execution upon real estate, and thereupon notice must be given as prescribed in section 30, Act June 30, 1864, as amended.

Any officer who shall demand or receive any fee, as above prescribed, without the actual performance of the service or work for which it is allowed, will thereby incur the penalties provided for extortion in section 36, Act June 30, 1864.

In cases where distraint for non-payment of taxes may be legally resorted to, but where the officer collects the taxes in person, without actually seizing property, his right to mileage fee for actual travel in going to make the distraint is not defeated by the manner of collection, provided that each collection or payment is made after the officer has gone to make the distraint. 6 I. R. R. 155.

An action in assumpsit may be maintained to recover money due to the government for taxes by the party sued. U. S. v. Cutting, 3 Wall, 441; U. S. v. Fisk, 3 Wall, 445.

The remedy by distraint given by the statute is not the exclusive remedy. Taxes constitute a personal debt due to the United States from the taxpayer independently of any lien therefor. U. S. v. Washington Mills, 6 I. R. R. 146.

Property seized for a tax under an act of Congress, and by virtue of a warrant regular upon its face, cannot be replevied. Such suits would delay if not wholly defeat the collection of the internal revenue. O'Reilly v. Good, 42 Barb. 521.

Internal revenue taxes do not become a lien upon the property of the taxpayer until they are due; and when they do become a lien, such lien does not take priority of pre-existing liens. 6 I. R. R. 195.

The levying of an attachment on personal property owned by a person who owes an internal revenue tax, does not affect the lien of the government for the tax, if the same was due when the attachment was served. 6 I. R. R. 195.

When Returns shall be made.

[SEC. 11. (July 13, 1868.) *And be it further enacted,* That all lists or returns required to be made monthly, by any person, firm, company, corporation, or party whatsoever, liable to tax, shall be made on or before the tenth day of each and every month, and the tax assessed or due thereon shall be certified or returned by the assessor to the collector on or before the last day of each and every month. And all lists or returns required to be made quarterly, and all other lists or returns for which no provision is otherwise made, shall be made on or before the tenth day of each and every month in which said list or return is required to be made, or succeeding the time when the tax may be due and liable to be assessed, and the tax thereon shall be certified or returned as herein provided for monthly lists or returns. And the tax shall be due and payable on or before the last day of each and every month. And in case said tax is not paid on or before the last day of each and every month, the collector shall add ten per centum thereto:

Provided, That notice (a) of the time when said tax shall become due and payable shall be given in such manner as shall be prescribed by the Commissioner of Internal Revenue; and if said tax shall not be paid on or before the last day of the month as aforesaid, it shall be the duty of said collector to demand payment thereof, with ten per centum additional thereto, in the manner prescribed by law; and if said tax and ten per centum additional are not paid within ten days from and after such demand thereof, it shall be lawful for the collector or his deputy to make distraint therefor, as provided by law, and so much of section eighty-three of the act of June thirtieth, eighteen hundred and sixty-four, as amended by the act of March third, eighteen hundred and sixty-five, as relates to the time of payment and collection of tax, is hereby repealed; and in all cases of neglect to make such lists or returns, or in case of false and fraudulent returns, the provisions of existing law, as amended by this act, shall be applicable thereto.]

(a) Unless notice is given, and demand for payment is made prior to the day on which a monthly tax falls due, there is no liability to a penalty for non-payment. 5 I. R. R. 148.

Penalty for Failure to pay Tax.

[SEC. 8. (March 2, 1867.) *And be it further enacted,* That hereafter for any failure to pay any internal revenue tax at the time and in the manner required by law, where such failure creates a liability to pay a penalty of ten per centum additional upon the amount of tax so due and unpaid, the person or persons so failing or neglecting to pay said tax, instead of ten percentum as aforesaid, shall pay a penalty of five per centum, together with interest at the rate of one per centum per month upon said tax from the time the same became due, but no interest for any fraction of a month shall be demanded.]

Proceedings in Case of Sale.

Sec. 29. (Amended July 13, 1866, § 9.) *And be it further enacted,* That in all cases where property liable to distraint for taxes may not be divisible, so as to enable the collector by a sale of part thereof to raise the whole amount of the tax, with all costs, charges, and commissions, the whole of such property shall be sold, and the surplus of the proceeds of the sale, after satisfying the tax, costs, and charges, shall be paid to the person legally entitled to receive the same; or if he cannot be found, or refuse to receive the same, then such surplus shall be deposited in the treasury of the United States, to be there held for the use of the person legally entitled to receive the same, until he shall make application therefor to the Secretary of the Treasury, who, upon such application and satisfactory proofs in support thereof, shall, by warrant on the treasury, cause the same to be paid to the applicant. And if any of the property advertised for sale as aforesaid is of a kind subject to tax, and such tax has not been paid, and the amount bid for such property is not equal to the amount of such tax, the collector may purchase the same in behalf of the United States for an amount not exceeding the said tax.

And in all cases where property subject to tax, but upon which the tax has not been paid, shall be seized upon distraint and sold, the amount of such tax shall, after deducting the expenses of such sale, be first appropriated out of the proceeds thereof to the payment of said tax. And if no assessment of tax has been made upon such property, the collector shall make a return thereof in the form required by law, and the assessor shall assess the tax thereon, And all property so purchased may be sold by said collector, under such regulations as may be prescribed by the Commissioner of Internal Revenue. And the collector shall render a distinct account of all charges incurred in the sale of such property to the Commissioner of Internal Revenue, who shall by regulation determine the fees and charges to be allowed in all cases of distraint and other seizures; or where necessary expenses for making such distraint or seizure have been incurred, and in case of sale, the said collector shall pay into the treasury the surplus, if any there be, after defraying such fees and charges.

Sale of Real Estate.

Sec. 30. (Amended July 13, 1866, § 9.) *And be it further enacted*, That in any case where goods, chattels, or effects sufficient to satisfy the taxes imposed by law upon any person liable to pay the same, shall not be found by the collector or deputy collector, whose duty it may be to collect the same, he is hereby authorized to collect the same by seizure and sale of real estate; (*a*) and the officer making such seizure and sale shall give notice to the person whose estate is proposed to be sold, by giving him in hand, or leaving at his last or usual place of abode, if he has any such within the collection district where said estate is situated, a notice, in writing, stating what particular estate is proposed to be sold, describing the same with reasonable certainty, and the time when and place where said officer proposes to sell the same; which time shall not be less than twenty nor more than forty days from the time of giving said notice.

And the said officer shall also cause a notification to the same effect to be published in some newspaper within the county where such seizure is made, if any such there be, and shall also cause a like notice to be posted at the post-office nearest to the estate to be seized, and in two other public places within the county; and the place of said sale shall not be more than five miles distant from the estate seized, except by special order of the Commissioner of Internal Revenue. At the time and place appointed, the officer making such seizure shall proceed to sell the said estate at public auction, offering the same at a minimum price, (*b*) including the expense of making such levy, and all charges for advertising, and an officer's fee of ten dollars. And in case the real estate so seized as aforesaid, shall consist of several distinct tracts or parcels, the officer making sale thereof shall offer each tract or parcel for sale separately, and shall, if he deem it advisable, apportion the expenses, charges, and fees aforesaid, to such several tracts or parcels, or to any of them, in estimating the minimum price aforesaid.

And if no person offers for said estate the amount of said minimum price, the officer shall declare the same to be purchased by him for the United States, and shall deposit with the District Attorney of the United States a deed thereof, as hereinafter specified and provided; otherwise, the same shall be declared to be sold to the highest bidder. And said sale may be adjourned from time to time by said officer, for not exceeding thirty days in all, if he shall think it advisable so to do. If the amount bid shall not be then and there paid, the officer shall forthwith proceed to again sell said estate in the same manner; and, upon any sale and the payment of the purchase money, shall give to the purchaser a certificate of purchase, which shall set forth the real estate purchased, for whose taxes the same was sold, the name of the purchaser, and the price paid therefor; and if the said real estate be not redeemed in the manner and within the time hereinafter provided, then the said collector or deputy collector shall execute to the said purchaser, upon his surrender of said certificate, a deed of the real estate purchased by him as aforesaid, reciting the facts set forth in said certificate, and in accordance with the laws of the State in which such real estate is situate, upon the subject of sales of real estate under execution, which said deed shall be prima facie evidence of the facts therein stated; and if the proceedings of the officer as set forth have been substantially in accordance with the provisions of law, shall be considered and operate as a conveyance of all the right, title, and interest the party delinquent had in and to the real estate thus sold at the time the lien of the United States attached thereto.

Any person, whose estate may be proceeded against as aforesaid, shall have the right to pay the amount due, together with the costs and charges thereon, to the collector or deputy collector at any time prior to the sale thereof, and all further proceedings shall cease from the time of such payment. The owners of any real estate sold as aforesaid, their heirs, executors, or administrators, or any person having any interest therein, or a lien thereon, or any person in their behalf, shall be permitted to redeem the land sold as aforesaid, or any particular tract thereof, at any time within one year after the sale thereof, upon payment to the purchaser, or, in case he cannot be found in the county in which the land is to be redeemed is situate, then to the collector of the district in which the land is situate, for the use of the purchaser, his heirs or assigns, the amount paid by the said purchaser and interest thereon at the rate of twenty per centum per annum.

And any collector or deputy collector may, for the collection of taxes imposed upon any person, or for which any person may be liable, and committed to him for collection, seize and sell the lands of such person situated in any other collection district within the State in which said officer resides; and his proceedings in relation thereto shall have the same effect as if the same were had in his proper collection district.

And it shall be the duty of every collector to keep a record of all sales of land made in his collection district, whether by himself or his deputies, or by another collector, in which shall be set forth the tax for which any such sale was made, the dates of seizure and sale, the name of the party assessed, and all proceedings in making said sale, the amount of fees and expenses, the name of the purchaser, and the date of the deed; which record shall be certified by the officer making the sale. And it shall be the duty of any deputy making sale as aforesaid, to return a statement of all his proceedings to the collector, and to certify the record thereof. And in case of the death or removal of the collector, or the expiration of his term of office from any other cause, said record shall be delivered to his successor in office; and a copy of every such record, certified by the collector, shall be evidence in any court of the truth of the facts therein stated. And when any lands sold, as aforesaid, shall be redeemed as hereinbefore provided, the collector shall make an entry of the fact upon the record aforesaid, and the said entry shall be evidence of such redemption.

And when any property, personal or real, seized and sold by virtue of the foregoing provisions, shall not be sufficient to satisfy the claim of the United States for which distraint or seizure may be made against any person whose property may be so seized and sold, the collector may, thereafter, and as often as the same may be necessary, proceed to seize and sell, in like manner, any other property liable to seizure of such person until the amount due from him, together with all expenses, shall be fully paid:

Provided, That the word "county," wherever the same occurs in this act, or the acts of which this is amendatory, shall be construed to mean also a parish or any other equivalent subdivision of a State or Territory.

(a) Real estate seized for the payment of internal revenue taxes, must be sold within five miles of where it is located, unless the Commissioner by special order in each case permits a sale to be made at a greater distance. 6 I. R. R. 195.

(b) The minimum price fixed by this section does not include the tax, but simply the expense of making the levy and the charges and fees for effecting the sale. 6 I. R. R. 195.

When a collector is selling lands for internal revenue taxes, he should bid for and in behalf of the United States, a sum equal to one half of the cash value of the property he is selling, and if no person bids more he should declare the property to be purchased by him for the United States. 10 I. R. R. 5.

Whenever and as often as property is purchased by the United States under the provisions of this section, the collector should report the following particulars:

The names of the parties assessed; the amount, date, and character of the tax; the date and cause of seizure and sale; all proceedings of the sale, including the place of the sale, and, if sold more than five miles from the property, the reason therefor and a reference by date, &c., to the Commissioner's special order; the sum for which sold and the items comprised in it; all entries made in the collector's books or accounts in regard to the sale; a full description of the property and minutes of the deed, including dates, names of parties, consideration, &c.; with what district attorney the deed is deposited; whether it is recorded, and, if so, when and where, naming book and page; when redeemed, the full particulars of the redemption; when sold, the full particulars of such sale, the use and occupation of the property since seizure and sale, and an estimate of its value. 8 I. R. R. 203.

When a deed is made after the time for redemption has elapsed, it should contain a recital of the facts set forth in the certificate, and in form be in accordance with the laws of the State in which the real estate is situate, on the subject of sales of real estate under execution. 6 I. R. R. 138.

Commissioner to have Charge of Real Estate.

[SEC. 4. (March 2, 1867.) *And be it further enacted,* That the Commissioner of Internal Revenue shall have charge of all real estate which has been or shall be assigned, set off, or conveyed, by purchase or otherwise, to the United States, in payment of debts arising under the laws relating to internal revenue, and of all trusts created for the use of the United States, in payment of such debts due them; and, with the approval of the Secretary of the Treasury, may sell and dispose of, at public vendue, upon not less than twenty days' notice, lands assigned or set off to the United States in payment of such debts, or vested in them by mortgage or other security, for the payment of such debts; and in cases where real estate has already become the property of the United States by conveyance or otherwise, in payment of or as security for a debt arising under the laws relating to internal revenue, and such debt shall have been paid, together with the interest thereon, at the rate of one per centum per month, to the United States, within two years from the date of the acquisition of such real estate, it shall be lawful for the Commissioner of Internal Revenue, with the approval of the Secretary of the Treasury, to release by deed, or otherwise convey, such real estate to the debtor from whom it was taken, or to his heirs or other legal representatives.]

Property of Persons not residing in the District.

SEC. 31. *And be it further enacted,* That if any collector shall find, upon any list of taxes returned to him for collection, property lying within his district which is charged with any specific or ad valorem tax or duty, but which is not owned, occupied, or superintended by some person known to such collector to reside or to have some place of business within the United States, and upon which the duty or tax has not been paid within the time required by law, such collector shall forthwith take such property into his custody, and shall advertise the same, and the tax charged upon the same, in some newspaper published in his district, if any shall be published therein; otherwise, in some newspaper in an adjoining district, for the space of thirty days; and if the taxes thereon, with all charges for advertising, shall not be paid within said thirty days, such collector shall proceed to sell the same, or so much as is necessary, in the manner provided for the sale of other goods distrained for the nonpayment of taxes, and out of the proceeds shall satisfy all taxes charged upon such property with the cost of advertising and selling the same.

And like proceedings to those provided in the preceding section for the purchase and resale of property which cannot be sold for the amount of duty or tax due thereon, shall be had with regard to property sold under the provisions of this section. And any surplus arising from any sale herein provided for shall be paid into the treasury for the benefit of the owner of the property. And the Secretary of the Treasury is authorized, in any case where money shall be paid into the treasury for the benefit of any owner of property sold as aforesaid, to repay the same, on proper proof being furnished that the person applying therefor is entitled to receive the same.

Collection of Taxes from Persons not having Property in the District.

Sec. 32. *And be it further enacted,* That whenever a collector shall have on any list duly returned to him the name of any person not within his collection district who is liable to tax, or of any person so liable to tax who shall have, in the collection district in which he resides, no sufficient property subject to seizure or distraint from which the money due for duties or tax can be collected, it shall and may be lawful for such collector to transmit a copy or statement containing the name of the person liable to such duty or tax aforesaid, with the amount and nature thereof, duly certified under his hand, to the collector of any district to which said person shall have removed, or in which he shall have property, real or personal, liable to be seized and sold for duty or tax, and the collector of the district to whom the said certified copy or statement shall be transmitted shall proceed to collect the said duty or tax in the same way as if the name of the person and objects of tax contained in the said certified copy or statement were on any list furnished to him by the assessor of his own collection district; and the said collector, upon receiving said certified copy or statement as aforesaid, shall transmit his receipt for it to the collector sending the same to him.

Report of Collections.

Sec. 33. *And be it further enacted,* That the several collectors shall, at the expiration of each and every month after they shall, respectively, commence their collections, transmit to the Commissioner of Internal Revenue a statement of the collections made by them, respectively, within the month, and pay over monthly, or at such time or times as may be required by the Commissioner of Internal Revenue, the moneys by them respectively collected within the said term, and at such places as may be designated and required by the Commissioner of Internal Revenue; and each of the said collectors shall complete the collection of all sums assigned to him for collection as aforesaid, shall pay over the same into the treasury, and shall render his accounts to the Treasury Department as often as he may be required. And the Secretary of the Treasury is authorized to designate one or more depositories in each State, for the deposit and safe-keeping of the money collected by virtue of this act; and the receipt of the proper officer of such depository to a collector for the money deposited by him shall be a sufficient voucher for such collector in the settlement of his accounts at the Treasury Department. And the Commissioner of Internal Revenue may, under the direction of the Secretary of the Treasury, prescribe such regulations with reference to such deposits as he may deem necessary.

Collectors charged with Taxes.

Sec. 34. (Amended July 13, 1866, § 9.) *And be it further enacted*, That each collector shall be charged (*a*) with the whole amount of taxes, whether contained in lists delivered to him by the assessors, respectively, or delivered or transmitted to him by assistant assessors from time to time, or by other collectors, or by his predecessor in office, and with the additions thereto, with the par value of all stamps deposited with him, and with all moneys collected for passports, penalties, forfeitures, fees, or costs, and he shall be credited with all payments into the treasury made as provided by law, with all stamps returned by him uncancelled to the treasury, and with the amount of taxes contained in the lists transmitted in the manner above provided to other collectors, and by them receipted as aforesaid; and also, with the amount of the taxes of such persons as may have absconded, or become insolvent, prior to the day when the tax ought, according to the provisions of law, to have been collected, and with all uncollected taxes transferred by him, or by his deputy acting as collector, to his successor in office:

Provided, That it shall be proved to the satisfaction of the Commissioner of Internal Revenue that due diligence was used by the collector, who shall certify the facts to the First Comptroller of the Treasury. And each collector shall also be credited with the amount of all property purchased by him for the use of the United States, provided he shall faithfully account for and pay over the proceeds thereof upon the resale of the same as required by law. In case of the death, resignation, or removal of the collector, all lists and accounts of taxes uncollected shall be transferred to his successor in office as soon as such successor shall be appointed and qualified, and it shall be the duty of such successor to collect the same.

(a) Collectors are charged with the stamps sold by them, as shown by their reports on Forms 76, 90, and 103, and should enter each month on Form 51 the collections shown by Forms 76, 90, and 103, each separately, as well as their receipts on Form 23½ and the collections thereon.

All packages of internal revenue stamps forwarded by the direction of the Commissioner, should, as soon as received, be opened and counted in the presence of two competent witnesses; and should a deficiency exist, duplicate affidavits of the facts should at once be forwarded to the Commissioner. No claim for any alleged deficiency will be considered unless this regulation has been complied with.

At the close of each quarter, collectors must render their final accounts for all lists which they may have held for six months or more. No credit will be allowed for lists which have been held for six months and longer; and at the close of each quarter thereafter collectors should deposit the money for all amounts remaining uncollected on such lists for which no claims have been presented to the Commissioner.

Claims on account of insolvency or absconding of the parties taxed must be made on Form 53, and sustained by the affidavit of the deputy collector. A collector making his own collections in any division should use Form 53, making his affidavit thereon, and treating the schedule in all respects as if made by a deputy.

Collectors or deputy collectors, using Form 53, should state, in a concise but clear manner, the reason for non-collection under the head of "Cause of inability to collect." For example: "Insolvent before demand could legally be made," "Died before receipt of list, and estate insolvent," "Left for parts unknown before the tax could be collected," "No property liable to seizure under the law," "Property would not pay expense of distraint." The dates should be given when the taxes were found to be uncollectible; and, when this cannot be done, it should be stated, in each case, that the inability to collect existed prior to the receipt of the list, or before legal demand could be made.

At intervals of not less than one month all taxes claimed to be uncollectible, either from error or insolvency, should be put into a single schedule on Form 48, grouped under captions designating the lists to which they belong, whether annual or monthly. The natural order of the months should be strictly observed. The captions should be written in red ink across the center of the schedule. The amount claimed should be placed only in the column headed "Amount claimed." The other two columns, ruled for dollars and cents, must be left blank. Each schedule must be verified by the certificate of the assessor and collector, and accompanied in all cases by affidavits on Form 47 or 53.

Affidavits should be numbered by the collectors to correspond to the claims in the schedule supported by them. Those covering several claims should be marked on their backs with the numbers of those claims Before transmitting any schedule, the collector should compare it with his lists, and check on the lists each claim contained in the schedule with intelligible abbreviations, showing the date of the application and its nature, whether for insolvency or error; and when notice of action is received, checks should be applied to the lists, showing the nature and date of such action in each case. In designating page and line, the collector and assessor should each have reference to the pages and lines of the lists as found in his own office.

The numbering of the claims should be carefully attended to for convenience of reference, and all claims presented at one time should be numbered as on one schedule, and the claims in each numbered from one to the last in that schedule. 8 I. R. R. 203.

1st. The powers and duties of the Commissioner extend to abating taxes that shall have been erroneously or illegally assessed. These powers and duties are conferred upon him for the benefit of the taxpayer, and not of the collector, to whom it is immaterial which way the Commissioner may decide. Of this class of cases are double and excessive assessments.

2d. His duties and powers extend also to allowing the collector for uncollectible taxes, in which a collector is directly interested. This class of credits properly appertain to accounting, and is placed under the direction of the Commissioner by law. But,

3d. Where a collector is twice charged with the same assessment, his relief is to be had upon proper evidence through the action of the accounting officers. This is simply the correction of errors in accounts, and involves no question as to the legality of the tax nor of the ability of the taxpayer to pay. 11 I. R. R. 58.

Where the same item of tax is charged on more than one list, or where the tax or assessed penalty has been changed in amount, or made specific penalty by a compromise with the taxpayer, the errors or differences are matters of account to be passed upon by the accounting officers of the Treasury Department, and are not subject to abatement by the Commissioner.

Collectors should present all such claims with their revenue accounts, and accompany them with evidence of the facts in the case.

1st. In cases of double charges where the same item appears upon more than one list, the collector should make extracts containing the tax from each assessment list; procure the affidavit of the assessor showing that he has personally compared the extracts with the originals and finds them true and correct, naming each list, page, and line where they appear, the amount of the tax and the amount of the footings of each list; that the said tax on each list was identical, and was included in the footings in both lists, and twice receipted for by the collector on Form 28$\frac{1}{4}$, or in case it was receipted for on any other Form or Forms, state the facts, referring to the Form by the number. The collector should himself make a similar affidavit proving the same facts, with the additional statement that the item of double charges has never been abated or remitted by the Commissioner; and that the said tax was only once paid by the taxpayer, and that neither the whole nor any part of the duplicate charge has been collected.

2d. In cases where the tax or assessed penalty has been changed in amount, or the assessed penalty made specific penalty by compromise with the taxpayer, the collector should make an extract, containing the tax and assessed penalty, from the assessment list; procure the affidavit of the assessor or assistant assessor that he has personally compared the extract with the original and finds it true and correct, naming the list, page, and line wherein it appears, the amount of the tax and assessed penalty, and the amount of the footings of the list; and that the said tax and assessed penalty are included in the footings of said list and receipted for on Form 28$\frac{1}{4}$ (or any other Form as the case may be), and that the extract contains the identical tax and assessed penalty that was afterward compromised, or the assessed penalty treated as specific penalty by the Commissioner. In cases where one person does not know all the facts, as many affidavits as may be necessary to prove them may be furnished. The collector should make his own affidavit to the same facts, and add thereto a further statement showing the terms of the compromise, and that the amount received from the taxpayer, naming the amount, was in lieu of and in full for said original tax and assessed penalty; and that the assessed penalty (or tax, as the case may be) has never been abated or remitted by the Commissioner, and that no part of it has been collected except as above stated. 11 I. R. R. 9.

It is the duty of the accounting officers to withhold the compensation of a collector until he has discharged his apparent liability for uncollected lists. 5 I. R. R. 46.

When a collector goes out of office he must make a list of all taxes in his hands which are collectible, and take a receipt therefor in duplicate from his successor, which must show the amount belonging to each assessment list. One copy of this receipt must be transmitted to the Commissioner. The outgoing collector will not receive credit in the Office of Internal Revenue for the taxes thus transferred to his successor until they have actually been collected. The new collector will report the amounts collected by him on the list received from his predecessor, when he has collected all that he can, specifying the several assessment lists on which they were originally returned. On receipt of this report, the old collector will be credited and the new collector charged with the amounts collected.

For relief from taxes received from his predecessor which are found to be uncollectible, the new collector must furnish to his predecessor affidavits on Form 33 that said taxes were uncollectible when they came into his hands. The old collector must furnish similar affidavits and certificates on Form 48 to the Office of Internal Revenue before the taxes will be abated in his account.

The public property, consisting of all annual and monthly lists of taxes, all official letters and records, stationery, forms, blank-books, laws, circulars, specials, decisions, pamphlets containing instructions, postage stamps, hydrometers and manuals, or receipts of gaugers for the same, and whatever there is furnished or paid for by the Government, must be delivered by the outgoing collector to his successor, together with an inventory of all such property in his possession. After obtaining the receipt of his successor to his inventory, he will transmit it to the Commissioner with his account of expenses on Form 91. 8 I. R. R. 205.

Proceedings against Delinquent Collectors.

Sec. 35. *And be it further enacted,* That if any collector shall fail either to collect or to render his account, or to pay over in the manner or within the times hereinbefore provided, it shall be the duty of the First Comptroller of the Treasury, and he is hereby authorized and required, immediately after evidence of such delinquency, to report the same to the Solicitor of the Treasury, who shall issue a warrant of distress against such delinquent collector, directed to the marshal of the district, therein expressing the amount with which the said collector is chargeable, and the sums, if any, which have been paid over by him, so far as the same are ascertainable. And the said marshal shall himself, or by his deputy, immediately proceed to levy and collect the sum which may remain due, with five per centum thereon, and all the expenses and charges of collection, by distress and sale of the goods and chattels or any personal effects of the delinquent collector, giving at least five days' notice of the time and place of sale, in the manner provided by law for advertising sales of personal property on execution in the State wherein such collector resides.

And the bill of sale of the officer of any goods, chattels, or other personal property distrained and sold as aforesaid, shall be conclusive evidence of title to the purchaser, and prima facie evidence of the right of the officer to make such sale, and of the correctness of his proceedings in selling the same. And for want of goods and chattels, or other personal effects of such collector, sufficient to satisfy any warrant of distress, issued pursuant to the preceding section of this act, the lands and real estate of such collector, or so much thereof as may be necessary for satisfying the said warrant, after being advertised for at least three weeks in not less than three public places in the collection district, and in one newspaper printed in the county or district, if any there be, prior to the proposed time of sale, shall be sold at public auction by the marshal or his deputy, who, upon such sale, shall, as such marshal or deputy marshal, make and deliver to the purchaser of the premises so sold a deed of conveyance thereof, to be executed and acknowledged in the manner and form prescribed by the laws of the State in which said lands are situated, which said deeds so made shall invest the purchaser with all the title and interest of the defendant or defendants named in said warrant existing at the time of the seizure thereof. And all moneys that may remain of the proceeds of such sale, after satisfying the said warrant of distress, and paying the reasonable costs and charges of sale, shall be returned to the proprietor of the lands or real estate sold as aforesaid.

Penalty for Extortion.

Sec. 36. *And be it further enacted*, That each and every collector, or his deputy, who shall be guilty of any extortion or wilful oppression, under color of law, or shall knowingly demand other or greater sums than shall be authorized by law, or shall receive any fee, compensation, or reward, except as herein prescribed, for the performance of any duty, or shall wilfully neglect to perform any of the duties enjoined by this act, shall, upon conviction, be subject to a fine of not exceeding one thousand dollars, or to be imprisoned for not exceeding one year, or both, at the discretion of the court, and be dismissed from office, and be forever thereafter incapable of holding any office under the government; and one-half of the fine so imposed shall be for the use of the United States, and the other half for the use of the informer, who shall be ascertained by the judgment of the court; and the said court shall also render judgment against said collector or deputy collector for the amount of damages accruing to the party injured, to be collected by execution. And each and every collector, or his deputies, shall give receipts for all sums by them collected.

Officers may enter Buildings.

Sec. 37. *And be it further enacted,* That a collector or deputy collector, assessor, assistant assessor, revenue agent, or inspector, shall be authorized to enter, in the day-time, any brewery, distillery, manufactory, building, or place where any property, articles, or objects, subject to duty or taxation under the provisions of this act, are made, produced, or kept, within his district, so far as it may be necessary for the purpose of examining said property, articles, or objects, or inspecting the accounts required by this act from time to time to be made or kept by any manufacturer, or producer, relating to such property, articles, or objects. And every owner of such brewery, distillery, manufactory, building, or place, or persons having the agency or superintendence of the same, who shall refuse to admit such officer, or to suffer him to examine said property, articles, or objects, or to inspect said accounts, shall, for every such refusal, forfeit and pay the sum of five hundred dollars:

Provided, however, That when such premises shall be open at night, such officers may enter while so open in the performance of their official duties.

Penalty for obstructing Officers.

Sec. 38. *And be it further enacted,* That if any person shall forcibly obstruct or hinder any assessor or assistant assessor, or any collector or deputy collector, revenue agent or inspector, in the execution of this act, or of any power and authority hereby vested in him, or shall forcibly rescue, or cause to be rescued, any property, articles, or objects, after the same shall have been seized by him, or shall attempt or endeavor so to do, the person so offending shall, upon conviction thereof, for every such offence, forfeit and pay the sum of five hundred dollars, or double the value of property so rescued, or be imprisoned for a term not exceeding two years, at the discretion of the court:

Provided, That if any such officer shall divulge to any party, or make known in any manner other than is provided in this act, the operations, style of work or apparatus of any manufacturer or producer visited by him in the discharge of his official duties, he shall be subject to the penalties prescribed in section thirty-six of this act.

Penalty for Compounding Offences.

[SEC. 26. (March 2, 1867.) *And be it further enacted*, That, if any collector, deputy collector, assessor, assistant assessor, inspector, district-attorney, marshal, or other officer, agent, or person charged with the execution, or supervision of the execution, of any of the provisions of this act, or of the act to which this is amendatory, shall demand, or accept, or attempt to collect, directly or indirectly, as payment or gift or otherwise, any sum of money or other property of value for the compromise, adjustment, or settlement of any charge or complaint for any violation or alleged violation of any of the said provisions, except as expressly authorized by law so to do, he shall be held to be guilty of a misdemeanor, and shall for every such offence be liable to indictment and trial in any court of the United States having competent jurisdiction, and on conviction thereof shall be fined in double the sum or value of the money or property received or demanded, and be imprisoned for a period of not less than one year nor more than ten years.]

Penalty for Assuming to be an Officer.

[SEC. 28. (March 2, 1867.) *And be it further enacted*, That if any person shall falsely represent himself to be a revenue officer of the United States, and shall in such assumed character demand or receive any money or other article of value from any person for any duty or tax due to the United States, or for any violation or pretended violation of any revenue law of the United States, such person shall be deemed guilty of a felony, and on conviction thereof shall be liable to a fine of five hundred dollars, and to imprisonment not less than six months, and not exceeding two years, at the discretion of the court.]

Penalty for Conspiracy.

[SEC. 30. (March 2, 1867.) *And be it further enacted*, That if two or more persons conspire (a) either to commit any offence against the laws of the United States, or to defraud the United States in any manner whatever, and one or more of said parties to said conspiracy shall do any act to effect the object thereof, the parties to said conspiracy shall be deemed guilty of a misdemeanor, and on conviction thereof shall be liable to a penalty of not less than one thousand dollars and not more than ten thousand dollars, and to imprisonment not exceeding two years. And when any offence shall be begun in one judicial district of the United States and completed in another, every such offence shall be deemed to have been committed in either of the said districts, and may be dealt with, inquired of, tried, determined, and punished in either of the said districts, in the same manner as if it had been actually and wholly committed therein.]

(*a*) Conspiracy is an agreement by two or more persons to commit an unlawful act or acts. It is sometimes defined to be an agreement to commit an act in itself unlawful, or to do an act lawful in itself by unlawful means. Either the final result or the means are to be unlawful. There is no special force in this division, inasmuch as something unlawful is to be done. This is the common-law definition independent of the statute, and, if the statute spoke simply of a conspiracy, it ought perhaps to be construed with reference to the common-law definition. But in this statute the word has a more comprehensive meaning, because it includes defrauding the United States in any manner whatever, whether the fraud had been declared a crime by any statute or not. It is therefore immaterial to consider whether the acts were a crime independent of the statute, if there is shown to have been a conspiracy to defraud the government. U. S. *v.* Whalan, 7 I. R. R. 161; s. c. 1 A. L. T. (C. R.) 68; In re Callicott, 8 I. R. R. 169.

Whether there has been such a conspiracy as the law requires, the jury are to gather from all the circumstances of the case. It is not necessary that there should have been a pecuniary consideration, a definite, absolute contract; but there must have been between the parties charged a concert of action, a concert of intent, which makes the offence. U. S. *v.* Allen et al. 7 I. R. R. 163; U. S. *v.* Sultzberger et al 7 I. R. R. 201.

The conspiracy to defraud with any one act by either of the parties constitutes the offence. The mere combining or confederating to commit the fraud is sufficient without any actual perpetration of it, or loss or damage to the Government, if any one of them has taken a step toward its execution, toward carrying the scheme into effect. The law strikes at the incipient steps, the germ of the offence, with a view the more effectually to deter persons from entering upon fraud, and lays hold of them before its consummation. U. S. *v.* Perry et al. 10 I. R. R. 205; U. S. *v.* Callicott, 7 I. R. R. 177; U. S. *v.* Allen et al. 7 I. R. R. 163.

When an overt act in furtherance of the object of the conspiracy is committed within the jurisdictional limits of the court, the court has jurisdiction to try the parties for the offence. U. S. *v.* Sperry et al. 10 I. R. R. 205.

The act charged may be stated in various ways, to be adapted to the various phases of a case which may be developed by the evidence. It is not necessary that the jury should discriminate between the various counts. If any count is good, it will support a general verdict. U. S. *v.*

Whalan et al. 7 I. R. R. 161; s. c. 1. A. L. T. (C. R.) 63; In re Callicott, 8 I. R. R. 169; s. c. 1 A. L. T. (C. R.) 129.

When there are several counts in an indictment, a verdict of not guilty is a verdict of not guilty under all the counts. If the jury find the accused guilty under any of the counts, they should except from their verdict whatever of the counts they find not to be proven. U. S. *v.* Allen et al. 7 I. R. R. 163; U. S. *v.* Callicott, 7 I. R. R. 177.

The practice of postponing the trial of a cause until the circuit judge can sit with the district judge is confined, with few exceptions, to capital cases. A division of opinion may be certified on motions in arrest of judgment, though it cannot on a motion for a new trial. But where there is a difference of opinion on a motion for a new trial, such direction will be given to the case as will enable the defendant to obtain a certificate of division under the statute. A new trial will be granted, and the cause again submitted to the jury in the presence of the two judges, and the question or questions regularly certified. U. S. *v.* Fullerton, 9 I. R. R. 3.

A witness who declares himself upon the stand to be guilty of the crime charged, holds such a relation to the case as to render it unsafe to convict upon his testimony alone, unless confirmed upon material points by evidence to which no suspicion attaches. It is sometimes necessary to call such witnesses, but they stand before a jury under a strong bias and confessing their own infamy. A witness who thus testifies will not be punished unless he tells an entirely different story on the stand from what he has told out of court. When a number of parties have been arrested, there is always a strong temptation to throw the blame on each other, and to buy immunity by evidence; and the stronger the suspicions are against one, the greater is the temptation, because he has less chances of escape in any other way; so that juries look for corroboration from independent witnesses who testify to material facts in the case; and these facts must tend to show not only his own knowledge of the crime which he admits, but the complicity of the others. U. S. *v.* Whalan et al. 7 I. R. R. 161; s. c. 1 A. L. T. (C. R.) 63; U. S. *v.* Callicott, 7 I. R. R. 177; s. c. 1 A. L. T. (C. R.) 129.

When other acts similar to those charged in the indictment are proved, they are only to be considered as throwing some light upon the question of the guilty intent and knowledge of the parties They tend to show a state of mind in the parties, and afford more or less evidence of the corrupt intent which with the commission of the act constitute the offence. There must be a criminal intent and it must be carried out by some act. U. S. *v.* Allen et al. 7 I. R. R. 163.

The defendants are entitled to the benefit of every reasonable doubt. If there is any reasonable doubt of their guilt, they should have the benefit of it and be acquitted. If the evidence shows that they are guilty beyond any reasonable doubt of an intelligent man, they should be acquitted. U. S. *v.* Whalan et al. 7 I. R. R. 161; s. c. 1 A. L. T. (C. R.) 63; U. S. *v.* Allen et al. 7 I. R. R. 163.

To constitute the offence, there must be a criminal intent, or such an amount of carelessness and total indifference in the discharge of official duties as amounts to criminality. U. S. *v.* Allen et al. 7 I. R. R. 163.

It would not be remarkable nor singular, if, in the multitude of business in the office of a collector, occasionally an imposition should be pressed upon him. But when a large number of fraudulent bonds, forged both as to principal and as to surety, or otherwise tainted with fraud, are accepted in succession within a limited period, it is sufficient to excite surprise, if not suspicion, and to call for an explanation. U. S. *v.* Callicott, 7 I. R. R. 177; s. c. 1 A. L. T. (C. R.) 129.

When parties are out on bail, they are entitled to their liberty until the case is disposed of. They cannot, after the cause has been submitted to the jury, be remanded to the custody of the marshal to await the result of the verdict. U. S. *v.* Sultzberger et al. 7 I. R. R. 201.

Penalty for Bribery.

[SEC. 62. (July 13, 1866.) *And be it further enacted,* That if any person or persons shall, directly or indirectly, promise, offer or give, or cause or procure to be promised, offered, or given, any money, goods, right in action, bribe, present, or reward, or any promise, contract, undertaking, obligation, or security for the payment or delivery of any money, goods, right in action, bribe, present, or reward, or any other valuable thing whatever, to any officer of the United States, or person holding any place of trust or profit, or discharging any official function under, or in connection with, any department of the government of the United States, after the passage of this act, with intent to influence his decision or action on any question, matter, cause, or thing which may then be pending, or may by law be brought before him in his official capacity, or in his place of trust or profit, or with intent to influence any such officer or person to commit, or aid or abet in committing, any fraud on the revenue of the United States, or to connive at or collude in, or to allow or permit, or make opportunity for the commission of any such fraud, and shall be thereof convicted, (*a*) such person or persons so offering, promising, or giving, or causing, or procuring to be promised, offered, or given, any such money, goods, right in action, bribe, present, or reward, or any promise, contract, undertaking, obligation, or security for the payment or delivery of any money, goods, right in action, bribe, present, or reward, or other valuable thing whatever, and the officer or person who shall in anywise accept or receive the same, or any part, respectively, shall be liable to indictment in any court of the United States having jurisdiction, and shall, upon conviction thereof, be fined not exceeding three times the amount so offered, promised, given, accepted, or received, and imprisoned not exceeding three years; and the person convicted of so accepting or receiving the same, or any part thereof, if an officer or person holding any such place of trust or profit, shall forfeit his office or place; and any person so convicted under this section shall forever be disqualified to hold any office of honor, trust, or profit under the United States.]

(*a*) If any effect is to be given to the words "and shall be thereof convicted," the section would be inoperative and impossible to be executed, since, by express words, a previous conviction is made necessary before an indictment can be found. The section must therefore read as if these words, which are without meaning as they are used, were not present. They should be treated as surplusage and of no effect. U. S. *v*. Stern, 6 I. R. R. 169.

Deputy may Act as Collector during Temporary Disability.

Sec. 39. *And be it further enacted*, That in case of the sickness or temporary disability of a collector to discharge such of his duties as cannot under existing laws be discharged by a deputy, they may be devolved (*a*) by him upon one of his deputies; and for the official acts and defaults of such deputy the collector or his sureties shall be held responsible to the United States.

(*a*) Proper evidence that the duties of the collector have been thus devolved upon the deputy collector should be filed in the Office of Internal Revenue, and the fact of sickness or other disability of the collector must appear upon papers signed by the deputy. 2 I. R. R. 2.

Deputy may Act as Collector in case of Vacancy.

Sec. 40. (Amended, March 3, 1865, § 1; March 2, 1867, § 9.) *And be it further enacted*, That in case of a vacancy occurring in the office of collector by reason of death, or any other cause, the deputies of such collector shall continue to act until his successor is appointed; and the deputy of such collector longest in service at the time immediately preceding shall, until a successor shall be appointed, discharge all the duties of said collector; and for the official acts and default of such deputy a remedy shall be had on the official bond of the collector, as in other cases; and of two or more deputy collectors, appointed on the same day, the one residing nearest the residence of the collector at the time of his death, resignation, or removal, shall discharge the said duties until the appointment of a successor:

Provided, That in case it shall appear to the Secretary of the Treasury that the interest of the government shall so require, he may, by his order, direct said duties to be performed by such other one of the said deputies as he may in such order designate. And any bond or security taken from a deputy by such collector, pursuant to this act, shall be available to his legal representatives and sureties to indemnify them for loss or damage accruing from any act of the deputy so continuing or succeeding to the duties of such collector.

Deputy to receive Compensation of Collector.

[SEC. 1. (March 1, 1869.) *Be it enacted by the Senate and House of Representatives of the United States of America in Congress assembled*, That any deputy collector of internal revenue who has performed, or may hereafter perform, under authority or requirement of law, the duties of collector of internal revenue, in consequence of any vacancy in the office of such collector, shall be entitled to and receive so much of the same pay and compensation as is provided by law for such collector; but no such payment shall in any case be made when the collector has received or is entitled to receive compensation for services rendered during the same period of time.]

[SEC. 2. (July 1, 1870.) *Be it enacted by the Senate and House of Representatives of the United States of America in Congress assembled*, That the true intent and meaning of an act approved March one, eighteen hundred and sixty-nine, entitled "An act to allow deputy collectors of internal revenue acting as collectors the pay of collectors and for other purposes," is as follows, to wit: That any deputy collector of internal revenue who has performed, or may hereafter perform, under authority of law, the duties of collector of internal revenue, in consequence of any vacancy in the office of said collector, shall be entitled to, and shall receive, the salary and commissions allowed by law to such collector, or the allowance in lieu of said salary and commissions allowed by the Secretary of the Treasury to such collector, and that the Secretary of the Treasury is authorized to make to the said deputy collector such allowance in lieu of salary and commissions as he would by law be authorized to make to said collector. And said deputy collector shall not be debarred from receiving said salary and commissions, or allowance in lieu thereof, by reason of the holding of another federal office by said collector during the time for which said deputy collector acts as collector: *Provided*, That all payments to said deputy collector shall be upon duly audited vouchers.]

Collectors to prosecute Suits.

Sec. 41. (Amended July 13, 1866, § 9.) *And be it further enacted*, That it shall be the duty of the collectors aforesaid, or their deputies, in their respective districts, and they are hereby authorized to collect all the taxes imposed by law, however the same may be designated, and to prosecute for the recovery of any sum or sums which may be forfeited by law; and all fines, penalties, and forfeitures which may be incurred or imposed by law shall be sued for and recovered, in the name of the United States, in any proper form of action, or by any appropriate form of proceeding, *qui tam* or otherwise, before any circuit or district court of the United States for the district within which said fine, penalty, or forfeiture may have been incurred, or before any other court of competent jurisdiction. And taxes may be sued for and recovered, in the name of the United States, in any proper form of action before any circuit or district court of the United States for the district within which the liability to such tax may have been or shall be incurred or where the party from whom such tax is due may reside at the time of the commencement of said action. But no such suit shall be commenced unless the Commissioner of Internal Revenue shall authorize or sanction the proceedings:

Provided, That in case of any suit for penalties or forfeitures brought upon information received from any person, other than a collector, deputy collector, assessor, assistant assessor, revenue agent, or inspector of internal revenue, the United States shall not be subject to any costs of suit, nor shall the fees of any attorney or counsel employed by any such officer be allowed in the settlement of his account, unless the employment of such attorney or counsel shall be authorized by the Commissioner of Internal Revenue, either expressly or by general regulations.

Commissioner to prescribe Regulations.

[SEC. 3. (March 2, 1867.) *And be it further enacted*, That in all suits or proceedings arising under the internal revenue laws, to which the United States is party, and in all suits or proceedings against a collector or other officer of the internal revenue, wherein a district attorney shall appear for the purpose of prosecuting or defending, it shall be the duty of said attorney, instead of reporting to the Solicitor of the Treasury, immediately at the end of every term of the court in which said suit or proceeding is or shall be instituted, to forward to the Commissioner of Internal Revenue a full and particular statement of the condition of all such suits or proceedings appearing upon the docket of said court: *Provided*, That upon the institution of any such suit or proceeding it shall be the duty of said attorney to report to said Commissioner the full particulars relating to such suit or proceeding; and it shall be the duty of the Commissioner of Internal Revenue (with the approval of the Secretary of the Treasury) to establish such rules and regulations, (*a*) not inconsistent with law, for the observance of revenue officers, district attorneys, and marshals, respecting suits arising under the internal revenue laws, in which the United States is a party, as may be deemed necessary for the just responsibility of those officers and the prompt collection of all revenues and debts due and accruing to the United States under such laws.]

(*a*) 1. Each district attorney should procure a well-bound docket and letter-book, labeled as follows: " The property of the United States, Internal Revenue Cases," each being provided with a suitable index.

These books will be carefully preserved and handed to the successor of such officers. Full and minute entries will be made in these dockets of the time of issuing and receiving papers and process, and of whatsoever is done by said officers in United States internal revenue cases of all kinds, with correct dates. The letter-book will contain full and true copies of all letters written by them officially concerning internal revenue suits or matters relating thereto, in which the United States is interested.

2. All official letters relating to cases under the internal revenue laws, received by district attorneys, will be preserved as public property, and delivered to their successors. Whenever such letters accumulate sufficiently to make a volume, the officer having them in possession will cause the same to be indexed and bound according to their dates.

All papers and documents used by, or coming to the possession of, any district attorney during the progress of a suit, and relating thereto, must be properly filed and kept in a bundle with the other papers relating to the cause, and delivered by him to his successor.

3. No district attorney will commence a suit or proceeding in court arising under the internal revenue laws, in the name, or for the benefit of, the United States, without instructions from the Commissioner, or by direction from some person or court authorized by law so to direct.

4. Whenever any district attorney shall in any manner become possessed of information which shall lead him to believe that a trespass upon the property of the United States (of which possession is held by virtue of the internal revenue law), or an infraction of the internal revenue law, has been committed, he will immediately report such information to the collector of internal revenue for the district in which the offence was committed, and, if the collector shall agree as to its propriety, suit shall be immediately commenced. If the collector shall not so agree, the district attorney will immediately report the circumstances of the case to the Commissioner, and await his instructions.

5. On the receipt of the papers on which to commence suit, the district attorney will closely examine and see if there is any defect in them, or if any explanation is wanted; and, if so, he will immediately report the same to the person from whom the papers were received, with such suggestions as shall seem to him proper. If, before the commencement, or during the progress of a cause, questions shall arise in the mind of the district attorney, in relation to which it may, in his opinion, be desirable that he should take counsel, he shall state such questions to the Commissioner, with the authorities bearing upon them, and also his own views.

6. The commencement of all suits must be reported by district attorneys, on Form 112, to the Commissioner, immediately after process shall be issued, and at the end of every term of the district and circuit courts, they will make a general report, on Form 113, containing a list of all

internal revenue suits commenced by them since the close of the last preceding term of such court, with a full statement of the cause of the action and all the proceedings therein; and also of all proceedings since the close of the last preceding term, in causes previously commenced, so as to furnish to the Commissioner a full history of what has been done in all causes since the previous term, including any trial, verdict, decision, or judgment, and the issuing of any execution, with the time when issued.

7. When a suit shall have been commenced, either by direction of a public officer or otherwise, it will be the duty of the district attorney having such suit in charge, to press the same to a judgment at as early a day as possible, consistent with the interest of the United States. When a cause shall have been continued, the district attorney will, in his next return to the Commissioner, state upon whose motion and upon what grounds the continuance was directed. No district attorney will discontinue a suit, or consent to a dismissal or discontinuance thereof, or suspend proceedings, or argue that a judgment or decree shall be taken for a less amount than the United States is entitled to claim, in view of the violation of the law committed by the defendant, without express instruction from the Commissioner, except that when such attorney shall be of opinion that the suit has been improperly brought, that an error has been committed in the pleadings or proceedings which may be fatal or hazardous to the interests of the Government, or that the evidence in his power to produce is insufficient to support the action, and there shall not be sufficient time to communicate with and receive instruction from the Commissioner, he may consent to suspend proceedings, or to a continuance. In all such cases the district attorney will immediately report the facts and his reasons for his action to the Commissioner.

8. As early as practicable after the perfecting of judgment, execution will be placed in the hands of the marshal by the district attorney, who will take duplicate receipts therefor, one of which he will transmit to the Commissioner. At the commencement of every term of court, the district attorney will carefully examine and ascertain whether the marshal has properly returned all process placed in his hands, the return of which is due. If he shall find that the proper return has not been made, it will be his duty to take prompt and efficient measures to compel action; in which case he will report the steps taken and their result to the Commissioner.

9. All records of cases in error, or on appeals to the Supreme Court, together with the points of both parties, the brief of the district attorney, the authorities cited by the opposing counsel, and the opinion of the judge, when it can be obtained, whether intended for the Attorney General, the clerk of the Supreme Court, or the Commissioner, must be enclosed to the Commissioner, when the proper disposition of the papers will be made.

10. In case of any change of the fee bills or rules of court in either of the districts, the proper district attorney is requested to advise the Commissioner of such alteration.

11. After process is placed in the hand of a marshal, district attorneys will not attempt to control or interfere with the execution of the same, as therein commanded, without special directions from the Commissioner.

MARSHALS.

1. Marshals will each procure a well-bound docket, day-book, ledger, and letter-book, labelled and marked as follows: "The Property of the United States—Internal Revenue Cases," with suitable index for each. These books will be carefully preserved by the marshals and handed to their successors. They will make minute entries in their dockets of the time of receiving and serving papers and process, and of whatever is done

by them in cases arising under the internal revenue laws, with correct dates. The letter-book will contain full and true copies of all letters written by such officers, officially relating to such suits or matters in which the United States are interested. In the day-book and letter-book full and accurate accounts will be kept of all moneys received and paid out for the United States, on account of these cases. The entries in docket and account-books will be so full, clear, and definite that they can be easily understood.

2. All official letters relating to United States internal revenue cases, received by marshals, not needed by them as vouchers for the payment of money, will be preserved as public property, and delivered to their successors. Where the originals are essential to them as vouchers, they will leave copies of them in their places. Whenever such letters accumulate sufficiently to make a volume, the officer having them in possession will cause the same to be indexed and bound according to their date.

3. On receipt of every process, mesne and final, in United States internal revenue cases (except subpœnas), marshals will notify the Commissioner thereof on Forms 114 and 115 respectively, stating the title and nature of the suit, the name of the process, and, if an execution, distress warrant, or otherwise requiring the collection of money, or sale or seizure of property, the amount of the debt, or a description of the property to be sold or seized, and the amount of the costs, with the time from which they are directed to collect interest. They will also give to the district attorney duplicate receipts expressing the above particulars.

4. Where a marshal, in an United States internal revenue case, makes a seizure or levy, he will report to the Commissioner, giving a full description of the property seized or levied upon, in whose possession found, where, how, and by whom, and upon what terms kept, and how long it will be necessary to keep it. If, at the time of sale, no one bids to the amount of the execution, or one-half the cash value of the property offered, he will postpone the sale and give notice to the Commissioner—except in cases where, by such postponement, the lien would be lost or the interest of the Government seriously jeopardized. In the latter case, if he shall deem it necessary to save the debt, he will consider the United States as bidding such an amount not greater than one-half the cash value of the property as he shall deem proper for their interests. Should the United States become the purchaser of the property, the marshal will take care of the same, and will make an immediate report of his action in relation thereto to the Commissioner.

5. When real estate shall be purchased at a marshal's sale by or for the United States, the marshal will immediately transmit to the office of the Commissioner his certificate of sale, according to the law and usages in his district; and when the purchaser shall be entitled thereto, said marshal shall execute his deed for the property to the United States, and cause the same to be placed on record, and immediately thereafter he will transmit such deed to the Commissioner.

6. On the return of process in cases arising under the internal revenue laws, the marshal will report in writing to the district attorney, and also to the Commissioner of Internal Revenue, what they have done on each. In cases where the marshal returns in substance "no property found," he will also specially report to the district attorney and the Commissioner the situation, residence, and circumstances of the party against whom the process was issued, and whether the debtor has any means within or out of the district, which can be reached by the United States, or whether the debt is valueless.

7. In all cases where the money is made by the marshal on execution, or where it shall come into his hands in any other manner, he will pay the entire gross proceeds into the registry of the court, and will immediately re-

port to the district attorney, and to the Commissioner, on Form 116, fully and particularly, stating when, from whom, and on what account the same was received.

8. On the first day of March in each year, marshals will report to the Commissioner the situation of all judgment debtors of the United States, under the internal revenue laws, within their respective districts, so far as they have any knowledge upon the subject, and will advise such proceedings in the premises as they shall deem proper.

Documents, books, and papers relating to internal revenue cases, coming into the possession of district attorneys and marshals, must be kept separate and distinct from those relating to other cases, and matters in which the United States are interested.

COLLECTORS.

1. Each collector will keep a record or docket of the seizures made in his district, and show therein the date of the seizure, at whose instance it was made, the kind, quality, and estimated value of the property, the name of the informer, if any, the name and address of the owner of the property, the reason for such seizure, where stored, or by whom taken care of, the nature of the proceedings instituted, and the final disposition of the case. On making a seizure the collector will at once notify the Commissioner, on Form 117, stating all the facts pertaining to the same then in his possession.

2. Where small seizures made by collectors shall be appraised at less than three hundred dollars, district attorneys will not proceed against them, but collectors will sell such articles in the manner prescribed by law.

3. All property seized by collectors or transferred to them, where practicable, will be stored and kept in the United States warehouse, or warehouses, used and occupied under the internal revenue laws by the officers of the Government.

4. When a collector of internal revenue directs the commencement of a suit for any cause, he will do so in writing addressed to the proper district attorney. If it is for a fine, penalty, or forfeiture, he will communicate all the facts which he expects to be able to prove, and the names and residences of the witnesses by whom such facts can be shown, and the name of the informer, if any. He will distinctly state what law he believes has been violated, and the amount of the penalty claimed. In cases of seizure, he will state what property has been seized, and for what cause; also, how and upon what terms the property so seized is kept. A copy of such direction and communication, the person ordering the suit will immediately send to the Commissioner.

MISCELLANEOUS.

1. District attorneys, marshals, and collectors of internal revenue will report to the Commissioner the existence and situation of any property belonging to the United States, by reason of violation of the internal revenue laws, which is not in the care of any officer or agent of the Government, to the end that it may be protected and preserved. If either of them shall discover that any claim in favor of the Government, not in his hands, can be collected, he will report to the Commissioner, and recommend the best mode for proceeding. They will also report immediately to the Commissioner any default of a district attorney, clerk, marshal, or collector, or other person engaged in the collection of any debt due to the United States under the internal revenue laws, or in the disbursement of any money collected in such cases. All reports will be made substantially

in the form furnished from the Commissioner's office, which will be exclusively used when applicable.

2. Whenever any suit shall be brought against any officer of the United States in the internal revenue service, for any act done or omitted in his official capacity, and in the defence of which he may desire the aid of the district attorney, or by the determination of which the interests of the United States may be in any wise affected, such officer shall, as soon as practicable, transmit to the district attorney the process served upon him, together with a clear statement of the circumstances out of which the suit shall have arisen; whereupon the district attorney will either assume the defence of such suit, or apply for instruction in relation thereto to the Commissioner, as may be required by the nature of the case.

3. Every officer (other than a collector of internal revenue in his own district) who makes a seizure, will at once report the fact to the collector of the district in which the seized property is located, and turn over the same to the said collector as soon as possible, forwarding to the Commissioner at once a report embodying all the facts concerning the same which are then known to him.

4. The receipt of all communications from the office of the Commissioner will be acknowledged by the first mail

5. In all cases where receipts, notices, returns, or other papers are required to be sent to the office of the Commissioner, they must be forwarded at the earliest practicable moment.

6. In all cases, where desired, duplicate receipts for moneys or papers received, will be executed by the party receiving them.

7. Letters to the Commissioner will be on ordinary sized letter paper, with ample margin on all sides. All letters will be enclosed in envelopes, and each distinct subject will be communicated within a separate letter. All letters will be endorsed on the back with the name of the party writing, official designation, residence, date of letter, and brief of contents.

8. None of the foregoing instructions to district attorneys, marshals, collectors, and other officers of internal revenue, are to be deemed to apply to any cases except those arising under the internal revenue laws. 5 I. R. R. 155.

When a marshal takes possession of a distillery by virtue of a process issued for a violation of the internal revenue laws, he should immediately cause the head of the still to be taken off, or the machinery to be disconnected in such a manner as to render it impossible for distillation to be carried on. Admission to such premises should at all times be permitted to any internal revenue officer who would be entitled to admission were the same put in the custody of the marshal. 7 I. R. R. 74.

Penalty for Perjury.

Sec. 42. *And be it further enacted,* That if any person, in any case, matter, hearing, or other proceeding in which an oath or affirmation shall be required to be taken or administered under and by virtue of this act, shall, upon the taking of such oath or affirmation, knowingly and wilfully swear or affirm falsely, every person so offending shall be deemed guilty of perjury, (a) and shall, on conviction thereof, be subject to the like punishment and penalties now provided by the laws of the United States for the crime of perjury.

(a) An indictment for perjury is good without any averment of materiality, when it appears upon its face that the fact alleged to have been falsely sworn to was a material one. It is not necessary that the facts sworn to should constitute full proof of the matter at issue; they are material, if it can be seen that they would necessarily tend to prove it. U. S. *v.* McHenry, 10 I. R. R. 42.

Separate Accounts to be Kept.

Sec. 43. *And be it further enacted,* That separate accounts shall be kept at the treasury of all moneys received from internal duties or taxes in each of the respective States, Territories, and collection districts; and that separate accounts shall be kept of the amount of each species of duty or tax that shall accrue, so as to exhibit, as far as may be, the amount collected from each source of revenue, with the moneys paid as compensation and for allowances to the collectors and deputy collectors, assessors and assistant assessors, inspectors, and other officers employed in each of the respective States, Territories, and collection districts, an abstract in tabular form of which accounts it shall be the duty of the Secretary of the Treasury annually, in the month of December, to lay before Congress.

Appeals to Commissioner.

Sec. 44. (Amended July 13, 1866, § 9.) *And be it further enacted,* That the Commissioner of Internal Revenue, subject to regulations prescribed by the Secretary of the Treasury, shall be, and is hereby, authorized, on appeal to him made, to remit, refund, (*a*) and pay back all taxes erroneously or illegally assessed or collected, all penalties collected without authority, and all taxes that shall appear to be unjustly assessed or excessive in amount, or in any manner wrongfully collected, and also repay to collectors or deputy collectors the full amount of such sums of money as shall or may be recovered against them, or any of them, in any court, for any internal taxes or licenses collected by them, with the costs and expenses of suit, and all damages and costs recovered against assessors, assistant assessors, collectors, deputy collectors, and inspectors, in any suit which shall be brought against them, or any of them, by reason of any thing that shall or may be done in the due performance of their official duties; and all judgments and moneys recovered or received for taxes, costs, forfeitures, and penalties, shall be paid to the collector as internal taxes are required to be paid.

Provided, That where a second assessment may have been made in case of a list, statement, or return which in the opinion of the assessor or assistant assessor was false or fraudulent, or contained any understatement or undervaluation, such assessment shall not be remitted, nor shall taxes ecollcted under such assessment be recovered, refunded, or paid back, unless it is proved that said list, statement, or return was not false or fraudulent, and did not contain any understatement or undervaluation.

(*a*) Claims for refunding must be made on forms 46, verified by affidavits like claims for abatement, and by certificates of the assistant assessor, assessor and collector. The collector must certify to the date of payment of the amount claimed. Claims for refunding should not be entered in schedules and may be presented as often as desired; but unless they are presented to the proper revenue officers within six months from the date of the payment of the tax, the Commissioner will not be bound to investigate them, and may refer the claimants to their remedy at law. The post-office address of parties making claims for refunding should be given; otherwise, the claims cannot be paid if allowed.

Both the assessor and collector should keep a perfect record in the book furnished for the purpose, of all claims presented to the Commissioner, and must certify that each claim has not been before presented. If any claim on Form 46 or 47 is presented without the certificate of the assistant assessor, the reason for the omission must be given.

If in any case, after a full investigation, the assessor and collector, either or both, cannot certify to the facts set forth in the affidavits, they should state the reason for their dissent, and allow the party to corroborate his statements by such other proof as he is able to furnish.

Members of firms making affidavits must swear, each for himself, to the fact set forth, including that of membership, and subscribed his own name and not that of the firm.

Affidavits may be made before any internal revenue officer, or before the chief clerk of an assessor, without fee; but when made before the chief clerk, must be accompanied by the assessor's or collector's certificate, verifying the chief clerkship and the absence of the assessor at the time. Any other person administering an oath or affirmation must show, by seal, or certificate from the proper authority, that he is qualified to do so, and the certificate must be stamped.

Credits should not be taken by collectors for taxes supposed to be uncollectible until notice of abatement is received from the Commissioner. When taxes are abated, the amounts are at once credited to the collectors upon the books in the office of the Commissioner, and schedules of the same are sent to them with authority to take credit for the sums abated in their next quarterly accounts.

When credit is given on account of insolvent or absconding persons, although the collector is thereby released from the obligation created by receipting for the amount credited, the obligation to pay still remains upon the assessed persons, of whom a record must be kept in the book furnished from the office of the Commissioner. Collectors should bear this fact in mind, and not consider themselves as released from the obligation to collect in such cases whenever it shall be in their power. If, pending action for abatement of an erroneous assessment, the tax should be collected, the collector, upon receiving an order for abating the same, will return the amount to the assessor on Form 58, and will make affidavit on Form 46, giving the date of the payment, and naming the assessment list upon which it is returned a second time, and have it properly certified to by the assessor and assistant assessor, when a draft for the amount will be drawn in favor of the person assessed. If a claim for an uncollectible tax should be paid, pending action, or after it has been abated, it should be returned as above on Form 58. Schedules of all taxes abated, refunded, or allowed as uncollectible, will be sent to assessors to be kept on file for public inspection. 8 I. R. R. 204.

No claim or application for the refunding of taxes will be entitled to consideration unless the same shall be filed with the Commissioner within two years from the date of the payment of the tax, or in the case of claims that accrued prior to August 3, 1866, within two years after that date. 10 I. R. R. 41.

The Commissioner is required to make application from time to time to the Secretary of the Treasury to have the necessary sums placed to his credit with the assistant treasurer at New York, on which he draws in like manner as if the moneys were in the hands of the collectors. 2 I. R. R. 68.

Whenever a proposition for a compromise is made by a delinquent taxpayer, it is forwarded to the Commissioner of Internal Revenue with the indorsement of the collector and assessor. A copy of an assessment made out by the assessor from the best information that he can obtain should accompany it. 3 I. R. R. 94.

When Suits for Taxes may be Commenced.

[SEC. 19. (July 13, 1866; as amended March 2, 1867, § 10). *And be it further enacted,* That no suit shall be maintained in any court for the recovery of any tax alleged to have been erroneously or illegally assessed or collected, until appeal (a) shall have been duly made to the Commissioner of Internal Revenue, according to the provisions of law in that regard, and the regulations of the Secretary of the Treasury established in pursuance thereof, and a decision of said Commissioner be had thereon, unless such suit shall be brought within six months from the time of said decision, or within six months from the time this act takes effect:

Provided, That if said decision shall be delayed more than six months from the date of said appeal, then said suit may be brought at any time within twelve months from the date of such appeal, and no suit for the purpose of restraining the assessment or collection of tax shall be maintained in any court.]

(a) Under the provisions of this section appeals may be made:

1. From the decision of an assessor when a person feels aggrieved by the assessment. This appeal may be presented on Form 47 for the abatement of the tax.

2. For refunding on Form 46.

In either case the applicant should specify the date of the assessment; if monthly, for what month or months; if annually, the year or part of the year for which the assessment was made, the subject matter upon which the assessment was imposed; and, in cases for refunding, the date of payment; and should give a clear and concise statement of the facts upon which he bases his application. When he refers to correspondence with the office of Internal Revenue, the date and subject of the letters should be given with the name of the writer, if to the office, or of the person addressed, if from the office, to facilitate the finding of the correspondence, or copies of all such letters, or the originals may be furnished when in the power of the applicant.

The officers should make the certificates on those Forms in the manner hereinbefore required for claims for abatement or refunding. 8 I. R. R. 204.

The jurisdiction of the courts to give redress to a party aggrieved by an erroneous or illegal assessment, has often been denied because the party may appeal to the Commissioner for redress, and because he may also pursue his remedy by petition to Congress or present it in the Court of Claims. Such a theory finds no substantial support in any act of Congress upon the subject or in any decided case. On the contrary, the several acts of Congress for the assessment and collection of internal revenue duties, contain many provisions wholly inconsistent with any such theory, and which, when considered together, afford an entirely satisfactory basis for the opposite conclusion. City of Philadelphia v. Collector, 5 Wall. 720; Nelson v. Carman, 6 I. R. R. 181; s. c. 5 Blatch. 511; Pacific Ins. Co. v. Soule, 7 Wall. 443; Mandell v. Pierce, 7 I. R. R. 193; s. c. 1 A. L. T. (C. R.) 123; Shaefer v. Ketchum, 6 I. R. R. 4; Blake v. McCartney, 10 I. R. R. 131.

A verbal protest noted by the collector upon the back of the receipt, given to the taxpayer, is sufficient. Shaefer et al. v. Ketchum, 6 I. R. R. 4.

Neither a Federal nor a State tribunal have any right to restrain the collection of a federal tax assessed by an officer having jurisdiction of the subject, be it ever so irregular or erroneous. By the common law, a citizen could not replevin property seized for taxes. It was deemed impolitic to suffer such a remedy. According to English equity, an injunction could not be issued in such a case. Wide as the departures are from these principles in some of the State courts, all disclaim the jurisdiction *per se*. By the rarity and exceptional character of their interposition, they authorize the assertion of the general rule that there was no remedy by injunction to prevent the collection of an illegal tax. Irrespective of all legislation, there was neither replevin nor injunction. The wrong must be submitted to, and suit at law brought to recover damages for its infliction. Whenever the government seeks the property of a citizen, exercising the right of eminent domain, or by taxation in any of its numerous forms, the processes for seizure and assessment are, in the most plenary sense, within the discretion of the legislature. Pullan et al. v. Kinsinger et al. 11 I. R. R. 197; Grover et al. v. King, 8 I. R. R. 157; s. c. 3 A. L. Rev. 169; Roback v. Taylor, 4 I. R. R. 170; Cutting et al. v. Gibert, 2 I. R. R. 93; s. c. 5 Blatch. 259; Clark et al. v. Gilbert, 4 I. R. R. 42; s. c. 5 Blatch. 330.

Bill of Sale to be Evidence.

Sec. 45. *And be it further enacted,* That in all cases of distraint and sale of goods or chattels for non-payment of taxes, duties, or licenses, as provided for, the bill of sale of such goods or chattels given by the officer making such sale, to the purchaser thereof, shall be *prima facie* evidence of the right of the officer to make such sale, and conclusive evidence of the regularity of his proceedings in selling the same.

Enforcement in Insurrectionary Districts.

Sec. 46. *And be it further enacted,* That if, for any cause, at any time after this act goes into operation, the laws of the United States cannot be executed in a State or Territory of the United States, or any part thereof, or within the District of Columbia, it shall be the duty of the President, and he is hereby authorized, to proceed to execute the provisions of this act within the limits of such State or Territory, or part thereof, or District of Columbia, so soon as the authority of the United States therein shall be re-established, and to collect the taxes, duties, and licenses in such States and Territories, under the regulations prescribed in this act, so far as applicable; and where not applicable, the assessment and levy shall be made, and the time and manner of collection regulated, by the instructions and directions of the Commissioner of Internal Revenue, under the direction of the Secretary of the Treasury.

When Officers shall collect Direct Tax.

Sec. 47. *And be it further enacted,* That the officers who may be appointed under this act, except within those districts within any State or Territory which have been or may be otherwise especially provided for by law, shall be, and hereby are, authorized, in all cases where the payment of such tax shall not have been assumed by the State, to perform all the duties relating to or regarding the assessment and collection of any direct tax imposed or which may be imposed by law.

Seizure of Property used for Fraudulent Purposes.

Sec. 48. (Amended July 13, 1866, § 9.) *And be it further enacted,* That all goods, wares, merchandise, articles, or objects, on which taxes are imposed by the provisions of law, which shall be found in the possession, or custody, or within the control of any person or persons, for the purpose of being sold or removed by such person or persons in fraud of the internal revenue laws, or with design to avoid payment of said taxes, may be seized (*a*) by the collector or deputy collector of the proper district, or by such other collector or deputy collector as may be specially authorized by the Commissioner of Internal Revenue for that purpose, and the same shall be forfeited to the United States; and also all raw materials found in the possession of any person or persons intending to manufacture the same into articles of a kind subject to tax for the purpose of fraudulently selling such manufactured articles, or with design to evade the payment of said tax; and also all tools, implements, instruments, and personal property whatsoever, in the place or building or within any yard or enclosure where such articles or such raw materials shall be found, may also be seized by any collector or deputy collector as aforesaid, and the same shall be forfeited as aforesaid; and the proceedings to enforce said forfeiture shall be in the nature of a proceeding *in rem* (*b*) in the circuit or district court of the United States for the district where such seizure is made, or in any other court of competent jurisdiction.

And any person who shall have in his custody or possession any such goods, wares, merchandise, articles, or objects, subject to tax as aforesaid, for the purpose of selling the same with the design of avoiding payment of the taxes imposed thereon, shall be liable to a penalty (*c*) of five hundred dollars, or not less than double the amount of taxes fraudulently attempted to be evaded, to be recovered in any court of competent jurisdiction; and the goods, wares, merchandise, articles, or objects, which shall be so seized by any collector or deputy collector, may, at the option of the collector, be delivered to the marshal of said district, and remain in the care and custody of said marshal, and under his control, until he shall obtain possession by process of law, and the cost of seizure made before process issues shall be taxable by the court: (*d*)

Provided, That when the property so seized may be liable to perish or become greatly reduced in price or value by keeping, or when it cannot be kept without great expense, the owner thereof, the collector, or the marshal of the district, may apply to the assessor of the district to examine said property; and if, in the opinion of said assessor, it shall be necessary that the said property should be sold to prevent such waste or expense, he shall appraise the same; and the owner thereupon shall have said property returned to him upon giving bond in such form as may be prescribed by the Commissioner of Internal Revenue, and in an amount equal to the appraised value, with such sureties as the said assessor shall deem good and sufficient, to abide the final order, decree, or judgment of the court having cognizance of the case, and to pay the amount of said appraised value to the collector, marshal, or otherwise, as he may be ordered and directed by the court, which bond shall be filed by said assessor with the United States district attorney for the district in which said proceedings *in rem* may be commenced.

Provided further, That in case said bond shall have been executed and the property returned before seizure thereof, by virtue of the process aforesaid, the marshal shall give notice of the pendency of proceedings in court to the parties executing said bond, by personal service or publication, and in manner and form as the court may direct, and the court shall thereupon have jurisdiction of said matter and parties in the same manner as if such property had been seized by virtue of the process aforesaid. But if said owner shall neglect or refuse to give said bond, the assessor shall issue to the collector or marshal aforesaid an order to sell the same; and the said collector or marshal shall thereupon advertise and sell the said property at public auction in the same manner as goods may be sold on final execution in said district; and the proceeds of the sale, after deducting the reasonable costs of the seizure and sale, shall be paid to the court aforesaid, to abide its final order, decree, or judgment.

(a) Where a seizure is made under this section, or any other section authorizing a seizure for fraud or violation of law, and is followed by proceedings *in rem*, if a decree is obtained and sale made by order of court, the collector cannot, of course, receive a commission on proceeds of sale. The same rule must govern if the case is compromised pending the suit.

In some cases, where taxes are due and fraud is suspected, it may be advisable to seize under this section or some other section authorizing seizure for fraud. In a case of this kind, if the seizure is converted into a distraint for taxes, and the goods or property are sold, the collector will, of course, charge the commission of five per cent. allowed by section 28. But if, after distraint in such case, and before sale, payment is made, or the case is compromised, the collector cannot charge a commission. 8 I. R. R. 202.

In order to avoid giving cause of complaint to transportation companies, warehousemen, or other persons having a lien on the property, collectors, when they seize property in the custody of such companies or persons, should address and deliver to them a written statement, giving, for the purpose of identifying the property seized, an inventory of the different articles, mentioning the brands, numbers, and marks thereon, including, when they are known, the name and residence of the ostensible owner.

They should also, in the same statement, specify in general terms that the property is seized for violation of the internal revenue laws.

If the property is removed from the custody of the company or bailee, that fact should be stated in the paper, that they may be able to show that the property has properly passed from their possession. This statement should be signed by the seizing officer, or collector, or deputy collector, giving his full address. Where it is required, the seizing officer should show that he is an officer authorized by law to make seizures.

When property is forfeited, the collector should inform the company or bailee. If, however, it is released, upon compromise or otherwise, it should be returned to the company or bailee, unless their consent is given that it be delivered directly to the claimant. 8 I. R. R. 203.

The Commissioner is not confined to designating one collector to make general seizures, but may designate any collector or deputy collector not of the proper district, whenever in his opinion, the exercise of such authority becomes necessary and expedient. 5 I. R. R. 44.

No property seized by any internal revenue officer will be released by order of the Commissioner until the officer who made the seizure and the assessor and collector of the district have reported the facts in the case, with their recommendation, or have had ample opportunity to make such report or recommendation. 10 I. R. R. 5.

The main question under this section is contained in the words, "for the purpose of being sold or removed by such person or persons in fraud of the internal revenue laws, or with the design to avoid the payment of said taxes." The circumstances attending the acquisition or receipt of the property liable to taxes are to be taken into consideration by the jury upon the question as to what the design of the parties was in regard to it, and in regard to selling and removing it. The claimants knew these circumstances, and it is for them to show these; and if there is any doubt, embarrassment, or difficulty, the point must be decided against them. The presumption is that the tax has not been paid. The government must show that the claimants knew, or had reasonable cause to believe, that the tax had not been paid. If a person, at the time he purchases and receives property, has reasonable ground to believe that the tax has been paid, and afterward finds out that the tax has not been paid, the property will be liable to seizure. In such case, after he finds out that the tax has not been paid, the property is in his possession with notice that the tax has not been paid. U. S. *v.* Quantity of Spirits, 9 I. R. R. 9; s. c. 2, A. L. T. (C. R.) 23; U. S. *v.* 36 Bbls. 12 I. R. R. 40.

The statute should receive a reasonable, not a strict, construction, so as to accomplish the intention of Congress. Distilled spirits in a distillery warehouse are in the possession of the owner of the spirits and warehouse. U. S. *v.* 86 Bbls. 12 I. R. R. 40.

This section is very comprehensive. It embraces: 1st. All goods, articles, or objects on which taxes are imposed by law, found in possession or within the control of any person for the purpose of being sold or removed, in fraud of the internal revenue, with intent to avoid payment of the taxes. 2d. All raw materials found in like possession or control, intended to be manufactured into articles of a kind subject to taxes, with the intent to sell the same, in fraud of the revenue; and, 3d. All personal property whatsoever found in the place or building, or within the yard or enclosure, where the articles or raw materials previously referred to were found or seized. The seizure of the articles in the third class stands on the ground of association with the guilty classes or articles. The fraudulent intent or purpose of the person in the possession or having the control of the articles do not constitute the element of the offence or ground of forfeiture. Personal property thus situated is frequently used to facilitate the accomplishment of the frauds provided against in the forepart of the section. Evidence is admissible to remove the guilt that arises from the condition of the property. The burden of proof rests upon the claimant, to make out to the satisfaction of the court and jury that the situation of the property is consistent with entire innocence on his part. When the evidence as to whether the articles claimed were within the place, building, yard, or enclosure, are all one way, the court need not submit the question to the jury. U. S. *v.* One still, 5 I. R. R. 188; s. c. 5 Blatch 403; U. S. *v.* 153 Bbls. 6 I. R. R. 203; U. S. *v.* Quantity of Rags, 7 I. R. R. 123.

Contra. By reason and analogy, as well as by the context, it is plain that some real connection with the fraud is intended to be attached to the property that is liable to seizure. The untaxed articles and the raw materials intended to be manufactured are the principal things, and the tools, implements, instruments, and personal property are only the connected incidents. By the familiar rule of construction, *noscitur a sociis*, the general words, "personal property," must be restricted by the more particular and immediately preceding words, "tools, implements, and instruments." The statute only forfeits the tools, implements, instruments, and personal property connected with the illegal business, and found within the building, yard, or enclosure where that business is carried on. U. S. *v.* 33 Bbls. 7 I. R. R. 55.

(*b*) The proceeding is only required to be in the nature of a proceeding *in rem*. It is left to the courts by rules and regulations to establish the practice to be observed in conducting such proceedings, which practice, however, must conform in nature to the well-known proceedings *in rem* and which must, of course, be subject to any general statutory regulations thereto. U. S. *v.* 7 Bbls. 8 I. R. R. 162.

The promulgation by the Supreme Court of rules for practice and pleadings superseded such rules of the district courts as were in conflict therewith. An information, as mentioned in Rule XXII., is a proceeding against property liable to seizure and condemnation, where the proceedings fall on the exchequer or common law side of the court. The old mode of proceeding was very much like a declaration, where each cause of action was set out in a distinct count, subject, of course, to all the rules governing such technical modes of pleading. When the pleading, however, was required to be done by articulation instead of the old common forms of counts, it was brought within the general modes used for libels in admiralty. It saves the pleader from needless repetition in connection with each of the several causes of forfeiture. The first proceeds to a general averment, which is applicable all the way through to each articulation. The original pleading being by articulation, the issues should take the form of an answer instead of a plea proper. The design of the Supreme Court was to have a uniform mode of pleading in the three classes of cases, informations, libels of information, and libels pure. The defendant, in pleading by answer, should affirm, admit, or controvert the allegations contained in each article, or admit part and controvert part, as the case may be. The necessity for a formal conclusion does not exist. The technical conclusion, if there be any for adoption in such cases, should be at the close of the answer to the various articles in the information, and that springs from the very nature of the case. The cause being a suit *in rem*, there is no defendant, properly speaking; any one within the rules of law who has the right to appear and claim such property, may appear. Hence, so far as the conclusion is concerned, it may be the ordinary form of conclusion, "wherefore he prays that the said property may be delivered to him"—a simple prayer for restitution. The answer should aver that the charge made in a particular article is not true, if it is to be controverted; or if it is to be admitted, say it is true, &c. Sometimes it may happen that there are many matters in one articulation, which the party pleading for the claimant may wish to separate. Then he can state: As to so and so, they are true; as to other matters, they are not true; or he may take still the third form, and may deny that they are any of them true, except as hereinafter stated, and then begin and state what he alleges to be the actual truth in regard to them. The averments of the answer must be positive. The pleadings must make issues. The information and belief should only be stated in the verification. There the party is not required to state of his own knowledge that what he has stated in the answer is true; but he must state that he knows, or that he has been informed, or that he believes it to be true. U. S. v. 25 Bbls. 10 I. R. R. 17.

A motion to quash an information does not lie. A demurrer is the proper mode of reaching technical or substantial defects.

Informations by United States district attorneys are amendable even after pleas filed, and in substance; and such amendments may be allowed even by the judge at chambers. Counts can be stricken out and new ones inserted.

Informations *in rem* in the exchequer side are not criminal proceedings. They are *civiliter non criminaliter*.

The broad distinction between informations by the attorney-general and informations by private persons are well settled and uniformly recognized.

Amendments can be made in the appellate court only when the suits are on the admiralty side of the court.

Although the technical precision of an indictment is not necessary, yet the allegations must be sufficiently specific to enable the claimant to traverse them, and the court to see that, if true, a violation of the statute exists. The violation may be charged in the words of the statute, but a general averment that the statute has been violated is not sufficient.

Charges may be averred in the alternative, but each alternative ought to contain in itself a complete and substantive charge. The court may order a repleader, so that each charge may be pleaded in a separate article.

A new *res* cannot be covered by way of amendment, for that would introduce a new subject or party, and change the nature of the proceedings. But when a *res* is before the court for an alleged forfeiture, the court will permit, by way of amendment, any new cause of forfeiture, consistent with the original nature of the suit, to be introduced by amendment.

When, on the hearing, it appears that the *res* is not forfeited for any of the causes alleged, but for some other cause not charged, the court will alter the *res* to be detained to await further proceedings.

Only one action *in rem* by the United States against the same *res* should be pending at the same time. If, on the hearing of that cause, it should appear that the forfeiture had been incurred on other than the grounds alleged, or if other causes of forfeiture existed which called for further proof, then, on the motion for restitution, the United States could object, and, on a petition or otherwise, ask for the detention of the *res* to await further proceedings.

The formal mode of disputing the claimant's right to be heard, or *status*, is by exception, in the nature of a plea in abatement. U. S. v. 396 Bbls. 3 I. R. R. 123.

If any one count in an information *in rem* is good in form and applicable to the case proved, objectious to other counts are disregarded. An amendment cannot be allowed without giving the claimant the option of a continuance. U. S. *v.* Whisky &c. 11 I. R. R. 109.

The government may procure an order requiring the claimant to produce his books. This order may be served upon the claimant's attorney. The order must be complied with at the time of the trial, or an excuse given under oath by the party himself for a non-compliance with it. If the order is not complied with, nor a sufficient excuse given, the government may claim a judgment by default, and a forfeiture of the property. The sufficiency or insufficiency of the excuse has to be determined when it is produced. The court may postpone the case to allow the claimant to make the affidavit. U. S. *v.* 469 Bbls. 10 I. R. R. 265.

The pendency of another information does not affect the question of the admissibility of evidence of other fraudulent acts similar to that charged. The range of such an inquiry must be determined according to the circumstances of each case. The period of time and its limit must be fixed in the discretion of the court. U. S. *v.* 36 Bbls. 12 I. R. R. 41.

If there is any reasonable doubt arising upon the evidence, as to whether the government has established its case, within the rules of law applicable to the subject, the verdict should be for the claimant. The government must make out its case by a preponderance of evidence. It is not like a criminal case, where the defendant is entitled to the benefit of a reasonable doubt of guilt. U. S. *v.* Quantity of Spirits, 9 I. R. R. 9.

The merits of the controversy do not depend upon the state of things existing at the time of the detention or seizure, but upon the question whether a forfeiture had previously been incurred. If it had been incurred, the title of the United States will have relation to the time when it was incurred; and the causes of forfeiture supposed by the seizing officer to have existed are in that case immaterial, if any sufficient cause alleged in the information is established by the evidence. In such cases the property is not forfeitable because it has been seized, but is seized because it was previously forfeited. It is wholly immaterial who makes the seizure, or whether it is irregularly made or not, or whether the cause assigned originally for the seizure is that for which the condemnation takes place, provided the adjudication is for a sufficient cause. U. S. *v.* Whisky &c. 11 I. R. R. 109; U. S. *v.* 56 Bbls. 4 I. R. R. 106.

The prosecution cannot be maintained except for the substantial causes which the information specifies; and these cannot be supplied by evidence defining or adding to the specification of them in the evidence. U. S. *v.* Whisky &c. 11 I. R. R. 109.

It is the offending thing that is forfeited. The entire right of property of all the world in the thing is cut off. The proceeding is *in rem*, and it is not the right of property therein of a mortgagor any more than the right of a mortgagee that is cut off. The thing is the offender, and the mortgagee, by suffering the thing to be in such a position that the offence can be committed in respect of it, is just as much, in a legal sense, a participant in the offence, so far as the thing is concerned, as is the mortgagor, who actively uses the thing to commit the offence. The good or bad faith of the mortgagee is immaterial. U. S. v. Distilled Spirits, 8 I. R. R. 81; s. c. 1 A. L. T. (C. R.) 103; U. S. v. 21 Bhls. 6 I. R. R. 213; U. S. v. 20 Bbls. 9 I. R. R. 4; U. S. v. 395 Bbls. 3 I. R. R. 135; Blair's Distillery, 3 I. R. R. 67.

When forfeited spirits are mixed with other spirits owned by the claimant, the amount of the mixture that will be forfeited depends upon the intent with which the mixture was made. Whenever goods of a similar kind are innocently mixed, so that they cannot be distinguished, and they are not substantially destroyed by the production of something of a different species, the several owners may reclaim their respective shares, and may take possession of the same wherever they can find their goods—if they can do so without a breach of the peace—or they may bring trover for the value of their respective shares against the person in possession, after demand and notice. When the intermixture is made wilfully, and not by mutual consent, the common law, to guard against fraud, gives the entire mixture to him whose property was originally invaded and its distinct character destroyed. There is a distinction between an innocent and a fraudulent act. Rectification does not change the species of the spirits. U. S. v. 56 Bhls. 4 I. R. R. 106; U. S. v. 278 Bbls. 10 I. R. R. 164; s. c. 16 Pitts. L. J. 250; U. S. v. 54 Bbls. 9 I. R. R. 121.

When a statute denounces a forfeiture of property as the penalty for the commission of a crime, if the denunciation is in direct terms, and not in the alternative, the forfeiture takes place at the time the offence is committed, and operates as a statutory transfer of the right of property to the government. The *bona fides* of a purchase made subsequent to the forfeiture is immaterial. If the forfeiture took place prior to the purchase, the right of property was immediately transferred to the United States, and that right must prevail over the right of the purchaser, notwithstanding the purchase was made in good faith. U. S. v. 56 Bbls. 4 I. R. R. 106; U. S. v. 46 Casks, 5 I. R. R. 161.

If an agent is cognizant of fraud at the time of the purchase of the spirits claimed, the principal is bound by that knowledge, whether the knowledge of the agent was acquired at that time or the day before. The principal is affected by the antecedent knowledge of the agent, if that knowledge is present in the mind of the agent at the time he makes the purchase. U. S. v. 278 Bbls. 10 I. R. R. 164; s. c. 16 Pitts. L. J. 250.

The word "defendant," as used in the act May 8, 1792 (1 St it. 277), must be held to include a claimant in an action *in rem* for a forfeiture. No other party is before the court in such a proceeding to whom the word defendant can be applied. According to the act, when a verdict is rendered in favor of the government, a judgment must be entered condemning the property as forfeited to the United States, and condemning the claimant to pay the costs; and such decree will cover all the costs of the cause. The act makes no allusion to any exceptions, nor does it permit the court to exercise any discretion in the premises. The claimant is made by law subject to the costs, and to all the costs incurred in the cause. The amount is not limited to the amount fixed in the stipulation for costs. The fact that the claimant signed the stipulation did not increase his liability, nor can the stipulation have the effect to diminish that liability which the statute imposes upon him. As to the stipulator, the case is different. He is only liable by virtue of his stipulation, and that liability cannot exceed the amount of the stipulation. U. S. v. 7 Bbls. 8 I. R. R. 162.

When the collector has seized property, and, on trial, a verdict has been rendered for the claimant, but certificate of probable cause is granted by the court, the collector must nevertheless return the property, or he will be liable to the owner. The certificate can only operate as a bar when the property is restored. The return of the property forthwith after judgment is a condition precedent to an exemption from liability. The court can only require the marshal to release the property from arrest. If the marshal neglects his duty, to the injury of the seizing officer, the latter must seek his remedy against the marshal. The collector is liable to a warehouseman for the storage of the goods during the time that they are under seizure. Smith v. Averill, 10 I. R. R. 156; s. c. 2 A. L. T. (C. R.) 1.

(c) The penalty pronounced by this section may be recovered by an indictment. The indictment need not aver that the property was found in the possession of the defendant, nor need the jury find the quantity of property held by the defendant. U. S. v. Mattingly, 6 I. R. R. 19.

The court has no discretion, but must always impose upon the convict, under this section, a penalty at least equal to double the amount of taxes fraudulently attempted to be evaded. The penalty cannot in any case be less than five hundred dollars, but may, and must, exceed this sum when double the amount of taxes fraudulently attempted to be evaded exceeds it. U. S. v. Smock, 4 I. R. R. 202.

The government, in an action of debt for the penalty, must establish its case beyond all reasonable doubts. Yet, the course of the defendant may supply, in the presumptions of law, all which this stringent rule demands. The opening proof, unexplained and uncontradicted, must enable the jury to find against the defendant for the claim of the government, or some material part of it. Then the defendant assumes the burden of proof. In the end all reasonable doubt must be removed. If the defendant has the means of explanation in his power, the burden rests upon him. Where a party has proof in his power which, if produced, would throw light upon certain material facts, the law presumes against the party who omits to produce it, and authorizes the jury to resolve all doubts adversely to his defence. The same rule is applicable where a party once had proof in his power which has been voluntarily destroyed or placed beyond his reach. When the defendant omits to produce his books and to testify himself, the presumption of law is that he has deliberately and with full knowledge of the law and all its presumptions, elected to withhold the proof. The presumption of law is that the defendant did keep the accounts usual and necessary for the correct understanding of his business. The law also presumes them to be in existence and accessible to the defendant. If any additions have been made, by or with the concurrence of the defendant, to the books, for the purpose of creating evidence contrary to the truth, it also raises a strong presumption against him. U. S. *v.* Chaffe et al. 11 I. R. R. 110.

(*d*) Although the act does not by express terms confer upon the court the power to deliver to the claimant on bail, pending the proceedings, the property claimed to be forfeited to the United States, under its provisions, it is apparent that the intention of the act is that proceedings under it shall conform in this respect to the methods heretofore pursued in cases of seizure under previous revenue laws. The power of releasing property upon bail, pending the proceedings, has been in constant exercise in most, if not all, cases of seizure under the import acts, and been deemed to be one of the inherent powers of the court over property in its custody. Indeed, it would seem to be a power necessary to the proper exercise of the jurisdiction of the court in most cases *in rem*, for in such cases the proceedings might sometimes prove futile, and the decree, when made, a barren one, without the exercise of such a power. Any other practice would be likely to entail upon the government large expense for the storage, custody, and care of all property seized as forfeited. Property held during long periods, to await the result of litigation, is necessarily subject to great risk of loss by fire, thieves, &c. U. S. *v.* 800 Bbls. 4 I. R. R. 165 ; U. S. *v.* 69 Bbls. 2 I. R. R. 45; U. S. *v.* 2 Tons of Coal, 5 Blatch. 386.

An application for permission to bail the property is an application for favor, and terms may be imposed. The claimant should be required to pay into the registry a sum of money equal to the amount of tax upon the property seized, to insure the liquidation of the tax in case of an acquittal of the property upon the charge in the information. U. S. *v.* Lot of Tobacco, 6 I. R. R. 222; s c. 2 Bt. 76.

A distillery will not be bonded where there is reasonable ground to believe that the law has been violated. The court will withhold from parties who have deliberately provided themselves with the means of committing frauds, the opportunity of carrying out their manifest intentions. U. S. *v.* Quantity of Spirits, 7 I. R. R. 29; s. c. 2 Bt. 101.

Penalty for Fraudulent Removal or Concealment.

[SEC. 14. (July 13, 1866.) *And be it further enacted*, That in case any goods or commodities for or in respect whereof any tax is or shall be imposed, or any materials, utensils, or vessels proper or intended to be made use of for or in the making of such goods or commodities shall be removed, or shall be deposited or concealed in any place, with intent to defraud the United States of such tax, or any part thereof, all such goods and commodities, and all such materials, utensils, and vessels, respectively, shall be forfeited ; and in every such case, and in every case where any goods or commodities shall be forfeited under this act, or any other act of Congress relating to the internal revenue, all and singular the casks, vessels, cases, or other packages whatsoever, containing, or which shall have contained, such goods or commodities, respectively, and every vessel, boat, cart, carriage, or other conveyance whatsoever, and all horses or other animals, and all things used in the removal or for the deposit or concealment thereof, respectively, shall be forfeited; and every person who shall remove, deposit, or conceal, or be concerned in removing, depositing, or concealing any goods or commodities for or in respect whereof any tax is or shall be imposed, with intent to defraud the United States of such tax or any part thereof, shall be liable to a fine or penalty of not exceeding five hundred dollars.]

Issuing of Search Warrants.

[SEC. 15. (July 13, 1866.) *And be it further enacted*, That the judge of any circuit or district court of the United States, or any commissioner thereof, may issue a search warrant, authorizing any internal revenue officer to search any premises, if such officer shall make oath in writing that he has reason to believe, and does believe, that a fraud upon the revenue has been or is being committed upon or by the use of said premises.]

Proceedings when Property is Worth Less than $300.

[SEC. 63. (July 13, 1866. *And be it further enacted*, That hereafter in all cases of seizure of any goods, wares, or merchandise which shall, in the opinion of the collector or deputy collector making such seizure, be of the appraised value of three hundred dollars or less, and which shall have been so seized as being subject to forfeiture under any of the provisions of this act, or of any act to which this is an amendment, excepting in cases otherwise provided, the said collector or deputy collector shall proceed as follows, (*a*) that is to say: He shall cause a list containing a particular description of the goods, wares, or merchandise seized to be prepared in duplicate, and an appraisement of the same to be made by three sworn appraisers, to be selected by him for said purpose, who shall be respectable and disinterested citizens of the United States residing within the collection district wherein the seizure was made. The aforesaid list and appraisement shall be properly attested by such collector or deputy collector and the persons making the appraisement, for which service said appraisers shall be allowed the sum of one dollar and fifty cents per day each, to be paid as other necessary charges to collectors according to law. If the said goods shall be found by such appraisers to be of the value of three hundred dollars or less, the said collector or deputy collector shall publish a notice, for the space of three weeks, in some newspaper of the district where the seizure was made, describing the articles and stating the time, place, and cause of their seizure, and requiring any person or persons claiming them to appear and make such claim within thirty days of the date of the first publication of such notice.

Provided, That any person or persons claiming the goods,

wares, or merchandise, so seized, within the time specified in the notice, may file with such collector or deputy collector a claim, stating his or their interest in the articles seized, and may execute a bond to the United States in the penal sum of two hundred and fifty dollars, with sureties, to be approved by said collector or deputy collector, conditioned that, in case of condemnation of the articles so seized, the obligors will pay all the costs and expenses of the proceedings, to obtain such condemnation; and upon the delivery of such bond to the collector or deputy collector, he shall transmit the same, with the duplicate list or description of the goods seized, to the United States district attorney for the district, who shall proceed thereon in the ordinary manner prescribed by law.

And provided also, That if there shall be no claim interposed, and no bond given within the time above specified, the collector or deputy collector, as the case may be, shall give ten days' notice of the sale of the goods, wares, or merchandise, by publication, and at the time and place specified in said notice shall sell the article so seized at public auction, and after deducting the expense of appraisement and sale he shall deposit the proceeds to the credit of the Secretary of the Treasury. And within one year after the sale of any goods, wares, or merchandise, as aforesaid, any person or persons claiming to be interested in the goods, wares, or merchandise so sold may apply to the Secretary of the Treasury for a remission of the forfeiture thereof, or any of them, and a restoration of the proceeds of the said sale, which may be granted by the said Secretary upon satisfactory proof, to be furnished in such manner as he shall prescribe:

Provided, That it shall be satisfactorily shown that the applicant, at the time of the seizure and sale of the goods in question, and during the intervening time, was absent out of the United States, or in such circumstances as prevented him from knowing of such seizure, and that he did not know of the same; and also that the said forfeiture was incurred without willful negligence or any intention of fraud on the part of the owner or owners of such goods. If no application for such restoration be made within one year, as hereinbefore prescribed, then, at the expiration of the said time, the Secretary of the Treasury shall cause the proceeds of the sale of the said goods, wares, or merchandise to be distributed according to law, as in the case of goods, wares, or merchandise condemned and sold pursuant to the decree of a competent court.]

(*a*) The provisions of this section are imperative, and must be strictly followed, as far as appraisement is concerned, in all cases where the property seized is, in the first instance, in the opinion of the collector or deputy collector making the seizure, of the value of three hundred dollars or less, and is finally so found upon appraisement.

Immediately after the seizure and appraisement provided for, the collector will report such seizure to the Office of Internal Revenue, in Form 117, stating what proceedings have been taken.

After a sale has been effected (which sale should be made as early as practicable after the seizure, provided the claimants do not give the required bond, and thus take the case into the United States Court), the collector will forward to the Commissioner a full and particular account of his action, giving each item of expense incurred, supported by proper vouchers, when it is possible to obtain them. No item of expense will be allowed unless it is shown that the same was necessarily incurred. A collector is expected to exercise the same care in the above regard that he would in the conduct of similar affairs of his own, incurring no expense that can be avoided.

Collectors are entitled to no commissions upon sales made under this section.

The entire net proceeds of sales should at once, after payment of the expenses, be deposited to the credit of the Secretary of the Treasury, and the duplicate certificate of deposit forwarded to the Commissioner, accompanied by a letter of transmittal, stating the section of law under which the proceedings had been taken, which information should also appear upon the face of the certificate.

Should the claimants give bond, as provided in this section, the collector will advise the Office of Internal Revenue. It will be observed, however, that the execution of such bond does not entitle the claimants to the possession of the property seized.

The three weeks' notice requiring the parties to appear, make claims, &c., and the ten days' notice of sale, need appear only in the weekly issues of the paper advertising such notices.

In cases where the value of the property seized is so small that it will not warrant proceedings for its sale by itself, under the section mentioned, the property may be stored in the least expensive manner possible until such time as a sufficient amount of property similarly situated has accumulated to warrant the expense of sale, when the several lots may be sold together, and treated as a unit, so far as incurring expense is concerned; but in the notice to appear, &c., each particular lot should be so distinctly described as to render it capable of identification by any person desiring to make claims thereto. And, in finally returning the cases to the Commissioner, separate and distinct reports of each must be made. In such cases the total expense incurred must be divided among the several lots of property, and to the account of each must be charged its proportionate share of such expense. The collector should see that the expenses in no particular case exceed the gross proceeds of sale, as in that event he would be the loser, as there is no provision of law for the payment of such excess. The action of a collector will not in any case be approved by the Commissioner unless in strict compliance with these regulations.

If, at the expiration of, or after the sale, no application has been made and granted for the restoration of the proceeds, the same will be distributed according to law by the Secretary of the Treasury, and no consideration will be given to the claim of an informer prior to the expiration of such period.

The provisions of section 58, Act of July 20, 1868, requiring that distilled spirits which have been forfeited to the government be sold subject to tax, have no application to sales under this section. The former section refers to sales after a decree of forfeiture and of property adjudged to belong to the government, in which no one else has an interest; while, under the latter section, the sale is made while the title to the property is yet in doubt, and when the government has no ascertained right to it further than to effect a sale. Spirits may, therefore, be sold under this section to the highest bidder, whatever his offer may be. 8 I. R. R. 203.

Provisions relating to Returns to Apply to all Persons liable to Tax.

Sec. 49. *And be it further enacted*, That all the provisions hereinafter made for the delivery of returns, lists, statements, and valuations, or for additions to the duty in case of false or fraudulent lists or returns, or in case of undervaluation or understatement on lists or returns, or in case of refusal or neglect to deliver lists or returns, and for the imposition of fines, penalties, and forfeitures, shall be held and taken to apply to all persons, associations, corporations, or companies liable to pay duty or tax; and any additions to duties, fines, penalties, or forfeitures hereinafter imposed for failure to perform any duty required to be performed, shall be held and taken to be additional to those hereinbefore provided.

Sec. 50. *Repealed* July 13, 1866, § 68.

Adoption of Act August 6, 1846.

Sec. 51. *And be it further enacted*, That the provisions of the sixteenth section of the act approved August sixth, eighteen hundred and forty-six, entitled "An act to provide for the better organization of the treasury, and for the collection, safe-keeping, transfer, and disbursement of the public revenue," are hereby applied to, and shall be construed to include all officers of the internal revenue charged with the safe-keeping, transfer, or disbursement of the public moneys arising therefrom, and to all other persons having actual charge, custody, or control of moneys or accounts arising from the administration of the internal revenue.

Penalty for Embezzlement.

[SEC. 16. (August 6, 1846.) *And be it further enacted*, That all officers and other persons charged by this act, or any other act, with the safe keeping, transfer, and disbursement of the public moneys, other than those connected with the post-office department, are hereby required to keep an accurate entry of each sum received, and of each payment or transfer; and that if any one of the said officers, or of those connected with the post-office department, shall convert to his own use, in any way whatever, or shall use, by way of investment in any kind of property or merchandise, or shall loan, with or without interest, or shall deposit in any bank, or shall exchange for other funds, except as allowed by this act, any portion of the public moneys intrusted to him for safe-keeping, disbursement, or transfer, or for any other purpose, every such act shall be deemed and adjudged to be an embezzlement (a) of so much of the said moneys as shall be thus taken, converted, invested, used, loaned, deposited, or exchanged, which is hereby declared to be a felony; and any failure to pay over or to produce the public moneys entrusted to such person shall be held and taken to be *prima facie* evidence of such embezzlement, and if any officer charged with the disbursements of public moneys shall accept, or receive, or transmit to the Treasury Department to be allowed in his favor, any receipt or voucher from a creditor of the United States, without having paid to such creditor, in such funds as the said officer may have received for disbursement, or such other funds as he may be authorized by this act to take in exchange, the full amount specified in such receipt or voucher, every such act shall be deemed to be a conversion by such officer to his own use of the amount specified in such receipt or voucher; and any officer or agent of the United States, and all persons advising or participating in such act, being convicted thereof before any court of the United States of competent jurisdiction, shall be sentenced to imprisonment for a term of not less than six months nor more than ten years, and to a fine equal to the amount of the money embezzled.

And upon the trial of any indictment against any person for embezzling public money under the provisions of this act, it shall be sufficient evidence, for the purpose of showing a balance against such person, to produce a transcript from the books and proceedings of the treasury, as required in civil cases, under the provisions of the act entitled "An act to provide more effectually for the settlement of accounts between the United States and receivers of public money," approved March third, one thousand seven hundred and ninety-seven; and the provisions of this act shall be so construed as to apply to all persons charged with the safe keeping, transfer, or disbursement of the public money, whether such persons be indicted as receivers or depositaries of the same; and the refusal of such person, whether in or out of office, to pay any draft, order, or warrant which may be drawn upon him by the proper officer of the Treasury Department, for any public money in his hands belonging to the United States, no matter in what capacity the same may have been received or may be held, or to transfer or disburse any such money promptly, upon the legal requirement of any authorized officer of the United States, shall be deemed and taken, upon the trial of any indictment against such person for embezzlement, as *prima facie* evidence of such embezzlement.]

(a) When, with the sanction of the head of a department, a person is appointed an officer of the United States for the safe keeping of public money, such appointment constitutes him such officer within the meaning of the constitution of the United States, and of the statutes of the United States, in regard to officers charged with the safe keeping of public money. U. S. *v.* Hartwell, 7 I. R. R. 100; U. S. *v.* Blumgart, 7 I. R. R. 148.

This clause is to be taken distributively. It applies, and was clearly intended to apply, to all the acts of embezzlement specified in the section;

to those relating to moneys in the first category as well as to those relating to vouchers in the second. The only effect of the provisions and requirements which are only applicable to the higher officers is that they only operate, according to their terms, where such higher officers are concerned. They are without effect as to subordinates to whom they are inapplicable. They do not take offenders of that class out of the penal and other provisions of the statute. U. S. *v.* Hartwell et al. 7 I. R. R. 100.

Objections to the action of the grand jury, when an indictment is found, ought to be made as early as practicable. Admitted rights may be waived by laches even in criminal cases. The court will not postpone sentence for the purpose of giving the defendant an opportunity to obtain a pardon. It is a part of the duty of the district attorney, and not of the court, to determine whether the public interest requires that the testimony of an accomplice shall be received, and whether his conduct is such as constitutes a compliance with the legal conditions which give him an equitable right to executive clemency. Cases may arise where the court would defer sentence. U. S. *v.* Hartwell et al. 12 I. R. R. 50.

On an application for a commitment, the government is not required to produce that proof which would be necessary to convict the person to be committed on a trial in chief, nor to absolutely convince the committing officer of the guilt of the accused. It is only necessary that probable cause be shown. Probable cause means a case made out by proof furnishing good reason to believe that the crime alleged has been committed by the person charged with having committed it. U. S. *v.* Blumgart, 7 I. R. R. 148.

Suits to Recover Money Withheld by Officers.

[SEC. 1. (March 3, 1797.) *Be it enacted by the Senate and House of Representatives of the United States of America in Congress assembled,* That when any revenue officer, or other person accountable for public money, shall neglect or refuse to pay into the treasury the sum or balance reported to be due to the United States upon the adjustment of his account, it shall be the duty of the Comptroller, and he is hereby required, to institute suit for the recovery of the same, adding to the sum stated to be due on such account the commissions of the delinquent, which shall be forfeited in every instance where suit is commenced and judgment obtained thereon, and an interest of six per cent. per annum, from the time of receiving the money, until it shall be repaid into the treasury.]

Transcripts to be Evidence.

SEC. 2. (March 3, 1797.) *And be it further enacted,* That in every case of delinquency, where suit has been or shall be instituted, a transcript from the books and proceedings of the treasury, certified by the register, and authenticated under the seal of the department, shall be admitted as evidence, and the court trying the cause shall be thereupon authorized to grant judgment and award execution accordingly. And all copies of bonds, contracts, or other papers relating to or connected with the settlement of any account between the United States and an individual, when certified by the register to be true copies of the originals on file, and authenticated under the seal of the department, as aforesaid, may be annexed to such transcripts, and shall have equal validity and be entitled to the same degree of credit which would be due to the original papers if produced and authenticated in court:

Provided, That where suit is brought upon a bond, or other sealed instrument, and the defendant shall plead "*non est factum*," or upon motion to the court, such plea or motion being verified by the oath or affirmation of the defendant, it shall be lawful for the court to take the same into consideration and (if it shall appear to be necessary for the attainment of justice) to require the production of the original bond, contract, or other paper specified in such affidavit.]

Who May Administer Oaths.

Sec. 52. (Amended March 3, 1865, § 1.) *And be it further enacted*, That all assessors and their assistants, all collectors and their deputies, revenue agents, and all inspectors, are hereby authorized to administer oaths (*a*) and take evidence touching any part of the administration of this law with which they are respectively charged, or where such oaths and evidence are by law authorized to be taken; and any perjury therein shall be punished in the like manner, and to the same degree, as in the case of perjury committed in proceedings in the courts of the United States.

(*a*) The authority to administer oaths is not general as to all matters connected with the revenue, but is limited to matters connected with the official discharge of some duty imposed by law upon the officer administering it.

An assessor is authorized to administer the proper oath to persons making to him a return for taxation; to his deputies in making their returns, and in verifying their accounts for services and expenses; and to his own clerks in verifying their accounts; but he is not authorized to administer such oath or affirmation to a collector, his deputies or clerks, nor in any case except where such oath or affirmation is necessary to the discharge of his own duties.

A collector is authorized to administer oaths and affirmations where they are required to returns or reports made to him; and to his own deputies and clerks in matters connected with the discharge of his official duties; but he is not authorized to administer them to an assessor, his assistants or clerks; nor can his deputies administer them to the collector or his clerks, or each other; nor to the assessor, his assistants or clerks. 1 I. R. R. 2.

In verifying accounts it is necessary that the same should be sworn to before an assessor, an assistant assessor, collector, deputy collector, United States commissioner, clerk of court, notary public, judge, or justice of the peace. In cases of verification before the last two mentioned officers, a clerk's certificate of the official character of the person administering the oath must be properly attached. When either of the above-named officers have an official seal, an impression thereof should accompany the jurat. 11 I. R. R. 80.

Official Communications to be Franked.

[SEC. 65. (July 13, 1866.) *And be it further enacted*, That all official communications made by assessors to collectors, assessors to assessors, or by collectors to collectors, or by collectors to assessors, or by assessors to assistant assessors, or by assistant assessors to assessors, or by collectors to their deputies, or by deputy collectors to collectors, may be officially franked by the writers thereof, and shall, when so franked, be transmitted by mail free of postage.]

Officers Not to be Interested in Distilleries, etc.

[SEC. 59. (July 13, 1866.) *And be it further enacted*, That any inspector or revenue agent who shall hereafter become interested, directly or indirectly, in the manufacture of tobacco, snuff, or cigars, and any assessor, collector, inspector, or revenue agent, who shall hereafter become interested, directly or indirectly, in the production, by distillation or by other process, of spirits, ale, or beer, or other fermented liquors, shall, on conviction before any court of the United States of competent jurisdiction, pay a penalty not less than five hundred dollars nor more than five thousand dollars, in the discretion of the court. And any such officer, interested as aforesaid in any such manufacture at the time this act takes effect, who shall fail to divest himself of such interest within sixty days thereafter, shall be held and declared to have become so interested after this act takes effect.]

Officers to Render an Account of Fees to Commissioner.

[SEC. 60. (July 13, 1866.) *And be it further enacted*, That every internal revenue officer, whose payment, charges, salary, or compensation shall be composed, either wholly or in part, of fees, commissions, allowances, or rewards, from whatever source derived, shall be required to render to the Commissioner of Internal Revenue, under regulations to be approved by the Secretary of the Treasury, a statement under oath setting forth the entire amount of such fees, commissions, emoluments, allowances or rewards of whatever nature, or from whatever source received, during the time for which said statement is rendered; and any false statement knowingly and willfully rendered under the requirements of this section, or regulations established in accordance therewith, shall be deemed willful perjury, and punished on conviction thereof, as provided in section forty-two of the act of June thirty, eighteen hundred and sixty-four, to which this act is an amendment; and any neglect or omission to render such statement when required shall be punished on conviction therefor by a fine of not less than two hundred dollars nor more than five hundred dollars, in the discretion of the court.]

SECS. 53, 54, 55, 56, 57, *Repealed* July 13, 1866, § 9.

Appointment of Inspectors.

Sec. 58. (Amended July 13, 1866, § 30.) *And be it further enacted*, That there shall be appointed by the Secretary of the Treasury, in every collection district where the same may be necessary, one or more inspectors of spirits, refined coal oil or other oil, tobacco, cigars, and other articles, who shall take an oath faithfully to perform their duties, in such form as the Commissioner of Internal Revenue shall prescribe, and who shall be entitled to receive such fees as may be fixed and prescribed by said Commissioner, to be paid by the owner or manufacturer of the articles inspected, gauged, or proved. And any manufacturer of spirits, refined coal oil or other oil, tobacco, cigars, or other articles which may by law be required to be inspected, who shall refuse to admit an inspector upon his premises, so far as it may be necessary for the performance of his duties, or who shall obstruct an inspector in the performance of his duties, shall forfeit the sum of one hundred dollars, to be recovered in the manner provided for other penalties imposed by this act.

Commissioner to Designate Officers to Inspect Distilled Spirits.

[SEC. 17. (March 2, 1867.) *And be it further enacted*, That hereafter all distilled spirits, before being removed from the distillery, shall be inspected and gauged by a general inspector of spirits, who shall mark the barrels or packages in the manner required by law; and so much of the act approved July thirteen, eighteen hundred and sixty-six, as requires the appointment of an inspector for each distillery established according to law, is hereby repealed: *Provided*, That such other duties as have heretofore been imposed upon inspectors of distilleries may be performed by such other duly appointed officers as may be designated by the Commissioner of Internal Revenue.]

Inspectors to Give Bond.

[SEC. 31. (March 2, 1867.) *And be it further enacted*, That all inspectors appointed under the provisions of the act or acts of which this is amendatory shall be required to give bonds, with security, approved by the Secretary of the Treasury or assessor of the district, in a sum not less than five thousand dollars, conditioned for the faithful discharge of the duties of such inspector.]

Sec. 59. *Repealed* July 13, 1866, § 9.

Secs. 62, 63, 64, 65, 66, 67, 68, 69, 70, *Repealed* July 13, 1866, § 9.

FERMENTED LIQUORS.

Brewers to Give Notice.

[Sec. 46. (July 13, 1866.) *And be it further enacted*, That every brewer shall, before commencing or continuing business after this act takes effect, file with the assistant assessor of the assessment district in which he shall design to carry on his business, a notice (*a*) in writing, stating therein the name of the person, company, corporation, or firm, and the names of the members of any such company or firm, together with the place or places of residence of such person or persons, and a description of the premises on which the brewery is situated, and of his or their title thereto, and the name or names of the owner or owners thereof; and also the whole quantity of malt liquors annually made and sold or removed from the brewery for two years next preceding the date of filing such notice.]

(*a*) The notice required by this section should be in the following form:

BREWERS' NOTICE.

187–.

Notice is hereby given that (if a partnership, insert here the name of each person comprised in the firm, whether as general or special partner, with the place of residence of each), of ——— in the county of ——— and State of ——— under the firm ——— intend to carry on as heretofore ——— ha— done at ——— in the town of ——— in the county and State aforesaid, the business of brewing beer (lager beer, ale, porter, or other fermented liquors).

The premises on which our brewery is situated are bounded in general as follows: (boundaries of premises to be inserted here). The brewery consists of the following buildings: (buildings to be designated here). The other buildings on the premises are as follows: (the other buildings to be indicated here).

The premises are owned by (or leased to) us (by a lease from ———, who are the owners thereof). For the two years next preceding the date the whole quantity of malt liquors annually made and sold or removed from the brewery has been as follows:

For the year ending ——— 1869, ——— bbls.
For the year ending ——— 1870, ——— bbls.
(Signed)

The assistant assessor with whom this notice is filed will immediately forward a certified copy thereof to both the assessor and collector of the district. 4 I. R. R. 84.

Bonds to be Given.

[Sec. 47. (July 13, 1866.) *And be it further enacted*, That every brewer shall execute a bond (*a*) to the United States, to be approved by the collector of the district, in a sum equal to twice the amount of tax which, in the opinion of the assessor, said brewer will be liable to pay during any one month, which bond shall be renewed on the first day of May in each year, and shall be conditioned that he will pay, or cause to be paid, as herein provided, the tax required by law on all beer, lager beer, ale, porter, and other fermented liquors aforesaid made by him, or for him, before the same is sold or removed for consumption or sale, except as hereinafter provided ; and that he will keep, or cause to be kept, a book in the manner and for the purposes hereinafter specified, which shall be open to inspection by the proper officers as by law required, and that he will in all respects faithfully comply, without fraud or evasion, with all requirements of law relating to the manufacture and sale of any malt liquors before mentioned:

Provided, That no brewer shall be required to pay a special tax as a wholesale dealer, by reason of selling at wholesale, at a place other than his brewery, malt liquors manufactured by him.]

(*a*) The bond required by this section must be renewed on the first day of May in each year, after Form 20, and in compliance with instructions therein.

Amount of Tax.

[SEC. 48. (July 13, 1866; amended March 2, 1867, § 10.) *And be it further enacted*, That there shall be paid on all beer, lager beer, ale, porter, and other similar fermented liquors, by whatever name such liquors may be called, a tax (*a*) of one dollar for every barrel containing not more than thirty-one gallons; and at a like rate for any other quantity or for any fractional part of a barrel which shall be brewed or manufactured and sold, or removed for consumption or sale, within the United States; which tax shall be paid by the owner, agent, or superintendent of the brewery or premises in which such fermented liquors shall be made, in the manner and at the time hereinafter specified:

Provided, That fractional parts of a barrel shall be halves, thirds, quarters, sixths, and eighths; and any fractional part of a barrel containing less than one-eighth shall be accounted one-eighth; more than one-eighth and not more than one-sixth, shall be accounted one-sixth; more than one sixth and not more than one-quarter, shall be accounted one-quarter; more than one-quarter and not more than one-third, shall be accounted one-third; and more than one-third and less than one-half, shall be accounted one-half; more than one-half and not more than one barrel, shall be accounted one barrel; and more than one barrel and not more than sixty-three gallons, shall be accounted two barrels, or a hogshead:

Provided, That fractional parts of barrels containing more than one-quarter and not more than one-half, shall be accounted one-half; and pay tax as such until June first, eighteen hundred and sixty-seven.]

(*a*) The tax mentioned in this section is to be paid by the owner, agent, or superintendent of the brewery or premises in which such fermented liquors shall be made; and stamps for that purpose are to be purchased and used as hereinafter required. 4 I. R. R. 84.

A beer containing not more than 2¼ per cent. of alcohol is properly denominated small beer, and is exempt. Weiss beer is exempt. Whenever a fermented liquor is put up in barrels it is subject to tax. 12 I. R. R. 29.

Cider, beer, ale and wine contain alcohol, but they are produced by fermentation; and inasmuch as they are not produced by distillation they are not subject to the tax on distilled spirits. 5 I. R. R. 59.

If a brewer purchase his products from another brewer before they have fermented and mixes them with flat beer for the purpose of creating a new fermentation, the purchaser who thus manufactures a salable article of beer, must pay a tax on the full amount sold by him, or removed for consumption or sale; but such products sold before fermentation need not be included in the monthly account of beer, &c., sold by the person who sells it. 5 I. R. R. 45.

Brewers may be allowed to deduct the amount of beer which has become sour on their hands, or which has been returned to them in that condition; but no deductions can be allowed for the amount of beer consumed by their workmen, or for the amount which may be presented as a gift to their customers. That which leaks before removal from the brewery is not to be holden for the tax. 1 I. R. R. 196; 3 I. R. R. 28.

The words "removed for consumption or sale," are separated by the disjunctive " or " from the words " manufactured and sold," as they must have been, in order to make the provision intelligible. The obvious intent of the law is to subject all of this class of beverages in the hands of the manufacturer made after the first day of September, 1862, to a uniform tax, and the time when such tax shall become payable is fixed at the date when the same shall be sold, or removed for consumption or sale. When the manufacturer sells it, then the tax will become payable. When he sends it to any place owned by himself or another for consumption, then the tax will become payab'e. When he removes it to a commission house or any other place for sale, then it will become payable. The law intends to make removal for consumption or sale equivalent to a sale, and requires the manufacturer, when he shall either sell or remove for consumption or future sale, to at once pay the tax. Shaefer *v.* Ketchum, 6 I. R. R. 4.

Books to be kept.

[SEC. 49. (July 13, 1866.) *And be it further enacted*, That every person owning or occupying any brewery or premises used, or intended to be used, for the purpose of brewing or making such fermented liquors, or who shall have such premises under his control or superintendence as agent for the owner or occupant, or shall have in his possession or custody any brewing materials, utensils, or apparatus, used or intended to be used on said premises in the manufacture of beer, lager beer, ale, porter, or other similar fermented liquors, either as owner, agent, or superintendent, shall, from day to day, enter or cause to be entered, in a book (a) to be kept by him for that purpose, the kind of such fermented liquors, the description of packages, and number of barrels and fractional parts of barrels of fermented liquors made, and also the quantity sold or removed for consumption or sale, and shall also, from day to day, enter or cause to be entered, in a separate book, to be kept by him for that purpose, an account of all material by him purchased for the purpose of producing such fermented liquors, including grain and malt; and shall render to said assessor or assistant assessor, on or before the tenth day of each month, a true statement in writing, taken from his books, of the whole quantity or number of barrels and fractional parts of barrels of fermented liquors brewed and sold, or removed for consumption or sale, during the preceding month; and shall verify, or cause to be verified, the said statement, and the facts therein set forth, by oath or affirmation to be taken before the assessor or assistant assessor of the district, according to the form required by law, and shall immediately forward to the collector of the district a duplicate of said statement, duly certified by the assessor or assistant assessor. And said books shall be open at all times for the inspection of any assessor or assistant assessor, collector, deputy collector, inspector, or revenue agent, who may take memoranda and transcripts therefrom.]

(a) Two books are required to be kept by every person engaged in the production of fermented liquors. Form 104 is recommended for the book for recording the qualities made, removed, and sold.

In a separate book is to be entered, from day to day, an account of all materials purchased by him for the purpose of producing fermented liquors, including grain and malt, in such form as shall be distinct, and explicit, and convenient for reference.

The entries made in this book must, on or before the tenth day of each month, be verified by the oath or affirmation of the person or persons by whom such entries shall have been made, which oath or affirmation must be written in the books respectively, at the end of such entries, and be certified by the officer administering the same; and said books are required to be open at all times for the inspection of any assessor, or assistant assessor, collector, deputy collector, inspector, or revenue agent who may take memoranda therefrom.

For verification of the book containing the entries of materials purchased, the same form is to be used as given in Form 104, except that for the words, "fermented liquors brewed, the quantity sold, and the quantity removed from," the words, "material purchased for the purpose of producing fermented liquors in," should be substituted, and the owner, agent, or superintendent, when the entries are not made by himself, must further verify them in the manner shown by Form 104.

Every person owning or occupying, or having under his control or superintendence as agent for the owner or occupant any brewery or premises used for making fermented liquors, or having in his possession or custody, as agent, owner, or superintendent, any brewing materials, utensils, or apparatus used or intended to be used on such premises in the manufacture of fermented liquors, is liable to punishment if these books are not kept as required by law.

On or before the tenth day of each month there must be rendered to the assessor or assistant assessor a true statement in writing (Form 18) of the whole quantity or number of barrels and fractional parts of barrels of fermented liquors brewed and sold, or removed for consumption and sale, during the preceding month, verified by oath, and a duplicate of said statement, duly certified by the assessor or assistant assessor, must be immediately forwarded to the collector of the district.

Every brewer who sells fermented liquors at retail, besides affixing and cancelling the proper stamps on the vessels in which the same is contained, is required to keep an account of the quantity so sold by him, and of the number and size of the vessels in which the same may have been contained, and to make a report thereof, verified by oath, monthly to the assessor, and forward a duplicate of the same to the collector.

All returns made by brewers to the assessor must be forwarded by that officer to the assistant assessor within whose division the brewery is located for which any return has been so rendered, for the purpose of placing the assistant assessor in possession of all facts necessary to the proper performance of his duties. 4 I. R. R. 84.

An indictment need not be founded upon a previous information, arrest, hearing and binding over, but may be sent up solely at the instance and in the discretion of the prosecuting officer of the government. U. S. v. Fuers, 12 I. R. R. 43.

Verification of Entries.

[SEC. 50. (July 13, 1866.) *And be it further enacted,* That the entries made in such books shall, on or before the tenth day of each month, be verified by the oath or affirmation of the person or persons by whom such entries shall have been made, which oath or affirmation shall be written in the book at the end of such entries, and be certified by the officer administering the same, and shall be in form as follows: "I do swear (or affirm) that the foregoing entries were made by me, and that they state truly, according to the best of my knowledge and belief, the whole quantity of fermented liquors brewed, the quantity sold, and the quantity removed from the brewery owned by ———, in the county of ———. And further, that I have no knowledge of any matter or thing, required by law to be stated in said entries, which has been omitted therefrom." And the owner, agent, or superintendent aforesaid, shall also, in case the original entries made in his books shall not have been made by himself, subjoin thereto the following oath or affirmation, to be taken in manner as aforesaid: "I do swear (or affirm) that, to the best of my knowledge and belief, the foregoing entries fully set forth all the matters therein required by law, and that the same are just and true, and that I have taken all the means in my power to make them so."]

Penalty for Illicit Brewing.

[SEC. 51. (July 13, 1866.) *And be it further enacted*, That the owner, agent, or superintendent of any brewery, vessels, or utensils used in making fermented liquors, who shall evade or attempt to evade the payment of the .tax thereon, or fraudulently neglect or refuse to make true and exact entry and report of the same in the manner required by law, or to do or cause to be done any of the things by law required to be done by him as aforesaid, or who shall intentionally make false entry in said book or in said statement, or knowingly allow or procure the same to be done, shall forfeit, for every such offence, all the liquors made by him or for him, and all the vessels, utensils, and apparatus used in making the same, and be liable to a penalty of not less than five hundred nor more than one thousand dollars, to be recovered with costs of suit, and shall be deemed guilty of a misdemeanor, and shall be imprisoned for a term not exceeding one year. And any brewer who shall neglect to keep the books, or refuse to furnish the account and duplicate thereof as provided by law, or who shall refuse to permit the proper officer to examine the books in the manner provided, shall, for every such refusal or neglect, forfeit and pay the sum of three hundred dollars.]

Stamps to be used.

[SEC. 52. (July 13, 1866.) *And be it further enacted*, That the Commissioner of Internal Revenue shall cause to be prepared, for the payment of the tax aforesaid, suitable stamps (*a*) denoting the amount of tax required to be paid on the hogshead, barrels, and halves, quarters, sixths, and eighths of a barrel of such fermented liquors, and shall furnish the same to the collectors of internal revenue, who shall each be required to keep on hand, at all times, a supply equal in amount to two months' sales thereof, if there shall be any brewery or brewery warehouse in his district, and the same shall be sold by such collectors only to the brewers of their districts, respectively; and such collectors shall keep an account of the number and values of the stamps sold by them to each of such brewers, respectively; and the Commissioner of Internal Revenue shall allow upon all sales of such stamps to any brewer, and by him used in his business, a deduction of seven and one-half per centum. And the amount paid into the treasury by any collector on account of the sale of such stamps to brewers shall be included in.estimating the commissions of such collector and of the assessor of the same district.]

(*a*) The collector of internal revenue, in any district in which there shall be a brewery or brewery warehouse, will be furnished by the Commissioner with stamps denoting the tax on fermented liquors; will keep the same for sale to the brewers of his own district alone for use in their business; and will allow to such brewers a deduction of seven and one-half per centum of the value denoted by the stamps which he sells to them.

Every brewer desiring to obtain stamps denoting payment of the tax on fermented liquors, will first apply to the collector of the district in which his brewery is situated; failing to obtain them of such collector, he may apply to the collector of any other district, and the last-named collector, upon satisfying himself of a previous application and refusal, as before specified, may furnish to him the desired stamps; these stamps are to be affixed upon every vessel containing fermented liquor when sold or removed from the brewery or warehouse; this requirement is also obligatory upon brewers selling at retail at their breweries.

It is necessary that the stamps should be well secured to the vessels, and not easily removed therefrom, except by intentional effort for that purpose. The following method of affixing them is prescribed:

A hole, $2\frac{3}{4}$ inches in diameter, $\frac{1}{8}$ inch deep, should be countersunk in the head of the barrel in such position as will bring the spigot at the lower edge of the stamp where the perforations are made. The stamp is to be pasted on this countersunk hole, with the perforated portion over the spigot-hole, with strong paste; and, if the barrels are to be exposed to the action of the weather, or to be stored in damp places for considerable periods, should also be secured by four tacks to prevent its peeling off.

In renewing the stamp upon a barrel, used the second time, the tacks should be withdrawn and the stamp carefully scraped off to prevent the hole from being filled with the scraps of the former stamp.

The stamps, at the time of being affixed, are to be cancelled by writing or imprinting thereon the name of the person, firm, or corporation by whom such liquor may have been made, or the initial letters of such name and the date of such cancellation. 4 I. R. R. 84.

The purpose of countersinking for beer stamps is to protect the brewer by preventing the stamp from becoming detached; if brewers prefer to affix their stamps without countersinking, there is no legal objection to the practice. 5 I. R. R. 44.

It is contrary to the spirit and intention, if not to the letter, of the law for any person other than a collector to sell revenue stamps for fermented liquors. The restrictions as to the sale and purchase of such stamps are prescribed with the obvious purpose of aiding in the ascertainment of the true product of the articles upon which the stamps are used. 11 I. R. R. 57.

Every collector is required to report, on or before the fifteenth day of each month, upon Form 103, the full value of the stamps of each denomination on hand on the first day of the month for which the report is made, the full value of the stamps received during the month, the full value of the stamps sold during the month, the full value of the stamps remaining on hand at the close of the month, and the aggregate value of all denominations in each of the above subdivisions in one column, and the value less seven and one-half per centum in another.

This report will be required for each month, although no sale may have been made; every collector is also required to keep a record corresponding with the monthly report, and, also, an account with each brewer in his district, showing the denominations and entire value of all stamps sold to him each month, and the value thereof less seven and one-half per centum.

Upon the sale of stamps, the collector will enter the amount received upon his record of daily collections, and include the same in his certificate of deposit for that day or for any period in which he is required by the Secretary of the Treasury to deposit collections.

The amount received from sales will be entered in his abstract of collections, Form 22, under the appropriate number, as though collected upon assessor's list.

In reporting on Form 51, beer stamps will form a separate title for each month, and should be designated—Beer stamps for month of ———. Only the amount received for stamps sold should be entered in the first column, as for a list, and also entered in the collection and total columns.

Wherever a change of assessor shall occur during any month, the collector will specify upon his report the value of the stamps sold during the respective periods of office of each, so that each one may receive his proper amount of commissions upon sales.

Affixing and Cancellation of Stamps.

[SEC. 53. (July 13, 1866.) *And be it further enacted,* That every brewer shall obtain from the collector of the district in which his brewery or brewery warehouse may be situated, and not otherwise, unless said collector shall fail to furnish the same upon application to him, the proper stamp or stamps, and shall affix upon the spigot-hole or tap (of which there shall be but one) (*a*) of each and every hogshead, barrel, keg, or other receptacle, in which any fermented liquor shall be contained, when sold or removed from such brewery or warehouse, a stamp denoting the amount of the tax required upon such fermented liquor, in such a way that the said stamp or stamps will be destroyed upon the withdrawal of the liquor from such hogshead, barrel, keg, or other vessel, or upon the introduction of a faucet or other instrument for that purpose; and shall also, at the time of affixing such stamp or stamps as aforesaid, cancel the same by writing or imprinting thereon the name of the person, firm, or corporation by whom such liquor may have been made, or the initial letters thereof, and the date when cancelled. Every brewer who shall refuse or neglect to affix and cancel the stamp or stamps required by law in the manner aforesaid, or who shall affix a false or fraudulent stamp thereto, or knowingly permit the same to be done, shall be liable to pay a penalty of one hundred dollars for each barrel or package on which such omission or fraud occurs, and shall be liable to imprisonment for not more than one year.]

(*a*) This section requires the tax upon fermented liquors to be paid in every case by the use of a single stamp upon each package. 5 I. R. R. 100.

Penalty for Fraudulent Removal.

[SEC. 54. (July 13, 1866.) *And be it further enacted,* That any brewer, carman, agent for transportation, or other person, who shall sell, remove, receive, or purchase, or in any way aid in the sale, removal, receipt, or purchase of any fermented liquor contained in any hogshead, barrel, keg, or other vessel from any brewery or brewery warehouse, upon which the stamp required by law shall not have been affixed, or on which a false or fraudulent stamp is affixed, with knowledge that it is such, or on which a stamp once cancelled is used a second time; and any retail dealer or other person, who shall withdraw or aid in the withdrawal of any fermented liquor from any hogshead, barrel, keg, or other vessel containing the same, without destroying or defacing the stamp affixed upon the same, or shall withdraw or aid in the withdrawal of any fermented liquor from any hogshead, barrel, keg, or other vessel, upon which the proper stamp shall not have been affixed, or on which a false or fraudulent stamp is affixed, shall be liable to a fine of one hundred dollars, and to imprisonment not more than one year. Every person who shall make, sell, or use any false or counterfeit stamp or die for printing or making stamps which shall be in imitation of or purport to be a lawful stamp or die of the kind before mentioned, or who shall procure the same to be done, shall be imprisoned for not less than one nor more than five years.

Provided, That every brewer, who sells fermented liquor at retail at the brewery or other place where the same is made, shall affix and cancel the proper stamp or stamps upon the hogsheads, barrels, kegs, or other vessels in which the same is contained, and shall keep an account of the quantity so sold by him, and of the number and size of the hogsheads, barrels, kegs, or other vessels in which the same may have been contained, and shall make a report thereof, verified by oath, monthly to the assessor, and forward a duplicate of the same to the collector of the district.

And provided further, That brewers may remove (*a*) malt liquors of their own manufacture from their breweries or other places of manufacture to a warehouse or other place of storage occupied by them within the same district, in quantities of not less than six barrels in one vessel without affixing the proper stamp or stamps, but shall affix the same upon such liquor when sold or removed from such warehouse or other place of storage. But when the manufacturer of any ale or porter manufactures the same in one collection district, and owns, occupies, or hires a depot or warehouse for the storage and sale of such ale or porter in another collection district, he may, without affixing the stamps on the casks at the brewery, as herein provided for, remove or transport, or cause to be removed or transported, said ale or porter, in quantities not less than one hundred barrels at a time, under a permit from the collector of the district wherein said ale or porter is manufactured, to said depot or warehouse, but to no other place, under such rules and regulations as the Commissioner of Internal Revenue may prescribe, and thereafter the manufacturer of the ale or porter so removed shall stamp the same when it leaves such depot or warehouse, in the same manner and under the same penalties and liabilities as when stamped at the brewery as herein provided; and the collector of the district in which such depot or warehouse is situated shall furnish the manufacturer with the stamps for stamping the same, as if the said ale or porter had been manufactured in his district.

And provided further, That where fermented liquor has become sour or damaged, so as to be incapable of use as such, brewers may sell the same for manufacturing purposes, and may remove the same to places where it may be used for such purposes, in casks, or other vessels, unlike those ordinarily used for fermented liquors, containing respectively not less than one barrel each, and having the nature of their contents marked upon them, without affixing thereon the stamp or stamps required.]

(*a*) Brewers may, without affixing the required stamp, remove their fermented liquors from their breweries to their places of storage within the same district, in quantities of not less than six barrels in one vessel; In this case, the stamps are to be affixed when the liquor is sold or removed from the places of storage.

Persons manufacturing ale or porter in one district, and owning, occupying, or hiring a place for the storage and sale of the same in another district, may, without affixing the required stamps, remove their ale or porter in any quantity not less than one hundred barrels to such place of storage and sale; the stamps in this case, also, to be affixed when the liquor leaves the warehouse.

For this removal of ale or porter a permit (Form 29) must be obtained from the collector of the district wherein such liquor was manufactured, on application to that officer, which application is to be made in the following form:

"Application for Permit to remove Ale or Porter from Brewery to Warehouse.

To the Collector of Internal Revenue:

——————— 187

——————— Collection District, State of ———————————.

The undersigned, manufacturer of ale (or porter) at ——————— in said District, owning (or occupying or hiring) a depot or warehouse for the storage and sale of the same in another, viz., the ——————— District of the State of ——————— to wit, at ——————— in the ——————— of ——————— and County of ——————— hereby applies for a permit to remove ——————— hundred barrels from his brewery aforesaid to his place of storage and sale aforesaid without affixing stamps thereto.

The quantity of liquor now at said brewery is as follows: (quantity stated here) and the quantity of the same at said warehouse is as follows: (quantity at warehouse stated here).

(Signed.) ———————————."

A duplicate of the permit will be forwarded by the collector to the collector of the district to which the removal is to be made; and the brewer will promptly notify the last-named collector of the receipt at his store or warehouse of such fermented liquors. If this last notice is not seasonably received, information of this fact will be given to the collector who granted the permit.

A record of all permits granted must be kept by the collector granting them.

Stamps for use at the place of storage, in these cases, should be obtained of the collector of the district within which the warehouse is situated.

Sour or damaged fermented liquor, incapable of use as such, may be sold for manufacturing purposes and may be removed to places of use for such purposes without the use of stamps; but the vessels in which it is so removed are to be unlike those ordinarily used for fermented liquors, and are to contain not less than one barrel each, and the nature of their contents is to be marked thereon. 4 I. R. R. 84.

Collectors will compare the monthly returns made by brewers with their own account of the stamps sold to the same brewers, and will take special care, when applications are made for permits to remove fermented liquors from one collection district to another, to satisfy themselves that no fraud is intended, and that none is permitted in case permits are granted.

The collector will take suitable measures, including seizure, if necessary, for the prevention of fraud in the sale and removal of fermented liquor alleged to be sour or damaged.

The collector will, from time to time, examine the barrels and other vessels used in the sale of fermented liquors, to see if they are properly marked as required by law.

Assessors and assistant assessors will use similar vigilance, and make diligent examination of returns made to them and of the facts involved in such returns; they will make frequent inspections of breweries, and, when satisfied that the government is deprived of its just amount of tax by concealment of the quantity of liquor brewed and sold, or removed from the brewery, or otherwise, the deficiency should be assessed, and payment required. 4 I. R. R. 85.

Marks on Vessels.

[SEC. 55. (July 13, 1866.) *And be it further enacted*, That every brewer shall mark or cause to be marked, in such manner as shall be prescribed by the Commissioner of Internal Revenue, upon every hogshead, barrel, keg, or other vessel containing the fermented liquor made by him, or before it is sold or removed from the brewery, or brewery warehouse, or other place of manufacture, the name of the person, firm, or corporation by whom such liquor was manufactured, and the place where the same shall have been made; and any person, other than the owner thereof, or his agent, who shall intentionally remove or deface such mark therefrom, shall be liable to a penalty of fifty dollars for each cask from which the mark is so removed or defaced.]

Penalty for Fraudulently Removing Stamps.

[SEC. 56. (July 13, 1866.) *And be it further enacted*, That every person, other than the purchaser or owner of any fermented liquor, or person acting on his behalf, or as his agent, who shall intentionally remove or deface the stamp affixed upon the hogshead, barrel, keg, or other vessel in which the same may be contained, shall be liable to a fine of fifty dollars for each such vessel from which the stamp is so removed or defaced, and to render compensation to such purchaser or owner for all damages sustained by him therefrom.]

Forfeiture for Non-payment of Tax.

[SEC. 57. (July 13, 1866.) *And be it further enacted*, That the ownership or possession by any person of any fermented liquor after its sale or removal from brewery or warehouse, or other place where it was made, upon which the tax required shall not have been paid, shall render the same liable to seizure wherever found, and to forfeiture; and that the want of the proper stamp or stamps upon any hogshead, barrel, keg, or other vessel in which fermented liquor may be contained after its sale or removal from the brewery where the same was made, or warehouse as aforesaid, shall be notice to all persons that the tax has not been paid thereon, and shall be prima facie evidence of the non-payment thereof.]

Business of Bottling Fermented Liquor.

[SEC. 58. (July 13, 1866.) *And be it further enacted*, That every person who shall withdraw any fermented liquor from (*a*) any hogshead, barrel, keg, or other vessel upon which the proper stamp or stamps shall not have been affixed, for the purpose of bottling the same, or who shall carry on, or attempt to carry on, the business of bottling fermented liquor in any brewery or other place in which fermented liquor is made, or upon any premises having communication with such brewery or any warehouse, shall be liable to a fine of five hundred dollars, and the property used in such bottling or business shall be liable to forfeiture.]

(*a*) The requirements of the law respecting stamps are to be observed in the business of bottling fermented liquors. The requirements of this section must be complied with. 4 I. R. R. 85.

DISTILLED SPIRITS.

Amount of Tax.

[SEC. 1. (July 20, 1868.) *Be it enacted by the Senate and House of Representatives of the United States of America in Congress assembled*, That there shall be levied and collected on all distilled spirits on which the tax prescribed by law has not been paid, a tax of fifty cents (*a*) on each and every proof gallon, to be paid by the distiller, owner, or person having possession thereof before removal from distillery warehouse; and the tax on such spirits shall be collected on the whole number of gauge or wine gallons when below proof, and shall be increased in proportion for any greater strength than the strength of proof spirit as defined in this act; and any fractional part of a gallon in excess of the number of gallons in a cask or package shall be taxed as a gallon. Every proprietor or possessor of a still, distillery, or distilling apparatus, and every person in any manner interested in the use of any such still, distillery, or distilling apparatus, shall be jointly and severally liable for the taxes imposed by law on the distilled spirits produced therefrom, and the tax shall be a first lien on the spirits distilled, the distillery used for distilling the same, the stills, vessels, fixtures, and tools therein, and on the lot or tract of land whereon the said distillery is situated, together with any building thereon, from the time said spirits are distilled until the said tax shall be paid.]

(*a*) A tax of 50 cents per gallon is to be collected on the whole number of gauge or wine gallons when the spirits are below proof, and upon the proof gallon when of greater strength than proof. The tax of $4 per barrel of 40 proof gallons is upon the proof gallons. 9 I. R. R. 147.

The product of stills, though medicated by distilling drugs, roots, &c., is nevertheless liable to a tax. 5 I. R. R. 45.

Bitters sold or used as beverages, made by mixing spirits, wine, or other liquor with any materials, to be sold under the name of "wine bitters," or any other name, are liable to tax. 10 I. R. R. 65; 11 I. R. R. 137.

The intention of this section is to make the tax on distilled spirits a lien on the lot or tract of land whereon the distillery is situated, whether the distiller has, or has not, any interest therein. 6 I. R. R. 194.

Definition of Proof Spirit.

[SEC. 2. (July 20, 1868.) *And be it further enacted*, That proof spirit shall be held and taken to be that alcoholic liquor which contains one-half its volume of alcohol of a specific gravity of seven thousand nine hundred and thirty-nine ten-thousandths (.7939) at sixty degrees Fahrenheit; and the Commissioner of Internal Revenue, for the prevention and detection of frauds by distillers of spirits, is hereby authorized to adopt and prescribe for use such hydrometers, (*a*) saccharometers, weighing and gauging instruments, meters, or other means for ascertaining the quantity, gravity, and producing capacity of any mash, wort, or beer used or to be used in the production of distilled spirits, and the strength and quantity of spirits subject to tax, as he may deem necessary; and he may prescribe rules and regulations to secure a uniform and correct system of inspection, weighing, marking, and gauging of spirits. And in all sales of spirits hereafter made, a gallon (*b*) shall be taken to be a gallon of proof spirit, according to the foregoing standard set forth and declared for the inspection and gauging of spirits throughout the United States. The tax on brandy made from grapes shall be the same and no higher than that upon other distilled spirits; and the Commissioner of Internal Revenue is hereby authorized, with the approval of the Secretary of the Treasury, to exempt (*c*) distillers of brandy from apples, peaches, or grapes exclusively, from such other of the provisions of this act relating to the manufacture of spirits as in his judgment may seem expedient.]

(*a*) Hydrometers are the only instruments furnished by the government for gaugers. Every gauger must obtain calipers, bung rods, head rods, sliding scales, and wantage rods, at his own expense.

Collectors who have not been supplied with a sufficient number of hydrometers, or manuals for inspectors, containing correction tables, &c., should send their orders for the same, with proper explanations, to the Commissioner.

No saccharometers having yet been adopted, distillers may use such saccharometers for ascertaining the gravity of beer as are in good repute and general use among brewers and distillers. The name of the scale used should, however, always be noted on the yeasting book. 9 I. R. R. 156.

The hydrometers adopted by the Commissioner are essentially the same as Tralles' hydrometers, except that while the latter show per cents. of alcohol, the former show per cents. of proof spirits, and to this end the scale is greatly lengthened, and broken up into five separate parts. By this means, the stem of each hydrometer is shorter than the stem of Tralles'; and at the same time, the division marks on the stem are widened so that the indication of proof can be readily and easily distinguished. Number one reads from 0 to 100, number two from 80 to 120, number three from 10 to 140, number four from 130 to 170, and number five from 160 to 200. These divisions were adopted as being the most convenient for practice, ranging from water mark 0 to alcohol mark 200, the proof point being 100 instead of 50, as in the Tralles' scale, or in other words, the indications are the same as Tralles' multiplied by two.

These hydrometers show distinctly the number of proof gallons contained in 100 gallons of a given spirit. Thus, in spirits of a strength usually called 40 over proof, Tralles' hydrometer shows 70, this hydrometer 140 (at the standard temperature of 60° Fahr.), indicating that 100 gallons of the liquor are equivalent to 140 proof gallons. Similarly, in whiskey of a strength usually called 10 below proof, Tralles' hydrometer shows 45, this hydrometer 90, because 100 gallons of the liquor are equivalent to 90 proof gallons.

When the proof is taken at any temperature different from 60° Fahr., the indication of the hydrometer is too high for higher, and too low for lower temperatures. The true per cent., or corrected proof, must be found in the manual, as is fully explained in the introduction to the same.

In reading the indication of the United States standard hydrometer, the first line under the liquid should be taken for the true reading, but the fraction of a per cent. above that line should be remembered; and if this fraction, with the fraction found in the correction table, make a whole per cent., it should be added accordingly.

When the temperature of the spirit to be inspected is different from the surrounding atmosphere, the hydrometer cup should be emptied and refilled several times prior to making the inspection.

In taking samples from the barrels to test the proof, care should be taken not to let the thief go to the bottom of the barrel, as often ice or water will settle at the bottom, if the barrels have been but recently filled, and the proof shown will not be correct.

In using the hydrometer, care should be taken to keep the part which is out of the spirit perfectly dry. The cup should always be filled full, as the indication is more readily seen, and there is less liability to make an error in reading it.

A manual for inspectors of spirits will be furnished to collectors for the use of inspectors. The tables in this manual, as well as the hydrometer, must, in all cases, as soon as received by collectors, be used for proving the strength of spirits.

The instruments for gauging casks consist of a caliper, a bung rod, a head rod, and a sliding scale for ascertaining the capacity of casks after the measures have been taken.

The caliper is used for taking the length of casks, and consists of a pair of rods, with an arm on the end of each. The rods are attached to each other, so as to clasp a cask between the two arms, and the length is read in inches and tenths on the top of the rod, and is so marked as to allow for the usual thickness of the heads, which for casks of the usual size of whiskey barrels is one and a-half inch, or three-fourths of an inch for each head.

The bung rod is used for ascertaining the inside diameter of a cask at the bung, and is simply a straight rod marked in inches and tenths, with a slide attached, on the lower end of which is a lip to slip under the stave.

The head rod is used for taking the diameter of a cask at the head. It is a straight rod, with a projecting point at the lower end, to slip readily under the chime on the opposite side of the head. The diameter is read in inches and tenths at the lower end of the slide.

After the measures are taken with these instruments, the capacity of the cask is found as follows: subtract the head diameter from the bung diameter, find the difference on the upper line of the second variety on the edge of the scale, and on the lower line is found the number to be added to the head diameter, which gives the mean diameter of the barrel. Then set the end of the slide of the scale at the figures representing the length of the barrel, and find the mean diameter on the slide, over which will be found the capacity of the barrel.

This rule will do for all whiskey barrels of ordinary shape.

The second variety scale is found by multiplying the difference between the head and bung by 0.63.

Should the inspector wish to gauge barrels or casks with a great curvature, for instance a port wine cask, he should use the first variety found on the face of the scale, or multiply the difference by 0.7; and if a very flat cask, multiply by 0.55, and add the product to the head for the mean diameter.

In taking the length of the cask, the caliper should be held in a horizontal line with the cask, about one inch above the top, the ends touching the heads at a point about equally distant from the center and the chime.

The bung diameter is taken by placing the rod perpendicular to the stave opposite to the bung, and care should be taken to observe any irregularity or unevenness in the bottom or in the thickness of the bung stave.

In taking the head diameter, the head rod should be applied diagonally across the grain of the wood. The upper end of the rod should be moved gently up and down, and the largest diameter indicated will be the correct diameter.

All dimensions should be taken with the greatest care and precision, and the rods should be moved gently and with ease, and not with quick strong jerks. All fractions of tenths of inches should be noticed. For example: if the caliper shows the length to be twenty-seven, one-tenth and half a-tenth inches, it should be written with a dash, thus, 27.1—, denoting that it is more than 27.1. A fraction on each dimension will often make a full half gallon. There is often, also, a fraction in the mean diameter, as for example: suppose the bung diameter to be 22.1 inches, and the head diameter 19 inches, the difference is 3.1 inches, which, by the second variety on the edge of the scale, gives one inch and nine and a-half tenths, which, added to the head diameter, gives 20.95 for the mean diameter.

The half-tenth, or 5-100, will often, with a fraction in the length, or other dimension, make a full half gallon, that would be lost if all fractions be disregarded.

The wantage rod, should the barrel not be full, is used for ascertaining the quantity required to fill the barrel, or the quantity to be deducted from its capacity, in order to obtain its actual contents. No larger allowance for wantage than a half wine gallon shall be made, unless ascertained by measurement with the wantage rod. When the wantage is found, by actual measurement, to exceed a half gallon, the actual wantage shall be allowed, and no more. The common wantage rod is to be used, taking the corrections as marked for casks of forty-two gallons, and bung depth of twenty-two inches. 5 I. R. R. 83.

Each gauger is held responsible for breakages of hydrometer stems in his possession, and new ones must be obtained at his expense. The stems required should be described in the order by the numbers.

All gaugers who have been supplied with the standard glass hydrometers are prohibited from using any other hydrometers for government inspections in any case whatever. Collectors should see that this regulation is strictly enforced.

Hydrometer stems sent by the Commissioner to collectors by express, which are found to be broken on arrival, will be replaced by the Commissioner on receiving a description of the broken stems from the collectors. Manuals and hydrometers should only be furnished to those gaugers who have given bond, and supplied themselves at their own expense with calipers and the other gauging instruments. 6 I. R. R. 35.

Hydrometers and manuals will be furnished to collectors for gaugers upon application to the Commissioner. These will be delivered by inspectors to gaugers, and each gauger must give his receipt therefor. They must be treated as the property of the United States, and returned to the collector of the district whenever a gauger having them goes out of office. 5 I. R. R. 83.

(*b*) Every person may legally contract for any degree of proof, as he may for wheat weighing more or less than the standard fixed by law.

The clear, obvious import of the sentence is that where a transaction has no other element than the mere sale of five wine gallons of whiskey, they shall be considered and taken to be five proof gallons; and that, too, whether they are above or below proof; that throughout the United States a wine or gauge gallon of spirits sold shall be taken and adjudged to be a proof gallon sold; that in a contract for the sale and delivery of one hundred gallons of whiskey merely, the contract is fulfilled by the delivery of one hundred wine gallons, above or below proof. It declares, in effect, that in any suits growing out of such sales where this question is involved, the courts shall allow neither buyer nor seller to dispute this fact, this conclusive presumption of law. U. S. *v*. Waugerien, 11 I. R. R. 181.

(*c*) All distillers of brandy from apples, peaches, or grapes exclusively, are exempted from the following provisions of the act of July 20, 1868, and the acts amendatory thereof, to wit:

From all of the provisions of sections 3, 8, 9, 15, 18, 21, 22, 24, and 45, of the act of July 20, 1868, and so much of the act of April 10, 1869, as is amendatory to section 8 of said act; and from portions of the following-named sections of said act of July 20, 1868, to wit:

So much of section 6 as requires the distiller to state in his notice the number of mash tubs and fermenting tubs, and the cubic contents of each tub, the number of receiving cisterns, and the cubic contents of each cistern, and the number of hours in which the distiller will ferment each tub of mash or beer. So much of section 7 as provides that in no case shall the distiller's bond be for a less sum than five thousand dollars. So much of section 12 as provides that no person shall use any still, boiler, or other vessel for the purpose of distilling, in any shed, yard, or inclosure connected with any dwelling-house. From all of the provisions of section 17, except so much thereof as provides that "no assessor shall approve the bond of any distiller until all the requirements of law and all regulations made by the Commissioner in relation to distilleries, in pursuance thereof, shall have been complied with," and the penalty relating thereto. From all of section 19, except so much thereof as provides for the keeping of a book or books, in the manner to be prescribed by the Commissioner, the preservation of such book or books for the inspection of revenue officers, and the penalties pertaining thereto, and the making of such returns: *Provided, however*, That the manner of making such returns shall be as prescribed in these regulations.

So much of section 20 as provides that forty-five gallons of mash or beer brewed or fermented from grain shall represent not less than one bushel of grain, and seven gallons of mash or beer, brewed or fermented from molasses, shall represent not less than one gallon of molasses; and so much of section 1 of the act approved April 10, 1869, as is amendatory thereof.

From all of the provisions of section 23, except so much thereof as requires that all distilled spirits shall be drawn into casks, and shall be gauged, proved, and marked by a United States gauger, by cutting on the cask containing such spirits, in a manner to be prescribed by the Commissioner, the quantity in wine gallons and in proof gallons of the contents of such cask, and the serial number of the package, in progressive order.

From so much of section 25 as provides for the receiving of an order from the collector for the removal of spirits from distillery warehouse; and from so much thereof as requires that the affixing of the tax-paid stamp, and the cutting or the burning of the serial number of the stamp, shall be done by a gauger.

From so much of section 1, act April 10, 1869, as requires that spirits purified or refined in the original course of manufacture must be by continuous distillation through continuous closed vessels and pipes until the manufacture thereof is complete.

Distillation from the aforesaid fruits, or from the undistilled products of either or all of these fruits, exclusively, is regarded as a distillation from the fruit. ·12 I. R. R. 1.

The authority conferred upon the Commissioner is ample. It is true that he can exempt the distillers from only such provisions of the act as relate to the manufacture of spirits, but all the provisions of the act which relate to spirits do, in the sense of Congress, relate to the manufacture of spirits. It is the distillers, that is, the manufacturers of brandy, who are to be exempt, and they are to be exempt from such provisions of the act as relate to the manufacture of spirits, that is, such as relate to them as manufacturers of spirits. The Commissioner is not authorized to exempt distillers of brandy from all the provisions of the act which relate to the manufacture of spirits. This is plainly implied by the term "other" used in the very sentence in which the authority is found. The provision from which he cannot exempt them is that which imposes a tax on them. U. S. v. 37 Bbls. 11 I. R. R. 125.

Meters Attached at Expense of Owners.

[SEC. 3. (July 20, 1868.) *And be it further enacted,* That whenever the Commissioner of Internal Revenue shall adopt and prescribe for use any meter, (*a*) meters, or meter safes, it shall be the duty of every owner, agent, or superintendent of a distillery to furnish and attach, at his own expense, such meter, meters, or meter safes as may have been prescribed for use at his distillery, and to furnish all the pipes, materials, labor and facilities necessary to complete such attachment in accordance with the regulations of the Commissioner of Internal Revenue, who is hereby further authorized to order and require such changes of or additions to distilling apparatus, connecting pipes, pumps, or cisterns, or any [machinery connected with or used in or on the distillery premises, or may require to be put on any of the stills, tubs, cisterns, pipes or other vessels, such fastenings, locks, (*b*) or seals as he may deem necessary.]

(*a*) The spirit meter, invented by Mr. Isaac P. Tice, has been adopted. The system which has been adopted involves the use of two meters; the first will be attached to the end of the worm, and will register the entire product of the still; the second will be placed upon the doubler in such a position as to register the quantity of low wines carried back to the doubler for redistillation. If the still is provided with such attachments that no low wines are discharged, and the distiller is prepared to report as taxable the entire product of the still, only one meter need be used.

Distillers, in making their applications for such meters, must state the capacity of the still in cubic feet, and its utmost possible producing capacity per minute,—that is, the greatest possible quantity of spirits that will pass from the worm in that time. The producing capacity here referred to must not be confined to high wines merely, but must show the entire quantity of spirits, whether high or low wines, which can or will pass from the worm in the time specified.

The application must also show the cubic contents of the doubler; the outside diameter of the worm at its lower extremity; the height and diameter of the tank in which it is placed, and the material of which the still, doubler, and tank are constructed; the diameter of the main pipe leading from the still to the doubler as well as of the charging and discharging and blow-off pipes, including the pipe used for discharging the doubler, must also be given. There is also required a description of the foundations upon which the still, doubler, and condenser are respectively supported. If the cylinder is provided with collapse valves, their number and diameter must also be stated.

This application will be made on Form 7, which will be furnished by the collectors of the several districts. At the time of making the application, the applicant will furnish the collector of his district a certificate of deposit in a United States depositary for the amount of the price of the meter or meters, payable to the order of Mr. Tice, and the collector will certify upon such application that he has received such certificate, and forward the application to the Office of Internal Revenue. The applicant should also state the means of access to the distillery, whether by railroad, steamboat, or canal, and with what points the distillery is connected by either of these modes of communication. If there is any person carrying on the trade of copper-smith in the immediate vicinity, the collector will state the fact, and if not, he will state the distance to the nearest point at which the services of such artisan can be procured. Upon the receipt of the bill of lading, the collector will immediately transmit the certificate of deposit to Mr. Tice, at his address, 314 Third Avenue, New York.

Whenever a certificate of deposit is forwarded, the collector will report the fact to the Office of Internal Revenue, giving the amount, and the name of the distiller who made the deposit. When collectors deposit their collections in a depositary bank, the meter deposit will be made in bank; but where they are required to deposit collections with an assistant treasurer or designated depositary the meter deposits will be made in some responsible bank.

The meters are constructed of six different sizes, the prices and capacities being as follows:

Sample meter A.
    Capacity, four gallons per minute..........................$200
Sample meter B.
    Capacity, eight gallons per minute.. 250
These are intended for attachment to small copper stills.
Meter No. 2.
    Capacity, three gallons per minute.........................600
Meter No. 3.
    Capacity, six gallons per minute...........................800
Meter No. 4.
    Capacity, eighteen gallons per minute....................1,000

The expenses of transportation and attachment of the meters, and of any changes required to be made in the distillery, are to be paid by the distiller.

When meters are being attached to several neighboring distilleries at the same time, the expenses incurred by Mr. Tice and his workmen will be apportioned among the several distilleries, according to the time employed in each. Whenever it is practicable, an officer detailed by the Commissioner will supervise the attachment; and, when no such detail is made, the assessor will detail one of his assistants for that purpose. When the attachment of a meter is completed, it must be promptly reported to the Office of Internal Revenue by such officer or assistant assessor. The presence of such officer, however, will not be understood as relieving either the collector or assessor of the district from the responsibility properly belonging to them.

A daily report must be made by the storekeeper in charge of each distillery to the assessor of the district, setting forth the indications shown by the meter at the hour of twelve, midnight, or at the time when the distillery ceases to operate for the day; and each assistant assessor, who has a distillery in his division, will examine each meter whenever he visits the distillery, and report to his assessor the indications of the meter above indicated; and assessors, in making their monthly computation on Form 89, will use the information thus given in determining the production. When but one meter is attached, they will charge the distiller with the full product of the worm, making no deduction for low wines returned to the still or doubler.

In distilleries where the product of the first distillation is singlings only, no meter will be required for the singling still; but each doubling still will require one or two meters, depending upon the fact whether there is a separation of the low wines. It must be understood that there must be a close connection between the singling and doubling stills in all cases, so that no access can be had by the distiller to the low wines at any point during their passage from the singling to the doubling still.

There are two classes of these spirit meters made. In one of these, all the liquor is weighed, and a small sample of each can-full reserved for future inspection. In the other class, all the liquor is likewise weighed; and, besides, the volume and weight of a certain portion of it is registered, from which the proof can be computed; in addition to which a small sample is taken, which serves to verify the proof deduced from the automatic register, and affords the means of applying a correction for temperature.

The first-class or sample meters are made of two sizes, marked A and B. The former weighs five pounds, and the latter ten pounds at one registration. To ascertain, at any time, how many proof gallons have run through one of these meters since a previous inspection, read the index, withdraw all the reserved sample, and ascertain its strength by the hydrometer in the usual way. Subtracting the previous reading of the register from that now observed, and multiplying the difference by five for sample meter A, or by ten for sample meter B, the product will be the number of pounds of liquor that have been run through the meter. The number of pounds and average proof being thus found, Table II. of the Manual for Gaugers will give the corresponding number of gallons. The number of proof gallons is then found in the usual way by multiplying the number of gallons by the per cent. of proof contained in them.

The second class, or complete meters, are made of four different sizes, marked respectively No. 2, No. 3, No. 4, and No. 5. In each meter the lower register counts every discharge of a weighing can, into which all the liquor runs. At each discharge, this can weighs—

        In No. 2, 5 pounds.
        In No. 3, 10 pounds.
        In No. 4, 30 pounds.
        In No. 5, 50 pounds.

The discharge of this weighing can at the same time empties a measuring can holding exactly a quart, and the spirits so emptied are weighed in a three pound weighing can, which is registered on the upper register; the number of quarts being taken from the lower register, as well as the total weight of the spirits. That portion of the spirits which was reserved in the weighing can passes, after being weighed in the three pounds can, into the large or lower weighing can. The quart and three pounds can are alike in all the sizes of meters.

In this way the whole weight of the spirits that have passed through the meter, and also the weight of a certain number of representative quarts are ascertained, from which, by appropriate tables, the strength and quantity, and consequently, the number of proof gallons can be found. It is convenient to convert the quarts into gallons, as the tables have been constructed for that unit.

When two meters are used, one at the worm and the other at the doubler, the proof gallons returned to the still, as shown by the latter, are to be deducted from the gross amount shown by the former, in order to ascertain the amount on which the tax is to be assessed.

These calculations all suppose that the liquor has been measured in the meter, at a temperature of 60° Fahrenheit, for which the tables are constructed. If the spirits have passed through the meter at a higher temperature, the proof derived from its indications would be higher than the actual strength; and if at a lower temperature, it would be lower than the actual strength, in precisely the same degree as if the proof had been taken by a hydrometer.

The receiver, in which the small samples are collected, contains a hydrometer and thermometer exposed to iron. By these the average strength of the spirits distilled since the receiver was last emptied can be ascertained by observation; and their indications should be recorded at each reading of the meter. The proof so obtained should not differ from that derived from the automatic register by more than what is due to the difference between 60° Fahrenheit and the temperature at which the spirits may have passed through the meter. The receiver should be emptied after the verification of each report of the indications of the meter. A difference of 6 or 7 per cent. is reasonable and usual. The computation of the proof gallons is made from the weight, and proof by samples according to Table II. of Manual.

The most reliable way to test the meters is to ascertain the weight by actual weighing, and by testing with the hydrometer the strength of a considerable quantity of spirits, both high and low wines, discharged from the meter, and compare the same with the registration on the meter.

To this end it would be necessary to disconnect the discharge pipes for high and low wines, and to let the spirits be run into tanks provided for the purpose, and sufficiently large to receive the product of a charge of high and low wines respectively. Each tank should be mounted on a platform scale, and means provided to empty the tanks into the receivers between the runs of the still. The weighing is preferred to measuring because the weight is not changed by heat, while the volume is. After weighing each tank, its contents should be well stirred, and the proof then taken with a hydrometer; the actual indication and temperature being set down, together with the weight and the corresponding index readings of the meter. Not less than 500 registrations of the weighing can should be used in the test. This will give an accurate and correct test of the rate of the meter.

A less accurate test may be made by comparing the result of the meter indications with the quantity and strength of the spirits actually delivered into the receiving cisterns for high wines. In adopting this method, the officer making the test must assure himself that there is no communication with the receiving cisterns, except that from the meter, and that the receiving cisterns are empty when he commences the test. He should measure all, and none but the spirits that have passed through the meter, and been delivered during this test. He will record the index readings of the meter at the commencement of the test, and at the close of each run of the still, and draw off, measure, and test the proof of the spirits delivered into the receiving cisterns during each run. The measuring may be done by means of sealed gallon or five gallon measures, or by barrels, the capacity of which has been ascertained by actual measurement with sealed measures, or by weighing the water they will hold, allowing 12 gallons for 100 pounds. The officer should see to the measurement personally, as well as to obtaining the average proof of each run. 9 I. R. R. 114.

(b) The register seal lock has been prescribed by the Commissioner. The party desiring it will pay the price, $3.50, to the collector or assessor of his district, who, on the receipt thereof, will remit the same to the collector at Buffalo, N. Y., by whom the money will be paid to the manufacturer, and the lock, with printed instructions, will be shipped to the officer ordering it, the expenses of shipping to be paid by the party. Collectors will see that the register seal lock is furnished in all cases where locks are to be applied under their supervision. The storekeeper, or other proper officer, must retain the custody of the keys of the locks in use, never suffering them to go out of his possession, except to the collector or assessor of his district. 10 I. R. R. 118.

Definition of Distilled Spirits.

[SEC. 4. (July 20, 1868.) *And be it further enacted*, That distilled spirits, spirits, alcohol, and alcoholic spirit, within the true intent and meaning of this act, is that substance known as ethyl alcohol, hydrated oxide of ethyl, or spirit of wine, which is commonly produced by the fermentation of grain, starch, molasses, or sugar, including all dilutions and mixtures of this substance; and the tax shall attach to this substance as soon as it is in existence as such, whether it be subsequently separated as pure or impure spirit, or be immediately, or at any subsequent time, transferred into any other substance, either in the process of original production or by any subsequent process; and no mash, wort, or wash (a) fit for distillation or the production of spirits or alcohol shall be made or fermented in any building or on any premises other than a distillery duly authorized according to law; and no mash, wort, or wash so made and fermented shall be sold or removed from any distillery before being distilled; and no person other than an authorized distiller shall by distillation, or by any other process, separate the alcoholic spirits from any fermented mash, wort, or wash; and no person shall use spirits or alcohol, or any vapor of alcoholic spirits, in manufacturing vinegar or any other article, or in any process of manufacture whatever, unless the spirits or alcohol so used shall have been produced in an authorized distillery, and the tax thereon paid. Any person who shall violate any of the provisions of this section shall be fined, for every offence, not less than five hundred dollars nor more than five thousand dollars, and imprisoned for not less than six months nor more than two years : *Provided*, That nothing in this section shall be construed to apply to fermented liquors.]

(*a*) Distillation of spirits from "drop beer" or "slops" may be carried on subject to the same requirements that apply to distillation from any material other than grapes and apples. 11 I. R. R. 58.

Under this section, no article into which alcoholic spirits, or alcoholic vapors enter as an ingredient, can be lawfully manufactured, unless such spirits or alcohol have been produced in an authorized distillery, and have paid the tax. The largest class of cases affected by it is that of manufacturers of vinegar by various processes of distillation. 8 I. R. R. 45. U. S. *v.* Vaporizer, 7 I. R. R. 205; U. S. *v.* 1 Still, 6 I. R. R. 220; U. S. *v.* 2 Bbls. 6 I. R. R. 44.

The phrase "fit for distillation" is not synonymous with the phrase "fit for profitable distillation," but means capable of distillation, and of the production of pure or impure alcoholic spirits. The obvious intent of the law is to levy a tax upon all alcohol and alcoholic spirits entering into the composition of any of the known articles of manufacture in the country, and to require that the alcohol thus produced shall be produced in authorized distilleries. The saving clause applying to fermented liquors is intended only to apply to manufacturers of ale, beer, &c. U. S. *v.* Prussing et al. 12 I. R. R. 34.

Registration of Still.

[SEC. 5. (July 20, 1868.) *And be it further enacted*, That every person having in his possession or custody, or under his control, any still or distilling apparatus set up, shall register (*a*) the same with the assistant assessor of the division in which said still or distilling apparatus shall be, by filing with him duplicate statements, in writing, subscribed by such person, setting forth the particular place where such still or distilling apparatus is set up, the kind of still and its cubic contents, the owner thereof, his place of residence, and the purpose for which said still or distilling apparatus has been or is intended to be used ; one of which statements shall be retained and preserved by the assistant assessor, and the other transmitted to the assessor of the district. Stills and distilling apparatus now set up shall be so registered within sixty days from the time this act takes effect, and those hereafter set up shall be so registered immediately upon their being set up. Any still or distilling apparatus not so registered, together with all personal property in the possession, or custody, or under the control of such person and found in the building, or in any yard or inclosure connected with the building, in which the same shall be set up, shall be forfeited. And any person having in his possession or custody, or under his control, any still or distilling apparatus set up which is not so registered, shall pay a penalty of five hundred dollars, and on conviction shall be fined not less than one hundred dollars nor more than one thousand dollars, and imprisoned for not less than one month nor more than two years.]

(a) The application for registry will be in duplicate on Form 26, one of which will be retained and preserved by the assistant assessor, and the other transmitted by him to the assessor of the district, and a copy thereof immediately sent by the assessor to the Commissioner. All stills and distilling apparatus set up must be registered, whether they are intended to be used or not. Each assessor will enter the registry of all stills in a book to be kept in his office, and open to inspection, denoting each distillery by its number. Every assessor must furnish the Office of Internal Revenue with a list of stills or distilling apparatus registered in his district, giving the names of the owners, the location, and whether or not the same are intended to be used, together with the registered number of the distillery. Where the distiller is not the owner of the fee, that fact should also be stated, and whether the consent, or stipulation, or leaseholder's bond has been filed with him. 9 I. R. R. 147.

Notice to be Given by Distillers.

[SEC. 6. (July 20, 1868.) *And be it further enacted*, That every person engaged in, or intending to be engaged in, the business of a distiller or rectifier, shall give notice (a) in writing, subscribed by him, to the assessor of the district within which such business is to be carried on, stating his name and place of residence, and if a company or firm, the name and place of residence of each member thereof, the place where said business is to be carried on, and whether of distilling or rectifying. And if such business be carried on in a city, the residence and place of business shall be indicated by the name of the street and number of the building.

In case of a distiller the notice shall also state the kind of stills, and the cubic contents thereof, the number and kind of boilers, the number of mash tubs and fermenting tubs, and the cubic contents of each tub, the number of receiving cisterns, and the cubic contents of each cistern, together with a particular description of the lot or tract of land on which the distillery is situated, with the size and description of the buildings thereon, and of what material constructed. The notice shall also state the number of hours in which the distiller will ferment each tub of mash or beer, the estimated quantity of distilled spirits which the apparatus is capable of distilling every twenty-four hours, and the names and residence of every person interested or to be interested in the business, and that said distillery and the premises connected therewith are not within six hundred feet of any premises authorized to be used for rectifying or refining distilled spirits by any process.

In case of a rectifier, the notice shall state the precise location of the premises where such business is to be carried on, the name and residence of every person interested or to be interested in the business, by what process the applicant intends to rectify, purify, or refine distilled spirits, the kind and cubic contents of any still used or to be used for such purpose, and the estimated quantity of spirits which can be rectified, purified, or refined every twenty-four hours in such establishment, and that said rectifying establishment is not within six hundred feet of the premises of any distillery registered for the distillation of spirits.

In case of any change in the location, form, capacity, ownership, agency, superintendency, or in the persons interested in the business of such distillery or rectifying establishment, or in the time of fermenting the mash or beer, notice thereof, in writing, shall be given to the said assessor or to the assistant assessor of the division within twenty-four hours of said change. And any assistant assessor receiving such notice shall immediately transmit the same to the assessor of the district. Every notice required by this section shall be in such form and shall contain such additional particulars as the Commissioner of Internal Revenue may from time to time prescribe. Any person failing or refusing to give such notice shall pay a penalty of one thousand dollars, and on conviction shall be fined not less than one hundred dollars nor more than two thousand dollars; and any person giving a false or fraudulent notice shall, on conviction, in addition to such penalty or fine, be imprisoned not less than six months nor more than two years.]

(*a*) Every person engaged in the business of a distiller, or intending to engage therein, must give notice on Form 27, over his own signature, to the assessor of the district in which such business is, or is to be, carried on, who will furnish a copy thereof to the collector. Like notice of any change in the location, form, capacity, ownership, agency, or superintendence; or in the persons interested in the business of said distillery, or in the time of fermenting the mash or beer, is to be given within twenty-four hours of such change, and a copy of such notice will be immediately transmitted to the Commissioner.

The notice (Form 27) should be prepared in strict conformity to sections 6 and 15 of the act July 20, 1868. The description of the distillery premises should be limited to the lot or parcel of land actually used in connection with the distillery, and for that purpose alone, and should be as particular as in a deed. The size and description of each building situated thereon, and of what material constructed, should be given; and the building used or intended to be used as a distillery warehouse, should be indicated, with an additional statement that no door, window, or other opening is in the walls of such warehouse leading into the distillery or any other room or building; and that said warehouse is on and constitutes a part of said distillery premises. The precise nature of the title to the distillery building, apparatus, and premises, should be stated; and where the written consent of the owner of the fee, or holder of liens or bonds s substituted in lieu of unencumbered fee simple, that fact should appear. The distiller must name in his notice (Form 27) the number of hours in which he will ferment each tub or mash of beer, and will be required to operate his distillery upon this fermenting period; but assessments will be made against him on the basis of the survey, a copy of the report of which was last delivered to him. 11 I. R. R. 121.

Each person having a still, and intending to use the same for the distillation of brandy from apples, peaches, or grapes, must, before commencing distillation, give notice, on Form 27½, to the assessor of his district, direct or through the assistant assessor of his division, of his intention to distil, stating in such notice his name and place of residence, and, if a company or firm, the name and place of residence of each member thereof; the place where said business is to be carried on; the number and kind of stills; the total capacity of each in gallons; the manner in which the same is to be boiled, whether by steam or furnace heat; the kind of fruit proposed to be used; the building or place on the premises where the distillery is situated in which he will deposit and keep the brandy to be distilled by him until the tax is paid thereon and the tax-paid stamps attached thereto; and that such still or stills are not within six hundred feet of any premises authorized to be used for rectifying or refining distilled spirits by any process. 12 I. R. R. 1.

Bonds of Distillers.

[SEC. 7. (July 20, 1868.) *And be it further enacted*, That every distiller shall, on filing his notice of intention to continue or commence business with the assessor before proceeding with such business, after the passage of this act and on the first day of May of each succeeding year, make and execute a bond (*a*) in form prescribed by the Commissioner of Internal Revenue, with at least two sureties, to be approved by the assessor of the district. The penal sum of said bond shall not be less than double the amount of tax on the spirits that can be distilled in his distillery during a period of fifteen days; but in no case shall such bond be for a less sum than five thousand dollars. The condition of the bond shall be that the principal shall faithfully comply with all the provisions of law in relation to the duties and business of distillers, and will pay all penalties incurred or fines imposed on him for violation of any of the said provisions; that he will not suffer the lot or tract of land on which the distillery stands, or any part thereof, or any of the distilling apparatus, to be encumbered by mortgage, judgment, or other lien, during the time in which he shall carry on said business. The assessor may refuse to approve said bond, when, in his judgment, the situation of the distillery is such as would enable the distiller to defraud the United States; and in case of such refusal, the distiller may appeal to the Commissioner of Internal Revenue, whose decision in the matter shall be final. A new bond may be required in case of the death, insolvency, or removal of either of the sureties, and in any other contingency, at the discretion of the assessor or Commissioner of Internal

Revenue. Any person failing or refusing to give the bond hereinbefore required, or to renew the same, or giving any false, forged, or fraudulent bond, shall forfeit the distillery, distilling apparatus, and all real estate and premises connected therewith, and on conviction shall be fined not less than five hundred dollars nor more than five thousand dollars, and imprisoned not less than six months nor more than two years.]

(*a*) Every distiller, on filing his notice with the assessor, must, before continuing or commencing business, on the first day of May in each succeeding year, make and execute a bond on Form 80, with at least two sureties to be approved by the assessor of the district; assessors will give special attention to the instructions printed thereon, and will require the sureties to justify, on Form 83, in double the amount of the penal sum of the bond. No distiller's bond should be approved until his distillery warehouse has been approved and established, and a storekeeper assigned thereto by the Commissioner, nor until all the requirements of law and the regulations in relation to distilleries have been complied with. The bonds of distillers, when approved by assessors, will be filed with the collector of the district; assessors will also forward to the Office of Internal Revenue information of the date when the bond was approved, if approved, and the time when the distiller commenced work. 9 I. R. R. 147.

Distillers should understand that with the last day of April their rights as distillers cease; and those intending then to discontinue distilling must so arrange their business as to terminate all work at their distillery on the last day of April, and not have beer on hand to be distilled in the first days of May; in such cases, the parties must be treated as illicit distillers. Distillers intending to discontinue business, should, on the thirtieth day of April, register their stills as not for use. A distiller desiring to continue his business, can only do so legally by giving his notice (Form 27), and executing his bond on the first day of May. Such distiller should have his bond complete and ready for execution with his notice (Form 27) prepared and presented to the assessor a sufficient length of time in advance of the first day of May, to enable him to make the necessary investigations by that day, so that he may, on the first day of May, when the bond is executed, approve or disapprove such bond. When the bond is approved on the first day of May, the distiller may continue his work at his distillery; but where the bond is disapproved, the mere fact of having presented it confers no rights upon the distiller, but he will be regarded as having failed to give bond as required, and must cease all work at his distillery. The assessor, in approving the bond, should endorse his approval thereon, giving the date of such approval, and sign his name thereto, officially. Where bonds are not approved until after the first day of May, or where presented for approval on the first day of May by those commencing business, the approval should not be made until the assessor is advised, by the Office of Internal Revenue, that the (Form 27) report of survey, plan, and warehouse are approved, and storekeeper assigned; but in the case of those offering bond for approval on the first day of May, with a view of continuing business, the approval will be made without awaiting advices from the Office of Internal Revenue, as, in such cases, the papers alluded to must have already had official approval. 11 I. R. R. 121.

The bonds should not be surrendered at the close of the special tax year, nor at any other time, but should be retained as security for any liabilities which may be discovered to have been incurred during the period covered by it. 8 I. R. R. 171.

Bonds of a distiller of brandy from apples, etc., so given, expire on the last day of April of each year, and parties must renew their bonds before continuing or again engaging in distillation after that date. 12 I. R. R. 1.

A distiller, who has prepared and delivered a bond to the assessor, and been notified of its approval, will not forfeit his property because he has omitted to hand in a plan of his distillery, and otherwise comply with the provisions of the ninth section. Whether the bond has been approved in point of fact is immaterial. Whenever the Commissioner did prescribe a form of bond, then it was the duty of the distiller to give it in that form; and until he did so prescribe a form, it was sufficient if the distiller gave a bond in the form and with the condition contained in the statute. U. S. *v.* 35 Bbls. 9 I. R. R. 67.

A bond voluntarily given to the United States to secure the performance of any lawful act, or the discharge of any public, official, or private duty, is valid and binding, if the United States, in its political and corporate capacity, has a legal pecuniary interest in the performance of the condition of such bond; although such bond is not required by any act of Congress, The United States, the different States of the Union, and all municipal corporations may legally take a bond with sureties for the faithful performance, by an individual, of all lawful contracts made with them, and in the performance of which they have a direct pecuniary corporate interest. In this respect they may take the same measures for their security as might be taken by an individual for his own security in similar cases; and whenever any tax is legally imposed by the United States, it may take security by bond for the payment of such tax, or for the proper accounting therefor by the officer who collects it, in the absence of any Congressional legislation upon the subject of such security. U. S. *v.* Garlinghouse et al. 11 I. R. R. 11.

The capacity of a party to make a contract is governed by the *lex loci contractus*, or the law of the place where the contract is made. When the laws of a State authorize a femme covert to engage in and carry on the business of a distiller upon her own account and for her sole benefit, separate from the business of her husband, and to make with an individual any contract for the procurement or use of a warehouse, to enable her to carry on such business, she may execute a bond with sureties as required by this act. By requiring such bond of a married woman, who might carry on the business of a distiller for her sole and separate benefit, Congress incidentally and necessarily conferred upon her the legal capacity to bind herself by such bond; for, otherwise, the execution of the bond would be a nugatory act, and the object and purpose of Congress in requiring such bond would be defeated. U. S. *v.* Garlinghouse et al. 11 I. R. R. 11.

The courts of the United States are governed by the rules of the common law, because the common law is in force in the State or Territory where the cause of action arose or is to be enforced, and not because the common law has been adopted by the United States, or has, under the laws of the United States, any binding force except as being the law of some State, Territory, or district. U. S. *v.* Garlinghouse et al. 11 I. R. R. 11.

A party who resorts to the practice of hiring sureties upon his bond, is bound to know that the sureties are good. He may pay money to another to become his surety, but it must be under such circumstances as to show an honest effort to procure good ones. U. S. *v.* O'Brien et al. 7 I. R. R. 63.

This act is a revenue law within the meaning of the act March 26, 1804, 2 Stat. 290, and the limitation for the prosecution, trial, and punishment of persons guilty of offences under it is extended to five years. U. S. *v.* Wright et al. 11 I. R. R. 35 ; s. c. 3 A. L. T. (C. R.) 17.

The lot or tract of land of which a description is to be given, or which is required to be unencumbered, or for the value of which a bond is to be given, and which is not allowed to be encumbered, is the real estate and premises connected with the distillery; that is, used in connection therewith to facilitate the carrying on of the business, and directly or indirectly conductive or contributory to that end. It will include all buildings, yards, inclosures, offices, stables, wine-cellars, &c., used in the business; but it ought not to include dwelling houses, pasture or sowing lots, &c., or village lots and leases, which, though owned by the distiller, and not in any way employed in his business as a distiller, which may be rented or occupied by other persons, and which, so far as the manufacture of distilled spirits is concerned, might as well have belonged to any one else. U. S. *v.* Piece of Land, 11 I. R. R. 126.

Approval of Bonds—Priority of Lien.

[SEC. 8. (July 20, 1868.) *And be it further enacted,* That no bond of a distiller shall be approved unless he is the owner in fee, unencumbered by any mortgage, judgment, or other lien, of the lot or tract of land on which the distillery is situated, or unless he files with the assessor, in connection with his notice, the written consent (*a*) of the owner of the fee, and of any mortgagee, judgment creditor, or other person having a lien thereon, duly acknowledged, that the premises may be used for the purpose of distilling spirits, subject to the provisions of law, and expressly stipulating that the lien of the United States for taxes and penalties shall have priority of such mortgage, judgment, or other encumbrance, and that in case of the forfeiture of the distillery premises, or any part thereof, the title of the same shall vest in the United States, discharged from any such mortgage, judgment, or other encumbrance.

In any case where the owner of a distillery or distilling apparatus, erected prior to the passage of this act, has an estate for a term of years only, in the lot or tract of land on which the distillery is situated, the lease or other evidence of title to which shall have been duly recorded prior to the passage of this act, the value of such lot or tract of land, together with the building and distilling apparatus, shall be appraised in the manner to be prescribed by the Commissioner of Internal Revenue; and the assessor is hereby authorized to accept, in lieu of the said written consent of the owner of the fee, the bond of said distiller with not less than two sureties, who shall be residents of the collection district or county, or an adjoining county in the same State, in which the distillery is situated, and shall be the owners of unencumbered real estate in said district or county, or adjoining county, equal to such appraised value. The penal sum of said bond shall be equal to the appraised value of said lot or tract of land, together with the buildings and distilling apparatus, and such bond shall be conditioned that in case the distillery, distilling apparatus, or any part thereof, shall, by final judgment, be forfeited for the violation of any of the provisions of law, the obligors will pay the amount stated in said bond. Said bond shall be in such form as the Commissioner of Internal Revenue shall prescribe.]

(a) The consent of the owner of the fee, or mortgagee, judgment creditor, or other person having a lien on the premises, must be duly acknowledged and executed with all the formalities required in conveyances of real estate, and must be duly recorded before the same is filed with the assessor. As the question as to the title to the real estate is material, the assessor should require of the distiller a properly certified statement, or search of the title to such to be exhibited to him, and full evidence as to what, if any, liens or encumbrances exist thereon.

Where the distiller's estate is for a term of years only, under a lease or other evidence of title recorded before the passage of this act, the distillery, or distilling apparatus, having also been erected prior to that date, the distiller may, in lieu of the consent and stipulation aforesaid, give an additional bond, on Form 3, with not less than two sureties, residents of the district or county, or adjoining county, and owners of unencumbered real estate in said district or county, equal to the penal sum of the bond. In such case the assessor will cause the value of the lot, or tract of land, together with the buildings and distilling apparatus, to be appraised by two or more competent persons to be designated by him, and the said appraisal may be increased by the assessor, if, in his judgment, the same is too low, and the penal sum of said bond must be equal to such appraised value.

This is in addition to the distiller's bond, required by section 7, and a substitute for the ownership in fee of the distillery premises; and if the same sureties should be offered upon both bonds, the assessor will see that they are the owners of unencumbered real estate, as aforesaid, sufficient in value to cover their liability upon both bonds. 9 I. R. R. 147.

The written consent required of the owner of the fee is one which has been given since the passage of the act, and should be filed with the assessor. 8 I. R. R. 72.

The filing of an original lease, or copies thereof, in the offices of the collector and assessor, is not such a record thereof as is contemplated by this section. If there is no public record for leases, or if for any other reason the lease has not been recorded, the general rule must be enforced. 8 I. R. R. 171.

If a distillery stands upon premises so situated that the portion where the distillery is located fronts upon the public highway, or is directly accessible from it, and is so inclosed and set apart from the rest of the premises as to be readily sold at public sale as separate property, such portion may be regarded as the distillery premises. 8 I. R. R. 172.

When Consent of Owner of Fee Not Required.

[SEC. 1. (April 10, 1869.) That section eight be amended so that in case of a distiller or distilling apparatus erected prior to the twentieth of July, eighteen hundred and sixty-eight, on a tract or lot of land held under a lease or other evidence of title less than fee simple, which was not required by the laws of the State to be recorded in order to be valid at the time of its execution, or in any case where the title was then and has continued to be in litigation, or where the owner is possessed of the fee but encumbered with a mortgage executed and duly recorded prior to the said twentieth of July, eighteen hundred and sixty-eight, and not due, or where the fee is held by a femme covert, minor, person of unsound mind, or other person incapable of giving consent as required by said act, a bond may be taken at the discretion of the Commissioner, as provided for in said section, for a distillery erected on land the lease or other evidence of title to which was duly recorded prior to the passage of this act: *Provided*, That nothing herein contained shall be so construed as to apply to any distillery or distilling apparatus not erected prior to the twentieth of July, eighteen hundred and sixty-eight.]

Any person desiring to avail himself of these provisions must make application to the Commissioner, showing, in case of a lease, that there was a valid subsisting lease on or before July 20, 1868, under which he holds, and that the same was not required to be recorded by the laws of the State. If the title is in litigation, in what court the proceedings are pending; the parties thereto, and the nature of their claims; and that such litigation was pending July 20, 1868; if a mortgage, the date and amount of the same; when recorded; by whom held, and when the same is due; and in case of incapacity to consent, the nature of said incapacity. In all cases, a full and clear statement of the title to the estate should be given; and such application should have endorsed thereon the certificate of the assessor of the district that he has personally investigated the case, and finds that the statements made are correct. 9 I. R. R. 148.

Where the title to the estate upon which an authorized distillery is located is changed by a sale, judicial or otherwise, or there is any change of ownership in the premises or distilling apparatus, or where the lot or tract of land on which the distillery stands, or any part thereof, or any of the distilling apparatus, subsequent to the approval of the bond, becomes subject to, or encumbered by, any mortgage, judgment, or other lien; or any person becomes interested in the business other than those stated on Form 27, it is no longer an authorized distillery. In such case, there must be a new notice on Form 27, and all the steps taken the same as in the case of a new distillery, except that the distiller may adopt or assent in writing to the correctness of the plan and survey on file, and the proper correction should be made upon the registry of the still. 9 I. R. R. 158.

Plan of Distillery.

[SEC. 9. (July 20, 1868.) *And be it further enacted,* That every distiller and person intending to engage in the business of a distiller shall, previous to the approval of his bond, cause to be made, under the direction of the assessor of the district, an accurate plan (a) and description, in triplicate, of the distillery and distilling apparatus, distinctly showing the location of every still, boiler, doubler, worm tub, and receiving cistern, the course and construction of all fixed pipes used or to be used in the distillery, and of every branch thereof, and of every cock or joint thereof, and of every valve therein, together with every place, vessel, tub, or utensil from and to which any such pipe shall lead, or with which it communicates. Such plan and description shall also show the number and location and cubic contents of every still, mash tub, and fermenting tub, together with the cubic contents of every receiving cistern, and the color of each fixed pipe, as required in this act. One copy of said plan and description shall be kept displayed in some conspicuous place in the distillery; two copies shall be furnished to the assessor of the district, one of which shall be kept by him and the other transmitted to the Commissioner of Internal Revenue. The accuracy of every such plan and description shall be verified by the assessor, the draughtsman, and the distiller; and no alteration shall be made in such distillery without the consent, in writing, of the assessor, which alteration shall be shown on the original or by a supplemental plan and description, and a reference thereto noted on the original, as the assessor may direct; and any supplemental plan and description shall be executed and preserved in the same manner as the original.]

(a) Previous to the approval of his bond, every person intending to engage in the business of a distiller, must, under the direction of the assessor, cause to be made an accurate plan and description in triplicate of the distillery and distilling apparatus. Such plan must be on good paper or tracing cloth, fifteen by twenty inches in size, with a margin of at least one inch on each side of the drawing. And where the distiller or distilling apparatus occupies more than one floor or story, each floor or story should be represented on a separate sheet. The assessor must, by personal examination, test the accuracy of such plan when made, and none but competent draughtsmen should be employed to make it. The capacity of each tub or vessel should be marked on the plan in gallons.

After such plan is made, no alterations can be made in such distillery or distilling apparatus without the written consent of the assessor, and such alteration must be shown by a supplemental plan and description, which should also be made in triplicate like the original. One of said plans is to be kept displayed in some conspicuous place in the distillery, one kept by the assessor, and one transmitted by him to the Commissioner, rolled and not folded; and any supplemental plan will be disposed of in the same way. The accuracy of every plan must be verified by the assessor, the draughtsman, and the distiller; and the assessor will note a reference to such supplemental plan on the copy in his possession, and on that of the distiller, and send a copy of such memorandum with such supplemental plan to the Commissioner.

In case a distiller desires to increase his capacity after his plans are furnished, the survey made, and his bond approved, he must give notice under section 6; and, if such change necessitates any alteration in his distillery, as the introduction of additional mash or fermenting tubs, a supplemental plan must be furnished, showing the alterations. If such alterations are confined to one floor, a supplemental plan of that floor properly certified will be received. 9 I. R. R. 148.

Survey of Distilleries.

[SEC. 10. (July 20, 1868.) *And be it further enacted*, That immediately after the passage of this act every assessor shall proceed, at the expense of the United States, with the aid of some competent and skillful person, to be designated by the Commissioner of Internal Revenue, to make survey (*a*) of each distillery registered or intended to be registered for the production of spirits in his district, to estimate and determine its true producing capacity, and in like manner shall estimate and determine the capacity of any such distillery as may hereafter be so registered in said district, a written report of which shall be made in triplicate, signed by the assessor and the person aiding in making the same, one copy of which shall be furnished to the distiller, one retained by the assessor, and the other immediately transmitted to the Commissioner of Internal Revenue. If the Commissioner of Internal Revenue shall at any time be satisfied that such report of the capacity of a distillery is in any respect incorrect or needs revision, he shall direct the assessor to make in like manner another survey of said distillery; the report of said survey shall be executed in triplicate and deposited as hereinbefore provided.]

(*a*) The object of this survey is to determine the true producing capacity of each distillery, *i. e.*, the quantity of spirits which may be produced in such distillery in twenty-four hours. In addition to this, the report should state the aggregate mashing and fermenting capacity in bushels or gallons, *i. e.*, the number of bushels of grain or gallons of molasses that may be mashed and fermented in twenty-four hours. As this is one of the tests by which the amount of tax due is to be determined, it should be carefully and correctly made. The report should be immediately forwarded to the Commissioner, who, if he shall at any time be satisfied that it is incorrect or needs revision, may direct a new survey to be made. 9 I. R. R. 148.

The assessor, and person designated to aid him, are to estimate the true producing capacity of each distillery, and make report thereof in writing. In performing this duty, they will assume that the distiller will put his machinery and apparatus in good working order, use good material, employ competent and skillful workmen, and so manage his business as to produce the most favorable results. And the question to be determined is, what, under such circumstances, is the number of bushels of grain, or gallons, that can be mashed and fermented in twenty-four hours, and the quantity of spirits that can be produced in the same time.

The true producing capacity of a distillery is not limited to what the distiller may produce by following a particular course which he has marked out, but what may be produced under favorable circumstances.

The true producing capacity of a distillery is not the amount so proposed to be produced, but the amount which can be produced, using all the machinery and apparatus under competent and skillful management, taking as a basis for the calculation such premises as will produce the best practical results.

In order to estimate and determine the true producing capacity of a distillery, it is necessary to ascertain the capacity of the mash and fermenting tubs. This should be done by actual and careful measurement, and the report must show the greatest diameter, least diameter, and depth of each tub; its form, whether round, oval, or square; its full capacity in gallons; the number of dry inches allowed for working or fermenting; its working capacity—the fermenting tubs in gallons, the mash tubs in bushels—estimating not less than one bushel to twenty-five gallons of mash.

The fermenting capacity, however, may limit the mashing capacity, because the distiller cannot mash more than he has capacity to ferment. If it should be found that a distiller has an excess of mash tubs, as compared with his fermenters, due regard will be had to this fact, as mash tubs may be used as fermenters.

Having ascertained the diameter and depth of each tub, the cubical contents will be found by the following rule: multiply the square of the mean diameter in inches, by the decimal, .0034, and the product will be the number of gallons in one inch of depth; multiply this product by the number of inches of depth in the tub, and the product will be the cubical contents or capacity of the tub in gallons.

Having found the aggregate capacity of the fermenters, the number of bushels which it will take to fill such fermenters is found by dividing that quantity by the number of gallons of mash made from a bushel of grain. Under the provisions of section 20, this divisor cannot exceed forty-five, except in case of a distillery having a producing capacity of less than one hundred gallons in twenty-four hours, and in which grain or meal is mashed by hand, and without the use of steam, in which case it cannot exceed sixty. These are the maximum limits, and if in either case the distiller makes a thicker mash, using less water to the bushel, the divisor will be proportionately less.

Having found the number of bushels which are required to fill the fermenters, the assessor and person designated to aid him will determine what, under all the circumstances, is a reasonable period to be allowed for fermenting, and in so doing they are not bound by the period stated in the distiller's notice, but are to take such period as will, under ordinary circumstances and with good management, produce the best results. From the best information, it is believed that a fermenting period of sixty hours is as long a period as can be used consistently with good management or a profitable conduct of the business, and where a greater period than this is assumed, it must be accompanied with such a statement of the circumstances as will show it to be justified as an exceptional case.

Having thus determined the fermenting period, the twenty-four hours during which the fermenting tubs are to remain empty are to be added, and with this sum divide the number of bushels which it requires to fill all the fermenters, and the result will show the number of bushels that can be mashed in one hour or in one day, according as the divisor is in hours or days, and, if in hours, multiply by twenty-four to find the quantity for one day of twenty-four hours.

Having thus found the number of bushels which can be mashed and fermented in twenty-four hours, the next point to be determined is, what quantity of spirits can, under all the circumstances, be produced from a bushel of grain—that is, what quantity of spirits can a practical distiller, with good management, produce from a bushel of good grain; and, while no fixed rule can be laid down upon the subject, it may be suggested that in ordinary distilleries this varies from three to four gallons, and in some cases over four gallons, or an average of three and a-half gallons to the bushel. It may be safely assumed that it would require a strong case to justify an estimate of less than three gallons, and in such case the reasons for such an allowance must be fully reported to the Commissioner; and in all cases where the estimate is below the average (three and a-half gallons), an explanation will be required. Having determined this product, multiply the number of bushels that can be fermented in twenty-four hours by it, and the result will be the quantity of spirits that can be produced in twenty-four hours.

The capacity of a molasses distillery is estimated upon the same principle. Having found the working fermenting capacity of the fermenters in gallons, as above stated, divide this by the number of gallons of mash which the distiller makes from a gallon of molasses, and it will give the number of gallons of molasses required to fill the fermenters. Take the fermenting period plus the twenty-four hours, and divide the amount found as above, and it will give the quantity which can be fermented in twenty-four hours.

The quantity of spirit which can be produced from a gallon of molasses varies, of course, with the completeness of the apparatus and the quality of the material, from 80 to 95 per cent., this probably being a fair average; and in no case should a less allowance than this average be made without first submitting a full report of the reasons therefor to the Commissioner.

In case any question arises as to the correctness of the survey, the assessor will forward a draft of his report to the Commissioner before it is signed, in order that such questions may be determined.

In estimating the number of dry inches to be allowed for fermentation, the assessor and person designated to aid him must, of course, be governed in a great measure by the depth of the fermenting tubs. From the best information received, it is believed that a fair allowance will be from three to seven dry inches for corn and any mixture of corn and rye not exceeding one-half rye to one-half corn, and from seven to twelve dry inches for rye and any mixture of rye exceeding one-half. While it is perhaps natural that the distiller should claim the maximum allowance as most advantageous to him, it is incumbent upon the officers making the survey to make such allowance only as is fair and equitable, having regard to the interests of the government as well as of the distiller. Should the allowance in any district in all cases equal the maximum allowance, or in most cases exceed the average between the two extremes given, the survey should be accompanied by some explanations to rebut the inference that might be drawn from such action.

Under the provisions of section 6 the distiller is required to state the fermenting period which he proposes to use, and the quantity of spirits which he will produce. This may or may not be the true producing capacity of his distillery, but having so stated it, he cannot change his fermenting period without notice to the assessor; if he does be renders himself liable to heavy penalties. This is his own statement, entirely distinct from and independent of the true producing capacity as estimated and determined under this section. It is to be made and filed before any action is taken under this section. If, after his true producing capacity is determined, he chooses to adopt a fermenting period corresponding to that assumed by the assessor and person designated to aid him, he may do so by giving the proper notice. If he does it without such notice, he subjects himself to heavy penalties. 10 I. R. R. 84.

The true spirit-producing capacity of a grain distillery is mainly determined by its fermenting capacity; but as this is sometimes affected by the modes of mashing and distilling, these are, therefore, to be considered in such cases. The surveyor having ascertained by measurement the cubic contents of the fermenting tubs, finds it necessary to determine: 1st. The number of dry inches to be allowed each tub for fermentation. 2d. The period necessary to enable the distiller to ferment each tub of mash. 3d. The number of gallons of spirits that can be produced from a bushel of grain.

These are questions coming within the discretion and judgment of the assessor and his skillful assistant, with which the Office of Internal Revenue has no disposition to interfere. But it has been thought proper for the guidance of the surveyor to prescribe certain rules on these three points. Surveyors are, therefore, to be governed by the following rules in fixing the capacity of a distillery, except where they find that they do not correctly determine its capacity.

If the capacity is different from that indicated by these rules, they are to report it according to the fact, and, if smaller, assigning in the report the reasons therefor; and if such reasons are not satisfactory to the Commissioner, he will order a new survey to be made. It is believed that no reasons exist to justify the fixing of a less capacity than that arrived at by these rules, except in one case hereinafter mentioned. The rule for determining the amount of dry inches is as follows:

For fermenting tubs five feet in depth and under, an allowance of seven inches for rye and three inches for corn. For each foot in excess of five feet, one-half inch for rye and four-tenths of an inch for corn. Forty-eight hours is prescribed as the maximum period to be allowed for fermentation in sweet mash distilleries.

The only exception to this rule that is thought to be justified by sufficient reasons is where the mashing is done by hand, where hot water is the only heating agent, and the distillation is in copper by furnace heat. It is believed that with this imperfect mode of stirring and regulating the temperature, such a perfectly fermented beer cannot be uniformly produced as is necessary for distillation in copper, with furnace heat, to prevent occasional burning of the still. In such cases seventy-two hours will be allowed for fermentation.

This is the only instance in which the mode of distillation is considered as affecting the period to be allowed for fermentation. Seventy-two hours is the maximum period to be allowed for fermentation in sour mash distilleries. This is based on the fact that where open beer, or beer in process of fermentation, or both, are the only fermenting agents used, fermentation is not so rapid as where yeast is used: and, therefore, this rule applies to all sour mash distilleries, whatever the mode of heating, stirring, and distilling may be.

The period is estimated from the time of yeasting or breaking up. An exception is made to this rule in the case of hand mash distilleries, where the mashing and distilling is done in the same tubs. In such cases the time will be estimated from the time of the first scalding of the meal. All the tubs will be embraced in the estimate of the capacity, and ninety-six hours will be allowed for fermentation, as in each case it necessarily includes the twenty-four hours used for mashing. Where the distiller prefers, he may set aside certain of his tubs to be used exclusively for mashing, marking them distinctly as such; and in such cases the computation will be made on the tubs used for fermenting, and the period be fixed from the time of yeasting or breaking up, instead of from the time of commencing the mashing.

In estimating the yield per bushel the minimum prescribed is three and a-half gallons where the distillation is by steam, without the use of the coil; where the coil is used, three gallons; and where the distillation is in copper, by furnace heat, two and a-half gallons.

In many instances it is found that the actual production exceeds these amounts. Where that is the case, the survey should be based upon the amount which it is found can be actually produced.

The amount of grain that can be used in a distillery is ascertained under the rule prescribed in section 20, act of July 20, 1868, and in the amendment thereto, section 1, act of April 10, 1869.

Where, however, it is found that the distiller uses a thicker mash, the estimate will be made according to the fact; but when a thinner mash is used, the estimate will be according to the statutory rule.

The capacity to be determined is not the capacity to make this or that particular kind or brand of distilled spirits, but the capacity to make distilled spirits, as described in section 4, act July 20, 1868.

Distillers sometimes insist that they cannot produce the particular kind or brand of spirits which they are in the habit of manufacturing without using a longer fermenting period than is allowed by these rules. Section 6 of said act affords the distiller ample opportunity to take any period he may desire by specifying such period in his Form 27; but as taxation is based upon capacity to produce spirits, as described in section 4, and not to produce this or that particular brand; and as the spirit described in section 4 is successfully produced within the period named, surveys are, therefore, made accordingly, and the taxation is thereby rendered uniform.

What is above stated is not fully applicable to the three other classes of distillation in use in the United States; to wit, gin, rum, and fruit brandy distilled from apples, peaches, or grapes exclusively. The gin and rum distilleries, being few in number, have been made the subject of special instruction to officers in whose districts they are located.

The attention of assessors is especially directed to the importance of correctly reporting their surveys. The reports must be signed by the assessor of the district and his designated assistant. An assistant assessor can only sign when he is acting assessor, and must then sign as such.

The assessor, in transmitting a copy of the report of survey to the Office of Internal Revenue, should accompany it with his certificate, showing the day upon which he delivered the copy thereof to the distiller. This delivery must be actual, and the assessor must be able to verify the fact of such delivery, and the particular day thereof.

The distiller is assessed upon such survey from and after the day of the delivery of the copy to him; and the day of the delivery must, therefore, be known.

When the report of the capacity of any distiller is in any respect incorrect, or needs revision, the Commissioner will direct the assessor to make another survey. It will be observed that the Commissioner alone has authority to order a resurvey for the correction of errors. This will be done in every case where, on an examination of the reports in the Office of Internal Revenue, they are found to be, in any respect, incorrect, or needing revision, or where so shown to be on the application of the distiller for a resurvey.

The corrections will, therefore, always be made on the order of the Commissioner for a resurvey; but when the corrections do not render a remeasurement necessary, it need not be done.

The copy of the report of resurvey will be delivered and certified the same as in other cases. Assessment will always be made on the survey a copy of which was last delivered to the distiller.

Assessors sometimes deem it necessary to make a resurvey on the reduction or increase of capacity. By referring to regulations it will be seen that the resurvey is not necessary either on the reduction or increase of capacity, except it be where, by the increase, new tubs are added; in such cases the assessor should call his designated assistant to make the required survey. 11 I. R. R. 129.

Fruit distilleries having no ascertainable mashing or fermenting capacity, the true producing capacity thereof is determined solely on the capacity for distillation. This is arrived at by determining, first, the capacity in gallons of each still, making proper deduction for boiling space; second, the number of boilings of each still that can be effected in twenty-four hours, of each condition of the material to be used; and, third, the spirit-producing capacity of the material in each condition.

The capacity in gallons of each still may be ascertained either by arithmetical calculation, or by filling the same and measuring the contents. When done by filling and measuring the contents, the columns in Form 99 for diameters may be left blank, and a note entered on the face of the report showing that the capacity was ascertained by measurement of contents. Twenty per cent. must be deducted from the total capacity of each still as an allowance of space for boiling. For instance, a still holding one hundred gallons will boil eighty gallons.

The number of boilings that can be effected of each material in twenty-four hours is to be determined in view of the appliances in use for that purpose. When steam is used, a greater number of boilings can be ordinarily effected than where furnace heat is used; and the number of boilings that can be effected with furnace heat depends on the shape of the still and the amount of surface exposed to the action of the heat, and the manner in which the still is set. It is believed that ordinarily seven boilings of fruit, in any of the conditions in which it is used, may be had in twenty-four hours.

The total number of boilings that can be had having been ascertained, proper deduction should be made for doubling; as, for instance, a still that can be boiled off seven times in twenty-four hours may require two boilings to double the singlings produced, thus leaving a capacity of five boilings in twenty-four hours.

Apples, peaches, and grapes, from which brandy is distilled, are used in such a variety of conditions, in different sections of the country, that it is difficult to give a classification of these materials which will embrace every condition in which they may be used. The following classification will, however, be found sufficiently comprehensive to embrace any of the ordinary conditions in which the fruit is distilled, viz.: pomace, cider, must, sour wine, wash, cheese, and lees. The blanks will be found to contain a column for "other material," in which to embrace material not clearly coming under either of the above classifications.

By pomace is meant the crushed fruit without the juice expressed therefrom; cider, the expressed juice of the apple; must, the unfermented juice of the grape; sour wine, the fermented juice of the grape; cheese, the residue of the fruit after the juice has been expressed therefrom; wash, is the liquid expressed from the cheese of apples or grapes, after adding water thereto; lees, or "*piquette*," the dregs or settlings of wine. The spirit-yielding capacity of these several conditions of the fruits is so variable that it is difficult for this office to lay down any fixed rules on the subject, but it must necessarily leave the determination of the amount of spirits to be produced from a given quantity of each of these materials to the judgment of the assessor and his designated assistants, they acting upon the most reliable information that can be obtained from past experiences in the particular locality in which they are making the surveys.

From the information contained in the records of this office, and derived from other reliable sources, it is believed that proof brandy may be distilled from these materials as follows: One gallon from every 17 gallons of apple or peach pomace; one gallon from every 8 gallons of grape pomace; one gallon from every 12 gallons of cider; one gallon from every 5 gallons of must; one gallon from every 7 gallons of sour wine.

The spirit strength of the other materials must be determined solely in the light of experience in each particular locality. This office is not prepared to give any rules relative thereto.

Having thus ascertained the number of gallons of each material that can be distilled in twenty-four hours, and the spirit strength thereof, the capacity of the still or stills for twenty-four hours is readily arrived at. 12 I. R. R. 1.

Distilling not to commence until Bond is given.

[SEC. 11. (July 20, 1868.) *And be it further enacted*, That after the passage of this act it shall not be lawful for any assessor to assess a special tax upon any distiller, or for the collector to collect the same, or for any distiller who has heretofore paid a special tax as such to continue the business of distilling until such distiller shall have given the bond required by this act, and shall have complied with the provisions of law having reference to the registration and survey of distilleries, and having reference to the arrangement and construction of distilleries, and the premises connected therewith, in manner and as required by this act; nor shall it be lawful for any assessor of internal revenue to assess, or for any collector to collect, any special tax for distilling on any premises distant less than six hundred feet (*a*) from any premises used for rectifying, nor shall any assessor assess or collector collect any special tax for rectifying distilled spirits on any premises distant less than six hundred feet from any distillery when the distillery and rectifying establishments are occupied and used by different persons; nor shall the process of distillation and rectification both be carried on within the distance of six hundred feet. In all cases where a distillery and rectifying establishment, distant the one from the other less than six hundred feet, are occupied and used by the same person, said person shall have the right to elect which business shall be discontinued at that place. In all cases where rectifying or distilling shall be discontinued under the provisions of this section, and the time for which the special tax for rectifying or distilling was paid remains unexpired, the Secretary of the Treasury is hereby authorized to refund out of any money in the treasury not otherwise appropriated, on requisition of the Commissioner of Internal Revenue, a proportionate part of any sum originally paid for special tax therefor, which shall be in such ratio to the whole sum paid as the unexpired time for which special tax was paid shall bear to the whole term for which the same was paid. Any collector or assessor of internal revenue who shall fail to perform any duty imposed by this section, or shall assess or collect any special tax in violation of its provisions, shall be liable to a penalty of five thousand dollars for each offence.]

(a) Where two establishments owned by different persons are within the prohibited distance of each other, the first party who in good faith gives the notice required by section six, would acquire a right of preference subject to be divested by laches, fraud, or failure to complete his compliance with the law in other respects. 8 I. R. R. 73.

Where Stills may be used.

[SEC. 12. (July 20, 1868.) *And be it further enacted*, That no person shall use any still, boiler, or other vessel for the purpose of distilling in any dwelling-house, nor in any shed, yard, or inclosure connected with any dwelling-house, nor on board of any vessel or boat, nor in any building, or on any premises where beer, lager beer, ale, porter, or other fermented liquors, vinegar or ether are manufactured or produced, or where sugars or sirups are refined, or where liquors of any description are retailed, or where any other business is carried on, nor within six hundred feet from any premises authorized to be used for rectifying; and every person who shall use any still, boiler, or other vessel for the purpose of distilling, as aforesaid, in any building or other premises where the above specified articles are manufactured, produced, refined, or retailed, or other business is carried on, or on board of any vessel or boat, or in any dwelling-house, or other place as aforesaid, or shall aid or assist therein, or who shall cause or procure the same to be done, shall, on conviction, (a) be fined one thousand dollars and imprisoned for not less than six months nor more than two years, in the discretion of the court: *Provided*, That saleratus may be manufactured, or meal or flour ground (b) from grain, in any building or on any premises where spirits are distilled; but such meal or flour only to be used for distillation on the premises.]

(a) A party who has been indicted, tried, and acquitted, on the charge of carrying on the business of a distiller without paying tax, may be indicted for using a still in a dwelling-house. The defendant could not, under the former indictment, have been convicted of the offence embraced in the latter, nor would the evidence necessary to support the latter indictment have been sufficient to warrant a conviction under the earlier one. U. S. *v.* Flecke et al. 7 I. R. R. 206.

(*b*) Where there are mills attached to a distillery, they must be so entirely separated by solid walls and otherwise as to be, in fact, independent premises; although both establishments may be driven by the same power, they must be so arranged that the description of the distillery premises on Form 27 does not include the mill. 9 I. R. R. 147.

Capacity Tax.

[SEC. 13. (July 20, 1868.) *And be it further enacted*, That there shall be assessed and collected monthly, from every authorized distiller whose distillery has an aggregate capacity for mashing and fermenting twenty bushels of grain or less, or sixty gallons of molasses or less, in twenty-four hours, a tax (*a*) of two dollars per day, Sundays excepted; and a tax of two dollars per day for every twenty bushels of grain or sixty gallons of molasses of said capacity in excess of twenty bushels of grain or sixty gallons of molasses in twenty-four hours. But any distiller who shall suspend work, as provided by this act, shall pay only two dollars per day during the time the work shall be so suspended in his distillery.]

(*a*) The per diem capacity tax will commence on the third day after the approval of the bond, and the full capacity tax will be assessed for every calendar day thereafter, Sundays excepted, reckoning the third day after the approval of the bond as a whole day, unless work shall be suspended as provided in section 22. But, should the distiller commence distilling at any time prior to the third day after the approval of the bond, the capacity tax will be assessed from the time when the production of spirits begins. 9 I. R. R. 149.

A distiller of brandy from apples, peaches, or grapes exclusively, is subject to the per diem capacity tax until the distillery is closed for the season, except for those days on which he proves, to the satisfaction of the assessor, the distillery was not in operation. 8 I. R. R. 171.

Duties of Manufacturers of Stills.

[SEC. 14. (July 20, 1868.) *And be it further enacted*, That any person (*a*) who shall manufacture any still, boiler, or other vessel, to be used for the purpose of distilling, shall, before the same is removed from the place of manufacture, notify in writing the assessor of the district in which such still, boiler, or other vessel is to be used or set up, by whom it is to be used, its capacity, and the time when the same is to be removed from the place of manufacture; and no such still, boiler, or other vessel shall be set up without the permit in writing of the said assessor for that purpose; and any person who shall set up any such still, boiler, or other vessel, without first obtaining a permit from the said assessor of the district in which such still, boiler, or other vessel is intended to be used, or who shall fail to give such notice, shall pay in either case the sum of five hundred dollars, and shall forfeit the distilling apparatus thus removed or set up in violation of law.]

(*a*) The manufacturer should inform himself of the use for which each boiler or other vessel is designed, or he may notify the collector in every case indiscriminately. 5 I. R. R. 163.

The term "for distilling" will be construed to mean "for distilling spirits." This limitation of the construction of the term does not furnish sufficient grounds upon which any tax, assessed under a more literal construction, will be refunded. 9 I. R. R. 157.

Distillery Warehouses.

[SEC. 15. (July 20, 1868.) *And be it further enacted*, That every distiller shall provide, at his own expense, a warehouse, (*a*) to be situated on and to constitute a part of his distillery premises, to be used only for the storage of distilled spirits, of his own manufacture; but no dwelling-house shall be used for such purpose, and no door, window, or other opening shall be made or permitted in the walls of such warehouse leading into the distillery or into any other room or building; and such warehouse, when approved by the Commissioner of Internal Revenue, on report of the collector, is hereby declared to be a bonded warehouse of the United States, to be known as a distillery warehouse, and shall be under the direction and control of the collector of the district, and in charge of an internal revenue storekeeper assigned thereto by the Commissioner of Internal Revenue; and the tax on spirits stored in such warehouse shall be paid before removal from such warehouse.]

(*a*) A portion of the distillery may be used as a distillery warehouse; but in such case it must be separated from the distillery by a solid brick or plank partition; and collectors will, when such warehouse is applied for, make a careful examination as to the sufficiency of the division walls; but the entrance to such room must be from the street or yard. If the distiller elects, such warehouse may be a separate building, but it must be upon the premises actually occupied for the distillery. It must be a portion of the distillery, adjoining the distillery building, or within, or adjoining the distillery yard.

Each distiller will make application in writing to the collector of the district, stating fully the precise location, size, description, and construction of the room or building desired for such warehouse, specifying its location on, or by reference to, the plan of the distillery; and upon receipt of such application, the collector will, by himself or one of his deputies, make a full and careful examination thereof, and, if the same is approved by him, will transmit said application to the Commissioner, with his report thereon, for his approval, stating the estimated storage capacity of such warehouse; and when approved by the Commissioner, a storekeeper will be assigned to such warehouse. Such warehouse must be established for each distillery before any spirits are distilled, and all expenses connected with such warehouse must be paid by the distiller. 9 I. R. R. 150.

A distillery warehouse will only be established for an authorized distiller, and at an authorized distillery; yet having been so established, the distiller has acquired the right under the law to have his spirits remain in bond according to the condition of his warehousing bond, which is that the tax shall be paid thereon before removal from such distillery warehouse, and within one year from the date of the bond. The failure of the distiller to renew his distiller's bond does not work a discontinuance of his bonded warehouse. The distillery warehouse will be continued as such in charge of the storekeeper assigned thereto, until all the spirits stored therein are withdrawn, and the tax paid thereon, the distiller, of course, being liable upon his bond for refunding to the government the compensation of such storekeeper. 11 I. R. R. 121.

Whenever the Commissioner shall be of opinion that any warehouse is unsafe, or unfit for use, or the merchandise therein liable to loss or great wastage, he may discontinue such warehouse, and require the merchandise therein to be transferred to such other warehouse as he may designate, within a time to be prescribed by him, and at the expense of the owner of the merchandise. If such transfer is not made, or such expenses not paid by the owner, the merchandise will be seized and sold by the collector, as upon a distraint. 9 I. R. R. 157.

Receiving Cisterns.

[SEC. 16. (July 20, 1868.) *And be it further enacted*, That the owner, agent, or superintendent of any distillery, established as hereinbefore provided, shall erect, in a room or building to be provided and used for that purpose, and for no other, and to be constructed in the manner to be prescribed by the Commissioner of Internal Revenue, two or more receiving cisterns, (*a*) each to be at least of sufficient capacity to hold all the spirits distilled during the day of twenty-four hours, into which shall be conveyed all the spirits produced in said distillery; and each of such cisterns shall be so constructed as to leave an open space of at least three feet between the top thereof and the floor or roof above, and of not less than eighteen inches between the bottom thereof and the floor below, and shall be so situated that the officer can pass around the same, and shall be connected with the outlet of the worm or condenser by suitable pipes or other apparatus so constructed as always to be exposed to the view of the officer, and so connected and constructed as to prevent the abstraction of spirits while passing from the outlet of the worm or condenser back to the still or doubler, or forward to the receiving cistern; such cisterns, and the room in which they are contained, shall be in charge of and under the lock and seal of the internal revenue ganger designated for that duty; and on the third day after the spirits are conveyed into such cisterns, the same shall be drawn off into casks under the supervision of such gauger in the presence of the storekeeper, and be removed directly to the distillery warehouse; and on special application to the assessor or assistant assessor by the owner, agent, or superintendent of any distillery, the spirits may be drawn off from the said cisterns under the supervision of the gauger at any time previous to the third day. All locks and seals required by law shall be provided by the Commissioner of Internal Revenue at the expense of the owner of the distillery or warehouse; and the keys shall be in charge of the collector or such gauger as he may designate.]

(a) Each of the cisterns must be of a sufficient capacity to hold all the spirits distilled during the day of twenty-four hours. These cisterns must be so constructed as to leave an open space of at least three feet between the top and roof or floor above, and a space of not less than eighteen inches between the bottom and the floor below; and they must be separated so that the officer may pass around them; and the pipes, or other apparatus by which the cisterns are connected with the outlet of the still, boilers, or other vessels, must be so constructed as to be always exposed to the view of the officer, and so as to prevent the abstraction of spirits while passing from the outlet of the worm or condenser back to the still or doubler, or forward to the receiving cistern. These cisterns must not be connected with each other. Where a distiller draws off his spirits but once in three days, he must have three cisterns. He cannot, in any case, have less than two. The product of each day's distillation must be run into one cistern, and one only. If the distiller has not provided at least two separate cisterns, each of a capacity sufficient to hold a full day's product, the assessor has no right to approve his bonds. 9 I. R. R. 148.

A distiller may carry his product through as many processes of distillation as he pleases, provided the process is continuous, commencing with the distillation of the mash wort or wash, the product of the distillation of the mash being carried through continuous closed vessels and pipes, until the final product is deposited in the receiving cisterns. This does not authorize the leaching of the spirits through charcoal or any other substance; nor the purifying and refining of distilled spirits in any other mode of distillation; and no materials or substances whatever can be added during the process. The apparatus must be so constructed that there can be no access had to the spirits on its passage through the pipes and vessels connecting the beer still with the receiving cisterns. Under these restrictions, an alcohol column may be substituted for one of the doublers. 9 I. R. R. 158.

A separator must be provided, unless the distiller is willing to discharge both high and low wines into the receiving cistern and pay tax on the entire product. The separator must be kept in perfect order so that the officer and distiller alike can at any time view the processes of discharge and separation of the spirits. Open tubs for the separation of the low and the high wines are prohibited. 9 I. R. R. 43.

The storekeeper will see that all spirits manufactured each day are conveyed into one of the receiving cisterns on the same day.

The cisterns, and the room in which they are contained, must be in charge of and under the lock of the internal revenue gauger designated for that duty. The collector will designate the gauger to perform this duty. The supervisor, however, has power to transfer gaugers so designated from one distillery to another. In no case, however, will the storekeeper be allowed to hold the key or have charge of the cistern room. The cistern room must not be opened, or suffered to remain open, except when the designated gauger is present, nor will the key of the government at any time be suffered to pass into the possession of the distiller, or any person in his employ. 9 I R. R. 149.

The Register Seal Lock is prescribed. The locks may be obtained by application to the collector or assessor of the district. 10 I. R. R. 113.

The Monogram Seal must be used in connection with the Register Seal Lock. One set of pliers, together with one hundred lead plugs, will be required at each distillery, and at each warehouse separate from a distillery, and will be entrusted to the care of the storekeepers, who will permit the gaugers and assistant assessors, and others having custody of locks at each distillery or at each bonded warehouse, to use the same for the purpose of sealing these locks when required. These seals may be obtained by application to the collector or assessor of the district. 10 I. R. R. 153.

When the cisterns and apparatus have not been constructed in the mode required by the statute and the regulations, it is not necessary that this omission should have been made with intent to defraud. The penalty is incurred and the offence is complete when the defendants have left undone those things which they ought to have done, and done things which they ought not to have done, and this without any criminal or fraudulent intent. U. S. v. McKim & Co. 10 I. R. R. 74.

Construction of Doors, Tubs, Tanks, etc.

[SEC. 17. (July 20, 1868.) *And be it further enacted*, That the door of the furnace of every still or boiler used in any distillery shall be so constructed that it may be securely fastened and locked. The fermenting tubs shall be so placed as to be easily accessible to any revenue officer, and each tub shall have distinctly painted thereon in oil colors its cubic contents in gallons, and the number of the tub. There shall be a clear space of not less than one foot around every wood still, and not less than two feet around every doubler and worm tank. The doubler and worm tanks shall be elevated not less than one foot from the floor; and every fixed pipe to be used by the distiller, except for the conveyance of water, or of spent mash or beer only, shall be so fixed and placed as to be capable of being examined by the officer for the whole of its length or course, and shall be painted, and kept painted, as follows; that is to say: Every pipe (*a*) for the conveyance of mash or beer shall be painted of a red color; every pipe for the conveyance of low wines back into the still or doubler shall be painted blue; every pipe for the conveyance of spirits shall be painted black; and every pipe for the conveyance of water shall be painted white. If any fixed pipe shall be used by any distiller which shall not be painted or kept painted as herein directed, or which shall be painted otherwise than as herein directed, he shall forfeit the sum of one thousand dollars. No assessor shall approve the bond of any distiller until all the requirements of the law and all regulations made by the Commissioner of Internal Revenue in relation to distilleries, in pursuance thereof, shall have been complied with. Any assessor who shall violate the provisions of this section shall forfeit and pay two thousand dollars, and shall be dismissed from office.]

(a) The various pipes must be designated by these colors on the plan. 9 I. R. R. 148.

Regulations concerning Signs.

[SEC. 18. (July 20, 1868.) *And be it further enacted*, That every person (a) engaged in distilling or rectifying spirits, and every wholesale liquor dealer and compounder of liquors, shall place and keep conspicuously on the outside of his distillery, rectifying establishment, or place of business, a sign, in plain and legible letters, not less than three inches in length, painted in oil colors or gilded, and of·a proper and proportionate width, the name or firm of the distiller, rectifier, wholesale dealer, or compounder, with the words: "registered distillery," "rectifier of spirits," "wholesale liquor dealer," or "compounder of liquors," as the case may be; and no fence or wall of a height greater than five feet shall be erected or maintained around the premises of any distillery, so as to prevent easy and immediate access to said distillery; and every distiller shall furnish to the assessor of the district as many keys of the gates and doors of the distillery as may be required by the assessor, from time to time, for any revenue officer or other person who may be authorized to make survey or inspections of the premises or of the contents thereof; and said distillery shall be kept always accessible to any officer or other person having any such key.

Any person who shall violate any of the foregoing provisions of this section by negligence or refusal, or otherwise, shall pay a penalty of five hundred dollars. Any person not having paid the special tax, as required by law, who shall put up the sign required by this section, or any sign indicating that he may lawfully carry on the business of a distiller, rectifier, wholesale liquor dealer, or compounder of liquors, shall forfeit and pay one thousand dollars, and, on conviction, shall be imprisoned not less than one month nor more than six months; and any person who shall work in any distillery, rectifying establishment, wholesale liquor store, or in the store of any compounder of liquors, on which no sign shall be placed and kept as hereinbefore provided, and any person who shall knowingly receive at, carry or convey any distilled spirits to or from any such distillery, rectifying establishment, warehouse, or store, or who shall knowingly carry and deliver any grain, molasses, or other raw material to any distillery on which such sign shall not be placed and kept, shall forfeit all horses, carts, drays, wagons, or other vehicle or animal used in carrying or conveying of such property aforesaid, and, on conviction, shall be fined not less than one hundred dollars nor more than one thousand dollars, or be imprisoned not less than one month nor more than six months.]

(a) A compliance with the provisions of this section should be required of every person who is a wholesale liquor dealer, either in the popular senses or in the strict sense of the term, as defined in section 59. 9 I. R. R. 36.

Other words may be added to the sign, if desired, to show the precise character of the business, as for instance, "In alcohol only." 9 I. R. R. 5.

Books to be kept by Distillers.

[SEC. 19. (July 20, 1868.) *And be it further enacted,* That every person making or distilling spirits, or owning any still, boiler, or other vessel used for the purpose of distilling spirits, or having such still, boiler, or other vessel so used under his superintendence, either as agent or owner, or using any such still, boiler, or other vessel, shall, from day to day, make, or cause to be made, true and exact entry in a book (a) or books, to be kept by him, in such form as the Commissioner of Internal Revenue may prescribe, of the kind of materials, and the quantity in pounds, bushels, or gallons purchased by him for the production of spirits, from whom and when purchased, and by what conveyance delivered at said distillery, together with the amount paid *for* therefor, the kind and quantity of fuel purchased for use in the distillery, and from whom purchased, the amount paid for ice or water for use in the distillery, the repairs placed on said distillery or distilling apparatus, the cost thereof, and by whom and when made, and [of] the name and residence of each person employed in or about the distillery, and in what capacity employed; and in another book shall make like entry [of] the quantity of grain or other material used for the production of spirits, the time of day when any yeast or other composition is put into any mash or beer for the purpose of exciting fermentation, the quantity of mash in each tub, designating the same by the number of the tub, the number of dry inches, that is to say, the number of inches between the top of each tub and the surface of the mash or beer therein at the time of yeasting, the gravity and temperature of the beer at the time of yeasting, and on every day thereafter its quantity, gravity, and temperature at the hour of twelve meridian; also the time when any fermenting tub is emptied of ripe mash or beer, the number of gallons of spirits distilled, the number of gallons placed in warehouse, and the proof thereof, and the number of gallons sold or removed, with the proof thereof, and the name, place of business, and residence of the person to whom sold; and every fermenting tub shall be emptied at the end of the fermenting period, and shall remain empty for a period of twenty-four hours. On the first, eleventh, and twenty-first days of each month, or within five days thereafter, respectively, every distiller shall render to the assistant assessor an account in duplicate, taken from his books, stating the quantity and kind of materials used for the production of spirits each day, and the number of wine gallons and of proof gallons of spirits produced and placed in warehouse. And the distiller or the principal manager of the distillery shall make and subscribe the following oath, to be attached to said return:

"I, —— ——, distiller (or principal manager as the case may be), of the distillery at ——, do solemnly swear that, since the date of the last return of the business of said distillery, dated —— day of —— to —— day of ——, both inclusive, there was produced in said distillery, and withdrawn and placed in warehouse, the number of wine gallons and proof gallons of spirits, and there were actually mashed and used in said distillery, and consumed in the production of spirits therein, the several quantities of grain, sugar, molasses, and other materials, respectively, hereinbefore specified, and no more."

The said book shall always be kept at the distillery, and be always open to the inspection of any revenue officer, and, when filled up, shall be preserved by the distiller for a period not less than two years thereafter, and, whenever required, shall be produced for the inspection of any revenue officer. If any false entry shall be made in either of said books, or any entry required to be made therein shall be omitted therefrom, for every such false entry made, or omission, the distiller shall forfeit and pay a penalty of one thousand dollars. And if any such false entry shall be made, or any entry shall be omitted therefrom, with intent to defraud or to conceal from the revenue officers any fact or particular required to be stated and entered in either of said books, or to mislead in reference thereto, or if any distiller as aforesaid shall omit or refuse to provide either of said books, or shall cancel, obliterate, or destroy any part of either of such books, or any entry therein, with intent to defraud, or shall permit the same to be done, or such books, or either of them, be not produced when required by any revenue officer, the distillery, distilling apparatus, and the lot or tract of land on which it stands, and all personal property of every kind and description on said premises used in the business there carried on, shall be forfeited to the United States. And any person making such false entry or omitting to make any entry hereinbefore required to be made, with the intent aforesaid, or who shall cause or procure the same to be done, or who shall fraudulently cancel, obliterate, or destroy any part of said books, or any entry therein, or who shall wilfully fail to produce such books or either of them, on conviction shall be fined not less than five hundred dollars nor more than five thousand dollars, and imprisoned not less than six months nor more than two years.]

(a) Forms 12, 13, 25, and 28, are prescribed as the books to be used by distillers. The distiller must also render an account in duplicate, on Form 14, taken from such books, on the first, eleventh, and twenty-first days of each month, or within five days thereafter, to the assistant assessor. No materials of a kind for which a special column is provided in Form 13 should be entered under the head of other materials; and in Form 12 every kind of material purchased should be specified. Each account must be verified under oath or affirmation by the owner, agent, or superintendent of the distillery. The oath of a clerk or other employee is not sufficient. Upon the receipt of the return the assistant assessor should satisfy himself, by personal examination of the books and premises, of the accuracy of the entries made, and will then transmit the same to the assessor. 9 I. R. R. 156.

Every omission or neglect to comply with the requirements of this section in regard to keeping books, is a violation of law, which the officer to whose knowledge it may come is required to report in writing to his next superior officer, and also to the Commissioner, under penalty of fine and imprisonment. Neglect to make such a report will be deemed cause for a dismissal from office. The distiller is required to enter upon his yeasting book the time when the tub is filled; the quantity, gravity, and temperature of the mash at the time of yeasting, and in each day thereafter, and the time when emptied, and also the time when the tub is refilled. It is not sufficient that an entry be made in the book. The entry must be in accordance with the facts, and must show a strict compliance with the law. These instructions will also apply to the books and accounts required to be kept by brewers.

Where it is found that any party, who is required by law to keep books, has omitted any of the details required to be entered in such book, or neglected to make such entries daily, he should be at once required to comply with the law; and a full statement of the case must be submitted to the Commissioner for instructions as to what further action should be taken. It is no answer to a call for the books that they have been accidentally destroyed or lost. The distiller is required to preserve them for the time specified in this section, and must place them beyond the reach of ordinary casualties. 10 I. R. R. 121.

Distillers must use Form 52 in addition to the books now kept by them, and enter thereon an account of all spirits withdrawn from their distillery warehouses, and to whom and how such spirits are disposed of. 11 I. R. R. 18.

Every distiller from fruit must provide himself with a book in accordance with Form 25½, in which he shall, from day to day, make or cause to be made a true and exact entry of the hours between which the still is operated each day; the kind, quantity, and condition of the fruits used; the number of times each still has been boiled off during each day, and the quantity of singlings and of brandy produced thereby; which book must be always kept open to the inspection of any revenue officer, and, when filled up, shall be preserved by the distiller for the period of not less than two years thereafter, and whenever required shall be produced for the inspection of any revenue officer. Severe penalties are provided in the law for making false entry in such book, or for fraudulently altering any entry made therein, or for omitting to make or have made the entries required. 12 I. R. R. 1.

When the Commissioner does not prescribe the form of the book, that does not excuse the distiller from providing books, and making in the books the entries demanded by law. The only effect of this provision is that the Commissioner may prescribe the form, and when he does, that form is to be followed. U. S. v. 35 Bbls. 10 I. R. R. 67.

It is not enough that the distiller failed to provide and make the proper entries in the book; that failure and omission must be with the intent to defraud the United States. Fraud is not to be presumed. It must be established. But it may be established indirectly by circumstances as well as by direct evidence. But these circumstances must necessarily tend to the conclusion, namely, that of fraud. If they do, then they are often as satisfactory as positive direct evidence of the fraud. It is sufficient, if there is an omission, to make an entry with a view to defraud. There must be a proof of a fraudulent intent, a fraudulent purpose, or else the verdict ought not to be for the government. U. S. v. 35 Bbls. 9 I. R. R. 67; U. S. v. Furlong, 9 I. R. R. 35.

Computation of Actual Product of Distilleries.

[SEC. 20. (July 20, 1868.) *And be it further enacted*, That on receipt (a) of the distiller's first return in each month, the assessor shall inquire and determine whether said distiller has accounted in his returns for the preceding month for all the spirits produced by him; and to determine the quantity of spirits thus to be accounted for, the whole quantity of materials used for the production of spirits shall be ascertained; and forty-five gallons of mash or beer brewed or fermented from grain shall represent not less than one bushel of grain, and seven gallons of mash or beer brewed or fermented from molasses shall represent not less than one gallon of molasses. In case the return of the distiller shall have been less than the quantity thus ascertained, the distiller or other person liable shall be assessed for such deficiency at the rate of fifty cents for every proof gallon, together with the special tax of four dollars for every cask of forty proof gallons, and the collector shall proceed to collect the same as in cases of other assessments for deficiencies; but in no case shall the quantity of spirits returned by the distiller, together with the quantity so assessed, be for a less quantity of spirits than eighty per centum of the producing capacity of the distillery, as estimated under the provisions of this act.]

[SEC. 1. (April 10, 1869.) That section twenty be so amended that in case of distilleries having a producing capacity of less than one hundred gallons in twenty-four hours, and in which grain or meal is mashed by hand and without the use of steam, sixty gallons of mash or beer brewed or fermented from grain shall represent not less than one bushel of grain.]

(a) The only construction that can be given to this section, consistent with reason and the general scope and purpose of the law, is, that if the return is not equal to 80 per cent. of the producing capacity of the distillery, the assessor shall assume that it ought to have been, and the distiller shall then be assessed on that basis as a method of discovering the actual product. The object of this section is accomplished when the distiller has paid the proper tax on all the spirits he has manufactured. When the distiller proves that he has not produced 80 per cent, it is an answer to a claim set up under this section for an alleged deficiency, the fact then being that the deficiency does not exist. U. S. *v.* Singer et al. 18 Pitts. L. J. 5.

On the receipt of the distiller's first return in each month, assessors will promptly make the computation required by this section, and report their action to the Office of Internal Revenue, on Form 89, whether any additional assessment is made or not for any deficiency in the return of spirits produced. The additional special tax of $4 per barrel for each barrel in excess of 100 barrels is to be made, on Form 89, as determined by the production, and the per diem capacity tax is to be entered on the same form. The survey made under section 10 is the basis for the assessment of the per diem capacity tax, and no return is required of the distiller therefor, as the assessment is to be made from the assessor's official records. The assessments made on Form 89 will be entered on the monthly lists and transmitted to the collector for collection. Assessors and collectors will see that the various reports required to be made to them by storekeepers and other officers are promptly made, and any failure should be at once reported to the Commissioner.

In order to secure uniformity and correctness in the monthly reports of assessors, on Form 89, the following instructions have been issued:

The first question to be determined is whether or not the distiller has returned and accounted for all the spirits produced by him during the month. If the assessor finds that the distiller has not done this, then he will, from the best evidence he can obtain, estimate and determine the quantity of spirits produced over and above the quantity returned, and this added to the quantity returned will be the quantity which should be entered on Form 89, as the required product or amount to be accounted for. If the assessor finds that the whole quantity produced has been returned and accounted for, this will agree with the reported product. It cannot be less than the reported product, unless the assessor is prepared to certify that the distiller has actually returned and accounted for more than he has produced. The assessor will be understood to certify that the distiller has actually produced the quantity of spirits entered on Form 89, as the required product or amount to be accounted for.

Under the provisions of this section, the assessor is required to make this investigation personally, and in so doing he is not concluded by the reports of the distiller or storekeeper, but should use every other means in his power to test the correctness of the returns.

In ascertaining and determining the quantity of materials used from the quantity of mash made, the rule laid down in the law is that 45 gallons of mash from grain shall represent not less than one bushel of grain, and seven gallons of mash from molasses shall represent not less than one gallon of molasses; that is, 45 gallons of mash must represent not less than a bushel of grain, but may represent more. If the distiller actually makes but 35 or 40 gallons of mash from a bushel of grain, then 35 or 40 is the divisor to be used, instead of 45.

Under the amendatory act of April 10, 1869, in distilleries in which grain or meal is mashed by hand and without the use of steam, and which have a producing capacity of less than 100 gallons of spirits in 24 hours, 60 gallons of mash or beer brewed or fermented from grain will represent not less than one bushel of grain.

The number of distilleries within this provision is comparatively small, and in making the surveys or computations, on Form 89, assessors will follow the instructions hereinbefore given, starting with 60 instead of 45 gallons of mash as representing not less than a bushel of grain. In all cases the inquiry should be, what is the usual and average quantity of mash made from a bushel of grain?

It must be remembered that this provision applies only to distilleries where grain or meal is mashed by hand without the use of steam, the actual producing capacity of which is less than 100 gallons in 24 hours.

In ascertaining or testing the correctness of the quantity of spirits reported as produced, by comparison with the quantity of material found to have been used, the assessor, if he have no more definite means, will determine what quantity of spirits should be produced from a bushel of material of the kind and quality used. The importance of these computations as a means of testing the correctness of the returns of the distiller, can be readily seen, and they all contain elements material to be considered in the determination of the question—what is the quanti'y of spirits which has been actually produced by the distiller during the month?

After having determined this question the assessor will calculate the 80 per cent. of the capacity as estimated under the provisions of the act.

To determine the 80 per cent. of the capacity, the assessor will take the number of gallons fixed by the survey as the product for twenty-four hours, multiply this by the number of days for which the per diem capacity tax should be assessed; 80 per cent. of this product is 80 per cent. of the capacity determined by the survey, and should be entered as such, on Form 89. This is a matter of arithmetical computation, and errors are hardly excusable.

If the 80 per cent. exceeds the reported product, then an assessment must be made on the balance. If the amount actually produced is found to be correctly reported, and the amount so reported is less than 80 per cent. of the capacity as determined from the survey, the difference between the reported product and the 80 per cent. must be assessed. On this point the law is imperative. But if the amount actually produced, and reported, equals or exceeds the 80 per cent. the assessment is to be made upon the difference between the amount so found and the reported product, even though the reported product exceeds the 80 per cent., because the distiller should pay upon all the spirits produced by him.

When the difference between the actual product and the reported product is greater than the difference between the 80 per cent. and the reported product, the assessment will be upon the former quantity. When the reported product equals or exceeds the 80 per cent., but is less than the actual product as above found, the assessment will be made upon the difference between the actual and the reported product; but, if in any case the actual product and the reported product are less than the 80 per cent., the assessment must be made for the difference between the reported product and the 80 per cent.

To determine the number of barrels of 40 proof gallons each, to be reported, on Form 89, as assessed at $4 per barrel, the greatest number of proof gallons, whether the required production, the reported production, or 80 per cent. of the capacity, will be divided by 40, and the quotient less the number exempt under the special $4 tax will be the number so assessed.

Where there is a fractional number of gallons less than 40, the assessment will be made at the rate of 10 cents per gallon; this will save the necessity of carrying forward such fractional number of gallons to the next computation. The number of barrels is found from the quantity reported together with any deficiency that may be assessed.

The per diem capacity tax is $2 upon the first 20 bushels or less of grain, or 60 gallons or less of molasses; and, in addition thereto, $2 for each even 20 bushels of grain, or 60 gallons of molasses, in excess of the first 20 or 60. In this assessment, fractions in excess of the first 20 or 60 are to be discarded.

The number of days upon which the per diem capacity tax is to be assessed is the whole number since the date of commencement in the month inclusive, less Sundays and the days upon which operations have been legally suspended, due notice having been given thereof by the distiller, accompanied by the certificate of the assistant assessor, that, at the time the locks were placed upon the furnace doors, no mash, wort, or beer, was on hand on the premises; the rule will be strictly adhered to, and all deductions made which are not supported by the official records on file in the Office of Internal Revenue, will be stricken out, and the assessment returned for correction.

The computations, on Form 89, should be made promptly at the commencement of each month, and immediately forwarded to the Office of Internal Revenue. 9 I. R. R. 156.

On the receipt of the distiller's return for brandy from fruit, Form 15, in each month, the assessor shall inquire and determine whether said distiller has accounted in his return for the preceding month for all the brandy produced by him; and if the assessor is satisfied that the distiller has returned all the spirits produced by him, he will enter the quantity so reported, on Form 89, as the amount to be accounted for during that month. If the quantity so reported by the distiller is less than 80 per cent. of the surveyed capacity of the distillery for the time run and material used, the assessor will assess the distiller 50 cents per proof gallon for every gallon of such deficiency, together with the special tax of $4 per barrel, for every barrel of 40 proof gallons each, provided, that no tax of $4 per barrel shall be assessed until the number of barrels exempted under the special tax has been produced. If the assessor finds, upon an examination, that the distiller has not reported all spirits actually produced by him during the month, he will ascertain the quantity actually produced.

In determining the amount actually produced, the assessor shall ascertain the kind and quantity of materials used, and the time operated, and determine such amount therefrom, on the basis of the spirit-producing capacity of the materials used as fixed in the survey.

The time will be arrived at by aggregating the hours run and dividing by 24, counting any fraction as a whole day. In the absence of a satisfactory return of the materials used, and time operated, he may base his estimate of actual production upon the surveyed capacity of the distillery for the period which it is ascertained it was operated, fixing the production at the full capacity thereof.

Whenever the actual production of brandy within the year shall be equal to the number of barrels exempted under the special tax, there shall be an additional tax of four dollars per barrel, 40 proof gallons, for every barrel in excess of the number so exempted.

No assessment for per diem tax will hereafter be made against distillers of brandy from apples, peaches, or grapes, exclusively. 12 I. R. R. 1.

Daily Account to be Kept by Storekeepers.

[SEC. 21. (July 20, 1868.) *And be it further enacted,* That the storekeeper assigned to any distillery warehouse shall also have charge of the distillery connected therewith; and, in addition to the duties required of him as a storekeeper in charge of a warehouse, shall keep in a book to be provided for that purpose, and in the manner to be prescribed by the Commissioner of Internal Revenue, a daily account of all the meal and vegetable productions or other substances brought into said distillery, or on said premises, to be used for the purpose of producing spirits, from whom purchased, and when delivered at said distillery, the kind and quantity of all fuel used, and from whom purchased, and of all repairs made on said distillery, and by whom and when made, the names and places of residence of all persons employed in or about the distillery, of the materials put into the mash tub, or otherwise used for the production of spirits, the time when any fermenting tub is emptied of ripe mash or beer, recording the same by the number painted on said tub, and of all spirits drawn off from the receiving cistern, and the time (a) when the same were drawn off. Any distiller or person employed in any distillery who shall use, cause, or permit to be used any material for the purpose of making mash, wort, or beer, or for the production of spirits, or shall remove any spirits in the absence of the storekeeper or person designated to act as said storekeeper, shall forfeit and pay double the amount of taxes on the spirits so produced, distilled, or removed, and, in addition thereto, be liable to a penalty of one thousand dollars.]

(a) At the end of the fermenting period every fermenting tub must be emptied, and remain empty twenty-four hours. Under the heading "fermenting tub emptied of beer or mash," on Form 100, the storekeeper will enter, in the proper column, the number of the tub on the line opposite, the proper date entered in the left hand column. If four tubs are emptied on the same day, and but three lines are used for the description of the materials used, as corn, rye, malt, then one line should be left blank in the column on the day named. It is highly important that the day as well as the hour of the day in which each tub is emptied, should be accurately stated. 9 I. R. R. 149.

Suspension of Work.

[SEC. 22. (July 20, 1868.) *And be it further enacted*, That every distiller, at the hour of twelve meridian, on the third day after that on which his bond shall have been approved by the assessor, shall be deemed to have commenced, and thereafter to be continuously engaged in the production of distilled spirits in his distillery, except in the intervals when he shall have suspended work, as hereinafter authorized or provided. Any distiller desiring to suspend work in his distillery may give notice (a) in writing to the assistant assessor of his division, stating when he will suspend work; and on the day mentioned in said notice, said assistant assessor shall, at the expense of the distiller, proceed to fasten securely the door of every furnace, of every still or boiler in said distillery, by locks and otherwise, and shall adopt such other means as the Commissioner of *the* Internal Revenue shall prescribe to prevent the lighting of any fire in such furnace, or under such stills or boilers. The locks and seals, and other materials required for such purpose, shall be furnished to the assessor of the district by the Commissioner of Internal Revenue, to be duly accounted for by said assessor. Such notice by any distiller, and the action taken by the assistant assessor in pursuance thereof, shall be immediately reported to the assessor of the district, and by him transmitted to the Commissioner of Internal Revenue. No distiller, after having given such notice, shall, after the time stated therein, carry on the business of a distiller on said premises until he shall have given another notice in writing to said assessor, stating the time when he will resume work; and at the time so stated for resuming work, the assistant assessor shall attend at the distillery to remove said locks and other fastenings; and thereupon, and not before, work may be resumed in said distillery, which fact shall be immediately reported to the assessor of the district, and by him transmitted to the Commissioner of Internal Revenue. Any distiller, after the time fixed in said notice declaring his intention to suspend work, who shall carry on the business of a distiller on said premises, or shall have mash, wort, or beer in his distillery, or on any premises connected therewith, or who shall have in his possession or under his control any mash, wort, or beer, with intent to distil the same on said premises, shall incur the forfeitures and be subject to the same punishment as provided for persons who carry on the business of a distiller without having paid the special tax.]

(a) On the day mentioned in the notice the assistant assessor will, at the expense of the distiller, proceed to fasten securely every door of every furnace, still, or boiler, in said distillery, by securely locking the same so that they cannot be opened, or any fire lighted in such furnace. Such notice must be immediately reported to the assessor, and, also, the action taken thereon; and such notice and report must be transmitted to the Commissioner. No distiller can carry on the business of a distiller after the time stated in such notice until he shall have given another notice, in writing, to the assessor, stating the time when he shall resume work, at which time the assistant assessor must attend and remove the locks and other fastenings, which action must be immediately reported to the assessor, and by him to the Commissioner; and the report of the assistant assessor must distinctly state whether, or not, there was any mash, wort, or beer on hand at the time of such suspension.

No deduction is to be made for a suspension of work, unless the provisions of this section are strictly complied with. The distiller must give two notices in writing to the assistant assessor, 1st. of the time when he proposes to suspend work, 2d. a like notice of the time when he proposes to commence, at both of which times the assistant assessor must be present to secure the furnaces, or to remove the fastenings, as the case may be, and these two notices cannot be combined in one.

Unless the distiller chooses to destroy the mash on hand when he suspends work he must fix his time so that he will have time to run off the mash on hand before the notice takes effect; as, after the time stated, he can have no mash, wort, or beer on his distillery premises. If he does the business of a distiller on the premises, or has any mash, &c., therein, or in his possession, or under his control, with intent to distil the same therein, he cannot suspend work under this section, and is not entitled to any deduction of the per diem capacity tax. 9 I. R. R. 149.

The Register Seal Lock has been prescribed for use in distilleries. 10 I. R. R. 111.

The Monogram seals have been prescribed to be used in connection with the Register Seal Lock. 10 I. R. R. 153.

No allowance can be made for the suspension of work in a distillery by reason of a breakage, until a legal suspension under this section can be effected. The loss between the time of a breakage and such legal suspension must be borne by the distiller, as an incidental loss for which the present law affords him no relief. 8 I. R. R. 172.

Where a distiller resumes work after a suspension, with no mash on hand, he will be deemed to have commenced the distillation of spirits at 12 meridian on the third day after the assistant assessor unlocks the furnace doors. The full per diem capacity tax will be assessed from the time the furnace doors are unlocked until work is again legally suspended. The time for estimating the 80 per cent. of the capacity will commence on the third day after, unless distilling is commenced prior to that day.

If distillation commences on the second day after the furnace doors are unlocked, the time for which the 80 per cent. is computed will include the second day. Where such an allowance is made in computing the 80 per cent., the assessor will note the fact on Form 89, stating the number of days allowed. 9 I. R. R. 156.

When any authorized distiller proposes to discontinue the business permanently, he must give notice to the assessor of the time at which he proposes to discontinue, who, upon the receipt of such notice, will direct one of his assistants to close and secure the furnace doors, as in the case of suspension of work. The distiller will also re-register his still as not for use, and make application for the discontinuance of his warehouse, withdrawing all spirits stored therein, by the payment of the tax. The assessor will report the action taken to the Office of Internal Revenue, and the per diem capacity tax will cease from the time the distillery is so closed. 9 I. R. R. 158.

Ganging and Marking.

[SEC. 23. (July 20, 1868.) *And be it further enacted*, That all distilled spirits shall be drawn from the receiving cisterns into casks, each of not less capacity than twenty gallons wine measure, and shall thereupon be gauged, proved, and marked by an internal revenue gauger, by cutting on the cask containing such spirits, in a manner to be prescribed by the Commissioner of Internal Revenue, the quantity, in wine gallons and in proof gallons, of the contents of such cask, and shall be immediately removed into the distillery warehouse, (a) and the gauger shall, in presence of the storekeeper of the warehouse, place upon the head of the cask an engraved stamp, which shall be signed by the collector of the district and the storekeeper and gauger, and shall have written thereon the number of proof gallons contained therein, the name of the distiller, the date of the receipt in the warehouse, and the serial number of each cask, in progressive order, as the same shall be received from the distillery. Such serial number for every distillery shall begin with number one (No. 1) with the first cask deposited therein after this act takes effect, and no two or more casks warehoused at the same distillery shall be marked with the same number. The said stamp shall be as follows:

Distillery warehouse stamp No. ⎯⎯.

Issued by ⎯⎯ ⎯⎯, collector, ⎯⎯ district, State of ⎯⎯. Distillery warehouse of ⎯⎯, 18⎯. Cask No. ⎯⎯, contents ⎯⎯ gallons, proof spirit.

Attest: ⎯⎯⎯⎯⎯⎯,
United States Storekeeper.

⎯⎯⎯⎯⎯⎯,
United States Gauger.

And the distiller or owner of all spirits so removed to the distillery warehouse, shall, on the first, eleventh, and twenty-first days of each month, or within five days thereafter, enter the same for deposit in such warehouse, under such rules and regulations, not inconsistent herewith, as the Commissioner of Internal Revenue may prescribe; and said entry shall be in triplicate, and shall contain the name of the person making the entry, the designation of the warehouse in which the deposit is made, and the date thereof, and [shall] be in form as follows:

Entry for deposit in distillery warehouse.

Entry of distilled spirits deposited by ⎯⎯ ⎯⎯, in distillery warehouse ⎯⎯, in the ⎯⎯ district, State of ⎯⎯, on the ⎯⎯ day of ⎯⎯, anno Domini ⎯⎯.

And the entry shall specify the kind of spirits, the whole number of casks, the marks and serial numbers thereon, the number of gauge or wine gallons, and of proof gallons, and the amount of the tax on the spirits contained in them; all of which shall be verified by the oath or affirmation of the distiller or owner of the same attached to the entry; and the said distiller or owner shall give his bond in duplicate, with one or more sureties satisfactory to the collector of the district, conditioned that the principal named in said bond will pay the tax on the spirits, as specified in the entry, or cause the same to be paid, before removal from said distillery warehouse, and within one year from the date of said bond, and the penal sum of such bond shall not be less than double the amount of the tax on such distilled spirits. One of said entries shall be retained in the office of the collector of the district, one sent to the storekeeper in charge of the warehouse, to be retained and filed in the warehouse, and one sent with the duplicate of the bond to the Commissioner of Internal Revenue, to be filed in his office.]

(a) No allowance can be made for any loss occurring in warehouse from leakage or any other cause. The amount of tax named in the entry and secured by the bond must be paid within the time named, even though loss may occur by leakage, fire, or otherwise. In this regard, spirits placed in warehouse are placed on the same footing with tax-paid spirits.

Spirits in distillery warehouse are not required to be gauged and proved before withdrawal therefrom, nor before the entry for withdrawal is made. The entry for withdrawal must correspond precisely to the entry for deposit; the tax paid stamp must specify the amount of tax on the same number of gallons as are named on the distillery warehouse stamp, and this amount must be paid before withdrawal. The collector, instead of directing the gauger to gauge and inspect spirits in warehouse before the entry for withdrawal is made, will, upon receiving the entry made as above set forth, direct the gauger to proceed to the warehouse, and there, in the presence of the storekeeper, stamp and mark the casks as required by law and regulations. 9 I. R. R. 149; U. S. v. Barrow et al. 10 I. R. R. 86; Thayer v. U. S. 9 I. R. R. 91.

When drawn into casks, the spirits must be gauged and proved by the gauger himself, and in no case can he deputize another person to do it for him.

The serial number of every distillery must begin with number one (No. 1) with the first cask deposited, and continue the series until the last day of the year, commencing a new series on the first day of January in each year thereafter, and no two or more casks warehoused at the same distillery may be marked with the same numbers. The exact number of gallons must be ascertained, marked, and reported. Fractions of gallons must be indicated in all cases, but the tax will be collected on the fraction of a gallon as if it were a whole gallon. A fraction of a wine gallon, however, is not to be taken as a whole gallon in calculating the number of proof gallons in a cask. 9 I. R. R. 149.

When the spirits are drawn from the receiving cisterns, they must be gauged, proved, and marked, and, in addition to affixing the distillery warehouse stamp, the gauger must cut upon the bung-stave, in a legible manner, the number of wine gallons, the proof, and number of proof gallons contained in each cask. At the same time the gauger will cut with a die or burn upon the head of each cask its serial number, in figures not less than one inch in length, and the serial number of the distillery warehouse stamp in figures not less than half an inch in length, placing the same immediately under the serial number of the cask. 10 I. R. R. 83.

Take the dimensions of cisterns or tubs in inches or tenths of inches; add together the square of the top diameter and four times the square of the midway diameter (ascertained by adding the top and bottom diameters together and dividing by two), and divide the sum by six, which gives the square of the true mean diameter. Multiply this by the height of the cistern or tub, and the product will be the capacity in cylindrical inches. As there are 294 cylindrical inches in a gallon, divide this last product by 294, and the quotient is the number of gallons contained in the cistern or tub.

Should the cistern be full or warped, so as not to be a perfect circle, or otherwise in such a condition that the diameter of the bottom cannot be taken, the following rule, though not mathematically correct, is, for all practical purposes, sufficiently so, the difference being shown only in large cisterns where the difference between the top and bottom diameters is considerable:

Take the outside circumference of the cistern, half way between the bottom and top; divide this by 3.1416 (or multiply by seven and divide by 22), and the quotient will be the mean diameter on the outside; deduct from this twice the thickness of the staves, and the remainder will be the mean inside diameter. Multiply this amount by itself and then by the height, and the product by .0034; the resulting product is the capacity of the cistern in gallons.

After the gauger has gauged, proved, and marked the barrels, he should enter in his record book the name of the distiller or rectifier and the shipping marks on the barrels, the name of the person for whom done, and the place where done, the serial number, and, directly opposite that number, the gauge, outs, and proof of each barrel, with the date of inspection and the temperature of the spirits inspected. If the temperature of the spirit in the barrels inspected differs enough to change the per centage for volume, the entries in the record book should be so arranged as to keep together these barrels for which the same correction applies. Where there is a large number of barrels to be inspected, the amount of proof spirits at the temperature of 60° may be ascertained by either of the following rules:

1. Add together the wine gallons, and if there are any outs deduct them from the wine gallons; then, in the manual, find the proper per centage of correction for volume; add or deduct this, as the case may be, and the result is the true wine gallons at 60° temperature. Then add the proofs together, and divide the sum by the number of barrels, and the average per cent. is obtained. Multiply the wine gallons by this per cent., divide the product by one hundred, and the total proof gallons are obtained.

2. Instead of dividing the total amount of proofs by the number of barrels when that procedure would leave fractions, simply multiply the number of wine gallons by the proofs added together, and divide the product by the number of barrels, and proceed as before.

When the strengths of the spirits are very different, or the packages containing them vary considerably in size, the proofs should be calculated on each barrel or package separately.

The above rule for spirits below proof is to be used only for spirits which, having been withdrawn from bonded warehouse for the purpose of being rectified or redistilled, are returned to the warehouse below first proof. In all other cases, when spirits subject to tax are found on inspection to be below proof, the wine gallons must be taken and returned as so many proof gallons.

Gaugers should carefully examine the barrels or casks before commencing to gauge them, as they often, from natural causes, or in manufacturing, become imperfect in shape, and sometimes are purposely made to defraud. The following are the most common irregularities: When barrels are put up in tiers without dunnage, the bottom stave sometimes becomes flattened or compressed to such an extent as to make the bung diameter much less than it would otherwise be, and, consequently, the apparent capacity of the barrel will be too little if this flattening be disregarded. Sometimes the heads are warped, becoming concave or convex, and there will be great difference in the length as taken at different places. Regard should be had to particular cases of irregularity. Barrels that are made to defraud are sometimes made with unusually thick or thin head staves, as well as the bung stave and the one opposite. Sometimes the bung stave is reamed out on the inside, and the stave opposite chipped out. Whenever an unusual difference is found between the head and bung diameter, the barrel should be thoroughly examined.

Again, instead of being put together in a true circular truss hoop, oval truss hoops are used, giving the barrel an oval shape at the bung, the perpendicular diameter differing from the horizontal, as may best suit the interest of the distiller. When barrels are found that bear evidence of having been made purposely to defraud, the facts in the case should be promptly reported to the collector of the district, and to the Commissioner.

For the sake of greater security against errors in gauging, gaugers should always see that the barrels, before gauging, are so placed that the bungs shall be exactly uppermost. 5 I. R. R. 84.

Distillers' original packages must contain at least twenty wine gallons. This applies to all distillers, whether of fruit or otherwise. Smaller packages cannot be warehoused, or sold, or removed by the distiller. If he sells in smaller packages, he must do so as a dealer, and such packages must be filled from the original casks or packages, and such sale cannot be made on the distillery premises. 9 I. R. R. 157.

Serial numbers of packages should not change with change of proprietors of distilleries. 10 I. R. R. 98.

On completing the process of distillation, the distiller of brandy from fruit, etc., must draw the brandy distilled by him into casks, each of not less capacity than ten gallons, wine measure, and must retain the same at the designated place of deposit at the distillery until the tax is paid thereon, and the tax stamps attached thereto, as hereinafter directed. 12 I. R. R. 1.

If there is any irregularity or violation of law on the part of the distiller, the storekeeper must make immediate report of the same to the collector and to the Commissioner, and for any neglect to do so he will be dismissed. Where a distillery is closed on account of any violation of law which is reported by the storekeeper, such storekeeper will be promptly assigned to another warehouse.

The warehouse entry should be made in triplicate, one to be retained by the collector, one sent with the duplicate of the bond to the Commissioner, and the other sent to the storekeeper in charge of the warehouse; and at the time of making such entry, the distiller will give bond in duplicate on Form 80.

Entries for deposit are to be made tri-monthly only, and such entries must cover the total amount of spirits deposited during the entire tri-monthly period next preceding the entry, and no entry for deposit can be made in any other manner. 9 I. R. R. 154.

The storekeeper will have charge of the warehouse to which he may be assigned, under the direction of the collector controlling the same. The warehouse will be in the joint custody of the storekeeper and the proprietor thereof, and kept securely locked. The storekeeper will retain the key of the government lock, and will not permit the same at any time to go into the possession of such proprietor; and the warehouse must at no time be unlocked or remain open, unless in the presence of the storekeeper. 9 I. R. R. 155.

The storekeeper in charge of each warehouse will keep a correct account of all goods received into his warehouse and delivered therefrom, specifying in detail the date of the receipt, original and warehouse marks and numbers, number and description of packages and contents, date of receipt of permit for delivery. date of delivery, to whom delivered, and for what purpose as specified in the permit; and shall enter in the warehouse book such further particulars as may be prescribed or found necessary for the identification of the packages to insure the correct delivery thereof. The book for this purpose must be furnished by the owner of the warehouse. Daily returns must be furnished to the collector of the district in which the warehouse is situate, of all goods received therein and delivered therefrom. These returns must be full, explicit, and correct in all details.

Accounts are also to be kept in the collector's office in each district with the several warehouses, of all goods received into and delivered from the same. This account will be debited with the goods received, as shown by the daily return of the officer in charge, and will be credited with the several permits or orders for removal as they issue from the collector's office. To test the accuracy of the daily returns made by the several storekeepers of goods received by them, their returns should be examined and compared with such other accounts in the collector's office as will furnish means of comparison, and, in case of any disagreement, the discrepancy must be immediately examined and corrected. All warehousing bonds should be numbered progressively from one upward for each calendar year. 9 I. R. R. 155; 6 I. R. R. 92.

Casks of spirits in a distillery warehouse cannot be filled up before withdrawal with spirits taken directly from the cistern. 9 I. R. R. 155.

Withdrawal from Warehouse.

[SEC. 24. (July 20, 1868.) *And be it further enacted*, That any distilled spirits may, on payment of the tax thereon, be withdrawn from warehouse on application to the collector of the district in charge of such warehouse, on making a withdrawal entry (*a*) in duplicate, and in form as follows:

Entry for withdrawal of distilled spirits from warehouse. Tax paid.

Entry of distilled spirits to be withdrawn, on payment of the tax, from —— warehouse by —— ——, deposited on the —— day of ——, anno Domini ——, by —— ——, in said warehouse.

And the entry shall specify the whole number of casks with the marks and serial numbers thereon, the number of gauge or wine gallons, and of proof gallons, and the amount of the tax on the distilled spirits contained in them; all of which shall be verified by the oath or affirmation of the person making such entry; and on payment of the tax the collector shall issue his order to the storekeeper in charge of the warehouse for the delivery. One of said entries shall be filed in the office of the collector, and the other transmitted by him to the Commissioner of Internal Revenue.]

(*a*) On the payment of the tax, the collector will indorse upon the back of a copy of said entry for withdrawal, an order to the storekeeper in charge of the warehouse for the delivery of the spirits specified in the entry in the following form, viz. :

Office of Collector of Internal Revenue.
———— District of the State of ————, 187—.

Sir: The full amount of taxes due and owing on the distilled spirits described in the within entry of withdrawal, having this day been paid to me, you are hereby directed to deliver said spirits to Mr. ————, after this order shall have been countersigned by the assessor of this district, or the assistant assessor, as directed by the regulations.

(Signed) ———— ————,
Collector.

This order will be countersigned by the proper assessor or the assistant assessor in the following form, viz.:

I hereby certify that the foregoing order has been presented to me, and that the amount of taxes certified therein to have been received has been entered in the bonded account of this district kept in my office.

(Signed) ———— ————,
Assessor.

This order must be presented to and signed only by the assessor in all city districts, as well as in all other districts where the warehouse from which the goods are withdrawn is situated in the same place or town with the assessor's office, or is within a convenient distance therefrom. In other districts the certificate may be signed by the assistant assessor of the division in which the warehouse is situated; and in such case he must immediately make an entry upon the assessment book of the items stated in the permit, and transmit to his assessor a duplicate of the entry, or a statement showing date, names, article, quantity, and amount of tax as given in the entry.

The collector will place one of said entries on file in his office, and transmit the other to the Commissioner.

Entries for withdrawal may be made at any time after the spirits have been stored in the warehouse and entered on the bonded account. All the spirits produced in any distillery must be removed to the distillery warehouse, even when they are immediately withdrawn therefrom on the payment of the tax. And the entry for deposit must be made at the regular tri-monthly period, although the spirits covered by it have been withdrawn. The bond to be given must cover all the spirits remaining in the warehouse at the end of the tri monthly period. If all the spirits deposited during that period have been withdrawn, no bond will be required; but the collector will, in such case, certify upon the entry that such spirits have been withdrawn upon the payment of the tax, giving the dates of the withdrawals, and the amount of the tax collected upon each. When a portion only of the spirits deposited during the tri monthly period is withdrawn prior to the entry for deposit, the bond will be taken for the quantity remaining in the warehouse at the end of the tri-monthly period, and the collector will make a like certificate covering the quantity withdrawn.

All warehousing bonds must be properly stamped, and the duplicate must be stamped as an original bond. Every entry for withdrawal (original and duplicate) must have affixed a 50 cent revenue stamp.

As the law requires the tax to be paid within one year from the date of the bond, collectors should keep the entries, accounts, and dates in such manner that the specified lots covered by each bond can be readily identified. 9 I. R. R. 155.

A party who purchases spirits sold under a distraint for unpaid taxes, is vested with the interest that the distiller had in the spirits so sold, and has the right to allow the same to remain in bond, or to withdraw the same on the usual form of entry for withdrawal in the same manner as the distiller might have done. 10 I. R. R. 113.

A sheriff cannot take goods from a warehouse until the taxes thereon have been paid. Upon payment of the taxes, the right of the sheriff to seize is determined by the State laws. 4 I. R. R. 109.

* **Payment of Tax Before Withdrawal.**

[SEC. 1. (Jan. 11, 1868.) *Be it enacted by the Senate and House of Representatives of the United States of America in Congress assembled*, That from and after the passage of this act, no distilled spirits shall be withdrawn or removed from any warehouse for the purpose of transportation, redistillation, rectification, change of package, exportation, or for any other purpose whatever, until the full tax on such spirits shall have been duly paid to the collector of the proper district. And all acts and parts of acts inconsistent with the provisions of this act be, and they are hereby, repealed.]

[SEC. 1. (June 25, 1868; as amended July 6, 1868.) *Be it enacted by the Senate and House of Representatives of the United States of America in Congress assembled*, That the act of January eleventh, eighteen hundred and sixty-eight, entitled "An act to prevent frauds in the collection of the tax on distilled spirits," be so construed as to permit rum, which at the date of the passage of said act was already distilled or redistilled and intended for export, or actually contracted for to be delivered for exportation, to be withdrawn, removed, and exported from the United States under such transportation and export bonds and regulations as were required therefor immediately prior to the passage of said act, and as shall be provided for hereafter: *Provided*, That all such spirits shall be actually exported within sixty days from the passage of this act; and that before any such exportation shall be permitted, proof in writing shall be furnished by sworn evidence, to the satisfaction of the Commissioner of Internal Revenue, that such rum was in fact at the date mentioned intended for export, and distilled or redistilled for that purpose, or actually contracted for to be so exported. And upon failure to so export the same within sixty days, the tax thereon shall become due and payable, and the bonds given for the transportation and export thereof shall be forfeited and collected, as in case of such bonds not canceled according to law.]

Stamping and Marking on Withdrawal.

[SEC. 25.   (July 20, 1868.)   *And be it further enacted,* That whenever an order is received from the collector for the removal from any distillery warehouse of any cask of distilled spirits, on which tax has been paid, it shall be the duty of the gauger by whom the same is gauged and inspected, in presence of the storekeeper, before such cask has left the warehouse, to place upon the head thereof, in such manner as to cover no portion of any brand or mark prescribed by law already placed thereon, a stamp (*a*) on which shall be engraved the number of proof gallons contained in said cask on which the tax has been paid, and which shall be signed by the collector of the district, storekeeper, and gauger, and which shall state the serial number of the cask, the name of the person by whom the tax was paid, and the person to whom and the place where it is to be delivered ; which stamp shall be as follows :

Tax-paid stamp No. ———.
Received ——— ———, 18—, from ——— ——— tax on ——— gallons proof spirit, cask No. —, ——— warehouse at ———, for delivery to ———, at ———.

                              ——————————,
Attest: *Collector* ——— *District, State of* ———.
——————————,
U. S. Storekeeper.
——————————,
U. S. Gauger.

And at the time of affixing the tax-paid stamp or stamps, the gauger shall, in the presence of the storekeeper, cut or burn upon each cask the name of the distiller, the district, the date of the payment of [the] tax, the number of proof gallons, and the number of the stamp, which cutting or burning shall be erased when such cask is emptied, by cutting or burning a canceling line across such marks or brands. Whenever any cask or package of rectified spirits shall be filled for shipment, sale, or delivery, on the premises of any rectifier, who shall have paid the special tax required by law, it shall be the duty of a United States gauger to gauge and inspect the same, and place thereon an engraved stamp, which shall be signed by the collector of the district and the said gauger, and state the date when affixed, and the number of proof gallons, which stamp shall be as follows :

Stamp for rectified spirits No. ——.

Issued by —— ——, collector, —— district, State of ——. —— ——, rectifier of spirits in the —— district, State of ——, —— ——, 18—, —— proof gallons.

—— ——,
U. S. Gauger.

Whenever any cask or package of distilled spirits shall be filled for shipment, sale, or delivery on the premises of any wholesale liquor dealer or compounder, it shall be the duty of a United States gauger to gauge and inspect the same, and place thereon an engraved stamp, signed by the collector of the district and the said gauger, stating the name of the compounder or dealer and the date when affixed, and the number of proof gallons, which stamp shall be as follows:

Wholesale liquor dealer's stamp No. ——.

Issued by —— ——, collector —— district, State of ——. —— ——, wholesale liquor dealer, of ——, —— district, State of ——, —— ——, 18—, —— proof gallons.

—— ——,
U. S. Gauger, —— *District, State of* ——.

All blanks in any of the above forms shall be duly filled in accordance with the facts in each case. And the stamps above designated shall be affixed so as to fasten the same securely to the cask or package and duly canceled, and shall then be immediately covered with a coating of transparent-varnish or other substance, so as to protect them from removal or damage by exposure; and such affixing, cancellation, and covering shall be done in such manner as the Commissioner of Internal Revenue shall by regulation prescribe; but such stamps shall in every case be affixed to a smooth surface of the cask or other package, which surface shall not have been previously painted or covered with any substance.]

(a) Whenever any person desires to withdraw spirits from a warehouse, he will notify the collector or deputy collector, who will, upon receipt of the tax, cut from the book, stamps, with the requisite coupons annexed, properly filled up and signed, which will be affixed by the gauger in presence of the storekeeper, to a smooth surface on the head of the respective casks.

At the time of affixing the tax-paid stamps, the gauger will, in presence of the storekeeper, brand the cask in accordance with the provisions of this section. A stencil plate cannot be used for this purpose. This brand must not be obliterated or canceled except by cutting or burning a canceling line across such brand or mark; and no stamp, mark, or brand must be defaced, or in any manner obliterated, until such cask is emptied, or its contents drawn off. 9 I. R. R. 158.

When withdrawn from warehouse, each cask must, in addition to the tax-paid stamp, have cut or burned upon it the name of the distiller, the district, the date of the payment of the tax, the number of proof gallons, and the number of the tax-paid stamp. This brand may be abridged in the following manner:

JOHN SMITH & CO.,
DISTILLERS,
6th District, O.,
T. P. Jan. 10, 1869, P. G. 44,
Stamp 39857.

All of this, except the date, number of proof gallons, and the number of the stamp, may be burned upon the cask prior to its being filled at the cisterns, and the date and numbers cut with a die at the time the tax-paid stamp is attached. The letters and figures constituting any brand or mark must in no case be less than half an inch in length. In addition to this, the cask must be conspicuously marked or branded with the particular name of the spirits as known to the trade, as, "Rye," "Bourbon," &c., as the case may be.

When it becomes necessary to change a package in a distillery, i. e., to draw off the contents of a cask bearing the distillery warehouse stamp and the accompanying marks and brands, and to place the same in a new cask, the spirits must be again inspected and gauged, the number of wine and proof gallons cut upon the bung stave and the head of each cask; the gauger will cut with a die, or burn with a branding iron, his name and office, the time and place of inspection, the proof of the spirits, the name of such spirits as known to the trade, the name of the distiller, the distillery where such spirits were produced, and the serial number of the original package, together with the serial number of the warehouse stamp.

When such change of package is made after the spirits have been withdrawn from warehouse and the tax-paid stamp attached, the cask will be marked and branded in the same manner, with the addition of the number of proof gallons, the date of the payment of the tax, and the serial number of the tax paid-stamp. 10 I. R. R. 83.

The fee for stamping and branding on withdrawal from a distillery warehouse is one-half of the fee for inspection into warehouse. 9 I. R. R. 51.

The original packages of a distiller, after removal from warehouse, must bear the distillery warehouse and tax-paid stamps. So long as the original package remains unchanged and bears these stamps, no other stamp is required. 10 I. R. R. 82.

Whenever any rectifier proposes to empty any spirits for the purpose of rectifying, purifying, refining, redistilling, or compounding the same, he will file with the collector a notice or statement, giving the number of casks or packages, the serial number of each, the number of wine and proof gallons in each, the kind of stamps and serial numbers of each, the particular name of such spirits as known to the trade, the proof, by whom produced, the district where produced, by whom inspected, and the date of inspection.

When the process of rectification (including compounding, &c.) has been completed, the rectifier will so notify the collector, giving the number of proof gallons so rectified, redistilled, or compounded, and request that the spirits may be gauged and inspected, and stamps issued for the same; and thereupon the collector will direct a gauger to gauge and inspect the same, and will issue stamps for rectified spirits covering the quantity of spirits, but not in any case to exceed the number of proof gallons stated in the notice of the rectifier as filed in his office. These notices will be preserved and filed by the collector, and a copy thereof furnished to the assessor, who, on the first of each month, will compare the same with the return of the rectifier.

Collectors will in no case issue stamps for rectified spirits to any rectifier until this notice is filed with him; and such stamps will be delivered to the gauger, who will attach the same to the barrels or packages.

Under the name rectified spirits are included all spirits which, after leaving the hands of the distiller, are leached through coal, redistilled, refined, compounded, or subjected to any process which would constitute the person using it a rectifier as defined by law.

Spirits subjected to any of these processes must be put up in casks, inspected and gauged, and, in addition to attaching the stamp for rectified spirits, the gauger will cut upon the bung stave the number of wine and proof gallons, and mark upon the head of each cask, with a stencil plate, in durable ink, his name and office, the date of inspection, the particular name of such spirits as known to the trade, the proof, the name and place of business of the rectifier, and the serial number of the stamp for rectified spirits affixed thereto.

To the mark or brand designated by the regulations, the rectifier may add any known trade-mark adopted and used by him; or where such trade-mark is the distinctive name of the spirits as known to the trade, it may be used as the name of the spirits.

The stamp for rectified spirits must not be removed until the cask is emptied. So long as the original cask remains unchanged no other stamp is required.

When the contents of a cask of rectified spirits are drawn from the original cask or package and placed in another cask or package containing not less than ten gallons, they must be again gauged and inspected, the number of wine and proof gallons cut upon the bung stave, and upon the head of each cask must be marked or branded the name of the gauger, the time and place of inspection, the proof of the spirits, the particular name of the spirits as known to the trade, the name and place of business of the rectifier, with the date of the original inspection and the serial number of the stamp for rectified spirits upon the original package. The absence of any stamp or brand required by law from any package of spirits containing more than five gallons, works a forfeiture of the package and contents. 10 I. R. R. 82.

Where wholesale liquor dealers purchase spirits regularly stamped and bearing the required marks and brands, and sell the same without change, no additional inspection or marking is required. Where, however, they draw from such stamped and branded packages, and fill other packages for shipment, sale, or delivery, the spirits must be again gauged and inspected, and the wholesale liquor dealer's stamp attached, and such packages must be marked with the name of the dealer and the particular name of the spirits as known to the trade. Where the package so filled contains ten gallons or more, it must also be branded or marked as required by section 47.

Retail liquor dealers are only authorized to sell in quantities less than five gallons, and no reinspection or stamping of the packages of spirits so sold by them is required. The spirits which they purchase must be in packages properly stamped, marked, or branded, and remain in the original casks or packages until drawn off for sale in retail packages, except where it becomes necessary, from leakage or other cause, to change the package. Where such change is made, the spirits must be again inspected and gauged, and the new packages branded. In all cases where spirits are inspected and gauged, the number of wine and proof gallons must be cut upon the bung stave. 10 I. R. R. 82.

All packages of five gallons or more sold must come from a wholesale dealer, and must be gauged and stamped; and packages of less than five gallons are not required to be gauged and stamped as such, and can only be sold by a retail dealer. Stand casks are forbidden. Dealers must draw from the stamped and branded packages they purchase directly into those in which the spirits are to be sold, and no other change of packages can be allowed, except when rendered necessary to prevent waste, and then the requirements of section 47 must be complied with. 10 I. R. R. 97.

Wholesale dealers must put up their spirits in such packages as are susceptible of receiving their stamps and marks or brands, and admitting of their proper cancellation. Hence they should not use glass vessels. Retail dealers may use packages of any material they please. 10 I. R. R. 98.

Imported spirits need not be stamped under this section. 9 I. R. R. 36.

The affixing, cancellation, and covering of stamps placed on casks or other packages containing distilled spirits must be done in the following manner:

The stamps are to be securely affixed to a smooth surface of the cask or package. That surface must not have been previously painted or covered with any substance. Transparent varnish, or any other adhesive material which will cause the stamp to stick securely and permanently, may be used for that purpose. The affixing will be done by the gauger, in the presence of the storekeeper.

The stamp, having been affixed, must be immediately cancelled. For this purpose the gauger will use a stencil plate of brass or copper, in which will be cut not less than five fine parallel waved lines long enough to extend not less than three-quarters of an inch beyond each side of the stamp on the wood of the cask; and the name of the gauger must be cut on one end of the plate, and his title, viz., "U. S. Gauger," on the other end, perpendicular to the lines. This plate must be imprinted with blacking or durable coloring material over and across the stamp as indicated, and in such a manner as not to deface the reading matter on the stamp—that is, so as not to daub and make it illegible.

The stamp, having been affixed and cancelled, must immediately be covered with a coating of transparent varnish, or other substance. Any transparent varnish, or other similar substance, may be used for this purpose.

Any neglect to mark and brand spirits, as required by the regulations, or any case of negligence or carelessness in attaching the stamps, should be at once reported to the Office of Internal Revenue, that the proper steps may be taken for the dismissal of the officer so doing; and collectors will also be justified in declining to assign any gauger to duty who shall be found guilty of such negligence, carelessness, or disregard of the regulations. 9 I. R. R. 159.

On or before the 25th day of each month, the distiller of brandy from apples, &c., shall notify the collector of his district, on Form A, stating the probable number of packages of brandy that will be distilled by him within the month, and probable number of wine gallons, with his request to have the same gauged and marked; and on the receipt of such notice, and after the last day of the month, the collector of the district shall cause the brandy produced during the month to be gauged, proved, and marked, as hereinafter directed, by a United States gauger, who, upon order of the collector, shall proceed at once to gauge, prove, and mark each package of such spirits as he may find at the distillery or designated place of deposit; and shall cut upon the bung stave of each package the wine gallons, the proof, and the proof gallons; and shall cut or burn on the head of each cask the name of such distiller, the district, the serial number of the cask, and kind of spirits; and shall mark thereon the date of such gauge, and the name of the gauger by whom made, placing such date and name on the head of the package in such way as to admit of the attaching of the tax-paid stamp between the same. The gauger, on completing each inspection, shall immediately make report thereof in triplicate, on Form 59 1-2, showing for whom gauged and where, the number of packages, the serial number of each, the proof, the wine gallons and the proof gallons of each, the kind of spirits and the amount of tax thereon, and sign the same, delivering one copy thereof to the distiller, and transmitting one copy thereof to the assessor, and one to the collector of the district. The fees for such gauging to be paid by the distiller, at such rates as are or may be prescribed by the Commissioner of Internal Revenue.

Immediately on the receipt of such return from the gauger, and on or before the 10th day of each month, the distiller shall make a return in triplicate, on Form 15, showing the number of days within the preceding month upon which the stills were operated; between what hours of each day operated; the kind, quantity, and condition of fruit used, and the number of times each still was boiled off each day; the quantity of singlings produced; the aggregate number of wine and of proof gallons of brandy distilled during the month, the quantity of singlings on hand at the end of the month; which return shall be signed by the distiller and sworn to by him before the assessor, assistant assessor, or some other officer having general power to administer oaths, and shall be transmitted to the assessor, who, on receipt thereof, shall forthwith transmit one copy to the Commissioner, and one copy to the collector of the district.

Having exempted distillers of brandy from apples, peaches, or grapes, exclusively, from the provisions of the law requiring that redistillation be carried on through continuous closed pipes and vessels, it is necessary that the distiller shall complete the process of distillation of his production within the month, so as to have no singlings on hand at the end of the month beyond the production of the last two days, and even this amount should be doubled, where it is possible to do so, within the month, and embraced in the return as brandy.

On payment of the tax upon the brandy as shown in the gauger's report, the collector shall prepare tax-paid stamps of the proper denomination, with all the blanks filled up according to the facts as appearing in such gauger's return, including the serial number of the package to which each stamp is to be attached, which stamps shall be signed by the collector, as well as by the gauger making the return, and delivered to the distiller.

Upon the receipt from the collector of the tax-paid stamps, the distiller shall affix the same to the packages in a secure and permanent manner, by pasting the same upon the head of the packages, at the place previously designated by the gauger, and by driving tacks, one in each corner, one in the center, and at each side of the stamp, making not less than seven in number; and shall cancel the same by writing across the face of the stamp his name, and the date upon which the stamp is affixed to the package, and varnish the stamp with a transparent varnish, so as to protect it from removal or damage by exposure; and shall cut or burn in legible figures, upon the head of each cask, the serial number of the stamp attached thereto, and the date of the payment of the tax. In attaching the stamps, the distiller must be careful to attach each stamp to the package the serial number of which is given in the stamp; and on having so attached stamps to each package, he shall make entry of the serial number of each package, and of the stamp attached thereto, in the proper column in his book, Form 25 1-2, together with the aggregate amount of tax paid; and on selling or disposing of the packages so stamped, shall enter on his book to whom sold or delivered.

Any distiller of brandy from apples, peaches, or grapes, desiring to avail himself of the privileges of a distillery warehouse, and of the bonding of the spirits of his own manufacture therein, may do so on complying with all the requirements of law in regard thereto, the same as if such provisions had not been included in the exemptions set forth in these regulations. 12 I. R. R. 1.

The gauging, inspecting, and stamping is to be done by the United States gauger; but the rectifier or dealer, when he has his casks filled, is to call upon the gauger to perform his duty, and he is not permitted to fill his casks without causing the same to be gauged, inspected, and stamped, as required by law. This section is confined to rectifiers and wholesale dealers, and is not limited to quantity, as in section 47. All sales of five gallons or more must be inspected, gauged, and stamped. All casks filled by rectifiers for shipment, sale, or delivery, must be inspected, gauged, and stamped. But to render the party liable, the filling of the casks, and the omission to cause the same to be so inspected, gauged, and stamped, must be alleged, and proved to have been knowingly and wilfully done, or neglected to be done, as the case may be. Two distinct offences for which a different penalty is imposed must not be included in the same count. The information need not set forth the number of gallons, or casks, or the number of gallons in each cask. U. S. v. Rectifying Establishment, 11 I. R. R. 45; U. S. v. 396 Bbls. 3 I. R. R. 135; U. S. v. 133 Casks, 11 I. R. R. 191; U. S. v. 37 Bbls. 11 I. R. R. 125.

Stamps to be in Book Form.

[SEC. 26. (July 20, 1868.) *And be it further enacted*, That all stamps required for distilled spirits shall be engraved in their several kinds in book form, and shall be issued by the Commissioner of Internal Revenue to any collector, upon his requisition, in such numbers as may be necessary in the several districts. Each stamp shall have an engraved stub attached thereto, with a number thereon corresponding with an engraved number on the stamp, and the stub shall not be removed from the book. And there shall be entered on the corresponding stub such memoranda of the contents of every stamp as shall be necessary to preserve a perfect record of the use of such stamp when detached.]

Stamps, how made.

[SEC. 27. (July 20, 1868.) *And be it further enacted*, That every stamp for the payment of tax on distilled spirits shall have engraved thereon words and figures representing a decimal number of gallons, and a similar number of gallons shall be engraved on the stub corresponding to such stamp, and between the stamp and the stub and connecting them shall be engraved nine coupons, which, beginning next to the stamp, shall indicate in succession the several numbers of gallons between the number named in the stamp and the decimal number next above. And whenever any collector shall receive the tax on the distilled spirits contained in any cask, he shall detach from the book a stamp representing the denominate quantity nearest to the quantity of proof spirits in such cask, as shown by the gauger's return, with such number of the coupons attached thereto as shall be necessary to make up the whole number of proof gallons in said cask, and any quantity in addition to the number of full gallons less than one gallon shall be regarded as a full gallon; and all unused coupons shall remain attached to the marginal stub; and no coupon shall have any value or significance whatever when detached from the stamp and stub. And the tax-paid stamps with the coupons may denote such number of gallons, not less than twenty, as the Commissioner of Internal Revenue may deem advisable.]

Collector's Stamp Account.

[SEC. 28. (July 20, 1868.) *And be it further enacted*, That the books of tax-paid stamps (a) issued to any collector shall be charged to his account at the full value of the tax on the number of gallons represented on the stamps and coupons contained in said books; and every collector shall make a monthly return to the Commissioner of Internal Revenue of all tax-paid stamps issued by him to be affixed to any cask or package containing distilled spirits, on which the tax has been paid, and account for the amount of the tax collected; and when the said collector shall return to the Commissioner of Internal Revenue any book of marginal stubs, which it shall be his duty to do as soon as all the stamps contained in the book, when issued to him from the Office of Internal Revenue, have been used, and shall have accounted for the tax on the number of gallons represented on the stamps and coupons that were contained in said book, there shall be allowed a commission of half of one per centum on the amount of the tax on spirits distilled after the passage of this act, in addition to any other commission by law allowed, which shall be equally divided between the collector receiving the tax and the assessor of the district in which the distilled spirits were produced. All stamps relating to distilled spirits other than the tax-paid stamps shall be charged to collectors as representing the value of twenty-five cents for each stamp; and the books containing such stamps may be intrusted by any collector to the gauger of the district, who shall make a daily report to the assessor and collector of all such stamps used by him and for whom used, and from these reports the assessor of the district shall assess the person for whom they were used, and the collector shall thereupon collect the amount due for such stamps at the rate of twenty-five cents for each stamp issued during the month; and when all the stamps contained in any such book shall have been issued, the gauger of the district shall return the book to the collector with all the marginal stubs therein.]

(a) The stamps will be issued to collectors upon their requisitions in such numbers as may be required, and will be charged to them at the full value of the stamps, or at the full value of the tax on the number of gallons represented on the stamps and coupons.

It is the duty of the collector to return to the Office of Internal Revenue any book of marginal stubs as soon as the stamps contained therein have been used; and when he has accounted for the tax on the number of gallons represented on the stamps and coupons that were contained in any book of tax-paid stamps, there will be allowed a commission of half of one per centum on the amount of the tax, to be equally divided between the assessor and collector.

The books containing any other than the tax-paid stamps may be entrusted by the collector to a gauger whenever he may deem it necessary so to do, and he may require such gauger to give security to return or account for all such stamps. Such gauger must make a daily report to the assessor and collector on Form 118 of all such stamps used by him and for whom used, and from these reports the assessor will, on the first day of each month, assess the person for whom they were used at the rate of twenty-five cents for each stamp used during the preceding month, and return the same to the collector for collection; these assessments should be transmitted to the collector with the monthly list, but should not be included in the aggregate of the list nor receipted for on Form 23½. When all the stamps contained in these books shall have been issued, the collector will return the books with marginal stubs therein to the Office of Internal Revenue.

The stubs must in no case be removed from any of the books, and all unused coupons must remain attached to the marginal stubs. No coupon will be of any value when detached from the stamp or stub. Collectors will be credited with the amount of the tax on the number of gallons represented by all coupons attached to the stubs returned to the Office of Internal Revenue.

The tax-paid stamps, as well as all other stamps, must be signed by the collector in his own handwriting, and the blanks in the stubs must be filled so as to preserve a perfect record of the use of the stamps when attached.

The amount actually received from all kinds of stamps for spirits should be reported monthly on Form 90, and also on Form 51, in the same manner that receipts from the sale of beer stamps are now reported.

If the book of stamps is not in the possession of the gauger, the collector or deputy collector will issue the stamps upon the report of the gauger in detail of his inspection, keeping an account of the number of stamps so furnished to each distiller, and will report to the assessor at the end of each month the number of stamps other than tax-paid stamps so issued by him and to whom issued. 9 I. R. R. 158.

It is contrary to the spirit and intention if not the letter of the law for any person other than a collector to sell stamps for distilled spirits. 11 I. R. R. 57.

Penalty for Fraudulently affixing Stamps.

[SEC. 29. (July 20, 1868.) *And be it further enacted,* That any revenue officer who shall affix or cancel, or cause or permit to be affixed or cancelled, any stamp relating to distilled spirits required or provided for in this act, in any other manner or in any other place, or who shall issue the same to any other person than as provided by law, or regulation made in pursuance thereof, or who shall knowingly affix or permit to be affixed any such stamp to any cask or package of spirits of which the whole or any part has been distilled, rectified, compounded, removed, or sold, in violation of law, or which has in any manner escaped payment of tax due thereon, shall, for every such offence, be fined not less than five hundred dollars nor more than three thousand dollars, and be imprisoned for not less than six months nor more than three years.]

Reduction of Producing Capacity.

[SEC. 30. (July 20, 1868.) *And be it further enacted,* That if any distiller shall desire to reduce (*a*) the producing capacity of his distillery, he shall give notice of such intention in writing to said assessor, stating the quantity of spirits which he desires thereafter to manufacture or produce every twenty-four hours, and thereupon said assessor shall proceed, at the expense of the distiller, to reduce and limit the producing capacity of the distillery to the quantity stated in said notice, by placing upon a sufficient number of the fermenting tubs close-fitting covers, which shall be securely fastened by nails, seals, and otherwise, and in such manner as to prevent the use of such tubs without removing said covers or breaking said seals, and shall adopt such other precautions as shall be prescribed by the Commissioner of Internal Revenue to reduce the capacity of said distillery. And any person who shall break, injure, or in any manner tamper with any lock, seal, or other fastening applied to any furnace, still, or fermenting tub, or other vessel, in pursuance of the provisions of this act, or who shall open or attempt to open any door, tub, or other vessel which shall have been locked or sealed, or otherwise closed or fastened as herein provided, or who shall use any furnace, still, or fermenting tub, or other vessel which shall be so locked, sealed, or fastened, shall be deemed guilty of a felony, and, on conviction, shall be fined not less than one thousand dollars nor more than five thousand dollars, and imprisoned for not less than one year nor more than three years.]

(a) Any distiller desiring to reduce the producing capacity of his distillery must give notice of such intention in writing to the assessor, stating the quantity of spirits which he desires thereafter to manufacture every twenty-four hours; and thereupon the assessor is required, at the expense of the distiller, to reduce and limit the producing capacity of the distillery to the quantity stated in his notice, by placing upon a sufficient number of tubs close-fitting covers securely fastened by nails, seals, and otherwise, so as to prevent the use of such tubs without removing said covers or breaking said seals; and whenever he shall be of opinion that other precautions are necessary, he will report the case to the Commissioner for instructions. Where a distiller desires to reduce his capacity without reducing the number of his tubs, it can only be done by cutting down his tubs to the size required. The mere cutting out of one or more staves is not sufficient, but the whole tub must be cut off. In all cases of a reduction of capacity, an immediate report will be made to the Commissioner by the assessor, showing what action has been taken and the proportionate reduction of capacity thereby effected. 9 I. R. R. 149.

Inspection of Worm Tubs.

[SEC. 31. (July 20, 1868.) *And be it further enacted*, That whenever any officer shall require that the water contained in any worm tub in a distillery, at any time when the still shall not be at work, shall be drawn off, and the tub and worm cleansed, the water shall forthwith be drawn off, and the tub and worm cleansed by the distiller or his workmen accordingly; and the water shall be kept and continued out of such worm tub for the space of two hours, or until the officer has finished his examination thereof; and for any refusal or neglect to comply with the requisition of the officer in this behalf, or the provision in this clause contained, the distiller shall forfeit the sum of one thousand dollars, and it shall be lawful for the officer to draw off such water, or any portion of it, and to keep the same drawn off for so long a time as he shall think necessary.]

Officers may enter Distillery by Day or Night.

[SEC. 32. (July 20, 1868.) *And be it further enacted*, That it shall be lawful for any revenue officer, at all times, as well by night as by day, to enter (a) into any distillery, or building, or place, used for the business of distilling, or in connection therewith, for storage or other purposes, and to examine, gauge, measure, and take an account of every still or other vessel or utensil of any kind, and of all low wines, and of the quantity and gravity of all mash, wort, or beer, and of all yeast, or other compositions for exciting or producing fermentation in any mash or beer, and of all spirits and of all materials for making or distilling spirits, which shall be in any such distillery or premises, or in the possession of the distiller; and if any revenue officer, or any person called by him to his aid, shall be hindered, obstructed, or prevented by any distiller or by any workman or other person acting for such distiller or in his employ, from entering into any such distillery, or building, or place as aforesaid; or if any such officer shall be, by the distiller, or his workman, or any person in his employ, prevented or hindered from, or opposed, or obstructed, or molested in the performance of his duty under this act, in any respect, the distiller shall forfeit the sum of one thousand dollars. If any officer, having demanded admittance into a distillery or premises of a distillery, and having declared his name and office, shall not be admitted into such distillery or premises by the distiller or other person having charge of the same, it shall be lawful for such officer, at all times, as well by night as by day, to break open by force any of the doors or windows, or to break through any of the walls of such distillery or premises necessary to be broken open or through, to enable him to enter the said distillery or premises; and the distiller shall forfeit the sum of one thousand dollars.]

(a) The law does not contemplate a forcible entry when the property is in the possession of the marshal. U. S. v. England, 7 I. R. R. 158.

Facilities for Examination to be Afforded.

[SEC. 33. (July 20, 1868.) *And be it further enacted*, That on the demand of any revenue officer, every distiller, rectifier, or compounder of spirits shall furnish strong, safe, and convenient ladders, of sufficient length to enable the officer to examine and gauge any vessel or utensil in such distillery or premises; and shall, at all times, when required, supply all assistance, lights, ladders, tools, staging, or other things necessary for inspecting the premises, stock, tools, and apparatus belonging to such person, and shall open all doors, and open for examination all boxes, packages, and all casks, barrels, and other vessels not under the control of a revenue officer in charge, under a penalty of five hundred dollars for every refusal or neglect so to do.]

Search to detect Fraudulent Distillation.

[SEC. 34. (July 20, 1868.) *And be it further enacted*, That it shall be lawful for any revenue officer, and any person acting in his aid, to break up the ground on any part of the distillery or premises of a distiller, rectifier, or compounder of liquors, or any ground adjoining or near to such distillery or premises, or any wall or partition thereof, or belonging thereto, or other place, to search for any pipe, cock, private conveyance, or utensil; and upon finding any such pipe or conveyance leading therefrom or thereto, he may break up any ground, house, wall, or other place through or into which such pipe or other conveyance shall lead, and break or cut away such pipe or other conveyance, and turn any cock, or examine whether such pipe or other conveyance may convey or conceal any mash, wort, or beer, or other liquor which may be used for distillation of low wines or spirits from the sight or view of the officer, so as to prevent or hinder him from taking a true account thereof.]

Work on Sunday Prohibited.

[SEC. 35. (July 20, 1868.) *And be it further enacted*, That no malt, corn, grain, or other material shall be mashed, nor any wash, wort, or beer brewed or made, nor any still used by a distiller at any time between the hour of eleven in the afternoon of any Saturday and the hour of one in the forenoon of the next succeeding Monday; and any person who shall violate the provisions of this section shall be liable to a penalty of one thousand dollars.]

Fraudulent Removal of Spirits.

[SEC. 36. (July 20, 1868.) *And be it further enacted*, That all distilled spirits found elsewhere than in a distillery or distillery warehouse, not having been removed therefrom according to law, shall be forfeited (a) to the United States. And in case of the seizure of any distilled spirits found elsewhere than in a distillery, distillery warehouse, or other warehouse for distilled spirits authorized by law, or in the store or place of business of a rectifier, or of a wholesale liquor dealer, or of a compounder of liquors, or in transit from any one of said places; and in case of the seizure of any distilled spirits found in any one of the places aforesaid, or in transit therefrom, which shall not have been received into or sent out therefrom in conformity to law, or in regard to which any of the entries required by law to be made in the books of the owner of such spirits or of the storekeeper, wholesale dealer, rectifier, or compounder, have not been made at the time or in the manner required, or in respect to which the owner or person having possession, control, or charge of said spirits shall have omitted to do any act required to be done, or shall have done or committed any act prohibited in regard to said spirits, the burden of proof shall be upon the claimant of said spirits to show that no fraud has been committed, and that all the requirements of the law in relation to the payment of the tax have been complied with. And any person who shall remove, or shall aid or abet in the removal of any distilled spirits on which the tax has not been paid, to a place other than the distillery warehouse provided by law, or who shall conceal or aid in the concealment of any spirits so removed, or who shall remove or shall aid or abet in the removal of any distilled spirits from any distillery warehouse, or other warehouse for distilled spirits authorized by law, in any manner other than is provided by law, or who shall conceal, or aid in the concealment of any spirits so removed, shall be liable to a penalty of double the tax imposed on such distilled spirits so removed or concealed, and shall, on conviction, be fined not less than two hundred dollars nor more than five thousand dollars, and imprisoned not less than three months nor more than three years.]

(*a*) Dealers in spirits must see that all spirits received by them are properly stamped and branded. The plea of innocence will not save spirits not properly stamped and branded from seizure. 9 I. R. R. 188.

This section does not apply to imported spirits. 9 I. R. R. 36.

The burden is upon the claimant to show that the requirements of the law to enable spirits to be removed from the warehouse have been complied with, and proof that the barrels appear to be properly marked and branded is not sufficient. The term "according to law" includes payment of the tax. U. S. *v.* 508 Bbls. 5 I. R. R. 190; s. c. 5 Blatch. 407; U. S. *v.* 6 Bbls. 6 I. R. R. 187; s. c. 5 Blatch. 542; U. S. *v.* 50 Bbls. 11 I. R. R. 94; U. S. *v.* 78 Bbls. 7 I. R. R. 4; U. S. *v.* 8 Casks, 7 I. R. R. 4.

The place where spirits are distilled is the distillery, not the tail of the worm nor the still itself, but the distillery premises. The removal which is made a crime by the statute is the removal of spirits from the distillery building otherwise than into a bonded warehouse. If any one of the defendants who had an interest in the establishment and in the profits of working it, directed, prescribed, ordered, or set on foot the removal of the spirits, then he may be convicted of such removal even though he was not personally present; and if any one of the defendants, whether he had a personal interest in the spirits or not, was personally concerned in handling, on any occasion, the means of removing the spirits, if he opened the door with the key, handled the hose, or screwed on the hose, and that was followed by the removal of the spirits by those means, then he is guilty of removing spirits and not merely of aiding and abetting in their removal. Any other help or assistance than this described, is an aiding in a removal. And giving any encouragement or instigation to commit a removal other than what has been defined to be a removal or an aiding in a removal, is an abetting in a removal. U. S. *v.* Blaisdell et al. 9 I. R. R. 82.

The court has authority in a criminal case to discharge a jury from giving a verdict, whenever there is a manifest necessity for the act, or when the ends of public justice would otherwise be defeated, and it may do this without the consent of the defendant; but the court is to exercise a sound discretion on the subject and to use the power with the greatest caution, under urgent circumstances, and for very plain and obvious causes. The court may discharge a jury with the consent of the defendant in a case which falls short of being one of manifest necessity. If the district attorney does not choose to proceed with the trial after a jury has been sworn and impannelled, the defendant has a right then and there to ask for a verdict of acquittal. The defendant is not bound to ask at the time for such a verdict. He has a right afterwards to claim that what took place was in effect such a verdict. In then determining whether the discharge of the jury was made from manifest necessity, or with the consent of the defendant, the court must he governed as to the facts by its own minutes. It would be very unsafe and lead to endless disputes and probable injustice for the court, in matters of this kind, to act upon its own recollection or on the affidavits of witnesses, especially after a lapse of time. U. S. *v.* Watson et al. 8 I. R. R. 170; s. c. 1 A. L. T. (C. R.) 131.

In making up the record of the evidence with a view to a motion for a new trial, the testimony should be reduced to the form of a narrative, and not taken by way of question and answer. U. S. *v.* 508 Bbls. 5 I. R. R. 190; s. c. 5 Blatch. 407.

Spirits to be Removed by Day.

[SEC. 37. (July 20, 1868.) *And be it further enacted,* That no person shall remove any distilled spirits at any other time than after sun-rising and before sun-setting, in any cask or package containing more than ten gallons, from any premises or building in which the same may have been distilled, redistilled, rectified, compounded, manufactured, or stored, and every person who shall violate this provision shall be liable to a penalty of one hundred dollars for each cask, barrel, or package of spirits so removed; and said spirits, together with any vessel containing the same, and any horse, cart, boat, or other conveyance used in the removal thereof, shall be forfeited to the United States.]

Penalty for creating Fictitious Proof.

[SEC. 38. (July 20, 1868.) *And be it further enacted,* That any person who shall add or cause to be added any ingredient or substance to any distilled spirits, before the tax imposed by law shall have been paid thereon, for the purpose of creating a fictitious proof, shall, on conviction, be fined not less than one hundred dollars nor more than one thousand dollars for each cask or package so adulterated, and imprisoned not less than three months nor more than two years, and every such cask or package, with its contents, shall be forfeited to the United States.]

Penalty for Evading Tax.

[SEC. 39. (July 20, 1868.) *And be it further enacted,* That any person who shall evade or attempt to evade the payment of the tax on any distilled spirits, in any manner whatever, shall forfeit and pay double the amount of the tax so evaded or attempted to be evaded; and any person who shall change or alter any stamp, mark, or brand on any cask or package containing distilled spirits, or who shall put into any cask or package spirits of greater strength than is indicated by the inspection mark thereon, or who shall fraudulently use any cask or package having any inspection mark or stamp thereon, for the purpose of selling other spirits or spirits of quantity or quality different from the spirits previously inspected therein, shall forfeit and pay the sum of two hundred dollars for every cask or package on which the stamp or mark is so changed or altered or which is so fraudulently used, and, on conviction, shall be fined for each such offence not less than one hundred dollars nor more than one thousand dollars, and imprisoned not less than one month nor more than one year.]

Penalty for using False Weights.

[SEC. 40. (July 20, 1868.) *And be it further enacted*, That any person who shall knowingly use any false weights or measures in ascertaining, weighing, or measuring the quantities of grain, meal, or vegetable materials, molasses, beer, or other substances to be used for distillation, or who shall destroy, break, injure, or tamper with any lock or seal which may be placed on any cistern-room or building, by the duly authorized officers of the revenue, or shall open said lock or seal, or the door to such cistern-room or building, or shall in any manner gain access to the contents therein in the absence of the proper officer, shall, on conviction, be fined not less than five hundred dollars nor more than five thousand dollars, and imprisoned not less than one year nor more than three years; and any person who shall use any molasses, beer, or other substance, whether fermented on the premises or elsewhere, for the purpose of producing spirits, before an account for the same shall have been registered in the proper record book provided for that purpose, shall forfeit and pay the sum of one thousand dollars for each and every offence so committed.]

Detention of Suspected Spirits.

[SEC. 41. (July 20, 1868.) *And be it further enacted*, That it shall be lawful for any internal revenue officer to detain any cask or package containing, or supposed to contain, distilled spirits, when such officer has reason to believe the tax imposed by law upon the same has not been paid, or that the same is being removed in violation of law; and every such cask or package may be held by such officer at a safe place until it shall be determined whether the property so detained is liable by law to be proceeded against for forfeiture; but such summary detention shall not continue in any case longer than forty-eight hours, without process of law or intervention of the officer to whom such detention is to be reported.]

Bonding Distilleries that have been seized.

[SEC. 42. (July 20, 1868.) *And be it further enacted*, That no distillery nor distilling apparatus seized for any violation of law shall be released to the claimant or any intervening party before judgment, except in case of a distillery for which the special tax had been paid, and which has a registered producing capacity of one hundred and fifty proof gallons, or more, per day, on showing by sufficient affidavits that there are hogs or other live stock, not less than fifty head in number, depending for their feed on the products of said distillery which would suffer injury if the business of such distillery is stopped; such distillery in that case may be released to the claimant, or any other intervening party, at the discretion of the court, on a bond to be given and approved in open court, with two or more sureties, for the full appraised value of all the property seized, which value shall be ascertained by three competent appraisers to be designated and appointed by the court. In case of the seizure of and judgment of forfeiture against any distillery used or fit for use in the production of distilled spirits, having a registered producing capacity of less than one hundred and fifty gallons per day, or of any distillery for the non-payment of the special tax, the still, stills, doubler, worm, worm tub, and all mash tubs and fermenting tubs shall be so destroyed as to prevent the use of the same, or any part thereof, for the purpose of distilling; and the materials shall be sold as in case of other forfeited property.]

Obliteration of Stamps, Marks, &c.

[SEC. 43. (July 20, 1868.) *And be it further enacted*, That it shall be the duty of every person who empties or draws off, or causes to be emptied or drawn off, any distilled spirits from a cask or package bearing any mark, brand, or stamp required by law, at the time of emptying such cask or package, to efface and obliterate (*a*) said mark, stamp, or brand. Any such cask or package from which said mark, brand, and stamp is not so effaced and obliterated, as herein required, shall be forfeited to the United States, and may be seized by any officer of internal revenue wherever found. Any railroad company, or other transportation company, or person, who shall receive, or transport, or have in possession with intent to transport, or with intent to cause or procure to be transported, any such empty cask or package, or any part thereof, having thereon any brand, mark, or stamp required by law to be placed on any cask or package containing distilled spirits, shall forfeit three hundred dollars for each such cask or package, or any part thereof, so received or transported, or had in possession with the intent aforesaid; and any boat, railroad car, cart, dray, wagon, or other vehicle, and all horses or other animals used in carrying or transporting the same, shall be forfeited to the United States.

Any person who shall fail or neglect to efface and obliterate said mark, stamp, or brand, at the time of emptying such cask or package, or who shall receive any such cask or package, or any part thereof, with the intent aforesaid, or who shall transport the same, or knowingly aid or assist therein, or who shall remove any stamp provided by this act from any cask or package containing or which had contained distilled spirits, without defacing and destroying the same at the time of such removal, or who shall aid or assist therein, or who shall have in his possession any such stamp so removed as aforesaid, or have in his possession any cancelled stamp, or any stamp which has been used, or which purports to have been used, upon any cask or package of distilled spirits, shall be deemed guilty of a felony, and, on conviction, shall be fined not less than five hundred dollars nor more than ten thousand dollars, and imprisoned not less than one year nor more than five years.]

(a) The essence of the requirement of this section is, that the stamp shall be effaced and obliterated at the time any distilled spirits are emptied or drawn off from the cask or package, so that there shall be no opportunity given for the commission of fraud. It is of no consequence what the intention of the defendant was. It is of no consequence that he himself never sold an empty barrel or parted with one until he had obliterated the stamps upon it. There is no discretion given to the court whether to fine or imprison for the offence. The offender must be fined and also imprisoned. U. S. v. Quantity of Spirits, 11 I. R. R. 3.

Where a clerk has emptied some barrels, carried them to a room where such are kept, and is in the act of effacing the stamps and obliterating the marks when the whole stock is seized by the revenue officer, and he is thus prevented from effacing the stamps and marks, in contemplation of law the stamps and brands are effaced. U. S. v. 10 Bbls. 11 I. R. R. 5.

Penalty for Distilling without paying Special Tax.

[SEC. 44. (July 20, 1868.) *And be it further enacted*, That any person who shall carry on the business of a distiller, rectifier, compounder of liquors, wholesale liquor dealer, retail liquor ufacturer of stills, without having paid the special tax (*a*) as required by law, or who shall carry on the business of a distiller without having given bond as required by law, or who shall engage in or carry on the business of a distiller, with intent to defraud the United States of the tax on the spirits distilled by him, or any part thereof, shall, for every such offence, be fined not less than one thousand dollars nor more than five thousand dollars, and imprisoned not less than six months nor more than two years.

And all distilled spirits or wines, and all stills or other apparatus, fit or intended to be used for the distillation or rectification of spirits, or for the compounding of liquors, owned by such person, wherever found, and all distilled spirits or wines, and personal property found in the distillery or rectifying establishment, or in the store or other place of business of the compounder, or in any building, room, yard, or inclosure connected therewith, and used with or constituting a part of the premises; and all the right, title, and interest of such person in the lot or tract of land on which such distillery is situated, and all right, title, and interest therein of every person who knowingly has suffered or permitted the business of a distiller to be there carried on, or has connived at the same; and all personal property owned by or in possession of any person who has permitted or suffered any building, yard, or inclosure, or any part thereof, to be used for purposes of ingress or egress to or from such distillery which shall be found in any such building, yard, or inclosure, and all the right, title, and interest of every person in any premises used for ingress or egress to or from such distillery, who has knowingly suffered or permitted such premises to be used for such ingress or egress, shall be forfeited to the United States.]

(*a*) To support the charge of violating this section, it is not necessary to aver or prove that the defendant had registered his still or given notice of his intention to distil, but only that he was engaged in the business of a distiller in any of the ways or by any of the means specified in the definition of a distiller as given by the law, without having paid the special tax or given the required bond. It applies to mere illicit distilling. U. S. *v.* Mathoit, 11 I. R. R. 158.

Three distinct offences are created by this section. The forfeiture of real estate is confined to distillers, but not so as to the spirits and apparatus for distillation, rectification or compounding of liquors found on the premises owned by the person carrying on either of the kinds of business enumerated. It is not necessary that the omission to pay the tax should have been done with an intent to defraud the United States. To constitute the offence but two things are necessary to be averred and proved: 1st, the carrying on the business; 2d, that the special tax was not paid as required by law. An averment that the defendant has not paid the special tax imposed by the act of July 20, 1868, is sufficient. U. S. *v.* Rectifying Establishment, 11 I. R. R. 46.

Congress can impose a tax on distilled spirits, and provide the processes and measures for collecting it. To make the defrauding of the government of the tax a cause of forfeiting the distillery premises is an obvious, suitable, and germane measure. The distillery is made a pledge to the amount of its value that the business of distilling in it shall be fairly carried on, and the owner by his written permit consents to this pledge. U. S. *v.* Distillery, 11 I. R. R. 174.

The forfeiture is limited to the distillery premises, *i. e.*, to such real estate and premises as were used in connection with or as auxiliary to the illicit business. It does not extend to adjoining lots and premises, though owned by the offender. U. S *v.* Lot of Land, 11 I. R. R. 126.

When separate offences are alleged, requiring a different judgment of forfeiture, they should be charged in different counts. U. S. *v.* Rectifying Establishment, 11 I. R. R. 45.

Books to be Kept by Rectifiers, Wholesale Dealers, &c.

[SEC. 45. (July 20, 1868.) *And be it further enacted,* That every rectifier, wholesale liquor dealer, and compounder of liquors, shall provide himself with a book, (*a*) to be prepared and kept in such form as shall be prescribed by the Commissioner of Internal Revenue, and shall, on the same day on which he receives any spirits, and before he shall draw off any part thereof, or add water or anything thereto, or in any respect alter the same, enter in such book, and in the proper columns respectively prepared for the purpose, the date when, the name of the person or firm from whom, and the place whence, the spirits were received, by whom distilled, rectified, or compounded, and when, and by whom, inspected, and, if in the original package, the serial number of each package, the number of wine gallons and proof gallons, the kind of spirit, and the number and kind of adhesive stamps thereon; and every such rectifier, compounder, and wholesale dealer, shall, at the time of sending out of his stock or possession any spirits, and before the same shall be removed from his premises, enter, in like manner, in the said book, the day when, and the name and place of business of the person or firm to whom, such spirits are to be sent, the quantity and the kind or quality of such spirits, and also the number of gallons and fractions of a gallon at proof; and, if in the original packages in which they were received, he shall enter the name of the distiller and the serial number of the package. And every such book shall be at all times kept in some public or open place on the premises of such rectifier, wholesale dealer, or compounder of liquors, respectively, for inspection; and any revenue officer may make an examination of such book and take an abstract therefrom; and every such book, when it has been filled up as aforesaid, shall be preserved by such rectifier, wholesale liquor dealer, or compounder of liquors, for a period not less than two years; and during such time it shall be produced by him to every revenue officer demanding the same; and if any rectifier, wholesale dealer, or compounder of liquors, shall refuse or neglect to provide such book, or to make entries therein as aforesaid, or shall cancel, alter, obliterate, or destroy, any part of such book, or any entry therein, or make any false entry therein, or hinder or obstruct any revenue officer from examining such book, or making an entry therein, or taking any abstract therefrom; or if such book shall not be preserved or not produced by any rectifier, or wholesale dealer, or compounder, as hereinbefore directed, he shall pay a penalty of one hundred dollars, and, on conviction, shall be fined not less than one hundred dollars nor more than five thousand dollars, and imprisoned not less than three months nor more than three years.]

(a) Imported spirits are subject to the requirements of this section. 9 I. R. R. 36.

Books in the Form of No. 52 must be used for keeping an account of all distilled spirits received and sent out. 11 I. R. R. 129.

This section applies to every case of removal, whether upon sale or otherwise, from the premises of a rectifier, compounder, or wholesale liquor dealer. It is sufficient to enter each and every package exceeding five gallons, and to enter daily in aggregate all lesser quantities removed. 8 I. R. R. 172.

The term "wholesale dealers" is used only in the popular sense of the term, and refers to all who are wholesale dealers in that sense, having reference to the general character, and not to the annual amount of their sales. This section does not apply to those who are not wholesale liquor dealers, in the popular sense, but who are classed as such in law only, because their retail sales exceed $25,000 per annum. 9 I. R. R. 36.

The requirements of this section are perfectly plain and unmistakable. The party must make the entries every day, day by day, as he receives the spirits, upon the day on which he receives them. U. S. v. Quantity of Spirits, 9 I. R. R. 9; s. c. 2 A. L. T. (C. R.) 23.

The proper entries must be made, but it is wholly immaterial by whom they are made. They may be made by a clerk. If they are in fact made, the law is satisfied. But a party cannot excuse himself from responsibility for the proper entries not being made, by showing that he employed some one specially to make them, and directed the person employed to make them. U. S. v. 50 Bbls. 11 I. R. R. 94; U. S. v. Quantity of Spirits, 11 I. R. R. 3; s. c. 3 A. L. T. (C. R.) 10.

The statute requires the rectifier and wholesale dealer to make the entries respecting all spirits which come into their respective establishments from all sources whatever. It is not limited to spirits purchased and sold. U. S. v. 50 Bbls. 11 I. R. R. 94; U. S. v. 1 Bbl. 4 I. R. R. 146.

It is not necessary that the party should know that the thing done or omitted to be done is a violation of the law, and that he should purposely intend to violate the law. No man is under obligation to engage in these pursuits, but if he does, he is under obligation to inform himself of what the law requires or forbids, and if he fails so to do, must bear the consequences of his acts. U. S. *v.* Rectifying Establishment, 11 I. R. R. 45; U. S. *v.* 39 Bbls. 7 I. R. R 38; U. S. *v.* Dutcher, 7 I. R. R. 122; s. c. 1 A. L. T. (C. R.) 60; U. S. *v.* 1 Cask, 10 I. R. R. 93.

The offence is not a continuing one. It was complete when the entry was not made in the proper book on the day the spirits were purchased and received. No entry on a subsequent day could condone or wipe out the offence already committed, nor would the failure to make the entry on such subsequent day be a new offence or a repetition of the old one. U. S. *v.* 1 Cask, 10 I. R. R. 93.

The entries must be accurate. The forfeiture does not depend upon the entry being fraudulent or wilfully false, but upon the neglect or refusal to make a correct entry. The amount lost by the process of rectification and redistillation should not be entered as sold and delivered. U. S. *v.* 50 Bbls. 11 I. R. R. 94.

It is not necessary to aver the time the liquors were received or sent out, or from whom received or to whom sent. U. S. *v.* Rectifying Establishment, 11 I. R. R. 46.

Purchases of Quantities Greater than Twenty Gallons.

[SEC. 46. (July 20, 1868.) *And be it further enacted,* That it shall not be lawful for any rectifier of distilled spirits, compounder of liquors, liquor dealer, wholesale or retail liquor dealer, to purchase or receive (*a*) any distilled spirits in quantities greater than twenty gallons from any person other than an authorized rectifier of distilled spirits, compounder of liquors, distiller, or wholesale liquor dealer. Any person violating this section shall forfeit and pay one thousand dollars: *Provided,* That this shall not be held to apply to judicial sales, nor to sales at public auction made by an auctioneer who has paid a special tax as such.]

(*a*) The word "receive," as used in this section, means received for sale. A party who receives for storage only, and not for sale, does not incur the penalty. U. S. *v.* Fridenburg, 11 L R. R. 5.

Reinspection on Change of Package.

[SEC. 47. (July 20, 1868.) *And be it further enacted,* That all distilled spirits drawn from any cask or other package and placed in any other cask or package containing not less than ten gallons, (*a*) and intended for sale, shall be again inspected and gauged, and the cask or package into which it is so transferred shall be marked or branded, and such marking and branding shall distinctly indicate the name of the gauger, the time and place of inspection, the proof of the spirits, the particular name of such spirits as known to the trade, together with the name and place of business of the dealer, rectifier, or compounder, as the case may be; and in all cases, except where such spirits have been rectified or compounded, the name also of the distiller, and the distillery where such spirits were produced, and the serial number of the original package; and the absence of such mark or brand shall be taken and held as sufficient cause and evidence for the forfeiture of such unmarked packages of spirits.]

(a) The provisions of this section apply to all cases where distilled spirits are drawn from any cask or package and placed in any other cask or package containing not less than ten gallons, and intended for sale, without regard to the person by whom or the place where such change is made. 10 I. R. R. 82.

This section does not apply to imported spirits. Imported spirits, when subjected to any of the processes of rectification in the United States, loses its foreign identity, and should thereafter be treated as domestic spirits. 10 I R. R. 105.

The addition of pure water to spirits does not constitute rectification. When part of the spirits are withdrawn from a package, and the package filled with water, such package must be gauged, stamped, and marked or branded, the same as if the spirits had been changed to an entirely different package 10 I. R. R. 153.

The spirits may be removed into packages containing less than five gallons, and the same need not be gauged, stamped, or branded. 9 I. R. R. 5; 10 L R. R. 154.

A dealer must not mix spirits of the same kind from different distillers, or distilleries or rectifiers, as by so doing he places it beyond his power to mark and brand the new packages as required by this section. 10 I. R. R. 121.

This section applies to distilled spirits drawn from one cask and placed in another cask containing not less than ten gallons, and intended for sale, no matter by whom done or where done. U. S. *v.* Rectifying Establishment, 11 I. R. R. 45; U. S. *v.* 8 Bbls. 6 I. R. R. 124.

Tax on Imitations of Sparkling Wine.

[SEC. 48. (July 20, 1868.) *And be it further enacted,* That on all wines, (a) liquors, or compounds, known or denominated as wine, and made in imitation of sparkling wine or champagne, but not made from grapes grown in the United States, and on all liquors not made from grapes, currants, rhubarb, or berries grown in the United States, but produced by being rectified or mixed with distilled spirits or by the infusion of any matter in spirits, to be sold as wine or by any other name, there shall be levied and paid a tax of six dollars per dozen bottles, each bottle containing more than one pint and not more than one quart; or three dollars per dozen bottles, each bottle containing not more than one pint, and at the same rate for any quantity of such merchandise, however the same may be put up or whatever be the package. And any person manufacturing, compounding, or putting up such wines, shall, without previous demand, make return, under oath or affirmation, to the assistant assessor, on the first and fifteenth day of each and every month, or within five days thereafter, of the entire amount of such wines manufactured and sold or put up and sold during the first fifteen days of the month and the residue of the month, respectively, except when the wines so manufactured or put up are used exclusively by the family of the person manufacturing the same; and the tax herein imposed shall be payable at the time such return is made. And in case such manufacturer shall neglect or refuse to make such return within the time specified, the assessor shall proceed to ascertain the amount of tax due, as provided in other cases of a refusal or neglect to make returns, and shall assess the tax, and add a penalty of fifty per centum to the amount; which said tax and also said penalty shall be collected in the manner provided for the collection of tax on monthly and other lists. Any person who shall fraudulently evade or attempt to evade the payment of the tax herein imposed shall, on conviction, be fined not less than five hundred dollars nor more than five thousand dollars, and imprisoned not less than six months nor more than two years.]

(a) In order to subject wines to this tax it is necessary that they should be made in imitation of sparkling wine or champagne; and further, that they should not be made from grapes grown in the United States. Parties who use native wine made from grapes grown in the United States, and convert the same into sparkling wine, need not pay the tax. The use, however, of any portion of foreign wine would make the product liable to a tax. 8 I. R. R. 71.

There is a process of producing sparkling wine by mixing with a still wine sugar, with or without a syrup, commonly of spirits, which mixture results in the evolution of carbonic acid gas, and this gas produces the appearance and effect which constitutes the sparkle of the wine, and makes the wine a sparkling or champagne wine. The sparkle may also be produced directly and immediately by the infusion into the wine or mixture of wine of carbonic acid gas. This latter process produces what is called an imitation of sparkling wine. 7 I. R. R. 106.

Bitters prepared as an imitation wine must be put up according to this section. 10 I. R. R. 166.

Supervisors of Internal Revenue.

[SEC. 49. (July 20, 1868.) *And be it further enacted,* That the Secretary of the Treasury, on the recommendation of the Commissioner of Internal Revenue, may appoint not exceeding twenty-five officers, to be called supervisors of internal revenue, each one of whom shall be assigned to a designated territorial district to be composed of one or more judicial districts and territories, and shall keep his office at some convenient place in his district to be designated by the Commissioner, and shall receive in addition to expenses necessarily incurred by him and allowed and certified by the said Commissioner, as a compensation for his services, such salary as the Commissioner of Internal Revenue may deem just and reasonable, not exceeding three thousand dollars per annum.

It shall be the duty of every supervisor of internal revenue, under the direction of the Commissioner, to see that all laws and regulations relating to the collection of internal taxes are faithfully executed and complied with; to aid in the prevention, detection, and punishment, of any frauds in relation thereto, and to examine into the efficiency and conduct of all officers of internal revenue within his district; and for such purposes he shall have power to examine all persons, books, papers, accounts, and premises, and to administer oaths and to summon any person to produce books and papers, or to appear and testify under oath before him, and to compel a compliance with such summons in the same manner as assessors may do.

It shall be the duty of every supervisor of internal revenue as aforesaid to report in writing to the Commissioner of Internal Revenue any neglect of duty, incompetency, delinquency, or malfeasance in office, of any internal revenue officer within his district of which he may obtain knowledge, with a statement of all the facts in each case, and any evidence sustaining the same; and he shall have power to transfer any inspector, gauger, or storekeeper, from one distillery or other place of duty to another, or from one collection district to another, within his district, and may, by notice in writing, suspend from duty any such inspector, gauger, or storekeeper, and in case of suspension shall immediately notify the collector of the proper district and the Commissioner of Internal Revenue, and within three days thereafter make report of his action, and his reasons therefor, in writing, to said Commissioner, who shall thereupon take such further action as he may deem proper.]

The form of the summons to be issued and the mode of enforcing obedience to the same is similar to that used and practiced by assessors. Perry *v.* Newcome, 10 I. R. R. 20 ; In re Meador & Brother, 10 I. R. R. 74 ; s. c. 2 A. L. T. (C. R.) 140 ; Stannard *v.* Green et. al. 11 I. R. R. 134 ; s. c. 3 A. L. T. (C. R.) 133.

Supervisors, detectives, and surveyors of distilleries should make out their bills for compensation and expenses monthly. In each case a clearly and carefully defined and itemized statement of every expenditure, under its proper date, must be made out, and except for fair by railroad, or other public conveyance, and for meals while travelling, must be accompanied by receipted bills as vouchers. Hotel bills must be in detail, stating the number of days paid for, and the price per day. Charges for washing will not be allowed.

Surveyors of distilleries must state the name and location of distilleries surveyed; the time employed in making each survey, its computations and reports, and in travelling to and from the distillery. As a general rule, more than two days' time, in each case, will not be allowed for the performance of the duties in making a survey of a single distillery.

Each account must be sworn to that the account is just and true in all respects; that the services were actually rendered; that the distances charged were actually travelled at the dates therein specified; that none of such distances were travelled under any free pass on any railroad, steamboat, or other conveyance; and that the expenses charged therein were actually paid, and were necessary for the proper discharge of the official duties of the officer. 11 I. R. R. 84.

Appointment of Detectives.

[SEC. 50. (July 20, 1868.) *And be it further enacted*, That the Commissioner of Internal Revenue shall have power, whenever in his judgment the necessities of the service may require, to employ competent detectives, not exceeding twenty-five in number at any one time, to be paid under the provisions of the seventh section of the "Act to amend existing laws relating to internal revenue, and for other purposes," approved March 2, 1867, and he may, at his discretion, assign any such detective to duty under the direction of any supervisor of internal revenue, or to such other special duty as he may deem necessary, and that from and after the passage of this act no general or special agent, or inspector, by whatever name or designation he may be known, of the Treasury Department in connection with the internal revenue, except inspectors of tobacco, snuff, and cigars, and except as provided for in this act, shall be appointed, commissioned, employed, or continued in office, and the term of office or employment of all such general or special agents or inspectors now authorized as aforesaid under employment at the time of the passage of this act shall expire ten days after this act shall take effect.]

Suspension of Collectors and Assessors for Fraud.

[SEC. 51. (July 20, 1868.) *And be it further enacted*, That from and after the passage of of this act no assessor or collector shall be detailed or authorized to discharge any duty imposed by law on any other collector or assessor, but a supervisor of internal revenue may, within his territorial district, suspend any collector or assessor for fraud, or gross neglect of duty, or abuse of power, and shall immediately report his action to the Commissioner of Internal Revenue, with his reasons therefor in writing, who shall thereupon take such further action as he may deem proper.]

Duties of Storekeepers.

[SEC. 52. (July 20, 1868.) *And be it further enacted*, That there shall be appointed by the Secretary of the Treasury such number of internal revenue storekeepers (a) as may be necessary, the compensation of each of whom shall be determined by the Commissioner of Internal Revenue, not exceeding five dollars per day, to be paid by the United States, one or more of whom shall be assigned by the Commissioner of Internal Revenue to every bonded or distillery warehouse established by law; and no such storekeeper shall be engaged in any other business while in the service of the United States without the written permission of the Commissioner of Internal Revenue. Every storekeeper shall take an oath faithfully to perform the duties of his office, and shall give a bond, to be approved by the Commissioner of Internal Revenue, for the faithful discharge of his duties, in such form and for such amount as the Commissioner may prescribe. Every storekeeper shall have charge of the warehouse to which he may be assigned, under the direction of the collector controlling the same, which warehouse shall be in the joint custody of such storekeeper and the proprietor thereof, and kept securely locked, and shall at no time be unlocked and opened, or remain open, unless in the presence of such storekeeper or other person who may be designated to act for him as hereinafter provided; and no articles shall be received in or delivered from such warehouse except on an order or permit addressed to the storekeeper, and signed by the collector having control of the warehouse. Every storekeeper shall keep a warehouse book, which shall at all times be open to the examination of any revenue officer, in which he shall enter an account of all articles deposited in the warehouse to which he is assigned, indicating in each case the date of the deposit, by whom manufactured or produced, the number and description of the packages and contents, the quantities therein, the marks and serial numbers thereon, and by whom gauged, inspected, or weighed, and, if distilled spirits, the number of gauge or wine gallons and of proof gallons; and before delivering any article from the warehouse, he shall enter in said book the date of the permit or order of the collector for the delivery of such articles, the number and description of the packages, the marks and serial numbers thereon, the date of delivery, to whom delivered, and for what purpose, which purpose shall be specified in the permit or order for delivery; and in case of delivery of any distilled spirits, the number of gauge or wine gallons, and of proof gallons, shall also be stated; and such further particulars shall be entered in the warehouse books as may be prescribed or found necessary for the identification of the packages, to insure the correct delivery thereof, and proper accountability *thereof* [therefor].

A daily return shall be furnished by every storekeeper to the collector of the district of all articles received in and delivered from the warehouse during the day preceding that on which the return is made, a copy of which shall be mailed by him at the same time to the Commissioner of Internal Revenue; and each storekeeper shall, on the first Monday of every month, make a report in triplicate of the number of packages of all articles, with the several descriptions thereof respectively, as above provided, which remained in the warehouse at the date of his last report, and of all articles received therein and delivered therefrom during the preceding month, and of all articles remaining therein at the end of said month; one of which reports shall be by him delivered to the assessor of the district, to be recorded and filed in his office; one delivered to the collector having control of the warehouse, to be recorded and filed in his office; and one transmitted to the Commissioner of Internal Revenue, to be recorded and filed in his office.

Any internal revenue storekeeper may be transferred by the supervisor of the district or by the Commissioner of Internal Revenue from one warehouse to any other. In case of the absence of any internal revenue storekeeper by sickness or from any other cause, the collector having control of the warehouse may designate a person to have temporary charge of such warehouse, who shall, during such absence, perform the duties and receive the pay of the storekeeper for the time he may be so employed; and for any violation of the law he shall be subject to the same punishment as storekeepers. Any storekeeper or other person in the employment of the United States having charge of a bonded warehouse, who shall remove or allow to be removed any cask or other package therefrom without an order or permit of the collector, or which has not been marked or stamped in the manner required by law, or shall remove or allow to be removed any part of the contents of any cask or package deposited therein, shall be immediately dismissed from office or employment, and, on conviction, be fined not less than five hundred dollars nor more than two thousand dollars, and imprisoned not less than three months nor more than two years.]

(a) The storekeeper will keep the warehouse book on Form 101, and make daily returns in duplicate to the collector and Commissioner, and triplicate monthly reports to the Commissioner, the collector, and the assessor; and will also keep the books required by section 21, on Form 100. The books must be furnished to the storekeeper by the distiller. 9 I. R. R. 150.

No material must be received upon the distillery premises, nor be allowed to be stored in the distillery building, without the storekeeper's personal knowledge, and without his recording the same in the appropriate book of accounts. The absence of scales or facilities for determining the weight and measure will not be received as a sufficient excuse for not performing this duty, unless the official files shall show that the storekeeper has reported their absence, and taken all reasonable steps to have them furnished. No material must be allowed by him to be put in the mash-tubs until he has ascertained and recorded its weight and measure. He should, from time time, test the accuracy of the scales set for weighing off the meal put into the mash-tub, and any want of accuracy should be immediately reported to the collector. He should also carefully note the character and condition of the distillery apparatus, and report at once any condition of the apparatus not in accordance with requirements.

He is required to record the hour and minute when the beer is set in the fermenting tubs, to measure the dry inches, and calculate the quantity in each tub at that time and at 12, noon, on each day thereafter, and enter the same in his book. He must, also, see that the tubs are not emptied before the end of the fermenting period fixed by the distiller, and, when emptied, that they remain empty the full 24 hours required by law; and any irregularity on the part of the distiller, in either of these respects, must be forthwith reported to the collector and Commissioner.

He has charge of, and is held responsible for, the care of spirits deposited in the warehouse while under his charge, and will not allow any person access thereto, except when necessary, and in his presence. The distiller and his employees will be allowed access to the warehouse for the purpose of examining the spirits, repairing the cooperage, or changing the packages to prevent waste. These things, when necessary, must be done under the immediate supervision of the storekeeper.

He is to note carefully each package of spirits received into or taken out of the warehouse, making entry on his books of the serial number of the package, the serial number of the warehouse stamp, and the wine and proof gallons as per the actual inspection in gallons and fractions of gallons, and make daily report of the same, on Form 86.

The same report of actual inspection, or of gallons and fractions of gallons, and not of taxable gallons, should be made in the monthly warehouse report, Form 87, and the storekeeper's monthly report, Form 88, care being taken, in all cases where required, that the serial number of the package and serial number of the warehouse stamps are given, and in no case will the serial number of the tax-paid stamp be reported.

Storekeepers must make a daily report (Sundays excepted), on Form 86, during all the time they are in charge of the distillery warehouse, whether any spirits are entered into or withdrawn from the warehouse or not, and in no case must the transactions of more than one day appear on Form 86. If the distillery shall be permanently closed, the storekeeper will continue to make a daily report until all the spirits are withdrawn from the warehouse.

The monthly return, Form 87, must show the quantity of spirits in warehouse on the first day of the month, the quantity entered and withdrawn during the month (which will, of course, agree with the footings on his warehouse book and the aggregate of his daily reports), and the quantity in warehouse on the last day of the month, after the close of business for that day.

In making the monthly abstracts, Form 88, storekeepers will enter, first, the amount of mash on hand at the close of the preceding month; under this they will enter the quantity of material used during the month, with the quantity of mash produced therefrom; and from the amount of these two items deduct the quantity of mash on hand at the end of the month.

All spirits should be drawn from the receiving cisterns after distillation ceases, on the last day of the month, or on the morning of the first day of the month, so that the full product of the month may be known and determined. If drawn off on the first day of the month, the quantity drawn off and warehoused on that day will be entered on the distiller's tri-monthly return, the storekeeper's abstract, Form 88, and on Form 89, in a separate item. Each return must contain the name of the distiller, the number of the distillery, district, and State, and be signed by the storekeeper, with his post-office address, and properly endorsed on the back.

The quantity of mash in a tub at the time it is emptied is not the subject of an estimate, but is to be determined by actual measurement; and the quantity made and used during the month, or on hand at its close, can and must be determined in the same way.

Storekeepers will make the several reports required of them for the whole time they are on duty, whether the distillery is in operation or not.

Collectors are required to report to the Office of Internal Revenue the day on which each storekeeper in that district enters upon actual duty, and the day on which he ceases to do duty under his assignment, and the storekeeper will be paid accordingly. Where a distillery is under suspension and all spirits withdrawn from the warehouse, the storekeeper will report to the collector the fact of the withdrawal of the last of the spirits, on the day on which it occurs, and he will be considered as relieved from duty after that day. Whenever the assignment of a storekeeper is revoked, his account for that month must bear the endorsement of the collector, showing the date on which the revocation was delivered to the storekeeper. 10 I. R. R. 185.

The collector may order the storekeeper under assignment to duty, on Sundays or Sunday nights, as the case may be, and in each case the storekeeper is expected to remain on duty, at his post, during the hours of his assignment, and will be entitled to receive the compensation allowed, the same as for other days and nights. 11 I. R. R. 43.

Storekeepers are not entitled to compensation until assigned to duty, at a warehouse, by the Commissioner; after their assignment, they will be entitled to the rate of compensation fixed in their assignment, for the time during which they are actually employed. Where, during the temporary absence of the regular storekeeper, the collector designates some person to act for him, the person so designated will be entitled to the same rate of compensation as the regular storekeeper, for the time he is so employed; and the regular storekeeper will not be entitled to compensation for such time. The provision forbidding storekeepers to engage in any other business does not apply to a storekeeper who is not under actual assignment for duty.

Whenever work is suspended or resumed in a distillery, the assessor will notify the storekeeper; and where such suspension is for an indefinite time, or for a period exceeding one week, the assessor will immediately report the fact to the Office of Internal Revenue, and whether or not the services of the storekeeper can be dispensed with. This must be in a separate report. 9 I. R. R. 150.

The fact that spirits are in bond calls for a day-storekeeper at least, whether the distillery is running or not, and he must be paid the same as if the distillery was running. 12 I. R. R. 5.

The bills of storekeepers must be made out in triplicate, on Form 107, with all the blanks properly filled, and should be scheduled, on Form 56. Separate bills should be rendered for the time served at each warehouse, when the storekeeper has been assigned to more than one warehouse in a month. Whenever an assignment of a storekeeper is revoked, the collector must endorse, on the bill, the date on which his services ceased. 11 I. R. R. 83.

Payment of Salaries and Expenses of Storekeepers.

[SEC. 1. March 29, 1869.) *Provided further*, That after the passage of this act the proprietors of all internal revenue bonded warehouses shall reimburse to the United States the expenses and salary of all storekeepers or other officers in charge of such warehouses, and the same shall be paid into the treasury and accounted for like other public moneys.]

Collection of Salaries and Expenses of Storekeepers.

[SEC. 1. (July 12, 1870.) *Provided*, That after the passage of this act, the proprietors of all internal revenue bonded warehouses shall pay to the collector the current expenses and salaries of storekeepers or other officers in charge of such warehouses; and the same, when not paid, may be collected by the same means provided for the collection of other taxes; and all sums so collected in the nature of reimbursements (a) to the United States for payments on account of expenses and salaries of storekeepers or other officers in charge of such warehouses, or that may hereafter be so collected, shall be carried to the credit of the appropriation for salaries and expenses of collectors, storekeepers, and so forth; and the Commissioner of Internal Revenue and the accounting officers of the treasury are hereby authorized and directed to take the necessary steps to carry this proviso into effect : *And provided further*, That the President may, at his discretion, divide the States and Territories respectively into convenient collection districts, or alter the same, or unite two or more districts or two or more States or Territories into one district, and may exercise said power from time to time as in his opinion the public interest may require.]

(a) The sureties upon a distiller's bond, who executed the same before the passage of this act, are not liable for a failure on the part of the principal to reimburse to the government the salary and expenses of a storekeeper placed in charge of his distillery. It was not within the contemplation of the sureties that their principal would be required to refund money which the government, by the law existing at the time of the execution of the bond, was obliged to pay. If it were otherwise, there would be no limit to the responsibility that might in this manner be cast upon a surety. U. S. *v.* Singer et al. 18 Pitts. L. J. 5.

Collectors should demand and collect, monthly, from owners of bonded warehouses situated in their districts, such sum as may have been paid to storekeepers, or other officers in charge of such warehouses, for salary and other expenses, and deposit the same to the credit of the Treasurer of the United States. The appropriation should be named on the face of the certificate of deposit. The certificate of the assistant treasurer, or designated depository, as the case may be, will be taken in triplicate, the original of which will be forwarded direct to the Secretary of the Treasury, the duplicate filed in the Office of Internal Revenue with Form 119, and the triplicate retained for their own protection. Storekeepers will be required to sign triplicate vouchers, the original and duplicate to be disposed of as required by existing regulations, and the triplicate to be presented to the owner of the bonded warehouse, with demand for reimbursement; and surrendered and receipted in his favor, when the amount thereof shall have been reimbursed to the United States. The amount of the reimbursement thus made will be entered to the credit of the United States, in a separate account current, upon Form 119. This account current will be supported by the duplicate certificate of deposit, and will be mailed to the Office of Internal Revenue within fifteen days after the close of the month in which the reimbursement and deposit may have been made. 9 I. R. R. 150.

Internal Revenue Gaugers.

[SEC. 53. (July 20, 1868.) *And be it further enacted*, That there shall be appointed by the Secretary of the Treasury, in every collection district where the same may be necessary, one or more internal revenue gaugers (*a*) who shall each take an oath faithfully to perform his duties, and shall give his bond, with one or more sureties satisfactory to the Commissioner of Internal Revenue, for the faithful discharge of the duties assigned to him by law or regulations; and the penal sum of said bond shall not be less than five thousand dollars, and said bond shall be renewed or strengthened as the Commissioner of Internal Revenue may require. The duties of every such gauger shall be performed under the supervision and direction of the collector of the district to which he may be assigned, or of the collector in charge of exports at any port of entry to which he may be assigned. Fees for gauging and inspecting shall be prescribed by the Commissioner of Internal Revenue, to be paid to the collector by the owner or producer of the articles to be gauged and inspected; and said collector shall retain all amounts so received as such fees until the last day of each month, when the aggregate amount of fees so paid that month shall, under regulation to be prescribed by the Commissioner of Internal Revenue, be paid to the gauger or gaugers performing the duty. In no case, however, shall the aggregate monthly fees of any gauger exceed the rate of three thousand dollars per annum. All necessary labor and expense attending the gauging of any article shall be borne by the owner or producer of such articles. Every gauger shall, under such regulations as may be prescribed by the Commissioner of Internal Revenue, make a daily return, in duplicate; one to be delivered to the assessor, and the other to the collector of his district, giving a true account, in detail, of all articles gauged and proved or inspected by him, and for whom, and the number and kind of stamps used by him. Any gauger who shall make any false or fraudulent inspection, gauging, or proof, shall pay a penalty of one thousand dollars, and, on conviction, shall be fined not less than five hundred dollars nor more than five thousand dollars, and imprisoned not less than three months nor more than three years.]

(*a*) No gauger can be appointed a storekeeper, nor can he deputize or allow another person to act for him. The fees for gauging are to be collected by the collector of the district; and on the first day of each month he will pay to each gauger the amount of fees due him, for the work done during the preceding month, not exceeding, however, $250 in any month. The accounts of the gaugers are to be settled, and closed, monthly. It was not intended that money earned by one gauger should be given to another, who did not earn so much; nor, if a gauger's fees amount to more than $250, in any one month, can the balance be carried forward and paid to him in any succeeding month, when the aggregate fees for the month do not amount to that sum.

The collector may require prepayment of the fees before issuing the order to the gauger to gauge and inspect. This may not be practicable in the case of inspection at the distillery, as the number of packages cannot be precisely known until they are filled from the cistern; but in such cases, prepayment will not generally be necessary in order to secure the fees; but in other cases, the number of packages may be known before the order for gauging is given. But whether this or any other course is pursued for collection of gauging fees, the collector is required to receive and retain all amounts received as such fees, until paid to the gaugers.

The collector will report, monthly, to the Office of Internal Revenue, the amount of fees collected by him during the month; the amounts paid to the several gaugers, accompanied by the receipt of each gauger for the amount paid him, and the balance in his hands on the last day of the month. The balance must be deposited to the credit of the Treasurer of the United States, with the general collections, and be reported on Form 51, in an item by itself, the same as the monthly list; and, on Form 22, using a new number, 168. The collector should charge himself with the balance thus deposited and reported, on his quarterly account, Form 79.

From the daily returns of the gaugers, on Form 59, the assessor will transmit, monthly, to the Office of Internal Revenue, a consolidated report, showing the number of packages gauged, and the fees earned by each gauger during the month. Both reports, from the collector and the assessor, must be made promptly at the end of each month. Whenever it is found that the amount received by the collector, for gaugers' fees, exceeds the amount paid, the collector should make a specific report of the fact, to the Commissioner, and recommend such change in the rate of fees as will bring the receipts, as near as possible, to balance the expenditures. 9 I. R. R. 155.

The labor of handling and moving barrels or packages, and the cost of branding irons, furnaces, brushes, paste, and varnish, used in marking and stamping, are to be borne by the owner or producer. Each distiller should keep the articles named on hand. Travelling expenses are not included, and gaugers cannot collect them as part of the expense of gauging. 9 I R. R. 156.

Drawback on Alcohol and Rum.

[SEC. 54. (July 20, 1868.) *And be it further enacted,* That a drawback (a) shall be allowed upon alcohol and rum exported to foreign countries on which taxes have been paid under the provisions of this act when exported as herein provided for. The drawback allowed shall include the taxes levied and paid upon the alcohol or rum exported, not, however, exceeding sixty cents per gallon proof spirits, which shall be due and payable only after the proper entries and bonds have been executed and filed, and all other conditions complied with as hereinafter required, and thirty days after the vessel has actually cleared and sailed on her voyage with such spirits on board; and the Secretary of the Treasury shall prescribe such rules and regulations in relation thereto as may be necessary to secure the treasury of the United States against frauds. And if any person shall fraudulently claim or seek to obtain an allowance of drawback on any alcohol or rum, or shall fraudulently claim any greater allowance or drawback than the tax actually paid thereon, such person shall forfeit and pay to the government of the United States triple the amount wrongfully and fraudulently sought to be obtained, and, on conviction, shall be imprisoned not less than one year nor more than ten years. And any owner, agent, or master, of any vessel who shall knowingly aid or abet in the fraudulent collection or fraudulent attempt to collect any drawback upon rum or alcohol, or shall knowingly aid or permit any fraudulent change in the spirits so shipped, shall, on conviction, be fined five thousand dollars and imprisoned not less than one year, and the ship or vessel on board of which such shipment was made, or pretended to be made, shall be forfeited to the United States, whether a conviction of the master or owner be had or otherwise, and proceedings may be had in admiralty by libel for such forfeiture.]

(a) The allowance of drawback is limited to alcohol and rum; and no drawback is to be allowed, except upon the articles of alcohol and rum as known to commerce. All exportations of alcohol, to be entitled to drawback, must be in quantities not less than two thousand gallons, and in casks actually containing not less than thirty gauge or wine gallons. Rum can only be exported, with privilege of drawback, in quantities not less than thirty gauge or wine gallons each; and drawback will be allowed only on the basis and number of proof gallons actually exported. 8 I. R. R. 41.

For regulations, see 8 I. R. R. 41.

The exporter is not entitled to drawback when the character of the article has been changed after the payment of the tax thereon, or when it is not shipped in the original casks in which it was delivered from the distillery warehouse. 10 I. R. R. 170.

The forging and altering of a bond, in a custom house, established since March 3, 1825, cannot be punished otherwise than is provided for in this section. U. S. v. Barney et al. 3 I. R. R. 46; s. c. 5 Blatch. 294.

Regulations for Exportation of Alcohol and Rum.

[SEC. 55. (July 20, 1868.) *And be it further enacted,* That alcohol and rum may be exported with the privilege of drawback, in quantities not less than two thousand gallons, and in packages containing not less than thirty gallons each, on application of the owner thereof to the collector of customs at any port of entry, and under such rules and regulations, and after making such entries, and executing such bonds, and giving such other additional security, as may be prescribed by law and by the Secretary of the Treasury. The entry for such exportation shall be in triplicate, and shall contain the name of the person applying to export, the name of the distiller; and of the district in which the spirits were distilled, and the name of the vessel by which, and the name of the port to which, they are to be exported; and the form of the entry shall be as follows:

Export entry of distilled spirits entitled to drawback.

Entry of spirits distilled by ——— ———, in ——— district, State of ———, to be exported by ——— ——— in the ———, whereof ——— ——— is master, bound to ———.

And the entry shall specify the whole number of casks or packages, the marks and serial numbers thereon, the quality or kind of spirits as known in commerce, the number of gauge or wine gallons and of proof gallons; and amount of the tax on such spirits shall be verified by the oath or affirmation of the owner of the spirits, and that the tax has been paid thereon, and that they are truly intended to be exported to the port of ———, and not to be relanded within the limits of the United States; and said owner shall give his bond executed in duplicate, with one or more sureties satisfactory to said collector, conditioned that the principal named in said bond will export the spirits as specified in said entry to the port of ———, and that the same shall not be landed within the jurisdiction of the United States. The penal sum named in said bond shall be equal to not less than double the amount of the drawback on such spirits. For the discharge of any such export bond the same time shall be allowed, and the same certificates of landing and other evidence shall be required, as is or may be provided and required for imported merchandise exported from the United States, that the said spirits have been landed at the port named, or at any other port, beyond the jurisdiction of the United States. One bill of lading, duly signed by the master of the vessel, shall be deposited with said collector, to be filed at his office with the entry retained by him; one of said entries shall be, when the shipment is completed, transmitted, with the duplicate of the bond, to the Secretary of the Treasury, to be recorded and filed in his office. The lading on board said vessel shall be only after the receipt of an order or permit signed by the collector of customs and directed to a customs gauger, and after each cask or package shall have been distinctly marked or branded, by said gauger, as follows: "For export from U. S. A." The casks or packages shall be inspected and gauged alongside of or on the vessel, by the gauger designated by said collector, under such rules and regulations as the Secretary of the Treasury may prescribe; and on application of the said collector, it shall be the duty of the surveyor of the port to designate and direct one of the custom-house inspectors to superintend such shipment. The gauger, as aforesaid, shall make a full return of such inspecting and gauging, certifying thereon that the shipment has been made, in his presence, on board the vessel named in the entry for export, which return shall be indorsed by said custom-house inspector, certifying that the casks or packages have been shipped under his supervision on board said vessel; and the said inspector shall make a similar certificate to the surveyor of the port, indorsed on, or to be attached to, the entry in possession of the custom-house: *Provided, however*, That no claim for drawback shall be allowed on either of the said articles which shall have been exported as aforesaid prior to the time at which this act shall take effect.]

Withdrawal of Spirits from Bonded Warehouse.

[SEC. 56. (July 20, 1868.) *And be it further enacted*, That all distilled spirits in any bonded warehouse shall within nine months after the passage of this act be withdrawn from such warehouse, and the taxes paid on the same; and the casks or packages containing said spirits shall be marked and stamped, and be subject in all respects to the same requirements as if manufactured after the passage of this act. And any distilled spirits remaining in any bonded warehouse for a period of more than nine months after the passage of this act shall be forfeited to the United States, and shall be sold or disposed of for the benefit of the same in such manner as shall be prescribed by the Commissioner of Internal Revenue, under the direction of the Secretary of the Treasury. And whenever in the opinion of the Commissioner of Internal Revenue any distillery or other warehouse shall become unsafe or unfit for use, or the merchandise therein shall for any reason be liable to loss or great wastage, the Commissioner may discontinue such warehouse, and require that the merchandise therein shall be transferred to such other warehouse as may be designated by him within such time as he shall prescribe. Such transfer shall be made under the supervision of the collector, or such other officer as may be designated by the Commissioner; and the expense thereof shall be paid by the owner of the merchandise; and if the owner of such merchandise shall fail to make such transfer within the time prescribed, or to pay the just and proper expense of such transfer, as ascertained and determined by the Commissioner, such merchandise may be seized and sold by the collector, in the same manner as goods are sold upon distraint for taxes, and the proceeds of such sale shall be applied to the payment of the taxes due thereon, and the costs and expenses of such sale and removal, and the balance paid over to the owner of such merchandise.]

Extension of Time for Withdrawal.

[SEC. 1. (April 10, 1869.) That section fifty-six be amended so as to extend the time for withdrawing distilled spirits from bonded warehouse until the thirtieth of June, eighteen hundred and sixty-nine, but subject to an additional tax on each proof gallon deposited and bonded in warehouse at the rate of one cent for each month after the twentieth of April, eighteen hundred and sixty-nine, and until withdrawn; and any distilled spirits remaining in bonded warehouse after the thirtieth day of June, eighteen hundred and sixty-nine, shall be forfeited to the United States and disposed of as provided in said section.]

Stamping of Stock on Hand.

[SEC. 57. (July 20, 1868.) *And be it further enacted*, That any person owning, or having in his possession, any distilled spirits intended for sale, exceeding in quantity fifty gallons, and not in a bonded warehouse at the time when this act takes effect, shall immediately make a return, under oath, to the collector of the district wherein such spirits may be held, stating the number and kind of packages, together with the marks and brands thereon, and the place where the same are stored, together with the quantity of spirits, as nearly as the owner can determine the same. Upon the receipt of such return the collector, being first satisfied that the tax on said spirits has been paid, shall immediately cause the same to be gauged and proved by an internal revenue gauger, who shall mark, by cutting, the contents and proof on each cask or package containing five wine gallons or more, and shall affix and cancel an engraved stamp thereon, which stamp shall be as follows:

Stamp for stock on hand. No. ——.
Issued by ———— ————.

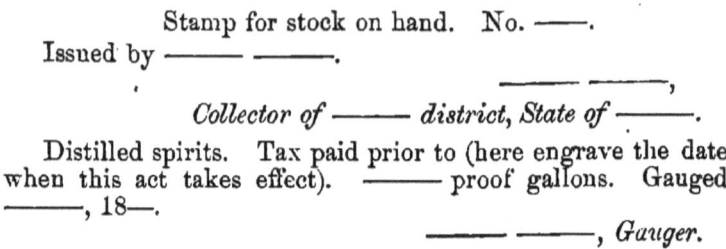

Collector of ———— *district, State of* ————.

Distilled spirits. Tax paid prior to (here engrave the date when this act takes effect). ———— proof gallons. Gauged ————, 18—.

———— ————, *Gauger.*

All distilled spirits owned or held by any person, as aforesaid, shall be included in the same return, and the gauging shall be continuous until all the spirits owned or held by such person are gauged and stamped, as aforesaid, and a report thereof in duplicate shall immediately be made by the gauger to the collector and assessor of the district, showing the number of packages, contents, and proof, of each package gauged and stamped; and one of said reports shall be transmitted by the collector to the Commissioner of Internal Revenue. No such spirits shall be gauged or stamped in any cistern or other stationary vessel. Any person owning or having in possession such spirits, and refusing or neglecting to make such return, shall forfeit the same; and all distilled spirits, found after thirty days from the time this act takes effect, in any cask or package containing more than five gallons (*a*), without having thereon each mark and stamp required therefor by this act, shall be forfeited to the United States. Any person who shall gauge, mark, or stamp, any cask or package of distilled spirits under the provisions of this section, or who shall cause or procure the same to be done, knowing that the same were manufactured or removed from warehouse subsequent to the taking effect of this act, or that the taxes thereon have not been paid, shall, on conviction, be fined not less than five hundred dollars nor more than five thousand dollars, and imprisoned not less than six months nor more than three years. All stamps required by this section shall be prepared, issued, and affixed upon casks and packages and cancelled in the same manner as provided for other stamps for distilled spirits in this act, and shall be charged at the rate of twenty-five cents for each stamp.]

(*a*) No package of spirits containing less than five proof gallons, whatever may be the number of wine gallons, is required to be stamped, unless the spirits are compounded in such a manner as that the compound will not admit of its strength being ascertained by the hydrometer, when five wine gallons will be taken to be five proof gallons. 11 I. R. R. 118; 10 I. R. R. 97.

The limitation, "found after thirty days from the time this act takes effect," shows that the spirits referred to are those which were on hand, and which were not in a bonded warehouse at the time the act took effect. These spirits the owner is allowed thirty days to have marked and stamped; besides, although the language of this provision is somewhat general, and might be applied to all distilled spirits literally, the connection in which it is found limits its application to the spirits mentioned in the section. As to distilled spirits generally, other sections of the statute must be consulted to ascertain the duties of distillers and others respecting them, and the forfeitures denounced against them. This section is confined by its spirit, and terms, to spirits intended for sale, on hand when the act took effect, and not in a bonded warehouse. U. S. v. 37 Bbls. 11 I. R. R. 125.

Sale of Forfeited Spirits.

[SEC. 58. (July 20, 1868.) *And be it further enacted,* That all distilled spirits forfeited to the United States, sold by order of court or under process of distraint, shall be sold subject to tax (*a*); and the purchaser shall immediately, and before he takes possession of said spirits, pay the tax thereon. And any distilled spirits condemned before the passage of this act, and in the possession of the United States, shall be sold as herein provided. And if any tax-paid stamps are affixed to any cask or package so condemned, such stamps shall be obliterated and destroyed by the collector or marshal after forfeiture and before such sale.]

(*a*) When a sale is made by the marshal, he will require the purchaser, before receiving possession of the spirits, to deliver to him the receipt of the collector of the district in which the sale is made, for the tax due upon the same, which receipt will be executed on Form 105. The purchaser, in order to obtain the receipt, will deliver to the collector a statement, to be signed by the United States marshal, giving the number of packages, the number of wine and proof gallons in each, with the date of sale, and the name of the purchaser; and the collector will issue, for every such cask or package, a tax-paid stamp, and cause the same to be affixed thereto. Upon the face of the receipt, Form 105, the collector will indorse the words "Tax-paid stamps issued," and upon the stamp "Tax on spirits sold by the United States marshal," with the date of the sale. Before the delivery of any spirits so sold, to the purchaser, the marshal will mark with a stencil plate, or brand with a branding iron, each cask or package, with his name, and official title, together with the date and place of sale, and the words "tax paid," and the number of proof gallons, with the name of the gauger who guaged the same, and the date of gauging.

The stamp, brand, or mark, which may be upon the barrels, at the time the spirits are condemned, is to be removed, or obliterated, except the tax-paid stamp, and the new tax-paid stamp, and mark of the marshal, should be so placed as not to cover, or deface, any of such stamps, marks, or brands. 10 I. R. R. 84.

Special Taxes.

[SEC. 59. (July 20, 1868; as amended April 10, 1869, § 1.) *And be it further enacted*, That the following special taxes shall be, and are hereby, imposed; that is to say:

Distillers producing one hundred barrels or less of distilled spirits, counting forty gallons of proof spirits to the barrel, within the year, shall each pay four hundred dollars; and if producing more than one hundred barrels, shall pay in addition four dollars for each such barrel produced in excess of one hundred barrels. And monthly returns of the number of barrels of spirits, as before described, distilled by him, shall be made by each distiller in the same manner as monthly returns of sales are made. Every person (*a*) who produces distilled spirits, or who brews or makes mash, wort, or wash, fit for distillation or for the production of spirits, or who by any process of evaporization separates alcoholic spirit from any fermented substance, or who, making or keeping mash, wort, or wash, has also in his possession or use a still, shall be regarded as a distiller: *Provided*, That a like tax of four dollars on each barrel, counting forty gallons of proof spirits to the barrel, shall be assessed and collected from the owner of any distilled spirits which may be in any bonded warehouse at the date of the taking effect of this act, to be paid whenever the same shall be withdrawn from such warehouse, under the provisions of the sixty-second section of this act: *Provided*, That no tax shall be imposed for any still, stills, or other apparatus, used by druggists and chemists for the recovery of alcohol for pharmaceutical and chemical or scientific purposes, which has been used in those processes.

Rectifiers (*b*) of distilled spirits, rectifying, purifying, or refining, two hundred barrels or less of distilled spirits, counting forty gallons of proof spirits to the barrel, within the year, shall each pay two hundred dollars, and shall pay fifty cents for each such barrel produced in excess of two hundred barrels. And monthly returns of the quantity and proof of all the spirits purchased and of the number of barrels of spirits, as before described, rectified, purified, or refined by him, shall be made by each rectifier in the same manner as monthly returns of sales are made. Every person who rectifies, purifies, or refines distilled spirits or wines by any process, and every wholesale or retail liquor dealer or compounder of liquors who has in his possession any still or leach tub, or who shall keep any other apparatus for the purpose of refining in any manner distilled spirits, shall be regarded as a rectifier.

Compounders of liquors shall each pay twenty-five dollars. Every person who, without rectifying, purifying, or refining distilled spirits, shall, by mixing such spirits, wine, or other liquor with any materials, manufacture any spurious, imitation, or compound liquors, for sale under the name of whiskey, brandy, gin, rum, wine, spirits, cordials, or wine bitters, or any other name, shall be regarded as a compounder of liquors.

[On and after the first day of May, eighteen hundred and sixty-nine, every person who rectifies, purifies, or refines distilled spirits or wines by any process other than by original and continuous distillation from mash, wort, or wash, through continuous closed vessels and pipes, until the manufacture thereof is complete, and every wholesale or retail liquor dealer who has in his possession any still or leach tub, or who shall keep any other apparatus for the purpose of refining in any manner distilled spirits, and every person who, without rectifying, purifying, or refining distilled spirits, shall, by mixing such spirits, wine, or other liquor, with any materials, manufacture any spurious, imitation, or compound liquors, for sale, under the name of whiskey, brandy, gin, rum, wine, spirits, cordials, or wine bitters, or any other name, shall be regarded as a rectifier, and as being engaged in the business of rectifying; and so much of the act, to which this is an amendment, as relates to compounders of liquors, and as is inconsistent with the provisions of the section hereby amended, be, and the same *are* [is] hereby, repealed.]

Retail dealers (*c*) in liquors shall pay twenty-five dollars. Every person who sells or offers for sale foreign or domestic distilled spirits, wines, or malt liquors, in less quantities than five gallons at the same time, shall be regarded as a retail dealer in liquors.

Wholesale liquor dealers shall each pay one hundred dollars. Every person who sells or offers for sale foreign or domestic distilled spirits, wines, or malt liquors in quantities of not less than five gallons at the same time, shall be regarded as a wholesale liquor dealer.

Dealers in liquors whose sales, including sales of all other merchandise, shall exceed twenty-five thousand dollars, shall each pay an additional tax at the rate of one dollar for every one hundred dollars of sales of liquors in excess of such twenty-five thousand dollars; and on every thousand dollars of sales of other merchandise shall pay at the same rate as a wholesale dealer; and such excess shall be returned, assessed, and paid in the same manner as required of wholesale dealers. But no distiller or brewer, who has paid his special tax as such, and who sells only distilled spirits or malt liquors of his own production, at the place of manufacture, in the original casks or packages to which the tax stamps are affixed, shall be required to pay the special tax of a wholesale dealer on account of such sales.

Distillers of brandy from grapes, peaches, and apples, exclusively, producing less than one hundred and fifty barrels annually, shall pay a special tax of fifty dollars, and, in addition thereto, the tax of four dollars per barrel of forty proof gallons.

But the payment of any special tax imposed by this act shall not be held or construed to exempt any person carrying on any trade, business, or profession from any penalty or punishment therefor provided by the laws of any State; nor to authorize the commencement or continuance of any such trade, business, or profession, contrary to the laws of any State, or in places prohibited by municipal law; nor shall the payment of any such tax be held or construed to prohibit or prevent any State from placing a duty or tax on the same trade, business, or profession for State or other purposes.

Manufacturers of stills shall each pay fifty dollars, and twenty dollars for each still or worm for distilling made by him. Any person who manufactures any still or worm to be used in distilling shall be deemed a manufacturer of stills.

(a) It is not only the person or persons who carry on the actual work of manufacturing distilled spirits that are distillers, but all persons having an interest in the business of distilling, or directly aiding the production of spirits for their use, or benefit, are considered distillers under the law, and are subject to, and amenable to, its provisions. The mere fact that a party knows that the law is violated is not sufficient; but if he has an interest in a mill, situated near the distillery, and the carrying on of the distillery would bring direct benefit to the mill in the way of toll; and if, in addition thereto, he has an interest in the land on which the distillery is erected, so as to give him the control of it, and knows that the law is violated, in the management thereof, then he may be considered a distiller. U. S. v. Howard, 11 I. R. R. 119.

Before a penalty can be visited upon the property or person of a distiller, the assessment must be made; and there should also be a demand for the tax, and a refusal by him. All that the law says is, that the special taxes shall be paid, and that they shall be paid as required by law. Precisely when they shall be paid is not distinctly set forth in the law; and the presumption is that they are payable when demanded by the proper officer. U. S. v. 35 Bbls. 9 I. R. R. 67; U. S. v. Trobe et al. 2 I. R. R. 133. Contra, U. S. v. Truesdell et al. 5 I. R. R. 102; U. S. v. Develin, 7 I. R. R. 45, 94; s. c. 1 A. L. T. (C. R.) 38; s. c. 6 Blatch. 71.

When a distiller has made an application to have the special tax assessed, he is not guilty of any offence under the law, unless it appears that he carried on the business of distilling after he was in default for non-payment. A distiller cannot be said to have carried on business without payment of the special tax, as required by law, so long as he has taken all necessary steps towards the ascertainment and payment of his special tax, and stands ready to pay it, as required by law. U. S. v. Shea, 6 I. R. R. 198; s. c. 1 A. L. T. (C. R.) 14; s. c. 5 Blatch, 545.

The use of a still by chemists to produce alcoholic spirits makes them liable. 6 I. R. R. 162.

The recovery of alcohol is not regarded by the law as distillation. It is not essential that the recovery should be made at the druggist's shop or place of business. 5 I. R. R. 168.

(b) A person becomes liable, not as a distiller but as a rectifier, by reason of passing whiskey upon which the tax has been paid through a still, for the sole purpose of improving it. 5 I. R. R. 59.

To mix distilled spirits, wines, or other liquors with any material, does constitute rectification, if by such mixing a spurious, imitation, or compound liquor is manufactured. To mix any material with distilled spirits, wine, or other liquor, which does not result in producing a spurious, imitation, or compound liquor, is not rectification. A spurious liquor is an imitation of, and held out to be, genuine. An imitation liquor is one that is an imitation of the genuine, and held out as such imitation. A compound liquor is any liquor composed of two or more kinds of spirits, or of one or more kinds of spirits mixed with any material which changes the original character of either, so as to produce a different kind, as known to the trade. The addition of water to spirits is not rectification. The mixing of spirits of different kinds is rectification. A party may become a rectifier by any manipulation of spirits which results in rectifying, purifying, or refining the same by any process other than by original and continuous distillation from mash, wort, or wash, through continuous closed vessels and pipes, until the manufacture thereof is complete. For instance, a party may mix a material with spirits, wine, or other liquor, which will not produce either a spurious, imitation, or compound liquor, but such mixing is nevertheless rectification, if it results in either purifying or refining the spirits, wine, or other liquors thus mixed. 10 I. R. R. 121.

A manufacturer of medicinal bitters who purchases raw or unrectified spirits, and rectifies the same prior to their use, is a rectifier. 10 I. R. R. 65.

Manufacturers of bitters who use rectified spirits, on which the tax has been paid, and who prefer to be taxed as rectifiers, must not put them up in the style of proprietary medicines, nor vend them as medicines. 11 I. R. R. 169.

(c) Brewers are exempt from special tax as dealers in liquors, with respect to their sales of liquors made at the brewery premises in the original casks or packages, to which the tax-paid stamps are required to be affixed. Brewers selling any other merchandise at their brewery should be assessed the proper special tax; but brewers who merely sell the refuse arising from the process of brewing, for the sake of getting rid of it, should not be required to pay special tax with respect to such sales. 10 I. R. R. 40.

Brewers are liable to special tax as liquor dealers with respect to their sales made at any other place than the brewery premises. 10 I. R. R. 177.

A distiller cannot sell his product in any way without paying tax therefor, after his tax receipt has expired. In such a case, the distiller would incur no liability on sales made through dealers on commission. 10 I. R. R. 154.

A rectifier cannot sell his distilled product at any place without paying tax as a liquor dealer. 10 I. R. R. 194.

A rectifier is not liable to tax as a dealer for simply transferring the liquor rectified by him to himself. His liability to tax as a dealer depends upon the character and amount of his sales to others. 11 I. R. R. 194.

218   U. S. INTERNAL REVENUE LAWS.

The words "five gallons," in this section, mean wine gallons, and not proof gallons. U. S. v. Wangarien et al. 11 I. R. R. 181; 11 I. R. R. 201.

A person who purchases liquor from a dealer in his own name, under an order from a customer, pays for the same, and ships it to the customer, and charges the amount on his bill, is a liquor dealer. But if he simply carries the order to the liquor dealer, who fills it, and ships the goods direct to the customer, no liability to tax as a liquor dealer is incurred. Persons who sell a mixture of soda-water, &c., and wine or other spirits, are regarded as liquor dealers. 11 I. R. R. 137.

Brewers who sell their products in any other manner than at the brewery premises, and in the original casks or packages, to which the tax-paid stamps are affixed, are liquor dealers. Brewers cannot sell their products from wagons about the streets. 11 I. R. R. 131.

No special tax as a liquor dealer is required of a town, city, or county agent appointed under what is popularly known as the "Maine Liquor Law," for sales made in strict accordance with the provisions of said law. 11 I. R. R. 145.

Persons who sell bitters and other alcoholic compounds, which are put up and sold as medicines, and which are properly stamped under Schedule C, are not liquor dealers. Persons selling bitters or other alcoholic compounds which are put up and stamped as rectified spirits should be held subject to tax as liquor dealers. 11 I. R. R. 1.

The liability to tax as a dealer depends upon sales. Every person who sells or offers for sale distilled spirits for himself or on commission is a dealer. 11 I. R. R. 17.

Auctioneers are liable to special tax as dealers in liquor with respect to their sales of liquor by auction. 10 I. R. R. 12.

Persons engaged in the manufacture of wine from grapes, berries, or fruits of their own growth are not subject to tax as liquor dealers for selling such wine at the place where the same is manufactured. Persons engaged in the manufacture of wine from grapes, berries, or fruits not of their own growth should pay special tax as liquor dealers when selling the same, whether their sales are made at the place of manufacture or otherwise. 10 I. R. R. 186.

Dealers in liquor cannot, under the payment of one special tax, sell at two or more places at the same time, nor can they delegate to another person as their agent the right of exemption from tax, except when selling at the place stated in their tax receipt. They will become liable to an additional and separate tax as dealers in liquors, if they also, at the same time, sell in the manner of a peddler. 10 I. R. R. 137.

A wholesale dealer cannot sell a package containing less than five gallons. The sale of several packages which separately contain less, but in the aggregate contain more, than five proof gallons cannot be made by a wholesale dealer. The sale of several packages of the same kind of spirits at the same time, each containing less than five proof gallons, but which in the aggregate contain more, cannot be made by a retail dealer; but he may sell several packages of different kinds of spirits, each containing less than five proof gallons, although the aggregate may be more. The sale of each different kind is considered as a separate sale. 10 I. R. R. 98.

The tax is to be imposed on all sales in excess of the amounts specified, at the proper rates, including not only units of hundreds and thousands, but fractions thereof. 10 I. R. R. 5.

Wholesale liquor dealers are entitled to a deduction from their returns of the sales made through other wholesale liquor dealers. 10 I. R. R 49.

A party who sells out his entire stock at one sale does not thereby become liable to tax as a wholesale dealer. 10 I. R. R. 169.

Dealers in liquor, whether wholesale or retail, whose sales, including sales of all other merchandise, exceed $25,000, are subject to an additional tax of one dollar for each hundred dollars of sales of liquors in excess of such $25,000, and at the same rate as a wholesale dealer on every thousand dollars of sales of other merchandise. When any liquor dealer's sales shall exceed $25,000, he must keep separate accounts of his sales of liquors and his sales of other merchandise, and must return them in separate items, and will be assessed one per cent. on his sales of liquors, and one-tenth of one per cent. on his sales of other merchandise, in excess of such $25,000. The exemption of distillers and brewers from special tax as dealers extends only to sales of liquors of their own production, made at the place of manufacture, and in the original casks or packages to which the tax-paid stamps are required to be affixed. The liquors must be delivered directly to the purchaser or his agent from the distillery or brewery premises. Dealers in liquors who sell in quantities less than five gallons, and also in quantities of five gallons and upward, must pay special tax both as wholesale and retail liquor dealers. 9 I. R. R. 157.

The additional tax of $1 on the sales of wholesale dealers in excess of $25,000 is a special tax, and not a tax on sales, and is not repealed. 12 I. R. R. 69.

TOBACCO, SNUFF, AND CIGARS.

Special Taxes.

Dealers (*d*) in leaf tobacco, whose annual sales do not exceed ten thousand dollars, shall each pay twenty-five dollars; and if their annual sales exceed ten thousand dollars, shall pay in addition two dollars for every thousand dollars in excess of ten thousand dollars. Every person shall be regarded as a dealer in leaf tobacco whose business it is for himself, or on commission, to sell, or offer for sale, leaf tobacco. And payment of a special tax as a wholesale dealer, tobacconist, manufacturer of cigars, or manufacturer of tobacco, shall not exempt any person dealing in leaf tobacco from the payment of the special tax therefor hereby required. But no farmer or planter shall be required to pay a special tax as a dealer in leaf tobacco for selling tobacco of his own production, or tobacco received by him as rent from tenants who have produced the same on his land.

Dealers in tobacco, whose annual sales exceed one hundred dollars and do not exceed one thousand dollars, shall each pay five dollars; and when their annual sales exceed one thousand dollars, shall pay in addition two dollars for each thousand dollars in excess of one thousand dollars. Every person whose business it is to sell or offer for sale manufactured tobacco, snuff, or cigars, shall be regarded as a dealer in tobacco. And any retail dealer, liquor dealer, or keeper of a hotel, inn, tavern, or eating-house, who sells tobacco, snuff, or cigars, shall pay, in addition to his special tax, the special tax as a dealer in tobacco.

Manufacturers of tobacco shall each pay ten dollars; and in addition thereto, where the amount of the penal sum of the bond of such manufacturer, required by this act to be given, shall exceed the sum of five thousand dollars, two dollars for each thousand dollars in excess of five thousand dollars of such penal sum. Every person whose business it is to manufacture tobacco or snuff for himself, or who shall employ others to manufacture tobacco or snuff, whether such manufacture shall be by cutting, pressing, grinding, crushing, or rubbing of any leaf or raw tobacco, or otherwise preparing raw or leaf tobacco or manufactured or partially manufactured tobacco or snuff, or the putting up for use or consumption of scraps, waste, clippings, stems, or deposits of tobacco, resulting from any process of handling tobacco, shall be regarded as a manufacturer of tobacco. But no manufacturer of tobacco shall be required to pay the special tax as a dealer in tobacco for selling the products of his own manufacture.

Manufacturers of cigars, whose annual sales shall not exceed five thousand dollars, shall each pay ten dollars, and when their annual sales exceed five thousand dollars, shall pay in addition two dollars for each thousand dollars in excess of five thousand dollars. Every person whose business it is to make or manufacture cigars for himself, or who shall employ others to make or manufacture cigars, shall be regarded as a manufacturer of cigars. No special tax receipt shall be issued to any manufacturer of cigars until he shall have given the bond required by law. Every person whose business it is to make cigars for others, either for pay, upon commission, on shares, or otherwise, from material furnished by others, shall be regarded as a cigar-maker. Every cigar-maker shall cause his name and residence to be registered, without previous demand, with the assistant assessor of the division in which such cigar-maker shall be employed; and any manufacturer of cigars employing any cigar-maker who shall have neglected or refused to make such registry shall, on conviction, be fined five dollars for each day that such cigar-maker so offending by neglect or refusal to register shall be employed by him.]

(*d*) Several partners buying and selling leaf tobacco at one place, as a or firm, are required to pay but one tax. 11 I. R. R. 98.

If a manufacturer of tobacco or a manufacturer of cigars sells at the same time the products of other manufacturers, he must pay a special tax as dealer. 9 I. R. R. 161.

A person who engages in the business of buying and selling leaf tobacco, though his sales are all made through an agent, factor. or commission merchant, is liable to this tax. 11 I. R. R. 49.

Every commission merchant selling leaf tobacco, and every other person who, as factor, agent, or consignee, sells tobacco on commission, is liable to this tax. 11 I. R. R. 17.

A peddler whose sales of manufactured tobacco, snuff, or cigars exceed $100 per annum is liable to a special tax as such, and also to the tax imposed by this section.

This tax is not in lieu of any other special tax, and the payment of another special tax—as, for instance, as commission merchant, manufacturer, auctioneer, &c.—does not relieve from the liability to pay this tax if the party also deals in tobacco. 10 I. R. R. 11.

A person who deals only in tobacco, snuff, or cigars, is only liable to this tax. 10 I. R. R. 25.

Retail dealers, keepers of hotels, inns, taverns, drinking or eating houses are liable to this tax, in addition to the other special taxes, if they sell tobacco, snuff, or cigars. 10 I. R. R. 58.

Every person whose business it is to make cigars for himself, or who employs others to make cigars, is a manufacturer of cigars. 10 I. R. R. 66.

Mode of Ascertaining Amount of Special Tax.

[SEC. 60. (July 20, 1868.) *And be it further enacted*, That in every case where it becomes necessary to ascertain the amount of annual or monthly sales made by any person on whom a special tax is imposed by this act, or to ascertain the excess of such sales above a given amount, such amounts and excesses shall be ascertained and returned (*a*) under such regulations and in such form as shall be prescribed by the Commissioner of Internal Revenue; and in any case where the amount of the tax has been increased by this act above the amount before paid by any person in that behalf, such person, except retail dealers, shall be again assessed and pay the amount of such increase from the taking effect of this act; and in any case where the amount of sales or receipts has been understated or underestimated by any person, such person shall be again assessed for such deficiency, and shall be required to pay the same, with any penalty or penalties that may by law have accrued or be chargeable thereon.]

(*a*) Dealers in leaf tobacco whose annual sales exceed $10,000, dealers in tobacco whose annual sales exceed $1,000, and manufacturers of cigars whose annual sales exceed $5,000, shall, on or before the 10th day of each month, make a return of the entire amount of their sales for the preceding month, and the tax on the excess of such sales above the given amount, as prescribed by law, will be assessed and returned for collection on or before the last day of the month. Whenever such sales are more or less than one thousand dollars, or an even number of thousand dollars, the fractional part of one thousand will be carried to the sales of the succeeding month.

Amount of Tax on Tobacco.

[SEC. 61. (July 20, 1868.) *And be it further enacted*, That upon tobacco and snuff which shall be manufactured and sold, or removed for consumption or use, there shall be assessed and collected the following taxes:

On snuff, manufactured of tobacco or any substitute for tobacco, ground, dry, damp, pickled, scented, or otherwise, of all descriptions, when prepared for use, a tax of thirty-two cents per pound. And snuff-flour, (*a*) when sold, or removed for use or consumption, shall be taxed as snuff, and shall be put up in packages and stamped in the same manner as snuff.

On all chewing tobacco, (*b*) fine-cut, plug, or twist; on all tobacco twisted by hand, or reduced from leaf into a condition to be consumed, or otherwise prepared, without the use of any machine or instrument, and without being pressed or sweetened; and on all other kinds of manufactured tobacco, not herein otherwise provided for, a tax of thirty-two cents per pound.

On all smoking tobacco, exclusively of stems, or of leaf, with all the stems in, and so sold, the leaf not having been previously stripped, butted, or rolled, and from which no part of the stems have been separated by sifting, stripping, dressing, or in any other manner, either before, during, or after the process of manufacturing; on all fine-cut shorts, the refuse of fine-cut chewing tobacco which has passed through a riddle of thirty-six meshes to the square inch by process of sifting, and on all refuse scraps and sweepings of tobacco, a tax of sixteen cents per pound.]

(*a*) The law taxes every kind of snuff or snuff flour prepared for use and sold or removed for use or consumption. It taxes snuff-flour prepared for use, and requires that it shall be put up in packages and the tax paid by stamps before it leaves the place of manufacture. 9 I. R. R. 57.

(*b*) The fact that a tax may have been paid on the cavendish or plug does not affect the liability of fine-cut tobacco manufactured from it. 9 I. R. R. 193.

The law does not require that there shall be any extended change in the natural leaf or any extended mode of preparation, or any process of reduction which cannot be performed by hand and without the aid of any machine or instrument. Therefore, all tobacco twisted by hand or prepared by any process, however simple, for consumption or use, must be packed as prescribed by law for manufactured tobacco; and the tax of 32 cents per pound paid thereon.

All scraps, waste, clippings, &c., put up for general sale and thrown upon the market for indiscriminate purchasers for use or consumption, will be regarded as manufactured tobacco, and will be required to be packed and the tax paid thereon. And any person purchasing scraps, waste, clippings, stems, sweepings, or broken and fragmentary tobacco, and manipulating the same by any process of cutting, pressing, grinding, crushing, rubbing, screening, or any other process, or putting up the same for use or consumption, will be held to be a manufacturer of tobacco. And any person who purchases raw or leaf tobacco, and in any way changes its condition and puts it up for use or consumption, will be held likewise to the special tax, and the specific tax payable by stamps.

Any process by which natural leaf tobacco is made into smoking tobacco which does not involve the stripping, butting, or rolling of the stems, or the separation of the stems from the leaf by sifting, stripping, dressing, or in any other manner, either before, during, or after the process of manufacturing may be employed, and the tobacco produced by such process will be liable to the tax of 16 cents.

But if the stems are stripped from the leaf, or butted or rolled, or if any portion of the stems are removed before, during or after the process of manufacturing, the tobacco produced by any process involving these conditions will be liable to a tax of 32 cents per pound. 10 I. R. R. 59.

All refuse of fine-cut chewing, or what are technically known as fine-cut shorts, to be entitled to the 16 cents per pound tax must actually have passed through a riddle of 36 meshes to the square inch.

The mixing of fine-cut shorts with other kinds of tobacco, whether chewing or smoking, renders the tobacco so mixed liable to a tax of 32 cents per pound.

Refuse, scraps, or sweepings, whether resulting from the manufacture of chewing tobacco or the manufacture of cigars, to be entitled to the tax of 16 cents per pound, must be put up and sold substantially in the ordinary condition in which they are made. If they are re-manufactured, the tobacco made therefrom, whether smoking or chewing, or capable of being used for either purpose, is liable to a tax of 32 cents per pound.

Tobacco prepared by processes generally employed in the manufacture of chewing tobacco, using sweetening, licorice or sweetened material, is liable to the tax of 32 cents per pound, though claimed to be sweetened smoking tobacco. 10 I. R. R. 130.

Packages for Manufactured Tobacco.

[SEC. 62. (July 20, 1868.) *And be it further enacted*, That from and after the passage of this act all manufactured tobacco shall be put up and prepared (*a*) by the manufacturer for sale, or removal for sale or consumption, in packages of the following description, and in no other manner:

All snuff in packages containing one, two, four, six, eight, and sixteen ounces, or in bladders containing not exceeding ten pounds each, or in jars containing not exceeding twenty pounds.

All fine-cut chewing tobacco, and all other kinds of tobacco not otherwise provided for, in packages containing one-half, one, two, four, eight, and sixteen ounces, except that fine-cut chewing tobacco may, at the option of the manufacturer, be put up in wooden packages containing ten, twenty, forty, and sixty pounds each.

All smoking tobacco, all fine-cut shorts which has passed through a riddle of thirty-six meshes to the square inch, and all refuse scraps and sweepings of tobacco, in packages containing two, four, eight, and sixteen ounces each.

All cavendish, plug, and twist tobacco in wooden packages not exceeding two hundred pounds net weight.

And every such wooden package shall have printed or marked thereon the manufacturer's name and place of manufacture or the proprietor's name and his trade-mark and the registered number of the manufactory, and the gross weight, the tare, and the net weight of the tobacco in each package: *Provided*, That these limitations and descriptions of packages shall not apply to tobacco and snuff transported in bond for exportation and actually exported.]

(*a*) Upon an application made by any manufacturer to the assessor of his district, accompanied by a suitable voucher that the party to whom he proposes to sell has given bonds as a manufacturer in accordance with law, and stating also the kind and quantity of the scraps, waste, or sweepings he proposes to sell, the assessor is authorized to give a permit for the removal of such scraps, &c., in bulk, and without the payment of any tax. But when the removal is made beyond his district, a list or schedule setting forth the name of the seller, and also the name of the purchaser, with the collection district from which the removal is made, and the number and kind of packages, and the quantity contained therein, should be forwarded to the assessor into whose district the removal is made. The purchaser will be held accountable for the quantity of scraps, &c., received, and must enter them in his monthly report as materials purchased. 10 I. R. R. 198.

Such sales can only be made to manufacturers of cigars, or to manufacturers of tobacco. 11 I. R. R. 138.

The label and notice required by section 68, and the marks and brands required by this section, must both appear upon each and every package. 8 I. R. R. 178.

Slight irregularities do not afford sufficient grounds for seizure. The goods should not be detained any longer than is necessary to obtain satisfactory explanation for any informality, and to satisfy the officers that no fraud has been committed or intended. 10 I. R. R. 81.

The law does not describe the form of wooden packages nor the size, within the limit of two hundred pounds, except for fine-cut chewing tobacco. The manufacturer may use kegs, barrels, drums, or pails. 12 I. R. R. 77.

Metallic Packages.

[SEC. 28. (July 14, 1870.) *And be it further enacted,* That in all cases where tobacco is required to be put up in wooden packages as provided by section sixty-two of an act entitled "An act imposing taxes on distilled spirits and tobacco, and for other purposes," approved July twenty, eighteen hundred and sixty-eight, it shall be lawful for the Commissioner of Internal Revenue to allow the same to be put up in metallic packages: *Provided,* That they shall be so constructed with such corrugations for receiving and protecting the revenue stamps as the Commissioner may approve.]

Manufacturers to furnish Statements, give Bonds, &c.

[SEC. 63. (July 20, 1868.) *And be it further enacted,* That every person before commencing, or, if already commenced, before continuing the manufacture of tobacco or snuff, shall, in addition to a compliance with all other provisions of law, furnish, without previous demand therefor, to the assessor or assistant assessor of the district where the manufacture is to be carried on, a statement, (a) in duplicate, subscribed under oath or affirmation, accurately setting forth the place, and, if in a city, the street and number of the street, where the manufacture is to be carried on; the number of cutting-machines, presses, snuff-mills, hand-mills, or other machines; the name, kind, and quality of the article manufactured, or proposed to be manufactured; and, if the same shall be manufactured for, or to be sold and delivered to, any other person, as agent, or under a special contract, the name and residence and business or occupation of the person for whom the said article is to be manufactured, or to whom it is to be delivered; and shall give a bond in conformity with the provisions of this act, to be approved by the collector of the district, in the sum of two thousand dollars, with an addition to said sum of three thousand dollars for each cutting-machine kept for use, of one thousand dollars for each screw press kept for use in making plug or pressed tobacco, of five thousand dollars for each hydraulic press kept for use, of one thousand dollars for each snuff mill kept for use, and of one thousand dollars for each hand-mill, or other mill or machine, kept for the grinding, cutting, or crushing of tobacco; that he will not engage in any attempt, by himself or by collusion with others, to defraud the government of any tax on his manufactures; that he will render truly and correctly all the returns, statements, and inventories prescribed by law or regulations; that whenever he shall add to the number of cutting-machines, presses, snuff-mills, hand-mills, or other mills or machines as aforesaid, he will immediately give notice thereof to the collector of the district; that he will stamp, in accordance with law, all tobacco and snuff manufactured by him before he removes any part thereof from the place of manufacture; that he will not knowingly sell, purchase, expose, or receive for sale any manufactured tobacco or snuff which has not been stamped as required by law; and that he will comply with all the requirements of law relating to the manufacture of tobacco or snuff. And the sum of the said bond may be increased from time to time, and additional sureties required by the collector, under the instructions of the Commissioner of Internal Revenue.

And every manufacturer shall obtain a certificate from the collector of the district, who is hereby authorized and directed to issue the same, setting forth the kind and number of machines, presses, snuff-mills, hand-mills, or other mills and machines, as aforesaid, for which the bond has been given, which certificate shall be posted in a conspicuous place within the manufactory. And any tobacco manufacturer who shall neglect or refuse to obtain such certificate, or to keep the same posted as hereinbefore provided, shall, on conviction, be fined not less than one hundred dollars nor more than five hundred dollars. And any person manufacturing tobacco or snuff of any description without first giving bond as herein required, shall, on conviction, be fined not less than one thousand dollars nor more than five thousand dollars, and imprisoned for not less than one year nor more than five years. And the working or preparation of any leaf tobacco, or tobacco stems, scraps, clippings, or waste, by sifting, twisting, screening, or any other process, shall be deemed manufacturing.]

(a) The manufacturer without demand must furnish the required statement on Form 36. Every assessor will see that these statements are properly furnished. The assessor will transmit to the collector one copy of each statement as soon as it is received by him. From these statements the collector will determine whether the bonds offered by manufacturers are in conformity to law. Before approving any bond the collector should require affidavits of the sureties to be made on Form 33 and filed in his office with the bond. The collector will issue the certificate, Form 41, to the manufacturer. 10 I. R. R. 58.

The sureties on the bond are not liable when the manufacturer continues business after the expiration of his license. U. S. *v.* Smith, 8 Wall. 587. Contra, U. S. *v.* Truesdell et al. 5 I. R. R. 102.

Manufacturers' Signs.

[SEC. 64. (July 20, 1868.) *And be it further enacted,* That within thirty days after the passage of this act every manufacturer of tobacco and snuff shall place and keep on the side or end of the building within which his business is carried on, so that it can be distinctly seen, a sign, with letters thereon not less than three inches in length, painted in oil colors or gilded, giving his full name and business. Any person neglecting to comply with the requirements of this section shall, on conviction, be fined not less than one hundred dollars nor more than five hundred dollars.]

Record of Manufactories.

[SEC. 65. (July 20, 1868.) *And be it further enacted,* That it shall be the duty of every assistant assessor to keep a record, (a) in a book or books to be provided for the purpose, to be open to the inspection of any person, of the name and residence of every person engaged in the manufacture of tobacco or snuff in his division, the place where such manufacture is carried on, and the number of the manufactory; and the assistant assessor shall enter in said record, under the name of each manufacturer, a copy of every inventory required by this act to be made by such manufacturer, and an abstract of his monthly returns; and each assessor shall keep a similar record for the district, and shall cause the several manufactories of tobacco or snuff in his district to be numbered consecutively, which numbers shall not thereafter be changed.]

(a) Every assistant assessor will keep the required record in a book, Form 74. In this book he will enter all inventories required by law to be made by tobacco manufacturers, and abstracts of all monthly returns, &c. Each assessor is required to keep a similar record for his district. Assesors should require their assistants as often as once every month to make a personal and careful inspection of every tobacco and cigar manufactory in his division and report the condition of each, what changes, if any, have been made in machinery or number of men, what factories are running on full time and employing their entire productive force, what factories are fully complying with all the requirements of the law, and which are not, and in what particulars they are not. 9 I. R. R. 59.

Manufacturer to Furnish Inventories and Keep Books.

[SEC. 66. (July 20, 1868.) *And be it further enacted*, That every person now or hereafter engaged in the manufacture of tobacco or snuff, shall make and deliver to the assistant assessor of the division a true inventory, in such form as shall be prescribed by the Commissioner of Internal Revenue, of the quantity of each of the different kinds of tobacco, snuff-flour, snuff, stems, scraps, clippings, waste, tinfoil, licorice, sugar, gum, and other materials held or owned by him on the first day of January of each year, or at the time of commencing and at the time of concluding business, if before or after the first of January, setting forth what portion of said goods and materials, and what kinds, were manufactured or produced by him, and what was purchased from others; which inventory shall be verified by his oath or affirmation; and the assistant assessor shall make personal examination of the stock sufficient to satisfy himself as to the correctness of the inventory, and shall verify the fact of such examination by oath or affirmation taken before the assessor, to be indorsed on or affixed to the inventory; and every such person shall keep a book or books, the forms of which shall be prescribed by the Commissioner of Internal Revenue, and enter therein daily an accurate account of all the articles aforesaid purchased by him, the quantity of tobacco, snuff, and snuff-flour, stems, scraps, clippings, waste, tinfoil, licorice, sugar, gum, and other materials, of whatever description, whether manufactured (and if plug tobacco the number of net pounds of lumps made in the lump-room, and the number of packages and pounds produced in the press-room each day), sold, consumed, or removed for consumption or sale, or removed from the place of manufacture in bond, and to what district; and shall, on or before the tenth day of each and every month, (*a*) furnish to the assistant assessor of the division a true and accurate abstract from such book of all such purchases, sales, and removals, made during the month next preceding, which abstract shall be verified by his oath or affirmation; and in case of refusal or wilful neglect to deliver the inventory, or keep the account, or furnish the abstract aforesaid, he shall, on conviction, be fined not less than five hundred dollars nor more than five thousand dollars, and imprisoned not less than six months nor more than three years.

And it shall be the duty of any dealer in leaf tobacco, or in any material used in manufacturing tobacco or snuff, on demand of any officer of internal revenue, to render a true and correct statement, verified by oath or affirmation, of the quantity and amount of such leaf tobacco or materials sold or delivered to any person named in such demand; and in case of refusal or neglect to render such statement, or if there is cause to believe such statement to be incorrect or fraudulent, the assessor shall make an examination of persons, books, and papers, in the same manner as provided in this act in relation to frauds and evasions.]

(*a*) The monthly returns must be made on Form 62, and must be verified by oath or affirmation. The inventory is to be made on Form 70. The book is to be kept on Form 77. 10 I. R. R. 59.

A manufacturer who has on hand stems, or waste, which is not worth the trouble of keeping, and who desires to destroy the same, may do so in the presence and under the supervision of an internal revenue officer, and the assessor will give him credit upon the proper books for the amount so destroyed. 10 I. R. R. 153.

Tobacco Stamps.

[SEC. 67. (July 20, 1868.) *And be it further enacted,* That the Commissioner of Internal Revenue shall cause to be prepared suitable and special revenue stamps (*a*) for payment of the tax on tobacco and snuff, which stamps shall indicate the weight and class of the article on which payment is to be made, and shall be affixed and cancelled in the mode prescribed by the Commissioner of Internal Revenue, and stamps when used on any wooden package shall be cancelled by sinking a portion of the same into the wood with a steel die, also such warehouse stamps as are required by this act, which stamps shall be furnished to the collectors of internal revenue requiring the same, who shall each keep at all times a supply equal in amount to three months' sales thereof, and shall sell the same only to the manufacturers of tobacco and snuff in their respective districts who have given bonds as required by law, to owners or consignees of tobacco or snuff, upon the requisition of the proper custom-house officer having the custody of such tobacco or snuff, and to persons required by law to affix the same to tobacco or snuff on hand on the first day of January, Anno Domini eighteen hundred and sixty-nine; and every collector shall keep an account of the number, amount, and denominate values of stamps sold by him to each manufacturer, and to other persons above described.]

(*a*) Stamps will be furnished to collectors upon requisition, and, with the exception of the exportation stamp, will be sold to manufacturers at their full value, as indicated by the tax on the quantity represented. For each exportation stamp 25 cents will be collected when the entry is made for the transportation of the tobacco to an export warehouse. The sales of the stamps must be reported monthly on Form 76, and also on Form 51, and are not to be entered on Form 23, nor receipted for on Form 23½. Collectors will procure from such manufacturers of tobacco in their respective districts as may desire to make use of stamped wrappers estimates of the quantities they will from time to time severally require for use, and will then forward to the Office of Internal Revenue a requisition for the stamped wrappers. The contractor will then be directed to print the required number for each manufacturer, and hold the same subject to the order of the collector. No order will be issued by the collector to any manufacturer, except upon the payment of the full amount of tax represented by the stamps. The printing of the stamps will be at the expense of the government, but the cost of the font and paper, and any additional printing that may be desired, must be paid by the manufacturer. Collectors will report each month on Form 76 the number of the stamped wrappers of each kind for which they have made requisitions, the amount collected during the month, and the balance remaining on hand on the last day of the month.

All packages of tobacco and snuff containing ten pounds or upward must have affixed a registered stamp, and the stamp must be of a denomination corresponding with the net weight of the package when the net weight of the package is an even number of pounds, and when such package can be fully covered by a single stamp. If the net weight of the package is such that no single stamp will suffice for the payment of the tax due thereon, then the manufacturer will affix a stamp of that denomination which approaches nearest to the net weight of the package and affix one, and, if necessary, more smaller stamps to fill up the complement and cover the amount of tax due. In stamping vendors' packages fractions of a pound less than one-half pound may be rejected.

Stamps must be affixed as follows:

1. Upon all kegs, half barrels and barrels of fine-cut chewing tobacco, the stamps shall be placed across the staves and be attached to as many staves as possible between the first and second tier of the hoops.

2. Upon ten or twenty pound boxes of fine-cut chewing and upon all boxes and caddies of plug or other descriptions of chewing tobacco, the stamp shall be affixed over one corner or angle of the box or caddy at equal distances from either end, attaching about equally to either side. And upon all such packages a groove of an inch deep shall be made to admit the stamp and prevent its being torn or rubbed off by transportation. If two serial stamps are used upon the same box, the second stamp shall be affixed in the same manner, only placed upon opposite sides of the box.

3. Strip stamps, whether used for packages of smoking tobacco, fine-cut chewing, snuff or cigars, must be so attached as to effectually seal the package and render it impossible to open the same or remove its contents without destroying the stamp.

4. The small stamps for cut tobacco and snuff must in like manner be so placed upon the package as to insure the destruction of the stamp upon opening the package.

The stamps are to be affixed to the packages by using an adhesive material that will cause them to stick to the wood, paper or other package securely and permanently. After the stamps on the wooden packages have become dry and have been properly cancelled, they must be varnished over thoroughly twice, allowing a short interval for the first coating to set.

The stamps must be cancelled in the following manner:

1. The stamps described under paragraph No. 1, including all the registered stamps with serial numbers, will be cancelled by the manufacturer

writing his name upon the stamp in the blank space left for that purpose, and also writing the date when the stamp was applied or used, in addition to the use of a steel die by which a portion of the stamp is to be sunk into the wood. The place for using the die is marked upon the stamp.

2. The small stamps for cut tobacco and snuff in packages of one-half ounce, one ounce and two ounces, and the stamped foil and paper wrappers must be cancelled by writing or imprinting upon each stamp the manufacturer's or proprietor's name and the date of cancellation.

3. The strip stamps for tobacco and snuff will be cancelled in the same manner, and in addition thereto each strip stamp must be so affixed on the package that in opening the same or using the contents thereof the stamp will be effectually destroyed.

4. The strip stamps for cigars in boxes will be cancelled by the use of a stencil plate of brass or copper, in which there shall be cut not less than six waved lines long enough to extend not less than three-quarters of an inch beyond each side of the stamp on the box. And in addition to the stencil plate of waved lines, the name of the manufacturer of domestic or of the owner of imported cigars, and the date of cancellation, must be written or imprinted upon each strip stamp used for cigars in boxes.

The strip stamps for cut and smoking tobacco are made sufficiently long to pass over both ends of the package and turn the opposite angles, thus effectually sealing the package, and they must be so affixed; and when applied to bags which only open at one end they must be affixed so as to effectually close that end. In cancelling stamps by writing or imprinting the manufacturer's or proprietor's name, where blank spaces are left on the stamps for that purpose they must always be used.

The regulations do not say where the unregistered stamps shall be placed. Manufacturers are permitted to attach the small stamps as they see fit, putting them into the groove, on the angle of the caddy or box, or attaching them to the sides or to the heads. 12 I. R. R. 85.

Collectors are to keep on hand at all times a supply of stamps equal in amount to three months' sales thereof. They can part with them only upon sale or upon payment therefor according to their representative value. They are authorized to sell stamps to the following parties in their own districts: 1st. To manufacturers who have given bond as required by law. 2d. To owners or consignees of tobacco and snuff or importers of cigars upon the requisition of the proper custom house officer. 3d. To persons required by law to affix the same to tobacco, snuff and cigars on hand unstamped, that is, to dealers in manufactured tobacco. They are limited in making sales to these three classes. The sale of stamps by any other person than a collector is not legal. 10 I. R. R. 60.

The manufacturer, not the proprietor, is required to affix and cancel stamps. The name may be written by himself or by some one authorized to sign for him. No particular form or device has been prescribed for the steel die. 10 I. R. R. 89.

Collectors must keep an account of sales of stamps in ledger form, opening a separate account with every manufacturer or other person purchasing stamps. Stamps are to be delivered only upon the written order of the person entitled to purchase the same. In signing his name to the order, the applicant will state whether he is a manufacturer, importer, or dealer in manufactured tobacco or cigars. The number, amount and denominate values of the stamps delivered will be entered on the ledger. The orders will be kept on file in the collector's office. At the end of each and every month, or on or before the 10th day of the following month, the collector will transmit to the assessor of his district a list or abstract of the number, amount, and denominate values of the stamps sold by him to each manufacturer or other person. Upon the receipt of these lists or abstracts, the assessor will enter them upon his account kept with the manufacturer, or his inventory account with the dealer in manufactured tobacco, &c., as the case may be. Whenever there is a discrepancy between the manufacturer's stamp account and his return of sales and products, the assessor will immediately make an investigation and report the result to the Office of Internal Revenue. 10 I. R. R. 129.

The collector's name in his own handwriting must appear in every registered stamp issued from his office, and the blanks in the body of the stamp must be filled with the number of the district, the State and the precise date of the issue. The blanks in the stubs must be filled in such manner as to preserve a perfect record of the following facts, viz.: the person to whom the stamp corresponding was issued, number of his factory, date when issued, and the collector by whom the stamp was issued. The stubs and coupons of registered tobacco stamps must be preserved in the same manner as the stubs and coupons of stamps used for distilled spirits. A deputy collector may be authorized to sign the stamps upon application to the Office of Internal Revenue setting forth the reasons for the application. 10 I. R. R. 185.

When stamps are once affixed to the packages they become a part thereof, and cannot be again used by the manufacturer nor redeemed by the government, even though the packages subsequently become spoiled and worthless. 10 I. R. R. 47.

The stamps may be affixed to the sides of drums and kits or tubs or pails of fine-cut chewing tobacco. 11 I. R. R. 43; 12 I. R. R. 77.

Proper internal revenue stamps are those, and only those, prepared by order of the Commissioner in pursuance of the authority given him by the 67th section, and furnished to collectors of internal revenue, who *alone* are authorized to sell and issue them. A package to be properly stamped must not only have genuine stamps affixed and cancelled, but the stamps must be of a denomination and value sufficient to pay the *entire amount* of tax to which the contents of the package is liable, and the stamps must not have been used previously to pay the tax on any other package of manufactured tobacco, nor the stamped portion of the package so used, nor the package filled or refilled after having been once emptied or partially emptied; hence it follows:

1. That all packages of tobacco short or insufficiently stamped are forfeited to the United States;

2. All packages of manufactured tobacco having affixed thereto false, forged, fraudulent, spurious, or counterfeit stamps, or imitations of stamps, are forfeited to the United States; and

3. All packages of manufactured tobacco with stamps which have been previously used, and all packages which have been emptied or partly emptied and refilled without the destruction of the stamps and the affixing of new stamps, and all packages having upon them the stamped portion of a package which has been previously used, are forfeited to the United States. 12 I. R. R. 77.

When there is a discrepancy between the collector's account of sales of stamps to a manufacturer and the manufacturer's returns, the assessor should make assessments for the deficiency. 11 I. R. R. 49.

Cigars made in State penitentiaries must be regularly stamped. 9 I. R. R. 188.

The manufacturer's name must in all cases be written upon the stamp, and in no case can the name of any other party be used, even though that other party is the proprietor of the brand. 10 I. R. R. 57.

Manufacturers' Labels.

[SEC. 68. (July 20, 1868.) *And be it further enacted*, That every manufacturer of tobacco or snuff shall, in addition to all other requirements of this act relating to tobacco, print on each package or securely affix by pasting on each package containing tobacco or snuff manufactured by or for him, a label on which shall be printed, together with the proprietor's or manufacturer's name, (*a*) the number of the manufactory, and the district and State in which it is situated, these words:

"NOTICE.—The manufacturer of this tobacco has complied with all the requirements of law. Every person is cautioned, under the penalties of law, not to use this package for tobacco again."

Any manufacturer of tobacco who shall neglect to print on or affix such label to any package containing tobacco made by or for him, or sold or offered for sale by or for him, or any person who shall remove any such label so affixed from any such package, shall, on conviction, be fined fifty dollars for each package in respect to which such offence shall be committed.]

(*a*) To facilitate the collection of the tax on tobacco, snuff, and cigars, to prevent and detect frauds thereon, to protect the trade at large—those who buy, sell, use, or consume these articles—all such labels and caution notices as are herein described, fraudulent in their design, and gotten up with an intent to mislead and deceive, are positively forbidden to be used; and by virtue of the authority conferred by section 101, the Secretary of the Treasury and the Commissioner prescribe that hereafter there shall be placed upon every keg, half-barrel, and barrel of fine-cut chewing tobacco, and upon every box, drum, caddy, or other package of fine-cut, cavendish, plug, twist, or other description of chewing tobacco, and upon every bladder and jar of snuff containing more than sixteen ounces, and upon every box of cigars, a *separate and distinct label*.

This label is required to be not less than four and not more than six inches long, and not less than two and one-half inches in width, and to contain in addition to the caution notice prescribed in sections 68 and 88 respectively, the following facts, printed in plain, open, and legible letters, viz.: (1) the manufacturer's or proprietor's name, (2) the number of the manufactory, (3) the collection district, and (4) the State. These labels will be in the following form, viz.:

FORM U.
FOR TOBACCO AND SNUFF.
A———————— B————————, *Manufacturer*.
Factory No. ———, ——— *District, State of* ———.

NOTICE.—The manufacturer of this tobacco has complied with all the requirements of law. Every person is cautioned, under the penalties of law, not to use this package for tobacco again.

FORM V.
FOR CIGAR BOXES.
A———————— B————————, *Manufacturer*.
Factory No. ———, ——— *District, State of* ———.

NOTICE.—The manufacturer of the cigars herein contained has complied with all the requirements of law. Every person is cautioned, under the penalties of law, not to use this box for cigars again.

The law allows the proprietor's name to be printed upon these labels instead of the manufacturer's. This, however, will only be allowed in those cases where the person claiming to be the proprietor is the owner of the factory, or has a legal right or title to the particular brand of goods manufactured, or where the tobacco, snuff, or cigars are made expressly for the person claiming such proprietorship. In either case, the labels must be affixed before the goods are removed from the place of manufacture, and when once so affixed they cannot be removed, or any others substituted therefor.

The labels must be affixed to the package in a conspicuous place, where they will be exposed as little as possible to be worn or rubbed off, and in a manner so as not to be covered up or concealed by any other labels or marks, and so as not to conceal by them any other marks or brands required by law to be placed upon the package.

A separate and distinct label will not be required on packages of tobacco and snuff containing sixteen ounces or less, provided the manufacturer shall cause to be printed on each such package his name or the proprietor's name and the number of his factory, collection district, and State, together with the caution notice, as required in section 68, in a clear, legible manner, where it will not be covered up by the stamp, or otherwise obscured or concealed.

All manufactured tobacco, snuff, and cigars imported from foreign countries, in addition to import duties, are made liable, by the act of July 20, 1868, to the same taxes as are imposed on like goods manufactured in the United States, and to have the same stamps, respectively, affixed and cancelled. Imported tobacco, snuff, and cigars are not required to have affixed to each box or other package a label and caution notice, as provided in the case of domestic manufactured tobacco, &c.

The act of July 28, 1866, authorized the Secretary of the Treasury to provide suitable stamps to be affixed to all imported cigars after they had been inspected, and before they were allowed to be withdrawn from a public store or bonded warehouse. These were not tax-paid stamps, but only indicated inspection, and showed that the cigars bearing the stamp had been properly entered at the custom-house and the duty paid, and that they were, therefore, not liable to seizure when found upon the market under the law then in force. The law authorizing the use of these inspector's stamps upon imported cigars has not been repealed, and the use of these stamps is still continued, under the instructions issued from the Secretary's Office, dated Sept. 5, 1866.

These stamps, when properly filled, show the inspector's name, the date of inspection, the port where the entry was made, and the name of the importer. They may subserve the same purpose with reference to imported cigars that the label and caution notice answer for domestic cigars. But these import stamps on boxes of cigars must never be mistaken for the internal revenue stamps. They are no more evidence of the payment of the internal revenue tax imposed *on all imported cigars* than the label or caution notice on boxes of domestic cigars would be in the absence of proper stamps. Series 5, No. 8, Supplement No. 3.

It is apparent that before tobacco can be removed for sale or consumption *in accordance with law*—

1. It must be put up in legal packages;
2. The package must have printed thereon or securely affixed a label with the manufacturer's name, the registered number of the factory, and the district and State, and if a wooden package, the manufacturer's name and place of manufacture, or the proprietor's name and his trade-mark, and the registered number of the manufactory, and the gross weight, the tare, and the net weight of each package, must be printed or marked *on the box*;

3. Every package must have affixed and cancelled a proper stamp or stamps to indicate the weight and class of the tobacco for which payment of tax is made; and

4. These stamps must be affixed and cancelled *in the mode prescribed by the Commissioner.*

Any removal of manufactured tobacco for sale or consumption without a compliance on the part of the manufacturer with all of these conditions is a "removal otherwise than as provided by law," and subjects the manufacturer to the forfeitures provided in section 69.

Manufactured tobacco found outside of a manufactory or export bonded warehouse, except the same shall be in transit from the manufactory to a bonded warehouse, without proper internal revenue stamps affixed to each package, is forfeited to the United States under section 70; and the person who removed the tobacco without proper stamps affixed and cancelled, and the person who uses or sells or offers for sale, or *has in his possession* such manufactured tobacco, becomes liable, on conviction, for the fines and penalties imposed by section 71. 12 I. R. R. 77.

Where the manufacturer inserts the name of the proprietor in the label instead of his own, it should read, "Manufactured for ———, at factory No. 1," &c. 10 I. R. R. 57.

When a manufacturer of tobacco, snuff, or cigars uses one part of a building for a salesroom, and another part as a place of manufacture, he must properly pack and stamp his goods before removal to the salesroom. 9 I. R. R. 161.

A manufacturer cannot cut his tobacco in one room of his store and retail it in an open box (whether previously stamped or not) in another room of the same store, except in the stamped packages or wrappers provided by law. U. S. *v.* Rosenfield, 9 I. R. R. 201.

Penalties Against Manufacturers.

[SEC. 69. (July 20, 1868.) *And be it further enacted*, That any manufacturer of tobacco or snuff who shall remove otherwise than as provided by law, or sell, any tobacco or snuff without the proper stamps denoting the tax thereon, or without having paid the special tax, or given bond as required by law, or who shall make false or fraudulent entries of manufactures or sales of tobacco or snuff, or who shall make false or fraudulent entries of the purchase or sales of leaf tobacco, tobacco stems, or other material, or who shall affix any false, forged, fraudulent, spurious, or counterfeit stamp, or imitation of any stamp required by this act, to any box or package containing any tobacco or snuff, shall, in addition to the penalties elsewhere provided in this act for such offences, forfeit (*a*) to the United States all the raw material and manufactured or partly manufactured tobacco and snuff, and all machinery, tools, implements, apparatus, fixtures, boxes, and barrels, and all other materials which shall be found in the possession of such person, in the manufactory of such person, or elsewhere.]

(*a*) It will be seen that this section provides for forfeiture by the manufacturer to the government of the property therein named, in case he commits any of the offences enumerated: 1. Removal of manufactured tobacco from the manufactory or place where it was made otherwise than as provided by law; 2. To sell tobacco or snuff without the proper stamps denoting the tax; 3. Without the payment of a special tax as manufacturer of tobacco; 4. Without having given bond as required by law; 5. The making by the manufacturer of false or fraudulent entries of manufactures or sales of tobacco or snuff; 6. The making of false or fraudulent entries of the purchase or sales of leaf tobacco, tobacco stems, or other material; and, 7. The affixing of any false, forged, fraudulent, spurious, or counterfeit stamp, or imitation of any stamp, to any box or package containing tobacco or snuff. The failure to do the things here specified, which the law requires to be done, or the doing of either of the things forbidden to be done, forfeits to the United States the property of the manufacturer as enumerated in said section 69. 12 I. R. R. 77.

The prepayment of tax by stamps on all tobacco, snuff, and cigars before the goods are removed from the manufactory or place where they are made, is the distinctive feature of the present law. 9 I. R. R. 43.

Inspectors will not be required to inspect tobacco, snuff, or cigars when the proper tax-paid stamps are affixed to the packages and duly cancelled before removed from the manufactory. 10 I. R. R. 60.

Absence of Stamp to be Evidence of Fraud.

[SEC. 70. (July 20, 1868.) *And be it further enacted*, That the absence of the proper stamp on any package of manufactured tobacco or snuff shall be notice to all persons that the tax has not been paid thereon, and shall be *prima facie* evidence of the non-payment thereof. And such tobacco or snuff shall be forfeited to the United States.]

Penalty for Evasion of the Law.

[SEC. 71. (July 20, 1868.) *And be it further enacted*, That any person who shall remove from any manufactory, or from any place where tobacco or snuff is made, any manufactured tobacco or snuff without the same being put up in proper packages, or without the proper stamp for the amount thereon being affixed and cancelled, as required by law; or if intended for export, without the proper warehouse stamp being affixed; or shall use, sell, or offer for sale, or have in possession, except in the manufactory, or in a bonded warehouse, any manufactured tobacco or snuff, without proper stamps being affixed and cancelled; or shall sell, or offer for sale, for consumption in the United States, or use, or have in possession, except in the manufactory or in a bonded warehouse, any manufactured tobacco or snuff on which only the warehouse stamp marking the same for export has been affixed, shall, on conviction thereof for each such offence, respectively, be fined not less than one thousand dollars nor more than five thousand dollars, and be imprisoned not less than six months nor more than two years. And any person who shall affix to any package containing tobacco or snuff any false, forged, fraudulent, spurious, or counterfeit stamp, or a stamp which has been before used, shall be deemed guilty of a felony, and on conviction shall be fined not less than one thousand dollars nor more than five thousand dollars, and imprisoned not less than two years nor more than five years.]

Stamps to be Destroyed on Emptying Packages.

[SEC. 72. (July 20, 1868.) *And be it further enacted*, That whenever any stamped box, bag, vessel, wrapper, or envelope of any kind, containing tobacco or snuff, shall be emptied, (*a*) the stamped portion thereof shall be destroyed by the person in whose hands the same may be. And any person who shall wilfully neglect or refuse so to do shall, for each such offence, on conviction, be fined fifty dollars, and imprisoned not less than ten days nor more than six months. And any person who shall sell or give away, or who shall buy or accept from another, any such empty stamped box, bag, vessel, wrapper, or envelope of any kind, or the stamped portion thereof, shall, for each such offence, on conviction, be fined one hundred dollars and imprisoned not less than twenty days and not more than one year. And any manufacturer or other person who shall put tobacco or snuff into any such box, bag, vessel, wrapper, or envelope, the same having been either emptied or partially emptied, shall, for each such offence, on conviction, be fined not less than one hundred nor more than five hundred dollars, and imprisoned for not less than one nor more than three years.]

(*a*) This section of the law applies not only to retail dealers who empty wooden packages by retailing their contents, but also to every person who purchases tobacco for his own use and empties such packages. He must destroy the stamped portion. The law in this respect will be sufficiently complied with if the stamp is thoroughly mutilated or destroyed without destroying the particular part of the jar, box, bladder, bag, or other inclosure used in packing tobacco, snuff, or cigars. 10 I. R. R. 61.

Bonded Warehouses.

[SEC. 73. (July 20, 1868.) *And be it further enacted*, That the Commissioner of Internal Revenue, upon the execution of such bonds as he may prescribe, may designate and establish, at any port of entry in the United States, bonded warehouses for the storage of manufactured tobacco and snuff in bond, intended for exportation, selecting suitable buildings for such purpose to be recommended by the collector in charge of exports at such port, to be known as export bonded warehouses, and used exclusively for the storage of manufactured tobacco and snuff in bond. Every such warehouse shall be under the control of the collector of internal revenue in charge of exports at the port where such warehouse is located, and shall be in charge of an internal revenue storekeeper assigned thereto by the Commissioner of Internal Revenue. No manufactured tobacco or snuff shall be withdrawn or removed (a) from any bonded warehouse without an order or permit from the collector in charge of exports at such port, which shall be issued only for the immediate transfer to a vessel by which such tobacco or snuff is to be exported to a foreign country, as hereinafter provided, or after the tax has been paid thereon. And such warehouse shall be under such further regulations as the Commissioner of Internal Revenue may prescribe. Any manufactured tobacco and snuff may be withdrawn once, and no more, from an export bonded warehouse for transportation to any other port of entry in the United States where an export bonded warehouse for the storage of manufactured tobacco and snuff may have been established, and such manufactured tobacco and snuff so withdrawn shall, on its arrival at the second port of entry, be immediately warehoused in an export bonded warehouse for the storage of manufactured tobacco and snuff, from which it shall be withdrawn only as provided by law.]

(a) The law makes no provision for the removal of tobacco in bond without payment of tax, except such tobacco and snuff as are intended for export. When properly stamped they may be removed in bond from the manufactory without payment of the tax, to be transported directly to an export bonded warehouse established at any port of entry of the United States for the storage of manufactured tobacco and snuff intended for exportation. The goods may be withdrawn either for immediate export to a foreign country or after the tax has been paid thereon. 10 I. R. R. 67.

An export bonded warehouse must be an entire building, with this exception, that as cellars are generally unsuitable for storing tobacco, the cellar of such premises may, if separated from the store above so that there shall be no means of inside communication therewith and the only entrance to the cellar is from the street, be used for other business purposes on request of the proprietor of the warehouse. Such a warehouse must be a first-class warehouse according to the classification of fire insurance companies of the city or place. or of the board of fire underwriters where such exist; and when adjoining other buildings it must be separated therefrom by a brick or stone wall, in which no door or other opening can be permitted. No goods whatever can be stored in the bonded premises except bonded tobacco and snuff.

No manufacturer of nor dealer in tobacco or snuff can be interested, directly or indirectly, in such a warehouse as owner or proprietor, and the collector who forwards the application must testify to these facts. The party desiring to establish such a warehouse will make application to the collector in charge of exports at the port of entry, describing the premises, the location, and capacity of the same, accompanying the application with a sketch or diagram showing the relative position of the warehouse and surrounding buildings. The application must be accompanied by a certificate properly stamped, signed by the officers of two or more insurance companies, that the premises offered are suitable, and may be insured at the usual rates for like property. The collector will thereupon, by himself or deputy, examine and inspect the premises; and if, in his opinion, the location, construction, dimensions, and the means provided for securing custody of the merchandise which may be stored in the same, are satisfactory, he will require the owner or applicant to give the proper bond. The penal sum in the bond should in no case be less than $10,000, and should always be sufficient to cover the tax on the total quantity of merchandise that can be stored in the warehouse at one time. The signers of this warehouse bond must be required to justify on Form 33, unless the ample sufficiency of principal and sureties is personally known to the collector who takes the bond.

The bond having been properly executed and delivered to the collector, he will report in writing concerning the application, stating the fact of personal inspection of the premises by himself, or deputy, and giving his opinion as to the necessity, capacity, and security of the warehouse.

No application for any export bonded warehouse will be granted unless accompanied by the collector's certificate, that the number of warehouses of that class already established in the district is not sufficient, and that the establishment of such additional warehouse is necessary for the storage of bonded tobacco and snuff intended for export. The collector must also certify that the building or premises offered are satisfactory in respect to location, construction, dimensions, and the means provided for securing the safe custody of the merchandise which may be stored therein, and are in every particular in accordance with law and regulations.

The collector having made his report, embracing the proper certificate as above directed, will mail the same to the Commissioner, together with 1st. The application and diagram; 2d. The insurance certificates; and 3d. A certified copy of the bond, on which the collector will indorse his certificate of the sufficiency of the penalty, and the responsibility of the obligors.

If the application for a warehouse is approved by the Commissioner, due notice will be given to the collector, and he will in no case allow the warehouse to be used as an export bonded warehouse until such notice is received by him, nor until all tax-paid or free goods are removed therefrom.

Export bonded warehouses will be numbered consecutively in each district. A conspicuous sign must be placed over the front entrance of each, or upon the outer wall, so that it can be plainly seen and read from the street. The sign must show the number of the district, the number and name of the proprietor, and must in substance be as follows:

Internal Revenue Export Bonded Warehouse,
—— District,
No. ——,
—— Proprietor.

Neglect to furnish and keep this sign in proper place will be cause for the discontinuance of the warehouse. Assessors and collectors will designate each warehouse by its number on the warehouse record.

Storekeepers are required to personally superintend the opening and closing of the doors and windows of the warehouses under their charge, and, unless by express permission of the Commissioner, to be in constant attendance at the warehouse from seven o'clock A. M. to sunset from April 1st to October 1st, and for the residue of the year from eight A. M. to sunset, except at the time necessary for dinner, not over one hour at noon, when the warehouse must be closed and locked.

An office for the accommodation of the owner or occupant may be allowed in export warehouses, but such office must be separated by a permanent partition from the rest of the store, so that the owner shall have no access to the goods except in the presence of the storekeeper, who, in such case, must be allowed such use of the office as may be necessary in the performance of his official duties.

An office may be allowed for the use of the owner or occupant for the exhibition of samples of goods stored in such warehouse, which sample room must be separated by a partition from the rest of the store, and so secured as to prevent access to the goods in other rooms in such store. The said sample room must not be used for retail business or trade.

Samples of tobacco and snuff stored in bond may be taken and exhibited in the sample room of the warehouse, according to the usages and customs of the tobacco trade; and no sample packages shall be removed from the bonded premises without proper stamps affixed and cancelled.

All merchandise in an export bonded warehouse may be examined during the business hours of the warehouse by the owner or consignee, or by an agent, upon the written order of the owner or consignee.

No samples can be taken, nor any goods be exhibited or examined, except under the immediate superintendence of the storekeeper, as well as that of the owner or proprietor; and the storekeeper must make a memorandum in the warehouse record of the date and description of such sampling opposite the entry of the lot thus sampled.

Collectors will in no case allow tobacco and snuff to be shipped in bond unless consigned to a collector, or his successor in office. Whenever additional warehouses are established, or any are discontinued, collectors will be duly notified thereof.

Export warehouses will be subject to such further rules as may be deemed necessary from time to time for the safekeeping of the goods and protection of the revenue, and may be discontinued as bonded warehouses by the Commissioner when, in his opinion, the public interests may require. In case of such discontinuance, if there should be any goods in store which it would be necessary to remove to another bonded warehouse, the expense of removal must be paid by the owner of the discontinued warehouse.

Should the owner or occupant of any building designated as an export bonded warehouse fail or refuse to comply with any law regulating the storage of merchandise, or any rules or regulations issued by the Commissioner, or by the collector, for the safety of the goods stored, the collector will refuse permission to deposit goods in such store, and report the facts at once to the Commissioner for his action. The proprietors or occupants of export warehouses, on ten days' notice from the collector, may be required to renew their bonds, and if they fail so to do, no more goods will be sent to such warehouses, and those within the same will be withdrawn at their expense.

The owner or occupant of any export warehouse will have the right to relinquish the business at any time, with the approval of the collector of the district, and on notice to the owners of the merchandise deposited therein, and paying the expenses of its removal to another export warehouse. Collectors will report the date and reasons for the discontinuance of such warehouse to the Commissioner as soon as such discontinuance takes place. But the bonds are not to be cancelled or delivered up to the bondsmen, but are to be retained and filed by the collector in his office. Collectors may, however, when the facts justify it, give a certificate that the warehouse has been discontinued, and surrendered to the owner, and that, so far as known to the collector, the conditions of the bond have been filled.

All labor on the goods deposited in these stores must be performed by the owner or proprietor of the warehouse under the supervision of the officer in charge of the same, and at the expense of the said owner or proprietor. All arrangements in regard to the rates of storage, and the price of labor, on goods deposited in export warehouses, must be made between the depositor and the owner or occupant of the store, but the Commissioner reserves the right to adjust these matters on appeal to him with due regard to the interests of all parties concerned. All amounts due for storage and labor must be collected by the owner or occupant of the store; the collector looking only to the custody of the merchandise for the security of the revenue.

Export warehouses must be under the joint custody of the owner or proprietor and the storekeeper appointed for the purpose, and must be under internal revenue locks, prescribed by the Commissioner, in addition to the locks of the owners, which latter must not open with the same key as the former. After stores or premises have been approved, and placed under internal revenue locks, the collector will retain the right of ordering additional fastenings, to be provided by and at the expense of the owners or occupants having charge of the premises.

It is the duty of the storekeeper always to keep in his own possession the keys of the government locks in use on the warehouse under his charge, never suffering them to go out of his custody, except to the collector or to his successor in office, upon the order of the collector. Nor must he allow any goods to be received or delivered except in his presence, nor must he be absent from the warehouse while it is unlocked. He should also be always present when goods are inspected, and see that none are unlawfully abstracted or taken away. The owner or proprietor of the warehouse will in no case be allowed to have access to it except in the presence of the storekeeper or collector having charge thereof, and the storekeeper will promptly inform the collector of any infraction of the warehouse rules and regulations by the owner or proprietor, any inspector or other person. Any storekeeper who is absent from the warehouse under his charge, while it is unlocked, will be discharged.

The storekeeper or officer in charge of each warehouse will keep a correct account of all goods received into his store and delivered therefrom, specifying in detail the date of receipt, original and warehouse marks and number; number and description of packages and contents; from what place received, and, when upon special order of the collector, the date thereof; also date of receipt of permit for delivery; date of delivery; to whom delivered, and for what purpose as specified in the permit or order for delivery; and will enter in the warehouse book such further particulars as may be prescribed or found necessary for the indentification of the packages to insure the correct delivery thereof. The book for this purpose must be furnished by the owner of the warehouse, and must be kept in such manner as to give all the information required by Form 121. The storekeeper will make daily returns in duplicate of the goods received into and delivered from the warehouse to the collector in charge thereof, and to the Commissioner on Form 121. These returns on Form 121 must be full, explicit, and correct in all details. In the column "For what purpose" should be written the words "Consumption," "Exportation," or the name of the owner of the export warehouse to which the goods are consigned, as the case may be. No goods are to be delivered from the warehouse by the storekeeper except upon the proper order or permit of the collector of the district. 10 I. R. R. 78.

Transportation in Bond to Bonded Warehouse.

[SEC. 74. (July 20, 1868.) *And be it further enacted,* That manufactured tobacco and snuff maybe removed (*a*) in bond from the manufactory, without payment of the tax, to be transported directly to an export bonded warehouse for the storage of manufactured tobacco or snuff established at a port of entry as hereinbefore provided; and the deposit in and withdrawal from any bonded warehouse, the transportation and exportation of manufactured tobacco and snuff, shall be made under such rules and regulations and after making such entries and executing such bonds and giving such other additional security as may be prescribed by the Commissioner of Internal Revenue, which shall in all respects, so far as applicable, conform to the provisions of law and regulations relating to distilled spirits to be deposited in or withdrawn from bonded warehouse or transported or exported. All tobacco and snuff intended for export, before being removed from the manufactory, shall have affixed to each package an engraved stamp indicative of such intention to be provided and furnished to the several collectors, as in the case of other stamps, and to be charged to them and accounted for in the same manner; and for the expense attending the providing and affixing such stamps, twenty-five cents for each package so stamped shall be paid to the collector on making the entry for such transportation; but the provisions of this section shall not limit the time for tobacco or snuff to remain in bond.]

(a) The party desiring to transport manufactured tobacco or snuff from a manufactory to an export bonded warehouse will give notice of his intention to the collector of the district in which the manufactory is situated, who will thereupon detail an inspector of tobacco to inspect, weigh, and mark the packages. The inspector will examine each package carefully, and see that the contents are such as the law requires. He will also see that each wooden package containing fine-cut chewing tobacco or cavendish, plug, or twist tobacco has printed or marked thereon the manufacturer's name and place of manufacture, or the proprietor's name and trademark, and the registered number of the manufactory. These marks and the label required by section 68 must be placed thereon by the manufacturer himself, or at his expense. The inspector will himself ascertain the gross weight, tare and net weight, and mark each upon the said wooden package, together with his own name and title, date of inspection, and collection district. If the packages are other than the above described wooden ones, the inspector will examine them carefully, and also see that each package has affixed thereto the label required by section 68.

In either case he will see that the export stamp is affixed to each package and cancelled, unless several small packages like caddies or papers of tobacco are put up in one package, in which case the export stamp will be affixed to the outer case or cask; and the inspector will also mark his brand upon such outer case, with date of inspection, collection, district, and kind of contents. The affixing and cancelling of the export stamp will be done by the manufacturer, or at his expense. When the case contains other than wooden packages, the inspector will, in addition to the foregoing, mark upon it the gross weight, tare, and net weight, which must also be stated in his report of inspections.

The collector will deliver to the inspector an order in triplicate on Form

A, upon complying with which the inspector will make a certificate of his inspections on each copy of the order, and leaving one copy with the owner of the goods, he will deliver the other copies to the collector. The manufacturer upon receiving this certificate will endorse upon it his entry for transportation from the manufactory to an export bonded warehouse. In the blank space of the entry after the words "to be conveyed by," the applicant must describe the entire route to be taken, stating, where transportation by land is intended, the name of the railroad or other transportation company to which the goods are first to be delivered; and, when transportation by water is intended, the name of the line or company, and the name of the particular vessel, or steamer, to which the goods are to be delivered, must be given.

At the time of filing the entry with the collector, the applicant is required to pay to the collector the sum of 25 cents for each package stamped as required by law. Each inspector will be entitled to receive from the manufacturer or owner a fee of five cents per package for inspecting, weighing, and marking tobacco or snuff at the manufactory or in export warehouse unless otherwise specially prescribed by the Commissioner. 10 I. R. R. 67, 186. For regulations, see 10 I. R. R. 67, 186.

Stamps to be Affixed by Actual Manufacturer.

[SEC. 75. (July 20, 1868.) *And be it further enacted,* That in all cases where tobacco or snuff of any description is manufactured, in whole or in part, upon commission or shares, or where the material from which any such articles are made, or are to be made, is furnished by one person and made or manufactured by another, or where the material is furnished or sold by one person with an understanding or agreement with another that the manufactured article is to be received in payment therefor or for any part thereof, the stamps required by law shall be fixed by the actual maker or manufacturer before the article passes from the place of making or manufacturing. And in case of fraud on the part of either of said persons in respect to said manufacture, or of any collusion on their part with intent to defraud the revenue, such material and manufactured articles shall be forfeited to the United States; and each party to such fraud or collusion shall be deemed guilty of a misdemeanor, and, on conviction, be fined not less than one hundred dollars nor more than five thousand dollars, and imprisoned for not less than six months nor more than three years.]

Books to be Kept by Dealers.

[SEC. 76. (July 20, 1868.) *And be it further enacted,* That every dealer in leaf tobacco shall enter daily in a book (*a*) kept for that purpose, under such regulations as the Commissioner of Internal Revenue may prescribe, the number of hogsheads, cases, and pounds of leaf tobacco purchased by him, and of whom purchased, and the number of hogsheads, cases, or pounds sold by him, with the name and residence, in each instance, of the person to whom sold, and if shipped, to whom shipped, and to what district. Such book shall be kept at his place of business, and shall be open at all hours to the inspection of any assessor, collector, or other revenue officer; and any dealer in leaf tobacco who shall neglect or refuse to keep such book shall be liable to a penalty of not less than five hundred dollars, and on conviction thereof shall be fined not less than one hundred dollars nor more than five thousand dollars, and imprisoned not less than six months nor more than two years.]

(*a*) Dealers must keep a book according to Form 77. 10 I. R. R. 59.

Auctioneers selling leaf tobacco must keep a book according to Form 77. 10 I. R. R. 41.

Any person who keeps leaf tobacco for sale is a dealer, and a single sale is sufficient to fix his character as such. In an action of debt under this section the jury cannot find a greater sum than five hundred dollars. U. S. *v.* Damiani & Co. 11 I. R. R. 5.

If the dealer delegates the duty of keeping the books to another person and such person neglects it, this will not excuse the dealer, and he must be held responsible for such omission. U. S. *v.* Auja, 10 I. R. R. 52.

Stamps on Imported Tobacco.

[SEC. 77. (July 20, 1868.) *And be it further enacted*, That from and after the passage of this act, and until the first day of October, eighteen hundred and sixty-eight, all manufactured tobacco and snuff (not including cigars) imported from foreign countries shall be placed by the owner, importer, or consignee thereof in a bonded warehouse of the United States at the place of importation, in the same manner and under rules as provided for warehousing goods imported into the United States, and shall not be withdrawn from such warehouse, nor be entered for consumption or transportation in the United States prior to the said first day of October, eighteen hundred and sixty-eight. All manufactured tobacco and snuff (not including cigars) imported from foreign countries, after the passage of this act, shall, in addition to the import duties imposed on the same, pay the tax prescribed in this act for like kinds of tobacco and snuff manufactured in the United States, and have the same stamps respectively affixed. Such stamps shall be affixed and cancelled on all such articles so imported by the owner or importer thereof, while such articles are in the custody of the proper custom-house officers, and such articles shall not pass out of the custody of such officers until the stamps have been affixed and cancelled. Such tobacco and snuff shall be put up in packages, as prescribed in this act for like articles manufactured in the United States before such stamps are affixed; and the owner or importer of such tobacco and snuff shall be liable to all the penal provisions of this act prescribed for manufacturers of tobacco and snuff manufactured in the United States.

Where it shall be necessary to take any such articles, so imported, to any place for the purpose of repacking (*a*), affixing, and cancelling such stamps, other than the public stores of the United States, the collector of customs of the port where such articles shall be entered shall designate a bonded warehouse to which such articles shall be taken, under the control of such customs officer as such collector may direct. And any officer of customs who shall permit any such articles to pass out of his custody or control without compliance by the owner or importer thereof with the provisions of this section relating thereto, shall be deemed guilty of a misdemeanor, and shall, on conviction, be fined not less than one thousand dollars nor more than five thousand dollars, and imprisoned not less than six months nor more than three years.]

(*a*) The law makes no provision for repacking domestic tobacco or snuff in bond. The original packages must be of the description and limitation prescribed by law. 10 I. R. R. 79.

Inventory to be Made—Packages to be Stamped.

[SEC. 78. (July 20, 1868; as amended December 22, 1868). *And be it further enacted,* That from and after the passage of this act it shall be the duty of every dealer in manufactured tobacco, having on hand more than twenty pounds, and every dealer in snuff, having on hand more than ten pounds, to immediately make a true and correct inventory of the amount of such tobacco and snuff, respectively, under oath or affirmation, and to deposit such inventory with the assistant assessor of the proper division, who shall immediately return the same to the assessor of the district, who shall immediately thereafter make an abstract of the several inventories, filed in his office, and transmit such abstract to the Commissioner of Internal Revenue, and a like inventory and return shall be made on the first day of every month thereafter, and a like abstract of inventories shall be transmitted while any such dealer has tobacco or snuff remaining on hand manufactured in the United States, or imported prior to the passage of this act, and not stamped. After the fifteenth day of February, eighteen hundred and sixty-nine, all smoking, fine-cut chewing tobacco, or snuff, and after the first day of July, eighteen hundred and sixty-nine, all other manufactured tobacco of every description, shall be taken and deemed as having been manufactured after the passage of this act, and shall not be sold or offered for sale unless put up in packages (a) and stamped as prescribed by this act, except at retail by retail dealers from wooden packages stamped as provided for in this act; and any person who shall sell, or offer for sale, after the fifteenth day of February, eighteen hundred and sixty-nine, any smoking, fine-cut chewing tobacco, or snuff, and after the first day of July, eighteen hundred and sixty-nine, any other manufactured tobacco not so put up in packages and stamped, shall, on conviction, be fined not less than five hundred dollars nor more than five thousand dollars, and imprisoned not less than six months nor more than two years.]

(a) Dealers in manufactured tobacco must sell in packages, each package bearing the properly cancelled stamp. Retail dealers are authorized to sell manufactured tobacco at retail from wooden packages legally stamped, or cigars from boxes packed, stamped and branded in the manner prescribed by law. The retail dealer must not withdraw the goods from the stamped package until the sale is made. The stamp upon the package from which he is retailing goods is *prima facie* evidence that the tax on such goods has been paid. 10 I. R. R. 61.

Snuff may be retailed from bladders or jars stamped according to law. 9 I. R. R. 68.

When the marshal sells forfeited tobacco, snuff, or cigars, the purchaser must affix the proper stamps. 9 I. R. R. 186, 203; 10 I. R. R. 10, 25.

Penalty for Fraudulent Representations on Sales of Tobacco or Snuff.

[SEC. 79. (July 20, 1868.) *And be it further enacted*, That any person who shall, after the passage of this act, sell, or offer for sale, any manufactured tobacco or snuff, representing the same to have been manufactured and the tax paid thereon prior to the passage of this act, when the same was not so manufactured, and the tax not so paid, shall be liable to a penalty of five hundred dollars for each offence, and shall be deemed guilty of a misdemeanor, and, on conviction, shall be fined not less than five hundred dollars nor more than five thousand dollars, and shall be imprisoned not less than six months nor more than two years.]

Sale of Tobacco or Snuff in Bond on Passage of this Act.

[SEC. 80. (July 20, 1868.) *And be it further enacted*, That all manufactured tobacco and snuff, manufactured prior to the passage of this act, and held in bond at the time of its passage, may be sold for consumption in the original packages, with the proper stamps for the amount of the tax thereon affixed and cancelled as required by law; and any person who shall, after the passage of this act, offer for sale any tobacco or snuff, in packages of a different size from those limited and prescribed by this act, representing the same to have been held in bond at the time of the passage of this act, when the same was not so held in bond, shall, on conviction, be fined fifty dollars for each package in respect to which such offence shall be committed: *Provided*, That after the first day of January, Anno Domini eighteen hundred and sixty-nine, no such tobacco or snuff shall be sold or removed for sale or consumption from any bonded warehouse, unless put up in packages and stamped as provided by this act.]

Tax on Cigars.

[SEC. 81. (July 20, 1868.) *And be it further enacted*, That upon cigars which shall be manufactured and sold, or removed for consumption or use, there shall be assessed and collected the following taxes, to be paid by the manufacturer thereof:

On cigars of all descriptions, made of tobacco or any substitute therefor, five dollars per thousand; on cigarettes weighing not exceeding three pounds per thousand, one dollar and fifty cents per thousand; when weighing exceeding three pounds per thousand, five dollars per thousand. And the Commissioner of Internal Revenue may prescribe such regulations for the inspection of cigars, cheroots, and cigarettes, and the collection of the tax thereon, as shall, in his judgment, be most effective for the prevention of frauds in the payment of such tax.]

Manufacturers of Cigars to Furnish Statement, Give Bonds, etc.

[SEC. 82. (July 20, 1868.) *And be it further enacted*, That every person before commencing, or, if already commenced, before continuing, the manufacture of cigars, shall furnish, without previous demand therefor, to the assistant assessor of the division a statement (*a*) in duplicate, subscribed under oath or affirmation, accurately setting forth the place, and if in a city, the street and number of the street where the manufacture is to be carried on; and if the same shall be manufactured for, or to be sold and delivered to any other person, the name and residence and business or occupation of the person for whom the cigars are to be manufactured, or to whom to be delivered; and shall give a bond in conformity with the provisions of this act, in such penal sum as the assessor of the district may require, not less than five hundred dollars, with an addition of one hundred dollars for each person proposed to be employed by him in making cigars, conditioned that he will not employ any person to manufacture cigars who has not been duly registered as a cigar-maker; that he will not engage in any attempt by himself, or by collusion with others, to defraud the government of any tax on his manufactures; that he will render truly and correctly all the returns, statements, and inventories prescribed; that whenever he shall add to the number of cigar-makers employed by him, he will immediately give notice thereof to the collector of the district; that he will stamp, in accordance with law, all cigars manufactured by him before he offers the same, or any part thereof, for sale, and before he removes any part thereof from the place of manufacture; that he will not knowingly sell, purchase, expose, or receive for sale any cigars which have not been stamped as required by law; and that he will comply with all the requirements of law relating to the manufacture of cigars. The sum of said bond may be increased from time to time, and additional sureties required at the discretion of the assessor, or under the instructions of the Commissioner of Internal Revenue.

Every cigar manufacturer shall obtain from the collector of the district, who is hereby required to issue the same, a certificate setting forth the number of cigar-makers for which the bond has been given, which certificate shall be posted in a conspicuous place within the manufactory; and any cigar manufacturer who shall neglect or refuse to obtain such certificate, or to keep the same posted as hereinbefore provided, shall, on conviction, be fined one hundred dollars. Any person manufacturing cigars of any description without first giving bond as herein required, shall, on conviction, be fined not less than one hundred dollars nor more than five thousand dollars, and imprisoned not less three months nor more than five years. Cigarettes and cheroots shall be held to be cigars under the meaning of this act.]

(a) The sworn statement must be furnished by the manufacturer in duplicate on Form 86 to the assistant assessor. As soon as received the assessor will transmit one of these statements to the collector, together with a list of the names of all cigar manufacturers and the amount of each one's bond as determined by him. Upon the filing of the bond the collector will issue to every cigar manufacturer a certificate, Form 41. 10 I. R. R. 66.

Manufacturers must give bond for all persons whom they employ in making cigars, whether as strippers, bunchers, or persons technically known as cigar-makers. 11 I. R. R. 10.

Signs of Cigar Manufacturers.

[SEC. 83. (July 20, 1868.) *And be it further enacted*, That within thirty days after the passage of this act every cigar manufacturer shall place and keep on the side or end of the building within which his buisness is carried on, so that it can be distinctly seen, a sign with letters thereon not less than three inches in length, painted in oil colors or gilded, giving his full name and business. Any person neglecting to comply with the requirements of this section shall, on conviction, be fined not less than one hundred dollars nor more than five hundred dollars.]

Record of Cigar Manufacturers and Cigar Manufactories.

[Sec. 84. (July 20, 1868.) *And be it further enacted*, That it shall be the duty of every assistant assessor to keep a record (*a*) in a book to be provided for the purpose, to be open to the inspection of any person, of the name and residence of every person engaged in the manufacture of cigars in his division, the place where such manufacture is carried on, and the number of the manufactory, together with the names and residences of every cigar-maker employed in his division, and the assistant assessor shall enter in said record, under the name of each manufacturer, an abstract of his inventories and monthly returns; and each assessor shall keep a similar record for the district, and shall cause the several manufactories of cigars in the district to be numbered consecutively, which number shall not thereafter be changed.]

(*a*) The numbering of cigar manufactories must not be confounded with the similar requirements in the case of tobacco and snuff manufactories, but a separate numbering of each is required. 10 I. R. R. 66.

Mode of Packing Cigars.

[Sec. 85. (July 20, 1868.) *And be it further enacted*, That from and after the passage of this act all cigars shall be packed in boxes, not before used for that purpose, containing respectively twenty-five, fifty, one hundred, two hundred and fifty, or five hundred cigars each; and any person who shall sell, or offer for sale, or deliver or offer to deliver, any cigars in any other form than in new boxes as above described, or who shall pack in any box any cigars in excess of the number provided by law to be put in each box, respectively, or who shall falsely brand any box, or shall affix a stamp on any box denoting a less amount of tax than that required by law, shall, upon conviction, for any of the above-described offences, be fined for each such offence not less than one hundred dollars nor more than one thousand dollars, and be imprisoned not less than six months nor more than two years: *Provided*, That nothing in this section shall be construed as preventing the sale of cigars at retail by retail dealers who have paid the special tax as such from boxes packed, stamped, and branded in the manner prescribed by law.]

Retail dealers are allowed to retail cigars from boxes packed, stamped and branded in the manner prescribed by law. They cannot retail cigars from show-cases. The presence of the revenue stamp is necessary to give currency to the goods. 10 I. R. R. 66.

Cigar Manufacturers to Furnish Statements, Keep Books, etc.

[Sec. 86. (July 20, 1868.) *And be it further enacted*, That every person now or hereafter engaged in the manufacture of cigars, shall make and deliver to the assistant assessor of the division a true inventory, in form prescribed by the Commissioner of Internal Revenue, of the quantity of leaf tobacco, cigars, stems, scraps, clippings, and waste, and the number of cigar-boxes and the capacity of each box, held or owned by him on the first day of January of each year, or at the time of commencing and at the time of concluding business, if before or after the first of January, setting forth what portion of said goods, and what kinds, were manufactured or produced by him, and what were purchased from others, which inventory shall be verified by his oath or affirmation indorsed on said inventory; and the assistant assessor shall make personal examination of the stock sufficient to satisfy himself as to the correctness of the inventory, and shall verify the fact of such examination by oath or affirmation taken before the assessor, also to be indorsed on the inventory; and every such person shall enter daily in a book, (*a*) the form of which shall be prescribed by the Commissioner of Internal Revenue, an accurate account of all the articles aforesaid purchased by him, the quantity of leaf tobacco, cigars, stems, or cigar boxes, of whatever description, manufactured, sold, consumed, or removed for consumption or sale, or removed from the place of manufacture; and shall, on or before the tenth day of each and every month, furnish to the assistant assessor of the division a true and accurate abstract from such book of all such purchases, sales, and removals made during the month next preceding, which abstract shall be verified by his oath or affirmation; and in case of refusal or wilful neglect to deliver the inventory, or keep the account, or furnish the abstract aforesaid, he shall, on conviction, be fined not less than five hundred dollars nor more than five thousand dollars, and imprisoned not less than six months nor more than three years.

It shall be the duty of any dealer in leaf tobacco or material used in manufacturing cigars, on demand of any Officer of Internal Revenue authorized by law, to render to such officer a true and correct statement, verified by oath or affirmation, of the quantity and amount of such leaf tobacco or materials sold or delivered to any person or persons named in such demand; and in case of refusal or neglect to render such statement, or if there is cause to believe such statement to be incorrect or fraudulent, the assessor shall make an examination of persons, books, and papers, in the same manner as provided in this act in relation to frauds and evasions.]

(*a*) Books must be kept by manufacturers according to Form 73. Their abstracts or monthly returns must be made on Form 72. 10 I. R. R. 66.

A cigar manufacturer who has on hand stems or waste which are not worth the trouble of keeping and who desires to destroy the same may do so in the presence and under the supervision of an internal revenue officer, and the assessor will give him credit upon the proper books for the amount destroyed. 10 I. R. R. 153.

The return must include sales of cigars that have been bought as well as of those that have been manufactured by the manufacturer. U. S. *v.* Cohn, 7 I. R. R. 69; U. S. *v.* Hoym, 7 I. R. R. 69.

Stamps for Cigars.

[SEC. 87. (July 20, 1868.) *And be it further enacted*, That the Commissioner of Internal Revenue shall cause to be prepared, for payment of the tax upon cigars, suitable stamps, (*a*) denoting the tax thereon; and all cigars shall be packed in quantities of twenty-five, fifty, one hundred, two hundred and fifty, and five hundred, and all such stamps shall be furnished to collectors requiring the same, who shall, if there be any cigar manufacturers within their respective districts, keep on hand at all times a supply equal in amount to two months' sales thereof, and shall sell the same only to the cigar manufacturers who have given bonds and paid the special tax, as required by law, in their districts respectively, and to importers of cigars who are required to affix the same to imported cigars in the custody of customs officers and to persons required by law to affix the same to cigars on hand on the first day of January, Anno Domini eighteen hundred and sixty-nine; and every collector shall keep an account of the number, amount, and denominate values of the stamps sold by him to each cigar manufacturer, and to other persons above described: *Provided*, That from and after the passage of this act, the duty on all cigars imported into the United States from foreign countries shall be two dollars and fifty cents [per] pound, and twenty-five per centum ad valorem.]

(*a*) Stamps are furnished to collectors to be sold only to cigar manufacturers who have given bonds and paid the special tax in their districts respectively. 10 I. R. R. 66.

Labels for Cigars.

[SEC. 88. (July 20, 1868.) *And be it further enacted*, That every manufacturer of cigars shall securely affix, by pasting on each box containing cigars manufactured by or for him, a label (*a*) on which shall be printed, together with the manufacturer's name, the number of his manufactory, and the district and State in which it is situated, these words:

"NOTICE.—The manufacturer of the cigars herein contained has complied with all the requirements of law. Every person is cautioned, under the penalties of law, not to use this box for cigars again."

Any manufacturer of cigars who shall neglect to affix such label to any box containing cigars made by or for him, or sold or offered for sale by or for him, or any person who shall remove any such label, so affixed, from any such box, shall, upon conviction thereof, be fined fifty dollars for each box in respect to which such offence shall be committed.]

(a) The law makes no provision for the removal of cigars in bond, or to a bonded warehouse, either for export or consumption. All cigars removed from the place of manufacture must be stamped. 10 I. R. R. 66.

Name on Cigar Labels.

[SEC. 1. (April 10, 1869.) That section eighty-eight be amended so that either the proprietor's name or the manufacturer's name shall be printed on the label for cigars provided for in said section.]

Penalty for Fraudulent Removal of Cigars.

[SEC. 89. (July 20, 1868.) *And be it further enacted,* That all cigars which shall be removed from any manufactory or place where cigars are made, without the same being packed in boxes as required by this act, or without the proper stamp thereon denoting the tax, or without burning into each box, with a branding iron, the number of the cigars contained therein, and the name of the manufacturer, and the number of the district, and the State, or without the stamp denoting the tax thereon being properly affixed and cancelled, or which shall be sold or offered for sale not properly boxed and stamped, shall be forfeited to the United States. And any person who shall commit any of the above-described offences shall, on conviction, be fined for each such offence not less than one hundred dollars nor more than one thousand dollars, and imprisoned not less than six months nor more than two years. And any person who shall pack cigars in any box bearing a false or fraudulent or counterfeit stamp, or who shall remove or cause to be removed any stamp denoting the tax on cigars from any box, with intent to use the same, or who shall use or permit any other person to use any stamp so removed, or who shall receive, buy, sell, give away, or have in his possession any stamp so removed, or who shall make any other fraudulent use of any stamp, or stamped box intended for cigars, or who shall remove from the place of manufacture any cigars not properly boxed and stamped as required by law, shall be deemed guilty of a felony, and, on conviction, shall be fined not less than one hundred dollars nor more than one thousand dollars, and imprisoned not less than six months nor more than three years.]

Absence of Stamp Evidence of Fraud.

[SEC. 90. (July 20, 1868.) *And be it further enacted*, That the absence of the proper revenue stamp on any box of cigars sold, or offered for sale, or kept for sale, shall be notice to all persons that the tax has not been paid thereon, and shall be prima facie evidence of the non-payment thereof; and such cigars shall be forfeited to the United States.]

Manufacture of Cigars on Commission.

[SEC. 91. (July 20, 1868.) *And be it further enacted*, That in all cases where cigars of any description are manufactured, in whole or in part, upon commission or shares, or where the material is furnished by one party and manufactured by another, or where the material is furnished or sold by one party with an understanding or agreement with another that the cigars are to be received in payment therefor, or for any part thereof, the stamps required by law shall be affixed by the actual maker before the cigars are removed from the place of manufacturing. And in case of fraud on the part of either of said parties in respect to said manufacture, or of any collusion on their part with intent to defraud the revenue, such material and cigars shall be forfeited to the United States, and every person engaged in such fraud or collusion shall, on conviction, be fined not less than one hundred dollars nor more than five thousand dollars, and imprisoned for not less than six months nor more than three years.]

Penalty for Fraud in the Manufacture or Sale of Cigars.

[SEC. 92. (July 20, 1868.) *And be it further enacted*, That any manufacturer of cigars, who shall remove or sell (*a*) any cigars without payment of the special tax as a cigar manufacturer, or without having given bond as such, or without the proper stamps denoting the tax thereon, or who shall make false or fraudulent entries of manufactures or sales of any cigars, or who shall make false or fraudulent entries of the purchase or sales of leaf tobacco, tobacco stems, or other material used in the manufacture of cigars, or who shall affix any false, forged, spurious, fraudulent, or counterfeit stamp, or imitation of any stamp required by law to any box containing any cigars, shall, in addition to the penalties elsewhere provided in this act for such offences, forfeit to the United States all raw material and manufactured or partly manufactured tobacco and cigars, and all machinery, tools, implements, apparatus, fixtures, boxes, barrels, and all other materials, which shall be found in the possession of such person, or in his manufactory, and used in his business as such manufacturer, together with his estate or interest in the building or factory and the lot or tract of ground on which such building or factory is located, and all appurtenances thereunto belonging.]

(a) Cigars kept for sale must be stamped. It is not sufficient that the owner intends to stamp before sale. U. S. v. Woolheim, 11 I. R. R. 78; Anon. 11 I. R. R. 10.

Stamps on Imported Cigars.

[SEC. 93. (July 20, 1868.) *And be it further enacted*, That all cigars imported from foreign countries after the passage of this act shall, in addition to the import duties imposed on the same, pay the tax prescribed in this act for cigars manufactured in the United States, and have the same stamps (a) affixed. Such stamps shall be affixed and cancelled by the owner or importer of cigars while they are in the custody of the proper customhouse officers; and such cigars shall not pass out of the custody of such officers until the stamps have been so affixed and cancelled, but shall be put up in boxes containing quantities as prescribed in this act for cigars manufactured in the United States before such stamps are affixed. And the owner or importer of such cigars shall be liable to all the penal provisions of this act prescribed for manufacturers of cigars manufactured in the United States. Where it shall be necessary to take any of such cigars, so imported, to any place for the purpose of affixing and cancelling such stamps, other than the public stores of the United States, the collector of customs of the port where such cigars shall be entered shall designate a bonded warehouse to which they shall be taken, under the control of such customs officer as such collector may direct. And any officer of customs who shall permit any such cigars to pass out of his custody or control without compliance by the owner or importer thereof with the provisions of this section relating thereto shall be deemed guilty of a misdemeanor, and shall, on conviction thereof, be fined not less than one thousand dollars nor more than five thousand dollars, and imprisoned not less than six months nor more than three years.]

(a) The work and labor of affixing and cancelling stamps on imported cigars can only be performed by sworn officers and employees of the customs, under the direction and control of the collector; and for such services there will be collected from importers a fee of twenty cents for each thousand cigars so stamped and cancelled, which shall be turned into the Treasury for the use of the United States and be accounted for by the collector as other customs fees. 10 I. R. R. 50.

Inventory of Cigars on Hand.

[SEC. 94. (July 20, 1868.) *And be it further enacted*, That from and after the passage of this act it shall be the duty of every dealer in cigars, either of foreign or domestic manufacture, having on hand more than five thousand thereof, imported or manufactured, or purporting or claimed to have been imported or manufactured, prior to the passage of this act, to immediately make a true and correct inventory of the quantity of such cigars in his possession, under oath or affirmation, and to deposit such inventory with the assistant assessor of the proper division, who shall immediately return the same to the assessor of the district, who shall immediately thereafter make an abstract of the several such inventories filed in his office, and transmit the same to the Commissioner of Internal Revenue ; and a like inventory and return shall be made on the first day of every month thereafter, and a like abstract of inventories shall be transmitted, while any such dealer has any such cigars remaining on hand, until the first day of April, eighteen hundred and sixty-nine. After the first day of April, eighteen hundred and sixty-nine, all cigars of every description shall be taken to have been either manufactured or imported after the passage of this act, and shall be stamped accordingly ; and any person who shall sell, or offer for sale, after the first day of April, eighteen hundred and sixty nine, any imported cigars, or cigars purporting or claimed to have been imported, not so put up in packages and stamped as provided by this act, shall, on conviction thereof, be fined not less than five hundred dollars nor more than five thousand dollars, and imprisoned not less than six months nor more than two years.]

Refunding Taxes on Cigars.

[SEC. 3. (April 10, 1869.) *And be it further enacted,* That any person having in his possession any tobacco, snuff, or cigars, manufactured and sold or removed from the manufactory, or from any place where tobacco, snuff, or cigars are made, since July twentieth, eighteen hundred and sixty-eight, or any person having in his possession cigars imported from foreign countries since July twentieth, eighteen hundred and sixty-eight, or withdrawn from a United States bonded warehouse since said date, such tobacco, snuff, and cigars having been put up in packages as prescribed in the act to which this act is an amendment, and all the other requirements of said act relating to tobacco, snuff and cigars having been complied with, and who, on the first day of February, eighteen hundred and sixty nine, filed with the assessor or assistant assessor of the district within which he resides, or has his place of business, the inventory required by the seventy-eighth and ninety-fourth sections of the act of July twentieth, eighteen hundred and sixty-eight, and who shall, prior to selling or offering such tobacco, snuff or cigars for sale, affix and cancel proper internal revenue stamps, shall be entitled to have refunded to him an amount of tax previously paid thereon equal to the value of the stamps affixed before sale as aforesaid; and the Commissioner of Internal Revenue shall be, and is hereby, authorized, on appeal to him made, to refund and pay back a sum of money equal to the value of the stamps so affixed, upon satisfactory evidence submitted to him that the tobacco and snuff were actually manufactured and removed from the place of manufacture, and that the cigars were so manufactured and removed, or imported and withdrawn from a United States bonded warehouse, and the several rates of tax imposed on such goods by the act of July twentieth, eighteen hundred and sixty-eight, as aforesaid, assessed and paid, and that the claimant had in all respects complied with the internal revenue laws as far as they have been or may be applicable to such articles. The Commissioner of Internal Revenue is hereby authorized and empowered to prescribe such rules and regulations for carrying out the provisions of this section as in his judgment shall be deemed proper and necessary; and the Commissioner may in any case, at his discretion, allow snuff and smoking tobacco manufactured prior to the twentieth of July, eighteen hundred and sixty-eight, not in wooden packages, to be stamped and sold in the original packages; and the rate of duty on cigars imported prior to July twentieth, eighteen hundred and sixty-eight, and now remaining in bond, shall be the same as on cigars imported after that date.]

Penalty for Fraudulent Representations on Sales of Cigars.

[SEC. 95. (July 20, 1868.) *And be it further enacted,* That any person who shall, after the passage of this act, sell or offer for sale any cigars, representing the same to have been manufactured and the tax paid thereon prior to the passage of this act, when the same were not so manufactured and the tax not so paid, shall be liable to a penalty of five hundred dollars for each offence, and shall be deemed guilty of a misdemeanor, and, on conviction, shall be fined not less than five hundred dollars nor more than five thousand dollars, and imprisoned not less than six months nor more than three years.]

Penalty for Wilful Violation of Law.

[SEC. 96. (July 20, 1868.) *And be it further enacted,* That if any distiller, rectifier, wholesale liquor dealer, componnder of liquors, or manufacturer of tobacco or cigars, shall knowingly and wilfully (*a*) omit, neglect, or refuse to do or cause to be done any of the things required by law in the carrying on or conducting of his business, or shall do anything by this act prohibited, if there be no specific penalty or punishment imposed by any other section of this act for the neglecting, omitting, or refusing to do, or for the doing or causing to be done the thing required or prohibited, he shall pay a penalty of one thousand dollars; and if the person so offending be a distiller, rectifier, wholesale liquor dealer, or compounder of liquors, all distilled spirits or liquors owned by him, or in which he has any interest as owner, and if he be a manufacturer of tobacco or cigars, all tobacco or cigars found in his manufactory, shall be forfeited to the United States.]

(*a*) When a specific penalty is imposed by other sections, whether the act or omission was a knowing or wilful one or not, such specified penalty alone is imposed, and this section is only intended to apply to those acts or omissions mentioned in the different sections for which no specific penalty is imposed, and only then when such act or omission was both knowing and wilful. U. S. *v.* Rectifying Establishment, 11 I. R. R. 45; U. S. *v.* Rectifying Establishment, 11 I. R. R. 46; U. S. *v.* 138 Casks, 11 I. R. R. 191; U. S. *v.* 87 Bbls. 11 I. R. R. 125. Contra, U. S. *v.* Quantity of Spirits, 11 I. R. R. 3; s. c. 3 A. L. T. (C. R.) 10.

The phrase "cause to be done" indicates the intention of Congress to make the omission to cause to be done any of the things required by law an offence in cases where it is not the duty of the offender himself to do them. The words "knowingly and wilfully" restrict the operation of the statute to those cases where the offender knowing what is required by law wilfully omits to cause it to be done. The offender is presumed to know the law. U. S. *v.* 133 Casks, 11 I. R. R. 191; U. S. *v.* Rectifying Establishment, 11 I. R. R. 3; U. S. *v.* 87 Bbls. 11 I. R. R. 125; U. S. *v.* Quantity of Spirits, 10 I. R. R. 206.

The forfeiture attaches only to the property owned by the offender at the time the act which causes the forfeiture was committed. It does not attach to property subsequently acquired. U. S. *v.* Cask, 10 I. R. R. 93.

A claimant may take advantage of the statute of limitations under an answer in the nature of a plea of the general issue. U. S. *v.* Six Tubs. 8 I. R. R. 9; s. c. 1 A. L. T. (C. R.) 126.

Penalty for Fraud in Distilling Spirits.

[SEC. 5. (March 31, 1868.) *And be it further enacted*, That every person engaged in carrying on the business of a distiller who shall defraud or attempt to defraud the United States of the tax on the spirits distilled by him, or any part thereof, shall forfeit the distillery and distilling apparatus used by him, and all distilled spirits and all raw material for the production of distilled spirits found in the distillery and on the distillery premises, and shall, on conviction, be fined not less than five hundred dollars nor more than five thousand dollars, and be imprisoned not less than six months nor more than three years.]

Penalty against Officers Interested in Distilleries, etc.

[Sec. 97. (July 20, 1868.) *And be it further enacted,* That any internal revenue officer who shall be or become interested, directly or indirectly, in the manufacture of tobacco, snuff, or cigars, or in the production, rectification, or redistillation of distilled spirits, shall be dismissed from office; and any such officer who shall become so interested in any such manufacture or production, rectification, or redistillation, shall, on conviction, be fined not less than five hundred dollars nor more than five thousand dollars.]

Penalty for Extortion, Fraud, etc.

[Sec. 98. (July 20, 1868.) *And be it further enacted,* That if any officer or agent appointed and acting under the authority of any revenue law of the United States shall be guilty of any extortion or wilful oppression, under color of law; or shall knowingly demand other or greater sums than shall be authorized by law; or shall receive any fee, compensation, or reward for the performance of any duty except as by law prescribed; or shall wilfuly neglect to perform any of the duties enjoined on him by law; or shall conspire or collude with any other person to defraud the United States; or shall make opportunity for any person to defraud the United States; or shall do, or omit to do, any act with intent to enable any other person to defraud the United States; or shall negligently or designedly permit any violation of the law by any other person; or shall make or sign any false entry in any book, or make or sign any false certificate or return in any case where he is by law or regulation required to make any entry, certificate, or return; or having knowledge or information of the violation of any revenue law by any person, or of fraud committed by any person against the United States under any revenue law of the United States, shall fail to report, in writing, such knowledge or information to his next superior officer, and to the Commissioner of Internal Revenue; or shall demand, or accept, or attempt to collect, directly or indirectly, as payment or gift or otherwise, any sum of money or other thing of value for the compromise, adjustment, or settlement of any charge or complaint for any violation or alleged violation of law, except as expressly authorized by law so to do, he shall be dismissed from office, and shall be held to be guilty of a misdemeanor, and shall, on conviction, be fined not less than one thousand dollars nor more than five thousand dollars, and imprisoned not less than six months nor more than three years. And one-half of the fine so imposed shall be for the use of the United States, and the other half for the use of the informer who shall be ascertained by the judgment of the court; and

Penalty for Fraudulent Bonds.

[SEC. 99. (July 20, 1863.) *And be it further enacted*, That any person who shall simulate or falsely or fraudulently execute or sign any bond, (*a*) permit, entry, or other document required by the provisions of this act, or by any regulation made in pursuance thereof, or who shall procure the same to be falsely or fraudulently executed; or who shall advise, aid in, or connive at the execution thereof, shall, on conviction, be imprisoned for a term not less than one year nor more than five years; and the property to which such false or fraudulent instrument relates shall be forfeited.]

(*a*) An officer cannot disregard a requirement of the law because he thinks it useless, or deems the government protected by other provisions. The duties of the citizen and of the officer in regard to the bonds are plainly set forth, and these duties must be peformed. The duty of one officer cannot be measured by the practice of some other officer. U. S. *v.* Allen et al., 7 I. R. R. 163; U. S. *v.* O'Brien, 7 I. R. R. 62; U. S. *v.* Callicott et al. 7 I. R. R. 177.

Penalty for Official Misconduct.

[SEC. 6. (March 31, 1868.) *And be it further enacted*, That if any officer or agent appointed and acting under the authority of any revenue law of the United States shall be guilty of gross neglect in the discharge of any of the duties of his office, or shall conspire or collude with any other person to defraud the United States, or shall make opportunity for any person to defraud the United States, or shall do or omit to do any act with intent to enable any other person to defraud the United States, or shall make or sign any false certificate or return, in any case where he is by law or regulation required to make a certificate or return, or having knowledge or information of the violation of any revenue law, by any person, or of fraud committed by any person against the United States under any revenue law of the United States, shall fail to report, in writing, such knowledge or information to his next superior officer and to the Commissioner of Internal Revenue, he shall, on conviction, be fined not less than one thousand dollars nor more than five thousand dollars, and shall be imprisoned not less than six months nor more than three years.]

Collector's Bonded Account.

[SEC. 100. (July 20, 1868.) *And be it further enacted*, That every collector having charge of any warehouse in which distilled spirits, tobacco, or other articles are stored in bond, shall render a monthly account of all such articles to the Commissioner of Internal Revenue, which account shall be examined and adjusted monthly by him, so as to exhibit a true statement of the liability and responsibility of every such collector on such account. In adjusting such account the collector shall be charged with all the articles which may have been deposited or received under the provisions of law, in any warehouse in his district and under his control, and shall be credited with all such articles shown to have been removed therefrom according to law, including transfers to other collectors and to his successor in office, and also whatever allowances may have been made in accordance with law to any owner of such goods or articles for leakage or other losses.]

Commissioner to make Regulations for Stamps, Labels and Marks.

[SEC. 101. (July 20, 1868.) *And be it further enacted*, That the Secretary of the Treasury and Commissioner of Internal Revenue are authorized and empowered to alter, renew, or change the form, style, and device of any stamp, mark, or label used under any provision of the laws relating to distilled spirits, tobacco, snuff, and cigars, when in their judgment necessary for the collection of revenue tax, or the prevention or detection of frauds thereon ; and to make and publish such regulations for the use of such mark, stamp, or label as they may find requisite. But in no case shall such renewal or change extend to an abandonment of the general character of the stamps provided for in this act, nor to the dispensing with any provisions requiring that such stamps shall be kept in book form and have thereon the signatures of revenue officers.]

Compromising Suits.

[SEC. 102. (July 20, 1868.) *And be it further enacted*, That in all cases arising under the internal revenue laws where, instead of commencing or proceeding with a suit in court, it may appear to the Commissioner of Internal Revenue to be for the interest of the United States to compromise (*a*) the same, he is empowered and authorized to make such compromise with the advice and consent of the Secretary of the Treasury; and in every case where a compromise is made there shall be placed on file in the office of the Commissioner the opinion of the solicitor of internal revenue, or officer acting as such, with his reasons therefor, together with a statement of the amount of tax assessed, the amount of additional tax or penalty imposed by law in consequence of the neglect or delinquency of the person against whom the tax is assessed, and the amount actually paid in accordance with the terms of the compromise; but no such compromise shall be made of any case after a suit or proceeding in court has been commenced, without the recommendation also of the Attorney General: *Provided*, That it shall be lawful for the court at any stage of such suit or criminal proceedings to continue the same for good cause shown on motion of the district attorney.]

(*a*) This section does not indicate the order in which the officers named shall act, but it does require, before any compromise shall be made of a pending suit, that the Commissioner, the Secretary of the Treasury, and the Attorney General shall concur in the opinion that a compromise would be advantageous to the United States. It is the Commissioner alone who can actually compromise a claim arising under the internal revenue laws. The functions of the Secretary of the Treasury and Attorney General are advisory. The Commissioner may compromise with their consent, but even in a case where both of them advise and consent to a proposed compromise, he may refuse to accept it. Before he submits a proposal to them it should appear to him that it would be for the interest of the United States that a compromise should be effected. If they both concur in the opinion that a compromise should be accepted, he will then be authorized to make it. If they agree that the proposed compromise would be inexpedient, or if they differ in opinion upon that question, he is not authorized to accept it. 8 I. R. R. 86.

This section includes all cases in which criminal proceedings have been or may be instituted, as well as those which may be prosecuted *civiliter*. Violations of the internal revenue laws, punishable by a fine in the discretion of the court, or by imprisonment with or without a fine, can be compromised, if no proceedings have been instituted, by the Commissioner, with the advice and consent of the Secretary of the Treasury; and if such proceedings have been commenced in court, then by these persons on the recommendation of the Attorney General. When proceedings have been begun before a Commissioner and the prisoner held to appear at the next term of court and that term has not expired, all propositions of compromise should be sent by the Commissioner to the Attorney General. District Attorneys may discontinue criminal proceedings before Commissioners, either without the payment of costs or on the payment of costs, when they are of the opinion that the public interests do not require any prosecution, —subject, however, to the general superintendence of the Attorney General or the head of any executive department or bureau to which the subject-matter belongs. Except in this case, district attorneys cannot discontinue or settle any case, whether civil or criminal, in court or out of court, by receiving for the United States any sum of money in the way of compromise or as a fine. 11 I. R. R. 18.

District attorneys cannot enter a *nolle prosequi* on payment of costs, without obtaining authority from either the Commissioner, the Secretary of the Treasury, or the Attorney-General, because such an entry is substantially a compromise. On receiving authority from either of these persons, it is to be presumed that all have been consulted, and have agreed to authorize a compromise. Attorneys should correspond in the first instance with the Commissioner. 11 I. R. R. 98.

Entering Nolle Prosequi.

[SEC. 7. (March 31, 1868.) *And be it further enacted*, That no compromise, or discontinuance, or nolle prosequi of any prosecution under this act shall be allowed without the permission in writing of the Secretary of the Treasury and the Attorney General.]

Regulations for Time of Assessment.

[SEC. 103. (July 20, 1868.) *And be it further enacted*, That when any tax (*a*) is imposed, and the mode or time of assessment or collection is not provided for, the same shall be established by regulation of the Commissioner of Internal Revenue; and the Commissioner is authorized to make all such regulations, not otherwise provided for, as may become necessary by reason of any change of law in relation to Internal Revenue made by this act.]

(*a*) The mode and practice of assessment and collection of taxes in the Indian Territory must be the same as in regular collection districts. 11 I. R. R. 43.

Meaning of Terms.

[SEC. 104. (July 20, 1868.) *And be it further enacted*, That where not otherwise distinctly expressed or manifestly incompatible with the intent thereof, the word "person," as used in this act, shall be construed to mean and include a firm, partnership, association, company, or corporation, as well as a natural person; and words of the masculine gender, as applied to persons, to mean and include the feminine gender; and the singular number to mean and include the plural number; and the word "State" to mean and include a Territory and District of Columbia; and the word "county" to mean and include parish, district, or other equivalent territorial subdivision of a State.]

Repeal of Prior Acts.

[SEC. 105. (July 20, 1868.) *And be it further enacted*, That all acts and parts of acts inconsistent with the provisions of this act are hereby repealed: *Provided*, That all the provisions of said acts shall be in force for levying and collecting all taxes properly assessed or liable to be assessed, or accruing under the provisions of former acts, the right to which has already accrued or which may hereafter accrue under said acts, and for maintaining, continuing, and enforcing liens, fines, penalties, and forfeitures incurred under and by virtue thereof. And this act shall not be construed to affect any act done, right accrued, or penalty incurred, under former acts, but every such right is hereby saved; and all suits and prosecutions for acts already done in violation of any former act or acts of Congress, relating to the subjects embraced in this act, may be commenced or proceeded with in like manner as if this act had not been passed: *And provided further*, That no office created by the said acts and continued by this act shall be vacated by reason of any provisions herein contained, but the officers heretofore appointed shall continue to hold the said offices without reappointment until their successors, or others officers to perform their duties, respectively, shall be appointed as provided in this act: *And provided further*, That whenever the duty imposed by any existing law shall cease in consequence of any limitation therein contained before the respective provisions of this act shall take effect, the same duty or tax shall be, and is hereby, continued until such provisions of this act shall take effect; and where any act is hereby repealed, no duty or tax imposed thereby shall be held to cease in consequence of such repeal, until the respective *correspective* corresponding provisions of this act shall take effect.]

The penalties imposed by previous laws are saved by this section. U. S. *v.* 6 Tubs, 8 I. R. R. 9.

Bill in Chancery to Enforce Lien for Taxes.

[SEC. 106. (July 20, 1868.) *And be it further enacted*, That in any case where there has been a refusal or neglect to pay any tax imposed by the Internal Revenue laws, and where it is lawful and has become necessary to seize and sell real estate to satisfy the tax, the Commissioner of Internal Revenue may, if he deems it expedient, direct that a bill in chancery be filed, in a district or circuit court of the United States, to enforce the lien of the United States for tax upon any real estate, or to subject any real estate owned by the delinquent, or in which he has any right, title, or interest, to the payment of such tax. And all persons having liens upon the real estate sought to be subjected to the payment of any tax as aforesaid, or claiming any ownership or interest therein, shall be made parties to such proceedings, and shall be brought into court as provided in other suits in chancery in said courts. And the said courts shall have, and are hereby given, jurisdiction in all such cases, and shall at the term next after such time as the parties shall be duly notified of the proceedings, unless otherwise ordered by the court, proceed to adjudicate all matters involved therein, and to pass upon and finally determine the merits of all claims to and liens upon the real estate in question, and shall, in all cases where a claim or interest of the United States therein shall be established, decree a sale, by the proper officer of the court, of such real estate, and a distribution of the proceeds of such sale according to the findings of the court in respect to the interests of the parties and of the United States.]

Tax Imposed on Articles Produced Anywhere in the United States.

[SEC. 107. (July 20, 1868.) *And be it further enacted,* That the Internal Revenue laws imposing taxes on distilled spirits, fermented liquors, tobacco, snuff, and cigars, shall be held and construed to extend to such articles produced anywhere within the exterior boundaries of the United States, whether the same shall be within a collection district or not.]

When Act takes Effect.

[SEC. 108. (July 20, 1868.) *And be it further enacted,* That all provisions of this act which require the use of stamps shall take effect at the end of sixty days from the passage of this act: *Provided,* That if at any time prior to the expiration of the said sixty days it shall be shown to the satisfaction of the Secretary of the Treasury that a longer delay is necessary for the preparation and due delivery of any of such stamps, he shall be authorized to fix a day not later than the first day of December next for putting said provisions, relative to the use of either of such stamps, into operation, and shall give public notice of the day so fixed and determined upon, which day shall then be held and taken to be the time when that portion of this act which requires the use of stamps shall have effect.]

SPECIAL TAXES.

Persons Liable to Special Tax.

Sec. 71. (Amended July 13, 1866, § 9.) *And be it further enacted,* That no person, firm, company, or corporation shall be engaged in, prosecute, or carry on any trade, business, or profession, hereinafter mentioned and described, until he or they shall have paid a special tax (*a*) therefor in the manner hereinafter provided.

(*a*) No liability to payment of special tax is incurred by any person with respect to business done on an Indian Reservation. 11 I. R. R. 177.

Every change of firm, whereby a former partner retires from the same, or a new partner is admitted, constitutes in contemplation of law a new firm, liable to new special tax for the unexpired portion of the year for which the same has been paid by the original firm, which should be assessed from the first day of the month in which the change occurs. A person retiring from business during the year for which he has paid the tax cannot transfer his receipt to the person succeeding him. 10 I. R. R. 78.

If any member of a firm transacts on his own private account a business for which a special tax is required, he should be assessed without reference to the fact that the firm to which he belongs has paid a tax for the same or any other kind of business. 6 I. R. R. 162.

The law is intended to operate upon the person and not upon the business. A contract is valid, even though the party making it has not paid a special tax. Aiken v. Blaisdell, 41 Vt. 655.

Registration of Persons Liable to Special Tax.

Sec. 72. (Amended July 13, 1866, § 9.) *And be it further enacted,* That every person, firm, company, or corporation engaged in any trade, business, or profession, on which a special tax is imposed by law, shall register with the assistant assessor of the assessment district, first, his or their name or style, and in case of a firm or company, the names of the several persons constituting such firm or company, and their places of residence; second, the trade, business, or profession, and the place where such trade, business, or profession is to be carried on; third, if a rectifier, the number of barrels he designs to rectify; if a peddler, whether he designs to travel on foot, or with one, two, or more horses or mules; if an inn-keeper, the yearly rental value of the house and property to be occupied for said purpose. All of which facts shall be returned duly certified by such assistant assessor, to both the assessor and collector of the district; and the special tax shall be paid to the collector or deputy collector of the district as hereinafter provided for such trade, business, or profession, who shall give a receipt therefor.

Penalty for Carrying on Business without Payment of the Special Tax.

Sec. 73. (Amended March 2, 1867, § 9.) *And be it further enacted,* That any person who shall exercise or carry on any trade, business, or profession, or do any act hereinafter mentioned, for the exercising, carrying on, or doing of which a special tax is imposed by law, without payment thereof, as in that behalf required, shall, for every such offence, (*a*) besides being liable to the payment of the tax, be subject to a fine or penalty of not less than ten nor more than five hundred dollars. And if such person shall be a manufacturer of tobacco, snuff, or cigars, or a wholesale or retail dealer in liquor, he shall be further liable to imprisonment for a term not less than sixty days and not exceeding two years.

(*a*) A party carrying on a business without having paid the special tax may be punished by indictment. U. S. v. Chappel, 26 Law Rep. 22; U. S. v. Simons 12 I. R. R. 10.

The offence may be charged to have been committed on divers other days between a day named and the finding of the bill. It is not charging divers acts, each constituting a distinct and different offence, but the same offence committed on a day certain and on a day between ascertained dates. A verdict under such a charge would conclude any further indictment for the offence during that period. U. S. *v.* Trobe et al 2 I. R. R. 188.

The offence created by this section is a misdemeanor. The defendant has no right of peremptory challenge. The burden of proof is upon the defendant. It is incumbent upon him to show that he has paid the special tax. U. S. *v.* Develin, 7 I. R. R. 94; s. c. 6 Blatch. 71; s. c. 1 A. L. T. (C. R.) 88.

Contents and Legal Effect of Receipt.

Sec. 74. (Amended July 13, 1866, § 9.) *And be it further enacted,* That the receipt for the payment of any special tax shall contain and set forth the purpose, trade, business, or profession for which such tax is paid, and the name and place of abode of the person or persons paying the same; if by a rectifier, the quantity of spirits intended to be rectified; if by a peddler, whether for travelling on foot or with one, or two, or more horses or mules, the time for which payment is made, the date or time of payment, and (except in case of auctioneers, produce brokers, commercial brokers, patent-right dealers, photographers, builders, insurance agents, insurance brokers, and peddlers) the place at which the trade, business, or profession for which the tax is paid shall be carried on:

Provided, That the payment of the special tax herein imposed shall not exempt from an additional special tax the person or persons (except lawyers, physicians, surgeons, dentists, cattle brokers, horse dealers, peddlers, produce brokers, commercial brokers, patent-right dealers, photographers, builders, insurance agents, insurance brokers, and auctioneers), or firm, company, or corporation doing business in any other place than that stated; but nothing herein contained shall require a special tax for the storage of goods, wares, or merchandise in other places than the place of business, nor for the sale (*a*) by manufacturers or producers of their own goods, wares, and merchandise, at the place of production or manufacture, and at their principal office or place of business, provided no goods, wares, or merchandise shall be kept except as samples, at said office or place of business. And every person exercising or carrying on any trade, business, or profession, or doing any act for which a special tax is imposed, shall, on demand of any officer of internal revenue, produce and exhibit the receipt for payment of the tax, and unless he shall do so may be taken and deemed not to have paid such tax. And in case any peddler shall refuse to exhibit his or her receipt, as aforesaid, when demanded by any officer of internal revenue, said officer may seize the horse or mule, wagon, and contents, or pack, bundle, or basket of any person so refusing, and the assessor of the district in which the seizure has occurred may, on ten days' notice, published in any newspaper in the district, or served personally on the peddler, or at his dwelling-house, require such peddler to show cause, if any he has, why the horses or mules, wagon, and contents, pack, bundle, or basket so seized, shall not be forfeited; and in case no sufficient cause is shown, the assessor may direct a forfeiture, and issue an order to the collector or to any deputy collector of the district for the sale of the property so forfeited; and the same, after payment of the expenses of the proceedings, shall be paid to the collector for the use of the United States. And all such special taxes shall become due on the first day of May in each year, or on commencing any trade, business, or profession upon which such tax is by law imposed. In the former case the tax shall be reckoned for one year; and in the latter case, proportionately for that part of the year from the first day of the month in which the liability to a special tax commenced, to the first day of May following.

(*a*) A manufacturer may sell his products at the place of manufacture, in the manner of an auctioneer, or in any other manner, without liability to special tax therefor. 11 I. R. R. 145.

No Additional Tax in Case of Death or Removal.

Sec. 75. (Amended July 13, 1866, § 9.) *And be it further enacted,* That upon the death of any person having paid the special tax for any trade, business, or profession, it may and shall be lawful for the executors or administrators, or the wife or child, or the legal representatives of such deceased person, to occupy the house or premises, and in like manner to exercise or carry on, for the residue of the term for which the tax shall have been paid, the same trade, business, or profession, as the deceased before exercised or carried on, in or upon the same houses or premises, without payment of any additional tax. And in case of the removal (*a*) of any person or persons from the house or premises for which any trade, business, or profession was taxed, it shall be lawful for the person or persons so removing to any other place to carry on the trade, business, or profession specified in the tax receipt at the place to which such person or persons may remove without payment of any additional tax:

Provided, That all cases of death, change, or removal, as aforesaid, shall be registered with the assistant assessor, and with the collector, together with the name or names of the person or persons making such change or removal, or successor to any person deceased, under regulations to be prescribed by the Commissioner of Internal Revenue.

(*a*) In case of the removal of a party the measure of whose liability to tax depends upon the amount of his sales, the assistant assessor or collector of the district from which the removal is made should endorse upon the special tax receipt the fact of the discontinuance, as well as the amount of sales up to the time of removal. 10 I. R. R. 49.

Additional Tax for More than One Pursuit for the Same Person.

Sec. 76. (Amended July 13, 1866, § 9.) *And be it further enacted*, That in every case where more than one of the pursuits, employments, or occupations, hereinafter described, shall be pursued or carried on in the same place by the same person at the same time, except as hereinafter provided, the tax shall be paid for each according to the rates severally prescribed:

Provided, That in cities and towns having a less population than six thousand persons according to the last preceding census, one special tax shall be held to embrace the business of land warrant brokers, claim agents, and real estate agents, upon payment of the highest rate of tax applicable to either one of said pursuits.

Sales by Auctioneers.

Sec. 77. (Amended July 13, 1866, § 9.) *And be it further enacted*, That no auctioneer shall, by virtue of having paid the special tax as an auctioneer, sell any goods or other property at private sale, nor shall he employ any other person to act as auctioneer in his behalf, except in his own store or warehouse or in his presence; and any auctioneer who shall sell goods or commodities otherwise than by auction, without having paid the special tax imposed upon such business, shall be subject and liable to the penalty imposed upon persons dealing in or retailing, trading or selling goods or commodities without payment of the special tax for exercising or carrying on such trade or business; and where goods or commodities are the property of any person or persons taxed to deal in or retail, or trade in or sell the same, it shall and may be lawful for any person exercising or carrying on the trade or business of an auctioneer to sell such goods or commodities for and on behalf of such person or persons in said house or premises.

Tax on Partnerships.

Sec. 78. (Amended July 13, 1866, § 9.) *And be it further enacted*, That any number of persons, except lawyers, conveyancers, claim agents, patent agents, physicians, surgeons, dentists, cattle brokers, horse dealers, and peddlers, doing business in copartnership at any one place, shall be required to pay but one special tax for such copartnership.

Special Taxes.

Sec. 79. (Amended July 13, 1866, § 9; July 14, 1870, § 1.) *And be it further enacted*, That a special tax shall be, and hereby is, imposed as follows, that is to say:

Brewers (*a*) shall pay one hundred dollars. Every person, firm, or corporation who manufactures fermented liquors of any name or description, for sale, from malt, wholly or in part, or from any substitute therefor, shall be deemed a brewer: *Provided*, That any person, firm, or corporation, who manufactures less than five hundred barrels per year, shall pay the sum of fifty dollars.

(*a*) Manufacturers of weiss beer are brewers, and liable to this tax. 12 I. R. R. 29.

The taxes under this section should be assessed the same as they were prior to July 14, 1870, until May 1, 1871. 12 I. R. R. 69.

Special Tax when Gross Receipts do not Exceed $1,000.

Sec. 80. (Amended July 13, 1866, § 9.) *And be it further enacted*, That the special tax shall not be imposed upon apothecaries, confectioners, butchers, keepers of eating houses, hotels, inns, or taverns, or retail dealers, except retail dealers in spirituous and malt liquors when their annual gross receipts shall not exceed the sum of one thousand dollars, any provision of law to the contrary notwithstanding; the amount of such annual receipts to be ascertained or estimated in such manner as the Commissioner of Internal Revenue shall prescribe, as well as the amount of all other annual sales or receipts where the tax is graduated by the amount of sales or receipts; and where the amount of the tax has been increased by law above the amount paid by any person, firm, or company, or has been understated or underestimated, such person, firm, or company shall be again assessed, and pay the amount of such increase: *Provided*, That when any person, before the passage of this act, has been assessed for a license, the amount thus assessed being equal to the tax herein imposed for the business covered by such license, no special tax shall be assessed until the expiration of the period for which such license was assessed.

Wines of Native Growth.

Sec. 81. (Amended July 13, 1866, § 9.) *And be it further enacted*, That nothing contained in the preceding sections of this act shall be construed to impose a special tax upon vintners, who sell wine (*a*) of their own growth at the place where the same is made; nor upon apothecaries, as to wines or spirituous liquors which they use exclusively in the preparation or making up of medicines; nor shall physicians be taxed for keeping on hand medicines solely for the purpose of making up their own prescriptions for their own patients; nor shall farmers be taxed as manufacturers or producers, for making butter or cheese, with milk from their own cows, or for any other farm products:

Provided, That the payment of any tax imposed by law shall not be held or construed to exempt (*b*) any person carrying on any trade, business, or profession, from any penalty or punishment, provided by the laws of any State, for carrying on such trade, business, or profession within such State, or in any manner to authorize the commencement or continuance of such trade, business, or profession contrary to the laws of such State, or in places prohibited by municipal law; nor shall the payment of any tax herein provided be held or construed to prohibit or prevent any State from placing a duty or tax for State or other purposes, on any trade, business, or profession, upon which a tax is imposed by law.

(*a*) Manufacturers of wine from grapes, berries, or fruits of their own growth, are not liable to special tax as manufacturers or as liquor dealers for selling such wine at the place where the same is made. Where such wine is sold at any other place, liability to payment of tax as a liquor dealer is incurred. Where wines are manufactured from grapes, berries, or fruits not of the manufacturer's own growth, the manufacturer must pay special tax as a liquor dealer, whether he sells his products at the place of manufacture or otherwise. 12 I. R. R. 5.

(*b*) The internal revenue law does not, and cannot, give any authority to a party paying a special tax to carry on the business within the limits of a State. A party may be indicted, convicted, and condemned to pay the penalty imposed for not having paid the special tax, even though the business is prohibited by the laws of the State. License Tax Cases, 5 Wall. 46; s. c. 6 I. R. R. 96.

A party who has paid a special tax may be indicted and convicted under a State law for carrying on a business prohibited by that law, even though he has paid a special tax therefor. McGuire *v.* Commonwealth, 3 Wall. 382; Pervear *v.* Commonwealth, 5 Wall. 475; State *v.* Delano, 54 Me. 501; State *v.* Elder, 54 Me. 381; Commonwealth *v.* Keenan, 10 Allen, 262; Commonwealth *v.* Casey, 12 Allen, 214; Commonwealth *v.* Holbrook, 10 Allen, 200.

Refunding Excessive Taxes.

[SEC. 1. (July 27, 1866.) *Be it enacted by the Senate and House of Representatives of the United States of America in Congress assembled,* That where the license tax imposed upon any wholesale dealer has been calculated upon the amount of such dealer's sales for the previous year, in accordance with the terms of the seventy-ninth section of an act approved June thirtieth, eighteen hundred and sixty-four, and it shall be proved to the satisfaction of the Commissioner of Internal Revenue that the sales made under such license did not equal in amount the sales of such previous year, it shall be lawful for said Commsissioner to refund to such wholesale dealer so much of the amount paid for such license as may be in excess of the proper tax chargeable upon the amount of sales actually made under such license during the year for which the same was issued.]

ILLUMINATING GAS.

MANUFACTURES, ARTICLES, AND PRODUCTS.

Statements Furnished by Manufacturers.

Sec. 82. *And be it further enacted,* That every individual, partnership, firm, association, or corporation (and any word or words in this act indicating or referring to person or persons shall be taken to mean and include partnerships, firms, associations, or corporations, when not otherwise designated or manifestly incompatible with the intent thereof), shall comply with the following requirements, that is to say :

First. Before commencing, or, if already commenced, before continuing, any manufacture liable to be assessed under the provisions of this act, and which shall not be differently provided for elsewhere, every person shall furnish, without previous demand therefor, to the assistant assessor a statement, subscribed and sworn to, or affirmed, setting forth the place where the manufacture is to be carried on, and the principal place of business for sales, the name of the manufactured article, the proposed market for the same, whether foreign or domestic, and generally the kind and quality manufactured or proposed to be manufactured.

Second. He shall, within ten days after the first day of each and every month, or on or before a day prescribed by the Commissioner of Internal Revenue, make return under oath or affirmation of the products and sales, or delivery of such manufacture, in form and detail as may be required, from time to time, by the Commissioner of Internal Revenue.

Third. All such returns, statements, descriptions, memoranda, oaths, and affirmations shall be in form, scope and detail as may be prescribed, from time to time, by the Commissioner of Internal Revenue.

Time for Making Returns.

Sec. 83. (Amended March 3, 1865, § 1.) *And be it further enacted,* That upon the amounts, quantities, and values of produce, goods, wares, merchandise, and articles produced or manufactured, and sold or delivered, hereinafter enumerated, the manufacturer or producer thereof, whether manufactured or produced for himself or for others, shall pay to the collector of internal revenue within his district, monthly, within ten days from the twentieth day of each month, or on or before a day to be prescribed by the Commissioner of Internal Revenue, the duties on such products or manufactures. And for neglect to pay such duties within said ten days the amount of such duties, with the additions hereinbefore prescribed, may be levied upon the real and personal property of any such producer or manufacturer. And such duties and additions, and whatever shall be the expenses of levy, shall be a lien from the day prescribed by the Commissioner for their payment aforesaid, in favor of the United States, upon the said real and personal property of such producer or manufacturer; and such lien may be enforced by distraint, as provided in this act. And in all cases of goods manufactured or produced in whole or in part upon commission, or where the material is furnished by one party, and manufactured by another, if the manufacturer shall be required to pay under this act the tax hereby imposed, such person or persons so paying the same shall be entitled to collect the amount thereof of the owner or owners, and shall have a lien for the amount thus paid upon the produced or manufactured goods.

[This section is modified by act July 13, 1866, § 11. Vide ante page 64.—ED.]

Penalty for Refusal to Pay Taxes.

Sec. 84. (Amended March 3, 1865, § 1.) *And be it further enacted*, That for neglect or refusal to pay the duties provided by law on manufactured articles, or articles produced as aforesaid, the goods, wares, and merchandise, manufactured or produced and unsold by or not passed out of the possession of such manufacturer or producer, shall be forfeited to the United States, and may be sold or disposed of for the benefit of the same, in manner as shall be prescribed by the Commissioner of Internal Revenue, under the direction of the Secretary of the Treasury. In such case the collector or deputy collector may take possession of said articles, and may maintain such possession in the premises and buildings where they may have been manufactured, or deposited, or may be. He shall summon, giving notice of not less than two nor more than ten days, the parties in possession of said goods, enjoining them to appear before the assessor or assistant assessor, at a day and hour in such summons fixed, then and there to show cause, if any there be, why, for such neglect or refusal, such articles should not be declared forfeited to the United States.

The manufacturers or producers thereof shall be deemed to be the parties interested, if the articles shall be, at the time of taking such possession, upon the premises where manufactured or produced; if they shall at such time have been removed from the place of manufacture or production, the parties interested shall be deemed to be the persons or parties in whose custody or possession the articles shall be found. Such summons shall be served upon such parties in person, or by leaving a copy thereof at the place of abode or business of the party to whom the same may be directed. In case no such party or place can be found, which fact shall be determined by the collector's return on the summons, such notice, in the nature of a summons, shall be given by advertisement for the term of three weeks in one newspaper in the county nearest to the place of such sale.

If at or before such hearing such duties shall not have been paid, and the assessor or assistant assessor shall adjudge the summons and notice, service and return of the same to be sufficient, the said articles shall be by him declared forfeit, and shall be sold, disposed of, or turned over by the collector to the use of any department of the government as may be directed by the Secretary of the Treasury, who may require of any officer of the government into whose possession the same may be turned over the proper voucher therefor; and the proceeds of sale of said articles, if any there be after deducting the duties and additions thereon, together with the fees, costs, and expenses of all proceedings incident to the seizure and sale, to be determined by said Commissioner, shall be refunded and paid to the owner, or if he cannot be found, to the manufacturer or producer in whose custody the articles were when seized, as the said Commissioner may deem just, by draft on the same or some other collector; or if the said articles are turned over without sale to the use of any department of the government, the excess of the value of said articles, after deducting the amount of the duties, additions, fees, costs, and expenses accrued thereon when turned over as aforesaid, shall be refunded and paid by the said department to the owner, or, if he cannot be found, to the manufacturer or producer in whose custody or possession the said articles were when seized as aforesaid.

The Commissioner of Internal Revenue, with the approval of the Secretary of the Treasury, may review any such case of forfeiture and do justice in the premises. If the forfeiture shall have been wrongly declared, and sale made, the Secretary is hereby authorized, in case the specific articles cannot be restored to the party aggrieved in as good order and condition as when seized, to make up to such party in money his loss and damage from the contingent fund of his department. Immediate notice of any seizure of manufactured articles or products shall be given to the Commissioner of Internal Revenue by the collector or deputy collector, who shall also make return of his proceedings to the said Commissioner after he shall have sold or otherwise disposed of the articles or products so forfeited; and the assessor or assistant assessor shall also make return of his proceedings relating to such forfeitue to the said Commissioner.

And any violation of, or refusal to comply with, the provisions of the eighty-second section of this act, shall be good cause for seizure and forfeiture, substantially in manner as detailed in this section; but before forfeiture shall be declared by virtue of the provisions of this section, the amount of duties which may be due from the person whose manufactures or products are seized shall first be ascertained in the manner prescribed in the eighty-fifth section of this act; and such violation or refusal to comply shall further make any party so violating or refusing to comply liable to a fine or penalty of five hundred dollars, to be recovered in manner and form as provided in this act. Articles which the collector may adjudge perishable may be sold or disposed of before declaration of forfeiture. Said sales shall be made at public auction, and notice thereof shall be given as the said Commissioner shall prescribe.

Assessment in case of Fraudulent Evasion of Tax.

Sec. 85. *And be it further enacted,* That in case of the manufacture and sale or production and sale, consumption or delivery of any goods, wares, merchandise, or articles as hereinafter mentioned, without compliance on the part of the party manufacturing or producing the same with all the requirements and regulations prescribed by law in relation thereto, the assistant assessor may, upon such information as he may have, assume and estimate the amount and value of such manufactures or products, and upon such assumed amount assess the duties and add thereto fifty per centum; and said duties shall be collected in like manner as in case the provisions of this act in relation thereto had been complied with, and to such articles all the foregoing provisions for liens, fines, penalties, and forfeitures shall in like manner apply.

Statement must Contain the Full Amount of Actual Sales.

Sec. 86. (Amended July 13, 1866, § 9.) *And be it further enacted,* That any person, firm, company, or corporation, manufacturing or producing goods, wares, and merchandise, sold or removed for consumption or use, upon which taxes are imposed by law, shall, in their return of the value and quantity, render an account of the full amount of actual sales made by the manufacturer, producer, or agent thereof, and shall state whether any part, and if so, what part, of said goods, wares, and merchandise has been consumed or used by the owner, owners, or agent, or used for the production of another manufacture or product, together with the market value of the same at the time of such use or consumption; whether such goods, wares, and merchandise were shipped for a foreign port or consigned to auction or commission merchants, other than agents, for sale; and shall make a return according to the value at the place of shipment, when shipped for a foreign port, or according to the value at the place of manufacture or production, when removed for use or consumption, or consigned to others than agents of the manufacturer or producer.

The value and quantity of the goods, wares, and merchandise required to be stated as aforesaid shall be estimated by the actual sales made by the manufacturer or by his agent. And where such goods, wares, and merchandise have been removed for consumption, or for delivery to others, or placed on shipboard, or are no longer within the custody or control of the manufacturer or his agent, not being in his factory, store, or warehouse, the value shall be estimated at the average of the market value of the like goods, wares, and merchandise at the time when the same became liable to tax.

Tax on Illuminating Gas.

Sec. 94. (Amended July 13, 1866, § 9; March 2, 1867, § 9; March 31, 1868, § 1; July 20, 1868, § 109; July 14, 1870, § 2.) *And be it further enacted,* That upon the articles, goods, wares, and merchandise hereinafter mentioned, except where otherwise provided, which shall be produced and sold, or be manufactured or made and sold, or be consumed or used by the manufacturer or producer thereof, or removed for consumption, or use, or for delivery to others than agents of the manufacturer or producer within the United States or Territories thereof, there shall be assessed, collected, and paid the following taxes, to be paid by the producer or manufacturer thereof, that is to say: On gas (*a*), illuminating, made of coal wholly or in part, or any other material, when the product shall not be above two hundred thousand cubic feet per month, a tax of ten cents per one thousand cubic feet; when the product shall be above two and not exceeding five hundred thousand cubic feet per month, a tax of fifteen cents per one thousand cubic feet; when the product shall be above five hundred thousand and not exceeding five millions of cubic feet per month, a tax of twenty cents per one thousand cubic feet ; when the product shall be above five millions, a tax of twenty-five cents per one thousand cubic feet. And the general average of the monthly product for the year preceding the return required by law shall determine the rate of tax herein imposed. And where any gas-works have not been in operation for the next year preceding the return as aforesaid, then the rate shall be determined by the estimated average of the monthly product:

Provided, That the product required to be returned by law by any gas company shall be understood to be, in addition to the gas consumed by said company or other party, the product charged in the bills actually rendered by the gas company during the month preceding the return; all gas companies whose price is fixed by law are authorized to add the tax herein imposed to the price per thousand feet on gas sold; and all such companies which have heretofore contracted to furnish gas to municipal corporations are, in like manner and for the same period, authorized to add such tax to such contract price:

Provided further, That all gas furnished for lighting street lamps or for other purposes, and not measured, and all gas made for and used by any hotel, inn, tavern, and private dwelling-house, shall be subject to tax, whatever the amount of product, and may be estimated ; and if the returns in any case shall be understated or underestimated, it shall be the duty of the assistant assessor of the district to increase the same as he shall deem just and proper:

And provided further, That gas companies located within the corporate limits of any city or town, whether in the same district or otherwise, or so located as to compete with each other, shall pay the rate of tax imposed by law upon the company having the largest production :

And provided further, That coal tar and ammoniacal liquor produced in the manufacture of illuminating gas, and the products of the re-distillation of coal tar, and the products of the manufacture of ammoniacal liquor thus produced, shall be exempt from tax.

(a) A gas company managed and controlled by trustees elected by a municipal corporation, but of which private subscribers are the legal owners, is liable to tax under this section. City of Philadelphia *v.* Collector, 5 Wall. 720.

The tax on illuminating gas is not repealed. 12 I. R. R. 77.

Sec. 95. *Repealed* March 31, 1868, § 1.

Sec. 96. *Obsolete*, March 31, 1868, § 1 ; July 14, 1870, § 2.

Tax may be Added to Contract Price.

Sec. 97. *And be it further enacted*, That every person, firm, or corporation, who shall have made any contract prior to the passage of this act, and without other provision therein for the payment of duties imposed by law enacted subsequent thereto, upon articles to be delivered under such contract, is hereby authorized and empowered to add to the price thereof so much money as will be equivalent to the duty so subsequently imposed on said articles, and not previously paid by the vendee, and shall be entitled by virtue hereof to be paid and to sue for and recover the same accordingly: *Provided*, That where the United States is the purchaser under such prior contract, the certificate of the proper officer of the department by which the contract was made, showing, according to regulations to be prescribed by the Secretary of the Treasury, the articles so purchased by the United States, and liable to such subsequent duty, shall be taken and received, so far as the same is applicable, in discharge of such subsequent duties on articles so contracted to be delivered to the United States and actually delivered according to such contract.

Purchase of Goods Free from Tax.

[SEC. 17. (March 3, 1865.) *And be it further enacted*, That the privilege of purchasing supplies of goods imported from foreign countries for the use of the United States, duty free, which now does or hereafter shall exist by provision of law, shall be extended, under such regulations as the Secretary of the Treasury may prescribe, to all articles of domestic production which are subject to tax by the provisions of this act.]

Tax on Machinery.

[SEC. 2. (March 31, 1868.) *And be it further enacted*, That nothing in this act contained shall be construed to repeal or interfere with any law, regulation, or provision for the assessment or collection of any tax which, under existing laws, may accrue before the first day of April, Anno Domini eighteen hundred and sixty-eight. And nothing herein contained shall be construed as a repeal of any tax upon machinery or other articles which have been or may be delivered on contracts made with the United States prior to the passage of this act.]

Exemption of Naval Machinery.

[SEC. 1., (March 3, 1869.) *Be it enacted by the Senate and House of Representatives of the United States of America in Congress assembled*, That the act to exempt certain manufacturers from internal tax, and for other purposes, approved March thirty-one, eighteen hundred and sixty-eight, be, and hereby is, amended in the second section thereof so as to remit all taxes upon naval machinery which had not accrued prior to the first day of April, eighteen hundred and sixty-eight.]

Sec. 98. *Repealed* July 14, 1870, § 2.

BROKERS.

Sales made by Brokers, Banks, or Bankers.

Sec. 99. (Amended July 31, 1866, § 9; July 14, 1870, § 2.) *And be it further enacted*, That there shall be paid on all sales (a) made by brokers, banks, or bankers, whether made for the benefit of others or on their own account, the following taxes, that is to say: Upon all sales and contracts for the sale of stocks, bonds, gold and silver bullion and coin, promissory notes or other securities, a tax at the rate of one cent for every hundred dollars of the amount of such sales or contracts; and on all sales and contracts for sale negotiated and made by any person, firm or company not paying a special tax as a broker, bank, or banker, of any gold or silver bullion, coin, promissory notes, stocks, bonds or other securities, not his or their own property, there shall be paid a tax at the rate of five cents for every hundred dollars of the amount of such sales or contracts; and on every sale and contract for sale, as aforesaid, there shall be made and delivered by the seller to the buyer a bill or memorandum of such sale or contract, on which there shall be affixed a lawful stamp or stamps in value equal to the amount of tax on such sale, to be determined by the rates of tax before mentioned; and in computing the amount of the stamp tax in any case herein provided for, any fractional part of one hundred dollars of value or amount on which tax is computed shall be accounted at one hundred dollars. And every bill or memorandum of sale, or contract of sale, before mentioned, shall show the date thereof, the name of the seller, the amount of the sale or contract, and the matter or thing to which it refers. And any person or persons liable to pay the tax as herein provided, or any one who acts in the matter as agent or broker for such person or persons, who shall make any such sale or contract, or who shall, in pursuance of any sale or contract, deliver or receive any stocks, bonds, bullion, coin, promissory notes, or other securities, without a bill or memorandum thereof as herein required, or who shall deliver or receive such bill or memorandum without having the proper stamps affixed thereto, shall forfeit and pay to the United States a penalty of five hundred dollars for each and every offence where the tax so evaded, or attempted to be evaded, does not exceed one hundred dollars, and a penalty of one thousand dollars when such tax shall exceed one hundred dollars, which may be recovered with costs in any court of the United States of competent jurisdiction, at any time within one year after the liability to such penalty shall have been incurred; and the penalty recovered shall be awarded and distributed by the court between the United States and the informer, if there be any, as provided by law, who, in the judgment of the court, shall have first given the information of the violation of the law for which recovery is had: *Provided*, That where it shall appear that the omission to affix the proper stamp was not with intent to evade the provisions of this section, said penalty shall not be incurred. And the provisions of law in relation to stamp duties in Schedule B of this act shall apply to the stamp taxes herein imposed upon sales and contracts of sales made by brokers, banks, or bankers, and others as aforesaid.

(*a*) The law does not require that the sales of banks, bankers, and money or stock-brokers shall be returned monthly. Brokers cannot stamp their books instead of giving stamped memorandums. 4 I. R. R. 62.

The act subjects sales made by a broker for himself to the same tax as those made for others. U. S. *v.* Cutting, 3 Wall. 441; s. c. 3 I. R. R. 111.

A party who purchases stocks, bonds, &c., for others, but makes the purchases in his own name and advances his own money and takes the transfers in his own name and holds the stocks as security for the repayment of the money by the persons for whom the stocks are purchased, and, on receiving such repayment with interest and the customary charges, delivers the stocks, bonds, &c., as per agreement, or in default of repayment, sells the same to reimburse himself, is a broker and subject to tax under this section. Such business is outside of the business of a banker. So far as a banker does the business of a broker he is to be regarded as a broker and must pay the broker's tax. Clark *v.* Gilbert, 5 Blatch. 330; s. c. 4 I. R. R. 42.

A banker, prior to the amendment, July 13, 1866, § 9, was not subject to tax under this section for sales or purchases of stocks for himself. U. S. *v.* Fisk, 3 Wall. 445, s. c. 2 I. R. R. 103.

A banker is, both by express terms as well as by necessary implication, empowered to carry on the business authorized under his license to its practical and useful results. When he is authorized to lend or advance money on stocks, bonds, &c., he has the right, in case of default in the repayment, to convert the security into money by way of reimbursement; and when he is authorized to receive stocks, bonds, &c., for sale, he may sell the same without, in either instance, making himself a broker. Clark *v.* Gilbert, 5 Blatch. 330, s. c. 4 I. R. R. 42.

Sec. 100. *Repealed* July 14, 1870, § 2.

Secs. 101, 102. *Repealed* July 13, 1866, § 9.
Secs. 103, 104, 105, 106, 107, 108, 109. *Repealed* July 14, 1870, § 2.

BANKS AND BANKERS.
Tax on Deposits, Capital Stock, and Circulation.

Sec. 110. (Amended July 13, 1866, § 9.) *And be it further enacted,* That there shall be levied, collected, and paid a tax of one twenty-fourth of one per centum each month upon the average amount of the deposits (*a*) of money, subject to payment by check or draft, or represented by certificates of deposit or otherwise, whether payable on demand or at some future day, with any person, bank, association, company, or corporation engaged in the business of banking; and a tax of one twenty-fourth of one per centum each month, as aforesaid, upon the capital (*b*) of any bank, association, company, or corporation, and on the capital employed by any person in the business of banking beyond the average amount invested in United States bonds; and a tax of one-twelfth of one per centum each month upon the average amount of circulation (*c*) issued by any bank, association, corporation, company, or person, including as circulation all certified checks and all notes and other obligations calculated or intended to circulate or to be used as money, but not including that in the vault of the bank, or redeemed and on deposit for said bank; and an additional tax of one-sixth of one per centum, each month, upon the average amount of such circulation, issued as aforesaid, beyond the amount of ninety per centum of the capital of any such bank, association, corporation, company, or person.

And a true and accurate return of the amount of circulation, of deposit and of capital, as aforesaid, and the amount of notes of persons, State banks, or State banking associations paid out by them for the previous month, shall be made and rendered monthly by each of such banks, associations, corporations, companies, or persons to the assessor of the district in which any such bank, association, corporation, or company may be located, or in which such person has his place of business, with a declaration annexed thereto, and the oath or affirmation of such person, or of the president or cashier of such bank, association, corporation, or company, in such form and manner as may be prescribed by the Commissioner of Internal Revenue, that the same contains a true and faithful statement of the amounts subject to tax as aforesaid; and for any refusal or neglect to make or to render return and payment, any such bank, association, corporation, company, or person so in default shall be subject to and pay a penalty of two hundred dollars, besides the additional penalty and forfeitures in other cases provided by law; and the amount of circulation, deposit, capital, and notes of persons, State banks, and banking associations paid out, as aforesaid, in default of the proper return, shall be estimated by the assessor or assistant assessor of the district as aforesaid, upon the best information he can obtain ; and every such penalty may be recovered for the use of the United States in any court of competent jurisdiction.

And in the case of banks with branches, the tax herein provided for shall be assessed upon the circulation of each branch, severally, and the amount of capital of each branch shall be considered to be the amount allotted to such branch ; and so much of an act entitled "An act to provide ways and means for the support of the government," approved March three, eighteen hundred and sixty-three, as imposes any tax on banks, their circulation, capital, or deposits, other than is herein provided, is hereby repealed :

Provided, That this section shall not apply to associations which are taxed under and by virtue of the act "to provide a national currency secured by a pledge of United States bonds, and to provide for the circulation and redemption thereof." And the deposits in associations or companies known as provident institutions, savings banks, savings funds, or savings institutions, having no capital stock and doing no other business than receiving deposits to be loaned or invested for the sole benefit of the parties making such deposits, without profit or compensation to the association or company, shall be exempt from tax on so much of their deposits as they have invested in the securities of the United States, and on all deposits (*d*) less than five hundred dollars made in the name of any one person ; and the returns required to be made by such provident institutions and savings banks after July, eighteen hundred and sixty-six, shall be made on the first Monday of January and July of each year, in such form and manner as may be prescribed by the Commissioner of Internal Revenue.

(*a*) Where a savings bank credits its depositors with interest, the amount thus credited should be treated as a deposit. 2 I. R. R. 92.

The particular manner in which deposits are made does not affect the liability to tax. 1 I. R. R. 132.

The average amount of deposits held during the month, and not the average amount received during that time, should be taken as the correct amount subject to tax. 2 I. R. R. 29.

The liability to make returns exists as long as the deposits remain in the hands of the bank or its agents. 2 I. R. R. 29.

To ascertain the average amount of deposits, the amount of daily balances during the month should be divided by the number of business days in the month. 5 I. R. R. 74.

When bona fide deposits are made with a bank, it makes no difference whether the deposits are general or special, that is, subject to call, or redeemable at a future time designated. 11 I. R. R. 137.

If the assignee of a bank loans the funds as collected, he must make the returns and pay the tax on the deposits. 2 I. R. R. 92.

(*b*) The surplus funds of a savings bank should be treated as capital. 1 I. R. R. 172.

Banking capital invested in real estate or otherwise should be inserted in the monthly returns of capital, and a tax should be paid thereon. 5 I. R. R. 74.

Surplus earned by the bank is no part of the capital, nor does the statute, either expressly or impliedly, regard it as such. Capital of a bank and surplus earnings convey distinct and different ideas and meanings. Mechanics' and Farmers' Bank *v.* Townsend, 3 I. R. R. 143; s. c. 5 Blatch. 315.

(*c*) The tax must be paid as long as any portion of the circulation is outstanding. 2 I. R. R. 29.

The receiver of a bank should make monthly returns of the outstanding circulation, and pay the tax thereon. 6 I. R R. 66.

All certified checks are subject to this tax. All notes and other obligations are subject to this tax if, or when, they are intended to be used as circulation. 1 I. R. R. 155; 2 I. R. R. 18.

A State certificate of indebtedness which circulates as money is liable to this tax. 5 I. R. R. 148.

(*d*) In ascertaining the taxable amount of deposits, all sums of $500 and upwards in the name of any one person are to be included. In determining the average amount of deposits, these institutions will be allowed to take the amount on deposit on the first days of January and July of each year prior to the time of making their returns as the correct average deposit, or to take such period between these dates as may be satisfactory to the assessor. If the return is not satisfactory to the assessor, he may fix the time. The total amount of deposits at the date fixed upon should be stated in the return. 4 I. R. R. 102, 196.

A corporation receiving deposits from its employees alone, and paying interest thereon, is liable to this tax. 3 I. R. R. 93.

A company which receives deposits and loans or invests the same for the benefit of the depositors, is engaged in the business of banking. Throughout the section the distinction between deposits, capital, and circulation, as separate objects of taxation, is clearly maintained, both in respect to the monthly returns and the monthly payment of duties. All moneys received by a bank, whether for safe-keeping or investment, are deposits, and are liable to taxation as soon as received. The fact that they are invested as soon as received does not make them exempt from tax. Bank for Savings *v.* Collector, 3 Wall, 495; U. S. *v.* Farmers' Loan and Trust Company, 3 I. R. R. 62.

Circulation of State Banks.

[SEC. 6. (March 3, 1865; as amended July 13, 1866.) *And be it further enacted*, That every national banking association, State bank, or State banking association, shall pay a tax of ten per centum on the amount of notes of any person, State bank, or State banking association, used for circulation and paid out (*a*) by them after the first day of August, eighteen hundred and sixty-six, and such tax shall be assessed and paid in such manner as shall be prescribed by the Commissioner of Internal Revenue.]

(*a*) Savings banks are subject to the tax imposed by this section. 4 I. R. R. 33.

Passing notes into the hands of a broker is paying them out. The fact that the broker forwards the notes for redemption does not affect the liability of the bank to this tax. 5 I. R. R. 74.

This tax is not a direct tax. The object of taxation is not the franchise of the bank, but property created or contracts made and issued under the franchise. Notes issued by a State bank may be made contributory to the public revenue. Franchises which are not conferred for the purpose of giving effect to some reserved powers of a State are as properly objects of taxation as any other property. The judicial cannot prescribe to the legislative department of the government limitations on the exercise of acknowledged powers. Veazie Bank *v.* Fenno, 8 Wall. 533 ; s. c. 10 I. R. R. 195.

Tax on Notes of Municipal Corporations.

[SEC. 2. (March 26, 1867.) *And be it further enacted*, That every national banking association, State bank, or banker, or association shall pay a tax of ten per centum on the amount of notes of any town, city, or municipal corporation paid out by them after the first day of May, Anno Domini eighteen hundred and sixty-seven, to be collected in the mode and manner in which the tax on the notes of State banks is collected.]

When Circulation of State Banks is exempt.

[SEC. 14. (March 3, 1865; as amended July 13, 1866.) *And be it further enacted*, That the capital of any State bank or banking association which has ceased or shall cease to exist, or which has been or shall be converted into a national bank, shall be assumed to be the capital as it existed immediately before such bank ceased to exist, or was converted as aforesaid ; and whenever the outstanding circulation of any bank, association, corporation, company or person shall be reduced to an amount not exceeding five per centum of the chartered or declared capital existing at the time the same was issued, said circulation shall be free from taxation ; and whenever any bank which has ceased to issue notes for circulation shall deposit in the treasury of the United States, in lawful money, the amount of its outstanding circulation, to be redeemed at par, under such regulations as the Secretary of the Treasury shall prescribe, it shall be exempt from any tax upon such circulation ; and whenever any State bank or banking association has been converted into a national banking association, and such national banking association has assumed the liabilities of such State bank or banking association, including the redemption of its bills, by any agreement or understanding whatever with the representatives of such State bank or banking association, such national banking association shall be held to make the required return and payment on the circulation outstanding, so long as such circulation shall exceed five per centum of the capital before such conversion of such State bank or banking association.]

Secs. 111, 112, 113. *Repealed* July 14, 1870, § 2.
Sec. 114. *Repealed* March 2, 1867, § 34.

Collection of Tax where Person has more than one Place of Business.

Sec. 115. *And be it further enacted,* That whenever by this act any license, duty, or tax of any description has been imposed on any person or corporate body, or property of any person, or incorporated or unincorporated company, having more than one place of business, it shall be lawful for the Commissioner of Internal Revenue to prescribe and determine in what district such tax shall be assessed and collected, and to what officer thereof the official notices required in that behalf shall be given, and of whom payment of such tax shall be demanded:

Provided, That all taxes on manufactures, manufacturing companies, and manufacturing corporations, shall be assessed and the tax collected in the district within which the place of manufacture is located, unless otherwise provided.

INCOMES.

Secs. 116, 117, 118, 119, 120, 121, 122, 123. *Repealed* July 14, 1870, § 17, *and expired.*

Persons liable to Income Tax.

[SEC. 6. (July 14, 1870.) *And be it further enacted,* That there shall be levied and collected (*a*) annually as hereinafter provided, for the years eighteen hundred and seventy, and eighteen hundred and seventy-one, and no longer, a tax of two and one-half per centum upon the gains, profits, and income of every person residing in the United States, and of every citizen of the United States residing abroad, derived from any source whatever, whether within or without the United States, except as hereinafter provided, and a like tax annually upon the gains, profits, and income derived from any business, trade, or profession carried on in the United States, by any person residing without the United States and not a citizen thereof, or from rents of real estate within the United States owned by any person residing without the United States and not a citizen thereof.]

(a) A tax upon incomes is not a direct tax, but a duty or excise, and is constitutional. Pacific Ins. Co. v. Soule, 7 Wall, 433.

Residents should make return in the district where they reside at the time of making return. The residence required under this section for the purpose of taxing income is held to be a residence during the year for which income is derived. If any person subject to income tax resides abroad he should make his return in the district where he last resided. 7 I. R. R. 59.

The place where a person votes, or is entitled to vote, is deemed his residence. When not a voter, the place where tax on personal property is paid is held to be the place of residence. Bout. 273.

Citizens of the United States residing abroad are subject to tax in the same manner as citizens residing in this country, upon their entire incomes from all sources whatever; and the same is true of foreigners residing in this country. 7 I. R. R. 59.

The law provides that the income tax shall be levied, collected, and paid upon the gains, profits, and income of every business, trade, or profession carried on in the United States by persons residing without the United States, and not citizens thereof. 7 I. R. R. 59; 9 I. R. R. 113.

The wife of an alien is to be regarded as an alien herself for the purposes of taxation under the internal revenue law, though she were a citizen prior to her marriage. If she resides abroad, the profits and income arising from stock, &c., held for her by a trustee in this country need not be returned for taxation. If she resides here, she is liable to the income tax imposed upon "every person residing in the United States." 6 I. R. R. 66.

An alien who resides within the United States, and is therefore liable to a tax on his annual gains, profits, and income, is entitled to the exemption of $2,000 of that income, in the same manner and under the same circumstances as a native-born or naturalized citizen. 6 I. R. R. 18.

Income derived from personalty held by a trustee for the benefit of persons who are not citizens of, and who do not reside within, the United States, is not taxable. The mere fact that income is derived from this country and passes through the hands of a citizen or resident here cannot be held to make the recipient, who is both a foreigner and non-resident, liable to the income tax. 1 I. R. R. 171.

Income derived from an inherited estate in a foreign country by a person who had to become a citizen of that country before he could receive the estate, is taxable. 3 I. R. R. 140.

When an association is so formed that its gains are the sole property of the whole association, and are not divisible among its members, the association is a person within the meaning of the internal revenue law, and must make a return. 10 I. R. R. 39.

All gains, profits, or income received by a decedent within the income year prior to the day of his death are liable to taxation under the internal revenue law, subject to the deduction which those laws allow in ascertaining the aggregate amount as the basis for the computation of the tax. In ascertaining the aggregate amount of the gains, profits, or income liable to such taxation, the same deductions are required to be made as would have been if the decedent, instead of having deceased, had ceased on that day to be the owner of any property, and for the residue of the income year had received nothing as gains, profits, or income within the meaning of these laws. The only gains, profits, or income received by the decedent within the income year are those which occurred prior to his decease. It would be absurd to suppose that he continued to own property after that date, or that he sustained any loss subsequent to that time, within the meaning of those laws. His legal representatives should make the return. Mandell v. Pierce, 7 I. R. R. 193; s. c. 1. A. L. T. (C. R.) 123.

What is subject to Income Tax.

[SEC. 7. (July 14, 1870.) *And be it further enacted*, That in estimating the gains, profits, and income of any person, there shall be included all income derived (*a*) from any kind of property, rents, interest received or accrued upon all notes, bonds, and mortgages, or other forms of indebtedness bearing interest, whether paid or not, if good and collectible, interest upon notes, bonds, or other securities of the United States; and the amount of all premium on gold and coupons; the gains, profits, and income (*b*) of any business, profession, trade, employment, office, or vocation; including any amount received as salary or pay for services in the civil, military, naval, or other service of the United States, or as Senator, Representative, or Delegate in Congress; except that portion thereof from which, under authority of acts of Congress previous hereto, a tax of five per centum shall have been withheld; the share (*c*) of any person of the gains and profits, whether divided or not, of all companies, or partnerships, but not including the amount received from any corporations whose officers, as authorized by law, withhold and pay as taxes a per centum of the dividends made, and of interest or coupons paid by such corporations; profits realized within the year from sales (*d*) of real estate purchased within two years previous to the year for which income is estimated; the amount of sales (*e*) of live stock, sugar, wool, butter, cheese, pork, beef, mutton, or other meats, hay, and grain, fruits, vegetables, or other productions, being the growth or produce of the estate of such person, but not including any part thereof consumed directly by the family; and all other (*f*) gains, profits, and income drawn from any source whatever, but not including the rental value of the homestead used or occupied by any person or by his family.]

(*a*) The interest that has accrued during the previous year on United States securities should be returned. 7 I. R. 60.

Gold received as interest on United States securities should not be returned at its nominal value where such gold has not been sold. When it has been sold, the premium should also be returned. 2 I. R. R. 5.

If interest which has accrued during the income year on notes, bonds, etc., is good and collectible at the end of the year, it should be returned as income whether actually collected or not. 7 I. R. R. 59.

When an absolute deed is taken instead of a mortgage, and a stipulation given to reconvey upon the payment of a certain sum equal to the loan with interest thereon, the transaction is equivalent to a mortgage and the gain accruing to the lender must be returned as income. 3 I. R. R. 140.

Interest should be considered as income only when paid, unless it is collectible and remains unpaid by the consent or agreement of the creditor. Bout. 274.

Rent derived from coal mines is income. Bout. 274.

The rental value of property occupied by the owner is neither to be included in the owner's income nor deducted therefrom. 1 I. R. R. 171.

If a party rents his own house and is subjected to pay rent elsewhere on account thereof, he must return the rent received and will be allowed to deduct the amount of rent paid 4 I. R. R. 46; 5 I. R. R. 154.

When land is leased for a term of years under a contract that the lessee shall erect a building thereon, the title to which, subject to the lessee during the term, immediately vests in the lessor, the expense of erecting the building is in the nature of rent and is returnable as such in the income return of the lessor. 7 I. R. R. 60.

When a person cultivates the land of another under a contract, either written or oral, to pay for the use of the same in the produce thereof, the produce thus paid is in the nature of rent, and should be returned by the party receiving it. The expenses of managing the premises so leased are to be deducted from the income of the lessee only. 7 I. R. R. 60.

Incomes derived from coal mines must be returned. No deductions can be made on account of the diminished value, actual or supposed, of the coal vein or bed by the process of mining. Bout. 274.

Whenever scrip dividends are returnable as incomes, they should be returned at their market value. 7 I. R. R. 59.

The income tax is assessed upon the actual income of individuals. Firms, as such, will not make returns. Bout. 275.

Marriage fees, gifts from members of a congregation to their pastor, &c., are taxable as incomes when the gifts or donations are in the nature of compensation for services rendered, whether in accordance with an understanding to that effect at the time of settlement or with an annual custom. 7 I. R. R. 59.

When the earnings of a minor child are legally under the control of his father, the amount of such earnings is clearly to be included in estimating the father's income. If the child's income is entirely free from the father's control, the assessment will be separate and distinct. 1 I. R. R. 181.

If a taxpayer has a minor child in the service of the government, receiving a salary, such parent should include in his income-return so much of the salary of the child as is not subject to a salary-tax. 7 I. R R. 59.

Where a child is so emancipated as to cut off his parent's legal right to demand and receive his child's earnings as his own, the parent should not be required to return them. A parent's agreement with a minor child to relinquish to the child the right he has to his services and earnings, is, as between them, such an emancipation as to relieve the parent from treating those earnings as a part of his own income, whether such agreement be written or oral. Neither is it necessary, as between them, that such agreement should be made public. Upon this point assessors should not adhere to the strict rule of evidence by which no contract of emancipation is to be presumed, and which ordinarily requires evidence of an express contract; but should give the law and the rules of evidence a liberal construction, and presume that, when a parent allows a minor child to retain his wages and appropriate them to his own use, it is done in pursuance of such an agreement between them as is binding upon the parent and emancipates the child. 11 I. R. R. 122.

Pensions received from the United States government must be returned with other income subject to taxation. Bout. 274; 4 I. R. R. 55.

Legatees are not required to return their legacies as income. Bout. 275.

(*b*) Salaries, except where specially provided for by statute, are regarded as income from business. 3 I. R. R. 188.

The salary of a judge of a State court is not liable to this tax. Such a tax is as indefensible in principle as if levied upon the office, or directly upon the revenues of the State before they are paid out of the State treasury, as the tax levied and collected operates to that extent as a reduction of the compensation allowed to the officer. If Congress may tax one State office, it may tax every other office known to the constitution and laws of a State. It may tax the salary of the governor, and the mileage and *per diem* of the legislators. Such a theory would lead necessarily to the subjugation of all State authority. Day *v.* Buffington, 11 I. R. R. 205.

The salary of a State officer is liable to the income tax. 4 I. R. R. 4.

Soldiers honorably discharged are not exempt from taxation of incomes. The exemption given in the joint resolution of July 28, 1866, refers to the special income for the year 1863. 11 I. R. R. 123.

A person in making up his returns may include all debts which he considers absolutely good and throw out those which he regards as bad, doubtful or comparatively worthless. If a person has good accounts on his books which he permits to remain instead of collecting, or if they are real gains and profits, he must return them. The true rule is to impose and collect the tax on real gains, profits or income, and not on what is merely nominal. Debts must be gains or profits, and if they are not, they are no part of a man's taxable income. U. S. *v.* Frost, 9 I. R. R. 41; s. c. 1 C. L. N. 129.

Lawyers and physicians may return either the actual fees received during the income year without regard to the time when they accrued, or the amounts due to the business of the income year. 7 I. R. R. 59.

If a manufacturer or dealer has been in the practice of estimating his annual profits by taking inventories of stock, he may take the cost value or the market value. 7 I. R. R. 59.

When a taxpayer has adopted one method of estimating his income, he cannot subsequently be allowed to adopt the other. 7 I. R. R. 59.

There is no distinction between income derived from business and that derived from fixed investments. 7 I. R. R. 59.

Money received by A from a life insurance company upon a policy taken out by B for the benefit of A is not subject to a legacy or an income tax. 3 I. R. R. 140.

If an inventor sells his invention at once for a gross sum, he should return as income the whole amount, less the expenses actually incurred in perfecting the invention and in procuring a patent right. If he sells only a portion of his right during the year, he may deduct a proportionate amount of such expense. 7 I. R. R. 59.

A merchant's return should cover the business of the income year, excluding previous years. Uncollected accounts must be estimated. Bout. 273.

Dividends payable in the income year should be returned as income for that year, no matter when declared. Bout. 274.

Old debts formerly considered hopelessly lost, but paid during the income year, should be included in the return. Bout. 274.

The increased value given to a building by permanent improvements should be charged to capital—not to income. Bout. 275.

The profits of a manufacturer from his business are not exempt from income tax in consequence of his having paid the excise tax imposed by law upon his manufactures. Bout. 275.

Gifts of money, when clearly not in the nature of payment for services rendered, or other valuable consideration, are not liable to taxation as income. Amounts received on life insurance policies and damages recovered in actions of tort are exempt from income tax. 7 I. R. R. 59.

The payment of legacy or succession tax on the bequest of an annuity does not relieve the annuitant from liability to income tax on his annuity. 7 I. R. R. 60.

Where any portion of a legacy has been transferred by the executor to the legatee, so that the executor in his capacity of guardian or trustee has no longer any control of the profits arising from such legacy, the return of such profits as income must be required of the legatee. 7 I. R. R. 59.

(c) When a corporation goes into liquidation and distributes its assets among its stockholders, the difference between the price paid for the shares and the sum so received is taxable as profits. 2 I. R. R. 138.

The undistributed earnings of a corporation made previous to September 1st, 1862, whether the corporation is required to pay a tax on dividends or not, should not be considered as the income of the stockholders, nor should the corporation be required to make a return of such earnings. Bout. 275.

If a corporation takes any part of its earnings and adds it to the working capital and then makes a new division of stock, the stockholders must pay an income tax on the additional stock acquired. If, on the other hand, it divides to all its stockholders its net earnings during the year, and after so doing merely gives to each stockholder two certificates of stock for one which he held before, there is no liability for such additional certificate except upon the dividend. There is no tax on a nominal increase. 1 I. R. R. 188.

Such portions of a stock dividend as are made up of earnings acquired prior to July 1, 1862, need not be returned. 2 I. R. R. 61.

A person who would be entitled to a share in the gains and profits of a company, whether incorporated or partnership, if divided, should return the same as income, whether divided or otherwise. 7 I. R. R. 60; 1 I. R. R. 157.

All profits of the companies mentioned in this clause, accruing in the income year, are liable to be returned as income. If there has been a division, and no surplus remains at the end of the income year, only the amount divided should be returned. 1 I. R. R. 180.

Profits of a gas company which have been carried to construction account should be returned as income by the stockholders. The undistributed earnings of a corporation made subsequently to September, 1862, should have been returned as income by the stockholders for the various years in which the same accrued. 3 I. R. R. 164.

Where a stock dividend is in reality a division of the accumulated earnings of several years, so much of the amount as is clearly shown to be due to the profits of previous years may be omitted from the return, being returnable for those years, provided always that no omission be made for any year subsequent to December 31st, 1861, unless the income tax on such portion of the stock dividend as was due to the earnings of that particular year has already been paid, 1 I. R. R. 155.

The statute does not require the taxpayer to enter the dividends mentioned in this clause upon his return. By the regulations, however, he is required to enter the amounts received from such institutions or corporations upon the list, not for the purpose of having them taxed, for the tax has already been assessed and paid upon them, and the law, therefore, excepts them in its enumeration of income to be returned by the stockholder for taxation, but in order that there may be a detailed statement of the taxpayer's entire income, so that any mistake or fraud may be the more readily detected: and then, to avoid taxing them at all, they are also deducted. The tax paid thereon by the corporations may also be deducted. The tax is in reality paid by the stockholder. The payment by the corporation is merely a mode of collecting it. Hence the taxpayer may enter it on the list among the deductions under the head of taxes. 10 I. R. R. 9.

The depositors receiving dividends or interest from the savings banks, described in the proviso to section 110, act June 30, 1864, are required to return the same as taxable in their annual statement of income. 11 I. R. R. 73.

Wherever the salary or pay received by any person in government employ does not exceed the rate of $2,000 per annum, or is made up of fees, or is uncertain or irregular in the amount or time, and has not, therefore, been subjected to salary tax, it should be included with other taxable income. Where such salary exceeds the rate of $2,000 per annum, the amount of salary from which the tax has been deducted may be deducted from the gross income. 7. I. R. R. 59.

Extra pay granted to officers by special acts is liable to tax. 2 I. R. R. 108.

The tax should be withheld from all payments on account of prize money, without regard to the time when the captures were made. 7 I. R. R. 11.

(*d*) The profits that have been made on sales of real estate which has been purchased during the year for which the return is made, or within two years previous to that year, should be returned. 7 I. R. R. 60.

A sale of underlying coal should be treated as a sale of real estate. If A pay to B, who owns the underlying coal, so much for every ton mined, or buys the same from him after it has been brought to the surface, A should be regarded as purchasing and B as selling real estate. 7 I. R. R. 60 ; 5 I. R. R. 154.

The profit on the sale of mined coal by the miner is the difference between the amount received for the coal and the actual expense of producing the same (excluding all deductions for the personal service of the miner and his family), plus the actual amount paid for each ton to the owner or lessor of the mine. The profit of the owner or lessor of the mine thus receiving pay from the lessee or miner is the difference between the amount received for each ton and the estimated amount which he paid for each originally. 7 I. R. R. 60.

If a part of a piece of real estate purchased within the required time is sold, the excess of the sum received therefor over the sum paid for the same portion should be returned. 5 I. R. R. 138.

The fact that the real estate has been increased in value by the erection of buildings thereon, either within the prescribed time, or within some period previous to that time, does not render any part of the receipts of sale taxable. 1 I. R. R. 196.

The profit realized on a sale of standing timber, or felled timber, is returnable for taxation without reference to the time when the land was purchased. Timber is converted into personalty by severance from the land on which it grew, and profits arising from the sale thereof is just as liable to the income tax as the profits received from the sale of other products of the soil, or from mines. A farmer who keeps woodland for the express purpose of cutting and selling firewood, or a proprietor who sells to others the privilege of cutting and appropriating the timber on his land, should be required to estimate the receipts from that source as a part of their income. Bout 301 ; 1 I. R. R. 171.

When timber is sold, either standing or cut, the taxable profits are arrived at by estimating the value of the land after the timber is removed, and adding thereto the net amount received for the timber, and from this sum deducting the estimated value of the land at the commencement of the income year. 7 I. R. R. 58.

(*e*) A farmer should make return of all produce sold within the income year. But a mere executory contract for a sale is not a sale; delivery, either actual or constructive, is essential. 7 I. R. R. 59.

Produce raised during the income year, or previous years, which remains on hand unsold at the close of the income year, should not be required to be returned as income. 11 I. R. R. 113; 2 I. R. R. 90.

Farmers need not make a return of produce consumed in their own immediate families. 7 I. R. R. 58.

(*f*) Profits on sales of live stock are to be estimated by deducting the purchase money from the gross receipts received from the sale thereof. 7 I. R. R. 58.

Profits on the sales of personal property should be assessed without regard to the time when it was purchased. The rule relating to realty does not apply to personalty. 1 I. R. R. 139; 2 I. R. R. 44; 11 I. R. R. 66.

Leases are personal property under the Internal Revenue laws. 7 I. R. R. 59; 2 I. R. R. 44.

A mining claim arising from the location of a mine situated on the public mineral lands of the United States is personal property. The difference between the actual cost and the price received from the claim is the profits and gains. 4 I. R. R. 124.

Exemptions from Income Tax.

[SEC. 8. (July 14, 1870.) *And be it further enacted*, That military or naval pensions allowed to any person under the laws of the United States, and the sum of two thousand dollars of the gains, profits, and income of any person, shall be exempt from said income tax, in the manner hereinafter provided. Only one deduction of two thousand dollars shall be made from the aggregate income of all the members (*a*) of any family composed of one or both parents and one or more minor children, or of husband and wife; but when a wife has by law a separate income, beyond the control of her husband, and is living separate and apart from him, such deduction shall then be made from her income, gains, and profits; and guardians and trustees shall be allowed to make the deduction in favor of each ward or beneficiary except that in case of two or more wards or beneficiaries comprised in one family, having joint property interest, only one deduction shall be made in their favor. For the purpose of allowing said deduction from the income of any religious or social community, holding all their property and the income therefrom jointly, and in common, each five of the persons composing such society, and any remaining fractional number of such persons less than five over such groups of five, shall be held to constitute a family, and a deduction of two thousand dollars shall be allowed for each of said families. Any taxes on the incomes, gains, and profits of such societies now due and unpaid, shall be assessed and collected according to this provision, except that the deduction shall be only one thousand dollars for any year prior to eighteen hundred and seventy.]

(*a*) For the purpose of the exemption of $2,000, husband and wife are to be regarded as members of the same family, though living separate, unless separated by divorce or other operation of the law, so as to break up the family relation. Minor children and their parents should be counted as members of the same family, whether living together or not. Guardians can be allowed no special deduction in favor of their wards where such wards are members of any family composed of one or both parents, and one or more minor children, or husband and wife. 7 I. R. R. 59.

A family composed of the mother and her minor children are entitled to only one deduction, and the guardian of the minor children is entitled to deduct a ratable proportion of the same from the income of his wards. 11 I. R. R. 89.

If a minor child has a legally appointed guardian, who has been lawfully invested with the power of caring for, and managing his property and estate, the guardian should be allowed a deduction of $2,000 in favor of his ward, whether the ward lives with his parents or not, and also whether that legally appointed guardian be his parent or not. Only one deduction, however, should be allowed to two or more wards comprised in one and the same family when their property interest is joint. The property also must be under the control of some other guardian than the guardian by nature, *i. e.*, the father, or if he be dead, the mother; but the person who would be guardian by nature may also be duly appointed guardian, and then the deduction may be allowed when the property of the wards is several. 11 I. R. R. 153.

An association so formed that its gains are the property of the whole association, and are not divisible among the members, is only entitled to an exemption of $2,000. It is not entitled to an exemption of $2,000 for each member. 10 I. R. R. 39.

Deductions from Income Tax.

[SEC. 9. (July 14, 1870.) *And be it further enacted*, That in addition to the exemptions provided in the preceding section, there shall be deducted from the gains, profits, and income of any person, all national, State, county, and municipal taxes (*a*) paid by him within the year, whether such person be owner, tenant, or mortgager; all his losses (*b*) actually sustained during the year, arising from fires, floods, shipwreck, or incurred in trade, and debts ascertained to be worthless, but excluding all estimated depreciation of values, the amount of interest paid during the year, and the amount (*c*) paid for rent or labor to cultivate land, or to conduct any other business from which income is derived; the amount paid for the rent of the house or premises occupied as a residence for himself or his family, and the amount paid out for usual and ordinary repairs. No deduction shall be made for any amount (*d*) paid out for new buildings, permanent improvements, or betterments made to increase the value of any property or estate.]

(*a*) State and municipal taxes paid upon a homestead, and ordinary repairs made thereon, are deductible. 11 I. R. R. 89.

National, State, county, and municipal taxes actually paid are deductible from the income of the year in which such payment is made, even though they are paid upon property from which no income is derived. 11 I. R. R. 98.

National, State, county, and municipal taxes not actually paid until after the close of the income year, should not be deducted from the income for that year, even though they may have been then due and payable. 7 I. R. R. 60.

United States legacy and succession taxes are deductible from the income of the beneficiaries by or for whom they are paid, but from no other income. The same is true of State taxes paid by or for such beneficiaries. The tax due upon the income of the testator or intestate for the period previous to his death diminishes the amount of legacy only. 7 I. R. R. 59.

Assessments made by municipal corporations for the laying out and grading of streets, the construction of walks, sewers, &c., may be deducted from income where they are laid upon all taxpayers within the corporation. 1 I. R. R. 196.

Assessments made upon the property-holders of a certain locality, in a city or town, by the municipal authorities thereof, on account of special improvements in or upon the streets adjoining their premises, should be allowed as deductions from the income of persons so assessed. 5 I. R. R. 115; 3 I. R. R. 188, 204.

Where, by the laws of the State, stocks divided into shares are not taxable by cities and towns, but are taxed by the State to the companies, and the tax collected by the State is credited to the towns where the stockholders reside, the stockholder cannot deduct the tax from his income, since the deduction was made by the corporation before the dividend was declared. 1 I. R. R. 181; but see 10 l. R. R. 9.

The amount withheld by corporations from the dividends of the shareholder, in accordance with the provisions of the infernal revenue laws, should be allowed as a deduction, since the tax is in reality a tax upon the shareholder and its payment by the corporation is merely a mode of collecting it. 10 I. R. R. 9.

Taxes which have been deducted from the income of a previous year cannot be deducted again. 1 I. R. R. 181.

When the owner of property occupies the same, he is entitled to deduct the taxes paid on such property as if the same were rented and produced income. 1 I. R. R. 155.

(*b*) The original cost of property destroyed by fire during the income year, less the amount received as insurance thereon, may be deducted from the income for that year of the person to whom the loss occurred. 5 I. R. R. 154.

A person is not allowed to put the property in any better condition than that in which it was before, but he is allowed to devote the income to restoration only. 1 I. R. R. 180.

The loss of a stock company by fire or shipwreck, if such companies were liable to income tax, would be deductible from the income of such companies, not from the income of the stockholders thereof. The fact that such companies are not subject to income tax makes a loss of this character none the less a loss of the company. It cannot, therefore, be deducted from the income of the stockholder. 5 I. R. R 148.

The fact that income is devoted to the paying of debts does not release the same from liability to income tax. 7 I. R. R. 59.

No so-called loss incurred by a gift of property can be allowed as a deduction from income. 7 I. R. R. 59.

Losses incurred in the prosecution of one kind of business may be deducted from the gains in another or from the gross income of the year. Assessors should be careful not to allow the deduction of amounts claimed to have been lost in business when in reality they should be regarded as investments or expenditures. 3 I. R. R. 140; 7 I. R. R. 59.

Payment by a surety makes the principal his debtor. Then, and ordinarily not till then, there is a debt from the principal to the surety for which there is a right of action. Whether the debt is worthless or not, is a question to be determined in each particular case. The claim of the surety against his principal may be perfectly good. He may have full security; or the principal may simply be absent or only temporarily embarrassed. Money paid as surety is not therefore necessarily and invariably lost; but when it is found to be a loss it may be deducted under the head of "debts ascertained to be worthless." 9 I. R. R. 121.

Estimated appreciations or depreciations of the value of property are in no case to be considered in ascertaining amounts to be taxed as income. 5 I. R. R. 154.

The whole amount expended for fertilizers applied during the income year to the farmer's lands may be deducted, but no deduction is allowed for fertilizers produced on the farm. The cost of seed purchased for sowing or planting may be deducted. 7 I. R. R. 58.

No deduction can be allowed for the subsistence of laborers employed on a farm so far as they live upon the produce of the farm. 3 I. R. R. 140.

No deduction can in any case be allowed for depreciation in the value of stocks or other property until they are actually disposed of and a loss realized. The law expressly disallows deductions from income on account of any depreciation in the value of property still on hand. 7 I. R. R. 59.

Where stocks are sold for less than actual cost, the difference between such cost and the price at which the same are actually sold may be allowed as a deduction from income of the year of sale. 7 I. R. R. 59.

Losses during the income year on sales of real estate purchased during the income year or within a period of two years previous to that year may be deducted from the income for such income year. 7 I. R. R. 60.

Debts which had previously been considered good, but which have been found to be worthless during the income year, may be deducted from the income of the creditor for such income year, if never before deducted. 7 I. R. R. 60.

Losses of capital, such as losses by robbery, losses as surety, &c., cannot be deducted from income. 7 I. R. R. 60.

Losses sustained in business since the close of the income year cannot enter into the income assessments for that year. Bout. 275; 1 I. R. R. 181; 2 I. R. R. 68.

No deduction can be made from income for money paid on a judgment of any court against the taxpayer in an action of tort. 1 I. R. R. 155.

An officer of the army or navy cannot be allowed to deduct from his income the expense of servant hire nor of fuel unless the fuel is consumed in carrying on business. He may deduct house rent in the same manner as other persons. 1 I. R. R. 100.

The amount paid for a substitute by a party drafted cannot be deducted from income. 2 I. R. R. 92.

There must be a discretion given to a person making his returns, and, if that discretion is used fairly and honestly, there is no just ground of complaint. It is not necessary that the debt should be ascertained to be worthless by a suit at law or in equity, for that would be impracticable. U. S. v. Frost, 9 I. R. R. 41; s. c. 1 C. L. N. 129.

When a company has gone out of existence and the stock is absolutely worthless the loss sustained by investment in such stock should be allowed as a deduction from the income of the year in which the company ceased to exist and the loss thus became an absolute and ascertained loss. 11 I. R. R. 105.

When a farmer loses animals by death during the income year, he may deduct the sums actually paid as purchase money. If the animals were raised by the owner claiming the deduction, no deduction can be allowed. 3 I. R. R. 100.

The law expressly disallows deductions from income on account of estimated depreciations of value. The annual depreciation in the value of vessels cannot be deducted from the earnings. 1 I. R. R. 109, 197.

Unless the property has been sold, there is no ascertained but merely a speculative loss which cannot be deducted. 8 I. R. R. 109.

Where a person cannot be compelled to pay interest which nominally falls due in any year, it cannot be deducted from his income. Except where interest is paid in connection with the carrying on of a business from which income is derived, only such portion of the same as is not in excess of the amount of interest received or falling due to the taxpayer is to be offset against income. 7 I. R. R. 59.

(c) When deductions are claimed on the ground of expenses, the items should be specified, otherwise the assessor may disallow them if he doubts their legality. 1 I. R. R. 100.

Money paid for labor, except such as is used or employed in domestic service, or in the production of articles consumed in the family of the producer, may be deducted. 7 I. R. R. 58.

No deduction can be allowed in any case for the cost of unproductive labor. If house servants are employed a portion of the time in productive labor, such as the making of butter and cheese for sale, a proportionate amount of the wages paid to them may be deducted. 7 I. R. R. 58.

Costs of suits and other legal proceedings arising from ordinary business are to be treated as other expenses of such business and may be deducted from the gross profits thereof. 7 I. R. R. 59.

Expenses for medical expenses, store bills, etc., are not proper subjects for deductions. Expenses for repairs of implements, tools, etc., used in business may be deducted. 7 I. R. R. 59.

So far as insurance moneys are paid as an expense of business, they are deductible from income, but no insurance on the homestead of the taxpayer, nor on his life or other lives, nor on his rented property when paid by the tenant, can be allowed. Insurance paid by the tenant is deductible from the tenant's income as rent paid. 7 I. R. R. 59.

The expense of sinking wells which are worthless when they are exhausted is one of the necessary expenses of conducting the business of producing oil for sale, and may be deducted from the income of a person so engaged. Men who sink wells, not for the sake of working them, but for the purpose of selling them to others, should not be allowed this deduction. 11 I. R. R. 123.

The salary of a person employed to take care of real estate is deductible from such income of the person paying such salary as is derived from the estate in question. 3 I. R. R. 102.

When persons expend money in farming or gardening for recreation or adornment rather than for pecuniary profits, such expenditures cannot be deducted from income. 7 I. R. R. 60.

The expenses of conveyance necessarily incurred in traveling from place to place in the prosecution of business may be deducted in making a return of income. 7 I. R. R. 60.

Hotel bills incurred by persons traveling for the prosecution of business, or by persons temporarily residing in hotels while prosecuting business away from home, and actually paid during the income year, should be regarded as expenses and as such deductible from income. 11 I. R. R. 122.

The amount paid for the good-will of a business is capital invested, and not a loss to be deducted from income. 7 I. R. R. 60.

Where physicians are obliged to keep a horse for the transaction of business, they may deduct so much of the expense so incurred as is fairly referable to the business done. 7 I. R. R. 59.

So much of the expense of season tickets on railways, used by a person in going from his home to his place of business and returning again, as is fairly chargeable to expenses of business may be allowed as a deduction. 1 I. R. R. 172.

The proprietor's labor cannot be deducted. 1 I. R. R. 156.

No deduction can be made by a person for the value of the services of his minor children, whether he actually pays for such services or not. If his adult children work for him, and receive compensation for their labor, they are to be regarded as other hired laborers in determining his income. 7 I. R. R. 58.

Expenditures for labor in one calendar year cannot be deducted from the proceeds of the crop sold in a subsequent year. 4 I. R. R. 12.

Interest on borrowed capital used in business may be deducted from incomes. Bout. 275.

Interest paid on money which is invested in business or real estate, from which no income is derived, is not deductible from income; interest thus paid may be offset against interest received or falling due to the taxpayer. 11 I. R. R. 50; 7 I. R. R. 59.

If a mortgage on a homestead is given to secure the payment of money which is invested in business from which income is derived, the interest paid thereon is deductible from income. Where, however, the mortgage is given to secure the purchase price, or any part thereof, interest paid thereon is not deductible, except where it may be offset against interest received or falling due. If income has been received by renting any portion of the mortgaged premises, a ratable deduction of interest paid should be allowed. 11 I. R. R. 89.

The expenses of carrying on a farm or plantation may be deducted from the income of the year when it was paid, and from the income of that year only. 6 I. R. R. 3.

The subsistence of horses, mules, oxen, and cattle, used exclusively in carrying on the farm, may be deducted. Bout. 274.

No deduction can be allowed from the taxable income for compensation paid for the services of a minor son. Bout. 274.

Expenses on real or personal property from which no income is derived are not deductible from income. 11 I R. R. 50.

Rent of a homestead actually paid may be deducted, but the rental value of property owned by the taxpayer is not a subject of deduction; but where the taxpayer rents a furnished house, that portion of the rent paid in consideration of the use of the furniture should not be allowed as a deduction. 7 I. R. R. 59.

Any person claiming a deduction on account of expense for room rent must satisfy the assessor that the room or rooms occupied by him constitute his home, and that he has no residence elsewhere; and this being shown, he may be allowed to deduct what he actually pays for rent of such rooms, but nothing can be allowed for rent of furniture or care of rooms. When rent is included and deducted as an expense of business, it must not be again deducted as rent; nor should a person hiring a house, and subletting a portion of it, be allowed to deduct more than the excess of his payments over his receipts. 7 I. R. R 59.

Where a taxpayer pays a gross sum for rooms and board, and has no home elsewhere, he is entitled to deduct a fair allowance for rent of such rooms. The assessor should determine, from the best information that he can obtain, what proportion of the amount paid was considered as payment for the room only. No deduction should be allowed for rent of furniture, care of rooms, or for fuel or lights used. 11 I. R. R. 58.

When a mortgage is given on a homestead to secure the purchase price or any part thereof, the interest paid thereon is not deductible except where it may be offset against interest received or falling due. If income is received from the rental of any portion of the mortgaged premises, a ratable deduction of interest paid should be allowed. If a mortgage has been given on a homestead to secure the payment of money which has been invested in business, from which income is derived, the interest paid thereon is deductible from income. 11 I. R. R. 89, 97.

(*d*) Repairs should be distinguished from permanent improvements. 2 I. R. R. 61.

Amounts expended by the purchaser of a building in repairing injuries which occurred thereto prior to his purchase, are, so far as he is concerned, betterments made to increase the value of his property, and cannot be allowed as deductions from his income. 7 I. R. R. 60.

Expenses incurred in putting property in a better condition than when it was purchased, or, if purchased prior to January 1, 1862, than it was in on the above date, are not deductible. . 2 I. R. R. 61 ; 11 I. R. R. 50, 73.

The laying of a new floor, or putting on of a new roof, would usually be regarded as ordinary repairs ; but the replacing of a shingle roof by a slate roof, or a board floor by a tile floor, or in short, by substituting a higher priced article for an inferior, would not be regarded as ordinary repairs, and only the value of the inferior article would be deductible. 11 I. R. R. 50.

The removal of a roof of ancient design from a building, and the substitution of one of modern style, raising the walls of the building to conform thereto, should be regarded as an improvement rather than as repairs. Bout. 06.

Repairs are allowable without reference to the productive nature of the property. 1 I. R. R. 156.

The replacing of worn-out tools or machinery should be considered as repairs, so far as the new article equals the estimated value of the old on January 1, 1862, and as permanent improvements in the amount by which the value of the new article exceeds that of the old on that date. 2 I. R. R. 61.

"Permanent improvements" and "betterments," as used in this section, are very nearly synonymous in meaning, and refer to that class of improvements which permanently increase the value of the property upon which they are made, while "repairs" are understood to be those improvements made or work done upon property which serve merely to prevent its become useless or depreciating in value. In ascertaining the amount to be allowed for repairs, the assessor must determine, according to the circumstances of the case, how much of the improvements made are to prevent the depreciation of the value of the property, and how much for the purpose of giving it permanent additional value. 5 I. R. R. 130.

Expenses for ditching and clearing new land are plainly expenses for permanent improvements, and are not deductible. 7 I. R. R. 58.

For and during what Time Assessed.

[Sec. 10. (July 14, 1870.) *And be it further enacted,* That the tax hereinbefore provided shall be assessed upon the gains, profits, and income for the year ending on the thirty-first day of December next preceding the time for levying and collecting said tax, and shall be levied on the first day of March, eighteen hundred and seventy-one and eighteen hundred and seventy-two, and be due and payable on or before the thirtieth day of April in each of said years. And in addition to any sum annually due and unpaid after the thirtieth day of April, and for ten days after notice and demand thereof by the collector, there shall be levied and collected, as a penalty, the sum of five per centum on the amount unpaid, and interest on said amount at the rate of one per centum per month from the time the same became due, except from the estates of deceased, insane, or insolvent persons.]

Income Returns.

[Sec. 11. (July 14, 1870.) *And be it further enacted,* That it shall be the duty of every person of lawful age, whose gross income during the preceding year exceeded two thousand dollars, to make and render a return, (*a*) on or before the day designated by law, to the assistant assessor of the district in which he resides, of the gross amount of his income, gains, and profits as aforesaid; but not including the amount received from any corporation whose officers, as authorized by law, withhold and pay as taxes a per centum of the dividends made, and of the interest or coupons paid by such corporation, nor that portion of the salary or pay received for services in the civil, military, naval, or other service of the United States, or as Senator, Representative, or Delegate in Congress, from which tax has been deducted, nor the wages of minor children not received; and every guardian (*b*) and trustee, executor or administrator, and any person acting in any other fiduciary capacity, or as resident agent for, or copartner of, any non-resident alien, deriving income, gains, and profits from any business, trade, or profession carried on in the United States, or from rents of real estate situated therein, shall make and render a return as aforesaid to the assistant assessor of the district in which he resides, of the amount of income, gains, and profits of any minor or person for whom he acts.

The assistant assessor shall require every such return to be verified by the oath of the party rendering it, and may increase the amount of any return, after notice to such party, if he has reason to believe that the same is understated. In case any person having a gross income as above, of two thousand dollars or more, shall neglect or refuse to make and render such return, or shall render a false or fraudulent return, the assessor or the assistant assessor shall make such return, according to the best information he can obtain by the examination of said person, or of his books or accounts, or by any other evidence, and shall add, as a penalty, (c) to the amount of the tax due thereon, fifty per centum in all cases of wilful neglect or refusal to make and render a return, and one hundred per centum in all cases of a false or fraudulent return having been rendered.

The tax and the addition thereto as penalty shall be assessed and collected in the manner provided for in cases of wilful neglect or refusal to render a return, or of rendering a false or fraudulent return. But no penalty shall be assessed upon any person for such neglect or refusal, or for making or rendering a false or fraudulent return, except after reasonable notice of the time and place of hearing, to be regulated by the Commissioner of Internal Revenue, so as to give the person charged an opportunity to be heard:

Provided, That no collector, deputy collector, assessor, or assistant assessor, shall permit to be published in any manner such income returns, or any part thereof, except such general statistics, not specifying the names of individuals or firms, as he may make public, under such rules and regulations as the Commissioner of Internal Revenue shall prescribe.]

(*a*) Questions may be asked. It is not claimed that taxpayers are obliged to answer the same, but a refusal, unless a reason for such refusal is given, might lead the assessor to doubt the correctness of the return. It is not supposed that the mere putting of the interrogatories will be an effectual check upon fraud, but experience has shown that questions are of great convenience in refreshing the memory of a large class of honest taxpayers, who are not accustomed to keeping acounts, and who, in many instances, cannot recall all the sources of their income unless they are thus reminded. 1 I. R. R. 155.

The destruction or disappearance of books of account of persons whose returns are unsatisfactory is an event which is always a subject of just suspicion. It is hardly possible, consistently with the known business habits of a commercial or manufacturing community, to give a credible explanation of it; and, in most instances, assessors will be justified in assuming that it is *prima facie* evidence of fraud, and treating the returns accordingly. 1 I. R. R. 155.

The verification of returns before a notary public should not be permitted. Some exceptions to this rule should, doubtless, be allowed in cases, for instance, of Members of Congress, and State Legislatures, and others, whose business require them to be absent from home at the time when the income returns are required to be rendered, in whose cases it would seem to be proper to allow the returns to be verified before an assessor or assistant assessor of the place in which the party may be when the return is required to be made. 11 I. R. R. 145.

The form of the oath may be modified in the case of the returns of lawyers and physicians, so as to be appropriate to the manner in which they compute their income. 1 I. R. R. 180; 11 I. R. R. 138.

(*b*) The trustees of an association like that of the Shakers should make the return of the income of the association. 10 I. R. R. 39.

The parent, as natural guardian of a minor child, is required to make return for him. But where any other guardian or trustee has been appointed, the return should be made by the latter. If the minor has no guardian or trustee, he should make return himself. If he refuse or neglect, an independent assessment must be made as in other cases, omitting penalty. 11 I. R. R. 185; 7 I. R. R. 59.

Incomes of persons who died after the close of the income year are taxable, and should be returned by executors or administrators, and also of all income which accrued during the income year to persons who died within that year. Income which accrued in the income year from the estates of such persons after the date of decease, should be returned by the heirs or other persons who received the benefit of the same. 7 I. R. R. 59; Mandell v. Pierce, 7 I. R. R. 193.

Guardians and trustees. whether such trustees are so by virtue of their office as executors, administrators, or other fiduciary capacity, are required to make return of income belonging to minors or other persons which are held in trust as aforesaid, and the income tax will be assessed upon the amount returned. Bout. 258.

A guardian residing abroad should return the income of his ward in the district where the ward resides. But a guardian not residing abroad should return the income of his ward in the district where the guardian resides. 3 I. R. R. 172.

No person can take oath respecting his or his ward's income except as and according to the best of his knowledge and belief. Few cases can arise where the trustee has not, or cannot, readily obtain information respecting the income of the *cestui que* trust; yet it is expected of trustees that they will use all due efforts to arrive at just estimates in this regard. Nor can a trustee conscientiously take the oath required unless he has used such efforts. 1 I. R. R. 181.

(*c*) In all cases arising under those sections which declare it to be the duty of the assessor to impose the penalty, no alternative is left him, and he must invariably impose the penalty. But in other cases, where the language of the law is that he "may add the penalty," he should impose such penalty whenever incurred, unless he is satisfied that it was impossible for the taxpayer to comply with the requirements of the law, as in cases of sickness, unavoidable absence, or excusable ignorance of the law. 2 I. R. R. 36.

When a short return is made in fraud of the revenue, the penalty should be computed on the whole amount of tax chargeable, though the tax has been paid under the fraudulent return. 1 I. R. R. 172; 3 I. R. R. 14.

A notice according to the form prescribed, 9 I. R. R. 113, should be served upon the delinquent by delivering it, or causing it to be delivered, to him in hand, or by leaving it, or causing it to be left, at his last and usual place of abode at least fifteen days prior to the day for hearing. Where the return is to be made by a guardian, trustee, executor, administrator, attorney, agent, or partner of a non-resident alien, or by a person acting in any other fiduciary capacity, the notice should be served upon him instead of his ward, *cestui que* trust, &c., and there may be a change in the phraseology of the notice to suit the circumstances of the case. 9 I. R. R. 113.

Appeal to Assessors.

[SEC. 12. (July 14, 1870.) *And be it further enacted*, That when the return of any person is increased by the assistant assessor, such person may exhibit his books and accounts and be permitted to prove and declare, under oath, (a) the amount of income liable to be assessed; but such oath and evidence shall not be conclusive of the facts, and no deductions claimed in such cases shall be allowed until approved by the assistant assessor. Any person may appeal from the decision of the assistant assessor in such cases to the assessor of the district, and his decision, thereon, unless reversed by the Commissioner of Internal Revenue, shall be final. The form, time, and manner of proceedings shall be subject to regulations to be prescribed by the Commissioner of Internal Revenue.]

(a) The oath taken at the time of rendering the return cannot be made available for the purposes for which the oath prescribed by this section is to be made. Magee v. Denton, 5 Blatch. 180.

Declaration of no Income under Oath.

[SEC. 13. (July 14, 1870.) *And be it further enacted*, That any person, in his own behalf, or as such fiduciary or agent, shall be permitted to declare, under oath, that he, or his ward, beneficiary or principal, was not possessed of an income of two thousand dollars, liable to be assessed according to the provisions of this act; or may declare that an income tax has been assessed and paid elsewhere in the same year, under authority of the United States, upon his income, gains, and profits, or those of his ward, beneficiary or principal, as required by law; and if the assistant assessor shall be satisfied of the truth of the declaration, such person shall thereupon be exempt from income tax in the said district.]

Income of Foreign Consuls.

[SEC. 14. (July 14, 1870.) *And be it further enacted*, That consuls of foreign governments who are not citizens of the United States shall be exempt from any income tax imposed by this act which may be derived from their official emoluments, or from property in foreign countries: *Provided*, That the governments which such consuls may represent shall extend similar exemption to consuls of the United States.]

Dividends of Corporations.

[SEC. 15. (July 14, 1870.) *And be it further enacted*, That there shall be levied and collected for and during the year eighteen hundred and seventy-one a tax of two and one-half per centum on the amount of all interest or coupons paid on bonds or other evidences of debt issued and payable in one or more years after date, by any of the corporations in this section hereinafter enumerated, and on the amount of all dividends of earnings, income, or gains hereafter declared, by any bank, trust company, savings institution, insurance company, railroad company, canal company, turnpike company, canal navigation company, and slack-water company, whenever and wherever (*a*) the same shall be payable, and to whatsoever person the same may be due, including non-residents, whether citizens or aliens, and on all undivided profits of any such corporation which have accrued and been earned and added to any surplus, contingent, or other fund, and every such corporation having paid the tax as aforesaid is hereby authorized to deduct and withhold from any payment on account of interest, coupons, and dividends an amount equal to the tax of two and one-half per centum on the same; and the payment to the United States, as provided by law, of the amount of tax so deducted from the interest, coupons, and dividends aforesaid, shall discharge the corporation from any liability for that amount of said interest, coupons, or dividends, claimed as due to any person, except in cases where said corporations have provided otherwise by an express contract:

Provided, That the tax upon the dividends of insurance companies shall not be deemed due until such dividends are payable either in money or otherwise; and that the money returned by mutual insurance companies to their policy-holders, and the annual or semi-annual interest allowed or paid to the depositors in savings banks or savings institutions, shall not be considered as dividends; and that when any dividend is made, or interest as aforesaid is paid, which includes any part of the surplus or contingent fund of any corporation which has been assessed and the tax paid thereon, or which includes any part of the dividends, interest, or coupons received from other corporations whose officers are authorized by law to withhold a per centum on the same, the amount of tax so paid on that portion of the surplus or contingent fund, and the amount of tax which has been withheld and paid on dividends, interest, or coupons so received, may be deducted from the tax on such dividend or interest.]

(*a*) The tax is to be paid by the company whenever and wherever the interest is payable, *i. e.*, at the time when, and regardless of the place where, it is payable. To construe the word "wherever" to mean at the place where, would be to make the tax in some cases payable in a foreign country, where the government neither has nor can have laws and officers to assess and collect it. The company indebted for money for which bonds are issued must itself make return of coupons and interest, and pay the tax thereon, regardless of the place where such interest and coupons are payable. 10 I. R. R. 81.

When bonds are issued by a State, county, city, or town, in aid of a railroad company, whereof the interest is to be paid by the company, the tax must be withheld, although neither bond nor coupon may express the liability of the company, such an arrangement being virtually an indorsement of the company's bonds by the State, county, city, or town. Whether the interest is paid by the State, county, city or town, and received from the company, or paid directly by the company to the bondholders, is immaterial. In either case the managers of the company must account to the government for the tax. Bout. 254.

It is the intention of the law to tax the entire net gains of railroad companies; and the company is not relieved from making a return and paying a tax thereon of surplus earnings which may not be set aside in the particular manner mentioned. 3 I. R. R. 85.

A tax should be imposed upon the amount carried to the repair fund. 2 I. R. R. 100.

It is to be observed that the tax is not imposed upon all funds used for construction, but merely upon profits used for construction, so that it is not sufficient, as laying the basis of liability, to show that a company has expended money for construction, but it must also be shown that the money thus expended is a portion of the profits of the company. The excess of receipts over disbursements is not necessarily profits, unless the disbursements include an outlay for improving or repairing the property of the company sufficient to keep the property up to its original value. In determining, therefore, the amount on which a railroad company should be required to pay a tax, it is necessary to determine the amount of profits during the period. These profits are taxable, whether expended for contruction or retained to be expended thereafter. The percentage of depreciation must vary with different railroads, so as to prevent the adoption of any fixed percentage as a proper allowance, and the only practicable rule would seem to be that all sums expended for the purpose and with the result of keeping the property of the company up to its average value, or up to its average value at the beginning of the period under consideration, should be allowed as expenses. If any company has failed to expend a sum sufficient to keep its property up to such value, it should be allowed to set aside, as not properly included in the profits, such sum as would have been expended had such repairs been made. 8 I. R. R. 19.

The taxes are assessable without regard to whether the stockholders, bondholders, &c., are non-resident aliens or not. 9 I. R. R. 118; Jackson v. Northern Central R. R. Co. 9 I. R. R. 139; s. c. 7 Wall. 262.

The amount paid as premium upon United States bonds purchased by the corporation cannot be deducted as a loss from the gross earnings. It is a part of the investment, and should be so treated in ascertaining the sum liable to tax. 5 I. R. R. 74.

In determining the amount of taxable gains, only such losses as have been ascertained and settled during the period covered by the return should be deducted. The business of each period should stand by itself. 5 I. R. R. 74.

No deduction should be made on account of a part of the earnings being the interest upon railroad bonds owned by the corporation, and upon which a tax has been withheld, or on account of tax withheld, by other corporations from dividends payable to it. 5 I. R. R. 91.

The law provides that the portion of the premiums returned by mutual life insurance companies to their policy holders shall not be considered as dividends, unless the company pay to the policy holder more than the premiums received from him. Unless such excess is so paid, no tax is imposed. Where any mutual life insurance company has a capital stock, and the profits of the company are divided between the stockholders and the policy holders, the amount paid to the policy holders is exempt from tax, provided that it fall within the rule above stated. 6 I. R. R. 139.

The tax may be levied upon non-resident stockholders. 9 I. R. R. 113.

(a) The taxes due from all corporations mentioned in this section are made payable to the collector of the proper district, the same as other taxes. 4 I. R. R. 156.

When a bank declares a dividend in coin, it should be reduced to its value in legal tender currency at the time when, and the place where, the dividend is declared payable, and the tax should be ascertained upon the currency value thus ascertained. 5 I. R. R. 74.

The tax upon a scrip dividend should be assessed when the scrip is issued, and the dividend should be returned at its par value. 5 I. R. R. 91.

Under the provisions of this section, it is clear that although the surplus from which the dividend is declared was acquired prior to the passage of the revenue law, yet, if the same is divided after the law went into effect, it is taxable. The rule is that the tax must be withheld from the entire dividend whenever it becomes due and payable, without regard to the time when the profits or earnings were acquired. 4 I. R. R. 44, 68.

Interest paid to depositors by savings banks is considered a dividend within the meaning of this section. 2 I. R. R. 36.

The dates of the previous and present dividend must be inserted in the return, so that the whole year may be accounted for. Bout. 226.

The banks falling within the proviso to section 110, act June 30, 1864, as amended, are not required to pay any tax under this section; but the dividends of all other banks, savings, or otherwise, are subject to tax, as provided in said section. 11 I. R. R. 73.

The corporations included in this section are not allowed to hold their profits in reserve, even if the same are not carried to what is technically known as a fund, without returning and paying tax on the same as often as once in each year, provided that profits so returned and the tax paid need not be again returned until they are distributed, when the tax already paid may be deducted from the total amount of tax on such dividend. The tax is due upon the entire net earnings or profits, whether the same are distributed to the stockholders or remain undistributed in the custody of the corporation, either as an undistributed sum or as carried to the account of any fund. 11 I. R. R. 10.

The amount paid out by an insurance company for reinsurance may be deducted from the gross receipts in ascertaining the amount of earnings or profits subject to a tax under this section. 11 I. R. R. 122.

The amount paid by the corporation as a tax under the provisions of this section cannot be deducted as an expense of business. Such taxes are not deductible. 10 I. R. R. 57; 5 I. R. R. 74.

But the amount paid as taxes on the capital, circulation, and deposits during the period covered by the return may be deducted the same as other expenses. 5 I. R. R. 74.

Insurance Companies.

[SEC. 1. (July 13, 1870.) *Resolved by the Senate and House of Representatives of the United States of America in Congress assembled,* That the act entitled "An act to provide internal revenue to support the Government, to pay interest on the public debt, and for other purposes," approved June thirty, eighteen hundred and sixty-four, and the several amendments thereunto, shall not be construed so as to impose a tax on any undistributable sum added to the contingent fund of any fire, marine, inland, life, health, accident, or like insurance company, or any unearned premium or premiums received for risks assumed by such companies, or any moneys paid by mutual life insurance companies to their policy holders.]

Return of Dividends.

[SEC. 16. (July 14, 1870.) *And be it further enacted*, That every person, having the care or management of any corporation liable to be taxed under the last preceding section, shall make and render to the assessor or assistant assessor of the district in which such person has his office for conducting the business of such corporation, on or before the tenth day of the month following that in which any dividends or sums of money become due or payable as aforesaid, a true and complete return, in such form as the Commissioner of Internal Revenue may prescribe, of the amount of income and profits and of taxes as aforesaid; and there shall be annexed thereto a declaration of the president, cashier, or treasurer of the corporation, under oath, that the same contains a true and complete account of the income and profits and of taxes as aforesaid. And for any default in the making or rendering of such return, with such declaration annexed, the corporation so in default shall forfeit, as a penalty, the sum of one thousand dollars; and in case of any default in making or rendering said return, or of any default in the payment of the tax as required, or of any part thereof, the assessment and collection of the tax and penalty shall be in accordance with the general provisions of law in other cases of neglect and refusal.]

Repeal of Sections of Act June 30, 1864.

[SEC. 17. (July 14, 1870.) *And be it further enacted*, That sections one hundred and twenty, one hundred and twenty-one, one hundred and twenty-two, and one hundred and twenty-three of the act of June thirty, eighteen hundred and sixty-four, entitled "An act to provide internal revenue to support the Government, to pay interest on the public debt, and for other purposes," as amended by the act of July thirteen, eighteen hundred and sixty-six, and the act of March two, eighteen hundred and sixty-seven, shall be construed to impose the taxes therein mentioned to the first day of August, eighteen hundred and seventy, but after that date no further taxes shall be levied or assessed under said sections; and all acts and parts of acts relating to the taxes herein repealed, and all the provisions of said acts shall continue in full force for levying and collecting all taxes properly assessed, or liable to be assessed, or accruing under the provisions of former acts, or drawbacks, the right to which has already accrued or which may hereafter accrue, under said acts, and for maintaining and continuing liens, fines, penalties, and forfeitures incurred under and by virtue thereof. And this act shall not be construed to affect any act done, right accrued, or penalty incurred under former acts, but every such right is hereby saved. And for carrying out and completing all proceedings which have been already commenced or that may be commenced to enforce such fines, penalties, and forfeitures, or criminal proceedings under said acts, and for the punishment of crimes of which any party shall be or has been found guilty.]

Secs. 124 to **149,** inclusive, *Repealed* July 14, 1870, § 2.

Sec. 150. *Repealed* July 13, 1866, § 9.

STAMP TAXES.

Who Shall Affix Stamps.

Sec. 151. *And be it further enacted,* That all laws in force at the time of the passage of this act in relation to stamp duties shall continue in force until the first day of August, eighteen hundred and sixty-four; and on and after the first day of August, eighteen hundred and sixty-four, there shall be levied (*a*), collected, and paid, for and in respect of the several instruments, matters and things mentioned and described in the schedule (marked B) hereunto annexed, or for or in respect of the vellum, parchment, or paper upon which such instruments, matters, or things, or any of them, shall be written or printed, by any person (*b*) or persons, or party who shall make, sign, or issue the same, or for whose use or benefit the same shall be made, signed, or issued, the several duties or sums of money set down in figures against the same, respectively, or otherwise specified or set forth in the said schedule.

(*a*) Instruments issued in the States lately in insurrection are subject to the same taxes as similar ones issued at the same time in the other States. 9 I. R. R. 165.

The law does not designate which of the parties to an instrument shall furnish the necessary stamp. 9 I. R. R. 163.

Judicial process, being wholly under the control of the respective States when issuing from or used in their courts, and being indispensable in the execution of the powers of the State, is as far removed from interference by the taxing power of Congress as any instrumentalities of the general government created to carry into execution the powers with which it is vested are removed beyond the interference of the State authorities. If State process could be taxed by the United States, it could be absolutely prohibited and destroyed by such a power brought to bear upon it; and as the States are sovereign in respect to the matters committed to them, Congress cannot, by taxation or in any other manner, retard, burden, or control their operation within the field of their duty, nor impose a specific tax of any kind upon any of the indispensable governmental functions of the State. Craig *v.* Dimock, 9 I. R. R. 129; Warren *v.* Paul, 22 Ind. 276; Fifield *v.* Close, 15 Mich. 505; Jones et al. *v.* Keep, 19 Wis. 369; Union Bank *v.* Hill et al. 3 Cold. 325; Lewis *v.* Randall, 1 Abb. Pr. N. S. 135; s. c. 30 How. Pr. 378; Walton *v.* Bryenth, 24 How. Pr. 357; Musselman *v.* Mauk, 18 Iowa, 289; Botkins *v.* Spurgeon, 20 Iowa, 598; Ford *v.* Clinton, 25 Iowa, 157; Harper *v.* Clark, 17 Ohio, 190. *Contra,* Jackson *v.* Allen, 26 How. Pr. 119; German Liederkranz *v.* Schieman, 25 How. Pr. 388; Smith *v.* Short, 40 Ala. 385.

The law requiring stamps on writs and other judicial process was repealed March 2d, 1867. Colerick et al. *v.* Bowser et al. 30 Ind. 329.

The recognized rule of construing penal statutes strictly and giving a liberal interpretation to words of exception contained therein should be applied to the stamp laws. They are directly penal, and clearly in restraint of common right. While such charges upon the people should be imposed by clear and unambiguous words, yet no interpretation should be adopted which will defeat the purpose of law, if the language naturally and fairly admits of an interpretation which sustains that purpose. Hugus v. Strickler, 19 Iowa, 413 ; Dorris v. Grace, 24 Ark. 326 ; Celley v. Gray, 37 Vt. 136 ; Vail v. Knapp, 49 Barb. 299 ; Harper v. Clark, 17 Ohio, 190 ; Hitchcock v. Sawyer, 39 Vt. 412.

A tax law (and a stamp act for the purpose of revenue is such) cannot be extended by construction to things not named or described as the subject of taxation. Every charge must be imposed by clear, unambiguous words. Boyd v. Hood, 57 Penn. 98 ; Smith v. Waters, 25 Ind. 397.

The construction given to the statute, by the Commissioner, should be regarded, and is entitled to much weight, if for no other reason than that there may be no conflict between two departments of the government in applying and executing the law, yet it cannot have the force of a judicial construction. The law itself provides that the only case in which his opinion is to be final is where he decides that an instrument does not require a stamp. Hugus v. Strickler, 19 Iowa, 413; Smith v. Waters, 25 Ind. 397.

No stamp is necessary upon an instrument executed prior to the 1st of October, 1862. Bayly v. McKnight, 19 La. An. 321.

A slight examination of the act, and of the schedule forming a part of it, shows very clearly that the subjects of taxation are written instruments in general use, whose character and objects are well understood, and have a definite meaning. Jackson v. Allen, 26 How. Pr. 119.

The mere handing or delivery of an accommodation note to the payee is not an issuing of it within the meaning of the act. The note has no validity or effect, as against the maker, so long as it remains in the hands of the payee. Its delivery to the payee is not an issuing of the note, but for the purpose of its being issued. The payee, before issuing it to third persons, may affix and cancel the required stamp, in the mode prescribed by the act. Voight et al. v. McKaim, 12 Pitts. L. J. 98.

(b) It is wholly immaterial who affixes the stamp. Either party to the instrument may do it. Adams v. Dale, 29 Ind. 273 ; Voight v. McKaim et al. 12 Pitts. L. J. 98 ; Ballard v. Burnside, 49 Barb. 102.

When an instrument is withheld for two days after its date, for the purpose of affixing a stamp, it cannot be regarded as completed until the stamp is affixed. Mason v. Cheney, 47 N. H. 24.

Under a contract "to execute a good and sufficient deed," in a place where it has for many years been the custom that the purchaser shall furnish the deed, the purchaser must pay for the stamps. Such a contract is not that the vendor shall prepare, but execute the deed. If it had been the former, it would have over-ridden the custom. McCready *v.* Callahan, 3 A. L. Reg. (N. S.) 241; s. c. 11 Pitts. L. J. 187.

A final judgment by the highest court of law or equity of a State, that revenue stamps attached to a deed offered in evidence and objected to as not having stamps proportioned to the value of the land conveyed are sufficient, is not a subject for review by the Supreme Court. The only question the State court had to pass upon was the value of the land. Neither the validity nor construction of the statute was drawn in question. Lewis *v.* Campau, 3 Wall. 106.

Record of Unstamped Instruments.

Sec. 152. (Amended July 13, 1866, § 9.) *And be it further enacted*, That it shall not be lawful to record (*a*) any instrument, document, or paper required by law to be stamped, unless a stamp or stamps of the proper amount shall have been affixed, and cancelled in the manner required by law; and the record of any such instrument, upon which the proper stamp or stamps aforesaid shall not have been affixed and cancelled as aforesaid, shall be utterly void, and shall not be used in evidence.

(*a*) If the record of an instrument is desired, the instrument must be stamped before it is recorded; because, without the stamp, the record is utterly void. Harper *v.* Clark, 17 Ohio, 190.

A judgment is not included in the provisions of this section. Corry Nat'l Bank *v.* Rouse, 3 I. R. R. 31.

A mortgage of chattels that is merely filed and not recorded is not included in the provisions of this section. Vail *v.* Knapp, 49 Barb. 299.

A mortgage insufficiently stamped at the time of recording cannot be made valid by a subsequent re-stamping under the authority of the collector so as to interfere with intervening rights. McBride *v.* Doty, 23 Iowa, 122.

The mortgagee will not be permitted to prove that only a portion of the consideration named in the mortgage was actually paid, and that the balance remains unpaid. The consideration was an entirety. If the instrument is not stamped for the right amount, according to the consideration expressed upon its face, it is void. It is true that, under the revenue act, if the consideration of an instrument is merely nominal, and fails to express the real amount paid or agreed to be paid, it is competent to show that fact, if the same is not properly stamped; but this is allowable in order to show an evasion of the provisions of the revenue act. This case is not similar to that class of cases. McBride *v.* Doty, 23 Iowa, 122.

More than one Stamp may be used.

Sec. 153. *And be it further enacted*, That no instrument, document, writing, or paper of any description, required by law to be stamped, shall be deemed or held invalid and of no effect for the want of the particular kind or description of stamp designated for and denoting the duty charged on any such instrument, document, writing, or paper, provided a legal stamp, or stamps, denoting a duty of equal amount, shall have been duly affixed and used thereon: *Provided*, That the provisions of this section shall not apply to any stamp appropriated to denote the duty charged on proprietary articles, or articles enumerated in Schedule C.

Official Documents Exempt.

Sec. 154. (Amended July 13, 1866, § 9.) *And be it further enacted*, That all official instruments, documents, and papers issued by the officers of the United States government, or by the officers (*a*) of any State, county, town, or other municipal corporation, shall be, and hereby are, exempt from taxation: *Provided*, That it is the intent hereby to exempt from liability to taxation such State, county, town, or other municipal corporation, in the exercise only of functions strictly belonging to them in their ordinary governmental and municipal capacity.

(*a*) No stamp is required upon an instrument to which the United States is a party, if it is signed and executed by a person representing the government; if not signed by such a person, stamps should be affixed 5 I. R. R. 60.

A tax deed need not be stamped. Congress does not possess the constitutional power, without the assent of the States, to tax the means or instruments devised by the States for the purpose of collecting their own revenues. Sayles *v.* Davis, 22 Wis. 225.

County orders, drawn on the county treasurer, for the payment of money by the county auditor acting under a resolution passed by the county commissioners, are exempt. Nave et al. *v.* King, 27 Ind. 356.

No stamp is required upon a bond given by a sheriff to a State for the faithful performance of his official duties. The State has the power to select its agents to execute its laws, and is empowered to exact from them such pledge for the faithful discharge of their duties as may seem best calculated to secure their performance. In exacting such security, it is independent of all control as in enforcing the condition of the bond when forfeited. State *v.* Garton, 32 Ind. ; s. c. 4 A. L. Rev. 396.

Forged or Counterfeit Stamps.

Sec. 155. (Amended July 13, 1866, § 9; April 10, 1869, § 2.) *And be it further enacted*, That if any person shall forge or counterfeit, or cause or procure to be forged or counterfeited, any stamp, die, plate, or other instrument, or any part of any stamp, die, plate, or other instrument, which shall have been provided, or may hereafter be provided, made, or used in pursuance of this act, or shall forge, counterfeit, or resemble, or cause or procure to be forged, counterfeited, or resembled, the impression, or any part of the impression, of any such stamp, die, plate, or other instrument as aforesaid, upon any vellum, parchment, or paper, or shall stamp or mark, or cause or procure to be stamped or marked, any vellum, parchment, or paper, with any such forged or counterfeited stamp, die, plate, or other instrument, or part of any stamp, die, plate, or other instrument, as aforesaid, with intent to defraud the United States of any of the taxes hereby imposed, or any part thereof; or if any person shall utter, or sell, or expose to sale, any vellum, parchment, paper, article, or thing, having thereupon the impression of any such counterfeited stamp, die, plate, or other instrument, or any part of any stamp, die, plate, or other instrument, or any such forged, counterfeited, or resembled impression, or part of impression, as aforesaid, knowing the same to be forged, counterfeited, or resembled; or if any person shall knowingly use or permit the use of any stamp, die, plate, or other instrument, which shall have been so provided, made, or used, as aforesaid, with intent to defraud the United States; or if any person shall fraudulently cut, tear, or remove, or cause or procure to be cut, torn, or removed, the impression of any stamp, die, plate, or other instrument, which shall have been provided, made, or used, in pursuance of this act, from any vellum, parchment, or paper, or any instrument or writing charged or chargeable with any of the taxes imposed by law; or if any person shall fraudulently use, join, fix, or place, or cause to be used, joined, fixed, or placed, to, with, or upon any vellum, parchment, paper, or any instrument or writing charged or chargeable with any of the taxes hereby imposed, any adhesive stamp, or the impression of any stamp, die, plate, or other instrument, which shall have been provided, made, or used in pursuance of law, and which shall have been cut, torn, or removed from any other vellum, parchment, or paper, or any instrument or writing charged or chargeable with any of the taxes imposed by law; or if any person shall wilfully remove or cause to be removed, alter or cause to be altered, the cancelling or defacing marks on any adhesive stamp, with intent to use the same, or to cause the use of the same after it shall have been once used, or shall knowingly or wilfully sell or buy such washed or restored stamps, or offer the same for sale, or give or expose the same to any person for use, or knowingly use the same, or prepare the same with intent for the further use thereof; or if any person shall knowingly and without lawful excuse (the proof whereof shall lie on the person accused) have in his possession any washed, restored, or altered stamps, which have been removed from any vellum, parchment, paper, instrument, or writing, then, and in every such case, every person so offending, and every person knowingly and wilfully aiding, abetting, or assisting in committing any such offence as aforesaid, shall, on conviction thereof, forfeit the said counterfeit stamps and the articles upon which they are placed, and be punished by fine not exceeding one thousand dollars, or by imprisonment and confinement to hard labor not exceeding five years, or both, at the discretion of the court. And the fact that any adhesive stamp so bought, sold, offered for sale, used, or had in possession as aforesaid, has been washed or restored by removing or altering the cancelling or defacing marks thereon, shall be *prima facie* proof that such stamp has been once used and removed by the possessor thereof from some vellum, parchment, paper, instrument, or writing, charged with taxes imposed by law, in violation of the provisions of this section.

Mode of Cancellation.

Sec. 156. *And be it further enacted*, That in any and all cases where an adhesive stamp shall be used for denoting any duty imposed by this act, except as hereinafter provided, the person using or affixing the same shall write (*a*) thereupon the initials of his name and the date upon which the same shall be attached or used, so that the same may not again be used. And if any person shall fraudulently make use of an adhesive stamp to denote any duty imposed by this act without so effectually cancelling and obliterating such stamp, except as before mentioned, he, she, or they shall forfeit the sum of fifty dollars.

Provided, That any proprietor (*b*) or proprietors of proprietary articles, or articles subject to stamp duty under Schedule C of this act, shall have the privilege of furnishing, without expense to the United States, in suitable form, to be approved by the Commissioner of Internal Revenue, his or their own dies or designs for stamps to be used thereon, to be made under the direction and to be retained in the possession of the Commissioner of Internal Revenue for his or their separate use, which shall not be duplicated to any other person. That in all cases where such stamp is used, instead of his or their writing the date thereon, the said stamp shall be so affixed on the box, bottle, package, that in opening the same, or using the contents thereof, the said stamp shall be effectually destroyed; and in default thereof, shall be liable to the same penalty imposed for neglect to affix said stamp as hereinbefore prescribed in this act. Any person who shall fraudulently obtain or use any of the aforesaid stamps or designs therefor, and any person forging, or counterfeiting, or causing or procuring the forging or counterfeiting any representation, likeness, similitude, or colorable imitation of the said last-mentioned stamp, or any engraver or printer who shall sell or give away said stamps, or selling the same, or, being a merchant, broker, peddler, or person dealing, in whole or in part, in similar goods, wares, merchandise, manufactures, preparations, or articles, or those designed for similar objects or purposes, shall have knowingly or fraudulently in his, her, or their possession any such forged, counterfeited likeness, similitude, or colorable imitation of the said last-mentioned stamp, shall be deemed guilty of a felony, and upon conviction thereof shall be subject to all the penalties, fines, and forfeitures prescribed in the preceding section of this act.

(*a*) Revenue stamps may be used indiscriminately upon any of the matters or things enumerated in Schedule B, except proprietary and playing-card stamps, for which a special use has been provided. Postage stamps cannot be used in payment of the duty chargeable upon instruments.

Each stamp used must be cancelled with ink. When stamps are printed upon checks, &c., so that, in filling up the instrument, the face of the stamp is and must necessarily be written across, no other cancellation will be required. All cancellation must be distinct and legible.

The defect in the mode of cancelling the stamp is no valid ground of defence against the instrument. The mode of cancellation prescribed by the Statute is directory only. No penalty is provided for an innocent omission to comply with the requirements of the law in this particular. Desmond *v.* Norris, 10 Allen, 250.

When the instrument is executed by two parties, it is sufficient if only one of them affix and cancel the stamp. The object of the statute is to raise revenue, and the stamps are required to be cancelled to prevent their use a second time. This is fully accomplished if one of the parties cancel the stamp. Teagarden *v.* Grover et al. 24 Ind. 399.

The party executing the instrument which requires the stamp is the one to affix it; and, in any event, the stamp cannot be affixed, nor the cancellation made by another party, without the actual knowledge and express or implied assent of the party who issues the paper on which the stamp is placed. Myers *v.* Smith, 48 Barb. 614.

The omission to cancel the stamps will not invalidate the instrument. Ballard *v.* Burnside, 49 Barb. 102; Adams *v.* Dale, 29 Ind. 273; Corry National Bank *v.* Rouse, 3 I. R. R. 31.

When an instrument, by its terms, is to become the property of another upon delivery, it is not a completed obligation until the delivery is made, and, if an agent is entrusted with the duty of delivering it, he will be presumed to have the power to affix and cancel stamps thereon, in order that the instrument may be perfect and valid. Cedar Rapids & St. Paul R. R. Co. *v.* Stewart, 25 Iowa, 115.

(*b*) The proprietor will be entitled to the commissions allowed by law. If the designs do not exceed in superficial area 13-16 of an inch for the denomination of one and two cent stamps or ⅔ of an inch for the denomination of three and four cent stamps, these being the sizes established by the Office of Internal Revenue for the above specified denominations, there will be no additional charge to purchasers. If, however, proprietors desire to increase the size of the stamps for the denominations above-mentioned, then an additional charge will be made for the additional cost of paper and printing. This additional charge will be ten cents per thousand for stamps of $8\frac{1}{2}$ inches superficial area, and in the same proportion for other sizes. All dies and plates will be retained by and be under the exclusive control of the Government. The general stamp must be cancelled by writing or printing thereon in ink the initials of the proprietor of the stamped article and the date, day, month, and year of cancelling; while the private stamp must be so affixed on the package that in opening the same the stamp shall be effectually destroyed. Where printing in more than one color is desired, the additional expense must be borne by the proprietor. Each stamp must bear the words, or a proper abbreviation of them, "United States Internal Revenue," also in words and figures the denomination of the stamp. Manufacturers of proprietary articles will be required to use the general proprietary stamp until stamps are furnished from their own designs. All stamps denoting duties under Schedule C, excepting those from private designs, may be used indiscriminately upon proprietary articles. 9 I. R. R. 167.

Commissioner may Prescribe Mode of Cancellation.

Sec. 157. *And be it further enacted*, That the Commissioner of Internal Revenue be, and he is hereby, authorized to prescribe such method (*a*) for the cancellation of stamps, as substitute for or in addition to the method now prescribed by law, as he may deem expedient and effectual. And he is further authorized, in his discretion, to make the application of such method imperative upon the manufacturers of proprietary articles, or articles included in Schedule C, and upon stamps of a nominal value exceeding twenty-five cents each.

(*a*) The following mode is prescribed for cancelling stamps, to wit: The cutting and cancelling the same by a machine which shall affix the date and so cut and deface the stamp as to render it manifestly unfit for re-use, and at the same time shall not so deface the stamp as to prevent its denomination and genuineness from being readily determined. An instrument used in making cancellations according to this method must be so constructed that an ordinary blow of the hand or pressure by lever will at one operation produce the required cancellation. Any machine producing a perfect cancellation, according to this method, may be used. The use of any cancelling machines which simply imprint the initials and date without cutting the stamp as herein required are prohibited. Cancellations by pen and ink are authorized. 12 I. R. R. 30.

Penalty for Omission to Stamp. Collector may Stamp.

Sec. 158. (Amended July 13, 1866, § 9; July 14, 1870, § 5.) *And be it further enacted*, That any person or persons who shall make, sign, or issue, or who shall cause to be made, signed, or issued, any instrument, document, or paper of any kind or description whatsoever, or shall accept, negotiate, or pay, or cause to be accepted, negotiated, or paid, any bill of exchange, draft, or order, or promissory note for the payment of money, without the same being duly stamped, or having thereupon an adhesive stamp for denoting the tax chargeable thereon, and cancelled in the manner required by law, with intent to evade the provisions of this act, shall, for every such offence, forfeit the sum of fifty dollars, and such instrument, document, or paper, bill, draft, order, or note, not being stamped according to law, shall be deemed invalid (a) and of no effect.

Provided, That the title of a purchaser of land by deed duly stamped shall not be defeated or affected by the want of a proper stamp on any deed conveying said land by any person from, through, or under whom his grantor claims or holds title:

And provided further, That hereafter, in all cases where the party has not affixed to any instrument the stamp required by law thereon at the time of making or issuing the said instrument, and he or they, or any party having an interest therein, shall be subsequently desirous of affixing such stamp to said instrument, or if said instrument be lost, to a copy thereof, he (b) or they shall appear before the collector of the revenue of the proper district, who shall, upon the payment of the price of the proper stamp required by law, and of a penalty of double the amount of tax remaining unpaid, but in no case less than five dollars, and where the whole amount of the tax denoted by the stamp required shall exceed the sum of fifty dollars, on payment also of interest, at the rate of six per centum, on said tax, from the day on which such stamp ought to have been affixed, affix the proper stamp to such instrument or copy, and note upon the margin thereof the date of his so doing, and the fact that such penalty has been paid; and the same shall thereupon be deemed and held to be as valid (c), to all intents and purposes, as if stamped when made or issued:

And provided further, That where it shall appear to said collector, upon oath or otherwise, to his satisfaction, that any such instrument has not been duly stamped at the time of making or issuing the same, by reason of accident, mistake, inadvertence, or urgent necessity, and without any wilful design to defraud the United States of the stamp, or to evade or delay the payment thereof, then, and in such case, if such instrument or if the original be lost, a copy thereof, duly certified by the officer having charge of any records in which such original is required to be recorded, or otherwise duly proven to the satisfaction of the collector, shall, within twelve calendar months after the first day of August, eighteen hundred and seventy-one, or within twelve calendar months after the making or issuing thereof, be brought to the said collector of revenue to be stamped, and the stamp tax chargeable thereon shall be paid, it shall be lawful for the said collector to remit the penalty aforesaid, and to cause such instrument to be duly stamped. And when the original instrument, or a certified or duly proved copy thereof, as aforesaid, duly stamped so as to entitle the same to be recorded, shall be presented to the. clerk, register, recorder, or other officer having charge of the original record, it shall be lawful for such officer, upon the payment of the fee legally chargeable for the recording thereof, to make a new record thereof, or to note upon the original record the fact that the error or omission in the stamping of said original instrument has been corrected pursuant to law; and the original instrument or such certified copy or the record thereof may be used in all courts and places in the same manner and with like effect as if the instrument had been originally stamped:

And provided further, That in all cases where the party has not affixed the stamp required by law upon any instrument made, signed, or issued at a time when and at a place where no collection district (*d*) was established, it shall be lawful for him or them, or any party having an interest therein, to affix the proper stamp thereto, or, if the original be lost, to a copy thereof; and the instrument or copy to which the proper stamp has been thus affixed prior to the first day of January, one thousand eight hundred and seventy-two, and the record thereof, shall be as valid, to all intents and purposes, as if stamped by the collector in the manner hereinbefore provided. But no right acquired in good faith before the stamping of such instrument or copy thereof, and the recording thereof, as herein provided, if such record be required by law, shall in any manner be affected by such stamping as aforesaid.

(*a*) The mere making or signing of an instrument, document, or paper intended for circulation, or to operate by delivery, gives it no validity or effect. It is invalid and of no effect until issued. It could not, then, have been the intention of Congress to prohibit the making or signing; but it was their intention to prohibit the issue of any instrument, document, or paper, mentioned and described in the schedule. And we must, therefore, read the word "or" before "issue," and "issued," in this and *the preceding* section as if written "and." The offence declared and prohibited, then, consists in the making, signing, and issuing any instrument, document, or paper contrary to the provisions of the section; that is to say, without the same being duly stamped for denoting the duty imposed thereon, or having thereupon an adhesive stamp to denote said duty. Voight et al. *v.* McKaim, 12 Pitts. L. J. 98.

This section is penal in its character both as to the forfeiture of the pecuniary penalty and as to the forfeiture of the instrument, document, or paper. In order to the incurring of the penalty, it must appear that the offence has been committed. The act expressly makes the intent to evade the provisions of the act a necessary ingredient of the offence. The words "such instrument" mean an instrument in reference to which the offence has been committed. It is clear that an indictment, complaint or declaration for the pecuniary penalty would be bad without an allegation that the omission of the stamp was with intent to evade the provisions of the statute. The same construction applies to the forfeiture of the instrument as to the pecuniary penalty. The forfeiture of the $50 and the forfeiture of the instrument are both embraced in one entire, connected proposition, and both rest on the same facts—the omission of the stamp with intent to evade the provisions of the act. The offence is not committed without an intent to evade the provisions of the act, and the instrument or document is not declared forfeited unless the offence is committed. The object of the statute was to raise revenue, and whatever power Congress has to declare the instrument void is incidental to the power to raise revenue. The provision invalidating the instrument is punitory and cannot be extended beyond the expressed will of the legislature. It is a punishment visited upon the offender to ensure the payment of the duty imposed, and the offence is made to consist, not in the accidental, but in the intentional, omission of the stamp with the purpose of evading such duty. This is the import of the language of the act. The court cannot, for the purpose of enforcing a compliance with the statute, dispense with an element made by the act necessary to the forfeiture. Hitchcock *v.* Sawyer, 39 Vt. 412; Tobey *v.* Chipman, 13 Allen, 123; Govern *v.* Littlefield, 13 Allen, 127; Crocker *v.* Foley, 13 Allen, 376; Holyoke Machine Co. *v.* Franklin Paper Co., 97 Mass. 150; McGovern *v* Hoesbeck, 53 Penn. 176; Dudley *v.* Wells, 55 Me. 145; New Haven and Northampton Co. *v.* Quintard, 6 Abb. Pr. N. S. 128; Beebe *v.* Hutton, 47 Barb. 187; Voerheck *v.* Roe, 50 Barb. 302; Howe *v.* Carpenter, 53 Barb. 382; Baird *v.* Pridmore, 31 How. Pr. 359; Blunt *v.* Bates, 40 Ala 470; Hallock *v.* Jaudin, 34 Cal. 167; Whitehill *v.* Shickle, 43 Mo. 537; Dorris *v.* Grace, 24 Ark. 326; Corry National Bank *v.* Rouse, 3 I. R. R. 31; Goodwin *v.* Wands, 25 Ind. 101; Harper *v.* Clark, 17 Ohio 190; Craig *v.* Dimock et al. 9 I. R. R. 129; Latham *v.* Smith, 45 Ill. 29. Contra, Hugus *v.* Strickler, 19 Iowa 413; Maynard *v.* Johnson, 2 Nev. 16, 25; Wayman *v.* Torreson, 4 Nev. 124.

The omission to put the proper stamp upon any instrument should be deemed presumptive evidence of an intent to evade the statute, but nothing more. It is to be presumed that the parties were aware of the requirements of the statute. Thus knowing the law, their omission to obey it must, in the absence of any explanations, be deemed wilful and with intent to evade its requirements. This view is in accordance with the principle that every person is presumed to contemplate the ordinary and natural consequences of his own acts. The act of omitting the stamp was unlawful and injurious to the government, and the presumption is that it was so intended. It comes within the class of cases in which the proof of justification or excuse lies with the party transgressing; and on failure thereof the law implies criminal intent. Howe v. Carpenter, 53 Barb. 382; Miller v. Larmon, 38 How. Pr. 417; Beebe v. Hutton, 47 Barb. 187; U. S. v. Learned et al. 11 I. R. R. 149; Baird v Pridmore, 31 How. Pr. 359; Harper v. Clark, 17 Ohio, 190.

Contra. If it is objected that an instrument is void by reason of its not being stamped, the objector must show that the omission of the stamp was with intent to evade the revenue law. The mere failure or omission to affix the stamp is not evidence of such intent. New Haven and Northampton Co. v. Quintard, 6 Abb Pr. 128; Dudley v. Wells, 55 Me. 145; Corry National Bank v. Rouse, 3 I. R. R. 31; Sawyer et al. v. Parker, 57 Me.

It is competent for a party to show that the absence or insufficiency of the stamp arose from inadvertence or mistake, and without any intent to evade the provisions of the revenue laws. Beebe v. Hutton, 47 Barb. 187. Contra, Maynard v. Johnson, 2 Nev. 25.

An unstamped instrument is not legally available to a party until the proper stamp is affixed. Beebe v. Hutton, 47 Barb. 187; Harper v. Clark, 17 Ohio, 190. Contra, Schemerhorn v. Burgess, 38 How. Pr. 123.

When an instrument is issued by an agent of a corporation with the intent to evade the provisions of the law, such unlawful intent may be imputed to the corporation, and the corporation may be held criminally responsible for the unlawful act. U. S. v. Balt. & Ohio R. R. Co., 8 I. R. R. 148.

In the absence of any evidence showing the contrary, it will be presumed that a lost instrument was properly stamped. Thayer v. Barney, 12 Minn. 502.

Upon indictments for forgery, the existence of a stamp upon the forged instrument need not be averred or proved. State v. Haynes, 6 Cold. 550.

The declaration need not allege that the deed upon which the suit is brought was stamped. It is well settled that in pleading a deed, it is not necessary to aver that it was signed or sealed or attested; but that the allegation that a party made his deed, imported all these requisites without which there would have been no deed. If, then, the law has created a new requisite and made a stamp an essential part of the instrument, the allegation that a party made the instrument will now include the stamp, by the same reasoning that it before included the seal. If the stamp is not essential to the validity of the deed, it is not necessary to allege that the deed was stamped, because the deed is valid without it. Jones v Davis, 22 Wis. 421.

When a copy of an instrument is affixed to a declaration and thus made a part of it, the copy need not show that the original was stamped. Hitchcock v. Sawyer, 39 Vt. 412; Trull v. Moulton, 12 Allen, 396; Hallock v. Jaudin, 34 Cal. 167.

In order to defeat a recovery upon an unstamped instrument, it must appear not only that the note was unstamped, but that the stamp has been fraudulently omitted. Hence the objection cannot be taken by demurrer. Trull *v.* Moulton, 12 Allen, 396; Hallock *v.* Jaudin, 34 Cal. 167.

The objection that letters of administration are not stamped cannot be made by demurrer, because the stamp may either be affixed to the administration bond or the letters of administration, and, therefore, although there is no stamps affixed to the letters, it does not necessarily follow that the letters are invalid. By demurrer the facts are taken to be true, and since the letters would be as valid if the bond was stamped as if the stamp had been affixed to the letters, there is no necessary defect in the pleading. If the defendant wishes to question the validity of the letters of administration, he should do so by a plea *ne unques* administrator. Miller *v.* Henderson, 24 Ark. 344.

A plea should allege not only that the instrument is unstamped, but that the stamp was omitted with an intent to evade the provisions of the statute. Hitchcock *v.* Sawyer, 39 Vt. 412; New Haven & Northampton Co. *v.* Quintard, 6 Abb. Pr. N. S. 128; Latham *v.* Smith, 44 Ill. 25.

Whilst at the common law a party could not set up his own fraud or violation of law as a defence or protection to himself, there is no question but that when a statute declares an instrument void for any reason, the defendant who is sued upon such instrument may show the facts that make it void, although in so showing he also shows that he has been guilty of some crime, fraud, or violation of a penal statute. In such case, it is the policy of the law to prevent some particular practice, such as usury, gaming, violation of the revenue law, etc. To effect that object more completely, the law allows the defendant to plead and prove his own wrongful act, not so much to protect the defendant as to carry out the policy of the law in suppressing illegal acts. There is no doubt but that a defendant may plead and prove the want of a stamp or proper stamps to the instrument sued on, if the facts as pleaded and proved make the instrument invalid. Maynard *v.* Johnson, 2 Nev. 17; Jacquin *v.* Warren, 40 Ill. 459; McBride *v.* Doty, 23 Iowa, 122.

The affixing of the stamp is the last act essential to the validity of the instrument, and is as much the act of the maker as the signature. The law will not presume that the holder would affix and cancel a stamp any more than that he would attach the maker's name. If the stamp is attached and cancelled without authority, it cannot give validity to the instrument. Without the stamp the instrument is as incomplete as if it lacked the maker's signature, and to attach and cancel it without authority would be as ineffective as to write the maker's name to the instrument without authority. Latham *v.* Smith, 45 Ill. 25.

Where a statute prohibits an act to be done under a certain penalty, though no mention is made of indictment, the party offending may be indicted and fined to the amount of the penalty. If a statute enjoins an act to be done without pointing out any mode of punishment, an indictment will lie for disobeying the injunction of the legislature. But where it is merely provided that, if a person do a certain act, he shall forfeit a certain sum to be recovered by an action of debt, no indictment can be supported. U. S. *v.* Crosby et al. 26 Law Rep. 32; U. S. *v.* Balt. & Ohio R. R. Co., 8 I. R. R. 148; U. S. *v.* Learned et al. 11 I. R. R. 149.

No man has a right to set up a construction of the law for himself, and then plead it in justification of his violation of the law. When a party knows of the existence of the state of facts which make an instrument liable to a stamp and yet believes that the instrument is not so liable in point of law, such ignorance of the law will not excuse him. With a full knowledge of all the facts before him, and of the consequences of a violation of the law, he assumes to construe the law and the instrument for himself, and, in case of misconstruction, he must abide the consequences. U. S. *v.* Learned et al. 11 I. R. R. 149.

The rule in England is that if there is nothing on the face of the instrument to show that it was post-stamped, it, being negotiable, will be good in the hands of an indorser or holder for value who received it in ignorance of the fact that it was not stamped until after it was issued. The reasoning in favor of the rule in England is fair, just, and legitimate. It accords with the duty of the maker, protects the government, and, in consonance with the principles of the law-merchant, protects the holder of such paper from those defences that do not arise upon its face. Blackwell *v.* Denie, 23 Iowa, 63; Latham *v.* Smith, 45 Ill. 25. Contra, Pope *v.* Burns et al. 4 I. R. R. 133.

If the consideration of an unstamped note is valuable, the payee may sue upon that consideration. If the note is tainted with illegality from any cause and invalid, and the plaintiff is no way connected with the infirmity thus affecting it, this does not in legal effect amount to a payment of the plaintiff's claim for the consideration thus given to the defendant. The case in this particular stands upon the same ground upon which the cases are put and rest where it is held that payment of a debt in counterfeit bills or in the worthless bills of a broken bank is in legal effect no payment. In all such cases a party may fall back, under a declaration adapted to the facts, upon the original consideration, and recover upon the liability arising therefrom. Wilson *v.* Carey, 40 Vt. 179; Israel *v.* Redding, 40 Ill. 362; Jacquin *v.* Warren, 40 Ill. 459; Wayman *v.* Torreson, 4 Nev. 124.

The language of the act is that the instrument shall be void and of no effect. It does not declare the contract invalid. Applying the well-known rule that the statute being penal in its nature is to be strictly construed, there can be no warrant for so construing it as to include the contract as well as the instrument. The writing itself can neither give a right nor create an obligation—it cannot be used as an instrument of evidence, but the original contract remains unaffected; and if, by the rules of law, it is such as may be shown by parol, the attempt to reduce it to writing will not exclude the evidence. It would not be proper to prove by parol the contents of the invalid writing nor to prove a contract which the law requires to be in writing. McAfferty v. Hale, 24 Iowa, 355.

A subsequent valid agreement may be proved even though there is a prior unstamped memorandum. Sykes v. Bates, 26 Iowa, 521.

Although an unstamped instrument cannot be read in evidence *per se*, yet a witness may refer to it to refresh his memory. But when it is thus received, it has to be taken as a whole as well for one party as the other. Israel v. Redding, 40 Ill. 362.

A representation that a note would not be valid until the maker should affix a stamp, is not such a misrepresentation as will make the note void for fraud. The maker could and was bound to judge of the legal import of such an instrument. Latham v. Smith, 40 Ill. 25.

A court of equity will not interfere to declare an unstamped instrument void and cancel it. Harshaw v. McCombs, 63 N. C. 75.

An action can be maintained upon a note given for property the grantor of which fraudulently understated the actual consideration and improperly stamped the deed therefor with the intent to evade the provisions of the law and pass an imperfect title. Lambert v. Whitelock, 29 Ind. 26.

A party who has been indemnified by a bond against a mortgage and has been compelled to pay the same, may maintain an action upon the bond even though a promissory note which formed a part of the payment was not stamped. Whether the note which has thus been accepted in payment can be collected or not, either by reason of its inherent defects or the insolvency of the maker, is immaterial. The jury, however, must find that such note was accepted as payment of the mortgage debt. Hardin v. Branner, 25 Iowa, 364.

The delivery of an unstamped deed to a vendee, which he has the power to have stamped, is a good part performance of a contract and entitles the vendor to claim other land which the vendee agreed to convey to him. Jones v. Pease, 21 Wis. 644.

When a party is surprised by a ruling of the court construing an instrument to be different in character from what he supposed and to require a larger amount of stamps, and there is no evidence of an intent to evade the revenue law, he is entitled to a new trial. Hoppock v. Stone, 49 Barb. 524.

An assignee of a judgment debtor who has made an assignment of his estate for the benefit of creditors, cannot maintain a bill in equity to restrain the judgment debtor from issuing an execution on his judgment founded upon an unstamped or improperly stamped note. Ritter v. Brendlinger, 58 Penn. 68; Corry National Bank v. Rouse, 8 I. R. R. 31.

A party has no right to have an instrument permanently forbidden to be used as evidence by the revenue law, beyond the power of Congress to repeal or alter it so as to permit the instrument to be read in evidence.

A repealing statute is such an express enactment as necessarily divests all inchoate rights which have arisen under the statute which it destroys. These rights are incident to the statute and fall with it. Hoppock *v.* Stone, 49 Barb. 524; Hibbard *v.* Gibson, 13 Mich. 215.

A party upon discovering that an instrument is not properly stamped may return it to the maker for that reason; and then upon its being stamped and redelivered, it takes effect as a valid instrument from the time of such redelivery. Robbins *v.* Deverill, 20 Wis. 142; Green et al. *v.* Lowry, 38 Geo. 548; Wayman *v.* Torreson, 4 Nev. 124.

But the maker cannot stamp the note after the death of the payee so as to make it valid in the hands of his administrator. Wayman *v.* Torreson, 4 Nev. 124.

(*b*) The duty of stamping instruments under this section is obligatory upon the collector, and he has no legal right to refuse to perform it. The penalty may be remitted. Interest cannot be remitted. The collector's marginal note should be in substance as follows:

Internal revenue stamps to the amount of $—— affixed to this instrument and cancelled by me at the request of ——, this —— day of ——, 18—. Penalty $— and interest $— collected, or penalty remitted and interest $— collected (if that be the fact).

                                  Collector ——, District of ——.

Where there is a difference of opinion respecting the stamp proper to be affixed, the collector should affix such a one as the applicant prefers; the applicant takes the risk of the validity of the instrument. In such cases, however, it is advisable to refer the question to the Office of Internal Revenue. When the originals are lost, the necessary stamps may be affixed to copies.

Each collector must keep a record of all instruments stamped or impressed by him, in which must be given the names of the parties to each instrument, the date of its execution and a sufficient description of its nature to show the reason for impressing or affixing the particular stamp. A certified copy of this record must be transmitted to the Office of Internal Revenue at the close of each quarter. When none have been stamped during the quarter, the fact should be reported upon Form 8. If an instrument is presented for insufficiency of stamp the amount upon it when presented should be stated.

The whole amount of penalties, paid to collectors for validating unstamped instruments, should be reported on Form 58 with other unassessed penalties; the interest should be entered under the head of interest upon monthly abstract of collections, Form 22, and both penalties and interest should be deposited to the credit of the United States Treasurer with other collections A person who holds an unstamped conveyance founded upon a confederate currency consideration will be allowed to affix such stamps thereto as he may think sufficient. 9 I. R. R. 162.

The payment of a penalty for the purpose of having an instrument properly stamped by a collector relieves no one from his liability to indictment or other legal proceedings; nor does the payment of a penalty imposed by the court make the instrument valid. The two penalties are entirely distinct and the payment of one does not relieve from the necessity or liability to pay the other. 6 I. R. R. 218.

When the application is not made by the makers of the instrument, but by another party having an interest therein, as payee or holder of a note, or the like, the proper district in which the application is to be made is the district in which the applicant resides. The collector of such district is the only one who has jurisdiction of the person applying and of the instrument in his hands. Schermerhorn v. Burgess, 38 How. Pr. 123.

Any party having an interest in the instrument may appear before the collector and have it stamped. The maker may prefer to subject himself to a penalty rather than have the instrument made valid by a stamp. Hence it was highly proper to provide that any party interested therein might procure the stamp to be affixed. This is the fair grammatical construction of the sentence. The antecedent of "he or they" who may appear is any party previously specified in the sentence who may be desirous of affixing the stamp for any reason. This interpretation is consistent with justice and fairness to both parties to an instrument. Schermerhorn v. Burgess, 38 How. Pr. 123; Blunt v. Bates, 40 Ala. 470.

Contra. The person who is to appear before the collector to procure the stamping and cancelling is the person who issued the paper and who should have applied the stamp. He it is upon whom the penalty is imposed, and he can only be relieved by appearing and making the application, and securing the indemnity. If a party having an interest in a paper shall desire it to be thus stamped for his benefit, he can only effect it by procuring the maker or party to be affected by it to appear before the collector and procure the stamping and cancellation. Without his knowledge and against his presumed assent it cannot be done. Myers v. Smith, 48 Barb. 614.

A deputy collector, by virtue of his ordinary duties as such, has no power to remit penalties and to stamp or authorize the stamping of instruments when they have been left unstamped from inadvertence or mistake, except when from the inability or sickness of the collector he acts by special authority in his place. The best evidence that this special authority has been devolved upon the deputy is the collector's official seal affixed to the certificate which remits the penalty and shows the ground upon which the stamp has been subsequently affixed. Unless the act of the deputy is authenticated with the official seal of the collector, or it is shown by sufficient evidence aliunde, that the collector was sick or otherwise unable to act at the time and that he was authorized for the time being to exercise the power in question, the same should be disregarded and treated as a nullity. Brown v. Crandal, 23 Iowa, 112; McAfferty v. Hale, 24 Iowa, 355; Deskin v. Graham, 19 Iowa, 553; Beebe v. Hutton, 47 Barb. 187.

The authority entrusted to the collector by the statute is to be exercised in his discretion upon an examination of the facts of which he is constituted the exclusive judge; and in the absence of any controlling provisions, his decision upon those facts must be conclusive. His action is in a limited sense judicial, and certainly no collateral inquiry into the grounds of it could be permitted. Peoria Marine and Fire Ins. Co. v. Perkins, 16 Mich. 380; Hoppock v. Stone, 49 Barb. 524; Corry National Bank v. Rouse, 3 I. R. R. 81.

The collector's certificate partakes of the character of the act and more resembles the memorial of a judicial determination than an ordinary official certificate. It commands confidence from the circumstance that it is made by an authorized public officer in the ordinary discharge of his duty as such, and in a matter concerning the government. It is admissible in evidence on the principle that allows public documents, surveys, plats, entries and the like, to be given in evidence. Peoria Marine and Fire Ins. Co. v. Perkins, 16 Mich. 380.

It is not necessary that the certificate should state that the collector is satisfied that the failure to stamp, etc., was without any wilful design to defraud, etc. Dowd v. Wright, 22 Iowa, 336.

(c) The statute declares that an instrument thus stamped before the collector shall thereupon be deemed and held to be valid to all intents and purposes as if stamped when made or issued. No language could be clearer, and it should receive a liberal, rather than a strict construction, the better to effectuate justice and carry out the reason and policy of the law. An exception to that clause in the statute which declares that the instrument shall be invalid and of no effect is made by this proviso, which takes out of its operation cases where the collector of the revenue of the proper district shall affix the proper stamps. Dowd v. Wright, 22 Iowa, 336; Tripp et al. v. Bishop, 56 Penn. 424; Gibson v. Hibbard, 13 Mich. 215; Hugus v. Strickler, 19 Iowa, 413; Cooke v. England, 27 Ind. 14; Dowler v. Cushwa, 27 Ind. 354; Dorris v. Grace, 24 Ark. 326; Mason v. Cheney et al. 47 N. H, 24; Garland v. Lane, 46 N. H. 245; Wright v. Mc-Fadden, 25 Ind. 483; Holyoke Machine Co. v. Franklin Paper Co. 97 Mass. 150; Patterson v. Eames, 54 Me. 203; Day v. Baker et al. 36 Mo. 125; Killip v. Empire Mill Co. 2 Nev. 34.

When the original instrument is lost, the parties may take a copy before the collector and have that stamped. Dowler v. Cushwa, 27 Ind. 354.

An instrument not properly stamped, although recorded, is no notice to other parties, and the subsequent stamping thereof by the authority of the collector cannot cure the defect in such a sense as to interfere with rights that have intervened between the making and the stamping of the instrument. McBride v. Doty, 23 Iowa, 122; Miller et al. v. Morrow et al. 3 Cold. 587. Contra, Sauzer et al. v. Parker, 57 Me.

Where chattel mortgages are merely filed and an entry made in a book kept by the clerk of the names of the parties, the amount secured, the date, time of filing and when due, they are not included within this provision of the statute, as it contemplates mortgages which require to be recorded. Filing and recording are not synonymous. Vail v. Knapp, 49 Barb. 299.

A mortgage duly stamped by the collector in accordance with the provisions of the statute is valid against the mortgagor and an assignee who has obtained the mortgaged property without given a valuable consideration therefor. Hoppock v. Stone, 49 Barb. 524.

(*d*) The court will take notice that there was no collection district in the State at the date of the instrument. Mudd v. McElvain, 3 A. L. T. (C. R.) 116.

Foreign Bills of Exchange.

Sec. 159. *And be it further enacted*, That the acceptor or acceptors of any bill of exchange or order for the payment of any sum of money drawn, or purporting to be drawn, in any foreign country, but payable in the United States, shall, before paying or accepting the same, place thereupon a stamp indicating the duty upon the same, as the law requires for inland bills of exchange or promissory notes, and no bill of exchange shall be paid or negotiated without such stamp; and if any person shall pay or negotiate or offer in payment, or receive or take in payment any such draft or order, the person or persons so offending shall forfeit the sum of two hundred dollars.

Exemptions.

Sec. 160. (Amended March 3, 1865, § 1.) *And be it further enacted*, That no stamp duty shall be required on powers of attorney or any other paper relating to applications for bounties, arrearages of pay, or pensions, or to the receipt thereof from time to time, or upon tickets or contracts of insurance when limited to accidental injury to persons, nor on certificates of the measurement or weight of animals, wood, coal, or hay, nor on deposit notes to mutual insurance companies for insurance upon which policies subject to stamp duties have been or are to be issued; nor on any certificate of the record of a deed or other instrument in writing, or of the acknowledgment or proof thereof by attesting witnesses; nor to any indorsement of a negotiable instrument, or on any warrant of attorney accompanying a bond or note, when such bond or note shall have affixed thereto the stamp or stamps denoting the duty required; and whenever any bond or note shall be secured by a mortgage, but one stamp shall be required to be placed on such papers: *Provided*, That the stamp duty placed thereon shall be the highest rate required for said instruments or either of them.

Sale of Stamps.

Sec. 161. (Amended July 14, 1870, § 4.) *And be it further enacted*, That the Commissioner of Internal Revenue be, and is hereby, authorized to sell (*a*) to and supply collectors, deputy collectors, postmasters, stationers, or any other persons, at his discretion, with adhesive stamps, or stamped paper, vellum, or parchment, as herein provided for, in amounts of not less than fifty dollars, upon the payment, at the time of delivery, of the amount of duties said stamps, stamped paper, vellum, or parchment, so sold or supplied, represent, and may allow, upon the aggregate amount of such stamps, as aforesaid, the sum of not exceeding five per centum as commission to the collectors, postmasters, stationers, or other purchasers; but the cost of any paper, vellum, or parchment shall be paid by the purchaser of such stamped paper, vellum, or parchment, as aforesaid.

And the proprietor or proprietors of articles named in said Schedule C, who shall furnish his or their own die or design for stamps to be used especially for his or their proprietary articles, shall be allowed the following commissions, namely: On amounts purchased at one time of not less than fifty dollars nor more than five hundred dollars, five per centum; and on amounts over five hundred dollars, ten per centum on the whole amount purchased.

Provided, That the Commissioner of Internal Revenue may from to time make regulations, upon proper evidence of the facts, for the allowance of such of the stamps issued under the provisions of this act as may have been spoiled, destroyed, or rendered useless or unfit for the purpose intended, or for which the owner may have no use, or which, through mistake, may have been improperly or unnecessarily used, or where the rates or duties represented thereby have been paid in error or remitted; and such allowance shall be made either by giving other stamps in lieu of the stamps so allowed for, or by repaying the amount or value, after deducting therefrom, in case of repayment, the sum of five per centum to the owner thereof; but no allowance shall be made in any case until the stamps so spoiled or rendered useless shall have been returned to the Commissioner of Internal Revenue, or until satisfactory proof has been made showing the reason why said stamps cannot be so returned:

Provided, That the Commissioner of Internal Revenue may, from time to time, furnish, supply, and deliver to any manufacturer of friction or other matches, cigar lights, or wax tapers, a suitable quantity of adhesive or other stamps, such as may be prescribed for use in such cases, without prepayment therefor, on a credit not exceeding sixty days, requiring in advance such security as he may judge necessary to secure payment therefor to the Treasurer of the United States, within the time prescribed for such payment. And upon all bonds or other securities taken by said Commissioner, under the provisions of this act, suits may be maintained by said treasurer in the circuit or district court of the United States, in the several districts where any of the persons giving said bonds or other securities reside or may be found, in any appropriate form of action.

(a) Payments to the Office of Internal Revenue for stamps should be made in the form of a duplicate certificate of a United States assistant treasurer or designated depositary of a deposit made on account of stamps. Revenue stamps may likewise be obtained of any national bank which is a designated depositary, at the usual rates of commission. They will also be deposited with the assistant treasurers and designated depositaries other than national banks.

If any revenue stamps for which the owner has no use are returned to the Office of Internal Revenue in good order and free of expense, others will be given in exchange, at a discount of two and one half per cent. Stamps that have been improperly or unnecessarily used and cancelled, when returned to the Office of Internal Revenue for exchange should be attached to the instruments on which they were used, and accompanied by an affidavit setting forth the facts, when other stamps will be given for them, at a discount of two and one-half per cent. The papers to which the stamps are affixed will be retained by the office. If the papers cannot be sent, that fact and the reasons for it must appear by the affidavit, and there must be certificates from both the assessor and the collector that they have each made personal examination of the case, and find the facts to be as stated. Stamps spoiled in transportation, or rendered valueless by any modifications of the law, will be exchanged free of charge. When the affidavit is made before a person who has no official seal, his authority to administer oaths generally should be certified to by the clerk of a court of record under the seal of the court. 9 I. R. R. 167.

On application to the Office of Internal Revenue, manufacturers who desire to avail themselves of the provisions of this section will be furnished with a blank bond in proper form to be filled up and executed. 9 I. R. R. 167.

Collector may determine Stamp to be affixed.

Sec. 162. *And be it further enacted,* That it shall be lawful for any person to present to the collector of the district, subject to the rules and regulations of the Commissioner of Internal Revenue, any instrument not previously issued (a) or used, and require his opinion whether or not the same is chargeable with any stamp duty; and if the said collector shall be of opinion that such instrument is chargeable with any stamp duty, he shall, upon the payment therefor, affix and cancel the proper stamp; and if of the opinion that such instrument is not chargeable with any stamp duty, or is chargeable only with the duty by him designated, he is hereby required to impress thereon a particular stamp, to be provided for that purpose, with such words or device thereon as he shall judge proper, which shall denote that such instrument is not chargeable with any stamp duty, or is chargeable only with the duty denoted by the stamp affixed; and every such instrument upon which the said stamp shall be impressed shall be deemed to be not chargeable, or to be chargeable only with the duty denoted by the stamp so affixed, and shall be received in evidence in all courts of law or equity, notwithstanding any objections made to the same by reason of it being unstamped, or of it being insufficiently stamped.

(*a*) The provisions of this section can in no case be applied to an instrument after it has been issued or used. The collector should decline to stamp or impress an instrument until the stamp duty with which he thinks it chargeable has been paid. In cases of reasonable doubt he should obtain the opinion of the Commissioner before affixing his stamp, unless immediate action be essential to the interests of the parties concerned. Each collector must keep a record of all instruments stamped or impressed by him, in which must be given the names of the parties to each instrument, the date of its execution, and a sufficient description of its nature to show the reasons for impressing or affixing the particular stamp. A certified copy of this record will be transmitted to the Office of Internal Revenue at the close of each quarter. When none have been stamped during the quarter, that fact should be reported upon Form 8. 9 I. R. R. 162.

Unstamped Instruments inadmissible as Evidence.

Sec. 163. (Amended July 13, 1866, § 9.) *And be it further enacted*, That hereafter no deed, instrument, document, writing, or paper, required by law to be stamped, which has been signed or issued without being duly stamped, or with a deficient stamp, nor any copy thereof, shall be recorded, or admitted, or used as evidence in any court (*a*) until a legal stamp or stamps denoting the amount of tax shall have been affixed thereto, as prescribed by law :

Provided, That any power of attorney, conveyance, or document of any kind, made or purporting to be made in any foreign country to be used in the United States, shall pay the same tax as is required by law on similar instruments or documents when made or issued in the United States; and the party to whom the same is issued, or by whom it is to be used, shall, before using the same, affix thereon the stamp or stamps indicating the tax required.

(*a*) Congress has no power to declare by law what shall or shall not be evidence in a State court, nor what domestic contracts made by the people of a State, in virtue of its laws and having no connection with the federal government, shall be valid or the contrary. The general government is as powerless in this regard as a State would be which should attempt to interfere with the subjects and rights exclusively confided to the general government. Latham *v.* Smith, 45 Ill. 29 ; Carpenter et al. *v.* Snelling, 97 Mass. 452 ; Hunter *v.* Cobb, 1 Bush. 239 ; Craig *v.* Dimock, 9 I. R. R. 129 ; Mudd *v.* McElvain et al. 3 A. L. T. (C. R.) 116. Contra, Howe *v.* Carpenter, 53 Barb. 382.

· The provision of the statute does not in terms apply to the courts of the several States. It can have full operation and effect if construed as intended to apply to those courts only which have been established under the constitution of the United States, and by acts of Congress, and over which the federal legislature can legitimately exercise control, and to which they can properly prescribe rules regulating the course of justice and the mode of administering the law. A broader interpretation should not be given to the statute. Carpenter et al. *v.* Snelling, 97 Mass. 452; Griffin *v.* Ranney, 35 Ct.

The document should be stamped before it is offered in evidence. Plessinger *v.* Depuy, 25 Ind. 419.

When an instrument not properly stamped is admitted in evidence without objection, the objection cannot be raised by asking for an instruction to the jury. The proper time for such an objection is when the instrument is offered in evidence; if made afterwards it will not be heard. Thomson *v.* Wilson, 26 Iowa, 120.

When it does not appear by an objection taken at the trial, or bill of exception, or certificate of court, that the instrument was not properly stamped at the time when it was offered in evidence, the objection cannot be taken in the appellate court, as it does not arise on the record. Hawkins *v.* Wilson, 1 W. Va. 117; Roberts *v.* Murray, 18 La. An. 572; Towne *v.* Bossier, 19 La. An. 162; Burnap *v.* Losey, 1 Lans. 111.

A mere memorandum made by the clerk upon the record that no stamp was attached to the note offered in evidence is not sufficient. It is the duty of the clerk to copy all the proceedings and all the documents as he finds them in the suit, without adding to or subtracting from them one single word. His duty is to copy the note as it was filed, without making any remarks creating negative or affirmative evidence for either of the parties. If even the judge below states in his judgment that the note was not stamped as required by law, and dismisses the suit on that ground, it would be no evidence of that fact in the appellate court. No notice can, therefore, be taken of the memorandum. Stark *v.* Bossier, 19 La. An. 179.

Provisions extended to Schedule C.

Sec. 164. *And be it further enacted,* That all the provisions of this act relating to dies, stamps, (*a*) adhesive stamps, and stamp duties, shall extend to and include (except where manifestly impracticable) all the articles or objects enumerated in schedule marked C, subject to stamp duties, and apply to the provisions in relation thereto.

(*a*) Stamps appropriated to denote the duty charged upon articles named in Schedule C cannot be used for any other purpose; nor can stamps appropriated to denote the duty upon instruments be used in payment of the duties upon articles enumerated in this schedule. 9 I. R. R. 167.

Penalty for Omission to Stamp Articles in Schedule C.

Sec. 165. (Amended July 13, 1866, § 9; July 14, 1870, § 1.) *And be it further enacted,* That if any person, firm, company, or corporation shall make, prepare, and sell, or remove for consumption or sale, drugs, medicines, preparations, compositions, articles, or things, including perfumery, cosmetics, lucifer or friction matches, cigar lights, or wax tapers, and playing cards, and also including prepared mustard, sauces, sirups, jams, and jellies, when packed or sealed in cans, bottles, or other single packages, whether of domestic manufacture or imported, upon which a duty or tax is imposed by law, as enumerated and mentioned in Schedule C, without affixing thereto an adhesive stamp or label denoting the tax before mentioned, he or they shall incur a penalty (*a*) of fifty dollars for every omission to affix such stamp.

(*a*) If a statute prohibits a matter of public grievance or commands a matter of public convenience, all violations of the prohibitions or commands of the statute are at least misdemeanors, and as such are punishable by indictment, unless the statute specifies some other mode of proceeding. This rule of the common law can only be applied in the jurisprudence of the United States in cases where the offence is defined and the punishment is prescribed in the acts of Congress containing the prohibition or command, or in some other applicable to the same subject-matter. U. S. *v.* Abbott, 9 I. R. R. 186.

Where the cause is sufficiently set forth in the complaint in an action of debt, and the complaint is sworn to, and the cause of action and arrest are identical, there is no necessity for an additional or separate affidavit to authorize an order for the arrest of the defendant. The constitutional provision against imprisonment for debt only applies to debts that arise under contract, express or implied, and does not include a penalty. If a penalty can be considered as included, it may be deemed a fraudulent debt. U. S. *v.* Walsh, 6 I R. R. 212.

What constitutes an original package depends in a great measure upon the circumstances of each particular case. When the top of a box is taken off for the purpose of exhibiting the kind and quality of its contents, and put on again before sale and delivery thereof, with the contents unchanged in kind or quantity, the package is unbroken. The court may set aside a verdict in an action for a penalty. U. S. *v.* Fox et al. 11 I. R. R. 36.

Penalty for removing Stamps from Articles named in Schedule C.

Sec. 166. *And be it further enacted,* That every manufacturer or maker of any of the articles for sale mentioned in Schedule C, after the same shall have been so made, and the particulars hereinbefore required as to stamps have been complied with, who shall take off, remove, or detach, or cause, or permit, or suffer to be taken off, or removed, or detached, any stamp, or who shall use any stamp, or any wrapper or cover to which any stamp is affixed, to cover any other article or commodity than that originally contained in such wrapper or cover, with such stamp when first used, with the intent to evade the stamp duties, shall for every such article, respect- ively, in respect of which any such offence shall be committed, be subject to a penalty of fifty dollars, to be recovered together with the costs thereupon accruing; and every such article or commodity as aforesaid shall also be forfeited.

Penalty for Evasion of Tax on Articles in Schedule C.

Sec. 167. (Amended March 3, 1865, § 1.) *And be it further enacted,* That on and after the passage of this act, every maker or manufacturer of any of the articles or commodities mentioned in Schedule C, as aforesaid, who shall sell, expose for sale, send out, remove, or deliver any article or commodity, manufactured as aforesaid, before the duty thereon shall have been fully paid, by affixing thereon the proper stamp, as provided by law, or who shall hide, or conceal, or cause to be hidden or concealed, or who shall remove or convey away, or deposit, or cause to be removed or conveyed away from or deposited in any place, any such article or commodity to evade the duty chargeable thereon, or any part thereof, shall be subject to a penalty of one hundred dollars, together with the forfeiture of any such article or commodity.

Exportation of Articles in Schedule C.

Sec. 168. (Amended March 3, 1865, § 1.) *And be it further enacted,* That all medicines, preparations, compositions, perfumery, cosmetics, cordials, and other liquors manufactured wholly or in part of domestic spirits, intended for exportation, as provided for by law, in order to be manufactured and sold or removed, without being charged with duty and without having a stamp affixed thereto, shall, under such rules and regulations (a) as the Secretary of the Treasury may prescribe, be made and manufactured in warehouses similarly constructed to those known and designated in treasury regulations as bonded warehouses, class two:

Provided, That such manufacturer shall first give satisfactory bonds to the collector of internal revenue for the faithful observance of all the provisions of law and the rules and regulations as aforesaid, in amount not less than half of that required by the regulations of the Secretary of the Treasury from persons allowed bonded warehouses. Such goods, when manufactured in such warehouses, may be removed for exportation, under the direction of the proper officer having charge thereof, who shall be designated by the Secretary of the Treasury, without being charged with duty, and without having a stamp affixed thereto. Any manufacturer of the articles aforesaid, or of any of them, having such bonded warehouse, as aforesaid, shall be at liberty, under such rules and regulations as the Secretary of the Treasury may prescribe, to convey therein any materials to be used in such manufacture which are allowed by the provisions of law to be exported free from tax or duty, as well as the necessary materials, implements, packages, vessels, brands, and labels for the preparation, putting up, and export of the said manufactured articles; and every article so used shall be exempted from the payment of stamp and excise duty by such manufacturer. Articles and materials so to be used may be transferred from any bonded warehouse in which the same may be, under such regulations as the Secretary of the Treasury may prescribe, into any bonded warehouse in which such manufacture may be conducted, and may be used in such manufacture, and when so used shall be exempt from stamp and excise duty; and the receipt of the officer in charge, as aforesaid, shall be received as a voucher for the manufacture of such articles. Any materials imported into the United States may, under such rules as the Secretary of the Treasury may prescribe, and under the direction of the proper officer, be removed in original packages from on shipboard, or from the bonded warehouse in which the same may be, into the bonded warehouse in which such manufacture may be carried on, for the purpose of being used in such manufacture, without payment of duties thereon, and may there be used in such manufacture. No article so removed, nor any article manufactured in said bonded warehouse, shall be taken therefrom except for exportation, under the direction of the proper officer having charge thereof, as aforesaid, whose certificate, describing the articles by their marks, or otherwise, the quantity, the date of importation, and name of vessel, with such additional particulars as may from time to time be required, shall be received by the collector of customs in cancellation of the bonds, or return of the amount of foreign import duties. All labor performed and services rendered under these regulations shall be under the supervision of an officer of the customs, and at the expense of the manufacturer.

(a) For regulations see 9 I. R. R. 195.

Exportation of Matches, &c.

[SEC. 4. (July 14, 1870.) *Provided*, That lucifer or friction matches, and cigar lights, and wax tapers, may be removed from the place of manufacture for export to a foreign country without payment of tax or affixing stamps thereto, under such rules and regulations as the Commissioner of Internal Revenue may prescribe; and all provisions of existing laws inconsistent herewith are hereby repealed.]

Transfer of Matches, &c., to Bonded Warehouse.

[SEC. 11. (March 3, 1865.) *And be it further enacted*, That lucifer or friction matches, and cigar lights and wax tapers, may be transferred, without payment of duty, directly from the place of manufacture to a bonded warehouse established in conformity with law and treasury regulations, and upon the execution of such transportation bonds or other security as the Secretary of the Treasury may prescribe, said bonds to be taken by the collector in the district from which such removal is made, and may be withdrawn therefrom for consumption after affixing the stamps thereto, as provided by the act to which this act is an amendment, or may be removed therefrom for export to a foreign country without payment of duty or affixing stamps thereto, in conformity with the provisions of the act aforesaid, relating to the removal of distilled spirits, all the rules and regulations and conditions of which, as far as applicable, shall apply to lucifer or friction matches, cigar lights, and wax tapers in bonded warehouse. And no drawback shall in any case be allowed upon any lucifer or friction matches, cigar lights, or wax tapers, upon which any excise duty has been paid, or stamps affixed, either before or after they have been placed in bonded warehouse.]

Tax on Imported Articles Named in Schedule C.

Sec. 169. (Amended July 13, 1866, § 9.) *And be it further enacted*, That any person who shall offer or expose for sale any of the articles named in Schedule C, or in any amendments thereto, whether the articles so offered or exposed are imported or are of foreign or domestic manufacture, shall be deemed the manufacturer thereof, and subject to all the duties, liabilities, and penalties imposed by law in regard to the sale of domestic articles without the use of the proper stamp or stamps denoting the tax paid thereon, and all such articles imported, or of foreign manufacture, shall, in addition to the import duties imposed on the same, be subject to the stamp tax, respectively, prescribed in Schedule C, as aforesaid :

Provided, That when such imported articles, except playing cards, lucifer or friction matches, cigar lights, and wax tapers, shall be sold in the original and unbroken package in which the bottles or other enclosures were packed by the manufacturer, the person so selling said articles shall not be subject to any penalty on account of the want of the proper stamp.

Medicines Exempted.

[SEC. 13. (July 13, 1866.) *And be it further enacted*, That no stamp tax shall be imposed upon any uncompounded medicinal drug or chemical, nor upon any medicine compounded according to the United States or other national pharmacopœia, or of which the full and proper formula is published in any of the dispensatories now or hitherto in common use among physicians or apothecaries, or in any pharmaceutical journal now issued by any incorporated college of pharmacy, when not sold or offered for sale, or advertised under any other name, form, or guise than that under which they may be severally denominated and laid down in said pharmacopœias, dispensatories, or journals as aforesaid; nor upon medicines sold to or for the use of any person, which may be mixed and compounded for said person according to the written receipt or prescription of any physician or surgeon. But nothing in this section shall be construed to exempt from stamp tax any medicinal articles, whether simple or compounded by any rule, authority, or formula, published or unpublished, which are put up in a style or manner similar to that of patent or proprietary medicines in general, or advertised in newspapers or by public handbills for popular sale and use, as having any special proprietary claim to merit, or to any peculiar advantage in mode of preparation, quality, use, or effect, whether such claim be real or pretended.]

Certain Officers to be Furnished with Stamps.

Sec. 170. *And be it further enacted,* That in any collection district where, in the judgment of the Commissioner of Internal Revenue, the facilities for the procurement and distribution of stamped vellum, parchment, or paper, and adhesive stamps, are or shall be insufficient, the Commissioner, as aforesaid, is authorized to furnish, supply, and deliver to the collector and to the assessor of any such district, and to any assistant treasurer of the United States, or designated depositary thereof, or any postmaster, a suitable quantity or amount of stamped vellum, parchment, or paper, and adhesive stamps, without prepayment therefor, and shall allow the highest rate of commissions allowed by law to any other parties purchasing the same, and may in advance require of any such collector, assessor, assistant treasurer of the United States, or postmaster, a bond (*a*), with sufficient sureties, to an amount equal to the value of any stamped vellum, parchment, or paper, and adhesive stamps which may be placed in his hands and remain unaccounted for, conditioned for the faithful return, whenever so required, of all quantities or amounts undisposed of, and for the payment, monthly, of all quantities or amounts sold or not remaining on hand.

And it shall be the duty of such collector to supply his deputies with, or sell to other parties within his district who may make application therefor, stamped vellum, parchment, or paper, and adhesive stamps, upon the same terms allowed by law, or under the regulations of the Commissioner of Internal Revenue, who is hereby authorized to make such other regulations, not inconsistent herewith, for the security of the United States and the better accommodation of the public, in relation to the matters hereinbefore mentioned, as he may judge necessary and expedient. And the Secretary of the Treasury may from time to time make such regulations as he may find necessary to insure the safe-keeping or prevent the illegal use of all such stamped vellum, parchment, paper, and adhesive stamps.

(a) No bond will be accepted for a less sum than five hundred dollars. Persons to whom stamps shall be furnished under this section must conform to the following rules:

Agents for the sale of stamps must make return under oath to the Office of Internal Revenue, on Form 55, on the first day of each month, of the amount of stamps sold during the preceding month, and of the amount actually on hand and unsold, in each case making separate statements of proprietary and general stamps.

Each collector will supply his deputies with adhesive stamps, and sell them to other parties within his district who may make application therefor, allowing the usual commissions. The collector may require such security from his deputies as he sees fit for the stamps placed in their hands, as he alone is responsible, and is to make returns and payments for them to the Office of Internal Revenue.

Orders may be made from time to time for such stamps as are desired, in no case to exceed three-fourths of the penal sum designated in the bond. Every agent will be charged with the stamps furnished to him, and credited with the amount of each remittance for the sale of stamps and five per cent. commission on the same. 9 I. R. R. 167.

Collection of Tax in case of Omission to affix Stamps.

[SEC. 5. (March 2, 1867.) *And be it further enacted*, That if the manufacturer of any article upon which a tax is required to be paid by means of a stamp shall have sold or removed for sale any such articles without the use of the proper stamp, in addition to the penalties now imposed by law for such sale or removal, it shall be the duty of the proper assessor or assistant assessor, within a period of not more than two years after such removal or sale, upon such information as he can obtain, to estimate the amount of the tax which has been omitted to be paid, and to make an assessment therefor, and certify the same to the collector; and the subsequent proceedings for collection shall be in all respects like those for the collection of taxes upon manufactures and productions.]

This section is not repealed. 11 I. R. R. 49.

SCHEDULE B, *as amended March* 3, 1865, § 1; *July* 13, 1866, § 9; *March* 2, 1867, § 9; *July* 14, 1870, § 4.

STAMP DUTIES.

	Duty.
AGREEMENT (a) or contract, other domestic and inland bills of lading, and those specified in this schedule; any appraisement (b) of value or damage, or for any other purpose; for every sheet or piece of paper upon which either of the same shall be written, five cents...	$0 05

Provided, That if more than one appraisement, agreement, or contract shall be written upon one sheet or piece of paper, five cents for each and every additional appraisement, agreement, or contract.

(a) A slight examination of the act and the schedule shows very clearly that the subjects of taxation are written instruments in general use, whose character and objects are well understood and have a definite meaning. Jackson *v.* Allen, 26 How. Pr. 119.

When a contract is executed in duplicate, and only one of the duplicates stamped, the unstamped duplicate may be read in evidence after proper notice has been given to the other party to produce the stamped duplicate. The stamped agreement is a binding contract upon both parties, though the other duplicate may not be stamped, and for that reason not binding. Bondurant *v.* Crawford, 22 Iowa, 40.

A receipt given for the delivery of goods is not an agreement within the meaning of the law. It is a receipt for the property to be transported, and contains only a notice of the terms on which the party is willing to undertake the transportation. The whole course of legislation shows that such receipts are not intended to be charged. Belger *v.* Dinsmore, 51 Barb. 69; De Barre *v.* Livingstone, 48 Barb. 511; U. S. *v.* Balt. & Ohio R. R. Co. 8 I. R. R. 148.

When a party signs an instrument, and then a few moments afterwards signs a memorandum explaining that his previous signature was merely intended as a guaranty, such memorandum is not an agreement, and does not require a stamp. Capps *v.* Watts, 43 Ill. 60.

A power to collect contained in an absolute assignment of a *chose* in action is wholly nugatory, since the authority it assumes to give would have existed without it. The assignment need only be stamped according to the rate for an assignment of that particular kind. Peoria Marine & Fire Ins. Co. *v.* Perkins, 16 Mich. 380.

A joint and several agreement requires but one stamp. One stamp is sufficient in the following cases: When a number of persons severally bind themselves in a penalty by one bond conditioned that each and every of them shall perform the same matter; when a debtor compounds with his creditors, and each creditor signs the deed; when several mariners join in a bill of sale of their several shares of prize money; when an agreement is made by several for a subscription to one common fund, though several as to each subscriber; when several underwriters on the same policy all agree to refer the demand of the insured on such policy; when an apprentice is bound for seven years, the first four with A B, and the last three with his father, to learn different trades; when members of a mutual insurance company all execute the same power of attorney authorizing the person therein named to sign the club policies for them. Any other construction would lead to the greatest danger, and might result in the greatest injustice. The subdivision of a single instrument to see how many separate and distinct contracts can be carved out would be a work of great labor. Ballard *v.* Burnside, 49 Barb. 102.

The following instrument is an agreement, viz.: " Due the bearer, or J. L. Coy, seven dollars in merchandise out of our store." U. S. *v.* Learned et al. 11 I. R. R. 149.

A waiver of protest and notice of dishonor by an indorser is not an agreement, and need not be stamped. The act evidently refers to original agreements by which parties intend to bind each other, and not to a waiver of some condition of the contract, or some right thereunder. Guyther *v.* Boury, 20 La. An. 157; Pacific Bank *v.* De Ro, 37 Cal. 538.

The statute only contemplates contracts which are completed by the assent of the parties thereto. Doubtless a letter in form may be a note, a promise to pay money, or an order, or an assignment necessary to be stamped, wherever this is the intention and the use to be made of it. But clearly there is nothing in the law that requires letters as such, mere correspondence, to be stamped before they can be placed in evidence, although they may be used as the evidence of an authority or an instruction to do a particular act, such as to receive money and pay it over to another. A party may not use a letter in the character of a substantial instrument to evade taxation; but when it is really a mere communication by way of correspondence, and merely conveys an intention or purpose of the writer, and is not used otherwise, it need not be stamped. Boyd *v.* Hood, 57 Penn. 98; New Haven & Northampton Co. *v.* Quintard, 6 Abb. Pr. N. S. 128. Contra, Myers *v.* Smith, 48 Barb. 614.

A letter stating terms for an agreement is not a contract or agreement of itself. It is only a proposition or offer. No contract or agreement is entered into until the other party has signified his assent thereto. The letter is only one link in the chain of evidence tending to prove the contract. No stamp is required to render it admissible for such purpose. Crocker *v.* Foley, 13 Allen, 376.

If an agreement to submit to arbitration is properly stamped, the acknowledgment need not be stamped. The agreement with the certificate constitute but one paper. McKnight *v.* McCullough, 21 Iowa, 111.

An award rendered in pursuance of a covenant to submit to arbitration need not be stamped. Burnap *v.* Losey, 1 Lans. 111. *

No stamp is necessary upon an instrument executed prior to October 1, 1862, to make it admissible in evidence, or to entitle it to record. 9 I. R. R. 165.

When an instrument is executed and issued in duplicate, triplicate, &c., as in the case of a lease of two or more parts, each part has the same legal effect as the other, and each should be stamped as an original. 9 I. R. R. 166.

A guaranty indorsed upon a note, bond, mortgage, or contract, whether made at the time of the execution of the note, &c., or subsequently, should be stamped as an agreement. 9 I. R. R. 165.

Any document of any kind made and issued in foreign countries, which is to have effect in the United States, and which, if made and issued in the United States, would require a stamp, may be stamped, and the stamp cancelled by the maker at the time and place of issue, or by the party to whom the same is issued, or by whom it is to be used. Bout. 342.

A contract for the sale of land, or to make a title deed to the purchaser upon payment of the purchase money, requires a five cent stamp as an agreement for each sheet or piece of paper upon which it is written. 9 I. R. R. 165.

A permit issued by a life insurance company, changing the terms of a policy as to travel, residence, occupation, &c., should be stamped as a contract or agreement. 9 I. R. R. 166.

A waiver of protest, or of demand, and notice written upon negotiable paper and signed by the indorser, is an agreement. 9 I. R. R. 166.

When a subscription is for a purpose in which there is a community of interest among the subscribers, the list should be stamped as a contract or agreement, at the rate of five cents for each sheet or piece of paper upon which it is written. When the subscription is for a purpose in which there is no community of interest among the subscribers, and the subscription is conditional, each signer executes a separate contract requiring its appropriate amount of stamps. This amount depends upon the number of sheets or pieces of paper upon which the contract is written. 9 I. R. R. 166.

A bill of sale of personal property other than a ship or vessel should be stamped as a contract or agreement. 9 I. R. R. 166.

An assignment of real and personal property, or of both, for the benefit of the creditors, should be stamped as an agreement or contract. 9 I. R. R. 166.

An assignment of a government land warrant should be stamped as an agreement. 1 I. R. R. 26.

Written or printed assignments of agreements, bonds, notes not negotiable, and of all other instruments, the assignments of which are not particularly specified in the foregoing schedule, should be stamped as agreements. 9 I. R. R. 166.

A mortgage to a building association, in addition to the appropriate stamp as a mortgage, requires an agreement stamp, as securing other matters besides a certain and definite sum. 11 I. R. R. 65.

(b) Inventories of the property of deceased persons returned for record or otherwise, should be stamped as "appraisements of value," at the same rate as agreements. 6 I. R. R. 105.

An appraisement of property made by freeholders selected by the sheriff of the county, in accordance with a law pending for the sale of real estate under executions issued by a court, as well as appraisements of personal property taken in actions of replevin, are subject to stamp duty. Bout. 348.

A mortgage given to secure a surety from loss, or for any other purpose whatever other than as security for the payment of a certain and definite sum of money, is taxable only as an agreement or contract. 5 I. R. R. 60.

When a wife conveys real property without valuable consideration to her husband through the intervention of a trustee, neither her deed to the trustee, nor the trustee's deed to the husband, need be stamped as a conveyance of realty sold, but each should be stamped as a contract or agreement. 6 I. R. R. 210.

An agreement stamp is required for stipulations waiving protest, promising to pay fees, &c., in promissory notes, in addition to the stamps appropriate to the note itself. 11 I. R. R. 138.

A permit of a towing company upon a canal is a contract or agreement. 3 I. R. R. 204.

A deed from the trustee of a person formerly a slave to the *cestui que* trust does not require a stamp, unless the deed contain covenants, in which case it should be stamped as an agreement. A stamp duty is imposed only upon realty sold. In this case there is no sale. The purpose and effect of such a deed is merely to place the legal title where the equitable title is. 3 I. R. R. 78.

A pawnbroker's check, when duly signed and issued, is subject to a stamp duty of five cents. 2 I. R. R. 108.

A transfer of stocks is subject to a stamp duty as an agreement or contract. Sometimes this transfer is made upon the back of a cerfificate; and when that is the case, and it is duly stamped, the record of the transfer made in the books of the company does not require to be stamped. But if the actual transfer is made in the transfer book of the company, and no such instrument is executed upon the back of the certificate, then the instrument in the transfer book becomes more than a mere record of the transfer. It is a regular transfer of stock, and as such should be duly stamped. 2 I. R. R. 5.

The assignment or transfer of a judgment should be stamped as an agreement. 2 I. R. R. 44.

A receipt or memorandum given to an applicant by an insurance company, on application for insurance, and of the premium notes, should be stamped as an agreement. 3 I. R. R. 156.

Car tickets do not require stamps as agreements. 4 I. R. R. 70.

The renewal of an agreement should be stamped the same as the original instrument. 9 I. R. R. 161.

BANK CHECK (c), draft, or order for the payment of any sum of money whatsoever, drawn upon any bank, banker, or trust company, or for any sum exceeding ten dollars drawn upon any other person or persons, companies, or corporations, at sight or on demand, two cents... 2

(c) Checks drawn on a bank by one of its proprietors for his daily expenses, or by its employees for their wages, must be stamped. Bout. 344.

The check of a correspondent on money to his credit, to transfer an amount of money collected for him, must be stamped. Checks drawn by a state for moneys belonging to the state are exempt. Bout. 345.

When a note is made payable at a certain bank, and a check is drawn upon the same bank for the amount thereof, the check must be stamped. When the note is simply charged at the bank to the account of the promissor without the use of a check, no stamp is required. Bout. 347.

If a check upon a book-keeper is used merely as a memorandum to show the liability of the drawer to the firm of which he is a member, it is exempt; but if used for any other purpose, and especially if paid out or transferred, or negotiable to a third party, it should be stamped. Bout. 349.

BILL OF EXCHANGE (d) (inland), draft, or order for the payment of any sum of money not exceeding one hundred dollars, other-

wise than at sight or on demand, or any promissory note (except bank notes issued for circulation, and checks made and intended to be forthwith presented, and which shall be presented to a bank or banker for payment), or any memorandum, check, receipt, or other written or printed evidence of an amount of money to be paid on demand, or at a time designated, for a sum not exceeding one hundred dollars, five cents.   5
And for every additional hundred dollars, or fractional part thereof in excess of one hundred dollars, five cents............   5
Promissory notes for a less sum than one hundred dollars are exempt.

(*d*) A check payable at sight, but post dated, which has been put into circulation prior to the day of its date, should be stamped the same as a promissory note, and not as a check payable on demand. Pope *v.* Burnset et al. 4 I. R. R. 133.

An agreement jointly and severally to pay the sums set opposite to the respective names of the makers is a promissory note. Ballard *v.* Burnside, 49 Barb. 102.

A due bill is a promissory note under the Illinois statutes, and in that State should be so stamped. Jacquin *v.* Warren, 40 Ill. 459.

Certificates of loan, in which there shall appear any written or printed evidence of an amount of money to be paid on demand, or at a time designated, are subject to stamp duty as promissory notes. 9 I. R. R. 165.

A check, draft, or order, for the payment of a sum of money drawn otherwise than at sight or on demand, is liable to stamp tax at the rate fixed for promissory notes. 9 I. R. R. 165.

A note payable in corn is subject to a stamp duty. The parties must estimate the value of the corn. Bout. 342.

When a loan is obtained upon collateral security, and an instrument substantially as follows is given, *i. e.*, "Received of ——— Bank $10,000 advance on $10,000 United States bonds," it should be stamped at the same rate as a promissory note. 9 I. R. R. 165.

Deposit notes given to mutual insurance companies are exempt when the policy is subject to duty. 9 I. R. R. 162.

There is no stamp upon a promissory note until it is issued. A stamp is to be cancelled when it is "attached or used," and although a stamp may be affixed when a note is signed, it cannot be said to be used until the note is issued. 9 I. R. R. 165.

A negotiable promissory note, made, signed, and issued in a foreign country, and made payable there, may be negotiated by indorsement in this country without liability to any United States stamp tax. 9 I. R. R. 165.

Coupons are a part of a bond, and do not require an additional stamp. 6 I. R. R. 105.

Whenever a bond or note is secured by mortgage, but one stamp duty is required on such papers, such stamp duty being the highest rate required on such instruments or either of them. In such case, a note or memorandum of the value or denomination of the stamp affixed should be made upon the margin or acknowledgment of the instrument which is not stamped. 9 I. R. R. 165.

A note or bond given for a part of the consideration for realty sold and conveyed is not relieved from stamp tax by the fact that a lien to secure the payment thereof is retained in the conveyance. Such lien should be stamped as a mortgage. In that case, the note need not be stamped. 9 I. R. R. 165; 10 I. R. R. 57.

The acceptor of any bill of exchange or order for the payment of any sum of money, drawn or purporting to be drawn in any foreign country, but payable in the United States, must, before paying or accepting the same, place the proper stamp thereon. 9 I. R. R. 165.

A check drawn by an individual upon himself, or drawn upon a bank by its cashier, in his official capacity and in the discharge of his official duty, is in its legal effect "written or printed evidence of an amount of money to be paid on demand or at a designated time" and should be stamped at the same rate as a promissory note when designed for circulation. In other cases they are to be stamped like checks drawn by one person upon another. 9 I. R. R. 165; 11 I. R. R. 193.

A single bill, or bill obligatory, *i. e.*, an instrument in the form of a promissory note, under seal, should be stamped at the same rate as a promissory note. 9 I. R. R. 166.

Bonds issued by cities or towns to aid in the construction of railroads or to purchase stock therein, are not considered as issued by municipal officers in the exercise of their ordinary governmental and municipal functions, and are therefore liable to a stamp tax at the same rate as promissory notes. 6 I. R. R. 105; 11 I. R. R. 169.

When each of the subscribers to a subscription list contracts to pay a certain and definite sum of money on demand, or at a time designated, the separate contract of each should be stamped at the same rate as a promissory note. 9 I. R. R. 166.

When a bank borrows money, and instead of giving its note, gives a memorandum containing "evidence of an amount of money to be paid on demand or at a time designated," such memorandum should be stamped at the same rate as a promissory note, even though it is in the form of a certificate of deposit. 11 I. R. R. 48.

No stamp is necessary upon the indorsement of a negotiable instrument. 5 I. R. R. 60.

If a written agreement to sell and convey real estate contains the promise of one of the parties signing it to pay a certain amount of money on demand or at a time designated, in addition to the appropriate stamp as an agreement it should also be stamped at the same rate as a promissory note. 7 I. R. R. 11.

The endorsement of a partial payment on the back of a note is regarded as a new memorandum not subject to stamp duty, and the fact that by implication of law it operates as an extension of the time of payment does not affect the case. 4 L R. R. 55.

New notes substituted for other properly stamped notes that have been destroyed, and which are evidence of the same debt, and not renewals of the notes payable at different dates, do not require to be stamped. A memorandum of the circumstances should be made on the new notes. If, however, notes are taken up and new notes given in lieu thereof, payable at a different date or otherwise changed, the new notes are subject to stamp duty. 4 I. R. R. 182.

BILL OF EXCHANGE (*e*) (foreign), or letter of credit, drawn in but payable out of the United State, if drawn singly, or otherwise than in a set of three or more, according to the custom of merchants and bankers, shall pay the same rates of duty as inland bills of exchange or promissory notes.

If drawn in sets of three or more: For every bill of each set where the sum made payable shall not exceed one hundred dollars, or the equivalent thereof, in any foreign currency in

which such bills may be expressed, according to the standard of value fixed by the United States, two cents............... 2
And for every additional hundred dollars or fractional part thereof in excess of one hundred dollars, two cents.......... 2

(*e*) A foreign bill of exchange or letter of credit, drawn in, but payable out of, the United States, if drawn according to the custom of merchants and bankers, is liable to the same stamp tax as an inland bill of exchange, *i. e.*, if drawn at sight or on demand it is liable to a tax of two cents; if drawn otherwise than at sight or on demand, it should be stamped at the rate of five cents for each $100 or fractional part thereof. Duplicates require the same amount of stamps as the original. 9 I. R. R. 165.

The phrase "letter of credit" is construed to refer to such letters as are equivalent to a bill of exchange, the payment of which is not contingent upon any other transaction. Bout. 353.

BILL OF LADING (*f*) or receipt (other than charter-party), for any goods, merchandise, or effects, to be exported from a port or place in the United States to any foreign port or place, ten cents... 10

(*f*) An inland or domestic bill of lading is exempt. 9 I. R. R. 161. A bill of lading to any port in British North America is exempt. 9 I. R. R. 161.

BILL OF SALE (*g*) by which any ship or vessel, or any part thereof, shall be conveyed to or vested in any other person or persons, when the consideration shall not exceed five hundred dollars, fifty cents... 50
Exceeding five hundred and not exceeding one thousand dollars, one dollar... 1 00
Exceeding one thousand dollars, for every additional amount of five hundred dollars, or fractional part thereof, fifty cents..... 50

(*g*) The stamp tax upon a bill of sale by which any ship or vessel, or any part thereof, is conveyed or vested in any other person or persons, is at the same rate as that imposed upon realty sold. A bill of sale of any other personal property should be stamped as a contract or agreement. 9 I. R. R. 166.

BOND—For indemnifying any person for the payment of any sum of money, where the money ultimately recoverable thereupon is one thousand dollars or less, fifty cents.................. 50
Where the money ultimately recoverable thereupon exceeds one thousand dollars, for every additional one thousand dollars or fractional part thereof in excess of one thousand dollars, fifty cents... 50

BOND (*h*) for the due execution or performance of the duties of any office, one dollar... 1 00

A bond given by an administrator for the faithful performance of his duties should be stamped. Blake *v.* Hall et al. 19 La. An. 49.

A bond given by a sheriff, conditioned for the faithful performance of his duties, need not be stamped. State *v.* Garton, 32 Ind.

(*h*) The official bonds of administrators, executors, and guardians are subject to a stamp tax of one dollar each as bonds for the due execution or performance of the duties of an office. 5 I. R. R. 60; 9 I. R. R. 161.

The bond given by the guardian of the minor heirs of a deceased soldier, in order to apply for the pension, bounty, or arrearages of pay, is subject to stamp duty as a bond given for the due execution and performance of the duties of his office. 2 I. R. R. 77.

The bond given by an assignee in bankruptcy requires a stamp. 6 I. R. R. 68.

The bonds given by town and county officers require a stamp. 5 I. R. R. 130; 11 I. R. R. 113.

A bond given by a town supervisor for the proper disbursement of school money, after he has given his official bond and qualified as a public officer, is exempt. 11 I. R. R. 123.

The position of treasurer in the organization of "Odd Fellows," or in any similar organization, is not an office within the meaning of the statute. The bond given by a person holding such position is only subject to a stamp duty of twenty-five cents. 6 I. R. R. 202.

A bond for the faithful disposition of the proceeds of sale, &c., required by the court of an executor, administrator, guardian, or trustee, upon his application for leave to sell property, is exempt, being a bond required in legal proceedings. 6 I. R. R. 210.

BOND (*i*) of any description, other than such as may be required in legal proceedings, or used in connection with mortgage deeds, and not otherwise charged in this schedule, twenty-five cents. 25

(*i*) A bond given by an insolvent, conditioned that he will appear at the next term of court, and present his petition for the benefit of the insolvent law, need not be stamped. It is required by legal proceedings. McGovern *v.* Hoesbeck, 53 Penn. 176.

An appeal bond need not be stamped. Smith *v.* Waters, 25 Ind. 397; Violet *v.* Heath, 26 Ind. 178; Anderson *v.* Coble, 26 Ind. 329.

A bond given to release property held under an attachment is a bond given in a legal proceeding, and need not be stamped. Bowers *v.* Beck, 2 Nev. 189.

State and city securities are exempt from stamp duty. 1 I. R. R. 75; 3 I. R. R. 14.

Bonds given in an action of replevin, and in actions commenced by *capias* are held to be bonds required in legal proceedings, and are exempt. 2 I. R. R. 52.

A bond to convey real estate requires stamps to the amount of twenty-five cents. 9 I. R. R. 166.

The two forms of bonds given by masters of steamboats require a twenty-five cent stamp each 6 I. R. R. 105.

Warehouse and rewarehouse bonds require a twenty-five cent stamp. 6 I. R. R. 122.

Enrollment and license bonds require a twenty-five cent stamp. 6 I. R. R. 122.

CERTIFICATE of stock in any incorporated company, twenty-five cents 25

CERTIFICATE of profits, or any certificate or memorandum showing an interest in the property or accumulations of any incorpora-

ted company, if for a sum not less than ten dollars and not exceeding fifty dollars, ten cents....... 10
Exceeding fifty dollars and not exceeding one thousand dollars, twenty-five cents.............. 25
Exceeding one thousand dollars, for every additional one thousand dollars, or fractional part thereof, twenty-five cents...... 25

CERTIFICATE.—Any certificate of damage, or otherwise, and all other certificates or documents issued by any port warden, marine surveyor, or other person acting as such, twenty-five cents.. 25

CERTIFICATE (*j*) of deposit of any sum of money in any bank or trust company, or with any banker or person acting as such—
If for a sum not exceeding one hundred dollars, two cents...... 2
For a sum exceeding one hundred dollars, five cents........... 5

(*j*) When money is received as a bona fide deposit, against which the depositor may draw, the certificate need only be stamped with a two cent or a five cent stamp, according to whether the amount exceeds one hundred dollars or not, even though the deposit draws interest for part or for all the time it remains in bank. 11 I. R. R. 43.

CERTIFICATE (*k*) of any other description than those specified, five cents......... 5

(*k*) The certificate of an officer to depositions taken before him does not require a stamp. No tax is imposed upon depositions, and the certificate of the officer before whom they are taken is an act essential to their validity, and in that sense forms a part of them. Prather *v*. Pritchard, 26 Ind 65; Cardell *v*. Bridge, 9 Allen, 355.

The certificate of a justice of the peace to a certified copy of his record, to be used on appeal or to be filed in a superior court, need not be stamped. Toledo, Logansport and Burlington R. R. Co. *v*. Nordyke, 27 Ind. 95; Comm *v*. Hardiman, 9 Allen, 487.

The certificate of a justice of the peace to an order to be used as a summons need not be stamped. East Haven *v*. Derby, 38 Vt. 253.

The return of a constable of the service of a summons is a certificate in both the technical and liberal sense of the term, and should be stamped. Miller *v*. Larmon, 38 How. Pr. 417.

When the caption to a deposition contains other certificates in addition to the jurat to the affidavit of the deponent, such as a certificate that the parties were or were not notified, that they did or did not appear, that they did or did not object, it is subject to a stamp duty of five cents. 9 I. R. R. 166.

When an attested copy of a writ or other process is used by a sheriff or other person in making personal service or in attaching property, a five cent stamp should be affixed to the certificate of attestation. 9 I. R. R. 166.

A marriage certificate isssued by the officiating clergyman or magistrate to be returned to any officer of a state, county, city, town, or other municipal corporation, to constitute part of a public record, requires no stamp; but if it is to be retained by the parties, a five cent stamp should be affixed. 9 I. R. R. 166.

A county clerk's certificate respecting the authority of a person to administer oaths, &c., issued to he used by a private party for his own benefit, should be stamped. 9 I. R. R. 166.

Certificates of measurement or weight of animals, wood, coal, or hay, are exempt. 9 I. R. R. 162.

If possession of real estate is taken by a mortgagee, or surrendered by the mortgagor, the certificate of the witness should be stamped. Bout. 347.

Certificates of dismission and recommendation of church members are not subject to a stamp duty. Bout. 346.

A certificate from an insurance company, approving a change of tenants by the insured and confirming his policy, should be stamped. Bout. 267.

Steamboat inspectors' certificates are exempt. 6 I. R. R. 105.

Official receipts, or certificates of the nature of receipts, issued by custom-house officers, are exempt. 6 I. R. R. 122.

CHARTER-PARTY.—Contract or agreement for the charter of any ship or vessel, or steamer, or any letter, memorandum, or other writing between the captain, master, or owner, or person acting as agent of any ship or vessel, or steamer, and any other person or persons for or relating to the charter of such ship or vessel, or steamer, or any renewal or transfer thereof, if the registered tonnage of such ship or vessel, or steamer, does not exceed one hundred and fifty tons, one dollar................ 1 00

Exceeding one hundred and fifty tons and not exceeding three hundred tons, three dollars................................. 3 00

Exceeding three hundred tons and not exceeding six hundred tons, five dollars 5 00

Exceeding six hundred tons, ten dollars....................... 10 00

CONTRACT (*l*).—Broker's note, or memorandum, of sale of any goods or merchandise, real estate, or property of any kind or description, issued by brokers or persons acting as such, for each note or memorandum of sale, ten cents.................. 10

Bill or memorandum of the sale or contract for the sale of stocks, bonds, gold or silver bullion, coin, promissory notes, or other securities, shall pay a stamp tax at the rate provided in section ninety-nine.

(*l*) Memorandums of purchase and sale must be regarded as within the meaning of the clause pertaining to contracts or brokers' notes, and subject to a stamp. Bout. 344.

The original and the duplicate, the one issued to the seller as well as that given to the buyer, must be stamped. Bout. 346.

CONVEYANCE (*m*).—Deed, instrument, or writing, whereby any lands, tenements, or other realty sold shall be granted, assigned, transferred, or otherwise conveyed to, or vested in, the purchaser or purchasers, or any other person or persons, by his, her, or their direction, when the consideration or value does not exceed five hundred dollars, fifty cents.................. 50

When the consideration exceeds five hundred dollars and does not exceed one thousand dollars, one dollar................. 1 00

And for every additional five hundred dollars, or fractional part thereof, in excess of one thousand dollars, fifty cents......... 50

(*m*) The assessment of the stamp duty is to be made in respect of the consideration or value. When the present value of the subject is less than the conventional or actual amount of the consideration, the stamp duty is assessable upon the consideration, without any reference to the value. If the consideration, as conventionally estimated by the parties, is less than the actual consideration, the stamp duty must be assessed upon the actual consideration, without reference to the language of the writings. The words "consideration or value" do not mean the value of the consideration. The word "value" does not qualify the word "consideration." The consideration is to be understood as that of the conveyance; the value as that of the subject of conveyance. James *v.* Blauvelt et al. 26 Law Rep. 485.

When a conveyance is made of an unimproved lot, with a stipulation that the grantor will advance a certain sum towards the cost of stipulated improvements thereon, and the grantor takes a mortgage to secure the estimated value of the lot, his advances and his stipulated profits, the actual consideration of the conveyance is the amount secured by the mortgage. James *v.* Blauvelt et al. 26 Law Rep. 485.

A conveyance without consideration, from a person who acts as a mere middleman, to convey to the real purchaser, need not be stamped; a double stamp duty is not incurred by such duplication. Any deficiency in the amount of stamps required for the entire transaction should be assessed upon the first conveyance. James *v.* Blauvelt et al. 26 Law Rep. 485.

Testimony is admissible to show that there was no consideration for a deed. It opens the question of value, under the stamp act, and enables the sufficiency of the stamp to be investigated upon that basis. Where there is no actual consideration the stamp must be regulated by the value of the interest sold. Groesbeek *v.* Seeley, 13 Mich. 329.

A tax-deed for land sold for taxes need not be stamped. Sayles *v.* Davis, 22 Wis. 225.

A sealed instrument, which merely declares and acknowledges that the party holds a lot of ground merely in trust, is not a conveyance, and need not be stamped; it merely declares, under the solemnity of a seal, a pre-existing state of facts, which could not be proved without the assistance of such formal declaration. Sime et al. *v.* Howard et al. 4 Nev. 473.

It is only upon a conveyance of realty sold that conveyance stamps are necessary. A deed of real estate made without valuable consideration need not be stamped as a conveyance, but should be stamped as an agreement or contract. 9 I. R. R. 165.

When a person conveys real property, without valuable consideration, through the intervention of a trustee, neither the deed to the trustee nor the trustee's deed to the *cestui que* trust need be stamped as a conveyance of realty sold, but each should be stamped as a contract or agreement.

When a deed purporting to be a conveyance of realty sold, and stamped accordingly, is inoperative, a deed of confirmation, made simply to cure the defect, requires no stamp. In such case, the second deed should contain a recital of the facts, and should show the reasons for its execution. 9 I. R. R. 165.

Partition deeds, between tenants in common, need not be stamped as conveyances inasmuch as there is no sale of realty, but merely a marking out, or a defining of the boundaries of the part belonging to each, but should be stamped as agreements. Where money, however, or other valuable consideration is paid by one co-tenant to another, for equality of partition, there is a sale to the extent of such consideration, and the conveyance should be stamped accordingly. 9 I. R. R. 165.

Deeds between joint tenants should be stamped as conveyances of realty sold. In the case of tenants in common, each tenant owns the whole of a part and there is no sale, but merely a marking out, or defining of the part belonging to each; in the case of joint tenants, each owns a part of the whole, and in what is usually denominated a division, in such case, there is an exchange of lands. An exchange does not differ materially from bargain and sale. 9 I. R. R. 165.

Ground rent deeds should be stamped at the same rate as other deeds of realty sold. 9 I. R. R. 165.

When the property of a deceased person is sold under a decree of court, the deed, *proces verbal*, or other instrument whereby the transfer is made, should be stamped at the usual rate of conveyances of realty sold. 9 I. R. R. 165.

When a conveyance of realty is made upon an actual valuable consideration, which is manifestly and intentionally inadequate, the deed should be stamped according to the amount of valuable consideration. 9 I. R. R. 165.

When the members of a business firm obtain an act of incorporation, and the partnership realty is conveyed to the corporation, each partner receiving stock therein to the amount of the partnership interest, the deed from the partnership to the corporation should be stamped the same as ordinary deeds. 9 I. R. R. 165.

When a deed conveys both realty and personalty, it should be stamped at the same rate as other deeds, according to the consideration or value of the realty; and, also, as a contract or agreement on account of the personalty. 9 I. R. R. 165.

A conveyance of lands, sold for unpaid taxes, issued since August 1, 1866, by the officer of any county, town, or other municipal corporation, in the discharge of their strictly official duties, is exempt. 9 I. R. R. 165.

A conveyance of realty, sold subject to a mortgage, should be stamped according to the consideration or value of the property unencumbered. The consideration, in such a case, is to be found by adding the amount paid for the equity of redemption to the mortgage debt. The fact that one part of the consideration is paid to the mortgagor, and the other part to the mortgagee, does not change the liability of the conveyance. 9 I. R. R. 165.

The actual consideration, and not the mere nominal consideration, determines the amount of stamp-tax upon a conveyance of realty sold. 5 I. R. R. 60.

A deed executed prior to Sept. 1, 1862, requires no stamp, if delivered before that date; but should be stamped if delivered since that date. 2 I. R. R 52.

Deeds of lands made under the decree of a master in chancery are subject to a stamp duty as conveyances. Bout. 339.

When a mortgage is foreclosed, and special execution issues, and the land is sold the same as in a general execution, the deed made by the sheriff must be stamped the same as other deeds. 2 I. R. R. 45.

Deeds of real estate sold by a sheriff under process of law should be stamped. Bout. 347.

In several States it is the custom to discharge a mortgage or deed of trust by a quit-claim deed. Such deed does not operate to convey the estate; it is merely, in substance, a release of the mortgage, and is exempt from tax duty. Bout 347.

Certificates of burial lots, being in the nature of conveyances, are subject to stamp duty as such. 2 I. R. R. 45.

When a vendee fails to pay the stipulated consideration for land sold to him, and in consideration of a release from the payment thereof, and of an additional sum paid to him, he conveys the land to the vendor, the deed of conveyance should be stamped according to the amount of such stipulated consideration and such additional sum together with all interest that may be due. 4 I. R. R. 142.

A release by a tenant for life to the owner of the remainder should be stamped at the usual rates for conveyances of realty sold. 6 I. R. R. 186.

When a vendor's lien is specially reserved in a deed, such lien should be stamped at the rate of mortgages in addition to the conveyance stamps. 10 I. R. R. 57.

The deed of an assignee in bankruptcy to purchasers, should be stamped at the usual rate of deeds. 6 I. R. R. 68.

Extraordinary powers, special covenants, &c., sometimes inserted in deeds of various kinds, but not contained in the common forms. are liable to the same tax as if they were issued separately. 4 I. R. R. 171.

ENTRY (n) of any goods, wares or merchandise at any custom house,
either for consumption or warehousing, not exceeding one
hundred dollars in value, twenty-five cents.................. 25
Exceeding one hundred dollars and not exceeding five hundred
dollars in value, fifty cents............................. 50
Exceeding five hundred dollars in value, one dollar............ 1 00

(n) Stamps should be required on entries of goods coming from Canada as well as from foreign countries. Bout. 278.

A constructive entry, for warehousing, is considered the same as an actual one, as far as the stamp tax is concerned. This kind of entry is made for the benefit of the parties, and not of the government. When the entries for warehousing and withdrawal are simultaneous, stamp tax should be paid for both. 10 I. R. R. 11.

ENTRY for the withdrawal of any goods or merchandise from
bonded warehouse, fifty cents........................... 50

INSURANCE (LIFE) (o).—Policy of insurance, or other instrument, by
whatever name the same shall be called, whereby any insurance shall be made upon any life or lives—
When the amount insured shall not exceed one thousand dollars,
twenty-five cents....................................... 25
Exceeding one thousand dollars and not exceeding five thousand
dollars, fifty cents..................................... 50
Exceeding five thousand dollars, one dollar................... 1 00

(o) The word life is to be construed as relating to human life only. When a material change, such as a change of the property insured, or in the amount of insurance, is made in an insurance policy, by erasures, interlining or otherwise after it has been issued, the changed policy is a new contract of insurance and requires a new stamp. 6 I. R. R. 210.

When a policy, properly stamped but incorrectly written, is surrendered, and another substituted solely to cure the defect in the first, the new policy requires no stamp. In such case the new policy should contain a recital of the facts, and show the reasons of its execution. 6 I. R. R. 105.

INSURANCE (*p*) (MARINE, INLAND, AND FIRE).—Each policy of insurance or other instrument, by whatever name the same shall be called, by which insurance shall be made or renewed upon property of any description, whether against perils by the sea or by fire, or other peril of any kind, made by any insurance company, or its agents, or by any other company or person, the premium upon which does not exceed ten dollars, ten cents.. 10
Exceeding ten and not exceeding fifty dollars, twenty-five cents. 25
Exceeding fifty dollars, fifty cents 50

(*p*) The stamp-tax upon a fire insurance policy is based upon the premium. 9 I. R. R. 166.

Deposit notes, taken by a mutual fire insurance company, not as a payment of the premium, nor as evidence of indebtedness therefor, but to be used simply as a basis upon which to make ratable assessments to meet the losses incurred by the company, should not be reckoned as premium in determining the amount of stamp-tax upon the policy. 9 I. R. R. 166.

When a policy of insurance, properly stamped, has been issued and lost, no stamp is necessary upon another issued by the same company to the same party, covering the same property, time, &c., and designed simply to supply the loss. The second policy should recite the loss of the first. 9 I. R. R. 166.

An instrument which operates as the renewal of a policy of insurance is subject to the same stamp-tax as a policy. 9 I R. R. 166.

When a policy of insurance is issued for a certain time, whether it be for one year only or for a term of years, a receipt for premium, or any other instrument which has the legal effect to continue the contract, and extend its operation beyond that time, requires the same amount of revenue stamps as the policy itself; but such a receipt as is usually given for the payment of the monthly, quarterly, or annual premiums, is not a renewal, within the meaning of the statute. The payment simply prevents the policy from expiring, by reason of non-performance of its conditions. A receipt, given for such a payment, should be stamped the same as other receipts for money. When, however, the time for payment has passed, and a tender of the premium is not enough to bind the company, but a new policy, or a new contract in some form, with the mutuality essential to every contract, becomes necessary between the insurer and the insured, the same amount of stamps should be used as that required upon the original policy. 9 I. R. R. 166.

An application for a policy forms a part of the policy, and is not subject to a separate stamp Bout. 267.

Each insurance, re-insurance, and duplicate policy, must be stamped according to the prescribed rates Bout. 266.

When the contract of insurance is entered in a register, instead of issuing a policy, whether it is a new insurance, re-insurance, or renewal of a policy, each entry requires a stamp, at the usual rate, based upon the premium. It would not be legal or sufficient to estimate the tax in the sum total of the premiums entered at one date as if it were a single policy. 6 I. R. R. 105.

The law imposes no tax upon the policies of Health Insurance Companies. 6 I. R. R. 195.

LEASE (*q*), agreement, memorandum, or contract for the hire, use, or rent of any land, tenement, or portion thereof, where the rent or rental value is three hundred dollars per annum or less, fifty cents 50
Where the rent or rental value exceeds the sum of three hundred dollars per annum, for each additional two hundred dollars, or fractional part thereof in excess of three hundred dollars, fifty cents... 50

(*q*) The stamp duty upon a lease, agreement, memorandum, or contract for the hire, use, or rent of any land, tenement, or portion thereof, is based upon the annual rent or rental value of the property leased, and the duty is the same, whether the lease be for one year, for a term of years, or for the fractional part of a year only. 9 I. R. R. 165.

A lease of both realty and personalty should be stamped as a lease of lands and tenements as to the realty, and as an agreement as to the personalty. 9 I. R. R. 165.

In oil leases there is very rarely a fixed rental value in money agreed upon. They are analogous to leases of farms upon shares. Such leases are subject to stamp duty as leases, and a stamp as an agreement or contract is not sufficient. The parties should apply to the collector and have the stamp duty determined. 1 I. R. R. 2.

When duplicate leases are executed, both should be properly stamped. Bout. 341.

MANIFEST (*r*) for custom-house entry or clearance of the cargo of any ship, vessel, or steamer for a foreign port—
If the registered tonnage of such ship, vessel, or steamer, does not exceed three hundred tons, one dollar......... .... 1 00
Exceeding three hundred tons and not exceeding six hundred tons, three dollars 3 00
Exceeding six hundred tons, five dollars.................... 5 00

(*r*) The amount of this tax in each case depends upon the registered tonnage of the vessel. If a vessel clears in ballast and has no cargo whatever, no stamp is necessary; but if she has any cargo, however small the amount, a stamp should be used. 5 I. R. R. 74.

Stamps are not required on copies of manifests mentioned in sections 21 and 25 of the act of 1799, ch. 22, nor on copies of entries furnished to the several officers of customs under that law. 7 I. R. R. 173.

MORTGAGE (*s*) of lands, estate, or property, real or personal, heritable or movable, whatsoever, where the same shall be made as a security for the payment of any definite and certain sum of money lent at the time or previously due and owing or forborne to be paid, being payable; also any conveyance of any lands, estate, or property whatsoever, in trust, to be sold or otherwise converted into money, which shall be intended only as security, and shall be redeemable before the sale or other disposal thereof, either by express stipulation or otherwise; or any personal bond given as security for the payment of any definite or certain sum of money exceeding one hundred dollars, and not exceeding five hundred dollars, fifty cents..... 50
Exceeding five hundred dollars, and not exceeding one thousand dollars, one dollar. 1 00

And for every additional five hundred dollars, or fractional part thereof, in excess of one thousand dollars, fifty cents 50

Upon every assignment (*t*) or transfer of a mortgage, the same stamp tax upon the amount remaining unpaid thereon as is herein imposed upon a mortgage for the same amount: *Provided*, That upon each and every assignment (*u*) or transfer of a policy of insurance, or the renewal or continuance of any agreement, contract, or charter, by letter or otherwise, a stamp duty shall be required and paid equal to that imposed on the original instrument: *And provided further*, That upon each and every assignment (*v*) of any lease, a stamp duty shall be required and paid equal to that imposed on the original instrument, increased by a stamp duty on the consideration or value of the assignment equal to that imposed upon the conveyance of land for similar consideration or value.

And no stamp shall be required upon the transfer or assignment of a mortgage, where the mortgage or the instrument it secures has been once duly stamped.

(*s*) A mortgage to secure the mortgagee as drawer and indorser of certain drafts which have been drawn for the benefit of the mortgagor and are payable subsequent to the execution of the mortgage need not be stamped. Vail *v.* Knapp, 49 Barb. 299.

A mortgage to secure $10,000 and having only a five cent stamp thereon is void against an assignee claiming under a subsequent assignment of the property made for the benefit of creditors. 30 How. Pr. 120.

Quære. Can the statute be so applied as to render contracts which on their face bear adequate stamps inadmissible in evidence or inoperative, by showing that they were executed in connection with another paper, viz.: a defeasance, which is inadmissible for the want of a stamp, but which if admitted would give to them a different legal effect and operation from that which would result from them if constructed by themselves. Carpenter et al. *v.* Snelling, 97 Mass. 452.

The mortgage must be stamped according to the consideration expressed upon its face. When a mortgage note is taken for the full sum intended to be advanced, but only a portion is advanced, the mortgage must be stamped according to the full face of the note. McBride *v.* Doty, 23 Iowa, 122.

The stamp tax upon a mortgage is based upon the amount it is given to secure. The fact that the value of the property mortgaged is less than that amount, and that consequently the security is only partial, does not change the liability of the instrument. When, therefore, a second mortgage is given to secure the payment of a sum of money partially secured by a prior mortgage upon other property, or when two mortgages are given upon separate pieces of property at the same time to secure the payment of the same sum, each should be stamped as though it were the only one. 9 I. R. R. 165.

If two mortgages are given to secure one bond and the appropriate stamp is affixed to the bond, the bond will be valid though the mortgages might not be. 2 I. R. R. 11.

A mortgage given to secure a surety from loss, or given for any other purpose whatever than as security for the payment of a definite and certain sum of money, is taxable only as an agreement or contract. 9 I. R. R. 165.

The stamp tax upon a mortgage or trust deed is based upon the definite and certain sum of money originally secured thereby without including any interest that may accrue after the date of the instrument. 9 I. R. R. 165.

A mortgage securing less than $100 is not subject to stamp duty, but the liability of the bond or note which is evidence of the amount secured is the same as though there were no mortgage. The necessary stamp may be affixed either to the bond or note, or to the mortgage. 9 I. R. R. 165.

No stamp is necessary upon the registry of a judgment, even though the registry is such in its legal effect as to create a lien which operates as a mortgage upon the property of the judgment debtor. 9 I. R. R. 166.

When a vendor's lien is secured in a deed, the lien should be stamped as a mortgage in addition to the stamps upon the conveyance. 10 I. R. R. 57.

A mortgage to a building association should be stamped according to the amount expressly secured by them, *i. e.*, according to the nominal amount appearing upon the face of the mortgage, and not according to the amount actually advanced to the mortgagee. 11 I. R. R. 65.

The renewal of a chattel mortgage by a notice entered upon the record as provided by the laws of several States need not be stamped. Bout. 343.

When the mortgage secures other matters besides the payment of a certain and definite sum, it should also be stamped as an agreement. 11 I. R. R. 65.

The ordinary power of sale commonly inserted in a mortgage or in a trust deed given as security for the payment of money, is regarded as a part of the mortgage or deed, and requires no additional stamp. Extraordinary powers and agreements should be separately stamped. 6 I. R. R. 130; 3 I. R. R. 44; 4 I. R. R. 171.

Whenever a bond or note is secured by a mortgage but one stamp duty is required on such papers, such stamp duty being at the highest rate required for such instruments or either of them; in such case, a note or memorandum of the value or denomination of the stamp affixed, should be made upon the margin or in the acknowledgment of the instrument not stamped. 9 I. R. R. 165.

A mortgage given to secure bonds which are to be issued from time to time as sales of them can be made is valid, so far as stamp taxes are concerned, though no stamps are affixed thereto, if the bonds are properly stamped as they are issued. 9 I. R. R. 165.

A personal bond given as security for any definite or certain sum of money must be stamped at the same rate as a mortgage. 3 I. R. R. 45.

(*t*) Upon every assignment or transfer of a mortgage a stamp tax is required, equal to that imposed upon the mortgage, for the amount remaining unpaid. This tax is required upon every such transfer in writing, whether there is a sale of the mortgage or not. But no stamp is necessary upon the endorsement of a negotiable instrument, even though the legal effect of such endorsement is to transfer a mortgage by which the instrument is secured. 9 I. R. R. 166.

When a partial interest in a mortgage is assigned, as where one of two mortgagees assigns his interest, the assignment should be stamped according to the amount of interest transferred. 9 I. R. R. 166.

The fact that the transfer is made by an order of court does not exempt it from stamp duty. 10 I. R. R. 85.

An assignment of a mortgage executed years ago must be governed by the law now in force. If the mortgage has been reduced by payment, the amount of stamps to be affixed to the assignment depends upon the amount actually due on the mortgage when the assignment is made. 2 I. R. R. 29.

(*n*) An entry upon a policy of insurance, and in the book of the company, that a loss is payable to a trustee in a deed of trust in the nature of a mortgage, to the extent of his interest, is a transfer of a policy, and must be stamped accordingly. 12 I. R. R. 21.

(*o*) An assignment of a lease within the meaning and intent of Schedule B is an assignment of the leasehold, or of some portion thereof, by the lessee, or by some person claiming by, from or under him—such an assignment as subrogates to the rights or some portion of the rights of the lessee, or of the person standing in his place. 9 I. R. R. 166.

An assignment of a lease is subject to the same duty as the original lease, and if any consideration is paid for the assignment beyond the yearly rent, it will be subject to an additional stamp duty proportionate to such consideration. 1 I. R R 196.

When the consideration for an assignment of an oil lease is a certain proportion of the oil to be produced from the premises assigned, as a royalty, and a fixed bonus to be paid out of the money first realized from the sale of stocks, or upon bonuses on sub-leases, the stamp duty for such consideration depends upon the estimated value of such annual rent and of such bonus. These estimates, if made by any other person than a collector, are made at the risk of the party. 2 I. R. R. 132.

A bill of sale of a vessel given as security for money must be stamped as a mortgage. Bout. 347.

PASSAGE TICKET (*w*) by any vessel from a port in the United States
to a foreign port, not exceeding thirty-five dollars, fifty cents.. 50
Exceeding thirty-five dollars and not exceeding fifty dollars, one
dollar.. 1 00
And for every additional fifty dollars, or fractional part thereof,
in excess of fifty dollars, one dollar........................ 1 00

(*w*) Stamps placed upon the passage tickets of passengers leaving for foreign ports should be based upon the currency value of the tickets, and not upon the gold value. 6 I. R. R. 105, 185.

POWER OF ATTORNEY (*x*) for the sale or transfer of any stock, bonds,
or scrip, or for the collection of any dividends or interest thereon, twenty-five cents.. 25

(*x*) Any written authority, in whatever form drawn, made by a stockholder in a corporation, for the transfer of shares in such corporation, is regarded as a power of attorney. Bout. 247.

A power of attorney designed to be used in a foreign country, and so prepared and authenticated as to conform to the laws of that country, need not be stamped. Bout. 348.

When several stockholders, who are the owners of distinct shares, sign a power of attorney, each authorizing a person to act for him, the instrument is to be regarded as the separate power of each, and should be stamped accordingly. If the power relates to general business, and not merely to the election of officers, it should be stamped at the rate of fifty cents for each signer whether it is to be used at elections or not. 9 I. R. R. 166.

No stamp is required upon any warrant of attorney accompanying a bond or note when such bond or note has affixed thereto the stamp or stamps denoting the duty required. 9 I. R. R. 165.

The exemption in regard to bounties, &c., applies to those papers only which relate to United States bounties, pensions, &c., and does not extend to those relating to state, county, or town bounties, &c. A power of attorney to endorse the official check of a United States disbursing officer, issued for money, to be applied in payment of a United States bounty or pension, or in discharge of a claim against the United States for what is technically known as arrearages of pay, is exempt. 9 I. R. R. 165.

Power of Attorney or proxy for voting at any election for officers of any incorporated company or society, except religious, charitable, literary societies, or public cemeteries, ten cents............ 10

Power of Attorney to receive or collect rent, twenty-five cents.... 25

Power of Attorney to sell and convey real estate, or to rent or lease the same, one dollar....................................... 1 00

Power of Attorney (*y*) for any other purpose, fifty cents........ 50

(*y*) A power of attorney appointing an agent to vote for an assignee, in a case pending in bankruptcy, need not be stamped. In re Myrick, 3 B. R. 38; contra, 6 I. R. R. 68.

An order authorizing a person to draw and receipt for moneys that may thereafter become due, is a power of attorney, and requires a fifty cent stamp. 3 I. R. R. 60.

The written appointment, mentioned in section 25 of the act, commonly known as the National Currency Act, is a power of attorney, and requires a fifty cent stamp. 5 I. R. R. 204.

Probate of will (*z*) or letters of administration: Where the estate and effects for or in respect of which such probate or letters of administration applied for shall be sworn or declared not to exceed the value of two thousand dollars, one dollar... 1 00
Exceeding two thousand dollars, for every additional thousand dollars, or fractional part thereof, in excess of two thousand dollars, fifty cents............................... 50
Provided, That no stamp either for probate of wills, or letters testamentary, or of administration, or on administrator or guardian bond, shall be required when the value of the estate and effects, real and personal, does not exceed one thousand dollars: *Provided further*, That no stamp tax shall be required upon any papers necessary to be used for the collection from the government of claims by soldiers or their legal representatives of the United States, for pensions, back pay, bounty, or for property lost in the service.

(*z*) When neither the bond, nor appraisement, nor letters of administration are stamped, the appointment to the office of administrator is a nullity. Blake *v.* Hall et al. 19 La. An. 49.

The stamp may be affixed to the bond, or to the letters of administration. Miller *v.* Henderson, 24 Ark. 344.

The evident purpose of the act is to impose stamp duties upon the estates of deceased persons upon which letters testamentary or of administration shall be granted. It is not a tax upon either class of documents as such, as is evident from the fact that the duty varies with the value of the estate. It can make no substantial difference in the result whether the stamp is affixed to the will upon its being admitted to probate, or to the certificate of proof thereof attached, or to the letters testamentary, as they are parts of one judicial proceeding; and the object of the act—revenue—is attained if either document is duly stamped. The presumption, when the question arises in a collateral proceeding, is that the probate court passed upon the value of the estate on evidence, and such action of the probate court cannot be reviewed collaterally. The sufficiency of the stamp cannot be tested by the evidence of the value of the estate produced in another proceeding where the letters are offered in evidence. The validity of proceedings for the settlement of the estates of deceased persons and of rights acquired through such proceedings, cannot there be made dependent upon the contingency that another court will make the same estimate of the value of the estate as the probate court did, based upon evidence which, from its nature, must be conjectural and fluctuating. Satteree *v.* Bliss, 36 Cal. 489.

The stamp duty upon the probate of a will or upon letters of administration is based upon the sworn or declared value of all the estate and effects, real, personal, and mixed, undiminished by the debts of the estate for or in respect of which such probate or letters are applied for. 9 I. R. R. 166.

When the property belonging to a person deceased lies under different jurisdictions, and it becomes necessary to take out letters in two or more places, the letters should be stamped according to the value of the property, real, personal, and mixed, for or in respect of which the letters in each case are issued. 9 I. R. R. 166.

Letters *de bonis non* should be stamped according to the amount of property remaining to be administered upon thereunder, regardless of the stamps upon the original letters. 9 I. R. R. 166.

PROTEST (*aa*).—Upon the protest of every note, bill of exchange, acceptance, check, or draft, or any marine protest, whether protested by a notary public or by any other officer who may be authorized by the law of any state or states to make such protest, twenty-five cents.................................. 25

Provided, That when more than one signature is affixed to the same paper, one or more stamps may be affixed thereto representing the whole amount of the stamp required for such signatures; and that the term money, as herein used, shall be held to include drafts and other instruments given for the payment of money: *Provided*, That the stamp duty imposed by the foregoing schedule (B) on manifests, bills of lading, and passage tickets, shall not apply to steamboats or vessels plying between ports of the United States and ports of British North America: *And provided further*, That all affidavits shall be exempt from stamp duty.

(*aa*) A stamp duty of twenty five cents is imposed upon the protest of every note, bill of exchange, check, or draft, and upon every marine protest. If several notes, bills of exchange, drafts, &c., are protested at the same time, and all attached to one and the same certificate, stamps should be affixed to the amount of twenty-five cents for each note, bill, draft, &c., thus protested. 9 I. R. R. 166.

The certificate of notice to the parties usually appended to a notary's certificate of protest forms no part of the protest, and requires additional stamps to the amount of five cents. 9 I. R. R. 166.

EXEMPTIONS.

Accidental injuries to persons, tickets or contracts for insurance against. 9 I. R. R. 161.

Acknowledgment of a deed. 9 I. R. R. 162.

Affidavits. 9 I. R. R. 161.

Assignment of a mortgage, where it or the instrument it secures has been once duly stamped. July 14, 1870, § 4.

Bill of lading to any port in British North America. 9 I. R. R. 161.

Bill of lading, domestic or inland. 9 I. R. R. 161.

Bond of administrator or guardian when the value of the estate and effects, real and personal, does not exceed $1,000. 9 I. R. R. 161.

Certificate of weight or measurement of animals, wood, coal, or hay. 9 I. R. R. 162.

Certificate of record of a deed. 9 I. R. R. 162.

Endorsement upon a stamped obligation in acknowledgment of its fulfilment. 9 I. R. R. 162.

Endorsement of any negotiable instrument. 9 I. R. R. 162.

Enrollment and licenses of vessels. 6 I. R. R. 124.

Gaugers' returns. 9 I. R. R. 162.

Legal documents:

Writ or other original process by which any suit, either civil or criminal, is commenced in any court either of law or equity.

Confession of judgment or cognovit.

Writs or other process on appeals from justice courts or other courts of inferior jurisdiction to a court of record. 9 I. R. R. 162.

Letters testamentary when the value of the estate and effects, real and personal, does not exceed $1,000. 9 I. R. R. 162.

Measurers' returns. 9 I. R. R. 162.

Notice by landlord to tenant to quit. 9 I. R. R. 166.

Passage tickets to ports in British North America. 9 I. R. R. 162.

Probate of will or letters testamentary where the estate and effects for or in respect of which such probate or letters of administration are applied for do not exceed the value of $1,000. 9 I. R. R. 162.

Promissory notes used as deposit notes to mutual insurance companies when policy is subject to duty. 9 I. R. R. 162.

Promissory notes for a less sum than $100. July 14, 1870, § 4.

Receipt for the satisfaction of any mortgage, judgment or decree of any court. 9 I. R. R. 162.

Receipts for the delivery of property. 9 I. R. R. 162.

Sheriff's return on writ or other process. 9 I. R. R. 162.

Warehouse receipts. 9 I. R. R. 162.

Warrant of attorney accompanying a bond or note, if the bond or note is stamped. 9 I. R. R. 162.

Weighers' returns. 9 I. R. R. 162.

Official documents, instruments, and papers issued by officers of the United States Government. 9 I. R. R. 162.

Official documents, papers, and instruments issued by the officers of any state, county, town, or other municipal corporation, in the exercise of functions strictly belonging to them in their ordinary governmental or municipal capacity. 9 I. R. R. 162.

Papers necessary to be used for the collection from the United States government of claims by soldiers, or their legal representatives, for pensions, back pay, bounty, or for property lost in the service. 9 I. R. R. 162.

Receipts for any sum of money, or the payment of any debt. July 14, 1870, § 4.

SCHEDULE C, *as amended July* 13, 1866, § 9; *July* 14, 1870, § 1.

MEDICINES OR PREPARATIONS.

For and upon every packet, (a) box, bottle, pot, phial, or other enclosure, containing any pills, powders, tinctures, troches, lozenges, sirup, cordials, bitters, anodynes, tonics, plasters, liniments, salves, ointments, pastes, drops, waters, essences, spirits, oils, or other medicinal preparations or compositions whatsoever, made and sold, or removed for consumption and sale, by any person or persons whatever, wherein the person making or preparing the same has, or claims to have, any private formula or occult secret, or art for the making or preparing the same, or has or claims to have any exclusive right or title to the making or preparing the same, or which are prepared, uttered, vended, or exposed for sale under any letters patent, or held out or recommended to the public by the makers, venders or proprietors thereof as proprietary medicines, or as remedies or specifics for any disease, diseases, or affections whatever affecting the the human or animal body, as follows: Where such packet, box, bottle, pot, phial, or other enclosure, with its contents, shall not exceed, at retail price, or value, the sum of twenty-five cents, one cent 1

Where such packet, box, bottle, pot, phial, or other enclosure, with its contents, shall exceed the retail price or value of twenty-five cents, and not exceed the retail price or value of fifty cents, two cents 2

Where such packet, box, bottle, pot, phial, or other enclosure, with its contents, shall exceed the retail price or value of fifty cents, and shall not exceed the retail price or value of seventy-five cents three cents.................................. 3

Where such packet, box, bottle, pot, phial, or other enclosure, with its contents, shall exceed the retail price or value of seventy-five cents, and shall not exceed the retail price or value of one dollar, four cents.................................. 4

Where such package, box, bottle, pot, phial, or other enclosure, with its contents, shall exceed the retail price or value of one dollar, for each and every fifty cents or fractional part thereof over and above the one dollar, as before mentioned, an additional two cents. 2

(a) When proprietary stamps from a private die are used, if they are so affixed to the boxes, bottles, or packages that in opening the same, or in using the contents thereof, they shall and must be unavoidably and effectually destroyed, no cancellation is necessary; but if they cannot be so affixed, they shall be cancelled in the ordinary manner by writing or imprinting thereon the initials and date. When general proprietary stamps are used, they must be cancelled by writing or imprinting thereon the date and the initials of the party using or affixing them. When proprietary medicines and preparations, perfumery and cosmetics, are stamped according to their retail price or value in the immediate vicinity of the place of manufacture, no additional stamps are necessary upon them, whatever may be the price at which they are offered. 9 I. R. R. 167.

Every man who prepares or compounds bitters, using in their preparation rectified spirits on which the tax has been paid, may stamp the same according to the provisions of this Schedule. Those who prefer to be taxed as rectifiers must not put their bitters up in the style of proprietary medicines, nor vend them as medicines. 11 I. R. R. 169.

Bitters put up and sold in good faith only as a medicine should be stamped according to this Schedule, even though they may subsequently be sold and used to some extent as a beverage. 11 I. R. R 137.

When a manufacturer of medicinal bitters purchases raw or unrectified spirits and rectifies the same prior to their use in the manufacture of bitters, he is both manufacturer and rectifier, and liable for both taxes. 10 I. R. R. 65.

Cough candies are liable to stamp duty. 11 I. R. R. 123.

The manufacturer must determine the denomination and value of the stamp or stamps to be affixed to each original package of medicinal bitters by the price at which he sells the same He may sell his bitters in original packages, of any desired capacity, and purchasers may break the original packages and put the contents into phials or bottles for sale. A purchaser who thus breaks the original packages and puts the contents of the same up in phials, bottles, or other enclosures, and affixes the manufacturer's labels, or a label bearing his own name and trade-mark, and then offers the same for sale, must affix revenue stamps according to his retail price of such packages. 10 I. R. R. 193.

No stamp tax is imposed upon medicines sold to or for the use of any person which may be mixed and compounded for such person according to the written recipe or prescription of a physician or surgeon. But all medicinal articles, whether simple or compounded by any rule, authority, or formula, published or unpublished, which are put up in a style or manner similar to that of patent or proprietary medicines in general, or advertised in newspapers or by public handbills for popular sale and use as having any special proprietary claim to merit, or to any peculiar advantage in mode of preparation, quality, use, or effect, whether such claim be real or pretended, should be stamped. 9 I. R. R. 166 ; Bout 276.

Ink is not liable to stamp duty. 6 I. R. R. 162.

PERFUMERY AND COSMETICS.

For and upon every packet, (b) box, bottle, pot, phial, or other enclosure, containing an essence, extract, toilet water, cosmetic, hair oil, pomade, hair dressing, hair restorative, hair dye, tooth-wash, dentifrice, tooth-paste, aromatic cachous, or any similar articles, by whatsoever name the same heretofore have been, now are, or may hereafter be called, known or distinguished, used or applied. or to be used or applied as perfumes or applications to the hair, mouth, or skin, made, prepared, and sold or removed for consumption and sale in the United States, where such packet, box. bottle, pot, phial, or other enclosure, with its contents, shall not exceed, at the retail price or value, the sum of twenty-five cents, one cent...................... 1

Where such packet, box, bottle, pot, phial, or other enclosure, with its contents, shall exceed the retail price or value of twenty-five cents, and shall not exceed the retail price or value of fifty cents, two cents.. 2

Where such packet, box, bottle, pot, phial, or other enclosure, with its contents, shall exceed the retail price or value of fifty cents, and shall not exceed the retail price or value of seventy-five cents, three cents.................................... 3

Where such packet, box, bottle, pot, phial, or other enclosure, with its contents, shall exceed the retail price or value of seventy-five cents, and shall not exceed the retail price or value of one dollar, four cents... 4

Where such packet, box, bottle, pot, phial, or other enclosure, with its contents, shall exceed the retail price or value of one dollar, for each and every fifty cents or fractional part thereof over and above the one dollar, as before mentioned, an additional two cents.. 2

(*b*) Soap sold as a dentifrice must be stamped. 10 I. R. R. 5.

Fancy, scented, honey, cream, transparent, and shaving soaps, are to be regarded as toilet soaps and not as perfumery or cosmetics, and need not be stamped. 3 I. R. R. 85.

Bay rum is covered by the provision concerning toilet water, and is liable to stamp duty. 7 I. R. R. 11.

FRICTION MATCHES, (*c*) or lucifer matches, or other articles made in part of wood, and used for like purposes, in parcels or packages containing one hundred matches or less, for each parcel or package, one cent.. 1

When in parcels or packages containing more than one hundred and not more than two hundred matches, for each parcel or package, two cents... 2

And for every additional one hundred matches or fractional part thereof, one cent.. 1

For wax tapers, double the rates herein imposed upon friction or lucifer matches; on cigar lights, made in part of wood, wax, glass, paper, or other materials, in parcels or packages containing twenty-five lights or less in each parcel or package, one cent... 1

When in parcels or packages containing more than twenty-five and not more than fifty lights, two cents.................. 2

For every additional twenty-five lights or fractional part of that number, one cent additional............................... 1

(*c*) Matches sawed out in blocks and dipped in sulphur must be stamped. The fact that the phosphoric composition is put up in a separate bottle does not exempt them from liability. 3 I. R. R. 60.

A lighter which consists simply of a thin strip of wood not prepared in any way to light by friction, and which can only be used as a cigar lighter in the same way that any strip of wood or paper might be used, is not liable to stamp duty. 10 I. R. R. 201.

Cigar lights and playing cards should be stamped according to the law now in force. 9 I. R. R. 166.

PLAYING CARDS.—For and upon every pack not exceeding fifty-two cards in number, irrespective of price or value, five cents.... 5

CANNED MEATS, &c.—For and upon every can, bottle, or other single package, containing sauces, sirups, prepared mustard, jams, or jellies contained therein and packed or sealed, made, prepared, and sold, or offered for sale, or removed for con-

sumption in the United States, on and after the first day of October, eighteen hundred and sixty-six, when such can, bottle or other single package, with its contents, shall not exceed two pounds in weight, the sum of one cent 1
When such can, bottle, or other single package, with its contents, shall exceed two pounds in weight, for every additional pound or fractional part thereof, one cent................ 1

DRAWBACK.

Exportation of Articles on which Internal Revenue Tax has been Paid.

Sec. 171. (Amended March 3, 1865, § 1; July 13, 1866, § 1.) *And be it further enacted,* That from and after the date on which this act takes effect, there shall be an allowance of drawback (*a*) on all articles on which any internal duty or tax shall have been paid, except raw or unmanufactured cotton, crude petroleum or rock oil, refined coal oil, naphtha, benzine or benzole, distilled spirits, manufactured tobacco, snuff, and cigars of all descriptions, bullion, quicksilver, lucifer or friction matches, cigar lights, and wax tapers, equal in amount to the duty or tax paid thereon, and no more, when exported, the evidence that any such duty or tax has been paid to be furnished to the satisfaction of the Commissioner of Internal Revenue by such person or persons as shall claim the allowance of drawback, and the amount to be ascertained under such regulations as shall, from time to time, be prescribed by the Commissioner of Internal Revenue, under the direction of the Secretary of the Treasury, and the same shall be paid by the warrant of the Secretary of the Treasury or the Treasurer of the United States, out of any money arising from internal duties not otherwise appropriated:

Provided, That no allowance of drawback shall be made or had for any amount claimed or due less than ten dollars, anything in this act to the contrary notwithstanding:

And provided further, That any certificate of drawback for goods exported, issued in pursuance of the provisions of law, may, under such regulations as may be prescribed by the Secretary of the Treasury, be received by the collector or his deputy in payment of duties under this act. And the Secretary of the Treasury may make such regulations with regard to the form of said certificates and the issuing thereof as, in his judgment, may be necessary.

Provided also, That no claim for drawback on any articles of merchandise exported prior to June thirtieth, eighteen hundred and sixty-four, shall be allowed unless presented to the Commissioner of Internal Revenue within three months after this amendment takes effect.

(*a*) No drawback is allowed on any domestic manufactures unless at the time of exportation there is an internal tax on such manufactures. 9 I. R. R. 194.

The regulations for the exportation of goods under this section may be found in 6 I. R. R. 106.

Drawback upon Cotton Goods.

[SEC. 6. (July 13, 1866.) *And be it further enacted,* That upon articles manufactured exclusively from cotton, when exported, there shall be allowed as a drawback an amount equal to the internal tax which shall have been assessed and paid upon such articles in their finished condition, and in addition thereto a drawback or allowance of as many cents per pound upon the pound of cotton cloth, yarn, thread, or knit fabrics, manufactured exclusively from cotton and exported, as shall have been assessed and paid in the form of an internal tax upon the raw cotton entering into the manufacture of said cloth or other article, the amount of such allowance of drawback to be ascertained in such manner as may be prescribed by the Commissioner of Internal Revenue, under the direction of the Secretary of the Treasury; and so much of section one hundred and seventy-one of the act of June thirty, eighteen hundred and sixty-four, " to provide internal revenue to support the government, to pay interest on the public debt, and for other purposes," as now provides for a drawback on manufactured cotton, is hereby repealed.]

What Drawback may be allowed upon Cotton Goods.

[SEC. 1. (July 14, 1870.) *Be it resolved by the Senate and House of Representatives of the United States of America in Congress assembled,* That the act of March thirty-first, eighteen hundred and sixty-eight, chapter forty-one, shall be held and construed not to prohibit the drawback provided for by section six of the act of July thirteenth, eighteen hundred and sixty-six, chapter one hundred and eighty-four, of as many cents per pound of cotton cloth, yarn, thread, or knit articles, manufactured exclusively from cotton and exported prior to May first, eighteen hundred and sixty-nine, as shall have been assessed and paid in the form of an internal tax upon the raw cotton entering into the manufacture of said cloth or other article: *Provided,* That such drawbacks shall be limited to exportations made not more than six months after the date of supplemental regulations issued by the Commissioner of Internal Revenue, and approved by the Secretary of the Treasury May sixteen, eighteen hundred and sixty-eight.]

When Drawback may be Allowed.

[SEC. 3. (March 31, 1868.) *And be it further enacted,* That after the first day of June next, no drawback of internal taxes paid on manufactures shall be allowed on the exportation of any article of domestic manufacture on which there is no internal tax at the time of exportation; nor shall such drawback be allowed in any case unless it shall be proved by sworn evidence in writing, to the satisfaction of the Commissioner of Internal Revenue, that the tax had been paid, and that such articles of manufacture were, prior to the first day of April, eighteen hundred and sixty-eight, actually purchased or actually manufactured and contracted for, to be delivered for such exportation; and no claim for such drawback or for any drawback of internal tax on exportations made prior to the passage of this act shall be paid unless presented to the Commissioner of Internal Revenue before the first day of October, eighteen hundred and sixty-eight.]

Designation of Collector to Superintend Exportation.

[SEC. 15. (March 3, 1865; July 13, 1866, § 20.) *And be it further enacted*, That in any port of the United States in which there is more than one collector of internal revenue, the Secretary of the Treasury may designate one of said collectors to have charge of all matters relating to the exportation of articles subject to tax under the laws to provide internal revenue; and at such ports as the Secretary of the Treasury may deem it necessary, there shall be an officer appointed by him to superintend all matters of exportation and drawback, under the direction of the collector, whose compensation therefor shall be prescribed by the Secretary of the Treasury, but shall not exceed, in any case, an annual rate of two thousand dollars, excepting at New York, where the compensation shall be an annual rate of three thousand dollars. And all the books, papers, and documents in the bureau of drawback in the respective ports, relating to the drawback of taxes paid under the internal revenue laws, shall be delivered to said collector of internal revenue; and any collector of internal revenue, or superintendent of exports and drawbacks, shall have authority to administer such oaths and certify to such papers as may be necessary under any rules and regulations that may be prescribed under the authority herein conferred.]

Penalty for fraudulently claiming Drawback.

Sec. 172. *And be it further enacted*, That if any person or persons shall fraudulently claim or seek to obtain an allowance or drawback on goods, wares, or merchandise, on which no internal duty shall have been paid, or shall fraudulently claim any greater allowance or drawback than the duty actually paid, as aforesaid, such person or persons shall forfeit triple the amount wrongfully or fraudulently claimed or sought to be obtained, or the sum of five hundred dollars, at the election of the Secretary of the Treasury, to be recovered as in other cases of forfeiture provided for in the general provisions of this act.

Repeal of prior Acts.

Sec. 173. *And be it further enacted*, That the following acts of Congress are hereby repealed, to wit: The act of July first, eighteen hundred and sixty-two, entitled "An act to provide internal revenue to support the government and to pay interest on the public debt," except the one hundred and fifteenth and one hundred and nineteenth sections thereof; and excepting, further, all provisions of said act which create the offices of Commissioner of Internal Revenue, assessor, assistant assessor, collector, deputy collector, and inspector, and provide for the appointment and qualification of said officers. Also, the act of July sixteenth, eighteen hundred and sixty-two, entitled "An act to impose an additional duty on sugars produced in the United States." Also, the act of December twenty-fifth, eighteen hundred and sixty-two, entitled, "An act to amend an act entitled 'An act to provide internal revenue to support the government and to pay interest on the public debt,' approved July first, eighteen hundred and sixty-two." Also, the act of March third, eighteen hundred and sixty-three, entitled "An act to amend an act entitled 'An act to provide internal revenue to support the government and to pay interest on the public debt,' approved July first, eighteen hundred and sixty-two, and for other purposes," excepting the provisions of said act which create the offices of deputy commissioner and cashier of internal duties and revenue agents, and provide for the appointment and qualification of said officers. Also, the twenty-fourth and twenty-fifth sections of the act of July fourteenth, eighteen hundred and sixty-two, entitled "An act increasing temporarily the duties on imports, and for other purposes." Also, the second section of the act of March third, eighteen hundred and sixty three, entitled "An act to prevent and punish frauds upon the revenue, to provide for the more certain and speedy collection of claims in favor of the United States, and for other purposes," so far as the same applies to officers of internal revenue. And, also, the act of March seventh, eighteen hundred and sixty-four, entitled "An act to increase the internal revenue, and for other purposes;" together with all acts and parts of acts inconsistent herewith:

Provided, That all the provisions of said acts shall be in force for levying and collecting all taxes, duties, and licenses properly assessed or liable to be assessed, or accruing under the provisions of former acts, or drawbacks, the right to which has already accrued or which may hereafter accrue under said acts, and for maintaining and continuing liens, fines, penalties, and forfeitures incurred under and by virtue thereof. And for carrying out and completing all proceedings (*a*) which have been already commenced or that may be commenced to enforce such fines, penalties, and forfeitures, or criminal proceedings under said acts, and for the punishment of crimes of which any party shall be or has been found guilty.

And provided further, That no office created by the said acts and continued by this act shall be vacated by reason of any provisions herein contained, but the officers heretofore appointed shall continue to hold the said offices without reappointment.

And provided further, That whenever the duty imposed by any existing law shall cease in consequence of any limitation therein contained before the respective provisions of this act shall take effect, the same duty shall be, and is hereby, continued until such provisions of this act shall take effect; and where any act is hereby repealed, no duty imposed thereby shall be held to cease, in consequence of such repeal, until the respective corresponding provisions of this act shall take effect.

And provided further, That all manufactures and productions on which a duty was imposed by either of the acts repealed by this act, which shall be in the possession of the manufacturer or producer, or of his agent or agents, on the day when this act takes effect, the duty imposed by any such former act not having been paid, shall be held and deemed to have been manufactured or produced after such date; and whenever by the terms of this act a duty is imposed upon any articles, goods, wares, or merchandise manufactured or produced, upon which no duty was imposed by either of said former acts, it shall apply to such as were manufactured or produced and not removed from the place of manufacture or production, on the day when this act takes effect.

And provided further, That no direct tax whatsoever shall be assessed or collected under this or any other act of Congress heretofore passed, until Congress shall enact another law requiring such assessment and collection to be made; but this shall not be construed to repeal or postpone the assessment or collection of the first direct tax levied, or which should be levied, under the act entitled "An act to provide increased revenue from imports, to pay interest on the public debt, and for other purposes," approved August fifth, eighteen hundred and sixty-one, nor in any way to affect the legality of said tax or any process or remedy provided in said acts, or any other acts, for the enforcement or collection of the same in any State or States and Territories and the District of Columbia; but said first tax, and any such process or remedy, shall continue in all respects in force, anything in this act to the contrary notwithstanding.

(a) The proviso of this section does not apply to a suit instituted under the 4th and 5th sections of the act March 3, 1863, to recover money paid by the plaintiff to the defendant under an illegal contract. There is no ground for the recovery at common law, and the special remedy given by the statute is repealed. Kimbro v. Colgate, 5 Blatch. 229.

Repeal of Inconsistent Acts.

[SEC. 16. (March 3, 1865.) *And be it further enacted,* That all provisions of any former act inconsistent with the provisions of this act are hereby repealed: *Provided, however,* That no duty imposed by any previous act, which has become due or of which return has been or ought to be made, shall be remitted or released by this act, but the same shall be collected and paid, and all fines and penalties heretofore incurred shall be enforced and collected, and all offences heretofore committed shall be punished, as if this act had not been passed; and the Commissioner of Internal Revenue, under the direction of the Secretary of the Treasury, is authorized to make all necessary regulations and to prescribe all necessary forms and proceedings for the collection of such taxes and the enforcement of such fines and penalties for the execution of the provisions of this act.]

Commissioner may Make Regulations.

Sec. 174. *And be it further enacted,* That the said Commissioner of Internal Revenue, under the direction of the Secretary of the Treasury, is authorized to make all such regulations, not otherwise provided for, as may become necessary by reason of the alteration of the laws in relation to internal revenue, by virtue of this act.

Sec. 175. *Expired by limitation,* April 1, 1865.

Regulations for Assessment and Collection.

Sec. 176. *And be it further enacted,* That when any tax or duty is imposed by law, and the mode or time of assessment or collection is not therein provided, the same shall be established by regulation of the Secretary of the Treasury.

Sec. 177. *Repealed* July 13, 1866, §§ 1 to 8, *inclusive.*

Foreign Consuls.

Sec. 178. *And be it further enacted,* That consuls of foreign countries in the United States, who are not citizens thereof, shall be, and hereby are, exempt from any income tax imposed by this act which may be derived from their official emoluments, or from property in such countries: *Provided,* That the governments which such consuls may represent shall extend similar exemption to consuls of the United States.

Prosecutions of Suits. Informers' Shares.

Sec. 179. (Amended July 13, 1866.) *And be it further enacted*, That, where it is not otherwise provided for, it shall be the duty of the collectors, in their respective districts, and they are hereby authorized, to prosecute for the recovery of any sum or sums that may be forfeited; and all fines, penalties, and forfeitures which may be imposed or incurred shall and may be sued for and recovered, where not otherwise provided, in the name of the United States, in any proper form of action, or by any appropriate form of proceeding, before any circuit or district court of the United States for the district within which said fine, penalty, or forfeiture may have been incurred, or before any court of competent jurisdiction.

And where not otherwise provided for, such share (*a*) as the Secretary of the Treasury shall, by general regulations, provide, not exceeding one moiety nor more than five thousand dollars in any one case, shall be to the use of the person, to be ascertained by the court which shall have imposed or decreed any such fine, penalty, or forfeiture, who shall first inform of the cause, matter, or thing whereby such fine, penalty, or forfeiture shall have been incurred; and when any sum is paid without suit, or before judgment, in lieu of fine, *penlly*, [penalty,] or forfeiture, and a share of the same is claimed by any person as informer, the Secretary of the Treasury, under general regulations to be by him prescribed, shall determine whether any claimant is entitled to such share as above limited, and to whom the same shall be paid, and shall make payment accordingly. It is hereby declared to be the true intent and meaning of the present and all previous provisions of internal revenue acts granting shares to informers that no right accrues to or is vested in any informer in any case until the fine, penalty, or forfeiture in such case is fixed by judgment or compromise and the amount or proceeds shall have been paid, when the informer shall become entitled to his legal share of the sum adjudged or agreed upon and received.

Provided, That nothing herein contained shall be construed to limit or affect the power of remitting the whole or any portion of a fine, penalty, or forfeiture conferred on the Secretary of the Treasury by existing laws. The Commissioner of Internal Revenue shall be, and is hereby, authorized and empowered to compromise, under such regulations as the Secretary of the Treasury shall prescribe, any case arising under the internal revenue laws, whether pending in court or otherwise. The several circuit and district courts of the United States shall have jurisdiction of all offences against any of the provisions of this act committed within their several districts.

Provided, That whenever in any civil action for a penalty the informer may be a witness for the prosecution, the party against whom such penalty is claimed may be and shall be admitted as a witness on his own behalf. Every person who shall receive any money or other valuable thing under a threat of informing or as a consideration for not informing against any violation of this act, shall, on conviction thereof, be punished by a fine not exceeding two thousand dollars, or by imprisonment not exceeding one year, or both, at the discretion of the court, with costs of prosecution.

(a) The following schedule of informer's shares has been prescribed:

Of the first $500	50 per cent.
Of the next 1,500	40 "
Of the next 2,000	30 "
Of the next 2,000	25 "
Of the next 2,000	20 "
Of the next 2,000	15 "
Of the next 2,000	10 "
Of all above 12,000 and not exceeding 55,000	5 "

4 I. R. R. 62.

This schedule applies to all informers' shares of fines, penalties, forfeitures and proceeds of forfeitures accruing under the provisions of internal revenue laws. 4 I. R. R 109.

The shares allotted to informers shall in all cases be subject to a proportionate deduction for costs and charges properly payable from the fine, penalty, or forfeiture, and no such share shall be paid until such deduction is made. 6 I. R. R. 74.

Internal revenue officers may claim and receive informers' shares. The information given must be of the cause, matter, or thing whereby the fine, penalty or forfeiture shall have been incurred, and, in order to be declared an informer, a person must prove that he was the first to give substantially the information required by the statute. The information given must be voluntarily given for the purpose of having it acted upon in order to recover the fine, penalty, or forfeiture, and must be so far definite and relevant that the officer or person acting upon it can, with reasonable and ordinary diligence, find the property forfeited or the person who has incurred the fine, penalty, or forfeiture, as well as evidence sufficient to obtain judgment against either the person or property; and must actually, directly, and proximately lead to the recovery of the fine, penalty, or forfeiture, and be so far material that without it the fine, penalty, or forfeiture, would not have been recovered. The information must be given to the United *States, that is to some person representing the United States for the purpose of administering the internal revenue laws. A communication from one revenue officer to another, or from any revenue officer to a United States attorney, or *vice versa*, is not first informing within the meaning of the statute. If the officer who first learns the facts makes the discovery by his own diligence and investigation, then he is the first informer. So far as the information is discovered by process of law through the examination of witnesses, neither the witnesses nor the officers making the examination can be regarded as informers. 11 I. R. R. 188.

Neither a United States attorney nor his assistant should in any case accept a retainer or fee from any person claiming to be an informer, nor should they appear for an informer in any case in which the United States are a party or are interested. 12 I. R. R. 3.

The informer's share is not given to the person who first gives information on which the property is seized, but to the person who first informs of the cause, matter, or thing whereby the forfeiture was incurred. The statute intends that the reward shall be given to the person who gives information of the cause for which the government can condemn the property. The condemnation is what the government aims at. U. S. *v.* 100 Bbls. 6 I. R. R. 179; s. c. 2 Bt. 14; U. S. *v.* Four Cutting Machines, 9 I R. R. 145; U. S. *v.* Hook et al. 15 Pitts. L. J. 361.

Any person whatsoever may share in a fine, penalty, or forfeiture, provided it be made to appear that such person first informed of the cause, matter or thing whereby such fine, penalty or forfeiture shall have been incurred. Officers of the revenue are included in the general words of the act, and are enabled to participate in the distribution of fines, penalties, and forfeitures. As there exist in the act no words of limitation as to the persons who may become informers, so also there is no limitation in regard to the method by which the information shall have been acquired. To whom the information shall be imparted the act does not say, but its fair import is that the information must be imparted to some one authorized to and who does thereupon take official action to recover the fine or penalty or to enforce the forfeiture. An officer who of his own motion and by his own diligence acquires information and imparts the same to the proper official is entitled to an informer's share. U. S. *v.* Chassell, 9 I. R. R. 175; s. c. 6 Blatch. 421; U. S. *v.* 34 Bbls. 9 I. R. R. 169; U. S. *v.* 100 Bbls. 8 I. R. R. 20.

In many cases an officer cannot be considered an informer merely because he as an officer acquires information that may be useful to the government. If this knowledges is acquired in the ordinary discharge of his duty touching the very subject-matter, or under a special retainer to investigate that matter, he cannot be considered as entitled to an informer's share. U. S. *v.* Four Cutting Machines, 9 I. R. R. 145; U. S. *v.* 100 Bbls. 8 I. R. R. 20; U. S. *v.* 34 Bbls. 9 I. R. R. 169.

The regulation issued by the Secretary of the Treasury on Sept. 2, 1867 (6 I. R. R. 74), is valid. U. S. *v.* 12 Bbls. 6 I. R. R. 203.

The informer's share is to be determined by the regulations in force at the time when the proceeds are paid into the marshal's hands, and cannot be affected by any regulations subsequently made. U. S. *v.* 8 Bbls. 10 I. R. R. 157; s. c. 1 Bt. 472; U. S. *v.* 20 Bbls. 6 I. R. R. 140; U. S. *v.* 25,000 cigars, 5 Blatch. 500; U. S. *v.* 8 Bbls. 6 I. R. R. 140.

The informer's right does not attach until the case has passed into judgment. The striking out of a judgment leaves the case as if no judgment had been entered. The informer is only entitled to the share which is allowed by the law in force at the time when the final judgment is entered. U. S *v.* 25,000 Gallons of Spirits, 7 I. R. R. 206; s. c. 1 Bt. 367; U. S. *v.* One Still, 6 I. R. R. 59, 67; s. c. 1 Bt. 367.

Although informers may be considered parties in interest, they are not parties on the record, and it cannot be said with propriety that they have a vested right in the sense in which the law considers such rights. Their interest is conditional, and a judgment of condemnation only ascertains and determines the fact on which the right is consummated should no remission take place. The right does not become fixed until the receipt of the money by the collector. The power of the Secretary of the Treasury to remit a forfeiture extends to the shares of officers and others who were informers as well as to the interest of the United States. This power is not a judicial one, but one of mercy. It admits of no appeal to any court. It is the exercise of his discretion in a matter entrusted to him alone, and from this there can be no appeal. Dorsheimer et al. *v.* U. S. 7 Wall, 166 ; s. c. 10 I. R. R. 131; s. c. 2 A. L. T. (C. R.) 74; U. S. *v.* Harris, 5 I. R. R. 21.

Where the value of the forfeited property is less than $250, the portion that accrues to the United States must be applied to the costs of prosecution, as provided in the ninety-first section of the act of 1799, and the share of the informer is not subject to a proportionate reduction for costs. U. S. *v.* One Tub, 10 I. R. R. 139.

When the sum received by the government under a compromise is less than the amount due as taxes, convincing proof will be necessary to show that the informer is entitled to any share thereof. U. S. *v.* 95 Bbls. 8 I R. R. 105.

The marshal may charge for reasonable and necessary expenses incurred in the removal of the property when such removal is proper, and for premiums actually paid to insure the property at its market value, and for the sums actually paid to a keeper to watch the same. To sustain the last item the proof must satisfactorily show that a prudent precaution in regard to all concerned in the property, justified the marshal in placing a keeper over it; that the keeper actually continued in charge of it for the time specified; and that the sum charged therefor is reasonable for the service and has actually been paid. U. S. *v.* 300 Bbls. 8 I. R. R. 105 ; s. c. 1. Bt. 72.

Debt Contracted by Sale of Goods without Payment of Tax Invalid.

Sec. 180. *And be it further enacted,* That if any person liable and required to pay any tax upon any article, goods, wares, and merchandise, or manufactures, as herein provided, shall sell, or cause or allow the same to be sold, before the tax to which such article, goods, wares, merchandise, or manufacture is legally liable is paid, with intent to avoid such tax, or in fraud of the revenue herein provided, any debt contracted in the sale of such article, goods, wares, merchandise, or manufactures, or any security given therefor, unless the same shall have been *bona fide* transferred to the hands of an innocent holder, shall be entirely void, and the collection thereof shall not be enforced in any court. And if any such article, goods, wares, merchandise, or manufacture has been paid for, in whole or in part, the sum so paid shall be deemed forfeited, and any person who will sue for the same in an action of debt shall recover of the seller the amount so paid, one-half to his own use and the other half to the use of the United States.

Sec. 181. *Expired by limitation,* June 30, 1865.

Disbursing Agents.

[SEC. 4. (March 3, 1865.) *And be it further enacted,* That so much money as may be necessary for the payment of the lawful expenses incident to carrying into effect the various acts relative to the assessment and collection of the internal revenues after the thirtieth day of June, eighteen hundred and sixty-five, until the first day of July, eighteen hundred and sixty-six, and not otherwise provided for, be, and the same is hereby, appropriated from any money in the treasury not otherwise appropriated. And it shall be the duty of such of the collectors of internal revenue as the Secretary of the Treasury may direct to act as disbursing agents to pay the aforesaid expenses without increased compensation therefor, and to give good and sufficient bonds and sureties for the faithful performance of their duties as such disbursing agents, in such sum and form as shall be prescribed by the First Comptroller of the Treasury, and approved by the Secretary.]

Meaning of Terms.

Sec. 182. *And be it further enacted,* That wherever the word State is used in this act, it shall be construed to include the Territories and the District of Columbia, where such construction is necessary to carry out the provisions of this act.

Removal of Suits.   Seized Goods Irrepleviable.

[SEC. 67. (July 13, 1866; as amended July 14, 1870, § 20.) *And be it further enacted,* That in any case, civil or criminal, at law or in equity, where suit or prosecution shall be commenced in any court (a) of any State against any officer of the United States, appointed under or acting by authority of the act entitled "An act to provide internal revenue to support the government, to pay interest on the public debt, and for other purposes," passed June thirtieth, eighteen hundred and sixty-four, or of any act in addition thereto or in amendment thereof, or against any person acting under or by authority of any such officer, on account of any act done under color of his office, or against any person holding property or estate by title derived from any such officer, concerning such property or estate, and affecting the validity of this act or acts of which it is amendatory, it shall be lawful for the defendant, in such suit or prosecution, at any time before trial, upon a petition to the circuit court of the United States in and for the district in which the defendant shall have been served with process, setting forth the nature of said suit or prosecution, and verifying the said petition by affidavit, together with a certificate, signed by an attorney or counsellor at law of some court of record of the State in which such suit shall have been commenced, or of the United States, setting forth that, as counsel for the petitioner, he has examined the proceedings against him, and carefully inquired into all the matters set forth in the petition, and that he believes the same to be true; which petition, affidavit, and certificate shall be presented to the said circuit court if in session, and if not, to the clerk thereof, at his office, and shall be filed in said office, and the cause shall thereupon be entered on the docket of said court, and shall be thereafter proceeded in as a cause originally commenced in that court; and it shall be the duty of the clerk of said court, if the suit were commenced in the court below by summons, subpœna, petition, or by any other form of action, except as hereinafter provided, to issue a writ of certiorari to the State court, requiring said court to send to the said circuit court the record and proceedings in said cause ; or if it were commenced by capias, or by any similar form of proceeding by which a personal arrest is ordered, he shall issue a writ of habeas corpus cum causa, a duplicate of which said writ shall be delivered to the clerk of the State court, or left at his office, by the marshal of the district, or his deputy, or some person duly authorized thereto; and thereupon it shall be the duty of the said State court to stay all further proceedings in such cause, and the said suit or prosecution, upon delivery of such process, or leaving the same as aforesaid, shall be deemed and taken to be moved to the said circuit court, and any further proceedings, trial, or judgment therein in the State court shall be wholly null and void.

And if the defendant in any such suit be in actual custody on mesne process therein, it shall be the duty of the marshal, by virtue of the writ of habeas corpus cum causa, to take the body of the defendant into his custody, to be dealt with in the said cause according to the rules of law and the order of the circuit court, or of any judge thereof in vacation.

All attachments made and all bail and other security given upon such suit or prosecution shall be and continue in like force and effect as if the same suit or prosecution had proceeded to final judgment and execution in the State court ; and if, upon the removal of any such suit or prosecution, it shall be made to appear to the said circuit court that no copy of the record and proceedings therein in the State court can be obtained, it shall be lawful for said circuit court to allow and require the plaintiff to proceed de novo, and to file a declaration of his cause of action, and the parties may thereupon proceed as in action originally brought in said circuit court; and on failure of so proceeding, judgment of nolle prosequi may be entered against the plaintiff, with costs for the defendant:

Provided, That an act entitled "An act further to provide for the collection of duties on imports," passed March second, eighteen hundred and thirty-three, shall not be so construed as to apply to cases arising under an act entitled "An act to provide internal revenue to support the government, to pay interest on the public debt, and for other purposes," passed June thirtieth, eighteen hundred and sixty-four, or any act in addition thereto or in amendment thereof, nor to any case in which the validity or interpretation of said act or acts shall be in issue:

Provided further, That if any officer appointed under and by virtue of any act to provide internal revenue, or any person acting under or by authority of any such officer, shall receive any injury to his person or property, for or on account of any act by him done, under any law of the United States, for the collection of taxes, he shall be entitled to maintain suit for damage therefor in the circuit court of the United States, in the district wherein the party doing the injury may reside or shall be found. And all property taken or detained by any officer or other person under authority of any revenue law of the United States shall be irrepleviable, and shall be deemed to be in the custody of the law, and subject only to the orders and decrees of the courts of the United States having jurisdiction thereof. And if any person shall dispossess or rescue, or attempt to dispossess or rescue, any property so taken or detained as aforesaid, or shall aid or assist therein, such person shall be deemed guilty of a misdemeanor, and shall be liable to such punishment as is provided by the twenty-second section of the act for the punishment of certain crimes against the United States, approved the thirtieth day of April, Anno Domino one thousand seven hundred and ninety, for the wilful obstruction or resistance of officers in the service of process.]

(a) A marshal sued for the rent of premises held by him after the expiration of the lease of a tenant whose property he had seized, cannot remove the case under the provisions of this section. Kelsey *v.* Dallon, 7 I. R. R. 86.

Suits cannot be instituted against internal revenue officers in the United States courts for acts done in their official capacity under the internal revenue laws by citizens of the same State. Ins. Company *v.* Ritchie, 5 Wall. 541; s. c. 5 I. R. R. 198; Hornthal *v.* Collector, 9 Wall. 560.

Cases arising under the internal revenue laws, if commenced in a State court, against an officer appointed or acting under those laws, or against persons acting under such an officer, may be removed on petition of the defendant into the circuit court, and the jurisdiction of the circuit court over such controversies, when all the prescribed conditions for the removal concur in the case, is clear beyond a doubt, irrespective of the citizenship of the parties. City of Philadelphia *v.* Collector, 5 Wall. 720; Stevens *v.* Mack, 6 I. R. R. 181; s. c. 5 Blatch. 514; Cutting *v.* Gilbert, 2 I. R. R. 93; s. c. 5 Blatch. 259; Clark et al. *v.* Gilbert, 4 I. R. R. 42; s. c. 5 Blatch. 330.

Officers not to be sued in United States Courts.

[SEC. 68. (July 13, 1866.) *And be it further enacted,* That the fiftieth section of an act passed June thirtieth, eighteen hundred and sixty-four, entitled "An act to provide internal revenue to support the government, to pay interest on the public debt, and for other purposes," is hereby repealed:

Provided, That any case which may have been removed from the courts of any State, under said fiftieth section, to the courts of the United States shall be remanded to the State court from which it was so removed, with all the records relating to such cases, unless the justice of the circuit court of the United States in which such suit or prosecution is pending shall be of opinion that said case would be removable from the court of the State to the circuit court under and by virtue of the sixty-seventh section of this act. And in all cases which may have been removed from any court of any State under and by virtue of said fiftieth section of said act of June thirtieth, eighteen hundred and sixty-four, all attachments made, and all bail or other security given upon such suit or prosecution, shall be and continue in full force and effect until final judgment and execution, whether such suit shall be prosecuted to final judgment in the circuit court of the United States or remanded to the State court from which it was removed.]

Since the passage of this section, and the repeal of the fiftieth section of the act of June 30, 1864, the Circuit Courts have no jurisdiction of cases arising under the Internal Revenue laws to recover back duties illegally assessed, and paid under protest, unless the plaintiff and defendant therein are citizens of different States. Such actions must be commenced in the State courts, if the parties are citizens of the same State; but the defendant may, at any time before trial, upon petition to the Circuit Court of the district in which he is served with process, remove the cause, upon due proceedings therein, into such Circuit Court, and the provision is that the cause thereafter shall be heard and determined as a cause originally commenced in that court. Assessors may perhaps be liable for an illegal assessment, in cases where they have no jurisdiction to make any assessment. Assessor *r.* Osborne, 9 Wall. 567.

Proceedings upon the issuing of a Writ of Error.

[SEC. 69. (July 13, 1866.) *And be it further enacted,* That whenever a writ of error shall be issued for the revision of any judgment or decree in any criminal proceeding where is drawn in question the construction of any statute of the United States, in a court of any State, as is provided in the twenty-fifth section of an act entitled " An act to establish the judicial courts of the United States," passed September twenty-fourth, seventeen hundred and eighty-nine, the defendant, if charged with an offence bailable by the laws of such State, shall not be released from custody until a final judgment upon such writ, or until a bond, with sufficient sureties, in a reasonable sum, as ordered and approved by the State court, shall be given ; and if the offence is not so bailable, until a final judgment upon the writ of error. Writs of error in criminal cases shall have precedence upon the docket of the Supreme Court of all cases to which the government of the United States is not a party, excepting only such cases as the court, at their discretion, may decide to be of public importance.]

Repeal of Inconsistent Acts.

[SEC. 70. (July 13, 1866.) *And be it further enacted,* That this act shall take effect, where not otherwise provided, on the first day of August, eighteen hundred and sixty-six, and all provisions of any former act inconsistent with the provisions of this act are hereby repealed :

Provided, however, That all the provisions of said acts shall be in force for collecting all taxes, duties, and licenses properly assessed or liable to be assessed, or accruing under the provisions of acts, the right to which has already accrued, or which may hereafter accrue, under said acts, and for maintaining and continuing liens, fines, penalties, and forfeitures incurred under and by virtue thereof, and for carrying out and completing all proceedings which have been already commenced, or that may be commenced, to enforce such fines, penalties, and forfeitures, or criminal proceedings under said acts, and for the punishment of crimes of which any party shall be or has been found guilty :

And provided further, That whenever the duty imposed by any existing law shall cease in consequence of any limitation therein contained before the respective provisions of this act shall take effect, the same duty shall be, and is hereby, continued until such provisions of this act shall take effect; and where any act is hereby repealed, no duty imposed thereby shall be held to cease, in consequence of such repeal, until the respective corresponding provisions of this act shall take effect :

And provided further, That all manufactures and productions on which a duty was imposed by either of the acts repealed by this act, which shall be in the possession of the manufacturer or producer, or of his agent or agents, on the day when this act takes effect, the duty imposed by any such former act not having been paid, shall be held and deemed to have been manufactured or produced after such date; and whenever, by the terms of this act, a duty is imposed upon any articles, goods, wares, or merchandise, manufactured or produced, upon which no duty was imposed by either of said former acts, it shall apply to such as were manufactured or produced, and not removed from the place of manufacture or production, on the day when this act takes effect. And the Commissioner of Internal Revenue, under the direction of the Secretary of the Treasury, is authorized to make all necessary regulations and prescribe all necessary forms and proceedings for the collection of such taxes and the enforcement of such fines and penalties for the execution of the provisions of this act.]

Rewards for Detection and Punishment of Offenders.

[SEC. 7. (March 2, 1867.) *And be it further enacted*, That the Commissioner of Internal Revenue, with the approval of the Secretary of the Treasury, is hereby authorized to pay such sums, not exceeding in the aggregate the amount appropriated therefor, as may in his judgment be deemed necessary for detecting and bringing to trial and punishment persons guilty of violating the internal revenue laws, or conniving at the same, in cases where such expenses are not otherwise provided for by law. And for this purpose there is hereby appropriated one hundred thousand dollars, or so much thereof as may be necessary, out of any money in the treasury not otherwise appropriated.]

Penalty for Dealing in Fraudulent Wrappers, etc.

[SEC. 16. (July 13, 1866.) *And be it further enacted*, That in case any person shall sell, give, or purchase or receive any box, barrel, bag, or any vessel, package, wrapper, cover, or envelope of any kind, stamped, branded, or marked in any way so as to show that the contents or intended contents thereof have been duly inspected, or that the tax thereon has been paid, or that any provision of the internal revenue laws has been complied with, whether such stamping, branding, or marking may have been a duly authorized act or may be false and counterfeit, or otherwise without authority of law, said box, barrel, bag, vessel, package, wrapper, cover, or envelope being empty, or containing any thing else than the contents which were therein when said articles had been so lawfully stamped, branded, or marked by an officer of the revenue, such person shall be liable to a penalty of not less than fifty nor more than five hundred dollars.

And any person who shall make, manufacture, or produce any box, barrel, bag, vessel, package, wrapper, cover, or envelope, stamped, branded, or marked, as above described, or shall stamp, brand, or mark the same, as hereinbefore recited, shall, upon conviction thereof, be liable to penalty as before provided in this section. And any person who shall violate the foregoing provisions of this section, with intent to defraud the revenue, or to defraud any person, shall, upon conviction thereof, be liable to a fine of not less than one thousand nor more than five thousand dollars, or imprisonment for not less than six months nor more than five years, or both such fine and imprisonment, at the discretion of the court. And all articles sold, given, purchased, received, made, manufactured, produced, branded, stamped, or marked in violation of the provisions of this section, and all their contents shall be forfeited to the United States.]

Sales upon Distraint or Forfeiture.

[SEC. 17. (July 13, 1866.) *And be it further enacted,* That where any whiskey, oil, tobacco, or other articles of manufacture or produce requiring brands, stamps, or marks of whatever kind to be placed thereon, shall be sold upon distraint, forfeiture, or other process provided by law, the same not having been branded, stamped, or marked as required by law, the officer selling the same shall, upon sale thereof, fix or cause to be fixed the brands, stamps, or marks so required, and deduct the expense thereof from the proceeds of such sale.]

Repeal of Inconsistent Acts.

[SEC. 34. (March 2, 1867.) *And be it further enacted,* That all acts or parts of acts inconsistent with this act, and all acts and parts of acts imposing any tax upon advertisements, or the gross receipts of toll roads, are hereby repealed: *Provided,* That this act shall not be construed to affect any act done, right accrued, or penalty incurred under former acts, but every such right is hereby saved; and all suits and prosecutions for acts already done in violation of any former act or acts of Congress relating to the subjects embraced in this act may be commenced or proceeded with in like manner as if this act had not been passed; and all penal clauses and provisions in the existing laws, relating to the subjects embraced in this act, shall be deemed applicable thereto.]

TAXES REPEALED.

Repeal of Special Taxes.

[SEC. 1. (July 14, 1870.) *Be it enacted by the Senate and House of Representatives of the United States of America in Congress assembled*, That on and after the first day of May, eigteen hundred and seventy-one, the special taxes imposed by the seventy-ninth section of the act entitled "An act to provide internal revenue to support the government, to pay interest on the public debt, and for other purposes," approved June thirty, eighteen hundred and sixty-four, as amended by section nine of the internal revenue act approved July thirteen, eighteen hundred and sixty-six, and as amended by section two of the internal revenue act approved March two, eighteen hundred and sixty-seven, be, and the same are hereby, repealed; but this act shall not be held to repeal or in any way affect the special tax on brewers imposed by said section, or the special taxes imposed by the act approved July twenty, eighteen hundred and sixty-eight, entitled "An act imposing taxes on distilled spirits and tobacco, and for other purposes," or the acts amendatory thereof.]

Repeal of Tax on Sales.

[SEC. 2. (July 14, 1870.) *And be it further enacted*, That on and after the first day of October, eighteen hundred and seventy, the several taxes on sales imposed by the internal revenue laws now in force, saving and excepting such taxes on sales as are by existing law paid by stamps, and the taxes on sales of leaf tobacco, manufactured tobacco, snuff, cigars, foreign and domestic distilled spirits, and wines, imposed by said act, approved July twenty, eighteen hundred and sixty-eight, and acts amendatory thereof, be, and the same are hereby, repealed.]

Repeal of Various Taxes.

[SEC. 3. (July 14, 1870.) *And be it further enacted*, That on and after the first day of October, eighteen hundred and seventy, the taxes imposed by the internal revenue laws, now in force, herein specified, be, and the same are hereby, repealed, namely: on articles in Schedule A; the special tax on boats, barges, and flats; on legacies and successions; on passports; and on gross receipts.]

Repeal of Stamp Duty.

[SEC. 4. (July 14, 1870.) *And be it further enacted,* That on and after the first day of October, eighteen hundred and seventy, the stamp tax imposed in Schedule B, on promissory notes for a less sum than one hundred dollars, and on receipts for any sum of money, or for the payment of any debt, and the stamp tax imposed in Schedule C, on canned and preserved fish, be, and the same are hereby, repealed. And no stamp shall be required upon the transfer or assignment of a mortgage, where it or the instrument it secures has been once duly stamped. And the proprietor or proprietors of articles named in said Schedule C, who shall furnish his or their own die or design for stamps to be used especially for his or their own proprietary articles, shall be allowed the following commissions, namely: On amounts purchased at one time of not less than fifty dollars nor more than five hundred dollars, five per centum; and on amounts over five hundred dollars, ten per centum on the whole amount purchased: *Provided,* That lucifer or friction matches, and cigar lights, and wax tapers, may be removed from the place of manufacture for export to a foreign country without payment of tax, or affixing stamps thereto, under such rules and regulations as the Commissioner of Internal Revenue may prescribe; and all provisions of existing laws inconsistent herewith are hereby repealed.]

Repeal of Tax on Barges, &c.

[SEC. 25. (July 14, 1870.) *And be it further enacted,* That section fifteen of the act approved July fourteen, eighteen hundred and sixty-two, entitled "An act increasing, temporarily, the duties on imports, and for other purposes," and section four of the act in amendment thereof, approved March three, eighteen hundred and sixty-five, be, and the same are hereby, so amended that no ship, vessel, steamer, boat, barge, or flat belonging to any citizen of the United States, trading from one port or point within the United States, to another port or point within the United States, or employed in the bank, whale, or other fisheries, shall hereafter be subject to the tonnage tax or duty provided for in said acts; and the proviso in section one hundred and three of the "Act to provide internal revenue to support the Government and to pay the interest on the public debt, and for other purposes," approved June thirty, eighteen hundred and sixty-four, requiring an annual special tax to be paid by boats, barges, and flats, is hereby repealed.]

Repeal of Legacy and Succession Taxes.

[SEC. 27. (July 14, 1870.) *And be it further enacted,* That all provisions of existing laws whereby any tax or duty is laid upon bequests or devises, or transfers by deed, grant, or gift, made or intended to take effect after the death of the grantor, or any real or personal property, in trust or otherwise, for public uses of a literary, educational, or charitable character, or upon any real or personal estate which may become subject to any trust as aforesaid under any past or future disposition, which, if made in favor of an individual, would confer on him a succession, be, and the same are hereby, repealed, and no taxes heretofore levied thereunder, but not paid, shall be collected.]

Section 17 does not, however, apply to the taxes mentioned in section 27 of the act of July 14, 1870, which absolutely repeals all provisions of existing laws for the assessment and collection of legacy and succession taxes, whether accrued or not, upon bequests, devises, gifts, &c., for public uses of a literary, educational or charitable character, and provides that taxes levied thereon before the passage of said act, but unpaid, shall not be collected. The attention of assessors is hereby called to the fact that legacy and succession taxes accrue upon property passing by reason of the death of a person dying since June 30, 1864, and that they accrue at the time of such death without regard to the time when they become due and payable. A person dies September 30, 1870, leaving real and personal property, which, however, the successors, legatees, or distributees, do not come into posssession of until October 1. The tax is, nevertheless, to be assessed except in cases falling under section 27 of the act of July 14, 1870, and should be paid at the time it becomes due, under the provisions of sections 125 and 127 of the act of June 30, 1864, as amended. (Compilation of 1867, pp. 109 and 113.)

Assessors are hereby instructed to give their special attention to the assessment of this class of taxes, and of all other taxes accruing under the provisions of law repealed by the act of July 14, 1870. 12 I. R. R. 93, 102.

Provision Dealers.

[SEC. 1. (July 14, 1870.) *Be it enacted by the Senate and House of Representatives of the United States of America in Congress assembled,* That there shall not be assessed or collected, under or by virtue of section four of an act approved March thirty-one, eighteen hundred and sixty-eight, entitled "An act to exempt certain manufacturers from internal tax, and for other purposes," any internal tax upon pork-packers, lard-renderers, or those engaged in smoking hams, curing meats, or others known as in the provision trade, as manufacturers within the meaning of the said section; and if any such tax shall have been assessed, but not collected, the same is hereby remitted.]

ADDENDA.

OFFICE OF INTERNAL REVENUE, WASHINGTON,
September 7, 1870.

W. RAYMOND LEE, ESQ., *Assessor of Third District, Boston, Mass.*

SIR: Your letter of the 1st instant, respecting the assessment and collection of the tax imposed upon dividends by section 15 of the act of July 14, 1870, was received on the 5th. It is enacted in said section " that there shall be levied and collected, *for and during* the year 1871, a tax of two and one-half per centum on the amount of all interest or coupons paid on bonds or other evidence of debt issued and payable in one or more years after date, by any of the corporations in this section hereinafter enumerated, and on the amount of all dividends of earnings, income, or gains *hereafter declared* by any bank, trust company, savings institution, insurance company, railroad company, canal company, turnpike company, canal navigation company, and slack water company, whenever and wherever the same shall be payable, and to whatsoever person the same may be due, including non-residents, whether citizens or aliens, and on all undivided profits of any such corporation which have accrued and been added to any surplus, contingent, or other fund; and every such corporation, having paid the tax as aforesaid, is hereby authorized to deduct and withhold from any payment on account of interest, coupons, and dividends, an amount equal to the tax of two and one-half per centum on the same."

You will notice that by the terms of the section, the tax upon the *interest and coupons* paid upon bonds or other evidences of debt issued by the companies, corporations, &c., therein enumerated, is to be levied "*for and during* the year 1871 ;" that the tax upon the *dividends of earnings* of said companies, &c., is also to be levied and collected *during* the year 1871, but it is to be levied upon all dividends *declared after the passage of the act.*

It is, therefore, ruled that no tax is to be withheld from interest or coupons which fall due during the last five months of the present calendar year, but that they are to be returned, like interest from other sources, in the next annual income returns of the parties receiving them.

It is also held that although a tax of two and one-half per centum is imposed upon dividends declared by said companies, corporations, &c., on and after August 1, 1870, it is to be " levied and collected . . *during* the year 1871." It is not necessary to decide at present at what time in 1871 the taxes upon those dividends of the last five months of 1870 are to be levied. Further legislation may perhaps be required upon that point.

12 I. R. R. 93.

OFFICE OF INTERNAL REVENUE, WASHINGTON,
September 15, 1870.

W. H. THOMPSON, ESQ., *Assessor Eleventh District, Easton, Penn.*

SIR: Referring to the letter addressed to you on the 15th ultimo, respecting the tax on sales, and published in *The Internal Revenue Record,* vol. xii., page 70, I have to say that I have carefully re examined that part of it which relates to the tax on the sales of wholesale dealers, and am of the opinion that it is not in accordance with the intent of Congress. It is, therefore, now held that such sales are included among those exempted by section 2 of the act of July 14, 1870, and that no tax is to be assessed upon those made on and after October 1, 1870. Sales of leaf tobacco, manufactured tobacco, snuff, cigars, foreign and domestic distilled spirits and wines, will continue to be liable after that date.

J. W. DOUGLASS, *Acting Commissioner.*

12 I. R. R. 93.

The proprietor's name and his trade-mark have been allowed to be printed or marked on wooden packages of manufactured tobacco, put up and prepared by the manufacturer for sale, or removal for sale or consumption, and the proprietor's name has also been allowed on the printed label or caution-notice. The use, however, of the proprietor's name on packages and on labels is limited to those cases where the person claiming to be the proprietor is the owner of the factory, or has a legal right or title to the particular brand of goods manufactured, or where the tobacco, or snuff, or cigars are made expressly for the person claiming such proprietorship. Goods manufactured for general sale to any customer who will purchase them are not entitled to have the purchaser's name appear on them as proprietor. 12 I. R. R. 101.

Dealers cannot sell small quantities of cavendish or plug tobacco, and, after having received pay for the same, cut it up with a hand cutting machine without paying the tax of thirty-two cents per pound. The manufacturer can sell in original stamped packages only. A retail dealer is allowed to break wooden packages and retail therefrom; but he is not allowed to change the character or condition of the article by any process of manipulation, by cutting, pressing, grinding, crushing, rubbing, or otherwise preparing it, either before or after sale. 12 I. R. R. 101.

No other openings are necessary in a vessel for fermented liquor except the bung, the air vent, and the spigot-hole or tap. If other openings exist in the vessel, they are to be regarded as additional spigot-holes, and are disallowed. Where such surplus opening exists in the cask, it is not sufficient that the same shall be closed or plugged, but the portion of the cask containing it must be removed and replaced with a piece having no opening. 12 I. R. R. 102.

Parties desiring to produce spirits from pine-apples and bananas must comply with the regulations relating to distilled spirits, and are not entitled to the exemptions allowed to distillers of brandy from apples, peaches, or grapes. 12 I. R. R. 69.

A distiller's bond is not void because it does not follow the words of the section, but in lieu thereof employs general language having no greater actual meaning. When the bond prescribed by the act is conditioned in detail for the performance of all the duties imposed by the statute, the failure to enumerate all those duties in detail does not invalidate the bond. In such case the words "conformity to all the provisions of the act," are, in meaning and legal effect, the same as doing and performing the several things in detail enumerated. Grouping the various duties in one word, and describing them as "conformity to all the provisions of the act," is exactly equivalent to an enumeration of each in detail. The bond, moreover, is not invalid, even if the distiller might have claimed a license upon tender of a bond less comprehensive in its scope. The parts not required by the statute may be treated as surplusage. If the terms are so comprehensive as to embrace a duty which if separately specified would have been rejected therefrom as an excess of surplusage, the court will regard such requirement embodied in the general words used as not in point of law included, and hold that a breach which is clearly one that would be included in the terms of the bond described by the statute is covered by the conditions. U. S. *v.* Mynderse, 12 I. R. R. 94, 104.

INDEX.

ABATEMENT OF TAXES, 73.
    power of Commissioner to, 89, 91.
    form of application, 90, 91.
    erroneously or illegally assessed, 73.
    of uncollectible taxes, 73.
    of tax charged on more than one list, 73.
    tax changed in amount, 73.
    affidavits to application for, 90.
    when collectors may take credit for, 90.
    on account of insolvency or absconding, 71.
    does not release liability, 90.
    when tax is paid pending application, 90.
    claim for, on account of insolvency, &c., 72.
    not after six months, 72.
    to be put in schedules, 72.
    schedules of taxes abated to be filed, 90.
ACCEPTORS of Foreign Bills to stamp them, 324.
ACKNOWLEDGMENTS exempt from stamp duty, 324, 355.
ACCOUNTS, monthly, of Commissioner, 19.
    of assessors, 44.
        what shall contain, 44, 45.
        accompanied by vouchers, 46.
        final, 47.
        yearly, 53.
    assistant assessors, 47.
        what shall contain, 45, 47.
        to be rendered monthly, 47.
        form of, 48.
        referred to Commissioner, 48, 49.
    disbursing officers, 106.
        receipts and payments, 106.
        account current, 54.
            when transmitted, 55.
            what contain, 55.
            no appeal from decision on, 56.
    collectors, 50.
        form of revenue account, 50.
        compensation and expense account, 51.
        yearly, 53.
        bonded account, 259.
        of beer stamps, 118.
        distilled spirits stamps, 182, 183.
        tobacco stamps, 228.
        documentary stamps, 324, 326.
        gauger's fee, 207.

ACCOUNTS— *Continued.*
    storekeeper's fees and expenses, 205, 20 6.
    storekeepers, kept by, 201.
        furnished by, 202, 203.
        transactions in distillery, 164.
    supervisors, 199.
    detectives, 199.
    surveyors, 199.
    brewers, to be kept by, 115.
    distillers, to be kept by, 158.
    rectifiers, 194.
    wholesale liquor dealer, 194.
    compounder of liquors, 194.
    dealers in tobacco, 242.
    manufacturers of tobacco, 224.
        cigars, 248.
    separate, kept at treasury, 89.
ACTS, inconsistent repeal of, 261.
    construction of, July 20, 1868, 263.
    extended beyond collection districts, 263.
    meaning of terms in, 261.
    March 2d, 1833, not to apply, 373.
    Aug. 6th, 1846, adopted, 106.
    March 3d, 1797, adopted, 108.
AFFIDAVITS, exempt, 354, 355.
    jurat containing certificate stamped, 343,
    who may take under revenue law, 109.
    assessor's chief clerk, 44, 47.
    on claims for abatement, 72.
    on claims for refunding, 90.
AGENTS, revenue, 22.
    no more appointed, 200.
    knowledge of, is principal's, 100.
    may stamp documents, 312.
AGREEMENT, stamp duty on, 335,
    when in duplicate, 335, 337.
    assignment of, 337.
    insurance permit is, 337.
    waiver of protest is, 336, 337.
    what assignments are, 337.
ALCOHOL. *See* DISTILLED SPIRITS.
ALE. *See* FERMENTED LIQUORS.
ALIENS, when liable to income tax, 283, 284.
    liable to tax on dividends, 302.
APOTHECARIES may use still for pharmaceutical purposes, 214.
APPEALS to assessors, 40.
    when not allowed, 41.
    to commissioner, 89.
        how made, 90.
        no suit until made, 91.
        suit may be brought after, 92.
    none from judge in attachment, 34.
    in criminal cases, 374.
    motion for a new trial, 79.
        in arrest of judgment, 79.
APPRAISEMENT of value or damage, 335, 337.
ASSESSMENT districts, 24.

ASSESSMENT—*Continued.*
    districts, 24.
        assistant assessors, residents of, 24.
        how made, 28.
    when parties fail to make returns, 29.
    additional within fifteen months, 42.
    monthly, on capacity of distillery, 152.
    in case of deficiency in distiller's returns, 161.
    none where returns are correct, 162.
    mode of ascertaining deficiency, 162.
    on imitation wines, 197.
    on dealers in tobacco, 219, 221.
ASSESSORS, appointment of, 24.
    to divide districts into assessment districts, 24.
    by whom succeeded in case of vacancy, 24.
    salary of, 43.
    commissions of, 44.
    not to exceed $4,000, 44.
    certain expenses paid, 44.
    Secretary of Treasury may fix compensation, 45.
    in certain states and territories, 45.
    liability for erroneous approval of accounts, 48.
    assistant assessor's accounts, 48.
    apportionment of commission, 56.
    no payment to, without certificate of Commissioner, 56.
    communications of, franked, 110,
    penalty against, for fraud or extortion, 43.
        for taking money to appoint assistant assessors, 47.
    when to commence assessment, 28.
    to reduce returns to legal tender currency, 35.
    may issue summons, 29.
    appeal to, 40.
    to furnish lists to collectors, 41.
    may make additional lists within 15 months, 42.
    to list property owned by non-residents, 87.
    may administer oaths, 109.
    may enter distillery, &c., 76, 185.
    to approve distiller's bonds, 137.
    when not to approve distiller's bonds, 137, 156.
    to keep plan of distillery, 143.
    to make surveys of distilleries, 144.
    when not to assess special tax, 150.
    to assess distiller's capacity tax, 152.
    to examine distiller's returns, 161.
    to have charge of locks and seals, 166.
    to report suspension of work in distillery, 166.
    commissions on stamps for distilled spirits, 182.
    to reduce capacity of distillery, 184.
    suspended for fraud, 200.
    not to discharge duties of other assessor, 200.
    to register tobacco manufactories, 226.
    to keep abstract of tobacco manufacturer's returns, 227.
    may examine persons, books, &c., 30.
ASSISTANT ASSESSORS, appointment of, 24, 25.
    reduction of number, 25.
    Commissioner may assign to special duty, 25.
    to make assessments, 28.
    duty when parties fail to make out lists, 29.

ASSISTANT ASSESSORS—*Continued.*
    make lists of property of non-residents, 37.
    to classify lists, 38.
    salary of, 44.
    settlement of accounts of, 47.
    penalty for fraud and extortion, 43.
    may enter distillery, &c., 76, 185.
    may administer oaths, 109.
    to preserve distiller's notice, 134.
    to close distillery on suspension, 166.
    to keep record of tobacco manufactories, &c., 226.
    to examine tobacco dealer's stock, 244.
    to keep record of cigar manufactories, 248.
              maker, 220.
    to examine stock of cigar manufacturers, 253.
ASSIGNMENT, stamp duty on, of agreement, &c., 337.
              for benefit of creditors, 337.
              of land warrants, 337.
              of judgment, 338.
              of policy of insurance, 350.
              of lease, 350.
ATTACHMENT for refusal to obey assessor's summons, 30.
        proceedings in, 34.
        for refusal to obey supervisor's summons, 34, 199.
        no appeal from decision in, 34.
AUCTIONEERS liable as dealers in liquor, 218.
              dealers in tobacco, 243.

BANKS, tax on circulation, 279.
    average deposits, 279.
    capital, 279.
    savings, 280.
    state, 282.
    to make return, 279.
    lien in case of non-payment by, 59.
    to exhibit books, 60.
    or bankers doing business as brokers, 279.
BRANDS on vessels for fermented liquors, 122.
            distilled spirits, on entry into warehouse, 167.
                  on withdrawal from warehouse, 175.
                  rectified spirits, 175.
                  by wholesale dealers, &c., 176.
                  upon change of package, 196.
    on casks of distilled spirits to be effaced, 191.
BRANDY, distillers of, from apples, &c., 125.
          from what exempted, 128.
          form of notice, 137.
          bond of, 139.
          capacity of distillery of, 149.
          books of, 160.
          computation of actual product of, 164.
          placing of, by, into casks, 171.
          stamping by, 179.
          special tax on, 215.
BEER. *See* FERMENTED LIQUOR.
BREWERS, special tax of, 268.
    to give notice, 112.

BREWERS—*Continued.*
    bonds of, 113.
    books kept by, 114.
    verification of accounts of, 116.
    penalty for evasion of tax, 117, 119.
    removal of beer without stamps, 120.
    not to bottle liquors, 123.
    when liable to wholesale dealer's tax, 217.
    forfeiture for non-payment of tax, 123.
BRIBERY, penalty for, 60.
BILLS OF EXCHANGE, stamp duty on, 338, 340.
    drawn out of and payable in U. S., 324.
BILL OF LADING, stamp duty on, 341.
    from British North American ports, 341, 354, 355.
BILL OF SALE, of vessel, stamp duty on, 341.
    of other personal property, 341.
BONDS of Commissioner, 18.
    of collector, 25.
        as disbursing agent, 370.
    of deputy collector, 26.
    for property under seizure, 94, 102.
    for property worth less than $300, 103.
    of brewers, 112.
    of distillers, 137.
        approval of, 140.
    no distilling until given, 150.
    no withdrawal of distilled spirits on, 174.
    for seized distilleries, 191.
    of storekeepers, 201.
    of gaugers, 206.
    for exportation of spirits, 209.
    manufacturers of tobacco, 224.
    inspectors, 111.
    penalty for fraudulent, 258.
    sureties not liable after expiration of license, 226.
    stamp duty on, 341, 342.
    distillery warehouse, 168.
    when copies shall be evidence, 109.
    of state officers not liable to stamp duty, 309.
    of manufacturers of cigars, 246.
        manufacturers of matches, etc., for stamps, 325.
        officers selling documentary and other stamps, 338.
BROKERS, tax on sales of, 277.
BOOKS, kept by brewers, 114.
        distillers, 158.
        storekeepers, 164.
        rectifiers, wholesale dealers, &c., 194.
        warehouse by storekeeper, 201.
        tobacco manufacturers, 227.
        cigar manufacturers, 248.
    assessor may demand production of, 29.
    supervisors may demand production of, 199.
    kept by dealers in tobacco, 242.

CANCELLATION of beer stamps, 119.
        stamps for distilled spirits, 176, 179.
            tobacco, &c, 229.

CANCELLATION—*Continued.*
        of stamps for cigars, 250.
        documentary stamps, 311.
        proprietary stamps, 311.
CAPACITY, producing, of distillery, how determined, 144.
    tax on, 152.
    tax on production according to, 161.
    reduction of, 184.
CHAMPAGNE. *See* WINES.
CHARTER PARTY, stamp duty on, 344
CERTIFICATES of stock, stamp duty on, 342.
        profits, stamp duty on, 342.
        damage, stamp duty on, 343.
        deposits, stamp duty on, 343.
        other description, stamp duty on, 343.
        magistrate's record on appeal, stamp duty on, 343.
        marriage, stamp duty on, 343.
        clerk to instruments, 344.
        copies of instruments, 343.
        measurement or weight of animals, &c, 324, 355.
        record of deed, 324, 355.
        caption of deposition, 343.
        loan, 339.
CHECKS, stamp duty on, 338.
CRIMES. *See* PENALTIES.
CIGARS, tax on, 246.
    labels for, 232, 250.
    tax on imported, 253.
    inspection of, 246.
    how packed, 248.
    penalty for illegally packing, 248.
    how labels on, are affixed, 250.
    when forfeited, 251.
    manufactured on commission, 252.
    manufactories of, to be numbered, 248.
    makers of, to be registered, 220.
    manufacturers of, to pay special tax, 220.
CISTERNS, receiving, 154.
    construction of, 154.
    capacity of, 155.
    to be under lock, 154.
    withdrawal of spirits from, 154, 167.
COLLECTION DISTRICTS, creation of, 23.
    President may alter, 23.
    reduction of number, 24, 205.
    tax on articles outside of, 263.
COLLECTORS, appointment of, 24.
    reduction of number of, 24, 205.
    to give bond, 25.
    pay over money daily, 19.
    regulations for transmittal of money, 20.
    appointment of deputy, 26.
    to take bond from deputy, 26.
    lists to be furnished to, 41.
    salary of, 50.
    expenses of, 50.
    account of, 50.

INDEX. 389

COLLECTORS—*Continued.*
    disbursing agent, 54, 370.
    apportionment of commissions, 56.
    to receipt for lists, 57.
    advertise time to pay taxes, 57.
    to collect by distraint, 58.
    suit against, to recover taxes, 61.
    fees of, in distraint, 62.
    sale under distraint, 65.
    sale of real estate, 66.
    collect from property of non-residents, 69.
    transmit lists to other collectors, 70.
    report collections, 70.
    charged with taxes, 71.
    account for taxes, 72.
    claims for deduction on taxes, 72, 73.
    transfer U. S. property to successor, 74.
    delinquent proceedings against, 74.
    penalty for extortion, 75.
    may enter buildings, 76, 185.
    suspension of, 200.
    penalty for compounding offences, 77.
    devolve duties on deputy, 81.
    to prosecute suits, 82.
    regulations in regard to suits, 83, 87.
    docket of seizures, 87.
    bill of sale, evidence, 92.
    when collect direct tax, 93.
    seizures of property for fraud, 93.
    sale of perishable property, under seizure, 94.
    receipt to warehouse men, &c, on seizure, 95.
    to return property on verdict for claimant, 101.
    proceedings on seizures less than $300, 103.
    penalty for embezzlement, 106.
    suits for money withheld by, 108.
    administer oaths, 109.
    franking privilege, 110.
    not interested in distilleries, &c, 110.
    case of death, who may act, 81.
    to sell beer stamps, 118.
    permit removal of fermented liquors, 120.
    collect tax of distillers monthly, 152.
    to have charge of locks and keys of distillery, 165.
    to retain entries of spirits into warehouse, 169.
    permit withdrawal of spirits from warehouse, 172.
    account for stamps for distilled spirits, 182.
        documentary stamps, 325, 333.
    not to discharge duties of other collectors, 200.
    designate storekeeper temporarily, 202.
    collect storekeeper's salary, &c., 205.
    superintend gauging, 206.
    to collect gaugers' fees, 206.
    to sell tobacco stamps, 228.
    permit withdrawal of tobacco for export, 236.
    designate bonded warehouse for imported tobacco, 244.
    monthly account of articles in bond, 259.
    superintend exportation, 362.

COLLECTORS—*Continued.*
    disbursing agents, 370.
    pay expenses for assessments and collections, 370.
COLLECTOR, DEPUTY, appointment of, 26.
    bonds, 26.
    duties of, 27.
    penalty for extortion, 75.
    may enter buildings, 76, 185.
    penalty for obstructing. 76.
        compounding offences, 77.
    act as collector during temporary disability, 81.
        in case of vacancy, 81.
    salary of, when acting as collector, 82.
    may administer oaths, 109.
    bond of, available to representatives of collector, 82.
    compensation of, 26.
COMMISSIONER OF INTERNAL REVENUE superintends collection of taxes, 17.
    organization of office, 18.
    keep accounts, 18.
    give bond, 19.
    to have charge of real estate, 69.
    what claims for deduction presented to, 73.
    prescribed regulations for suits, 83.
    appeals to, for refunding, &c., 89.
    exempt distillers of brandy from regulations, 125.
    prescribe meters, 129.
    prescribe rules for inspection of spirits, &c., 124.
    make changes in distilling apparatus, 129.
    prescribe form of distiller's bond, 137.
    require new distiller's bond, 137.
    revise report of survey of distilleries, 144.
    prescribe mode of constructing room for cisterns, 154.
    provide locks and seals for distilleries, 155.
    approve distillery warehouse, 153.
    prescribe rules for entry of distilled spirits into warehouse, 168.
        brands on casks for distilled spirits, 167.
        mode of cancelling stamps for distilled spirits, 176.
            tobacco, &c., 67, 259.
        books for wholesale dealers, &c., 194.
        form and amount of storekeeper's bonds, 201.
    appoint detectives, 200.
    prescribe fees for gaugers, 206.
        regulations for return of sales of tobacco, &c., 221.
        yearly inventory of tobacco, 227.
        books of account for manufacturers of tobacco, 227.
    prepare stamps for tobacco, 228.
    establish tobacco bonded warehouse, 236.
    prescribe form of yearly inventory of cigars, 248.
        stamps for cigars, 250.
    change forms of stamps, labels, &c., 259.
    authorize compromise, 259.
    prescribe regulations for collection of tax, 261.
    authorize suit in equity to enforce tax, 262.
    give rewards for detection of frauds, 375.
    claims for drawback presented to, 360, 361.

COMPOUNDER OF LIQUORS, special tax of, 214.
 procure and keep sign, 157.
COMPROMISES, how made, 259.
 of penalties, 366.
COMMISSIONS of assessors, 44.
     collectors, 50.
 mode of computing, 52.
 apportionment of, 56.
 none on payments before sale in distraint, 62.
 to be reported to Commissioner, 110.
 on stamps for fermented liquors, 117.
    distilled spirits, 182.
 on documentary and other stamps, 325.
 to parties who furnish their own dies, 325.
CONSPIRACY, penalty for, 77.
 what is, 78.
 what constitutes, 80.
CONSTITUTIONAL LAW, assessor's power to summon, constitutional, 32, 33.
 income tax is constitutional, 284.
 Congress cannot tax judicial process of State courts, 306.
 cannot tax judge's salary, 287.
 Congress cannot make contracts invalid, 327.
    declare what shall be evidence in State courts, 327.
    tax deed for taxes, 309.
     bond of county officer, 309.
 power of assessors to appoint assistants, unconstitutional, 24.
CONTRACTS, broker's note, stamp on, 277, 344.
 not invalidated by non-payment of special tax, 264.
CONVEYANCE, stamp on, 344.
 what required, 345.
 only of realty sold, 345.
 how consideration computed, 345, 346.
 between tenants in common, 346.
 subject to mortgage, 346.
 from husband to wife through third person, 345.
 for unpaid taxes, 309.
 under judicial decree, 346.
 special covenants contained in, 347.
 duplicates, 337.
 of register in bankruptcy, 347.
 of assignee in bankruptcy, 347.
 of pew, 347.
COUNSEL, when collector may employ, 83.
   commissioner may employ, 83.

DEALERS in distilled spirits, special tax on, 215.
   tobacco, special tax on, 219.
   distilled spirits to keep books, 194.
    signs of, 157.
   tobacco to render statements of business, 221.
    to keep accounts, 242.
DEBTS to be void, 369.
DETECTIVES, appointment of, 200.
 accounts of, 199.
DRAWBACK on alcohol and rum, 208.
 on articles that have paid tax, 360.

DISTILLED SPIRITS, definition of, 133.
 proof defined, 124.
 tax on, 124.
 drawn off every third day, 154.
 removed to distillery warehouse, 154.
 account of amount manufactured, 158.
 to be kept, 158.
 manner of drawing from cisterns, 157.
 entry in warehouse, 168.
 withdrawn from warehouse on payment of tax, 172.
 branding, on withdrawal, 175.
 penalty for fraudulent removal of, 187.
 when seized, burden of proof on claimant, 187.
 purchase of more than 20 gals., 196.
 reinspection on change of package, 196.
 drawback on exportation of, 208.
 regulations for exportation of, 209.
 not to withdraw from warehouse until payment of tax, 174.
 stock on hand to be stamped, 211.
 forfeited to be sold subject to tax, 213.
 to be removed by day, 189.
DISTILLATION OF SPIRITS, definition of, 133.
 when prohibited, 150, 151.
 account of, to be kept by storekeeper, 164.
 suspension of, 165.
 officers may examine progress of, 185.
 prohibited on Sunday, 187.
 computation of amount of, 161.
 penalty for illicit, 192.
DISTILLER, definition of, 214.
 special tax on, 214.
 of brandy from grapes, special tax on, 215.
 what exempt from, 125, 128.
 liable for tax, 124.
 to attach meters, 124.
 to pay expense of meters, 129.
 to register still, 134.
 to give notice of intention to distil, 135.
 to give bond, 137.
 to furnish plan of distillery, 143.
 not to distil until bond given, 150.
 to pay $2 per day during suspension, 152.
 to provide distillery warehouse, 153.
 to erect cistern, 154.
 sign of, 157.
 to keep books, 158.
 when may suspend work, 165.
 to give bond for payment of tax, 137.
 on warehouse spirits, 168.
 how may reduce capacity, 184.
 furnish ladders, &c., to officers, 186.
 to make monthly returns, 214.
 penalty for illicit distilling, 192.
DISTILLERY, where may be located, 140, 142.
 to be registered, 134.
 plan of, 143.
 survey of, 144.

DISTILLERY—*Continued.*
    not within 600 feet of rectifying establishment, 161.
    where it may be, 151.
    warehouse for, 153.
    construction of cistern in, 154.
    construction of doors, &c., 156.
    signs on, 157.
    notice of change of ownership, 136.
    notice of change in, 136.
    tax to be lien on, 124.
    reduction of producing capacity, 184.
    inspection of tubs, &c., 185.
    officers may enter, 185.
    facilities to be furnished, 186.
    search for means of illicit distilling, 186.
    bonding of, seized, 191.
    what forfeited, 193, 194.
DISTILLING APPARATUS, only set up on permit, 152.
    destroyed when forfeited, 191.
DISTILLERY WAREHOUSE, how established, 153.
    entry of spirits in, 167.
    withdrawal from, 172.
    when discontinued, 210.
DISTRAINT, proceedings in case of, 57, 58.
    what exempt from, 60.
    officers' fees in, 62.
    property seized irrepleviable, 63.
    sales under, 65.
DISTRICT ATTORNEY reports suits to Commissioner, 83.
    regulations for conduct of suits, 84.
    keep docket, 84.
    give information to Commissioner, 86.
    compromise suits, 259.

EMBEZZLEMENT, penalty for, 106.
    proceedings in, 107.
ENTRY of spirits into warehouse, 168.
    for withdrawal from warehouse, 172.
    for export, 347.
    at custom house, stamp on, 347.
EVIDENCE of similar acts to prove fraud, 36, 79.
    range of such inquiry, 99.
    of accomplice, 79.
    collector's bill of sale, 92.
    deed of land, 67.
    principal bound by agent's knowledge, 100.
    when party omits to testify, 101.
    for commitment, 108.
    transcript of bonds, 108.
    of fraud, 161.
    burden of proof that tax has been paid, 187.
    testimony on motion for a new trial, 189.
    absence of stamp on packages of tobacco, 235.
            boxes of cigars, 252.
EXEMPTIONS from distraint, 60.
    of distillers of brandy, 125, 128.
    bonds on legal procedings, 342.
    official instruments, 309.

EXEMPTIONS—*Continued.*
    legal papers relating to bounties, &c., 324.
    other papers, &c., 324, 355.
    medicines, &c., 332.
EXPENSES of assessors, 44.
        vouchers for, 46.
    of collectors, 50.
        vouchers for, 52.
    supervisors, detectives, and surveyors, 199.
EXPORTATION, alcohol and rum, 208.
    tobacco and snuff, 236, 240.
    medicines, &c., 330.
    matches, &c., 331.
    articles subject to internal tax, 360.
EXTORTION by assessors and assistant assessors, 43.
    collectors and deputy collectors, 75.
    officers, 77, 257.

FRANKING PRIVILEGE of Commissioner, 18.
    of internal revenue officers, 110.
FERMENTED LIQUORS, notice given before manufacture of, 112.
    tax on, 113.
    accounts by manufacturers of, 114.
    penalty for illicit manufacture of, 117.
    stamps for, 117.
    cancellation of stamps, 119.
    fraudulent removal of, 119, 120.
    removal without payment of tax, 121.
    marks on vessels for, 122.
    penalty for removing stamps, 123.
    bottling of, 123.
FORFEITURES, property held or used for fraudulent purposes, 93.
    how enforced, 97.
    what interest forfeited, 99.
    of spirits mixed with others, 100.
    rights of purchaser after, 101.
    bonding of forfeited articles, 102.
    non-payment of tax on fermented liquors, 123.
    collector to prosecute for, 82.
    unregistered still, 134.
    for fraudulent bond, 138.
    distilling apparatus set up without notice, 152.
    for working during suspension, 166.
    fraudulent removal of spirits, 187.
    for removal at night, 189.
    creating fictitious proof, 189.
    evading tax on distilled spirits, 190.
    detention for, 190.
    for not obliterating marks, &c., 191.
    for distilling without paying special tax, 192.
    fraudulent claim of drawback, 208.
    on distilled spirits, 208.
    sale of forfeited spirits, 213.
    for fraudulent removal of tobacco, &c., 234.
    fraudulent representations on sale of tobacco, 245.
    of unstamped cigars, 252.
    fraudulent removal of cigars, 252.

INDEX. 395

FORFEITURES—*Continued.*
    for wilful violation of law, 255.
    for executing false instruments, 258.
    for omission of proprietary stamp, 350.
    sale of articles less than $300, 103.

FRAUD, fraudulent returns, 35.
    who subject to penalties for, 106.
    in entry in distiller's books, 158.
    in books of wholesale dealers, &c., 194.
    in use of weights, 190.
    in bonds, 258.
    in gauger's return, 306.
    in entries of manufacturers of tobacco, 224.
                                    cigars, 248.
    in manufacture of distilled spirits, 192.
                       imitation wines, 197.
                       tobacco on commission, 242.
                       cigars on commission, 252.
    in execution of bonds, 258.
    in use of cigar boxes, 375.
    collectors suspended for, 200.

GAUGERS, appointment of, 206.
    fees of, 206.
    instruments of, 124, 125.
    have charge cistern room, 164.
    draw off spirits, 164.
    gauge and brand spirits, 167.
    stamp and mark spirits, 175.
    may have charge of stamps, 182.
    make daily report of stamps used, 182.
    return marginal stubs to collector, 183.
    may be transferred by supervisor, 199.
    fees to be paid by owner of articles gauged, 206.

GAS, tax on, 274.

HYDROMETERS, what used, 124, 125.

INCOME TAX, who liable to, 283.
    what subject to, 285.
    exemptions from, 290.
    deductions from, 291.
    for what time assessed, 297.
    returns of, 297.
    by guardian, &c., 297.
    appeal from assessment, 299.
    declaration under oath, 300.
    foreign consuls, 300, 365.
    interest on bonds, 300.
    dividends of corporation, 301.
    undivided profits of corporation, 301.
    dividends of insurance companies, 301.
    contingent fund of fire insurance, &c., 303.
    returns by corporations, 304.
    where residents should make return, 284.
    of decedent, 284.

INCOME TAX—*Continued.*
    on interest, 285.
    services of minor child, 286.
    salaries, 286.
    rent, 286.
    debts, 287.
    gifts, 286, 288.
    profits of corporations, 288.
    sales of real estate, 289.
    deduction of taxes, 291.
        losses, 292.
        expenses, 294.
        repairs, 296.
    questions may be asked, 298.
    penalty for non-return, 297, 299.
    notice for return, 299.
    on funds of corporation, 302.
INFORMERS, shares of, 366.
    who may be, 367, 368.
    penalty for levying black-mail, 367.
INJUNCTION, none to restrain collection of tax, 91.
    none against assessor having jurisdiction, 92.
    assessor not having jurisdiction liable, 373.
INSPECTORS, appointment of general, 22.
    no more appointed, 200.
    of tobacco, 111, 200.
INSTRUMENTS, stamp duty on, 335.
INSURANCE, stamp on policy, 347, 348.
        new policy for one lost, 348.
        permit changing terms, 337.
        assignment of policy, 350.
        entry in register, 348.
    accidental, exempt, 324, 355.
INVENTORY of cigar manufacturer, yearly, 248.
    of tobacco manufacturer, 227.
INDICTMENT may be used to recover penalty, 264.
    for joint offence, 36.
    not on repealed statute, 36.
    may charge crime in various ways, 78.
    one good count will support verdict, 79.
    averment in, for perjury, 88.
    for penalty, under sec. 48, 101.
    objections to action of grand jury, when taken, 108.
    may be sent up by prosecuting officer, 116.
    limitation to, 140.
    distinct offences having different penalty, 181.
INFORMATION to enforce forfeitures, 97.
    pleading in, 97.
    motion to quash, does not lie, 98.
    amendment of, 98.
        not cover new *res*, 98.
        may cover new cause of forfeiture, 98.
    only one against same *res*, 98.
    mode of disputing claimant's right, 98.
    valid, if one count good, 99.
    not include two distinct offences in one count, 181.

INDEX. 397

LABELS for tobacco, 232.
    cigars, 232, 250.
LEASE, stamp on, 349.
    assignment of, 350.
LIENS for non-payment of taxes, 59.
    not until due, 63.
    deed of land takes effect from the time lien attached, 67.
    on distillery premises, 124. *Liquor Dealers 215*
LISTS, classification of, 37.
    mode of making, 38.
    assessors furnish collectors, 41.
    collectors' receipt for, 57.
    correction of errors in, 73.
LOCKS AND SEALS provided by Commissioner, 155.
    mode of obtaining, 133, 156.
    to be accounted for by assessor, 166.
    penalty for tampering with, 190.

MANUFACTURERS of cigars, definition of, 220.
        special tax on, 220.
        bond of, 246.
        yearly inventory of, 248.
    tobacco, definition of, 219.
        special tax on, 219.
        bond of, 224.
        when not taxed as dealer, 220.
        furnish statement of business, 224.
        sign of, 226.
        yearly inventory of, 227.
        books of, 227.
        labels of, 232.
    stills, definition of, 216.
        special tax on, 216.
        to give notice, 152.
MASH made only at distillery, 133.
    not removed from distillery, 133.
    45 gals. equal 1 bush. grain, 161.
    7 gals. equal 1 gal. molasses, 161.
    when 60 gallons equal 1 bush. grain, 161.
MANIFEST, stamp on, 349.
MATCHES, stamp on, 358.
    exportation of, 331.
MEDICINES, stamp duty on, 356.
    exportation of, 330.
    what exempt, 332.
MORTGAGES, stamp on, 349.
    assignment, 350.
    when record of, valid, 308.
    validated by stamping before collector, 323.
    restamping, not interfere with acquired rights, 415, 323.
METERS, attached at expense of owners, 129.
    what required, 129.
    mode of obtaining, 130.
    mode of testing, 132.

OATHS, who may administer, 109.
    to returns, 27.
    brewer's returns, 116.

OATHS—*Continued.*
    distiller's returns, 159.
    returns of manufacturers of tobacco, &c., 227.
                    cigars, &c., 249.
        for income tax, 297.
OFFICERS, render account of fees, 110.
    not to be interested in distilleries, &c., 110, 257.
    may administer oaths, 109.
    suits of money withheld by, 108.
    penalty for embezzlement by, 106.
    when collect direct tax, 103.
    penalty for bribery of, 80.
            levying black mail, 77.
            obstructing, 76.
    may enter buildings, 76, 185.
    penalty for extortion by, 43, 75.
    may inspect worm-tub, 185.
        demand facilities to examine distillery, 186.
        search for means of fraud, 186.
        detain suspected spirits, 190.
        examine books of wholesale dealer, &c., 194.
    penalty for being guilty of fraud, 257.
OFFICIAL INSTRUMENTS exempt from stamp, 309.

PASSAGE TICKET, stamp duty on, 352.
PLAYING CARDS, stamp duty on, 358.
PRACTICE, what assessor's summons should state, 32.
    attachment may be quashed, 34.
    postponement of cause for circuit judge, 79.
    when new trial granted, 79.
    parties out on bail cannot be committed until after verdict, 80.
    in informations, 97.
    of bonding seized property, 102.
    objections to action by grand jury, 108.
    commitment of offender, 108.
    presenting indictments, 116.
    discharging sworn panel, 188.
    making up evidence for new trial, 189.
PENALTIES for fraudulent return, 35.
    malfeasance in office by assessors, &c., 43.
    for receiving money for appointment of assistant assessor, 47.
    for failure to pay tax, 64.
    malfeasance in office by collector, &c., 75.
    obstructing officers, 76, 185.
    demanding money to settle violations of law, 77.
    for personating officer, 77.
        conspiracy, 77.
        bribery, 80.
        perjury, 88.
        fraudulent use of property, 93.
            concealment or removal of property, 102.
        embezzlement, 106.
    all, applicable to corporations, 106.
    for being interested in distilleries, &c., 110.
        fraudulent statement of fees, 110.
        not keeping brewer's books, 117.
            affixing and cancelling brewer's stamps, 119.

PENALTIES—*Continued.*
    for fraudulent removal of fermented liquors, 119.
                      brands on casks, 122.
    for fermented liquors, 122.
    for defacing brewers' stamps, 123.
    non-payment of tax on fermented liquors, 123.
    illicit bottling of fermented liquors, 123.
    for illicit distilling, 133, 151.
    non-registration of still, 134.
    omission to give distillers notice, 136.
    fraudulent distillers' bonds, 138.
    distilling without bond, 150.
    setting up still without notice, 152.
    fraudulent construction of distillery, 156.
    fraudulent putting up distillers' signs, 157.
    fraudulent entries in distillers' books, 159.
    using material for mash in absence of storekeeper, 165.
    working during legal suspension, 166.
    fraudulently using distillers' stamps, 184.
    tampering with locks on distillery, 184.
    refusing to cleanse worm tub, 185.
               allow examination of distillery, 186,
    fraudulent removal of distilled spirits, 187.
    removal of distilled spirits by night, 189.
    creating fictitious proofs, 189.
    evading tax on distilled spirits, 189.
    using false weights, &c., 190.
    omission to obliterate stamps on distilled spirits, 191.
    distilling without paying special tax, 192.
    fraudulent entries in books of rectifiers, &c., 195.
    sales of more than 20 gals. of distilled spirits, 196.
    omission to stamp on change of package, 196.
    evasion of tax on sparkling wines, 197.
    fraudulent removal of distilled spirits from warehouse, 202.
    malfeasance in office by gauger, 207.
    fraudulently claiming drawback on alcohol, &c., 208.
    for employing unregistered cigar makers, 220.
    manufacturers of tobacco, 224.
                not obtaining collector's certificate, 225.
                not giving bond, 225.
                putting up sign, 226.
                keeping books and making returns, 227.
                neglecting to affix labels, 232.
                fraudulent removal of tobacco, 234.
    removing tobacco without stamps, &c., 235.
    for omitting to destroy tobacco stamps, 236.
        fraud in manufacture of tobacco on commission, 242.
        omission to make entries by tobacco dealer, 242.
                stamp imported tobacco, 243.
    offering unstamped tobacco for sale, 245.
    false representation on sale of tobacco, 245.
    selling tobacco in unlawful packages, 245.
    manufacturers of cigars, 246.
                not obtaining collector's certificate, 247.
                giving bond, 247.
                putting up sign, 247.
                keeping accounts and making inventory, 248.

400 INDEX.

PENALTIES—*Continued.*
    manufacturers of cigars, neglecting to affix label, 250.
        fraudulent removal of cigars, 251.
        for removal without paying special tax or giving bond, 252.
    for putting up cigars in unlawful packages, 248.
    for fraud in manufacture of cigars on commission, 252.
    against officer for allowing removal of unstamped imported tobacco, 244.
    against officer for allowing removal of unstamped imported cigars, 253.
    for selling unstamped imported cigars, 253.
        false representations on sale of cigars, 255.
        wilful violation of law, 255.
        malfeasance in office, 257.
        fraudulent bonds, 258.
        fraud in distilling spirits, 256.
        failure to pay special tax, 264.
        refusal to pay tax on manufactures, 271.
        omission to stamp brokers' contracts, 277.
        refusal by banks and bankers to make returns, 279.
        making fraudulent income returns, 298.
        default by corporations to make return for incomes, 304.
        counterfeiting documentary stamps, 309.
        omission to cancel documentary stamp, 312.
            affix documentary stamp, 313.
        not affixing stamps to proprietary medicines, 330.
        fraudulent removal or use of proprietary stamps, 329.
        selling unstamped articles named in Schedule C, 330.
        selling unstamped imported articles named in Schedule C, 332.
        fraudulently claiming drawback on taxed articles, 332.
        using, selling, or making boxes, &c., fraudulently made, 375.
PERFUMERY, stamp duty on, 357.
POWER OF ATTORNEY, stamp duty on, 352.
    made here, but to be executed abroad, 352.
    when signed by several, 352.
    to receive and collect rent, 353.
    to sell and convey real estate, 353.
    contained in a mortgage, 324, 351.
    for other purposes, 353.
    accompanying bond or note, 324, 351.
    to collect bounty, &c., 324, 353.
    to represent creditor in bankruptcy, 353.
PROBATE OF WILL, stamp duty on, 353.
    how estimated, 353.
    when exempt, 353.
    letters *de bonis non*, 354.
PROMISSORY NOTE, stamp duty on, 339.
    new notes substituted for others, 340.
    renewals, 340.
    under seal, 340.
    given in part consideration of realty, 339.
    when secured by mortgage, 339.
PROPRIETARY ARTICLES, medicines, &c., stamp duty on, 356.
    manufacturers of, may furnish dies, 311.
    commission allowed on sales to, 325.
    exportation of, 330.
    tax on imported, 332.

PROPRIETARY ARTICLES—*Continued.*
    what subject to tax, 332, 356.
        exempt, 332
PROTEST, stamp duty on, 354.
        on waiver of, 336, 337.

REAL ESTATE, sale of, for taxes, 66.
    Commissioner to have charge of, 69.
REASSESSMENT may be made within 15 months, 42.
RECORD of unstamped instruments void, 308.
RECTIFIERS, definition of, 214.
    special tax on, 214.
    to give notice, 135.
    to keep books, 194.
    sign of, 157.
    to make returns, 214.
RETURNS, who shall make, 27.
    when to be made, 28, 64.
    when officer may make, 29.
    proceedings in case of failure to make, 29.
    to be in legal tender currency, 35.
    penalty for fraudulent, 35.
    property of non-residents, 37.
    by persons owning property out of district, 37.
    classification of, 37.
    revision of, by assessors, 40.
    by brewers, 115.
    monthly, of barrels manufactured by distiller, 214.
    when to be made by distillers, 158.
    of spirits produced, not less than 80 per cent., 161.
    by gauger, 206.
    monthly, by rectifier, 214.
    by storekeeper, 201.
    of manufacturers of tobacco, 227.
        dealers in tobacco, 227.
        manufacturers of cigars, 248.
        dealers in cigars, 249.
        manufacturers of sparkling wines, 197.
    by collector of tax-paid stamps, 182.
    for income, 297.
            by guardian, 297.
    by corporations of dividends, &c., 300.

SALES under distraint, 58, 62.
    when property not divisible, 65.
    of real estate, 66.
    forfeited spirits, 213.
    forfeited tobacco, 245.
STAMPS, fermented liquors, sale of, 117.
        affixing and cancellation of, 119.
        fraudulent removal or defacing of, 123.
    distilled spirits to be in book form, 181.
        how made, 181.
        sale of, 182.
        affixing and cancellation of, 175, 176.
        fraudulently affixing, 184.

STAMPS—*Continued*
    effacing of, 191.
    tobacco, &c., Commissioner to prepare, 228.
        sale of, 228.
        affixing and cancellation of, 229.
        absence, evidence of non-payment of tax, 235.
        penalty for removal without, 235.
        for tobacco for export, 241,
        Commissioner may change device of, 259.
    cigars, Commissioner to prepare, 250.
        sale of, 250.
        absence, evidence of non-payment of tax, 252.
        penalty for removal without, 252.
    proprietary, what used, 311, 328.
        penalty for removing, 329.
        penalty for sale without, 330.
        proprietors may furnish dies for, 311.
        commissions on sale of, 325.
        what articles are subject to, 356.
        sale of, 324, 333.
    documentary, who to affix, 306
        construction of, 307.
        record of unstamped, 308.
        use of more than one, 308.
        official documents, 309.
        tax deed, 309.
        bond of county officer, 309.
        penalty for forging or counterfeiting, 309.
        mode of cancellation, 311, 313.
        penalty for omission, 313.
        collector may stamp, 313.
        where no collection district, 315.
        proof of intent, 315.
        forged instrument unstamped, 317.
        declaration on instruments, 317.
        plea of omission, 318.
        demurrer for omission, 318.
        bona fide holder, 319.
        sue on original consideration, 319.
        who may apply to collector, 322.
        when deputy may stamp, 322.
        collector's act judicial, 322.
        unstamped, validated, 323.
        foreign bill of exchange, 324.
        exemptions, 324, 355.
        sale of, 324.
        collector may determine amount, 326.
        unstamped, no evidence, 327.
            may be evidence in State courts, 327.
        what liable to, 335.
        duplicates, 335, 337.
SPECIAL TAXES, on distillers, 214.
    rectifiers, 214.
    retail dealers in liquor, 215.
    wholesale dealers in liquor, 215.
    distillers of brandy from apples, &c., 215.
    dealers in tobacco, 219.

SPECIAL TAXES—*Continued.*
    manufacturers of tobacco, 219.
    manufacturers of cigars, 220.
    brewers, 268.
    on manufacturers of stills, 216.
    non-payment does not invalidate contract, 264.
SIGNS of distiller, rectifier, wholesale dealer, &c., 157.
    tobacco and snuff manufacturers, 226.
    cigar manufacturers, 247.
STILLS, manufacturers of, 216.
        special tax on, 216.
    registration of, 134.
    manufacture of, 152.
    for recovery of spirits used pharmaceutically, 214.
STORE-KEEPERS, appointment of, 201.
    duties of, 201, 202.
    payment of salary and expenses of, 205.
    to have charge of distillery, 164.
SNUFF, tax on, 221.
    packages of, 223.
    penalty for fraudulent removal of, 234.
    tax on imported, 243.
    inventory of stock on hand, 244.
    when tax thereon refunded, 254.
    flour, how taxed, 221.
SUPERVISORS, appointment of, 198.
    duties of, 199.
    accounts of, 199.
    when suspend collector or assessor, 206.
SURVEYORS, accounts of, 199.
SUITS, collector prosecute, for tax, 82.
    Commissioner regulates conduct of, 83.
    regulations for, 84.
    in equity to enforce lien, 262.
    no injunction against assessment or collection of tax, 91.
    assumpsit to recover tax, 63.
    against collector to recover tax collected illegally, 61, 91, 370.
    when brought in United States circuit court, 372.
        State court, 373.
    against assessor for illegal assessment, 373.

TAX on fermented liquors, 113.
    distilled spirits, 124, 161, 152.
    brandy made from apples, &c., 215.
    sparkling wine and champagne, 197.
    native wines, 268,
    tobacco, &c., 221.
    imported tobacco, 243.
    cigars, 246.
    imported cigars, 253.
    special, 263.
    on gas, 274.
        brokers' sales, 277.
        banks and bankers, 279.
        incomes, 288.
        instruments, 306.
        proprietary articles, 328.

TOBACCO, tax on, 221.
    special tax on manufacturer, of, 219.
    persons growing, not to pay tax on sales, 220.
    packages of, 223.
        for exporting, 223.
    manufacturer of, to make statement, 224.
    record of manufactory of, 226.
    inventory of, 227.
    stamp on, 228.
    labels on, 232.
    forfeited for non-payment of tax, 234.
    exportation of, 236.
    transportation of, to bonded warehouse, 240.
    manufacture of, on commission, 242.
    sale of, at retail, 245.
    tax on imported, 243.
    effacing stamps on, 236.

VINEGAR, how manufactured, 133, 134.

WARRANTS, issuing of search, 103.
WAREHOUSE distillery, 153.
        construction of, 153.
        when discontinued, 210.
        proprietors of to pay salary of storekeeper, 205.
        entry of spirits in, 167.
        withdrawal from, 172.
        payment of tax before withdrawal, 174.
  for export of tobacco, 236.
    storage of tobacco to be exported, 236.
    proprietary medicines, 330.
WINES, sparkling and champagne, tax on, 197.
    of native growth, 268.
WAREHOUSE RECEIPTS, stamp duty on, 347.
WEIGHER'S RETURNS, stamp duty on, 324, 355.

www.ingramcontent.com/pod-product-compliance
Lightning Source LLC
Chambersburg PA
CBHW050849300426
44111CB00010B/1193